Discourse and Cognition

DISCOURSE AND COGNITION

Derek Edwards

SAGE Publications

London · Thousand Oaks · New Delhi

SAGE Publications Ltd
6 Bonhill Street
London EC2A 4PU

SAGE Publications Inc
2455 Teller Road
Thousand Oaks, California 91320

SAGE Publications India Pvt Ltd
32, M-Block Market
Greater Kailash - I
New Delhi 110 048

British Library Cataloguing in Publication data

A catalogue record for this book is
available from the British Library.

ISBN 0 8039 7696 8
ISBN 0 8039 7697 6 (pbk)

Library of Congress catalog card number 96-71381

Typeset by Type Study, Scarborough, North Yorkshire
Printed in Great Britain by Redwood Books, Trowbridge,
Wiltshire

Contents

Acknowledgements

I wish to thank friends and colleagues who have helped me in writing this book. The Discourse and Rhetoric Group at Loughborough University has been a continuous source of challenge and inspiration. In particular, Malcolm Ashmore and Mick Billig have done all they can to stop me becoming too satisfied with anything I think or say. If I keep coming back for more it is all they deserve. Useful comments and suggestions on various draft chapters were provided by Charles Antaki, Jack Bilmes, Kathy Doherty, Alessandra Fasulo, Katie MacMillan, and David Middleton.

Several chapters provided the basis for a series of seminars in early 1996, at the Universitat Autònoma de Barcelona, organized by Lupicinio Iñiguez. I thank the participants at those seminars for helping me clarify things.

It will surprise nobody if I single out Jonathan Potter for a special mention. I owe him the greatest debt, not only for his comments on every chapter as it was written, but for his friendship and good humour throughout. People who know his work will recognize its influence on mine.

1

An Informal Introduction

This book is an exercise in discursive psychology. Its aim is to outline and illustrate an approach to the relations between language and cognition, in which the primary and defining thing about language is how it works as a kind of activity, as discourse. The focus on cognition is part of an abiding interest in discursive psychology, which has sought to establish itself in contrast to the dominant perspective of the discipline, which is cognitive psychology, while at the same time shifting the focus of analytic attention. It would be peculiar if the sorts of phenomena that discursive psychology manages to reveal, given its opposition to prevailing paradigms of method and explanation, fell neatly into the same set of categories (memory, reasoning, emotional states, causal attributions, etc.). When examining discourse, those categories of mind are blended, if identifiable at all, and they are mixed with a variety of concerns that have not traditionally been considered central to psychology. The discourse-based study of psychological themes looks both ways, then, to the nature of discourse, and to the established nature of psychology as a discipline. It does that in order to have something to say, and somebody to say it to.

Rules and representations

One way to approach the study of language and thinking is to focus on rules and representations. Words, sentences, ideas, and so on, can be said to *represent* the world in some way. That is to say, they are descriptive – they can be used to categorize and refer to things, activities, processes, both in the world 'outside' of us, and in the 'inner' world of consciousness and mind. The topic of study would then be how the linguistic representations, with which we communicate our thoughts, map onto our mental representations of the world, and onto the world itself. In fact, to anticipate my argument somewhat, this representational mapping metaphor for language–mind–world relations, and even the *communication* model of language, are not going to survive scrutiny in the way I have expressed them. But let us continue for a moment with the mapping metaphor.

The notion of *rules* is relevant in several senses. There are rules of thought and of language to consider: rules of reasoning, such as logic, and rules of language, such as grammar. There are also rules that seem to connect events in the world 'outside', and which would therefore have to be mirrored in some way, in the 'inner' world of representations which is our knowledge of that world. For example, there are the regular ways in which events in the world occur, how they follow each other sequentially, coherently, causally. Correspondingly, we *expect* things to happen one after another in some sensible order, both physical things (the effects of gravity, the passage of the seasons, life and death, the motion of objects, etc.) and social things (making friends, eating out in restaurants, career paths, international relations, etc.). If it were not that these kinds of things occurred in some regular way, we could not know them, anticipate them, recognize them, be surprised when unusual things happen, and we could not take part, nor learn to take part, in them.

Let us take it, then, that we shall be concerned in some way with rules and representations. However, the way I have set up these notions, of rules and representations, is not a particularly neutral way to start. It has the virtues of being fairly common sense, and also of fitting in with a great deal of academic theorizing on the subject, in psychology, philosophy, linguistics, and anthropology, for example. There is also the rather attractive alliteration – 'rules and representations' – which I am loath to abandon. But the way I have defined them so far does not fit very well with the perspective that will be taken in this book, and so we need to look more critically at various assumptions.

The notion of 'representation' requires caution in that, by using it, we easily enter a kind of hall of mirrors, where we encounter severe analytical problems with the relations between mind, world, and language. It would be convenient, maybe, if the ways we think or conceive of things were mapped straight onto the categories and structures of language, and both were mapped in turn onto the structures of the real world. But things are not so convenient. The world's languages differ in ways that, if they were reflections of a fixed and pre-coded 'reality', should not be possible. Even within a single language, individual events do not have to be described in the same way by different people, or even by the same person on different occasions. Anybody may confirm this who has been involved in a mundane argument about 'what happened' somewhere, let alone taken part in the delicate manoeuvrings of relationship counselling or courtroom cross-examinations. Similarly the difficulties we sometimes experience of saying what we think, expressing what we know, or finding the right, or the best, description of something all testify to the vagaries of mind, world, and language.

One approach to that 'it would be convenient' scenario, where the maps or mirrors reflect each other without distortion or variability, has been more or less to insist upon it, or *make* it so. I offer this as a way of thinking about many of the concerns, practices, and problems of cognitive psychology. Take, for example, the study of reasoning, the psychology of language, and the pursuit of artificial intelligence. The study of reasoning has proceeded largely in terms of the trials and tribulations of formal logic, as a possibly adequate (but evidently not) characterization of how people think, or should think. It was a founding principle of formal logic that ordinary language is too imperfect and confusing, its reasoning too obscure, its references to things too vague and ambiguous, for the requirements of logical thought. So a special language had to be invented, in which expressions such as 'if *p* then *q*' have a definitive meaning, as part of a set of rules and categories that are fixed and unambiguous. But the distance obtained from ordinary language is bought at a price, a trade-off between rigour and relevance. Inevitably, it becomes difficult to get back from those abstracted logical formulations to the study of ordinary human language and reasoning (Wason and Johnson-Laird, 1972).

In cognitive psychology the notion of 'ordinary human language' has been borrowed virtually wholesale from the science of linguistics, where language is treated predominantly as an abstract, idealized system of categories and rules. It is idealized in Noam Chomsky's (1968) sense, not by error or omission, but deliberately. Everyday conversation is considered to be full of errors, hesitations, false starts, and other 'performance' factors that only obscure the orderly, rule-governed workings of grammar. So language is approached as a system of rules and categories, not as how people talk, or how talk serves as a medium of social interaction. The idealized system is language as we *know* it, language as something about which we can express judgements, such as knowing that sentence (1) is ungrammatical, while sentence (2) obeys the rules of grammar:

(1)   cat mat the on sat the
(2)   the cat sat on the mat

This focus on *knowledge of* language (what Chomsky, 1968, calls 'competence'), rather than on everyday conversation ('performance'), has proved immensely attractive to cognitive psychologists, whose focus has also been on idealized mental rules and representations, rather than everyday activities. It is a focus born out of cognitive psychology's celebrated victory over behaviourism, in which Chomsky's notion of language competence, and his trenchant critique of performance-based behavioural conditioning approaches, played a decisive part (see, for example, Chomsky, 1959; Gardner, 1985; Hamlyn, 1990).

In a similar way, the project of artificial intelligence (AI), in seeking to simulate human thought using the exact categories and rules needed for computer programming, has had to restrict its domains of application. AI has achieved its best successes by restricting those domains to formal games such as chess, and to fixed artificial 'micro worlds' composed of logically separate objects such as large green triangles, small blue pyramids, and a fixed and discrete set of possible actions and spatial relations into which they can enter (for example, Winograd, 1972). Again, it is arguable that much of experimental cognitive psychology has proceeded in a similar way, by tidying up (using laboratory conditions, materials, and procedures) the messy, indeterminate nature of reality and language, in pursuit of the rules of thought. And the same kinds of problems have arisen; what do those tidied-up versions of cognition and reality tell us about everyday thought and language?[1]

The justifications that psychology has offered for dealing with *idealizations* of thought and language include an extension of Chomsky's worries about performance; the world of everyday, ordinary activities is considered much too messy and inconsistent to model or predict. We need to simplify it to see how it works. Although dealing with simplifications, the argument goes, we need not worry about the gap between our studies and the messy world of ordinary talk and action, as long as that messy world works on the same principles. The relationship here is something like the one that obtains, hopefully, between a simple physics experiment and the natural world. While the precise, moment-to-moment motion of a leaf falling from a tree would be exceedingly difficult to predict or describe, it presumably moves according to the various pulls and resistances of mass and energy, gravity and friction, wind motion and air resistance, that we could mimic variable-by-variable in the laboratory. It is hopefully the same with the dynamics of thought and language. Cognitive models and experiments surely capture what goes on in ordinary discourse; it is just that ordinary discourse has all those paraphernalia of rules and representations, grammar and knowledge, social and personal 'factors,' and so on, confusingly mixed together.

I have inserted 'hopefully', 'surely', or 'presumably' a few times in that last paragraph. There are two bases for such caution, the second being, for my argument, the more important. The first basis, which will not detain us, is the notion that leaves falling from trees may not be so straightforward after all; at least, not according to 'chaos' theories, if such motions are anything like large-scale weather systems or sub-atomic quantum emissions. The cause-and-effect world of the school physics experiment may leave something to be desired other than mere complexity when it comes to explaining complex physical events. Second, it may be that, outside of the laboratory (and perhaps inside it too), meaningful human actions are simply not organized on a factors-and-variables causal basis. It could be that experiments do not *reveal*, but rather *make it so*, that human actions can be fitted to predictable causal formats. That will be the position taken in this book, and it requires that we start again, and re-theorize how a study of thought and language might begin.

Rules, representations, and discourse

Let us begin again with rules and representations, and consider how we might give them a different status. One way to begin is to reject the notion that we need to start in the laboratory, or with formal models, but instead start trying to make sense of ordinary talk and actions. When we do that, in what sense are we looking at rules and representations, or their products? In what sense are our everyday actions and understandings guided or determined by (knowledge of) rules? There are, of course, various kinds of rules we might consider, ranging from the rules of logic or grammar, to social rules and conventions, or legal statutes. Let us take how traffic lights work. As an English visitor to Mexico City, I was struck by the fact that the Mexican friends who were driving me around kept going through red lights; not all of the time, but a lot of the time, and so did other drivers. Later, on a beach in Huatulco, people were openly hawking goods to tourists, in spite of clearly displayed notices forbidding it, and despite the occasional presence of officials who appeared to ignore the activity. It was not clear to me, in either case, what the rules were, or what their status was, or how they applied. Of course, we English are not above breaking a few rules, but the blatant way the Mexicans were doing it *on these occasions* was something I thought remarkable. So I remarked on it, seeking guidance from my friends.

The way I came to understand it, the traffic lights and the beach notice remained in force, but not in any way that was supposed to govern people's actions. If you went through a red light, and hit another car, then running the light could be invoked to say whose fault it was. If the beach hawkers got to be a nuisance, then the notices and by-laws were available to point to and say the hawkers should not be there. Such verbal and gestural pointings-out would not be automatic in their effects, however. It might be disputed not only that the light was red at that moment, but also that the rule applied in this case, that perhaps this was one of the 'less serious' red lights that everyone routinely goes through, and expects each other to go through, so you should always be careful and look to see what is coming and not rely on the light; just like how the beach notice might for some inventive reason not apply in some particular case. So this was the status of the rules – they were *available* and could be applied, but not definitively, nor without dispute.[2]

Now the interesting thing, of course, is that these kinds of rules are not so different from the ones I was more used to. The difference was in how used to them I was, how recognizable they were in operation, and how tightly they might apply. But however tightly they apply, they apply in the same kind of way as in Mexico, not as principles governing human actions, but as resources that actors might use, or make relevant, in accounting for actions, or in arguing about some event. This notion of rules as *available*, and available to actors themselves as part of their own descriptive and accounting practices, contrasts with a conception of rules as underlying or governing human actions, and needing to be discovered objectively by analysts. That is to say, the importance of rules-for-human-actions to actions themselves is not merely one of governance or of rule-following. It is something that depends on how the actors themselves, as part of their actions, and as part of how they account for their actions, treat rules as relevant.[3] This might involve participants *treating* rules as constraining, or needing to be followed, or, as inapplicable, or optional, or, indeed, there may be some dispute as to what the rule, or the relevant rule, actually is. In fact, the invocation of a rule is part of defining what kind of action it was to start with. So all this depends heavily on how things and events are *described*.

Take the law, for instance. As a practice, rather than as a set of written statutes, we need law courts (jurisprudence) to make it work. Laws are not written, and could not be written, in such a way as to specify exactly which actions they cover. The range of possible *illegal* actions is infinitely extendible, just as the range of possible actions of *any* kind is, when we take account of variations in persons, settings, behaviours, reactions, circumstances, methods, and so on: in other words, when we take account of the indefinitely many ways that human actions might be described. It is the necessary business of the courts to decide on a description of what actually happened in some case, decide the relevant law, decide how it applies, and categorize the offensive actions accordingly. The same can be said of game rules, such as those of football or cricket. The relevance of a set of rules is that they can be applied in particular circumstances, which have to be decided on in each case; was some specific event a 'foul', a 'goal', a case of 'offside', of 'ball tampering', or of 'leg before wicket'? Whereas laws and regulations can be written and revised to make their applications more effective, or their effects more desirable (at least to the law-makers), we never get to the point where applications of such rules become automatic. As Wittgenstein argued,[4] there can be no set of rules that are defined so as to cover all contingencies, all applications.

I do not want to pretend that a couple of stories from a trip to Mexico, or armchair thoughts about laws, are sufficient to ground an approach to thought and language, or rules and representations. These are issues for which there is a large and sophisticated literature, and a considerable body of empirical work, some of which will feature in later chapters. That literature includes the philosophical tradition of 'conceptual analysis' (Coulter, 1990a; Ryle, 1949; Wittgenstein, 1958), which analyses meanings by reference to how words are ordinarily used; and also ethnomethodology and conversation analysis (Garfinkel, 1967; Heritage, 1984a; Sacks, 1992), which explore these kinds of relations between rules, actions, and descriptions by conducting closely observed empirical studies of social practices. However, anecdotes are enough to begin to define a perspective on the relations between cognition and language, when these are studied not in the abstract but as features of situated human practices. Let us explore those relations a little further, then, with some more observational materials.

In his popular ethnography *Among the Thugs*, Bill Buford (1991) describes his involvement with groups of English football (soccer) 'hooligans' (as the press generally called them) during the notorious heyday of violent confrontations in the 1980s. From his perspective as participant observer, Buford provides a gripping and evocative series of narratives and analyses. The thing of interest, in this context, is how those descriptions *constitute* events as understandable sorts of human actions, and how that descriptive process involves imputing relations between social rules and mental processes. It is not that Buford's text is an especially appropriate one for this kind of treatment. Its usefulness is that it stands somewhere between anthropological ethnography, investigative journalism, and popular literature.

The kinds of descriptive practices at issue here are common to all those fields, as well as to mundane conversation, gossip, and other arenas of everyday discourse.

One of Buford's themes, echoing many popular treatments of crowd behaviour since Le Bon (1896; see also Reicher, in press), is the nature of 'riots', which he depicts as suspensions, or transgressions, of social order: 'when what is civilized ceases to be, when the structures of continuity – job, shelter, routine, responsibility, choice, right, wrong, the state of being a citizen – disappear', leaving 'nothingness in its beauty, its simplicity, its nihilistic purity' (Buford, 1991: 194–5). However, this notion of an absence of rules and meanings contrasts with Buford's own descriptions of crowd *cohesion* in the midst of those same breakdowns of order, such as the functions of 'leaders', and the *recognizable* (and describable) order of apparent chaos. Chaos is chaotic only in contrast to some other, outsider's view of order, and there is always a participants' orientation to that more normal, writer's and reader's conventional order that is part of its overt rejection: 'It has been planned . . . a riot by appointment' (1991: 203).

It becomes clear from Buford's account that participants themselves construct these events, in their actions and descriptions, as planned and orderly, or as a breakdown of order, and make use of a set of descriptive terms shared by both 'thugs' and police. These include how people were 'herded' into 'pens', the 'pit', 'cages', a whole range of animal images from the border categories of wild and domesticated, that Buford himself deploys as much as he analyses ('fear . . . it would have been a presence like a smell', 1991: 223). The rioting participants themselves display (that is, are reported by Buford as displaying) normative expectations of disorder, are accountable to it, and *recognize* and *name* what happens when the violence 'goes off' – 'the crack, the buzz and the fix' (1991: 206). As Jonathan Potter and Stephen Reicher (1987) have shown, 'riot' itself is a contentious descriptive category, applicable to events which other participants (or the same participants on other occasions) may describe differently.

Let us take stock of where we are concerning rules and representations. Our focus has shifted from notions of human actions as rule-governed and based on cognitive representations of the world, towards a concern with norms and descriptions. Further, we are becoming concerned with participants' own descriptions of their practices, and with how such actions and descriptions do not so much *obey* as *orient to* norms in some way. This is the suggestion that rules or norms do not govern actions, but that actions are done and described in ways that display their status with regard to some rule or expectation. The relation between actions, norms, and descriptions is clearly an intimate one.

When people describe events, they *attend to* accountability. That is to say, they attend to events in terms of what is normal, expectable, and proper; they attend to their own responsibility in events and in the reporting of events (cf. Edwards and Potter, 1992a: Buford's and my own earlier observations are given as first-hand, eye-witnessed and participation-based); and they *invoke* notions of motive, causation, justification, and cognition. As Emanuel Schegloff (1989a) has noted, accounts *of* actions are invariably, and at the same time, accounts *for* actions, and we shall return recurrently to that important ethnomethodological insight in later chapters. It will be one of our major routes into discourse and cognition, opening up possibilities for both theory and empirical work with regard to traditionally 'cognitive' phenomena such as memory and narrative reporting, causal attribution, schematic event knowledge (script theory), categorization, and what has been called 'folk psychology'.

Description, action, and rhetoric

One of the most important features of descriptions is their could-have-been-otherwise quality. No description of anything is the only one that is reasonable or possible. The importance of this as a feature of everyday descriptions, when people produce accounts of, and in, social practices, contrasts starkly with the use of descriptions in cognitive studies, where it is almost entirely overlooked. Where it is not overlooked, it is generally treated as a nuisance. In studies of event memory that use textual representations, for example, the nature of the events to be remembered, and of remembered events, are typically provided in the form of one-off descriptions. Things in the world, and memories of them, are *as described*. This holds whether we are dealing with sets of sentences, prose passages, textual scenarios, autobiographical memory, laboratory studies, or 'ecologically situated' ones. The notion that events might be differently described, in the sense that any event description is only one version, and a potentially variable and contentious one, is of little interest in such studies. It is something to be avoided, prevented, or methodically 'controlled for,' being a form of inconsistency or social contagion that might obscure our view of the workings of mind. Similarly, variability and inconsistency are systematically removed from cognitive studies of all kinds, not only of attitudes (Potter and Wetherell, 1987), but in studies ranging from causal reasoning to cognitive anthropology. So what happens when we find this could-have-been-otherwise feature of everyday talk and texts *interesting*?

It is not only that descriptions could have been otherwise; usually there is a fairly specific 'otherwise' that is at issue. That is to say, descriptions are selected and assembled with regard to *actual* alternatives, and sometimes specific counter-descriptions. They are not merely different from otherwise possible descriptions, but have a *rhetorical*, argumentative quality with regard to what somebody else might say (Billig, 1987). This is a feature not only of overt disagreements between people, but of discourse in general. We can always inspect a piece of discourse, even the most straightforwardly uncontroversial and descriptive (perhaps especially those! – see Chapters 3 and 8), and ask: what is being denied by that assertion? Or, what otherwise plausible world, or version of the world, is at issue?

One of the texts that Harvey Sacks analyses, in his marvellous *Lectures on Conversation*, is a *New York Times* report of a Navy pilot's remarks on serving in Vietnam. The article[5] included the following:

> Commander Jack H. Harris, leader of the Attack Squadron 155 aboard the Coral Sea was explaining how a carrier pilot feels about Vietnam: 'I certainly don't like getting shot at. But this is the top of my flying career and it's important I should know about it. I really feel I'm fortunate to get the opportunity after 21 years in the Navy of combat experience. I need it to be a real professional.'
> . . .
> How did he feel about knowing that even with all the care he took in aiming only at military targets someone was probably being killed by his bombs?
> 'I certainly don't like the idea that I might be killing anybody,' he replied. 'But I don't lose any sleep over it. You have to be impersonal in this business. Over North Vietnam I condition myself to think that I'm a military man being shot at by another military man like myself.'

Sacks (1992, vol. 1: 205) notes how the pilot 'takes it that there are alternative ways that he and those he is dealing with (bombing, being fired at), may be categorically formulated'. Sacks analyses in some detail how descriptions that denote group membership and institutional role (for example, 'a military man being shot at by another military man like myself') provide a warrant or justification for described actions, and attend rhetorically to alternative possible descriptions: 'the formulations have alternative imports, and . . . he is able to choose that formulation [of military action] . . . that permits him to do it without important moral consequences' (1992, vol. 1: 206).

Among the descriptive categories used in the extract are a variety of psychological terms, including expressions of feeling, liking, what some-body ought to know, grounds for 'losing sleep', and the strategic cognitive capacity to 'condition myself to think' something. Note how these ex-pressions occur within the trajectory of the discourse, and rhetorically, as part of providing norm-oriented accounts and justifications for actions. What is 'not liked' is 'getting shot at', and 'killing anybody', and these are 'certainly' not liked. The 'certainly' invokes what any reasonable person might be expected to dislike; it protests the point, against the morally dangerous possibility that the pilot might find these kinds of activities intrinsically appealing, and points us instead toward his professionalism. 'Combat experience' is necessary to being a 'real professional', a military man engaged with other military men (Sacks emphasizes the justificatory work done by this reciprocity of categories), where being 'impersonal' about killings is a requirement of 'this business'. It is a *profession* – a feature also used extensively in recruitment advertising for the British Army – 'Join the Professionals'. The various psychological descriptions that occur in the passage are marshalled within such accounts, so that, in this case at least, we would need to pay close attention to how such expressions work rhetorically, in such contexts, and in the creation of such texts, in order to appreciate their significance.

The basis of this book is that this is a fruitful way to proceed generally, to investigate relations between psychology and language within a study of situated discourse. The thought–language relationship is one that exists not only, or even primarily, in the heads of participants, within their linguistic systems or vocabularies, nor merely as the 'folk psychology' they use, but it is dealt with by participants as a practical matter, a concern *of theirs* that they handle in talk and text.

Cognition and reality: why intervene?

When ordinary discourse deals with psychological themes, with states of mind, thoughts, motives, personality, and so on, it does so not only by directly naming them, but also (and in close attendance) indirectly, by describing states of the world. In Sacks's 'Navy pilot' example, the pilot's various likes, preferences, impersonality, and feelings are intelligible in terms of their objective circumstances: killing and being shot at, twenty-one years in the Navy, 'military targets', flying over North Vietnam, being 'in this business'. In fact, this is a feature of both lay and professional psychologizing, that psychological states are defined with regard to an external world. The workings of memory, of causal reasoning (the domain of attribution theory), of perception, and their various schematic effects, distortions, or measures of accuracy, are all defined with regard to what *actually* happened, or what the original 'stimulus materials' were. It is similar with everyday discourse; we judge mental states and personal characteristics according to their circumstances. 'Forgetting', 'believing', and 'knowing' are things we can discriminate and talk about insofar as we can claim some purchase on what should have been remembered, or what the facts are.

Cognition and reality are like two sides of a coin. If we want to know about cognition, we need to take account of the world, hold reality constant, or vary it systematically, so that we can discern the workings of mind. If we want to know about reality, it is cognition and other human foibles that have to be held constant or under control. We have to assure ourselves that we are not deluded, mistaken, or misinformed, seeing what we expect or want to see, and this may require systematic methods for countering the vagaries of mind. Such methods include criminal and legal investigations, using multiple witnesses, standardized tests, large subject samples, or using scientific procedures with automatic, preferably machine-based measurements or 'inscription devices' (Latour and Woolgar, 1986). The interesting thing, of course, is what happens when we consider any such purchase on non-psychological reality to be *itself* a product of human perceptions, artefacts, practices, and accounts.

In everyday discourse, this is the realm of description, or of factual reporting. Given the intimate, mutually implicative relationship between reality and mind, it is possible to perform a lot of psychological business, invoking notions of motive, intent, memory, selfishness, or whatever, 'merely' by describing actions and their circumstances. The 'merely' is significant of course, not only because I want to signal the wariness that we must adopt for the category of objective descriptions, but because 'merely' is precisely what the rhetoric of cognition and reality calls for. It is the goal and achievement of objective descriptions, especially given that a lot of inferences may be riding on them, to have some specific formulation of things stand as 'merely' description, gloriously unnoticeable as a piece of discourse: mere, versionless, reality.

Sometimes everyday discourse touches on issues that are 'psychological' not only in the everyday sense, but in terms directly linked with academic psychology, such as intelligence testing, much of Freudian psychology, notions of child 'development', and so on. One of these links between academic and lay psychology is the phenomenon of 'bystander inter-vention', a celebrated theme of 1970s social psychology promoted largely by the work of Bibb Latané and John Darley (1970). The relation between formal psychology and everyday discourse was a particularly close one in this case. Although the term 'bystander intervention' remains a technical one, the research itself was closely linked to public concerns with, and descriptions of, the apparent apathy of onlookers who witnessed vicious personal attacks in public places but did not intervene. Although we shall not be taking a special interest in bystander intervention, nor reviewing a large amount of experimental evidence on the topic, the way it has been defined and treated by psychologists provides a useful basis for opening up issues of cognition and reality. It provides a basis for contrasting the ways in which a traditional cognition-and-action approach to any such phenomena would contrast with a discursive approach. It also offers the advantage of being a well-researched topic, one that picks up themes from our discussion of Bill Buford's descriptions of crowd violence, and those of Harvey Sacks's Navy pilot, and one which deals directly with relations between psychologi-cal explanations, descriptions, and real world events.

The emblematic case was the terrible story of Kitty Genovese, beaten to death over a period of more than half an hour in full view of a large number of her New York City neighbours, watching from their windows. This became a focus of heavy media attention, and it prompted a series of social psychological studies. A contemporary newspaper report described the event as follows:[6]

> For more than half an hour thirty-eight respectable, law-abiding citizens in Queens watched a killer stalk and stab a woman in three separate attacks in Kew Gardens.
> Twice the sound of their voices and the sudden glow of their bedroom lights interrupted him and frightened him off. Each time he returned, sought her out and stabbed her again. Not one person telephoned the police during the assault; one witness called after the woman was dead.

A variety of lay and professional explanations were offered for this and other similar (that is, categorized as similar) incidents. None of these explanations went uncontested, even the experimentally supported ones, for which other experiments could be adduced to disagree (Eiser, 1978).

Explanations included familiar notions of urban alienation and apathy, contrasted with helpful but nosy small town community life; sheer absence of any understandable basis (reminiscent of Buford's nihilistic breakdown of order); 'diffusion of responsibility' effects, used to explain why people in groups seemed less prone to help than individuals alone; cost–benefit theories, in which onlookers compute a series of personal costs and benefits as a condition for intervening (the explanation preferred by Latané and Darley, 1970); and other cognitive theories such as a failure to 'activate' an appropriate 'helping script' (Abelson, 1981).

Among the steps in such cognitive processes are *recognizing* and *interpreting* the event. In Latané and Darley's model, these are the early stages of a decision-making process. It begins as follows:

> Let us suppose that an emergency is actually taking place. A middle aged man walking down the street has a heart attack. He stops short, clutches his chest, and staggers to the nearest building wall, where he slowly slumps to the sidewalk in a sitting position. What determines whether a passer-by will come to his assistance? (Latané and Darley, 1970: 31)

According to the model, the 'determinants' of intervention are the five steps of a perception-and-action information processing sequence that might abort at any step: (1) noticing something wrong; (2) deciding the event is an emergency; (3) deciding on degree of personal responsibility; (4) deciding the specific mode of intervention; (5) implementing the intervention. It is an automatic sort of sequence, a kind of flow-diagram from reality, through perception, to action. The importance of step 2 is that an event might be 'ambiguous':

> To the extent that an emergency is ambiguous, the bystander is free to interpret it in a number of ways. Many things will probably help determine this choice of interpretation, including his past history, his personality, and his present mood, but two things are of special interest – the extent to which the individual is motivated to avoid belief that it is an emergency, and the way he is influenced by the reactions of other bystanders. (1970: 33)

This is the first point of contrast between cognitive and discursive psychology. As we have seen, the starting point for Latané and Darley, if not for their experimental (or imaginary) participants, is an unambiguous event, identified with a single, definitive description of it: 'Let us suppose that an emergency is actually taking place . . .' Like with the Kitty Genovese case, we know what happened, what kind of event it was (the man was having a heart attack), and we know equally well what the witnesses' responses were; the task is to explain them. Ambiguity arises in the model as a problem *for participants*, at which point a number of psychological factors and variables switch into operation, to 'determine' which way their decision processes will fall.

In contrast, discursive psychology starts with the descriptions. We examine *accounts* – both of and for the incident itself, and of and for whatever the witnesses did, including their own accounts. The status of those descriptions and accounts is not secondary to the 'event itself', but, rather, they constitute the nature of it, and set it up descriptively as some kind of problem to be solved, something that calls for one or another kind of explanation, and which may contain already, within the description, the seeds or implications of explanation. For example, the initial newspaper report already sets up the Kitty Genovese case as a puzzle, of how 'thirty-eight respectable, law-abiding citizens' could watch such an event 'for more than half an hour'.

This is not necessarily the kind of puzzle that police or forensic psychologists (or anyone else) might pose, which might be, say, 'how could a man do such a thing?' The focus is on the witnesses, and it is *rhetorically* posed. These are 'respectable, law-abiding citizens', a presumptive description (presumably not based on investigation) of ordinary folk like you or me, contrasting with, say, some bunch of callous criminal types from a rough neighbourhood. 'For more than half an hour' is relevant to the extent that, while not being very precise about time, it places restrictions on account-ability. It would be difficult to claim, for example, that it all happened so fast that there was no time to react. The narrative is of a drawn-out incident with the attacker returning several times. And the fact that he was 'frightened off' by bedroom lights coming on suggests that he could fairly easily be frightened off, if anyone had bothered to try. Similarly, 'not one person' intervened, in contrast to expectation, and the number who watched. The sheer number of witnesses, thirty-eight (the standard quoted number, cf. Rosenthal, 1964), is suggestive of some sort of generalized human phenom-enon, rather than something to be accounted for in terms of personality or individual differences.

This specific and recurrent (in the literature) number, thirty-eight, is itself interesting, given the implausibility that all of them were equivalent as witnesses to the event, that they all saw as much of it, for as long, from equivalent viewpoints, and that there were not some borderline cases who may have seen very little, maybe forty-three possible witnesses, with seventeen who watched for more than thirteen minutes, or whatever, where even those kinds of (invented) numbers would be categories obscuring differences. Instead the witnesses all figure (in this description) as a determinate and undifferentiated bunch, which again sets up the phenom-enon for explanation: what caused them (all) to (not) do what they did? Presumably, if this were a court case, the status of each of the witnesses, and of the event itself, would be concerns for legal cross-examination, rather than something to be taken as given from a newspaper report. Without having to accept such a court's findings as any guarantee of truth, the point is that these and all the rest of the details of the case are *as described*, where descriptions are things people produce on occasions, and are not (though they may be taken to be) the same thing as 'events'. Nor are they neutral with regard to explanations.

Let us turn now to the factors and variables, the 'determinants' of action. In Latané and Darley's work, the task of the experimental psychologist was to identify the causal factors and variables at work, and manipulate them in order to discover their relative importance and how they interact. Events such as the Kitty Genovese murder are like our leaf falling from its tree, a complex interweaving of factors that need to be differentiated under controlled conditions. Kay Deaux and Lawrence Wrightsman summarize three 'causes' that combine to produce the 'bystander effect', which is the statistically robust finding that potential helpers in emergencies are less likely to intervene when in the company of others than when alone:

> Through a *social influence* process, bystanders look to others to help them interpret the situation and may conclude that the need to help is not so great if others do not seem alarmed or are not taking action. Second, *audience inhibition*, or what is also called evaluation apprehension . . . may contribute to the bystander effect if a bystander is worried about how others will evaluate his or her behavior. . . . Or, in situations in which bystanders arrive at the scene of an accident after it has occurred and are not sure what caused it, potential helpers may even fear that arriving bystanders will mistakenly conclude that they caused the victim's plight if they get involved. . . . Finally, there is the process called *diffusion of responsibility*: when several potential helpers are available, responsibility for acting is divided, and so each individual may be less likely to assume personal responsibility for acting. (1988: 355)

In discursive psychology, the role of these sorts of considerations is that they may feature as parts of accounts. They are just the kinds of things people may say, or claim, or others may say, in accounting for why they did nothing, and they can be set against more blaming, *internal* attributions such as apathy or sadistic interest.[7] The analytic task with such accounts is not to decide amongst them as explanations, nor to add them together as strands in a complex causal weave, but to treat them as phenomena in their own right. We can investigate how they are constructed, on what kinds of occasions, within what sorts of discursive interactions, attending to what kinds of rhetorical business.

Though we should expect no one-to-one correspondence, the kinds of features that appear in experimental studies as *variables*, or *hypotheses*, are likely to appear in discursive studies as *accounts*. One consequence of this is that, from a discursive perspective, the problem does not arise of sorting out which of those accounts is correct, or most important; there is no embarrassment when such accounts conflict or contradict each other. Accounts can do that, being rhetorically loaded constructions that *participants* offer, for and on occasions. The analytical task is to see how those accounts are constructed, how and when they are produced as explanations, how they are designed and positioned with regard to alternative accounts, and in what kinds of interaction sequences they are produced. In experiments, on the other hand, conflicting accounts are likely to be turned into conflicting hypotheses that the *experimenter* holds, and the task is to test their causal efficacy, eliminate contradictions, and sort what remains into some kind of logical and consistent causal order. These are, clearly, highly contrasting ways of dealing, empirically and theoretically, with the issues of what people do and why.

Let us take a second, contrasting item on apparent bystander apathy in

New York City, this time a more recent, more distanced commentary from a British newspaper:

> New York is in one of its periodic frenzies of self-disgust. The latest spasm was exacerbated last week when a man raped his three-year-old niece in a park while several people stood and watched from the roadside. The event provoked something close to hysteria in the tabloids and on the television news, where – not so much the rape, but the passivity of the onlookers – was seen as yet more evidence of the city's terminal decadence. 'We are on a one-way seesaw going down,' declared the *New York Post*.
>
> Or perhaps not. A closer inspection of the event shows that the spectators, far from gazing curiously at the ghastly scene, were bellowing at the man to stop. They couldn't reach him because the park was separated from the road by an eight-foot-high fence, and a man who tried to climb it cut open his leg. His scream of pain scared the attacker, who scooped up the child and ran off.
>
> Then a truck driver backed up through rush-hour traffic to reach the off-ramp, while radioing for help. He caught up with the rapist and grabbed him till the police arrived. The man is now being held in Rikers Island jail. . . . The story shows that contrary to what they think, many New Yorkers are brave and resourceful folk who will take a lot of risks to help someone in trouble. (Simon Hoggart, *The Observer*, 21 July 1991)

The thing of interest in this report is that it focuses not only on violent events and the actions of witnesses, but on 'the story', on event reporting. It contrasts prevailing television news coverage and 'tabloid' press reporting with what can be known from some unspecified 'closer inspection of the event'. However, the added sophistication of this second newspaper report, in contrast to the more straightforward *New York Times* extract on Kitty Genovese, should not be taken as providing any kind of view of events over and beyond their description. The 'closer inspection' is itself, presumably for the journalist, and in any case for us, a contrasting set of reports, this second set being accepted at face value as 'the event'.

Again, it is a text we can analyse for its management of fact and accountability (or description and causation), and its rhetoric of reality and mind. New Yorkers' 'self-disgust' is given as something subject to 'periodic frenzies' and 'hysteria', of which this latest example (thus-counted) is a 'spasm'. This is a repertoire of irrational mass reactions,[8] contrasted with the writer's own 'closer inspection'. The counter-image, that of a community of concerned and active interveners, is graphically built with circumstantial detail and narrative sequence, in which the rapist was pursued by several people (one alone might be an exception) against adversity and cost (the high fence, personal injury, the scream, the heavy traffic), building a picture of New Yorkers (in general) as 'brave and resourceful folk', a conclusion set rhetorically 'contrary to what they think'. At the same time, and in the same process, the writer manages reflexively to provide for his *own* identity as a reliable news reporter, who takes the trouble to get the facts, in contrast to the 'tabloid' journalists responsible for all the 'hysteria'. This is an example of how, even in textual monologues such as newspaper reports, discourse is a species of social action.

I am not wanting to substitute journalism, nor this specific piece of journalism, for social psychological research. The point is that *all* sets of event descriptions are rhetorically organized, construct the nature of events, assemble description and narrative, and make attributional inferences available. This applies to so-called primary and secondary sources, accounts provided by witnesses and event participants, by newspaper reporters, and even by psychological investigators in their research reports and textbooks, who make use of those reports as well as producing their own. Experimental social psychology chose, in the case of bystander intervention, to focus not on the crimes but on the perceptions of witnesses. Discursive psychology treats both those things (the events, and what people make of them) as available in discourse.

Descriptions and accounts of the nature of the world, and of the things people do, are produced by participants themselves, as part of living their lives. By turning to accounts we do not ignore 'what really happened' in events, even such disturbing ones as the death of Kitty Genovese. Rather, we treat that as a live participants' concern,[9] and see how they deal with it. This may strike the reader as fence-sitting, relativist, uncommitted, and so on, in that analysts may themselves (ourselves) wish to adhere to a particular version of reality, or what happened, or what the world is like, and this is especially pertinent in harrowing cases of violence and murder. The point is that we can do so, and generally should do so, but only by *joining in* those kinds of processes, becoming participants in event construction, offering our own versions of things, choosing amongst accounts – to do that is not to avoid the discursive construction of reality and mind, but to engage in it, and inevitably to provide further materials for analysis.

Discourse, communication, and action

I have noted that the conception of language and thought as 'representation' makes use of a mapping metaphor, for relations between world, mind, and language. It is a metaphor that continues to underpin mainstream work in cognitive, social, and developmental psychology. One of the vices or virtues (whichever you choose) of that metaphor is that it helps to reduce language–thought relations to individuals and their mental processes. Nevertheless, 'representation' has other dictionary senses, including social ones, such as delegation, speaking-on-behalf-of, and political representation. These are inherently social categories, not reducible to individual sense-making, providing an alternative metaphor of 'representation' that points us in the direction of social practices. Whether or not we want an alternative metaphor, they are largely unavoidable in discourse (Lakoff, 1987), so let us try a couple more for size. One of them is 'communication'.

It may appear strange to think of communication as a metaphor – is it not a phenomenon, indeed *the* phenomenon, the very thing we need to study? In fact, I want to turn away from the notion of discourse as communication, and it is largely because of the unwanted metaphorical baggage it carries. The notion that discourse is a form of social action should not be equated with language as 'communication'. Certainly the notion of communication improves on the individualistic sense of 'representation', in that it introduces a necessary social dynamic to relations between thought and language. But it also invokes an image that is itself stubbornly individualistic. It stems from starting not with discourse as a phenomenon, but from psychology, where two (imagined) individuals, possessing thoughts, intentions, and so on, have the problem of having to get these thoughts and intentions across the airwaves via a communication channel. The metaphor of communication, then, gives rise to a host of apparent difficulties, such as how we can know the minds of others, how we can ensure that the world is accurately pictured, that the original message got transmitted, and so on.[10] One of the tasks of later chapters will be to elaborate a conception of discourse as an activity, which does not rely on the idea of message transmission between minds.

Let us try another analogy, or metaphor, that of a game such as tennis or cricket. If we think of discourse, or face-to-face conversation perhaps, as something like a game, then it will not be long before we find the analogy wanting – that is the fate of analogies, of course, in that they are always something different, necessarily, from whatever we are trying to illuminate with them. Nevertheless, the usefulness of thinking of conversation as being something like tennis or cricket (and perhaps this is the limit of its utility) is that it helps us get rid of the 'communication' metaphor, or at least to appreciate that it *is* a metaphor. Interactive games are forms of social interaction, like talk is; but it seems a bit stretched to think of them as 'communication'. They are activities people engage in, according to a more or less agreed set of rules (we have touched on ways in which rules might be thought to constrain actions), a little like (more analogies) driving in city traffic. They may involve exchanges of signals and shared meanings, but they are not very adequately described as 'means of communication'. But what a nuisance! Immediately I have denied it, I can't help starting to think of ways in which cricket can indeed be considered a means of communication. We can try to push any analogy, of course, as far as we can; but let us take it for now that discourse can be considered as a form of social activity like any other. It does not have to be conceived as a 'means' of doing something else, including being a means of transmitting messages between minds.

The earlier argument concerning rules concluded on the side of rules and norms being *considerations* that participants make relevant to their actions, and to other people's actions, rather than as principles underlying, generating, or governing actions themselves. People manage to bring off, describe, and account for their actions with regard to rules and norms, rather than simply following or breaking them. Now, one of the explanations considered and largely rejected by experimental psychologists for 'pro-social behaviours' such as helping people in distress is that this is a socially normative thing to do; we do things because we know and feel we ought to, and that would explain why we feel bad or shocked when people refuse to help. It is useful to appreciate why experimental social psychologists are not fond of norms as an explanation of actions, because it sharpens the contrast between norms as explanations of actions, and norms as *resources that participants use* in explaining actions.

Deaux and Wrightsman summarize the explanatory inadequacy of norms as follows:

> First, norms are so general that they may not tell us what to do in specific situations. Second, if most people in society subscribe to such norms, how can norms explain individual differences in helping behavior? Third, two conflicting norms may seem equally applicable in a situation. The norm of social responsibility, for example, is contradicted by a norm that says 'Don't meddle in other people's affairs.' And finally, people's behavior often is inconsistent with social norms. (1988: 346)

While all these observations about social norms pose problems for their status as causal explanations of behaviour, they are grist to the mill for their role as participants' resources.

The fact that norms do not provide instructions for *specific situations* is ideal, because that is what makes them flexibly applicable to whatever comes up. The 'specific' thing is precisely how, in accounts and descriptions, for actual instances, participants bring actions under the auspices of norms and rules. The flexibility permitted by the generality of rules and norms is just what is required for talk to perform its rhetorical, interactional, accountability-oriented business. The observation that generally held norms cannot explain *individual differences* in behaviour is granted by the fact that this is not the psychological status of norms, to 'cause' or 'explain' behaviour of any kind, even when that behaviour is classed as conventional. The notions that *norms conflict* with each other, and that people do not always act in *accordance* with them, are also features that make them discursively useful. Conflicting norms are the very stuff of rhetoric, permitting justifications and counter-justifications, permitting norms to be flexibly applied. As we noted when contrasting 'accounts' with 'hypotheses', contradiction is not a problem, but, rather, a valuable resource (Billig, Condor, Edwards, Gane, Middleton, and Radley, 1988). And from the same participants' resource perspective, the notion that some set of actions does or does not conform to a norm is precisely the thing at issue in their talk. That is how norms work; they are used in making such judgments.

We began this chapter with a notion of how convenient it might be if there was a one-to-one mapping between language, mind, and reality, or between rules and the actions they govern. Everything would work beautifully; actions would be coherent and orderly, descriptions would be definitive and accurate, explanations would be correct, and knowledge would be assured. But things are not like that, and it is time to count it not as a nuisance or inconvenience for psychological theorizing, but as a blessing. As we noted with the relation between norms and actions, it is precisely the general applicability of norms, their lack of precision with regard to specific occasions, their contradictory qualities and to-be-applied character, that provide the bases on which people use them. The same principle applies to descriptions, or language–mind–world relationships. The useful thing about them is how fuzzy, overlapping, indeterminate, and contradictory they are. Far from getting in the way of clear thinking, those are the foundations of our capacity to describe anything at all, to agree and disagree, to decide on what is best and true, and to perform all manner of rhetorical and interactional business in talk and text. The analytic focus, if any of this is to be taken seriously, has to shift from idealized or invented items of language and logic, tailored to fit factors-and-variables causal or representational models, to the study of discourse practices as natural phenomena.

Overview of the book

The chapters that follow develop a discourse-based perspective on language and cognition. Chapters 1 to 5 are foundational. As well as discussing specific topics, they set up the general analytic perspective that is used in subsequent chapters. Chapters 2 and 3 take up the discussion started here of how mind–world relations are discursively constituted and traded off against each other, in both everyday and scientific discourse, including academic psychology.

Chapter 2 ('Cognitivism and Cognition') deals with cognitivism, which is currently psychology's dominant theoretical and methodological perspective. Whereas *cognition* is a possible topic for investigation, *cognitivism* is a perspective that reduces all of psychological life, including discourse and social interaction, to the workings of cognitive, or even computational, mental processes. We explore how cognitivism inherited its aim, of specifying mechanical input–output processes, from the stimulus–response behaviourism that it sought to replace with the 'information processing' metaphor of mind. Chapter 2 also discusses how the focus on individual minds, rather than on cultural or discursive practices, was a consequence of that same inheritance, together with philosophical assumptions that encouraged a reduction of cognition and language to individual, and even innate, mental structures. The basic cognitivist position that we start with a given, external world, which is then perceived and processed, and *then put into words*, is addressed, undermined, and inverted in this and subsequent chapters. The categories and functions of 'mind' are reworked throughout the book as discourse categories that are coined and deployed in and for the business that talk and texts perform.

It is the business of discourse to formulate and deal with the nature of the world outside and the world within: with reality and mind, and the relations between them. Whereas Chapter 2 introduces cognition as a discourse topic, Chapter 3 ('Discourse and Reality') deals with how notions of an external world that is independent of what we think of it is sustained through discourse practices. Rather than discussing generalized and vacuous notions such as whether 'reality' exists, the focus is on how specific versions of the world are put into place, undermined, and defended. As in Chapter 2, which discusses not only cognition but also the cognition-defining practices of cognitive psychology, Chapter 3 focuses on studies of science as a reality-defining social practice. This entails a discussion of some of the principal features of the sociology of scientific knowledge (SSK), such as impartiality and symmetry, methodological relativism, ethnographies of laboratory practices, splitting and inversion, externalization, and the study of scientific discourse and rhetoric.

Chapter 3 also touches on ethnomethodology, social constructionism, and ethnography. The connection between these and SSK is a general concern with the ways in which both everyday and technical descriptions deal with the real world as something that gets defined in contrast to the workings of mind and human interests. We are concerned with the central importance of *description*, and with fact-versus-subjectivity as a discursively managed participants' concern, rather than as something that discourse analysis itself has to resolve. This in turn sets up later discussions, in Chapters 4 and 5, of discourse as a domain of social action. In these and subsequent chapters, mind and world are *at issue* in discourse, rather than discourse being an expression of mind or a reflection of the world.

Chapters 4 and 5 develop the notion, introduced in this first chapter, of an action performative, rather than 'communication model', of talk. Chapter 4 ('Talk as Action') focuses on conversation analysis (CA), which is the empirical study of how everyday (and any other) talk performs social actions. The outline of CA is tailored to this book's major concern with discourse and cognition. CA is defined as a non-cognitivist approach to discourse which makes problematical any approach that treats it as the expression and communication of speakers' intentions. Rather, mind and world (intentional states, and talk's topics) are analysed as participants' concerns, as matters at issue in talk itself, and as part and parcel of talk's practical business.

A key feature of CA is its insistence on dealing with carefully transcribed samples of tape-recorded talk. The assumption, endemic in cognitive psychology, that we more or less know how people talk, such that we can blithely invent examples of it and analyse *those*, is strongly refuted. Chapter 4 discusses the importance of studying descriptions and accounts as discursively situated phenomena. This is crucial if discourse is to be analysed as the performance of social actions. It is precisely the extraction of discourse from its occasions of production that encourages and sustains the misguided cognitivist treatment of it as a product of mind, an expression of understanding or intention, or a reflection of the world. Chapter 4 also introduces the notion of 'subversion', a term used by Harvey Sacks (1992) for the way talk and other social actions are designed with regard to how they will be received and responded to.

Taking up the discussion of conversational 'intersubjectivity' in Chapter 4, Chapter 5 ('Shared Knowledge') approaches mutual understanding as something *practically managed* in talk, rather than a series of actual mental states that precede and result from it. Chapter 5 criticizes the standard psycholinguistic approach to shared knowledge as a matter of matching up speakers' and hearers' knowledge states in a process of communicating information between minds. Rather, shared knowledge is analysed as discourse's business-in-hand, such that notions of what information is 'given' or 'new' at any juncture is approachable not as a matter of actual knowledge states, but, rather, as *a way of talking*. For example, 'given' and 'new' information feature as rhetorical categories that participants use and do things with, rather than being slots for things actually known in common, or even assumed by them to be known. The chapter goes on to examine how the *packaging* of descriptions as understood, as new, and even as 'information', figures in ordinary talk, advertising copy, propaganda, and in various institutional settings where what they have said up to that point is 'formulated' by participants. Agreement and consensus are also analysed as participants' practical concerns, rather than actual states of mind that the analyst has to try to discern.

Chapter 6 ('Scripts and Dispositions') puts into effect the perspective developed in earlier chapters, with regard to a fundamental feature of discourse, cognition, and social life. This is the notion that we understand the nature of events, and take part in them, in terms of how recognizably routine or exceptional they are. A contrast is developed between cognitive 'script theory' and discursive psychology. 'Script formulations' are kinds of talk which *describe* events *as* following a routine and predictable pattern. Chapter 6 analyses how script talk works and what it does; in particular, how it 'works up' events as scripted, or as exceptional or anomalous, how it treats specific events as instances of general patterns, and how those patterns are used as bases for drawing inferences about the personality, moral character, dispositions, or mental states of the actors.

A major theme of the analysis of script formulations is the contrast between scriptedness as something that producers of descriptions attend to, work up, undermine, and use to do things, and the cognitive approach in which the scriptedness of situations and events is something people merely *notice* about them. So Chapter 6 develops a contrast introduced in Chapters 1 to 5, between the action performative nature of discourse, and the cognitivist presumption of folk as basically disinterested perceivers of the world, figuring it all out, and then expressing that sense, or understanding, in their talk. In contrast to that, the study of script formulations takes us into the realm of locally constructed, interactionally occasioned, and rhetorically potent descriptions of actions and events, in which their routine and exceptional nature is built or countered with regard to at-issue alternative descriptions, and alternative causal inferences and upshots. As Chapter 4 argues, exploring how this fine-grained discursive business is done requires close attention to transcripts and textual details.

Chapter 7 ('Emotion') picks up Chapter 6's discussion of the relations between event descriptions and imputations of actors' mental states, and focuses on the rhetorical design and use of emotion categories. As well as looking at conversational transcripts, we examine various historical and anthropological perspectives on how emotions are conceived and invoked in everyday discourse. We consider not only the distinct uses of specific emotion terms, but also the status of 'the emotions' as a superordinate and explanatory category for human life, where it is contrasted (in both lay and academic discourse) with rational thought. Again, rather than accepting and working with that distinction, it is analysed as a rhetorically potent device that participants themselves may use.

In contrast to cognitivist and universalist approaches to emotion and its semantics, a discursive approach to emotion concepts is developed. This approach explores the rich repertoire of alternative, overlapping, somewhat inconsistent, opposable, and sometimes almost but not quite synonymous descriptive terms that permit us to talk flexibly and contentiously about ourselves and each other. Emotion words are approached as conceptual resources for discourse to do the things it does, rather than for folk to express their 'theories' of human life, or their once-and-for-all views of events. Emotion categories are not expressions of individual feelings, nor is their deployment in discourse reducible to a kind of detached, cognitive sense-making. Rather, they occur inside narrative and rhetorical sequences, like script formulations do, as *ways of talking* that perform social actions on and for the occasion of their production.

Chapter 7's approach to emotion categories and metaphors, as designed for and deployed in discourse, anticipates an extended discussion, in Chapters 8 and 9, of the cognitive and discursive bases of verbal categories – that is, of word meanings. Chapter 8 ('Categories I: Language and Perception') focuses on the nature, critique, and defence of the Sapir–Whorf hypothesis (SWH). The SWH claims that language categories, which vary profoundly from culture to culture, structure our understanding of the world. The current cognitivist consensus is against it, and emphasizes how 'basic' language categories derive mainly from realistic perceptual experience, and/or rest on innate principles of mental functioning. Chapter 8 critically explores the foundations of that consensus, both conceptually, and through an examination of the classic experimental studies of colour vocabulary and perception that helped establish it.

However, rather than merely reinstating the SWH, Chapter 8 argues for a shift towards the study of situated discourse. This entails a partial reinstatement of Whorf's (1956) original concerns, which psychologists have mostly lost sight of, with language *usage*. Psychological studies of the SWH effectively side-stepped looking at what people mean by what they say, and what they do, interactionally, with words. The colour experiments became tests of possibly universal features of human perception, rather than studies that sprang from an interest in how, why, and when people ordinarily describe things. As with emotion categories, the relentless logic of the cognitivist study of colour terms eventually came full circle, and 'discovered' a set of physiologically based universals, for which descriptions in English luckily seemed more or less adequate.

Chapter 9 ('Categories II: Bodily Experience and Folk Psychology') examines how the cognitivist approach to 'basic' and 'natural' categories has been extended into a general-purpose theory of categorization and metaphor. In contrast to the SWH, a cognitive 'Lakoff–Gibbs hypothesis' is identified, which suggests that word meanings and metaphors derive from bodily experience in a more or less realistically experienced world, and from the application of 'idealized cognitive models' (ICMs) which are culturally variable, but trade on bodily experiences. This approach manages to encompass and illuminate a large variety of everyday expressions and metaphors. But their sheer variety and specific nature are also significant, and point to their rhetorical and discursive usefulness. Verbal categories and metaphors do not merely exist and operate as convenient coding schemes for classifying our experiences and then talking about them, but, like emotion words, they serve as marvellously various and contrasting ways of talking and doing things with words.

Chapter 9 also develops a theme started in Chapters 2 and 3, and then picked up in 7 and 8, which is the danger of taking scientific descriptions as if they were non-descriptive, or indicative of a world prior to language, as if science was not itself a descriptive practice. As with colours and emotions, the Lakoff–Gibbs 'experiential realism' approach to meanings and metaphors starts from what science tells us the real world is like, and uses that as a 'pre-conceptual' bedrock for ordinary language. Not only are there various flaws in this approach, but it also says nothing about how and why a specific way of saying something is chosen, and does something, on the occasions it is used. The pursuit of cognitive idealizations misses a crucial, action-performative basis for the very existence of descriptions and metaphors as *ways of talking*, and therefore misses a crucial feature of their psychology.

A discursive approach to verbal categories, that they are designed for situated deployment, is explored through analysing samples of discourse of interpersonal violence; through a critical discussion of various efforts to extract a theoretical 'folk psychology' from how people talk; and through a discussion of the uses of proverbs and idioms. I argue that the practice of collecting, inventing, or remembering sets of decontextualized exemplars (lists of words, expressions, metaphors, etc.) reinforces a broader tendency to treat language in that way, as conceptual categories divorced from occasions of use. It is a practice that reinforces rather than resolves the deep problematics of cognitivism, in particular those that arise through approaching discourse as 'language', as 'mental representation', and as 'communication'. Discourse is not adequately conceived as a matter of coding experience and transmitting messages between minds.

Chapter 10 ('Narrative: Stories and Rememberings') develops a theme that is implicit in earlier chapters: the nature and uses of narratives, or stories. 'Narrative psychology' is allied to discursive psychology in its focus on talk and text, and it contributes a rich exploration of the relevance of fictional texts to the study of factual discourse, and to studying how people make sense of their lives. However, it tends to deal in *ideal types* of stories and story structures, derived largely from traditions of literary analysis of set-piece written texts such as diaries, novels, and autobiographies, or from theoretical dichotomies such as Bruner's (1986) narrative versus paradigmatic modes of thinking. The pursuit and use of literary genres and structures, linked to notions of narrative as a kind of universal mode of human understanding, tends to obscure the specific, action-performative nature of conversational story-telling. In some respects narrative psychology retains a cognitivist, person-centred notion of story-telling as a kind of detached sense-making, as psychological studies of 'autobiographical memory' more obviously do, rather than as a mode of situated social action.

Most studies of everyday narratives extract them from the occasions of their telling, or play down the importance of those occasions and performances by collecting stories via research interviews, or in the form of written autobiographies. Research practices of that kind tend to reinforce the literary, set-piece, 'sense-making' conception of narrative, as a form of understanding and reflection on life, rather than as a way of doing something in the telling. Chapter 10 discusses factuality, authenticity, accuracy and distortion, memory and confabulation as discursively managed concerns. The narrative–paradigmatic distinction is reviewed, and linked to the discussion in earlier chapters of how a philosophical, idealized notion of 'science' is pervasively used in psychological theory. The contrast between cognitive and discursive approaches to narratives is further illustrated (with links back to Chapters 4 to 6 on conversation, intersubjectivity, and script formulations) by a discussion of Harvey Sacks's (1992) work on 'second stories'. These are occasions on which, when a story is told, a recipient produces a second one that relates to it in some way.

Chapter 10 also defines three ways of approaching narratives that are applicable to discourse of almost any kind, and relevant to the rest of the book. The first approach (type 1) treats discourse as pictures of events, as a route to *what the talk is about*; this is the kind of thing ostensibly involved in obtaining witnesses' testimony, confessions, oral histories, ethnographic reports, and everyday event reporting. Type 2 treats discourse as pictures of mind, an 'expression' of how people *see and understand* things, which may also be considered a kind of distortion of type 1, a subjective veil that we have to get through in order to retrieve 'what actually happened'. Much of narrative psychology treats discourse in this type 2 fashion, as how people 'understand' things, as do some kinds of ethnography, counselling practice and theory, and much of developmental and cognitive psychology. Type 3 is the discursive approach, which treats discourse as *doing* something, as performing actions in and on the occasions of its production, as rhetorically oriented, and where the topics of types 1 and 2 (world and mind) are *at stake*. The discursive approach treats discourse as the primary domain, where world and mind are at issue.

Chapter 11 ('Membership: Children, Animals, and Machines') again deals with something that has remained implicit in previous chapters. When we analyse the discourse of competent cultural participants or 'members', we take for granted being a member, and how we get to be one. The membership, or 'socialization', issue is raised for extreme cases, 'marginal' members such as animals, human infants (discussed in Chapter 2), and computers. The discussion is designed to have broader relevance not only to language and thinking, but to issues such as animal rights, human rights, social categories, race, gender, children's rights, and so on, as matters of everyday common sense and its analysis. The approach taken here builds on the earlier discussions of the status of scientific knowledge (SSK); of discourse as fact-constructive, rhetorical, and action-oriented (CA); and of social–discursive actions as designed in a public fashion so that people can (learn to) see how to take part in them (ethnomethodology).

Chapter 11 does not attempt to define or resolve where 'membership' boundaries should properly fall, but, rather, discusses the ways in which such discussions and practices are conducted. The conceptual categories that are used in those boundary-maintaining procedures include notions such as imitation, anthropomorphism, intentionality, performance versus competence, and various kinds of rule-following. These are discussed alongside the familiar 'Mirror to Man' trope that has been used to justify various programmes of work on apes' capacities to learn human language, and in work on artificial intelligence (AI). Efforts to decide membership of the club of bona fide human participants and language users, by defining a set of technical criteria that grant it, are themselves analysed as the social and discursive practices of counting-as and dis-counting. They are instances of this book's major topic: the nature and uses of psychological descriptions.

Notes

1. Some idea of the ambition of early AI, in this regard, can be gleaned from this apparently non-ironic statement by John McCarthy, when head of Stanford University's prestigious AI laboratory: 'The only reason we have not yet succeeded in formalising every aspect of the real world is that we have been lacking a sufficiently powerful logical calculus. I am currently working on that problem' (quoted by Joseph Weizenbaum, 1984: 201). The shortfall between such ambitions and AI's actual achievements (Dreyfus, 1992) can be attributed to the inadequate assumptions about the role of rules and descriptions in *human* affairs that continue to underpin the cognitivist tradition (Button, Coulter, Lee, and Sharrock, 1995). See also Chapters 3, 4, 6, and 11 of this volume.
2. Wittgenstein also uses traffic rules as an example: 'The regulations of traffic in the streets permits and forbids certain actions on the part of drivers and pedestrians; but it does not attempt to guide the totality of their movements by prescription' (1967: §440, cited in Button et al., 1995). Although rules may be formulated and interpreted as *covering* what people do, and even, for some occasions, as *describing* what they do, that does not mean that rules actually *generate* what people do, nor that people are *following* them. Rather, it is a matter of how actions are produced and described (accounted for) so as to bring them under the auspices of one rule or another. 'Rule-following' is a kind of account we may produce for our actions, and it is an account that has its discursive uses, such as in explaining, blaming, defending, and mitigating what we do.
3. These ideas will be taken up in later chapters. On rule-following as preferable to causation as the basis of human actions, see Harré and Secord (1972). On rule-orientation and rule relevance as participants' concerns, and as preferable to rule-following explanations, see

Heritage (1984a). On rules and their applications as a matter of rhetoric and argument, and for a further critique of the rule-following model, see Billig (1987).

4. 'How should we have to imagine a complete list of rules for the employment of a word? – What do we mean by a complete list of rules for the employment of a piece in chess? Couldn't we always construct doubtful cases, in which the normal list of rules does not decide? Think, e.g., of such a question as: how to determine who moved last, if a doubt is raised about the reliability of the players' memories?' (Wittgenstein, 1967: §440). For related discussions of this indefinitely extendible, application-contingent feature of rules for human actions, see also Collins (1990), Coulter (1991), Dreyfus (1992), Garfinkel (1967), Heritage (1984a), Mulkay (1979a), and Zimmerman (1971).

5. Quoted by Sacks (1992, vol. 1: 205) from the *New York Times*, Saturday, 29 May 1965: 'A Navy Pilot Calls Vietnam Duty Peak Of Career', by Seth King.

6. From the *New York Times*, 27 March 1964. A variety of accounts, views, and quotations on the incident were subsequently assembled and discussed by an editor of the paper, A.M. Rosenthal (1964), in the book *Thirty-Eight Witnesses*.

7. A range of possible 'internal factors' in bystander intervention have been studied experimentally, including personality, mood, and various perceptual variables. Relations and contrasts between cognitive and discursive approaches to causal *attribution* are discussed in some detail in Edwards and Potter (1993).

8. It is a deployment of metaphor, of a kind notably explored by George Lakoff (1987; see also Edwards, 1991; Lakoff and Johnson, 1980; and Chapters 7–9 of this volume). The notion of the irrational crowd, mob rule, the contagion of mass reaction, and so on, is another meeting point of common-sense knowledge and professional social science, the latter exemplified by Gustave Le Bon's (1896) classic study, *The Crowd*.

9. See also the discussions of John Dean's testimony to the Watergate Committee, in terms of what it tells us about memory and events, in Edwards and Potter (1992b) and Neisser (1981).

10. The notion that these may be pseudo-problems, generated by metaphors such as 'representation' and 'communication', is discussed by philosophers such as Harris (1981), Rorty (1980), and Wittgenstein (1958; in contrast to his earlier representational model in the *Tractatus Logico-Philosophicus*, 1922/1972).

2

Cognitivism and Cognition

Cognitivism is both more and less than the study of cognition. It is *more* in that it covers not only topics such as knowledge, reasoning, and memory, but extends to most of the rest of psychology and cultural life, including social relationships and child development, and topics such as psychopathology and the emotions. That extension, beyond the more straightforwardly 'cognitive', is accomplished by treating knowledge-based processes (or even a particular, information processing version of them) as primary, the foundation of all the rest.[1] Social psychology, for example, becomes 'social cognition', in which the central explanatory framework is people's mental representations and understandings of each other; just as the psychology of children has become predominantly the study of their 'cognitive development'. Similarly, psychopathology is approached as a matter of people's pathological *understandings*, while even the emotions stem from how we understand the world and our place in it.

But cognitivism is also *less* than the study of cognition, in that its prime focus is psychological: the rules and representations of individual minds. Any interest in knowledge as something culturally realized – in written texts and social practices, in academic disciplines, in science, myth, or common sense – is quickly referred to individual understandings, to issues such as the relations between literacy and logical reasoning, to mental creativity and problem solving, and to the superiority of cognitive science itself over the inadequacies of 'folk theories' and common sense. If cognition is topic, cognitivism is theory.

That will do for an introduction to these terms, but we should note straight away an interesting complication. The distinctions between *topic* and *theory*, and therefore between *cognition* and *cognitivism*, are not as clear-cut as I have implied, even allowing for the rather loose sense of 'theory' I am using. This is because it is the business of theory, and of academic enterprises such as cognitive psychology, to define what their topic is. It is not the case that there is a proper, definitive set of cognitive processes sitting out there in the world, or in our heads, categorially separate from emotion and social life, waiting for psychologists to find and explain them. We might argue that, if the universe is what cosmologists tell us it is (see Chapter 3), and history is what historians tell us took place, then cognition is what cognitive psychologists tell us it is. We can not simply *point it out*, therefore, that cognitivism has overextended itself, nor that it omits to deal with many culturally based topics that it ought properly to consider. Those are things that have to be argued (as do the contributors to Still and Costall, 1991), and in doing so we enter into the definitions of what cognition is, or might be. The reason that this is a point worth making here, even though it starts to appear circular, is that it calls attention to something substantial about our topic. Cognition, like any other object of academic study, is brought into being by us, as soon as we start to define its nature and scope. That suits the rest of my argument, of course, in that cognition is already, before we have got very far, clearly a cultural and discursive matter.

History and rhetoric of cognitive psychology

The notion that cognitive psychology is an academic enterprise like any other, whose business is to construct its object or topic, rather than simply and neutrally 'finding' it, leads us to consider cognitivism historically. For example, David Hamlyn argues that cognitive psychology inherited some arbitrary and inadequate features of behaviourism, which it was designed to counter and replace, precisely *because* it was designed to counter and replace it. Specifically, it inherited a notion of 'human beings and animals as a kind of box with input and output' (Hamlyn, 1990: 8). In some respects, cognitive psychology is not as distant from stimulus–response (S–R) behaviourism as its proponents made out. While it replaces non-mentalism with mentalism, it retains the mechanistic notion of mind as an input–output conversion device, where the path between input and output is traced as information flow rather than S–R connections. In the classic text *Plans and the Structure of Behavior* (Miller, Galanter, and Pribram, 1960), the cognitive perception-and-action feedback unit TOTE (Test–Operate–Test–Exit) was explicitly designed to replace the S–R reflex arc as the basis of psychological explanation. In the same way, Chomsky's (1965) 'Language Acquisition Device' (LAD), an innate mechanism that converts linguistic input (what the child hears) into linguistic competence, was formulated as an alternative to Skinner's behavioural conditioning model of language learning. Where Skinner treated mind as opaque and inaccessible to study, and focused instead on behaviour, Chomsky considered behaviour (performance, talk, etc.) as opaque and incoherent, and shifted the focus to the relative clarity of mental rules and representations.

The interesting thing here is how cognitive psychology can be understood as a *rhetorical* exercise, taking on characteristics from its historical and argumentative position, being designed from the outset to oppose and replace behaviourism. The adoption of the input–process–output model of cognition was driven not only by the available computer metaphor (with its various input and output devices mediated by a central information processor running rules-and-representations software), but by the rhetorical requirement that it could handle the kinds of perception-and-action problems that behaviourism had (according to various arguments) tried and failed to explain. That is what made the computational metaphor so powerful and inviting. It provided a model for tracing a route through the mind, in the form of information data and program-rules, from stimulus (perception) to response (action):

A key notion in the Newell–Simon [artificial intelligence/AI] scheme is the production system, in which an operation will be carried out if a certain specific condition is met [cf. the TOTE]. Programs consist of long sequences of such production systems operating on the data base. As described by the theorists, the production system is kind of a computational stimulus–response link; so long as the stimuli (or conditions) are appropriate, the response (or production) will be executed. (Gardner, 1985: 150)

In fact, AI has retained its own almost behaviourist version of input–output 'functionalism', in the form of the Turing test (see also Chapter 11 below), named after its proposer, Alan Turing (1950). This is the controversial principle that artificial intelligence is achieved when, from a given input, the output (typed responses to questions, say) of an information processing device (computer) is indistinguishable from what a human would produce, *irrespective* of whatever mental machinations might be going on inside.

Howard Gardner (1985), in his clear and thorough account of the origins and foundations of cognitive science, lists some of its defining features. These include having a level of mental representation that is independent of either culture or biology, and also the requirement that psychological models of mind should be described in terms of computational processes. He adds:

. . . the deliberate decision to de-emphasize certain factors which may be important for cognitive functioning but whose inclusion at this point would unnecessarily complicate the cognitive-scientific enterprise. These factors include the influence of affective factors or emotions, the contribution of historical and cultural factors, and the role of the background context in which particular actions or thoughts occur. (1985: 6)

According to this formulation, context, culture, and the situated activities in which cognition comes into play are *assumed*, rather than shown, not to be central to any understanding of 'mind'. They could be safely omitted from consideration while the other, internal rules-and-representations stuff was sorted out first. In being set aside for future study, after the mentalistic basics are worked out, they are construed to be a set of contextual variables, peripheral factors, or specific local content that may clothe or distort the universals of thought. Of course, this contrasts sharply with the claims of those espousing culturally based and discourse-oriented approaches to language and cognition, for whom such assumptions are fundamentally mistaken.

The computation metaphor

Consider a statement by Ulric Neisser, one of the principal producers of cognitive psychology as a theoretically coherent discipline, rather than

merely a collection of cognitive studies.[2] Neisser recalls how it was that the
computer provided such an attractive model for cognitive psychology: 'It
was because the activities of the computer itself seemed in some ways akin
to cognitive processes. Computers accept information, manipulate symbols, store items in "memory" and retrieve them again, classify inputs,
recognize patterns and so on' (1976: 5). It should not escape our notice,
however, that this is a *description* of what computers do, and that it is
couched in terms that pre-date their invention (see also Button et al., 1995,
and Chapter 11 of this volume). It might be objected, for example, that
computers do none of those things, but merely perform fast electrical
switching (another description), while we *say* that they do all those things.

Why, for example, does Neisser place only the word 'memory' inside
quotation marks? What about 'accept', 'manipulate', 'recognize', and the
rest? The description of what computers do is arguably *full* of contentious
inferences, even in the description of its simple information-swapping
tasks, let alone when claims are made for what they may 'think' or 'understand'. Once the computer is described as doing all those things, the analogy with mind is unobjectionable – because human-like performances
have already been incorporated into the description of its basic functions.
Similarly, Gardner refers to a growing awareness of computers in the
1950s, when behaviourist rejections of mind were hardly tenable 'now that
"mere" mechanical gadgets could lay claim to such [mental] processes'
(1985: 119). But again, who was 'laying claim' here? The computers themselves are grammatically credited with doing that, a rhetoric that detaches
such claims from the cognitive scientists whose claims they presumably
were.

Howard Gardner and Ulric Neisser, in the quotations I have given, are
recounting rather than endorsing those cognitivist assumptions. They tell
of the foundation of a discipline, based on assumption and the rhetoric of
what it set out to replace, as much as on the metaphor of computer hard-
ware and software. And just as behaviourism sought to colonize into its
explanatory territory much more than its immediate empirical province,
the training schedules of rats and pigeons, so cognitive studies became the
basis of cognitiv*ism*, a manifesto for all psychology, or at least for all the
hard-nosed psychology whose rules and representations would be explicit
enough to be written as computer programs. Christopher Longuet-
Higgins, with ironic modesty, suggested that:

> It is perhaps time that the title 'artificial intelligence' were replaced by something
> more modest and less provisional. . . . Might one suggest, with due deference to
> the psychological community, that 'theoretical psychology' is really the right
> heading. . . . (1981: 200)

It is not at all unusual, for disciplines that flourish, that they take on a
presumptive reality-defining role in which what once were tentative claims,
useful metaphors, and 'deliberate' assumptions become part of the ontological furniture, and may be invoked as criteria by which to reject or

'discipline' alternative perspectives (Latour, 1987; cf. Bowers, 1991, on the politics of cognitive science).

The objection to cognitive science is not that it pursues a metaphor, that it pursues a study of human nature as if we were digital computers, but that it tends to proceed as if that were not metaphorical, as if we were, actually, even self-evidently, information processing devices. But metaphors themselves are *discursive* devices, and they can be both illuminating and restrictive. Metaphors join two discourse domains together, and the effects are mutual. They illuminate, draw attention to, points of contrast and similarity, generality and exception, that might otherwise be missed. What is dangerous is when the metaphorical nature of the enterprise is forgotten, and domain A is talked about in terms of domain B, as if it were not a metaphor at all. To take another, non-computational metaphor, it has proved useful to see human actions and understandings as a kind of theatre (role play, self-presentation, the use of scenes and scripts, 'backstage' domains, and so on), just as it has proved fruitful to see life as a series of games people play. But it is just as illuminating to see theatre, games, and so on, as restricted domains of everyday life; to consider how theatre is understandable, interesting, and engaging precisely by virtue of its non-theatricality (it has to be so, for its relevance, and issues of allegory and realism are pervasive in our understandings of how it works). In the same way, by showing how science is a socially organized, discursive, and cultural pursuit, sociological studies of science can profitably turn the metaphorical tables on pervasive notions of 'Man the scientist'.[3] One of the advantages of discursive psychology is that the rhetorical use of these kinds of metaphors and analogies can be topics of reflexive study. People are not examined 'as if' they produce discourse, though none of us who uses discourse, including discourse analysts, can be free of metaphor and analogy.

Cognition, nativism, and the *Meno*

One of the strongest sub-themes in cognitive psychology, though always a controversial one, has been *nativism*, the claim that our basic cognitive processes are biologically rather than culturally provided. Language (more specifically, grammatical competence) was the first and most influential example of the (then) new cognitive nativism. Chomsky's (1959) rejection of behaviourism was a critique not merely of behavioural conditioning, but of *empiricism* in general – the notion that human capacities are acquired rather than inborn. In place of Skinner's (1957) notion of language as conditioned 'verbal behaviour', Chomsky (1965) inserted, as we have noted, an innate 'Language Acquisition Device' (LAD). This was an information processing device, equipped with knowledge of human language universals, and with mechanisms for hypothesis testing and rule induction. Its supposed task was to perform pattern recognition and rule induction procedures on linguistic 'input', looking for how the innate universals of grammar are instantiated in whatever the local language happened to be (English, Samoan, Urdu, or whatever). The categories and rules that LAD inferred had the status of *hypotheses* about the structure of the input language that could be tested and refined against further input until the child's hypotheses conformed to a particular language's category-and-rule structure, or grammar: 'This device must search through the set of possible hypotheses G1, G2, . . . , which are available to it . . . and must select grammars that are compatible with the primary linguistic data' (Chomsky, 1965: 32).

As Howard Gardner (1985) pointed out, the adoption of this individual-istic, mentalistic, computational, and culture-minimal notion of language and mind as an approach to *cognition in general*, was more a 'deliberate decision' than a conclusion forced by evidence and argument. Nativism can be understood as a consequence of pushing individualist assumptions, and the hypothesis-testing 'Man the scientist' model, as far as they will go. If culture, function, and situated usage are first removed from consideration, then the only place to look for explanations is biology. Once again it is a decision that starts to produce ontological implications, a 'what else could it be' conclusion in favour of nativism.

For example, the developmental psychologist Frank Keil promotes a view of cognitive development as *having to be* innately constrained in its organizational principles: 'Under this view, acquiring complex knowledge would be impossible, if all of us did not share certain a priori constraints that restrict the range of hypotheses to be made about the structure of what is learned' (1986: 85). Similarly, Susan Carey cites the Chomskyan linguist and philosopher Jerry Fodor to the effect that 'given a hypothesis-testing model of learning, the child cannot possibly learn something he cannot represent' (1985: 107). In Fodor's words, 'one can't learn a conceptual system richer than the conceptual system that one starts with, where learning is construed as a process of hypothesis formation and confirmation' (1975: 97). That is to say, no hypothesis, no hypothesis testing, no learning.

The question is begged, of course, not only where the hypotheses might come from, but whether the prior assumption is necessary to start with, that cognition boils down to hypothesis testing. As Carey also notes:

> Representational theories of mind presuppose hypothesis-testing theories of learning. In explaining the acquisition of any body of knowledge, one must specify the class of hypotheses the organism entertains, the evidence that is taken as relevant to decisions among the hypotheses, and evaluation metrics for that evidence. . . . If the child is not a hypothesis generator, then representational theories of mind are false, and cognitive psychology is in trouble. My argument here [is] of the this-is-all-you've-got variety . . . given basic assumptions shared by all cognitive psychology. . . . (1985: 117)

Carey does not conclude, as she might, that cognitive psychology is indeed 'in trouble'. Rather, given its consensual status in psychology, backed by a great deal of experimental work within that paradigm, and given the lack of alternatives, we have to pursue its implications all the way from situated performances (including laboratory ones) back through the mental rules and representations that generate them, and back further from there to the realm of innate ideas. A counter-argument is that there *are* alternatives to what Costall and Still (1991: 2–3) call 'the "Fodor option" where one tries to keep a reasonably straight face while presenting the absurd consequences of the scheme', and that these alternatives are to be found in ecological, discursive, and cultural approaches to cognition. But are we just being circular in saying that they come from other people? Where would *they* get them from, if not innately?[4]

The cultural–discursive argument is not that they come from other people in a transmitted, baton-relay kind of way, since that would lead us straight back to individuals and the biology of mind. Rather, we require a conception of social life that does not reduce to the mental processes of individuals. On the contrary, perhaps it takes *multiple* perspectives in order to *have* concepts and conceptual problems, to propose that an explanation is wrong, or needs justification or testing, even to provide a basis for such a notion as 'explanation'. Hypothesis formation and testing can be understood as kinds of arguments, rather than kinds of pattern recognition. The process in individuals may be as plausibly derived from the social (from the rhetoric of disagreement, potential disagreement, justification, criticism, anticipated criticism, forestalling disagreement, backing claims, etc.), as the other way round. The usual counter to this is that intelligent cognitive processes can be observed in animals and infants, which/who operate without the benefit of language and culture; I shall return to that conundrum shortly, after a trip back to Plato.

The notion of the innate origin of ideas has its own historical and textual origins (ironically enough), notably in the philosophies of Plato, Descartes, and Kant. These philosophers are the cited sources of the assumptions of cognitive science, nativist linguistics, and even the categories of Piaget's developmental epistemology (Chomsky, 1966; Gardner, 1985; Piaget, 1971). For example,

> . . . no ideas of things, in the shape in which we envisage them by thought, are presented to us by the senses. So much so that in our ideas there is nothing which was not innate in the mind. . . . (Descartes, quoted in Chomsky, 1966: 67)

Gardner traces the key assumptions to Plato's dialogue *Meno*, in which Socrates questions a slave boy on his understanding of geometry, and reveals, despite the slave's initial apparent ignorance, that he 'knew' Pythagoras's theorem already, without being taught it. According to Gardner, 'through this interchange, the philosopher [Plato/Socrates] ultimately succeeds in drawing out from the boy the knowledge . . . [etc.]' (1985: 4). He needed only to be 'reminded of it' (*anamnesis*), to have the knowledge awakened in him, brought out of him, by a process of mental 'midwifery'.[5] The dialogue is provided by Plato as a demonstration of innate knowledge. It is instructive to examine exactly what, in the dialogue, this 'drawing out' consists of. Plato wrote it in the form of a demonstration by Socrates to Meno, the slave boy's master, of how the slave, initially ignorant

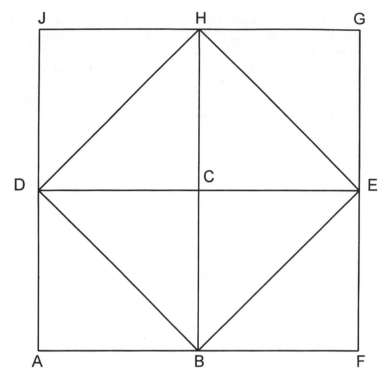

Figure 2.1   *Socrates's drawing*

of Pythagoras's theorem,[6] comes to demonstrate an understanding of it, even though Socrates merely asks a set of strategic questions, and claims to teach the boy nothing.

Socrates begins by drawing a square in the sand at his feet (Figure 2.1, the area ABCD), and establishes that the boy can calculate the square's area.

Socrates: Now if this side is two feet long, and this side the same, how many feet will the whole be? Put it this way. If it were two feet in this direction and only one in that, must not the area be two feet taken once?
Boy: Yes.
Socrates: But since it is two feet this way also, does it not become twice two feet?
Boy: Yes.
Socrates: And how many feet is twice two? Work it out and tell me.
Boy: Four.
(Guthrie, 1956: 131)

The boy's contributions to the dialogue are clearly minimal here, the first two being simple affirmations of propositions put to him by Socrates. If this were a transcript of natural dialogue, which it is not, we might guess that, before Socrates said 'put it this way . . .', the boy had probably paused, unable to answer the initial question. Indeed, several times during the complete dialogue, Socrates rephrases or breaks down the problem into simple steps, as he does here. But in doing so, he asks recognizably 'leading questions', providing the answers within his own questions, with even the restricted choice between 'yes' and 'no' cued by the form of the question – 'must not the area be . . .', 'does it not become . . .'. Furthermore, in breaking the problem down into a series of small steps, Socrates requires of the boy only that he performs small calculations; the boy's one substantive contribution is to work out that twice two is four, a calculation he could easily have made, or learned to recite, without reference to geometry. It is difficult not to read the dialogue as essentially Socrates's thought rather than the boy's, or, at best, as an interactional product rather than mere elicitation.

Socrates goes on to 'elicit' from the boy Pythagoras's theorem. I shall have to summarize much of it, but some key parts are given in the extracts below. First, he elicits from the boy the false judgment that if we double the length of the sides, to four feet, we will get a square of double the area, eight square feet. Of course, as we and Socrates already know, a square with sides of four feet is four squared – sixteen square feet, not eight. As the dialogue proceeds, Socrates builds in steps the geometrical diagram shown in Figure 2.1, having started with the simple square ABCD, moving sequentially through the alphabet as each new line is drawn. Through argument and demonstration he gains the boy's appreciation that doubling the sides of a square quadruples, rather than doubles, its area.

Socrates:	How big is it then? Won't it be four times as big?
Boy:	Of course.
Socrates:	And is four times the same as twice?
Boy:	Of course not.
Socrates:	So doubling the side has given us not a double but a fourfold figure?
Boy:	True.
Socrates:	And four times four are sixteen, are they not?
Boy:	Yes.

(Guthrie, 1956: 132–3)

Again the boy's role in the dialogue is to confirm the propositions put to him by Socrates: 'won't it be four times as big?' The sole exception is a minimal and tautological one, in which the boy is called upon to deny that 'four times' is the same as 'twice'. It is important to realize that the diagram drawn by Socrates does not simply exist for the boy as a natural object, to be learned from via untutored perceptual experience. It is constructed for him by Socrates, step by step, with the significance of each new part encapsulated in Socrates's descriptions, prompts, and questions. The diagram is itself, therefore, a significant and contextually embedded artefact, invoked by Socrates as a necessary context in terms of which his various propositions and questions make sense.

Socrates's questions reduce the boy to a state of apparent confusion. In pursuit of what the length of the *sides* must be, of a figure of eight square feet, Socrates points out that they 'must be longer than two feet but shorter than four' (Guthrie, 1956: 134). The boy suggests three feet, but is prompted to calculate that three squared gives not eight, but nine. He despairs: 'It's no use, Socrates, I just don't know' (1956: 135). Socrates proceeds to enlighten the boy by drawing more lines in the diagram and again exhorts his master, Meno, to 'notice what . . . he will *discover* by seeking the truth in company with me, though I simply ask him questions without teaching him' (1956: 135, emphasis added). Once more, 'in company with me' is a fairly minimal gloss on Socrates's role in the 'discovery'.

Socrates:	(Drawing in the diagonals.) Now does this line going from corner to corner cut each of these squares in half?
Boy:	Yes.
Socrates:	And these are four equal lines enclosing this area? (BEHD.)
Boy:	They are.
Socrates:	Now think. How big is this area?
Boy:	I don't understand.
Socrates:	Here are four squares. Has not each line cut off the inner half of each of them?
Boy:	Yes.
Socrates:	And how many such halves are there in this figure? (BEHD.)
Boy:	Four.
Socrates:	And how many in this one? (ABCD.)
Boy:	Two.
Socrates:	And what is the relation of four to two?
Boy:	Double.
Socrates:	How big is this figure then?
Boy:	Eight feet.
Socrates:	On what base?
Boy:	This one.
Socrates:	The line which goes from corner to corner of the square of four feet?
Boy:	Yes.
Socrates:	The technical name for it is 'diagonal'; so if we use that name, it is your personal opinion that the square on the diagonal of the original square is double its area.
Boy:	That is so, Socrates.

(Guthrie, 1956: 137)

Socrates goes on to conclude that, since the boy's understanding of the theorem was elicited by questions rather than directly drilled into him, 'these opinions were somewhere in him. . . . This knowledge will not come from teaching but from questioning. He will recover it for himself' (Guthrie, 1956: 138). The assumption behind the claim that Socrates was 'not teaching him anything, only asking' (1956: 132) is that questions do not carry information, that they may not inform and persuade, command and convince. Of course, this is a demonstrably false assumption, one unlikely to be made even by the pre-Socratic Sophists, the experts in rhetoric (Billig, 1987), let alone by modern scholars of pragmatics and speech acts, or of discourse comprehension. As Stephen Levinson remarks, 'questions will generally share the presuppositions of their assertive counterparts' (1983: 184). The boy's conclusions did indeed pre-exist Socrates's elicitation of them, not in the boy's innate understanding, but in Socrates's grasp of

Greek geometry, embodied in his discourse – that is to say, for the boy, they were available interactionally and culturally.

Whereas the *Meno* can be cited, as Plato presented it, as an argument for the doctrine of *innate ideas*, it is also claimed by Jerome Bruner (1986: 132) as a precursor of Vygotsky's (1934/1987) socio-cultural account of mental development. This is an account in which thought develops as an internalization of dialogue, through a process of *guided discovery*, between a child-apprentice and an older adult-expert.[7] Further, Plato's translator W.K.C. Guthrie, in a commentary, provides an *experiential learning* gloss that could have been written by a Piagetian:

> What shows him his errors, and the right answers, is not so much the questions as the diagrams themselves, and were he mathematically inclined he might, given time, draw the diagrams and deduce the truth from them, without an instructor. (1975: 255)

The same text/event clearly lends itself to multiple and conflicting readings; what is the *Meno* a document *of*? In all of the readings, including my own, the nature of experience, understanding, and events are accomplished discursively, in how they are described and narrated. Of course it may be considered unfair, or merely anachronistic, to treat the *Meno* in this way as grounds for a critique of cognitivism, even though it is claimed historically as cognitivism's precursor. The point of my analysis has been to open up some key issues in the relations between discourse and cognition, including the importance of the analyst's own discourse in constructing, through descriptions and interpretative glosses, what happened in some event, what was demonstrated, and what inferences to take. As we shall see, these themes recur in more recent work of a highly empirical and controlled nature, and not only in studies of dialogue.

Thought without language: infant cognition

When faced with claims about the importance of language in mental life, psychologists often point to counter-cases, where sophisticated cognitive processes appear to pre-exist, or exist independently of, language. The standard examples are the cognitive abilities of human infants, animals, language-impaired adults, computers, human visual–spatial reasoning, and the functions of the right-sided hemisphere of the brain. I do not propose to review all of that here (see Chapters 9 and 11 for some further discussion), but, rather, to take a couple of examples concerning infant cognition and see what a discourse-based approach might say about them. Note first, however, that discursive psychology, of the sort I am promoting here, is *not* primarily a claim concerning the importance of language in mental life, nor concerning the nature of mental representations. Its explanatory domain is not mental life, but discourse. It is an approach to how the various concepts and categories of mental life are described, invoked, and made relevant in talk and text. And that includes the things psychologists say and write, concerning the non-verbal origins of thought, for example, as well as everyday, non-specialist discourse. It is worth examining, therefore, some *studies* of 'thought without language' to see what status they may have with regard to a discursive approach to cognition.

Infant cognition was first described systematically by Jean Piaget (1952, 1954), in terms of pre-linguistic 'sensori-motor intelligence'. As a 'genetic epistemologist' it was Piaget's aim to discover the developmental origins of what he took to be the fundamental categories of (adult) human thought, and especially its highest achievements in scientific, mathematical, and logical thinking. Piaget is renowned for his counter-intuitive position, though this has become a psychological orthodoxy, that those achievements do not rest primarily upon language, but, rather, upon the coordination of actions and perceptions that begin in infancy and which continue afterwards in a staged series of reconstructions of mental organization. The roots of 'operational' thinking are in the infant's sensori-motor coordinations. In providing the foundations of logic, mathematics, and objectivity, infancy is also the period in which the basic categories of Kant's epistemology are developed, specifically those of Identity (object permanence), Space, Causality, and Time (Piaget, 1954). More recent studies of infant cognition have pushed such achievements back in developmental time, ever earlier in the child's life, and point much more to innate organizations. But the terms of reference for such studies, the agenda of what is to be found and explained in infant cognition (such as object perception, spatial organization, causality, temporal sequence, logical and mathematical categories, and the child's concept of 'mind'), have remained largely as Piaget defined them, though there has been an added emphasis on the infant's pre-verbal communicative abilities (Butterworth and Light, 1982; Tronick, 1982).

A strong feature of research on infant cognition is how it is always forward-referenced to later developments, and to adult cognition. Whatever infants can be shown to do is the development, or the first stages in the development, or first signs of, notions such as causality, a world of enduring objects, grammatical organization, 'speech act' functions, and so on. Piaget started with Kant's philosophy, with a conception of biological adaptation, and with a rather idealized picture of adult cognition. Empirical findings (what infants do) are described in such a way as to fit them to these categories, to show how they are present or absent, or present in prototypical form. This is inevitably a largely post hoc sort of enterprise. There is no suggestion that, given only what infants do, and knowledge of nothing later, it would be possible to *predict* the development of logic, mathematics, science, and such. Indeed, any such prediction would, in any case, itself be an example of those things. The entire practice of studying infant cognition rests on the notion that we know where it is going – at the very least, it requires some such 'we' to do the studies. This produces a twist to the Fodor thesis. It is not so much infants perhaps, but developmental psychologists, who must test hypotheses that they got from somewhere other than perceptual experience, even though their results are presented as 'findings', and even though there is no suggestion that Kant's or Plato's philosophy, or the history and epistemology of science, are pre-wired into *their* brains.

Some of the more recent experimental work on infant cognition has specifically addressed the notion of 'thought without language' (Weiskrantz, 1988). I shall deal briefly with two excellent examples of that work, by George Butterworth and Lesley Grover (1988), and by Alan Leslie (1988; cf. Leslie and Keeble, 1987). Butterworth and Grover provide an account of the 'origins of referential communication' that builds on earlier findings by Scaife and Bruner (1975) in which infants as young as two months, face-to-face with an adult (usually the mother), will follow the adult's line of regard when the adult looks away towards some object. A series of carefully controlled experimental studies is reported, in which conflicting available objects are eliminated from the field of view, precise angles of view are measured, and developmental progress is charted. These developments are presented as the likely origins of *linguistic reference* in which, by using words communicatively, we are able to bring the things or ideas that they refer to into joint focus as topics of conversation. The infant's behaviour is interpreted as follows:

> Since the baby adjusts the focus of visual attention contingent upon a change in the focus of attention of an adult, this would seem to suggest less than total egocentrism;[8] the baby perceives a change in another person's point of view. The observation is also important because it suggests that even the very young baby may be aware of an external, spatial objective of the mother's attention and this in turn may suggest that the infant perceives the mother's gaze as signalling the 'permanent possibility of an object' at the terminus of their joint lines of gaze. (Butterworth and Grover, 1988: 10)

Similar descriptions include how the infant's actions are performed 'to share in the focus of the mother's attention' (1988: 10), and that, at least prior to eight or nine months, 'the infant clearly takes the mother's action to signal the existence of a potentially interesting object somewhere in his own visual field' (1988: 21). The notable thing here, from a discourse-oriented perspective, is not what babies do, but what they are *described as* doing, or *counted as* doing, and, indeed, how that counted-as process is precisely what constructs the nature of their actions. Even without the intentionality implicit in descriptions such as 'to share in', there are the more explicit claims concerning such matters as 'another person's point of view', and object permanence. What are the grounds for attributing to the infant any kind of cognition, implied by the use of these words, of 'another person', and one who has a 'point of view'?

The same behaviour, of turning in response to the mother's face turning, could presumably be described as a kind of automatic servo-mechanism, as one might for a robot, or even an automatic door closer (Latour, 1988). Instead, the infant's actions are described in the same kind of as-if intentional language as we language-using adults use for our own actions.

And if they were not, then what is observed (coordinated head and eye movements, *let us say*) would have no relevance to the development of joint reference in language. The important linking work, the thing that builds the nature and pre-linguistic status of infant behaviour, is precisely these *descriptions*. There is some irony, therefore, in the notion that what we are doing is tracing the pre-linguistic nature of cognition, when this relies so heavily on the observer's descriptive practices to render it all as relevant.

There are two ways in which adult cognition, and adult language, may be 'read into' infant performances. One is the use of categories derived from philosophy and linguistics (grammar, predication, causality, speech act functions, etc.), the things the investigator is looking for or trying to trace developmentally, which are mapped onto pre-verbal actions in their various proto-forms, absences, and accomplishments (cf. Bruner, 1983; Edwards, 1973). The explanatory procedure, of course, is to invert that process, and claim for infants' actions the status of *preceding* those categories. The other way of reading-in is the more innocuous seeming, virtually inescapable use of ordinary descriptions, which are full of the intentional, agentive, mind-soaked terminology of common-sense discourse. These come into play at the crucial point at which findings are given theoretical significance, and they work irrespective of the technicalities of experimental equipment, measurements, and controls. On the contrary, the technicalities are of no interest at all (as we note also in Chapter 11) until they are made sense of in these terms, as something to do with intentionality, causality, and so on.

The status of 'technical findings' is not *prior* to their description. A sense of this can be gleaned from an exchange between Andrew Kertesz and George Butterworth at the symposium where these findings were discussed. Kertesz 'asked what duration of gaze was accepted as being directed towards a target location' (Weiskrantz, 1988: 66). Presumably the issue here is that an infant might look rather loosely off in some direction, its gaze sweeping casually past some object that the investigator has placed there, and the investigator may count this as 'looking at' the object. Butterworth's response was that this was a matter of 'inter-observer reliability', where 'in some cases the duration of gaze was very fleeting indeed, while in others it was more extended. Coding was based primarily on the direction . . . rather than on duration of gaze' (Weiskrantz, 1988: 66). Since direction and duration are presumably linked (the infant's eyes would have to get to the object, and may or may not have gone past it, over it, etc., on the way there or back), the question is not definitively answered. But in any case, the measure is given – 'inter-observer reliability', which is to say, the infant was counted as looking towards an object when a set of observers counted her as looking towards an object. My point here is not to criticize this study, nor to cast doubt on its findings, nor even on its basic conclusions. Rather, my aim is to see how it works as a piece of developmental psychology, to analyse it *as text*, examine its descriptions and interpretations, and to show what is involved in taking a piece of infant behaviour as the pre-linguistic origin of something that comes later, and comes with a label attached to it.

Alan Leslie's (1988) contribution to the same conference, on non-linguistic thought, described some rather brilliantly conceived studies of infants' perception of causality. These adapted the classic method used by Michotte (1963), who produced in adults an *illusion of causality* by showing them a filmed sequence in which a drawn object (a two-dimensional shape) appears to move toward and 'hit' another, and the other then moves, as if bumped like a billiard ball. In Leslie's experiments a variety of variables and controls were introduced, including changes in the direction of movement, and the shapes (rectangular figures) touching or not quite touching. There was also the crucial introduction of a 'delayed reaction' condition in which the second rectangle did not move immediately it was 'hit'. These variations helped gauge whether infants are susceptible to the same illusion, and whether it is indeed 'causality' that they see.

In order to test this with infants, given that they could not report verbally what they saw, a 'habituation' method was adopted. The infants first habituated to, that is, in some sense got used to and stopped attending to, a particular filmed sequence. Then, if a change introduced to that sequence managed to rekindle their 'interest', that would show that the infants could indeed perceive such a change, that in some way it called up a category in their cognitive architecture. The trick was to control and vary conditions in such a way as to specify 'causality'. Experiments with infants of twenty-seven weeks provided support for the conclusion that they did indeed possess a grasp of causality, and also for the more general claim that 'the main organizational features of the adult mind appear to be present in infancy' (Leslie, 1988: 207).

One of the features of these studies that makes Leslie's conclusion possible is that he was dealing with what, in adults, is classed as an illusion. It was possible to compare child and adult notions of 'causality' more parsimoniously than Butterworth could do with the precursors of 'referential communication' precisely because no 'actual' causality was involved. What was compared, given obvious differences of procedure and measurement, was susceptibility to a perceptual illusion. So, if we start to quibble that we have not been shown 'causality' in infants that compares with adult notions of causality, the strict comparison can be drawn with Michotte's experiments; the infants act like adults do. Of course, that strength is also a weakness. For us adults, the notion that what we see is an illusion of 'causality' can be confirmed by seeing it *ourselves*, and by *describing it* in those terms, and both those things are conflated with our *conceptions* of causality. We map the phenomenon onto common-sense notions of causation, and call it an illusion of causality, just as we might wish to distinguish such elementary perceptions from what might be called causal *explanation*.

Causal explanation is a discursive matter, in that we use it contrastively against other sorts of explanations, such as intentions, reasons, and coincidences; causality is an 'explanation' precisely because there are other kinds of explanations available. Interestingly, this availability of alternative explanations and descriptions is what makes the Michotte phenomenon an *illusion*. Further, the fact that we are able to call the Michotte phenomenon an illusion means we can also describe what 'actually' happens, on the projector screen, without resort to conceptions of causality. Of course, that in turn means that whatever the *infant* sees, and 'expects', and is 'surprised' at, or gets habituated to, can also be described without resort to conceptions of causality. Whatever the experimental conditions and variations, it is a pattern in which one kind of thing perceptively happens after another kind of thing, and we adults require Hume's philosophy and/or our common-sense linguistic practices, and conceptual contrasts, to call that 'causation'.

Infant conceptions of causality, whatever the experimental sophistication, are therefore observers' categories, examples of the descriptive practices I am calling *counts-as*. As noted with Piaget's work, Leslie's, and that of Butterworth and Grover, it involves an ineluctable procedure of post hoc description, involving the *reading-in* of linguistic, common-sense, or philosophical mental categories into infant performances – a kind of Whig history of child development. There may be good grounds for that, even unavoidable ones, just as historical objectivity is ultimately illusory (White, 1987). I am not criticizing the experiments themselves, nor suggesting that they could have been better controlled.[9] Rather, I am claiming that this is what is going on in these sorts of demonstrations of pre-linguistic cognitive abilities; that what they involve is reading-in, counting-as, or describing the non-linguistic in terms of the linguistic. In making this argument, I am opening up some room for discursive psychology, by widening its potential range of application, and suggesting that it can not easily be pushed into a corner by notions of non-linguistic or pre-linguistic intelligence.

This *attributional* character of the psychology of infant cognition is also evident from the fact that psychologists and linguists (if not the public at large) are often more reluctant to attribute the same kinds of proto-adult-human competencies to animals. This is something we shall return to in Chapter 11, because 'anthropomorphic' attributions are important and pervasive cognitive–discursive *practices*, that is to say, phenomena worthy of study, rather than merely issues of methodology and error. But it is worth noting at this point how the verbal abilities of apes that have been taught bits of human language have been dismissed on the grounds that what is called 'language' in apes, even when it is (in various claimed ways) similar to the language of children, does not properly count as language because the apes do not go on to acquire the rest. So, by the same token, what young *children* say is called 'language development' not because of its intrinsic properties but because of what comes later. In apes the same kind of thing is dismissed as merely a superficial copy, a false promise, an *illusion* of language (Brown, 1973; Chomsky, 1979; Edwards, 1994a). The notion that mental categories are attributed ones, resources for discourse practices that include everything from ordinary talk to the writing of experimental reports, brings us to the notion that this is how cognition needs to be studied, as a feature of human nature embedded in, or at least arising out of, cultural practices. One such project is named 'cultural psychology'.

Cultural psychology

The notion of 'thought without language' is a rhetorical one, cast in the form of a negation or denial. It argues against language-based explanations for cognitive achievements that can be found in pre-linguistic or non-linguistic humans or animals. I have suggested that there is much constructive, post hoc, discursive work being done in that notion of 'found in'. But there is also an inverse argument that we can apply. We should not expect the kinds of human cognition that discursive psychology deals with to be merely the same as, or reducible to, or extensions of, the perceptual achievements of animals and infants. There is a strong tradition of theory and empirical work, even in psychology (let alone sociology, anthropology, and philosophy), that asserts the novelty, in human evolution, of cultural, semiotically mediated, language-based cognition. This tradition includes the work of Wilhelm Wundt and Ivan Pavlov (the founders of experimental psychology) through Frederick Bartlett and others,[10] to the more recent social constructionists, and the thrust of it is to doubt the assumption of cognitive science (Gardner, 1985: 6) that culture and context can safely be left until later. But perhaps the major work was done by the Russian psychologist Lev Vygotsky, and his colleagues Alexander Luria and Alexei Leontiev, and this work has become a foundation for recent developments in 'cultural psychology', which include a variety of internationally organized projects and publications, and the launching of at least two new journals.[11]

I shall not attempt a systematic coverage of the Russian school of cultural psychology here, but, rather, pick out some features that bear on the relations between discourse and cognition, and between discursive and cognitive psychology. The usual point of departure for treatments of Vygotsky is a contrast with Piaget, which Vygotsky (1934/1987) himself initiated. Most of Piaget's work emphasized the non-linguistic basis of thought and reasoning, originating in the individual child's pre-linguistic actions and perceptions. In fact, the capacity to communicate effectively using language was supposedly severely hampered by 'egocentrism' (see notes 8 and 12), well into middle childhood. In contrast, Vygotsky suggested that the 'elementary' action-and-perception psychology of infancy is greatly transformed by the use of cultural tools and signs, and especially language. The development of 'inner speech' was seen as an important way of organizing perception, understanding, and voluntary action, with psychological development proceeding from the social–cultural to the individual and mental, rather than, in Piaget's[12] theory, from individual egocentrism towards social competence.

Vygotsky's conception of the role of language in mental development was part of a wide-reaching vision that linked *phylogeny* (the evolution of the human species), *history* (the development of cultural tools and sign systems, including languages, forms of literacy, mathematics, mythology, and science), *ontogeny* (psychological development), and *microgenesis* (the moment-to-moment changes of understanding when performing some task). The point at which these four 'developmental domains' (Wertsch, 1985) come together is in social interaction, when cultural learning occurs. Children's minds develop in a context of social guidance, called a 'zone of proximal development', in which the means (including language) by which social interactions are co-ordinated become the means by which the child's understandings are constructed. So, through a form of apprenticeship in cultural competence (cf. Lave, 1988; Rogoff, 1990), the social becomes mental, and language is the principal form of cultural 'mediation' through which both social interactions, and thence mental life, are organized. This is the process of guided discovery that Bruner compared to the *Meno*,[13] though clearly the pre-existence of the knowledge to be acquired can be cultural, invented historically and built into social interaction, rather than developed phylogenetically and built into our chromosomes.

The Vygotskian approach creates the possibility of a much more thoroughly social and cultural conception of mind than standard cognitivism provides. Mental contents and operations are at the same time both individual and social, forged developmentally through, and *for*, engagement in cultural life. Language, mind, and actions come to be organized on the same basic functional principles, which we might call socio-technological. Consider the implications of language as a *psychological tool* (rather than, say, a perceptual information-coding scheme for the conceptual library of our minds – see Chapters 8 and 9). The *tool* notion invokes function, usage, and construction. Like the technological parts of human cultures, language gets things done, performs actions, and can be viewed as a form of semiotic technology. It breaks the world down into its component parts and processes, as mining and metallurgy do, and puts them together again as in craft workshops and factory production, in new or imitative ways, in the form of sentences, propositions, versions.

An important feature of Vygotskian psychology is that the role of culture, in the formation of mind, is not merely that of *causal factors and variables*, nor of the 'influence' of social contexts on mental processes and contents. The relation is much more fundamental. Culture is in some sense *constitutive* of mind, and that means that standard forms of factors-and-variables cognitive experimentation, even when extended into real life contexts, are unlikely to do it justice. One of the reasons for pursuing discursive psychology is the requirement to re-conceptualize relations between language and mind, and to find alternative ways of dealing empirically with that 'constitutive' relationship.

For example, take some of the terms I have just used to define the 'socio-technological' nature of language and mind. To take seriously the idea that language 'performs actions' is to take as our object of study not 'language', in Chomsky's sense of an individual's idealized knowledge of the linguistic system, but, rather, discourse. It is in discourse, not in the dictionary, nor the grammar book, nor in the grammatical intuitions of an ideal speaker–hearer, that we find language *in use*. Similarly, the notion that *language* analyses-and-synthesizes[14] the world it describes is a shorthand for saying that *people* do that, on occasions, in talk and text – in discourse. It is a matter not of mapping the relations between semantic systems and reality, but of studying the practices of description. And this is where we require the kinds of theory and methods that have been developed in the study of rhetoric, of textual construction, of factual discourse, and conversational interaction.

Discursive and cultural psychology

Given that discursive and cultural psychology are related enterprises, a question of scope and relationship arises: why focus specifically on discourse? Why not broaden the scope to the study of cultural objects in general, to activities, history, cultural settings (not to say external reality), and the development of mind? Is discursive psychology a specific, language-focused branch of the wider field of cultural psychology; or is there a more interesting tension between them? I shall try to give a sense of why discourse can sensibly be made the prime focus of theory and investigation.

One of the justifications for such a focus is reflexive: discourse is primarily what *we* produce, we academics, researchers, and writers of books on cultural (and other) psychologies. We traffic in versions, descriptions, theories; even our pictures and diagrams require their captions and explanatory notes. Now, this sort of observation may appear both trivially obvious (though it can be disputed) and inward-looking. No sooner have we widened the psychological scope, from mental information processing to the world of cultural practices, history, and artefacts, than discursive psychology seeks to push us straight back to taking an egocentric interest in ourselves and our own works. But as anthropological writers such as Clifford Geertz (1988) have noted, and sociologists of science such as Michael Mulkay (1985) and Malcolm Ashmore (1989), and philosophers such as Richard Rorty (1980), there is no easy distinction to be had between our texts and the objects of our investigations. It is our texts, our discourses, our descriptive practices, that bring their objects into being. At least, they bring them into being as the objects of our understanding: the objects of a 'cultural psychology', for example. Part of that process, of bringing the world into being, is to assign to particular versions of it an external, prior-to-description existence (Latour and Woolgar, 1986; Potter, 1996), just as in the case of infant 'pre-linguistic' cognition. What we produce descriptively, when we do it convincingly, are versions of the world 'as it is', as if it possessed that *described* nature independently of those descriptions.

This focus on how particular versions of reality are discursively produced starts to break down the notion that reflexive concerns are merely inward-looking. This is because the world beyond the text, the world that includes cultural practices, activities, cognitive development, and mind, is precisely what texts are about. In producing the culture of cultural psychology, we understand the nature of those non-textual things through each other's writings. That is not to say that we do not also stand somewhere in the world, see things for ourselves, do field studies, think things through, and so on. But none of that becomes cultural psychology (or any other kind of human or social science) except by being publicly articulated and made relevant. But so what? What is the advantage of thinking/writing of it this way? How does it make a difference to what we do?

One thing it does (and I claim this as an advantage) is to encourage the notion that we are doing something similar to what the folk we study are doing. That is to say, rather than sitting outside of cultures and minds looking in, we are engaged in the same kind of thing they are doing, a form of cultural production of how the world is, and what people are like. This means that our own terms of reference, by which we describe and account for cultural-psychological phenomena, are themselves cultural productions. Take, for example, Vygotsky's domains of human development (phylogeny, history, ontology, microgenesis: Wertsch, 1985). These are, in the first instance, discursive categories; we coin and encounter them in the pages of cultural psychology. They are cultural psychology's terms of reference, and they may have correlates in other, including everyday, discourses. That being so, we can ask what they do, how they categorize things, what kinds of explanatory work they perform, and how they figure as categories produced by and in cultural practices.

For example, Michael Cole (1994: 38) inserts a fifth developmental domain, 'physical time', or 'the history of the universe that long precedes the appearance of life on earth', prior to phylogeny and history and human development. From a discourse perspective, this is the insertion prior to human practices of a *product* of those practices, a conception of an out-there, linear-time cosmic universe. The elision between reality and its description is nicely encapsulated in the twin senses of 'history' of the universe – either what happened, or some version of what happened. Similarly, cultural history, as the broader context of human development, is, from a discourse perspective, equivalent to the textual products of historiography and cultural anthropology. *In this sense* discourse is prior to, or constitutive of, the world it describes. So the relevance of a discourse-based perspective can be broadened to include all of the categorial distinctions of cultural psychology itself.

This is somewhat different from seeing things the other way round. If we start with the developmental domain categories, then discourse takes its place roughly as follows. In microgenetic time, people converse, read, and write. In ontogenetic time, they learn to do so. In historical time, languages and forms of literacy are invented with their various functions. In phylogenetic time, humans evolve a capacity for language. In cosmic time, well, there is no discourse before phylogeny and history get to work (as factual realities, that is, rather than as academic disciplines). What the discourse-based perspective does is not to deny any of that, but to recognize it all as cultural product.

The same kinds of arguments can be made for other examples of 'terms of reference': natural versus artificial, human versus non-human, and so on (see Edwards, 1994a; and Edwards, Ashmore, and Potter, 1995, for some discussion of these categories). Clearly the status of such distinctions is not taken for granted in cultural psychology, but, rather, it is the work of cultural psychologists and anthropologists that has made these sorts of distinctions productive and interesting. But what I want to pursue are some consequences of keeping them in focus as discourse categories rather than things in the world. Once we include the sciences as cultural–discursive practices, as surely we must, then what humans produce is not merely the artificial (while the natural is there already, beyond us), but that very distinction; and we produce also the nature of the natural. 'Nature' itself is science's product, just as the distinction between nature and culture is a dichotomy used within a range of cultural practices, including how we categorize, theorize, account for, and bring up our children, how we keep pets and zoos and wildernesses, conduct inter-ethnic relations, and worry about ecology and the food we eat.

This argument, that cultural psychology is in important ways the same kind of thing as cultural life in general, brings into focus a familiar kind of etic–emic[15] quandary for the discipline. If both cultural psychologists and *jpfs* ('just plain folks' – a descriptive category used ironically by Jean Lave, 1988) are engaged in discursive constructions of social and physical reality, then what should be the relation between those two realms of discourse? That is to say, how should cultural psychological accounts of human practices use, relate to, draw on, dispute, choose amongst (or whatever), the kinds of accounts that cultural participants themselves produce, as part of living their lives? It is a problem that might concern any branch of the human and social sciences, of course, but it arises much more obviously for cultural and discursive psychologists (cf. Clifford, 1988; Gilbert and Mulkay, 1984) than for traditional cognitive and experimental psychology – and, again, that can be taken as an encouraging sign. It is also the point at which these possibly arcane-looking issues of discourse, reflexivity, and ontology start to have substantial consequences for method and empirical work.

Discursive psychology offers a perspective and methodology for dealing with many of the topics that cultural psychology is also interested in, but there are differences in theory and method concerning how we conceive of relations between language, cognition, and reality. It may be useful to draw a crude distinction between two senses of 'social construction': *ontological* and *epistemic*. In much of cultural psychology, mind is 'socially constructed' ontologically, in the same sense as, for Piaget, it is constructed through the internalization of actions. In other words, mind is real for the theorist and analyst, and the analytic task is to explain how it is built within a real world of cultural settings and practices. In discursive psychology, the major sense of 'social construction' is epistemic; it is about the constructive nature of *descriptions*, rather than of the entities that (according to descriptions) exist beyond them.

Epistemic constructionism is the more radical kind, especially as it rebounds reflexively on itself; if texts constructively describe their objects, then so do the texts that say so (Ashmore, 1989). In prioritizing discourse, discursive psychology is almost inevitably more relativistic (Edwards et al., 1995; Shotter, 1993a, 1993b). Mind and reality are treated analytically as discourse's topics and business, the stuff the talk is about, and the analytic task is to examine how participants *descriptively* construct them. In treating cognitive categories as discursive ones, this locates the study of cognition as a matter that participants deal with and make relevant in discursive practices.

Where discursive and cultural psychology come together is in the recognition given to the primacy of public signs (discourse, symbolic mediation, etc.), and their social practicality, rather than abstracted mental models, or models of mental processes. In discursive psychology, as in cultural psychology, we recognize that culture should not be treated merely as a causal variable. But the same principle is extended to not treating 'mind' as a dependent one. We reject a product-and-process psychology of mental development, where mind is viewed as an objective developmental outcome. In its place is a discursive–constructive notion of mind as a range of participants' categories and ways of talking, deployed in descriptions and accounts of human conduct. Mind figures as a counts-as, described-as, kind of category (in all its glorious, overlapping, inconsistent sub-categories and oppositions), where the analytic interest is in how people assign and use those categories in and for social practices. Another advantage of the discursive approach is that it focuses us squarely onto cultural practices, rather than back to cognitive psychological notions of mind. Mind figures as a cultural construction in the discursive, described-as sense, rather than as an entity constructed like houses and other physical artefacts.

Given half a chance, one might suspect, relativistic discourse analysts (and epistemic constructionists generally) might want also to treat houses (ontology, external reality) and their physical construction as counts-as, described-as categories, and of course that is quite correct (Edwards et al., 1995; Woolgar, 1988a). The next couple of chapters are addressed to how this can be, that it makes sense to treat mind and reality as descriptive categories, or, as discourse and conversation analysts might say, participants' concerns. This will require a further foray into social constructionism, and a brief look at social studies of science, and will take us deeper, of course, into discursive psychology.

Notes

1. The influential textbook *Human Information Processing* by Peter Lindsay and Donald Norman (1972), for example, had as its sub-title *An Introduction to Psychology*. The notion

that psychological topics are reducible to information processing may become so institutionally dominant as to appear self-evident: e.g., Mahzarin Banaji (1992: 448) in a discussion on memory – 'What else can it be?'

2. Neisser's (1967) *Cognitive Psychology* was hugely influential in articulating the scope, nature, and sense of purpose of the new discipline, though in his later work Neisser has been at the forefront of criticism, promoting ecologically situated alternatives to cognitive psychology's narrow focus on information processing and computational modelling (e.g., Neisser, 1976, 1982).

3. The 'Man the scientist' metaphor is typically male, or male-posing-as-neutral. On psychology in general as a metaphorical pursuit, see Soyland (1994). Game and theatre metaphors are especially common in social and personality psychology and in micro-sociology (e.g., Berne, 1968; Goffman, 1959; Harré, 1979), while 'Man the scientist' is an explicit feature of George Kelly's (1955) personal construct theory, and of Fritz Heider's (1958) attribution theory (a well-established form of 'social cognition'), as well as of other cognition-based notions of human functioning. For a discursive–rhetorical treatment of the limitations of game and theatre metaphors, see Billig (1987). Social studies of science are briefly examined in Chapter 3.

4. In a sustained critique of cognitivism's philosophical assumptions, Button et al. unpick a variety of conceptual confusions that stem from the presumption that our 'minds' are full of propositions, hypotheses, and amateurish theories – 'a series of formulae for the truth conditions of word applications, as though one could conceive of human beings as creatures who did . . . precious little else, as not leading . . . an active life' (1995: 104).

5. This is Plato's term for it in his *Thaetetus*, the 'maieutic' method. Note that the words 'concept', 'conception', and 'conceive' have the same root, in images of becoming pregnant, so that minds can give birth to meanings latent within, given certain kinds of experience and Socratic dialogic midwifery. A fuller analysis of the dialogue, on which I have drawn heavily here, is provided as Chapter 3 of Billig et al. (1988).

6. Pythagoras's theorem is the one that states that the square on the hypotenuse of a right-angled triangle is equal to the sum of the squares on the other two sides – but then you knew that already, of course, without being taught, and needed only to be reminded, both now and when you first heard it!

7. It is ironic that this dialogue, extracting agreement from a compliant slave, has been taken not only to demonstrate the innate cognition hypothesis, but also as a basis for modern, liberal, child-centred education.

8. 'Egocentrism' is the term Piaget (1926, and subsequently) used for a currently unpopular claim that children up to the age of about seven years, or at least until well after acquiring the basics of language, remain ignorant of the fact that other people see and know different things than they themselves do, and, correspondingly, that they themselves actually have a 'point of view' at all.

9. In fact, I have selected what I judge to be exemplary studies. Further, the investigators themselves are often aware of the danger in the kind of explanatory mapping process that is involved in moving between infant capacities and the categories of adult cognition, though this is usually treated as an unfortunate technical problem, rather than a phenomenon that may itself be just as interesting as the one under investigation: 'perhaps all we can do is establish developmental pathways and make arguments about the genesis of language in terms of *family resemblances* between behaviors organized at different levels' (Butterworth, discussion in Weiskrantz 1988: 68, emphasis added).

10. I am referring here to Wilhelm Wundt's (1900–20) 10-volume *Volkerpsychologie*, and to Ivan Pavlov's (1941) notion of a 'second signalling system' based on language and conventional signs, which could override the workings of the stimulus–response reflexes and behavioural conditioning for which he is better known. Bartlett is cited as a founder of cognitive psychology (Neisser, 1967), though again this underplays his insistence on the socio-cultural bases of mental processes: see also Edwards and Middleton (1987) and Shotter (1990).

11. See, for examples, Bruner (1990); D'Andrade (1981); Holland and Quinn (1987); LCHC

(1983); Stigler, Shweder, and Herdt (1990); Wertsch (1991); and the journals *Culture and Psychology* and *Mind, Culture and Activity*.

12. Piaget's notion of infantile 'autism' and childhood 'egocentrism' were developments of a Freudian conception of persons as in the first place individuals, solipsistic and irrational, and only secondarily objective and socialized.

13. This can be compared to Vygotsky's own formulation of mental development, in which 'instruction is good only when it proceeds ahead of development. Then it *awakens and rouses to life* an entire set of functions which are in the stage of maturing, which lie in the zone of proximal development' (Vygotsky, cited in Wertsch, 1985: 71, emphasis added).

14. For a concise statement of this idea, applied to a comparison of human language with the linguistic achievements of apes, see Bronowski and Bellugi, for whom language 'expresses in miniature a deeper human capacity for analysing and manipulating the environment in the mind' (1980: 112).

15. This is a distinction introduced by Kenneth Pike (1954), derived from the linguistic categories 'phonetic' and 'phonemic'. An 'etic' approach attempts to describe cultural objects and activities in generalized, objective terms applicable to any culture. An 'emic' approach describes cultural practices in terms internal to that culture, and in relation to other parts of the culture rather than to generalized, cross-cultural criteria. These are idealized, though useful, distinctions.

3

Discourse and Reality

The real world of objects and events can be approached in what I have called a 'counts as' fashion – that is, as a discourse topic or concern. In defining the nature of mind–world or subject–object relations, factual reality is the obverse of mind. It is the thing known, the criterion of what counts as knowledge, as objectivity or subjectivity. The way we define knowledge's adequacy, and distinguish between categories such as knowledge or belief, perception or illusion, memory or confabulation, is by appealing to what is real. Making that kind of appeal is a feature both of professional psychology and of ordinary common sense. Of course, we can treat *the appeal itself* as an interesting activity, and this is the stance taken by 'constructionist' approaches to mind and reality. The real world is what counts as the real world, and this is a product or feature of, rather than something prior to, descriptive practices.

In this chapter I take a rather hurried look at a range of counts-as practices for defining objective reality: in science, social science, and common-sense reasoning. The interest of this topic, in a book on discourse and cognition, lies in how those practices involve *managing subjectivity*. The ways in which we produce definitive and specific versions of the world require that we also take account of, set aside, or otherwise control for the potentially subjective workings of cognition, perception, personality, and other biasing categories and vagaries of human interest. This is the case whatever reality-defining social apparatus we are dealing with; whether everyday stories and descriptions, or the workings of law courts, or the laboratory procedures and reporting practices of experimental psychology.

Social constructionism, as Kenneth Gergen (1985) has remarked, comes in many guises. Perhaps, of all the '-isms', it is the one that should. But is it one constructionism in many guises, or a variety of quite different constructionisms, or merely old issues dressed up in new jargon, or even new issues scholarly interpreted as old ones? In fact, this is begging the question. Social constructionism is all about that kind of issue, of how descriptions map onto, carve up, bring into being, or categorize and explain the things they describe. Of course, the objects of those descriptions are not usually (reflexively) 'social constructionism' itself, but the rest of the physical, social, and mental worlds. And now we have another set of distinctions – 'physical', 'social', and 'mental'. Are *these* categories distinct, inter-related, causally connected, arbitrary, necessary, or pre-descriptively real?

I shall offer, as a basic feature of the various social constructionisms, the assumption that knowledge and reality, those two sides of the epistemic coin, are provided and guaranteed not by a reality or 'nature' that exists independently of how we come to know it; nor by processes of knowing that are contained within the perceptual–cognitive apparatuses of individual minds or persons. Rather, knowledge and reality are cultural categories, elements of discourse, invented, used, and defended within social practices. Outside of philosophical discussions, but also very frequently within them, the topics of such discourse are not usually gross abstractions such as 'knowledge' and 'reality', but specific versions of the world, and specific claims about persons' mental processes and dispositions. Indeed, this is where a constructionist position starts to look less ridiculous. It is not a matter of denying, or of supporting, vacuous notions such as 'reality exists', but, rather, a matter of treating all efforts to specify it, all *actual descriptions or versions* of reality, as particular, discursive, socially occasioned productions. Even the gross generalizations are things that might be said or written at some juncture, performing, perhaps, some kind of generalizing work on whatever local matters are at issue.

Before allying social constructionism very closely with relativism, a further distinction must be made. It is the one with which we ended the previous chapter: some varieties of constructionism are more relativist than others. We can place them on a continuum. At the more realist end, various ontological limits or bottom-line criteria are introduced, which operate as constraints on the social invention of understandings. People may socially construct their understandings, but it remains possible (at this more realist end of the constructionist continuum) to say whether they get it right or not. Such ontological criteria may include the brute, undeniable reality of rocks and furniture, or the things that science's objective procedures tell us, and/or the macro social contexts of institutions and power relations within which any discourse takes place.[1] At the more relativist end of the continuum, saying whether they get it right or not can only ever be a matter of comparing one set of social constructions with a preferred alternative set. There are no ontological guarantees, no non-epistemic, non-social, non-constructionist ways of underwriting knowledge claims, no prospect of obtaining an irrefutable, just-so, non-descriptive description of reality, though every prospect of examining how and when, and as parts of what social practices, such appeals are made!

This chapter deals briefly with a set of reality-fixing practices, amongst the favourites available in Western cultures. These are the descriptive and explanatory practices of *science*, of *mundane common sense*, and those of observational descriptions or *ethnography* as used in the social sciences. These are huge topics in their own right, of course. The aim here is to sketch some of their features in a way that can be brought to bear upon the relations between discourse and cognition. The method is to treat science, common sense, and observational descriptions not as routes to the nature of phenomena (which of course, as practical enterprises, they *are*), but as themselves phenomena whose practical workings can be examined. The most fruitful ways of approaching them, as empirically available social practices, have been ethnomethodology, and what is called SSK (sociology of scientific knowledge).[2]

SSK: science as social construction

In the 1970s a loosely connected series of studies (for example, Barnes, 1977; Bloor, 1976; Collins, 1974; Latour and Woolgar, 1979, 1986; Mulkay, 1979b) began to emerge which treated scientific *knowledge* as something within the scope of social studies. This became known as the sociology of scientific knowledge (SSK). Until this time, social studies of science had been restricted to studies of the social organization of science, its institutions and practitioners, its historical development, and the shaping of its priorities and consequences.[3] But scientific knowledge itself had been left to the scientists themselves to resolve, and to philosophers to provide idealized (rather than empirical) descriptions of how science works. Science was left to take care of its own epistemology. Given that geology, say, was the discipline that told us about how rocks were formed, there was no need for sociologists, anthropologists, or psychologists to provide social or psychological accounts of geological knowledge.

So scientific knowledge itself was set aside, as beyond the scope of social or psychological investigation, leaving only scientific error available for social or psychological explanations (Bloor, 1976; see Lynch, 1993, for a useful discussion of these developments). The trouble with that was the way it compromised the entire enterprise of science studies. Social scientists interested in science were dependent upon whatever the current scientific consensus happened to be, before they knew what they were permitted to explain; and not only is scientific consensus a moving target, subject to revision, but it is itself likely to be a matter of dispute at any time, and indeed a consequence of the very kinds of social processes they wanted to study. They wanted to study the processes of science in-the-making (Latour, 1987), not just provide post hoc studies that depended on accepting what ought properly to be the very business under scrutiny. Those 'objects' should include scientists' accounts and descriptions of what they thought, knew, and did; and the nature and formation of scientific consensus itself (Gilbert and Mulkay, 1984; Mulkay, 1981).

David Bloor (1976) provided a widely influential definition of SSK, in the form of the four linked elements of a 'strong programme' for social studies of science: *causality, impartiality, symmetry*, and *reflexivity*. These four elements were considered necessary if social studies of science were to have any chance of a purchase upon scientific *knowledge*, rather than focusing only on more obviously 'social' themes such as institutional organizations, funding policies, and the personalities, biases, allegiances, commitments, and career moves of scientists.

Causality is the notion that scientific beliefs (and not only erroneous ones) are a function of social conditions, rather than an automatic product of the formal canons of scientific method. Indeed, the canons of scientific method themselves become available for study as discourse, in terms of how and when they are invoked.[4] *Impartiality* is the principle that social studies of science have to take a neutral stance on scientific truth and error, treating these as topics for study, rather than adopting a current scientific consensus on fact or correctness, and using that as a basis for defining the range of errors that are then amenable to 'social' kinds of explanations. Impartiality is the principle that brings 'scientific knowledge' within the reach of social studies. *Symmetry* states that the same kinds of explanation are to be provided for all knowledge claims, whether or not (some) scientists count them as valid or erroneous. So, extending the notion of impartiality, symmetry insists that we should not have, for example, a set of 'social' explanations for scientific errors, in contrast to a reserved set of 'scientific' canons that explain scientific facts. This principle is essential in ensuring that social studies of science do not merely reproduce the very phenomenon under investigation, which is the production of scientific knowledge. *Reflexivity* is the principle that whatever SSK finds to say about science ought to be applicable to social studies, and to SSK itself. Varieties of SSK can be distinguished according to how far they treat reflexivity as applicable-in-principle but not to be seriously pursued, or else as the basis for a serious (or indeed light-hearted), self-referential research programme (Ashmore, 1989; Woolgar, 1988b; see also Collins and Yearley, 1992).

So, the principles of impartiality and symmetry require that, in order to study how scientific knowledge is produced, we should not take a current scientific consensus and read back from that. Instead, we have to study 'science in action' (Latour, 1987), or science in-the-making, as if we did not know, or trust, the outcome. This is not to deny the validity of any particular scientific claim. Rather, it is a *methodological* precept for studying such claims, a feature of what Harry Collins (1982) calls 'methodological relativism', and of Bruno Latour's 'third rule of method' for SSK: 'we can never use the outcome – Nature – to explain how and why a controversy has been settled' (1987: 99). Current states of scientific knowledge are the *outcomes* or accomplishments of the processes under study, and are, in principle and in practice, open to further change. Using (current) outcomes as criteria for how knowledge got that way would be to adopt, rather than study, one of the features of (some) scientific discourse, which is to explain accepted findings and popular theories as being the way they are because they reflect the way the world is.

In Steve Woolgar's (1988a) version of SSK, the way the world is (ontology) must be equated with the way we understand the world to be (epistemology). The way the world is can therefore be studied as science's *product*, even though particular versions of the world may feature, in scientific discourse, as science's prior condition; nature rather than claim, science's 'discovery' rather than its 'construction'. So in SSK, 'discovery' becomes available as a discourse category, as a knowledge claim, and the analytic interest is in how 'findings' get to be categorized as such, as discoveries, rather than as errors, artefacts, glitches, or as phenomena of no importance (Brannigan, 1981; Lynch, 1985). Such practices involve 'externalization' (Woolgar, 1988a), which is the range of descriptive and explanatory devices that place 'out there' in the world, as objects prior to discovery, the accomplished-as-such objects of discovery, and the outcomes of argument.[5]

Latour and Woolgar (1979, 1986), in their influential study of laboratory practices in a biochemistry institute, invented the useful terms 'splitting' and 'inversion' to describe features of this process of externalization. Rather than having to live with the notion that SSK is uncomfortably inverting something rather obvious, which is that the nature of the universe precedes its scientific description, Latour and Woolgar disarmingly suggest that it is scientists themselves who perform the inversion. The argument runs roughly as follows.

What scientists possess is a series of observational 'documents' such as recordings, printouts, various machine-produced 'inscriptions', marks on paper, records on tape or film, and so on. Scientists' work involves the production and collection of such laboratory 'documents', and also the crucial work by which these are found interesting, and get counted as the documents *of* whatever out-there objects they 'represent'. The process called *splitting* is the separation of such documents from their objects, such that the objects are given an existence independent of whatever documentary evidence, and accounting practices, it took to establish their 'nature'. The notion of *inversion* places that independent existence prior to the discovery procedures that produced it, that is, prior to its documentary evidence. Woolgar (1988a: 68) characterizes splitting and inversion thus:

(1) document
(2) document → object
(3) document   object [independent existence]
(4) document ← object
(5) deny (or forget about) stages 1–3

A major achievement of this process is the removal of the scientist, as agent, from any active constructional work: science becomes a reflection of reality, 'as if observers merely stumble upon a pre-existing scene' (1988a: 69). The familiar use of passive voice, and the impersonal style of experimental reports, are among the devices that serve to delete human agency and productive practices from scientific facts, this being a pervasive feature of scientific rhetoric, and basic to the nature of the scientific enterprise, that of establishing 'the ontological robustness of the object itself' (1988a: 69).

This production of 'ontological robustness' is clearly a two-sided business. In constructing an object's 'out-there-ness' it has to be split from, and placed prior to, whatever human practices were involved in its identification, and which threaten, should they become the focus of attention, to relativize, or display as constructed, any such object. Those human practices include cognitive processes such as perceptual impressions, biases, descriptions, arguments, expectations, and such. Laboratory procedures and report-writing conventions can be understood as ways of controlling or eliminating those things. Data processing and recording equipment provide ways of mechanizing observations and inferences. Expectations are policed into hypotheses, and the potential for bias through expectancy effects is reversed (in *theories of* science, at least) into concerted efforts to falsify expectations rather than support them. In written reports, the author/experimenter's thoughts, expectations, and activities appear only as hypotheses and 'procedure', shorn of personality, motive, and subjectivity. The effort to

> place the source of action in the . . . method . . . provides the basic epistemologi-cal assumption; by use of the same method different observers must reach the same conclusions. . . . The author . . . means to persuade, but only by presenting an external world to the audience and allowing that external reality to do the persuading. Thus the language must be emptied of feeling and emotion. The tone must be clinical, detached, depersonalized. (Gusfield, 1976: 20)[6]

However, none of these features of science-as-activity have to be taken at face value. Without necessarily undermining their results, they can be studied as reality-fixing, cognition-policing practices, as forms of description and persuasion, however persuasive (Yearley, 1981).

As Bruno Latour (1987) has argued, the out-there independence of science's findings, from the conditions of production of those findings, is itself a function of distance. The closer we get to those conditions of production, to when and where and how things got decided, to laboratory and textual practices, the less 'independent' those findings become. They start to become matters of dispute and consensus (that is, socially provided-for),[7] matters of definition and agreement, where even the nature and workings of apparatus (data recording and processing machinery) are *counted as* working properly (or not), as measuring what they ought to, and were designed to measure, within some permissible margin, subject to some set of operational caveats, external criteria, and so on.

Karin Knorr-Cetina (1981), in an ethnographic study of laboratory practices, also suggests that instrumentation is fundamental to scientific claims and procedures. This works in a cumulative manner, such that any particular 'result' is always the product of layers and series of prior results, where prior results become the basis for certain technological procedures attaining the status of neutral, mechanical instruments that produce findings that are, in their current uses, treated as free of human interests and judgments. Paradoxically, the more we automatically *inscribe* (in Latour's and Woolgar's terms) external reality, or behaviour, or mental processes, the more links we need to maintain to relate those representations to the phenomena they are supposed to represent, providing further opportunities for distortions and errors. Beneath the mythology of 'inscription' ma-chinery's objectivity, its function in turning the world into data, is its human manufacture and calibration, the goals and criteria built into it, the knowledge thus embodied, the essentially descriptive and description-ready nature of its output, the function it has in sorting, ignoring, and deleting the 'data' it processes, and the place it necessarily has within a social nexus of usage, interpretation, criteria of adequacy and proper functioning, error accounting, and so on. Like descriptions, machine inscriptions are deconstructible as forms of representation and social practice; *more* social rather than less (Latour, 1987). Their robustness against such deconstructive efforts can be considered no kind of rebuttal either, since 'the stability of [a] particular factual claim is precisely a reflection of the enormous amount of work which is now required to deconstruct it' (Woolgar, 1988a: 59).

Rather than using the binary categories of truth and error, fact and opinion, or subject and object, Latour and Woolgar (1986) suggest an indefinitely graded set of 'modalities' in which knowledge claims are made more or less robust:

[. . .]
X
X is a fact
I know that X
I claim that X
I believe that X
I hypothesize that X
I think that X
I guess that X
X is possible

For any factual claim, 'negative modality' is provided by working down this list (or some such list), moving from greater to lesser certainty. Moving up the list provides 'positive modality', culminating in the mere existence of X, and, eventually, in a state of unquestioned familiarity such that X need not even be formulated. What we have are degrees of robustness, or of 'externality', where the status of facts-as-such amounts to the same thing as their articulation within modalities of factual description (cf. Edwards and Potter, 1992a; Potter, 1996).

The notable thing about these modalizing descriptions is how the factuality of a claim stands in inverse proportion to the introduction of 'human factors' such as understandings, thoughts, agency, interests, and motivation. Woolgar (1988a: 70) lists the following examples of increasingly negative modality:

(1) 'The glass transition temperature for this sample is 394 degrees C.'
(2) '*Giessen claims that* the glass transition temperature for this sample is 394 degrees C.'
(3) 'Giessen claims that the glass transition temperature for this sample is 394 degrees C *because he wants it to be consistent with his previous results.*'
(4) '*It's in Giessen's interests* to suggest that the glass transition temperature for this sample is 394 degrees C.'

The successive introduction of Giessen's involvement, as an actor and claimant, and then as one with interests and motives, serves to undermine the straightforward, impersonal, and factual status of statement (1).

This descriptively constructed opposition between, on the one hand, hard facts and the impersonal procedures that produce them, and, on the other hand, the activities, mental processes, and social settings of the people who produce them, recurs as a strong feature in studies of scientists' discourse. Nigel Gilbert and Michael Mulkay (1984) did the classic 'discourse analysis' study,[8] focusing on textual documents, technical reports, and the interview statements of various groups of biochemists, including a Nobel Prize winner, who conducted work on the chemical storage of cellular energy. The important features of Gilbert and Mulkay's study, for the purposes of this chapter, are the ways in which they deal with the status of scientists' accounts of their practices and findings, and the contrasting ways in which the scientists accounted for truth and error.

One of Gilbert and Mulkay's major claims was the discovery in scientists' discourse of two contrasting and functionally different kinds of explanation. There was an *empiricist repertoire* – the kind of impersonal, method-based, and data-driven account of findings and theory choice that is provided in experimental reports. This is the realm of objectivity and discovery, the production of factual knowledge through the operation of rule-governed formal procedures. There was also a *contingent repertoire* – an appeal to personal motives and thoughts, insights and biases, social settings and commitments, a realm in which speculative guesses and intuitions can operate, and where conclusions and theory choice may give rise to, rather than follow from, the empirical work that supports them. While the empiricist repertoire was used in making factual claims and in supporting favoured theories, the contingent repertoire was useful in accounting for how and when things go wrong, particularly in rival laboratories, and with regard to discredited findings. Contingent accounts of this kind were a feature of informal settings and interview talk, rather than of published scientific papers.

Again, then, the mind–world dichotomy features here as a participants' explanatory resource. It is important to emphasize two things; first this notion of a *participants' resource*, which I introduced in Chapter 1. It is not that Gilbert and Mulkay wanted to endorse these views of scientific fact and error. What they did was to investigate how scientists themselves construct and account for those categories. It was an exercise in methodological relativism, an exercise in the social study of science, neither an endorsement nor a refutation of current views on cellular chemistry. The second thing to emphasize is the central importance of the contingent repertoire. It might be assumed that this is an informal side-show to the proper arena of scientific discourse, which is the formal report, the empiricist repertoire. What scientists also say informally, in talk, might be thought a less important, neither here nor there, non-essential domain. This is not Gilbert and Mulkay's conclusion, nor apparently the view of the scientists they talked to.

What emerges[9] is that the empiricist repertoire alone is inadequate for science *in practice*. Like cognition and reality, scientific truth and error are mutually implicative, and one of the things that has to be done in practice is resolving disagreements or contrary claims. Since proper adherence to the idealized formal canons of method should not, *according to the empiricist repertoire itself*, produce errors, then some other, contingent form of accounting is required, particularly for persistent errors and entire research programmes. Error accounts are essential to the credibility of factual accounts, and include various kinds of stubbornness, interests, rivalries, and misguided allegiances. So, despite their absence from formal reports, 'in much informal talk among scientists such things are discussed, are taken to be an essential part of science, and are depicted as influencing the course of scientific development' (Gilbert and Mulkay, 1984: 110).

Gilbert and Mulkay discuss other things such as the TWOD, the 'Truth Will Out Device', which is a discursive way of rescuing the empiricist repertoire when a scientist's own position is under threat from a contingency account. It is a way of saying that the speaker's favoured position will win 'in the end', whatever its local and temporary difficulties, and the account for that eventual winning will be the empiricist repertoire. They also analyse scientists' humour. In humorous contexts the two repertoires may be juxtaposed, as in the kinds of spoof contrasts pinned up on many a department or laboratory noticeboard:

What he wrote	*What he meant*
It has long been known that . . .	I haven't bothered to look up the reference.
Three of the samples were chosen for detailed study . . .	The results on the others didn't make sense and were ignored.
Accidentally strained during mounting . . .	Dropped on the floor.
Handled with extreme care throughout the experiment . . .	Not dropped on the floor.
Typical results are shown . . .	The best results are shown, i.e. those that fit the dogma.
Correct within an order of magnitude.	Wrong.
It is suggested that . . . it is believed that . . . it appears that . . .	I think.
It is generally believed that . . .	A couple of other guys think so too.
Fascinating work . . .	Work by a member of our group.
Of doubtful significance . . .	Work by someone else.

(Abbreviated from Gilbert and Mulkay, 1984: 176–7)

Gilbert and Mulkay note that 'the long list of phrases, the continuation dots at the end of each formal phrase, and the absence of any specific speaker, all tell us that these are not isolated, idiosyncratic turns of speech, but that they represent distinct, coherent linguistic styles. The proto-joke is textually organized as a joke about interpretative repertoires' (1984: 177). Their point is that these repertoires are not merely their own, analysts' categories, imposed on scientists' talk, but appear to be oriented to by scientists themselves, across a range of activities including informal talk, error accounting, joking, and accounting for why a favoured line of research is correct despite not yet being able to convince everybody (the TWOD).

The work on science as a discursive practice throws into relief several important principles for work on discourse and cognition. First, there is the mutually implicative relation between (constructions of) reality and (constructions of) the minds, motives, and personalities of whoever may be perceiving, understanding, or making claims about the nature of the world. That 'whoever' includes the current speaker or writer, whose version of things may require protection from doubt or discounting; the speaker's possible 'stake' or 'interest' in that version may have to be managed (Edwards and Potter, 1992a, 1993). Reality is what we have when the vagaries of mind are under control; the workings of mind become visible when set against a somehow otherwise known (or constructed) backdrop of reality.

Second, there is the status of participants' accounts as resources for discourse analytical research. Gilbert and Mulkay did not find out about science simply by going and asking scientists to tell them about it, nor by simply reading their formal reports. Variability between and within those sources required that all such accounts be treated *as phenomena*. The insight here is to convert a troublesome methodological nuisance (what do we do about the messy, inconclusive, and inconsistent nature of participants' accounts?) into the basic topic under investigation. This is a crucial move that can be applied to any study of participants' accounts, in any context across the social and human sciences. We treat accounts as objects for investigation, as activities performed somewhere, rather than as inadequate sources of information about human practices, upon which we must improve by using 'tighter' methods such as formal questionnaires, cross-checking, and sampling.

Third, there is the importance, for analysts, of referring analytical categories back to participants' practices. The task is not only to bring to light the nature of participants' accounting practices, but to make sure that whatever analytic schemas come out of that analysis, such as Gilbert and Mulkay's empiricist and contingent repertoires, are not merely higher-order abstractions that the analyst constructs, but also categories that participants themselves may also treat as meaningful. This is the value of their analysis of humour, that the discourse of the scientist-participants is not only analysable into repertoires, but that the participants also seem to orient to the existence of those repertoires, or something very like them, even though they may not call them that.

These are the main principles we might take from social studies of science, then, as foundations for a discursive psychology of cognition:

1 *Methodological relativism*. We begin with no specific assumptions about the nature of mind and reality, neither those of common-sense reasoning, nor those of psychological texts, but treat them as participants' discursive concerns. This brings both folk psychology and its formal,

academic counterpart within our analytic scope, in that we can study how each is constructed, practically and discursively, without necessarily undermining the truth-claims of either. The thing to avoid is beginning with current assumptions about reality and mind, and working back from those for our explanations.

2   *The counts-as principle.* The nature of mind and external reality can be treated analytically, not as matters for direct investigation, but, rather, as whatever participants (in everyday settings, in schools and law courts, in consulting rooms and in psychological laboratories) count them as. The focus is on participants' descriptions, accounts, stories, criteria, explanations, and so on; how these are produced, made convincing, and undermined.

3   *The mutually constitutive mind–reality relationship.* Just as claims made about objective reality require independence from the workings of human subjectivity (via externalization devices, splitting and inversion, the empiricist repertoire, etc.), so we can expect that claims about the nature of human subjectivity, the workings of mind, the schemas of perception and cognition, will require (in both lay and professional psychological discourse) the establishment of guarantees concerning what is real and independent of mental processes. The object of our pursuit will be not just a discourse of mind, therefore, but a discourse of mind-and-reality.

4   *The merits of close empirical investigation.* In Latour's and Woolgar's sense, we need to get close to the conditions of production. In any set of human practices, not only formal science, we can expect the nature of mind and reality to be more robust and unquestionable the further we remain from the practices in which they are produced or at issue. We need to investigate the details of mundane and professional discourse, in the contexts in which they occur, at home and in schools, at work, in laboratories and law courts, clinics and dinner parties.

5   *The usefulness of focusing on error accounts.* In SSK, the prime site for scientists' invocations of human agency, subjectivity, social and mental factors, is in accounts of scientific errors. We may expect the same kind of fruitfulness in error accounts in other kinds of discourse, where error is analysed as a participants' category. The topics of cognition and reality might not even arise, except that there is (potential) disagreement, an alternative or preferred view, and a requirement for discounting some such alternative. Without distortion and forgetting, there need be no psychology of perception and memory. If witnessing were always accurate and reliable, we would not need cross-examination. If our friends and enemies, spouses and partners, and everyone else in the world always saw things the same way we do, then, apart from the world being infinitely more boring, we would have no recourse to the discourses of foolishness, jealousy, insight, pathology, and delusion; perhaps no discourse and no psychology at all.

Mundane reality: common sense as discursive practice

The principles that I have derived from SSK give an arguably false impression of cohesion in that field. Even the scope of what should count as SSK is disputable. The advantage of the particular summary I have offered is that it enables me to make close links with another major foundation for discursive psychology, which is *ethnomethodology*, effectively founded by Harold Garfinkel (1967). Ethnomethodology resists easy definition, which is to say that plenty of ethnomethodologists will deny the accuracy of any such effort. With similar caution, Jeff Coulter defines it as 'a range of inquiries into the achievement, intelligibility and organization of practical social actions' (1990c: ix). A central concern is with 'practical reasoning', that is to say, with 'societal members' methodical and sanctioned ways of sustaining a recognizable and real world' (Turner, 1974b: 11). Many of the principles that have been introduced in this and earlier chapters are echoed in, or derive directly from, ethnomethodological work. Among these principles are the particular notions of norms and rules that were introduced in Chapter 1: the pursuit of participants' categories and concerns; the counts-as principle, whereby participants' resources (mundane reason, causal explanation, etc.) become analysts' phenomena; the importance of close empirical investigation of participants' practices; and a useful (but not essential) focus on errors, breaches, and the definition and management of 'problems', also viewed as participants' concerns.

Ethnomethodology has played a significant part in the origins of SSK. This includes both self-avowed ethnomethodological studies such as those of Harold Garfinkel and Michael Lynch (for example, Garfinkel, Lynch, and Livingston, 1981; Lynch, 1985, 1993), but also a much wider range of studies of laboratory practices and scientific discourse. Further, there is important ethnomethodological work that helps us move from the nature of scientific discourse into a concern with other institutional and everyday settings where mind-and-reality definitions are at stake.[10] One such arena is conversation analysis (CA), the ethnomethodologically inspired study of ordinary conversation originated by Harvey Sacks, and the major topic of Chapters 4 and 5. But non-CA ethnomethodological work is also important to discursive psychology.

SSK's adoption of methodological relativism parallels ethnomethodology's efforts to 'point to some of the ways in which the world is rendered objectively available and is maintained as such' (Heritage, 1984a: 220). As in SSK, 'reality is temporarily placed in brackets' (Heritage, 1984a: 229), and that includes not only common-sense reality, but also whatever notions of society and mental life are currently endorsed by the human and social sciences. Adopting no particular prior stance on the nature of external reality, social reality, or the nature of mind, ethnomethodology sets out to examine how such notions are constructed and deployed within social life, as participants' practical concerns. Inevitably, the practices of *academic* sociology and psychology must also fall within its purview, along with those of everyday common sense, especially given that academic studies (including the sciences) rest upon a range of fundamental and intricate common-sense procedures that, prior to SSK and ethnomethodology, remained largely unexamined.

This is what is meant by the notion of 'ethnomethodological indifference' (Garfinkel and Sacks, 1970: 63). It is not, as is often falsely supposed, an uncaring indifference towards the values, knowledge, and practical concerns of ordinary people, nor even those of social scientists. Rather, it is the crucial methodological precept that, in order to study the workings of practical common sense, or of institutions, or of social science, then it is no use starting from an acceptance of (some of) them. Ethnomethodological indifference is merely a reiteration of ethnomethodology's basic project, to study rather than presume the workings of common-sense talk and practical actions. The social and natural sciences are viewed as arenas of practical actions and sense-making that are, as such, amenable to study.

One arena in which 'indifference' (in this sense) is applied is the use, in both academic and ordinary explanations of human conduct, of appeals to physical and social settings as causal factors or contextual determinants of action. For ethnomethodology any such appeals would be relevant only as empirical phenomena, as discursive actions by participants perhaps, and therefore as topics under study, but not as explanations to be adopted by the analyst. Such a methodological indifference to well-established academic explanations leads to tensions between ethnomethodology and other approaches that may be anything but indifferent when comparisons and contrasts are discussed in the academic literature.

Heritage (1984a: 132) contrasts a traditional notion of 'context', attributed to Talcott Parsons, with Garfinkel's approach:

> *Parsons:* The situation of action is a stable object of consensual identification prior to action. Such identification is essential if normatively co-ordinated conduct is to occur. Such situational identification is essentially a transcendent product of shared substantive knowledge of 'matters of fact' known in advance.

> *Garfinkel:* The situation of action is essentially transformable. It is identifiable as the reflexive product of the organized activities of the participants. As such, it is on-goingly 'discovered', maintained, and altered as a project and product of ordinary actions. Situational constitution is essentially a 'local' and immanent product of methodic procedure rather than a result of 'pre-existing' agreement on 'matters of fact'.

Garfinkel's position is that 'situational context' is best approached as what *participants treat as* such, and make relevant to their activities *as part of* their activities. The interest is in participants' public sense-making practices. Ethnomethodology has nothing *of its own* to say about whether, or how far, participants' descriptions or assumptions are accurate with respect to the situations they may describe or take for granted.

In contrast to this ethnomethodological approach, cognitive psychology has typically taken particular specifications of the external world not only as consensual and prior to action, as in Parsons, but as *unproblematically known by the analyst*, such that the nature of that 'given' world can be placed into the Method section of reports. Conclusions about cognitive processes – their accuracy, distortions, schematic representations, cognitive and perceptual coding, etc. – are based on the analyst's knowledge of 'input', rather than studied as participants' concerns. The real world is concretely given in the experimental design, or the field 'setting', in the choice of materials, the methodological procedure (trial 1, stachistoscopic presentation, stimulus materials and their removal from view and later use as test criteria, video records in eyewitness studies, the 'original text', etc.), including also analytic scoring procedures (counting the dots, the words recalled, the instances to be counted as reasonable paraphrases, the idea units, the correspondence judged to obtain between pictures and descriptions, etc.). All of these matters are prerogatives of the analyst, part of 'method' rather than the phenomenon under study, and are as reduced, reliable, and simple as possible, and preferably automated. The ethnomethodological perspective takes a different view. It seeks to open up all such 'methods', and more interestingly the methods of ordinary talk and reasoning, as participants' concerns, and make them available for empirical study.

Whereas in cognitive psychology, individual mental representations, intentions, and meanings have conventionally been treated as more tractable than the ostensibly more complex and mysterious-sounding 'shared/social/distributed/joint cognition', ethnomethodology supports the reverse view (see also Chapter 5). What are tractable, and available for study, are the public procedures by which the mutual intelligibility of human actions is accomplished, and these public procedures *include* imputations of individual dispositions and mental states (see Chapters 6 and 7).

Garfinkel's contribution, then, is to reinforce Wittgenstein's (1958) argument that the word–world relationship is best conceived in terms of action rather than representation, unless representation is itself considered a kind of social practice. Heritage draws attention to

> a pervasive and long-standing view which treats language exclusively in terms of its representative function. Within this view, the meaning of a word is what it references, corresponds with, or 'stands for' in the real world. Within this view the function of sentences is to express propositions, preferably true ones, about the world . . . this essentially pre-Wittgensteinian view of language has remained a tacit assumption for generations of social scientists. As such, it has permeated sociological activity at all its levels – empirical, theoretical and metatheoretical. (1984a: 137)

It is also the view prevalent in cognitive psychology, including social-cognitive and developmental psychology. If we switch to an action-based approach to cognition and language, then references to mental states, and states of the world, become available for study as situated descriptions.

> Descriptions . . . are not to be regarded as disembodied commentaries on states of affairs. Rather, in the ways in which they (1) make reference to states of affairs and (2) occur in particular interactional and situational contexts, they will unavoidably be understood as actions which are chosen and *consequential*. Like other actions, descriptions are '*indexical*' and are to be understood by reference to where and

when etc. they occur. Like other actions too, descriptions are '*reflexive*' in maintaining or altering the sense of the activities and unfolding circumstances in which they occur. (Heritage, 1984a: 140, emphasis added)

This focus on *indexicality* and *reflexivity*, together with participants' orientations to their talk and actions as accountably *consequential*, are key components of ethnomethodology, and of how ethnomethodology can inform discursive psychology.

According to Garfinkel, 'the activities whereby members produce and manage settings of organized everyday affairs are identical with members' procedures for making those settings "account-able"' (1967: 1). What Garfinkel means by 'account-able' includes both the nameable or describable (by participants), and the morally sanctionable (by participants), nature of actions. Since much of ethnomethodology is encapsulated in that epigrammatic statement by Garfinkel, it is worth repeating, this time in Heritage's words: 'the intersubjective intelligibility of actions ultimately rests on a symmetry between the production of actions on the one hand and their recognition on the other . . . this symmetry of method is both assumed and achieved by the actors' (1984a: 179). This is not to say that harmonious intersubjectivity is assumed to exist mentally, or is guaranteed, or even predominant statistically across conversations. Rather, it is to say that social actions, including the actions of talking and describing, agreeing and disagreeing, are produced and oriented to by participants as recognizable and interpretable within a pervasively relevant factual and moral order. The construction and maintenance of that factual and moral order requires (and is given) continuous effort, monitoring, and repair, including participants' orientations to difference and disagreement.

Consider three classic ethnomethodological studies: Harold Garfinkel's (1963) 'breaching experiments', Lawrence Wieder's (1974) study of the 'convict code', and Melvin Pollner's (1987) study of 'reality disjunctures' in a traffic court. I shall deal briefly and selectively with them here, in terms of their relevance to the study of discourse and cognition. In all three studies, reality and mind feature as matters at stake in participants' descriptions, which is to say, as participants' resources for managing accountability.

Garfinkel: norms, breaches, and accounts

Garfinkel's breaching experiments included exercises in which his students went into public and domestic settings and acted in ways that challenged conventional understandings. For example, they would engage in ordinary conversations and insist on clarifications of everything said, or go into shops, 'select a customer, and . . . treat the customer as a clerk [assistant] while giving no recognition that the clerk was any other person than the experimenter took him to be and without giving any indication that the experimenter's treatment was anything other than perfectly reasonable and legitimate' (Garfinkel, 1963: 223). Another ploy was 'to spend fifteen minutes to an hour in their own homes acting as if they were boarders'

(1963: 226). These activities produced from the 'subjects' (victims, or whatever) a range of efforts to correct their ruptured social worlds, to restore a normally interpretable order, and/or to treat whatever occurred as something interpretable within that order.

Garfinkel's analysis focused on how the variously evoked normative rules were *constitutive of the sense* of conduct, rather than regulative of conduct. That interpretative, description-dependent, counts-as-an-instance way in which norms were applied included a range of appeals to causal explanations, rational accountability, and the dispositional and mental characteristics of the various actors, both 'subjects' and 'experimenters'. Garfinkel cited a range of cases in which family members 'vigorously sought to make the strange actions intelligible, and to restore the situation to normal appearances' (1963: 226). For example,

> Reports were filled with accounts of astonishment, bewilderment, shock, anxiety, embarrassment, and anger as well as with charges by various family members that the student was mean, inconsiderate, selfish, nasty, and impolite. Family members demanded explanations: 'What's the matter?' 'What's gotten into you?' 'Did you get fired?' 'Are you sick?' 'What are you being so superior about?' 'Are you out of your mind or are you just stupid?'. . . . A father berated his daughter for being insufficiently concerned for the welfare of others and of acting like a spoiled child. . . . (1963: 226–7)

These and other studies demonstrated the situated and flexible character of participants' definitions and moral appeals to norms, and the importantly sense-constitutive work done by normative descriptions. 'Subjects' made strenuous efforts to render whatever happened interpretable and accountable, whether as exceptions to some normative order, or as instances of one. Constituting those efforts were a series of behavioural descriptions, causal and trait attributions, and moral judgments.

The value for discursive psychology of these studies is how they begin to throw light on the ordinary and pervasive ways in which everyday descriptions and psychological attributions, viewed in the contexts of their occurrence as discourse, perform normative, reality-defining, intersubjectivity-oriented work. That work includes the invocation of a range of psychological categories whose status is not so much definitive of the persons described, nor even of the person-perceptions of the describers, but, rather, constitutive of the interpersonal actions performed in using them.[11]

Wieder: rules as participants' categories

Lawrence Wieder (1974) studied how the 'convict code' worked in a residential 'halfway house' for the rehabilitation of paroled narcotic-addict felons. The 'code' was a set of norms or rules of conduct that Wieder (1974: 145–7) sets out in the form of eight maxims:

1   Above all do not snitch (to staff)
2   Do not cop out (i.e., confess to misdemeanours)
3   Do not take advantage of other residents

4 Share what you have
5 Help other residents
6 Do not mess with other residents' interests
7 Do not trust staff – staff is heat (i.e., they have a policing/detecting function)
8 Show your loyalty to the residents (versus the staff)

In some kinds of ethnographic and social psychological work, it is seen as *the analyst's job* to come up with a set of rules of this kind, on the basis that these are the kinds of rules that participants 'follow', that govern their actions, and underlie their perceptions and understandings of events. In contexts such as the halfway house, they constitute the inmates' social psychological counter-culture. The analyst's general task is to observe activities and construct appropriate descriptions; formulate the rules that appear to govern actions; interview participants and obtain reports, sets of definitions, and rule formulations, which then have to be checked against observations, cross-referred against other members' accounts, and sifted for reliability and error, such that a definitive picture could then be given of rules, understandings, and patterns of conduct.

Wieder's study called into question that kind of analysis, by treating all participants' references to rules, to instances of rules, to exceptions, and so on, as speech events in their own right. For example, the inmates used a set of code-referenced categories for describing persons and actions, such as 'kiss ass', 'snitch', and 'sniveler':

To be called a 'kiss ass' meant that one was too close to staff. The title 'snitch' was employed to designate another as an informer. 'Sniveler' was employed to designate another resident as one who chronically complained to staff and pleaded with staff for better treatment. (Wieder, 1974: 145)

Thus patterns of deviance, and the various sanctions enforced against it, could be identified in participants' (both inmates and staff) actions and discourse. However, rather than taking these kinds of descriptions of persons and events at face value, as participants' perceptions and understandings, Wieder's ethnomethodological move was to take them as a further set of actions performed in the 'telling', and essentially no different in explanatory status from the actions they described.

One of the features of participants' descriptions, to which Wieder drew attention, was the flexibility with which any particular action or event might be described. This meant that, by describing particular actions in terms of the code, and in terms of one feature of the code rather than another, participants could *render* the action in question as an instance or breach, and thus as morally accountable. Such descriptions were therefore actively constructive of the sense of events, and consequential in the telling, rather than merely reflective of how things were, or even of how they were definitively 'seen' or 'understood'. For example, reference to some maxim in the code ('telling the code') could serve as an acceptable reason for complying with or refusing a staff member's request, such as to organize a pool tournament ('It would look like I'm kissing ass', Wieder, 1974: 155), or talking about the local market in marijuana ('It would look like I'm joining your side', 1974: 155).

The staff would also 'tell the code', and as for the inmates, it was always rhetorically and interactionally 'consequential':

> It served to relieve staff members of some of their responsibilities for motivating residents to participate in the [rehabilitation] program. It tempered staff's obligation to be knowledgeable about the affairs of residents, since they could explain their ignorance by referring to residents' unwillingness to cop out or snitch. . . . It was also consequential in justifying staff's control over residents and staff's unwillingness to trust or give responsibilities to residents. (1974: 156)

It was precisely because these sorts of accounts, descriptions, and code-tellings functioned in this way for all participants, as situated actions performing their own interactional business, that Wieder could take them neither as straightforward descriptions of events, nor as equivalent to participants' event perceptions, nor, again, as explanations that he felt able to adopt as his own, analyst's account of why people did what they did.

The code functioned as a participants' explanatory resource, and for that reason, it could not have that status for Wieder. He had to treat it as the phenomenon under study. This is also the lesson for discursive psychology. *Discourse is the object of study*, to be examined in the contexts of its occurrence *as action*, as phenomenon, and only as such can it be treated as relevant to the nature of the events described, and to the nature of event perceptions and cognitions. It is an analytic principle that can be applied to a wide range of cognitive psychology's traditional topics, such as object, person and event categorization; 'script' cognitions; memory reports; causal explanations; children's understandings of the world; and much else.

Pollner: reality disjunctures and their resolutions

Melvin Pollner (1974, 1987) drew attention to the 'mundane reasoning' practices by which people in ordinary settings, such as traffic courts (but also anywhere else), maintained the sense of a commonly shared world that exists independently of them.[12] Pollner noted that 'When mundane inquiry reaches out for the "real", it is confronted by a paradox: the real is precisely that which is independent of its "grasp", and yet it is available only through some sort of grasping' (1987: 26). Rather than dealing with that paradox philosophically, or through the study of sensory mechanisms, Pollner dealt with it as a matter that people resolve practically in the course of their everyday lives. He focused on 'reality disjunctures' (those occasions when participants produce, or are faced with, more than one version of the world), and what people did to resolve them.

The first observation was that people do indeed treat such disjunctures as needing some kind of resolution. Without resolutions, conflicting versions would threaten the 'world in common', dissolving it into mere points of view, a world that exists 'only in the thinking . . . "evidence" of the absurd and radical subjectivity of the world' (Pollner, 1974: 46). The practices of mundane reason restored a world in common, establishing and maintaining a state of affairs in which there were definitive and singular truths, from which departures were errors. Reality itself, unlike versions of it, was kept incorrigible. Summarized examples of 'the solution of mundane puzzles' in traffic courts included:

> *Puzzle*:   How could a defendant claim that he did not exceed 68 miles an hour
> and an officer claim that he did?
> *Solution*:   Faulty speedometer.
>
> *Puzzle*:   How could a defendant claim that the vehicle in front of him and not
> his camper held up traffic and an officer claim that it was the camper?
> *Solution*:   The camper blocked the officer's vision.
>
> *Puzzle*:   How could a defendant claim that [illegal] drag racing did not occur
> at a specified time and place when an officer claims that it did?
> *Solution*:   The officer was actually referring to a different time.
>
> (Pollner, 1974: 49–50)

It is important to emphasize that what Pollner was investigating here were *members' methods*; he was not adjucating on these resolutions as factual guarantees. He neither accepted nor denied the particular versions of mundane reality that they produced. To do that would be to cease analysis and take on the business of the courtroom.

Pollner analysed various discursive procedures by which mundane factual reality was routinely maintained in the face of disagreements. Heritage (1984a: 214–15) organizes them into the following psychologically relevant list:

1 *Perceptual resolutions*: people who disagree are looking at different things, or from different angles, or from different vantage points, or with different perceptual capacities, or hallucinating, or whatever.
2 *Cognitive resolutions*: different interpretations are being put upon what is perceived.
3 *Reportage resolutions*: these include story discrepancies, lies, jokes, and incomplete or distorted verbal reports.

Heritage (1984a) and also Gilbert and Mulkay (1984) note how these mundane reasoning procedures for repairing or reinstating the existence of a single, definitively knowable world echo the workings of the 'contingent repertoire' in scientists' discourse. This is one sense in which science is a formalization of, rather than a basic contrast to, ordinary reasoning. The textual insulation[13] from each other of science's twin repertoires can be understood as a way of protecting scientific knowledge from the same danger that confronts mundane reason – of reality being dissolved into mere points of view.

Heritage's organization of Pollner's disjuncture resolutions into three 'contingent' categories (perceptual, cognitive, reportage) draws attention to the implications of this kind of list for discursive psychology. There are two broad kinds of implications concerning the nature of the categories and psychology's usual ways of dealing with them. First, the categories themselves are common-sense ones, available for empirical examination as features of participants' discourse. In fact, psychological processes and representations feature as ways not only of getting reality wrong, but also of getting it right, just as they do in cognitive psychology (Neisser, 1976).

> The 'objective out there' . . . implies a 'subjective in-here.' It implies as well certain modalities through which individuals may experience reality such as 'perception' or 'observation' and modalities in which individuals turn from the real to the subjective as in 'imagination,' 'hallucination' or 'dreams'. . . . We learn to use 'belief' in conditions when the 'objective facts' are unknown or problematic and we want to indicate the tenuous character of our claim. (Pollner, 1987: 21; cf. Coulter, 1990a)

So the question arises, *do* people systematically distinguish between perception, cognition, and reporting in interesting ways? That is to say, how are categories of mind and action, perception and reality, deployed in situated talk, as ways of performing the actions done in talk? How fixed or flexible are such uses? How do people distinguish and contrast psychological categories as part of reporting and attending to accountability?

A prima facie plausibility exists for viewing such practices functionally, given the familiarity of tropes such as 'seeing is believing' and their contrasts, 'you can't judge a book by its cover'. Such issues give rise to a large range of possible investigations into 'folk psychology', into the rhetoric and situated deployment of mental and behavioural categories within everyday descriptions. We can examine how people use categories and contrasts such as knowledge and belief, cognition and emotion, memory and imagination, and all manner of finer grained categorizations – indeed, the project is to examine *whatever such categories and contrasts we find* in situated practices.

The second implication of Heritage's list is that it permits an examination of academic psychology's traditional ways of dealing with such categories, typically as common-sense categories that can be improved and replaced by careful laboratory work, and by the production of a more rigorous and consistent technical vocabulary of mental life. In discursive psychology, the relation between folk and professional psychology is that the former can become the latter's prime topic, rather than a set of false beliefs, woolly descriptions, and confused practices that need to be amended and replaced. Both of these implications, the nature and deployment of folk psychological categories (for example, the status of perceptual experience), and the contrast between discursive and traditional cognitive psychology, will be developed further in subsequent chapters. But let us examine one such case here, which is the way in which states of knowledge are defined with regard to cognitive expectations, external reality, and what any ordinary person would think or see.

Pollner's traffic court studies focus on how 'what really happened' is decided in the presence of conflicting, implausible, or deemed-impossible accounts of events. The survival of a singular, objective characterization of events is maintained against the threat of multiple versions by undermining the objective status of one or more of those versions. One way (or category of ways) of doing that is to work upon the observer/reporter's psychology; to focus on perceptual errors, subjectivity, motive, memory, lies. In the face of actual or potential doubt or hostility, the producer of a report may take the option of presenting him- or herself as an 'ordinary perceiver', where 'ordinary' implies normal, just like anyone else, nothing remarkable or especially accountable, and therefore (by virtue of mundane realism's 'world in common') as truth-telling by default.

Harvey Sacks (1984) discusses the notion of ordinariness as a concerted interactional accomplishment, which he calls 'doing being ordinary'. His analytic concern is with how, as a recurrent pattern of social life,

> it is almost everybody's business to be occupationally ordinary; that people take on the job of keeping everything utterly mundane; that no matter what happens, pretty much everybody is engaged in finding only how it is that what is going on is usual, with every effort possible. (1984: 419)

As Gail Jefferson (1984) and Robin Wooffitt (1992) have shown, this pursuit of ordinariness is a routine feature of the reporting of unusual or dubious experiences. One discursive device for the production of ordinariness in such contexts is something along the lines of 'At first I thought (mundane X), but then I realized (extraordinary Y)'. Sacks gives several examples, including how 'the initial report of the assassination of President Kennedy was of having heard backfires' (1984: 419). Such reportings indexically display the reporter as normal, as not predisposed to witnessing unusual things, indeed as predisposed to seeing the ordinary world we all see.

Jefferson's (1984) 'At first I thought . . . but then I realized . . .' formula attends to the potential incredulity that may greet the recounting of an unusual experience. The 'first impression' formulation in the description reports a more innocuous event than the reappraisal then offers. It narrates how the reporter, a normal mundane reasoner in Pollner's sense, was not looking for extraordinariness, but tried hard to see things as ordinary, but then it was no use; reality could not be denied. Once again we have a participants' orientation to the mind–world dichotomy as an *attributional* issue, with deviance and normalcy at stake. The upshot of the formulation is: I am normal, it is the world that (on this occasion) was weird. It is an assertion that works rhetorically, as an *implicit denial*, set against any doubting of the reporter's rationality or reliability as a witness. The plausibility of that doubt is raised by the reporting of an unusual experience – and, indeed, the use of the formula further indexes the speaker's cognitive normalcy, in that it displays a sensitivity to the very plausibility of that normality being doubted!

Wooffitt (1992) shows how the fine-grained detail of an account of a *paranormal* experience also routinely contains discursive work that is functionally similar to this 'at first I thought' pattern. In the following example, the speaker places the paranormal event within a normal, everyday context, in which her initial efforts were directed towards finding a rational, 'material' cause:

Extract 3.1
1   every time I walked into the sitting room, (0.3) er:m. (0.7)
2   right by the window (0.3) and the same place always

```
 3   I heard a lovely (0.3) s:ound like de↑de↓dede↑dedede ↓ dededah
 4   just a happy (.) little tu:ne (0.5)
 5   a:nd >of course< I tore apart ma window
 6   I tore apart the window frame
 7   I >did Everything< to find out what the hell's causing that
 8   cos nobody else ever heard it .hhh (0.2) >y'know< (.)
 9   there could >be ten people in the room nobody'd hear it but me<
10   (0.7) er:m: and I wanted to know what was
11   the: (.) material cause of this
```
(Wooffitt, 1992: 74, altered line breaks)
(See Appendix for transcription symbols, and for how data sources are cited)

Wooffitt draws attention to many significant details in Extract 3.1, but let us note just a few features that are particularly relevant to the present discussion.

First, there is the descriptive work done in lines 5–7 and 10–11 that displays the speaker/actor as first pursuing, with some vigour, a 'material cause' of the sounds (before eventually concluding that they were of supernatural origin). The speaker is thus a normal, rational perceiver of the world, whose initial commitment to rational explanation was defeated only by force of evidence and experience. The efforts described in this case were energetic and sustained, and by no means token – 'I tore apart the window frame I >did Everything<'. Second, the experience is described as recurrent and reliable ('every time' and 'always', lines 1–2), rather than some kind of one-off perceptual anomaly. This kind of replicated reliability of phenomena is a key feature of factual, objectifying discourse, both in everyday talk (see Chapter 6, on script formulations) and in scientific accounts. It helps fix phenomena as in-the-world rather than in-the-head (or in the eye/mind/report, using the Heritage/Pollner list).

Third, there is the appeal (lines 8–9) to what other people could or could not hear. This entails some delicate work, given that appeals to other people's contrasting stories or experiences will generally cast doubt on a report.[14] If nobody else could hear it, that may stand as evidence for the unreliability of the report, as a mishearing, a lie, or even hallucination and pathology. In fact, not only are dissenting reports quoted here, but the reporting draws specific attention to the large number of them ('*nobody* else' and 'there could be *ten people*'), and their consistency ('*ever* heard it'). So, is the speaker undermining her own claims here? In fact, Wooffitt informs us that, prior this extract, the theme being developed was the speaker's special perceptual abilities. This is a report from a professional medium, at pains to demonstrate her clairvoyance. Further, as she shortly goes on to tell, her auditory experiences were later confirmed by another medium, who informed her 'that was Da:ve a ma:n who passed over quite long time ago' (Wooffitt, 1992: 74). So this is the delicacy being done; the speaker is an otherwise perfectly normal, rational, and reliable reporter, not given to false claims or gullibility, resistant to supernatural explanations, who neverthe-less finds herself to be possessed of extraordinary psychic abilities.

Let us consider a related example, just to get a sense of the range and variety of these kinds of discourse phenomena, and this kind of analysis. It is not something restricted to special domains such as supernatural or unusual experiences, nor to specific textual formulae such as 'I was just doing X when Y'. At the time of writing (autumn 1995), there is a television advertisement for Eurotunnel, the company that operates the recently constructed tunnel under the English Channel. Eurotunnel's advertising is aimed at persuading reluctant customers to use the new service in preference to a well-established alternative, the cross-Channel car ferries. The advert includes what purports to be a 'vox pop' comment from someone who has just used the tunnel:

> . . . *having been a <u>very</u> strong sceptic before, I would now recommend it. Yes.*

What we have here is a condensed little narrative of mind, experience, and world. The prior scepticism is important, in that it sets up the recommendation as unprejudiced, based on experience, and indeed counter to prior expectations. The speaker is no spokesperson for the company, but (ostensibly) an ordinary punter, a common-sense reasoner just like the sceptical target audience. Like Wooffitt's tales of the unexpected, it narrates a world-out-there, in the face of possible doubt, and fixes it as real and dependable. It does that by constructing the reporter not only as a common-sense reasoner just like the listener, but as initially sceptical, not *disposed* to thinking such things, but forced to do so by experiential evidence.

As Wooffitt does, we follow here the principle of methodological relativism. Wooffitt neither sides with, nor debunks, the various claims to paranormal experiences that he examines, but, rather, takes them apart to see how they are assembled, and how they work. And they work essentially like many other claims to experience, false experience, and reality. That is, they are interactionally oriented and sensitive to grounds for doubt and evidence. They discursively manage, sometimes very delicately, the mind–world dichotomy, holding the one constant so that the other can vary (for example, it wasn't the torn apart window frame so we have to believe something else; it wasn't illusory so it had to be real). And they attend to the attributional issues of causation and accountability, both in the reported events and in the activity of their reporting (cf. Edwards and Potter, 1992a, 1993). The upshot of all this is the possibility of examining accounts, reports from memory, scripted action formulations (for example, 'every time I walked into the sitting room . . .'), occasioned descriptions of mental states and dispositions, categorizations and generalizations, and so on, as *discursive phenomena*, played out against consideration of the external world, and oriented to considerations of what the audience might otherwise believe or think.[15] Those various topics and concerns (stories and accounts, event descriptions, mental state descriptions, categorizations, script formulations, shared knowledge, being a bona fide 'member') are the subject matter of the rest of this book.

Ethnographic description

Social studies of science, and of mundane reason, have often been
conducted as ethnographies, in which researchers venture into the exotic, or
to-be-rendered exotic, world of the laboratory, of ordinary talk, of traffic
courts or halfway houses, and write up what they find there as reports on
cultural practices. Wieder's (1974) ethnomethodological study, while
emphasizing participants' categories and their situated uses, was nevertheless an ethnographic report, based largely on participant observation, field
notes, and interviews. The systematic use of tape recordings and transcriptions of naturally occurring conversation is of course the business of
conversation analysis,[16] which is the topic of the next chapter of this book.
The topic here is ethnographic description, which is the observer's (or
participant-observer's) account of cultural activities. Observational descriptions are the business not only of cultural anthropologists, but of all kinds of
research where characterizations are offered, however brief, of the 'research setting', or 'context', or of participants' activities.

A recurrent feature of ethnographic studies is the depiction of a local,
closed-system logic of thought and action. This applies whether the object of
study is a scientific laboratory, the workings of the convict code, or a set of
tribal beliefs. As Pollner puts it, 'in the manner of an anthropologist
approaching a strange and alien tribe we shall attempt to specify in some
detail what a person assumes when he assumes an intersubjective world'
(1974: 35). The much celebrated logic of Azande witchcraft and oracles
(Evans-Pritchard, 1937), for example, which Pollner (1974: 41–8) enlists for
his discussion of mundane reason, is recruitable also for a discussion of the
social basis of scientific reasoning (for example, Latour, 1987: 186). As
Michael Polanyi remarks, in Evans-Pritchard fashion, 'any contradiction
between a particular scientific notion and the facts of experience will be
explained by other scientific notions; there is a ready reserve of possible
scientific hypotheses available to explain any conceivable event' (1964: 292).

Given that people's descriptive practices tend to constitute and defend a
local, ordered world, and that this is a feature both of scientific writing and of
mundane reason, we can also expect it to be a feature of the ethnographies
that report on them (Atkinson, 1990). Further, we can expect it to be a
feature of my own account, here, of what ethnography, science, and
mundane reason are like. Ethnography is, as James Clifford and others have
explored it (Clifford, 1988; Clifford and Marcus, 1986), and as Clifford
Geertz (1988) has eloquently discussed, a kind of writing whose quality as
'observation' is textually produced. Just as Wooffitt's witnesses of supernatural events deployed a variety of textual devices that warranted the
observed, 'out-there' status of their descriptions, so ethnographers have to
pull off what Geertz (1988) calls 'being there'. At the risk of misrepresenting
the broad debate in textually self-conscious anthropology, and with no claim
to be providing an overview, I focus here on Geertz.[17]

One of Geertz's topics is the writings (which he admires) of E.E.

Evans-Pritchard, the ethnographer of the Azande and of the Nuer of the Sudan and east Africa. What strikes Geertz is Evans-Pritchard's talent for naturalistic description:

> . . . this sort of 'of-course' discourse . . . [is] camouflaged by a studied air of unstudiedness . . . There is the suppression of any sign of the struggle with words. Everything that is said is clearly said, confidently and without fuss. Verbally, at any rate, there are no blanks to fill in or dots to join, what you see is what you get. (Geertz, 1988: 59–61)

Geertz shows how this can be analysed as a literary style. His depiction of Evans-Pritchard's textual ethnography (and also his pictures, sketches, and diagrams) as a 'slide show' emphasizes the *graphic* element of the descriptions, 'his enormous capacity to construct visualizable representations of cultural phenomena – anthropological transparencies' (1988: 64). Moreover, it is a style which projects a view of the descriptive availability of the world, where 'nothing, no matter how singular, resists reasoned description' (1988: 61).

Such ethnography manages also to *reflexively project its own adequacy* for the description of whatever forms of exotic 'others' one might encounter: 'that the established frames of social perception, those upon which we ourselves instinctively rely, are fully adequate to whatever oddities the transparencies [Evans-Pritchard's descriptive vignettes] may turn out to picture' (1988: 64). Thus, 'on the Akobo as on the Isis, men and women are brave and cowardly, kind and cruel, reasonable and foolish, loyal and perfidious, intelligent and stupid, vivid and boring, believing and indifferent, and better the one than the other' (1988: 71). What Evans-Pritchard manages to convey, therefore, is not merely an 'of-course' or 'just-so' picture of recognizable mundane (but culture-specific) reasoners, but 'a forceful argument for the general authority of a certain [British, Oxbridge] conception of life. If it could undarken Africa, it could undarken anything' (Geertz, 1988: 70).

So, paralleling the closed-system cultures of mundane reason and science, and of Azande oracles and witchcraft, is the world inhabited by the ethnographer, itself the criterion of what is found exotic, and the foundation of ethnography's descriptive adequacy. Topicalizing it like this calls to account the self-validating capacity of any academic scheme, including the physical and cognitive sciences, experimental psychology, attribution theory, constructionism, or discourse analysis; they are seen to work by their own candle, lit by their own light.

The shift Geertz exemplifies takes him from Malinowski's classic notion of an ethnography based on direct participation and empathy, 'soaking it up and writing it down' (Geertz, 1988: 83), to examining how any such basis for doing ethnography, *as a form of writing*, enjoys credibility. Malinowski's legacy turns out to be 'not, as so often thought, a research method, "Participant Observation" (that turns out to be a wish not a method), but a literary dilemma, "Participant Description"' (Geertz, 1988: 83). Participant observation itself, not only its reporting, is questioned. Geertz represents his own ethnographic studies in Morocco, Java, and Bali, as done

> not by imagining myself someone else, a rice peasant or a tribal sheikh, and then seeing what I thought, but by searching out and analysing the symbolic forms – words, images, institutions, behaviors – in terms of which, in each place, people actually represented themselves to themselves and to one another. (1983: 58)

Geertz's textual turn raises two features that I have identified as important in relation to ethnomethodology and SSK: the focus on participants' descriptions and other symbolic activities as the prime cultural phenomena under analysis, and, consistently with that, the reflexively constitutive status of the analyst's own writings, with regard to those phenomena.

However, the case has been made most convincingly by ethnomethodologists such as Lawrence Wieder and Harvey Sacks for examining the *situated and occasioned* nature of the kinds of 'representations' to which Geertz refers. This entails examining how participants' versions occur as *parts of* practices, rather than as reflections *on* them, produced for the record, in interview, or taken as indicative of a general cultural perspective. In an early commentary on ethnographic research, Sacks remarked that

> they're studying the categories that members use, to be sure, except at this point they're not investigating their categories by attempting to find them in the activities in which they're employed. And that, of course, is what I'm attempting to do. (1992, vol. 1: 27)

Sacks's method for doing that was to collect written texts and, mainly, audio-recordings of mundane talk, and present his analyses alongside transcripts, so that 'the reader has as much information as the author, and can reproduce the analysis' (1992, vol. 1: 27). This became what is now called conversation analysis.[18]

The second feature that I have picked out of Geertz's work is textual constructionism, and its purported dangers. Concerning ourselves with how ethnographies are written, rather than with the lives described in them, may be seen as 'time wasting at best, hypochondriacal at worst . . . an unanthropological sort of thing to do. What a proper ethnographer ought properly to be doing is going out to places, coming back with information about how people live there . . .' (Geertz, 1988: 1). More severely, there is the worry that analysing ethnographic texts is destructive of having anything to say at all, as if 'concentrating our gaze on the ways in which knowledge claims are advanced undermines our capacity to take any of those claims seriously . . . [as if] exposing how the thing is done is to suggest that, like the lady sawn in half, it isn't done at all' (1988: 2). The analytic principle we have to return to here is that of *methodological relativism*; it is not a matter of denying reality, any more than of saying that Malinowski or Evans-Pritchard were or were not, in their distinct ways, splendid ethnographers.

Social constructionism and reality in psychology

Geertz's general critique of positivist social science, what he calls 'laws-and-causes social physics' (1983: 3), resonates with the broad range of social constructionist approaches in psychology, including discursive and rhetorical psychology, and ethnomethodology's and SSK's demonstrations of the social constitution of 'facts' (Potter, 1996). Undermining of the scope of causal explanation with regard to human actions, and the preference for meaningful 'action' over mechanical 'behaviour', are also basic to social constructionism in psychology (cf. Harré and Secord, 1972: 3, on 'this antiquated framework' of positivist, causes-and-factors psychology).

The action–behaviour distinction has a long pedigree, its more recent history being the forceful arguments of Ludwig Wittgenstein (1958) and Peter Winch (1958), and developments of those arguments in the domain of psychology and artificial intelligence, by Jeff Coulter (1983, 1990a), Hubert Dreyfus (1992), and Harry Collins (1990). The classic distinction is between a blink and a wink, the former being behaviour, the latter a kind of culturally meaningful action. According to Coulter, for example, blinking is a mere 'physical event, and not an action', while 'the concept of "winking" must be shared in the culture within which the conduct so identified has occurred for it to have been rationally ascribed' (1990a: 15). Note the *constitutive* role of culture here, in defining a wink *as such*: it is not merely a matter of interpretation, following and imposed upon some neutrally describable event, and not only a matter of gaining intentional control of a pre-existing bit of behaviour, but one of social semiotics.

This deep penetration of cultural meaning into psychological life, as I noted in Chapter 2, is also a feature of Vygotsky's (1934/1987) social-developmental psychology. Vygotsky's psychology is often taken to provide a theory of the individual's mental development, with individual personality and mind being the final product of social–cultural learning and internalization, a socio-cultural theory *of mind* to be set against Piaget's primarily individualistic one. But a less mentalistic preoccupation, on our parts, might take from Vygotsky, as from Frederick Bartlett (1932; cf. Edwards and Middleton, 1987), a more socially constituted, socially embedded, and discursive notion of mind-in-interaction, something more like Coulter's. It is not only that cultural activities *produce* individual psychologies, but rather that psychological categories and explanations *remain* socially embedded, and ascribed, features of social practices.

From an ethnomethodological perspective, for example, it is not that, as analysts and theorists, we should go about substituting 'action' accounts for 'behavioural' ones. The very opposition between action and behaviour may itself feature as part of cultural practices, within the linguistic–conceptual apparatus of categories and oppositions that participants use in accounting for conduct. It is the kind of distinction that figures in Erving Goffman's (1971) celebrated study of 'face-threatening' occasions such as 'remedial interchanges', when people bump into each other in the street, for example, and apologize.[19] Accident and intention, behaviour and action, are salient oppositions *inside* the accounting practices of ordinary conversation, courts of law, and all manner of discourses of pathology and morality (Jayyusi, 1993). So it is not for analysts to declare, for instance, that human cultures are full of actions, while behaviour is for the birds and bees (see also Chapter 11 on this). As Coulter remarks, opposed categories such as intentional action versus mechanical behaviour are 'phenomena of communicative praxis in their own right' (1990a: 153). Presumably what human infants have to learn is how to recognize and use these sorts of distinctions.

The use of the term 'social constructionism' in psychology is strongly associated with the related but distinct work of Kenneth Gergen, Rom Harré, and John Shotter.[20] The major domain of these reality-and-mind constructing practices is discourse: 'Social constructionism is principally concerned with elucidating the processes by which people come to describe, explain, or otherwise account for the world in which they live' (Gergen, 1985: 3–4). Similarly, Shotter declares that

> Central to the social constructionist ontology I want to outline, is the view (shared . . . with Gergen, 1985; Harré, 1983, 1990) that the primary human reality is conversational or responsively relational, that one's 'person–world' dimension of interaction or being exists within a whole mêlée of 'self–other' relationships or dimensions of interaction. (1993b: 161)

As Shotter's statement illustrates, much of this work has pursued theoretical and meta-methodological positions on selfhood and agency, where notions of 'discourse' or 'conversation' may refer not only to text and talk, but to those notions as a kind of metaphor for social life in general. Nevertheless, the thrust of social constructionist psychology has been toward an increasing emphasis on discourse, incorporating developments in rhetorical and discursive psychology, and ethnomethodology (Shotter, 1993a).

Whereas Shotter and Gergen tend toward relativism, Harré is an avowed realist: 'conversation is to be thought of as creating a social world just as causality generates a physical one' (Harré, 1983: 65). In contrast, SSK, and a more thoroughgoing, relativistic constructionism, might include 'causality' and the physical world also as social constructions, as features of the descriptive practices of science and common sense. In Shotter's apt phrase, realism boils down to the notion that we can 'know the essential nature of the world ahead of time' (1993a: 150); that is, prior to whatever practices and criteria are involved in what counts as real. Those practices are not only evidential, but argumentative, whether in the 'agonistic field' of science in-the-making (Woolgar, 1988a), or in Michael Billig's (1987: 91) notion of a more everyday realm of 'argumentative meaning'. This is the idea that, in order to understand any stretch of discourse, and especially anything that looks merely descriptive, monological, 'just so', or objective, it is necessary to consider what alternative or counter-versions are being (implicitly) denied or criticized. All discourse can be considered to be not only dialogically, but *rhetorically* organized, with regard to actual or potential alternatives.

In an earlier conception of people as 'rule-following agents', Harré's proposed social science of *ethogenics* sought to identify 'the generative "mechanisms" that give rise to behaviour' (Harré and Secord, 1972: 9). So ethogenics was close to cognitivism, in that it sought a kind of generative grammar of social action:

> It is the self-monitored following of rules and plans that we believe to be the social scientific analogue of the working of generative causal mechanisms in the processes which produce the non-random patterns studied by natural scientists. (Harré and Secord, 1972: 12)

This notion of self-monitored rule-following is retained in more recent statements: 'the essence of psychological activity is rule following' (Harré and Gillett, 1994: 120), though the process is not automatic but intentional – actors perform an action '*so that* it realizes a rule' (Harré and Gillett, 1994: 117).

Despite that ethnomethodological-looking notion of actions and rules, an important difference is that, for Harré, the *explanation* of social behaviour remains *his* business, while for ethnomethodology the task is to examine and *explicate* the bases on which social life is made recognizable and intelligible to, and by, *participants*. This may seem a rather subtle or forced distinction, but it grows in importance as we start to engage in empirical work. For example, when it comes to analysing 'accounts', there is a significant distinction to be made, between treating these as the ways participants see things, and treating them as forms of situated social action. In ethogenics, persons' accounts of their actions are the primary data:

> At the heart of the explanation of social behaviour is the identification of the meanings that underlie it. Part of the approach to discovering them involves the obtaining of *accounts* – the actor's own statements about why he performed the acts in question, what social meanings he gave to the actions of himself and others. These must be collected and analysed, often leading to the discovery of the rules that underlie the behaviour. The explanation is not complete, however, until differing accounts are negotiated and, further, put into the context of an *episode* structure. (Harré and Secord, 1972: 9, original emphasis)

In contrast, the ethnomethodological move is to treat those accounts themselves as actions that occur in and for their own sequential contexts. That is different from collecting accounts in interview, say, and checking them against the episodes they are *about*, or against the generalized structure of other similar episodes, as described by the analyst. In ethogenics the relation between accounts and episodes is that they are assumed to be produced by the same underlying mechanisms and rules. If accounts can be taken to be generated by the same principles as social actions in general, they can therefore be taken as the basis for psychologists to formulate explanations of why people do what they (say they) do. Roughly speaking, with due process of sifting and 'negotiation', you ask people and they tell you. The ethogenic psychologist's goal is to provide his/her own explanation of social behaviour, based on people's accounts; it is not to investigate account production as a social activity – that is what ethnomethodology and conversation analysts do, and in doing so provide, in my view, a sounder basis for discursive psychology.[21]

So how are *episodes* structured? Ethogenics draws a contrast between everyday life and formal ceremonies, where everyday episodes are less easily described:

> Most episodes cannot be clearly classified: they are *enigmatic*, having neither an explicit set of rules, nor produced by well-established causal mechanisms. Enigmatic episodes are explained by applying to them concepts used in the explanation of those paradigmatic episodes which themselves have clear explanations, be they formal [rule-governed] or causal. (Harré and Secord, 1972: 12, original emphasis)

This is rather like the 'leaf falling from the tree' image that was used in Chapter 1, where a controlled laboratory science of forces and resistance might hope to provide all the explanatory principles required for that complex natural event, just as laboratory experiments on animal conditioning were expected by behaviourists to provide all we need for explaining the more complex phenomena of human language and social interactions.

Unfortunately, as Harré and Gillett (1994: 34) recognize, that hope is probably forlorn; we can no longer expect to model everyday interaction on the 'clearer' pattern of rituals and ceremonies. Ethnomethodology emphasizes how the orderliness of mundane social life is a moment-by-moment concerted accomplishment. It is not the case that it is generated by rules of the sort that govern marriage ceremonies, but too mixed up or messy to see. Rather, once we see how mundane interactions work, we may start to see that formal ceremonies are more like *those*. Even in ceremonies the rules are not generative of actions (either causally *or* formally, like in grammar), but available, and *treated as relevant*, and always open to situated and alternative 'counts-as' applications and definitions.

This is all very applicable to a discursive psychology of reality and cognition. Issues of accuracy and error in descriptions and accounts, their correspondence to some actual state of affairs, can be approached as participants' business, or discursive accomplishments. We can 'bracket off' prevailing theories of reality and mind, whether those of common-sense reasoning or of cognitive science, just as SSK has done for science generally ('methodological relativism'), and Garfinkel and Sacks have done for common sense and standard sociology ('ethnomethodological indifference'). The task for discursive psychology is to investigate how notions of mind-and-reality feature in everyday and professional discourse. Of course, cognitive psychologists may choose to respond with their own indifference to the fruits of any such studies, but it is not clear that they have any principled grounds for doing so. To the extent that everyday 'representations' (descriptions, explanations, stories, accounts, etc.) are found to be systematically variable, interactionally designed, contextually occasioned, and rhetorically oriented elements of social actions, then such findings must have a bearing on what psychological theories purport to be theories *of*. The next chapter looks at conversation analysis, which is the most highly developed study of discourse-as-social-action available.

Notes

1. As Clifford Geertz puts it, 'there may be things that anybody properly put together cannot help but think – that rocks arc hard and death inevitable' (1983: 10–11). See Edwards et al. (1995) for a defence of relativist constructionism against 'death and furniture arguments', which are invocations of simple material reality such as tables and rocks (what 'can not be denied'), and of various kinds of death, violence, and suffering (what also *'should* not be denied'). Our argument is that these are themselves analysable as constructions and rhetorical devices – as 'arguments'. The notion that we can leave it to science, to macro-sociology, to common sense, or to ethnographic descriptions of 'context' to place constraints on discursive constructions is countered by the application of discursive and constructionist methods and principles to those very things.
2. Ethnomethodology and SSK will be fleshed out rather briefly in this chapter. Heritage (1984a) provides an excellent overview of the ethnomethodological perspective; see also Button (1991), Coulter (1990b), Garfinkel (1967), and Turner (1974a). SSK includes a variety of approaches; see, for example, Ashmore (1989), Bloor (1976), Collins (1985), Latour (1987), Pickering (1992), and Woolgar (1988a, 1988b). Science, common sense, and observational description are also major topics of concern in philosophical analysis, and some of that work, such as Husserl (1965), Rorty (1980), and Wittgenstein (1958), is in important ways akin to the kinds of perspectives taken in SSK and ethnomethodology.
3. I am constructing here a brief version of what has become a standard story in SSK, of its origins and justification, and its break with the older 'Mertonian' sociology of science (Merton, 1973). This story is itself worthy of analysis, for how 'SSK' has been constituted and accounted for by its members (Ashmore, 1989) 'Origin' stories arc, of course, a classic topic in cultural anthropology.
4. For example, drawing on a range of observational and textual studies of scientific practices, Lynch and Bogen conclude that 'methods accounts are written to respect proper canons of scientific reportage and not to describe what scientists actually do' (1994: 88). This echoes the discussion in Chapter 1 of the *oriented-to* nature of norms and rules, and brings scientific practices closer to ordinary ones. Similarly, Woolgar treats standard method accounts as 'a resource for the characterization and evaluation of research practice' (1988a: 49) and even suggests that 'much scientific practice proceeds in spite of the canons of scientific method rather than because of them. At least one philosopher (Feyerabend) argues that we are unlikely to produce reliable knowledge *unless* we deliberately flout the rules of science' (1988a: 12, original emphasis).
5. Bruno Latour distinguishes between a 'ready-made' perspective on science, and SSK's 'in the making' view, in terms of contrasting propositions such as: 'Nature is the cause that allowed controversies to be settled' (the ready-made view), and 'Nature will be the consequence of the settlement' (the in-the-making view) (1987: 99).
6. 'The style of non-style is itself the style of science' (Gusfield, 1976: 17). With ironically conscious style, Gusfield concludes that 'Art and Rhetoric have not been sent into perpetual exile to live outside the walls of Science and Knowledge. With or without passport, they steal back into the havens of clinical and antiseptic scholarship and operate from underground stations to lead forays into the headquarters of the enemy' (1976: 22).
7. Gusfield's notion, quoted earlier, that what methods accounts display is that 'by use of the same method different observers must reach the same conclusions' can be viewed as a form of consensus warranting, this being a general discursive practice for objectifying accounts and protecting them from doubt (Edwards and Potter, 1992b; Potter, 1996).
8. See also Mulkay (1985); Mulkay and Gilbert (1982); and the development of this variety of

discourse analysis (DA) by Potter and Wetherell (1987) into a broadly applicable approach to language and cognition in social psychology.

9. My own use of an empiricist repertoire here, for Gilbert and Mulkay's 'findings' about scientists' discourse, gives those findings positive modality. Negative modality could be introduced via a more contingent treatment, in which Gilbert and Mulkay's two repertoires are not so much emergent features of their data as, rather, idealized schemas which they make their data fit. While relativizing the two repertoires, however, such a move would also manage to bolster further the basic point concerning how any such relativizing, or modalizing, gets done discursively.

10. Such a move is not too difficult to make, given that one of SSK's claims is that science, contrary to some popular and scientific opinion, is not essentially different from other forms of socially embedded knowledge production (see, for example, Woolgar, 1988a).

11. A notable omission from Garfinkel's (1963) discussion of these findings is any interest in the status of the students' reports as, themselves, activities oriented to the students' accountability for producing the kind of work that Garfinkel required of them – nor indeed of the possibly 'strenuous' efforts required to render those occurrences descriptively, as bases for ethnomethodological insight. Although ethnomethodological studies place a strong emphasis on 'reflexivity' as an endogenous feature of participants' actions and descriptions, in that descriptions are themselves actions that constitute the sense of the activities they are part of, ethnomethodologists have mostly avoided SSK's further extension of reflexivity, which is the systematic application of one's analytical apparatus to one's own analytical and descriptive activities (Ashmore, 1989; Woolgar, 1988a). Pollner (1991) argues that this avoidance is a feature of later rather than earlier ethnomethodology, and especially of conversation analysis, and recommends the use of 'radical referential reflexivity' by ethnomethodologists towards their own research practices, where it should have the same revealing, 'unsettling' function as the breaching experiments did for ordinary life. Pollner's studies, reviewed below, have started to be cited as 'constructivist' and non-ethnomethodological (Watson, 1994).

12. Pollner's studies illustrate how ethnomethodology builds on the phenomenological work of Husserl and Schutz, whose notions of an everyday 'fact-world' or 'natural standpoint' are investigated empirically as the practical and accountable accomplishments of ordinary activities. See also Heritage (1984a).

13. Mulkay and Gilbert (1983: 179) note the operation of an 'embargo' on open use of the contingent repertoire, such as in formal scientific texts.

14. The provision and undermining of corroborating reports is a standard feature of courtroom practice, as well as of mundane talk; see Atkinson and Drew (1979) on courtroom discourse, and Edwards and Potter (1992a) on the rhetoric of 'consensus' as a factual warrant. Pomerantz (1986) also discusses the conversational rhetoric of 'extreme case formulations' of which there are several in Extract 3.1: 'every time' (line 1), 'always' (line 2), 'everything' (line 7), 'nobody' (lines 8 and 9), such devices being used notably on occasions when the factual status of a report is interactionally in doubt.

15. Wooffitt notes the significance of the fact that psychology (including parapsychology) is the major academic domain of study of the paranormal, in that the whole issue is defined as a *mind* rather than a *world* phenomenon. Cultural anthropology typically takes the same approach: it studies exotic belief systems, rather than simply reporting the exotic phenomena believed.

16. In fact, Pollner and some other ethnomethodologists are not always entirely happy about the status of CA as ethnomethodology, drawing attention to some of CA's 'positivist' tendencies, or else treating CA itself as worthy of ethnomethodological study. See, for example, Lynch and Bogen (1994), Pollner (1991), and Wieder (1988). I follow Heritage (1984a) and others in defining CA as an essentially ethnomethodological pursuit.

17. Geertz's work (e.g., 1973, 1983, 1988) is perhaps the best known, but still only part of a sophisticated body of work in cultural anthropology on the textual nature of ethnography. James Clifford's work largely analyses ethnographies themselves, as textual–cultural practices (cf. Rabinow, 1986), rather than analysing cultures, and he incorporates

perspectives and texts from literature and history. Hence he is 'often referred to as "the voice from the campus library" by scholars distinguished for their foreign travels' (Pearce and Chen, 1989: 123; cf. Rabinow, 1986: 243).

18. For a discussions of the *importance* of ethnographic assumptions and descriptions to conversation analysis and ethnomethodology, rather than ethnography being superseded by them, see Moerman (1988) and Nelson (1994).

19. Goffman's (1971) analysis is not ethnomethodological, but focuses on the 'ritual' and dramatic (face-oriented and role-enacting) elements of a set of largely idealized and invented interchanges.

20. Social constructionism, even within psychology, is a diverse body of work united mainly by its critique of mainstream psychology and its pursuit of a range of cultural and discourse-based alternatives. Typical resources that social constructionists might draw on include the traditions of hermeneutic and phenomenological philosophy; the later Wittgenstein (forms of life, language games, the rejection of mirror theories of mind); Rorty's (1980) relativistic rewriting of the philosophy of knowledge; ethnomethodology; conversation analysis; feminist and related critiques of the manipulative and alienating nature of positivistic psychology (Henriques, Hollway, Urwin, Venn, and Walkerdine, 1984; Jaggar, 1983; Parker, 1992); the various forms of SSK; Foucault's historical studies of discourse and power; and the post-structuralist philosophy, literary criticism, and cultural analysis of Roland Barthes, Jacques Derrida, and others. Varieties of constructionism can be identified by the varying weights they accord to such sources.

21. Harré (1995) clearly disagrees on this point, preferring his own more common-sense 'accounts analysis' to the 'rebarbative' language of ethnomethodology used in Edwards and Potter (1992a), such as the notion of accounts as 'occasioned' phenomena. The position I take here, in this and subsequent chapters, is that accounts (etc.) are discursive actions produced *on and for the occasions when they occur*, and that it is only by examining them as such that the social actions that they perform can be investigated.

4

Talk as Action

The approach to language taken in this book is that it is, in the first instance, a medium of *social action* rather than a code for representing thoughts and ideas, as psychologists have generally conceived it, or a grammatical system, as linguists generally conceive it. Of course, language does code knowledge and experience (the sense in which this is so is taken up in subsequent chapters), and is also properly studied in terms of grammatical categories and rules. The claim that it is social action 'in the first instance', or primarily, is an assumption about what humans are doing in possession of such a system. It has been argued, from a variety of perspectives (for example, Bruner, 1983; Halliday, 1970; Schegloff, 1989b, 1991; Vygotsky, 1934/ 1987), that languages have evolved and developed in the performance of social activities, such that the requirements of social life are what generate the necessity for languages to be grammatical, together with the basic conditions under which words, utterances, talk, texts, or whatever other units we look at, may be taken to 'code experience'. In other words, the psychological structures and functions of language have been shaped by language's primary social functions.

The major discipline which studies language primarily as a medium of social action is conversation analysis (henceforth CA). CA is the application of ethnomethodological principles to the empirical study of talk.[1] Its origins are in the inspirational lectures of Harvey Sacks (1989, 1992; originally delivered in 1964–72), and in the associated work of Sacks's colleagues Emanuel Schegloff and Gail Jefferson. Examples and extensions of that work can be found in numerous journal articles, edited collections, and summaries.[2] Although the term 'conversation analysis' is now standard, and will be used here, a more accurate term for this work is Schegloff's (1989a) 'talk-in-interaction'. This avoids the common but false impression that CA is exclusively concerned with casual and inconsequential chat, while also rejecting the notion that 'chat' is an adequate analytic characterization of ordinary talk. In fact, since its origins, CA has focused on both casual and institutional talk, much recent work being on talk in institutional settings (for example, Boden, 1995; Boden and Zimmerman, 1991; Drew and Heritage, 1992), and a small number of Sacks's (1992) earliest analyses and illustrations used dialogues taken from written texts, such as newspapers or the Bible.

Nevertheless, there is a kind of primacy given in CA to casual talk. Let us use the notion of 'casual talk' as a common-sense category for a moment, because it may not be easy to define technically, nor easy to find a pure, unadulterated example of it. Casual conversation is talk where there are no obviously asymmetrical or pre-assigned turns at talking (as there generally are in courts of law, interviews, interrogations, lectures, church services, and the like); and where participants are more free than in those kinds of settings to choose and change topic; and where topics are often local and personal, if not to say (from an outsider's point of view) trivial. The primacy of mundane talk in CA is not that CA focuses on it all the time. Rather, it is considered to be the primordial kind of talk, from which other kinds of talk-in-interaction are derived or deviate (see Heritage, 1984a, 1995; Sacks, Schegloff and Jefferson, 1974; Schegloff, 1989b, 1992a). It is the kind of talk everybody can do, that everybody first learns to do, where the complexities of turn-taking, and the management of intersubjectivity, have to be accomplished on-the-fly rather than folk being able to rely on some pre-formed script or arrangement. Indeed, it is usually noted by conversation analysts that informal conversation is talk at its most complex.

As I have suggested, it may not be possible to specify pure examples of mundane talk. Even the notion that this is primordial in evolutionary, historical, or ontogenetic terms (Heritage, 1984a: 239) may require qualification, in that it may well be the experience of many children, and of early language-using humans, that talk is/was embedded in highly organized, ritualized, and asymmetrical social relationships. Yet there remains an important *analytical* sense in which casual talk is foundational. When people have no pre-structured conversational script to fall back on, they have to manage turns and topics themselves, there and then. Classic studies in CA have illuminated how people do that, but also how, in more formal or pre-structured kinds of 'speech exchange systems', participants themselves may acknowledge and mark their talk as talk-in-a-setting, as contextually appropriate, as orienting to pre-established roles and privileges, and generally as deviating from some common-sense notion of ordinary talk.

Indeed, the nature of situations and their constraints can be analysed in this way, not by *adding in* the analyst's notions of social structure (or 'context') as a means of explaining talk, but by examining how participants, in their talk, make such settings and organizations relevant for their current activities (Drew and Heritage, 1992; Schegloff, 1992a). In other words, the primacy of casual talk may occur *as a participants' concern*, as something they may *treat as* normal when deviating from it,[3] rather than being some kind of arbitrary decision by the analyst to relate all analyses to what 'chat' is like. That is another reason why we can entertain the idea of the primacy of casual talk, without having to be able to point to objectively unambiguous examples of it, nor even study it all the time.

So, what has all this to do with cognition? CA is a *non*-cognitive approach to talk-in-interaction, in that it avoids attempting to explain talk in terms of the mental states that precede it, generate it, or result from it. It may even be an *anti*-cognitive enterprise, in that it not only sets aside such cognitive questions, as tasks for others (such as psychologists and philosophers) to consider, but offers an alternative way of dealing with talk that renders those questions fundamentally problematical. CA's talk-as-action approach conflicts with what I have called the communication model, which is the underlying metaphor assumed in most cognitive and social-cognitive theory and methodology.[4] As we noted in Chapter 1, the communication model is based on the notion that talk is a means of expressing speakers' intentions, a medium by which thoughts can traverse the airwaves between the minds of speaker and hearer. In CA, on the other hand, talk is a species of social activity, in which intentional states are the kinds of things that are at issue for participants, as part of talk's business, rather than being the actual mental states that precede and follow message transmission. It may be that those mental states are not strictly beyond the reach of observational study, as both behaviourists and cognitivists have assumed (Hamlyn, 1990), but are approachable as the kind of business that is invoked and managed in talk-in-interaction (cf. Coulter, 1990a). The sense in which mental states are 'at issue' in talk will be fleshed out in this and subsequent chapters.

Another relevance of CA for cognition is easily overlooked, given CA's primary focus on the *sequential organization* of talk, rather than on its verbal or *conceptual content*. In fact, CA provides a powerful methodology for dealing with talk's content. Certainly proponents of CA, especially when arguing for its distinctive achievements, have emphasized its discovery of content-free principles of sequential organization (Psathas, 1995; Sacks et al., 1974).[5] But that is not to say that CA has scant interest in content. On the contrary, a reading of specific content is an essential, though often implicit, part of any effort to understand sequential organizations; a question–answer *pair* is identifiable as such only through its content, even if it is then possible to formulate for such pairs normative rules that operate irrespective of specific content. Moreover, a great deal of research in CA focuses directly on content (such as the work on categories, various kinds of 'formulations', and so on, that will be discussed in later chapters).

The key here is that content occurs in talk as an *occasioned* phenomenon – that is, situated in, and relative to, its sequential occurrence. When psychological categories such as memories, causal explanations, mental states, or actors' understandings of events arise in talk, then they are found within talk's sequential organizations, and it is these sequential organizations that are the key both to the *specific selection* of those categories, and to whatever *interactional business* is being done with them. Talk's sequential organizations provide the contexts in which content and topic are produced and, therefore, the interaction frames within which reality and cognition are managed as participants' concerns. Later chapters will focus on particular studies of this kind of psychological content-in-sequence, when we examine categorization, emotion talk, script formulations, personality attributions, event reports (rememberings), and stories.

The rest of this chapter will provide an outline of some of CA's main features, particularly those which are most significant for a discursive approach to psychological topics. Summaries of CA, written for other purposes, include: Goodwin and Heritage (1990), Heritage (1984a, 1989), Heritage and Atkinson (1984), Nofsinger (1991), Psathas (1995), Wooffitt (1990), and Zimmerman (1988). The major themes considered here are: the empirical study of talk; the status of speakers' communicative intentions; the action orientation of descriptions; some basic features of sequential organization, conditional relevance, and repair; accounts and accountability; and the practical management of intersubjectivity. The latter issue is further extended in Chapter 5, on 'shared knowledge.'

The empirical study of talk

It has been a common misapprehension across the social and human sciences and in philosophy that we already know, intuitively, how people talk. We search for the psychological *mechanisms* of talk, the processes of speech production, the relations between conceptual thought and linguistic categories (grammar and semantics), and the ways in which utterances realize speakers' intentions, and are comprehended by hearers. But it has generally been assumed, outside of conversation analysis, that we know *what talk is like* – and that we know it well enough to invent our own examples of it, or simulations of it, and treat those synthetic objects as worthy of analysis, or as illustrations of theoretical models. This has been the case even with studies of the social nature of talk, including some of Erving Goffman's (1971) and Basil Bernstein's (1971) work, cognitive models of 'discourse processing' (for example, Kintsch and Van Dijk, 1983), and most of 'speech act' theory (Searle, 1979).

CA, on the other hand, is based on the notion that we do not know what talk is like, except through careful empirical study of tape-recorded samples. When we examine such samples, our competence as speakers, or as more or less co-members or knowledgeable observers of the culture and interaction under study, surely provides a major basis for doing analysis. But that cultural competence does not mean that we can invent samples of talk, or simply intuit its empirical nature. CA is founded on the principle that the object under study is actually occurring situated talk, rather than our intuitions, or some set of idealized and invented illustrations of it.

The notion that we intuitively know the nature of talk, like we 'know' grammar,[6] is a foundation of speech act theory (Searle, 1969, 1983), and of a great deal of research on speech production and comprehension in cognitive psychology and artificial intelligence. It also echoes an assumption embedded in ethnographic practices, where talk by 'informants' is rendered into remembered versions of, or on-the-spot notes on, what they say. The empirically available details of talk have mostly been treated, outside of CA, as 'specifically uninteresting'.[7] Reasons for this include the following:

1　There is a long tradition in the psychology of language and cognition, and in philosophy and linguistics, prior to the invention and use of audio recording equipment. This coincides with a tradition of dealing with linguistic items (sentences, dialogues, narratives) that are specially invented for the purposes of analysis, and based on the norms of written text (Linell, 1988), though even then rather stilted.[8]

2   There are various strong theoretical justifications for treating language *as* an idealization – for example, Noam Chomsky's (1965) 'competence–performance' distinction, and Ferdinand de Saussure's (1922/1974) '*langue*' and '*parole*'.[9] Sophisticated developments in theoretical linguistics are founded on making up examples of sentences[10] and judging whether or not they are grammatical. This may help to underpin, without actually working it out rationally, the practice in psychology of making up samples of *discourse* (utterances) to serve as stand-in empirical phenomena, and treating those inventions as adequate exemplars.

3   There is our long familiarity with literary scripts in novels and plays, and in philosophy since Plato, where dialogue is more or less 'realistically' and recognizably thought up and written out – though there has always been the requirement for actors and directors to 'interpret' and bring such dialogues to life, or else to replace them with actors' improvisations, in the pursuit of naturalism.

4   There is a notion that, since somebody *could* have said it, and there is nothing obviously wrong with it, an invented example of dialogue will do. The trouble here is that recordings of talk are not much like the kinds of invented examples used prior to and outside of CA, while many of CA's empirical discoveries require detailed transcripts and, though recognizable once pointed out, were not obvious before that.

5   There is our sheer familiarity with talk itself – we produce and understand it all the time, routinely, and mostly without trouble. It is tempting to assume, therefore, that we are *already* experts on it. Of course, the same is equally true and false of all the rest of our conscious mental and behavioural lives. The issue is, what role should that presumptive knowledge play in analysis? In CA the role it plays is crucial, but in explicating actual samples of talk, where it is answerable to talk's particulars. Those particulars, the precise words said (even those are not as easy to faithfully transcribe as might be assumed), and also the emphases, pauses, and pronunciational details that CA transcripts usually include (see Appendix), may at first appear over-detailed and unnecessary. But that is because of our unfamiliarity with seeing those details *in print*, even though we use them routinely in conversation. When talking, those mundane particulars are used *there and then*, on the spot, rather than being retained in our general notions of what we were saying and doing. We become analytic victims of talk's familiarity.

So conversation analysis deals with recorded and transcribed samples of talk. The task it sets itself is *not* to look for expected kinds of phenomena, such as how categories borrowed from linguistic theory or speech act theory are 'expressed' in talk, or how teachers, policemen, or counsellors dominate interactions with pupils and clients. Rather, it is what George Psathas and others call 'unmotivated looking':

> Data may be obtained from any available source, the only requirement being that these should be naturally occurring, rather than produced for the purpose of study, as in the case of laboratory experiments or controlled observations. In practice, this has meant interactional phenomena that would have occurred regardless of whether the researcher had come upon the scene; therefore, conversations, news interviews, therapy sessions, telephone calls, dinner table talk, police calls, as well as all manner of interactional phenomena that the researcher may be able to come upon and record are potential data sources. (Psathas, 1995: 45)

While this seems to rule out studies that use experimental procedures or interviews, it does not strictly do so. Any interactional phenomenon can be *naturalized* by *treating it as* natural. So if what you have are interview data, then that is how to treat them, as a species of talk-in-interaction, as 'interview', rather than treating the questioner as researcher, the question schedule as 'method', and only the responses as 'data' (cf. Wetherell and Potter, 1992; Widdicombe and Wooffitt, 1995; Wooffitt, 1992). Nevertheless, what Psathas calls naturally occurring discourse is preferable, if research is not always going to find its own practices the most interesting the world has to offer. Furthermore, the collection of corpora of natural data has started to produce an accumulation of resources that can sustain indefinitely many further analytic forays, which contrasts with more artificial methods where data tend strictly to 'belong to' the specific study that produced them, and to date rather rapidly in analytic interest.

The notion of 'unmotivated looking' sounds an implausibly naïve and empiricist one, and in any case, researchers are soon engaged in looking for and analysing further instances of phenomena in which they have started to take an interest.[11] But the phrase encapsulates an important analytic principle. That principle is to avoid 'reading into' the data a set of ready-made analytic categories; to avoid being disappointed with the data available, and to allow 'interesting' to be a matter of whatever analysis can produce, rather than something built into who is talking, or what momentous things they are talking about. For example, rather than start from some ready-made issue such as 'how attitudes to authority develop' and looking for them in conversational materials, Sacks recommended that 'the first rule is to learn to be interested in what you've got. I take it that what you want to do is *pose those problems that the data bears*' (1992, vol. 1: 471, emphasis added). As Sacks's own analyses clearly demonstrate, that is precisely what opens up, rather than prevents, the possibility of empirical work on participants' categories of the ostensibly non-discursive, including everything from group membership to personal identity, institutional setting, matters of belief, cognition, and constructions of what is routine and exceptional in life.

Conversation, communication, and intention

The 'communication model' of discourse sits most happily with a minds–goals–intentions version of what people are doing when they are talking, writing, reading, conversing, and so on. The starting point is two individuals, two minds that begin in Cartesian isolation from each other, but which/who set out to know and influence each other's contents. Each mind contains (or is partly made up of) knowledge, in the form of images, semantic organizations, propositions, hypotheses, inferences, and so on, and these include notions about the content of other minds. On the basis of those notions, messages are formulated to achieve a variety of communicative goals, such as informing, persuading, and finding things out. For the analyst who assumes such a model, having started with an a priori notion of individual minds, various problems logically arise. The prime problems are those of 'communication' (how does it work?) and of 'knowledge of other minds' (how is it possible?). These problems, in their various guises, have generated much of the taken-for-granted problematics of cognitive, social, and developmental psychology, and of epistemic philosophy. However, by conceiving of the communication model *as* a model, rather than an obvious reality or necessity,[12] it is possible to reconsider the empirical and theoretical status of a large range of psychological issues. This is essentially the enterprise that Jonathan Potter and I have called 'discursive psychology' (Edwards and Potter, 1992a), which draws on CA's fundamental reconception of discourse as action, not communication (Schegloff, 1995).

One reason for being suspicious of the communication model is that folk do not always use it. Whereas it is certainly a recognizable component of common sense, it is (1) not everybody's common sense, and (2) not always common sense for those who use it. In ethnomethodology and CA, the status of common sense is that it is the object under analysis. It is the analyst's business neither to adopt it as theory, nor to replace it with something better – more objective, technically specified, or consistent, for example. The claims that the communication model is *not everybody's* common sense, nor *consistently* used by those who use it, are sustained by anthropological and social constructionist analyses of categories such as communicative intentions, agency, and the sense of self.[13]

For example, Alessandro Duranti (1988) analyses the interactionally accomplished nature of meanings in Samoan *fono* (politico-judiciary meetings). He rejects the universality of 'personalist' notions of meaning, and argues for the generality of socially accomplished, shared, and consequences-oriented meanings in Polynesian societies; for the importance of 'local theories of Self and task accomplishment'; and for how the significance of 'the role of the audience in shaping utterances and (re)defining meanings must be an integral part of any model of verbal communication' (1988: 14). Thus,

> Rather than taking words as representations of privately owned meanings, Samoans practice interpretation as a way of publicly controlling social relationships rather

than as a way of figuring out what a given person 'meant to say.' Once uttered in a given context, words are interpreted with respect to some new reality they help to fashion rather than with respect to the supposedly intended subjective content . . . in Samoa a speaker must usually directly deal with the circumstances created by his words and cannot hide behind his alleged original intentions. In Samoan, one cannot say 'I didn't mean it.' (1988: 15–17)

However, if we consider our own, more familiar kinds of discursive practices, then this dichotomy between Polynesia and the West starts to look more like an interesting generalization than an absolute difference. When English speakers address issues of what they 'meant to say', these may also, if viewed in context as discursive activities, turn out to be ways of publicly controlling social relationships.[14] Certainly Duranti's concern is not only with the distinctive features of Samoan talk, but with what they can tell us about the socially accomplished and context-contingent nature of *all* talk *anywhere*.

Although Duranti argues for a Samoan, or more generally Polynesian, lack of public concern with selfhood and intentionality, he also suggests that 'Samoans, like any other people in the world, *must* interpret each other's doings as having certain ends with respect to which those doings should be evaluated and dealt with' (1988: 30, emphasis added). So, 'one of the reasons for having orators speak first or on behalf of a chief, a fairly common practice on Polynesia . . . is that of allowing the chief to change his opinion without loss of face. The chiefs' "wrongs" are assumed, in the public arena, by the orators who spoke on their behalf . . . ' (1988: 22). It would seem, then, that a 'face'-oriented, goals–intentions–actions model remains applicable to Samoans' talk (whether we wish to apply such a model is another matter), even while participants are treating their talk and actions as non-intentional. Even for Samoans, communicative intentionality may be something that is *socially managed*, rather than merely absent: systematically avoided in such settings, perhaps, rather than conceptually unrecognizable.

Given that strategic 'reasons' can (if not 'must') be adduced by the analyst for such patterns of talk (cf. Goffman, 1955 and 1979, on 'face work', and on 'footing'), we ought not perhaps to conceive of those kinds of talk as demonstrating a *presence* or *absence* of intentionality, or even of participants' conceptions of intentionality. Rather, it may be more fruitful to consider how notions of agency, intentionality, responsibility, and so on, may be *managed* by participants in talk. This allows for notions of agency and intentionality to be made relevant or not, affirmed or denied, treated (by participants) as individually based or socially distributed, at particular junctures in any stretch of talk and interaction. This alternative notion, of speakers' and actors' goals and intentions being interactionally managed (where analytically relevant at all), brings Polynesian practices closer to those of Western conversations,[15] where such matters are also interactionally managed, rather than merely pervasively present.

A rather extreme example of the rhetorical management of intentionality occurred in the 'Scott report'. This was commissioned by the British Prime Minister, John Major, to provide an 'independent' judgment on allegations concerning the role of government ministers in possibly deceiving parliament, and in allowing innocent men to risk being jailed for illegal, though quietly condoned, arms exports to Iraq shortly before the Gulf War of 1992. The report, when it finally appeared in February 1996, became notorious for how it permitted both favourable and unfavourable conclusions to be drawn concerning the role of ministers:

> The Scott report reveals that William Waldegrave, now Treasury Chief Secretary, bombarded MPs with misleading information on more than 30 occasions, even though he knew first hand that the guidelines on arms sales had changed. But while Scott charges him with *deliberately misleading* Parliament, he also allows that he did not *intend to deceive*. Can both these accounts be true? (Editorial commentary, *The Observer*, 18 February 1996, Review section, p. 3, emphases added)

It is a feature of ordinary language, which we shall return to many times, that it provides a range of almost identical, possibly synonymous, but slightly different, or somewhat contradictory, terms of reference for all kinds of things in the world, in social relations, and in our mental lives. These include the nuances available between 'deliberate' and 'intend', or between 'misleading' and 'deceive' (and of course there are plenty of others: lie, confabulate, misinform, mistake, etc.). Rather than viewing these as evidence of the incoherent and inadequate nature of common-sense language, they are to be celebrated as just the kinds of resources that permit everyday discourse to do what it does.

Consider now the following brief exchange (see appendix for transcription symbols):

Extract 4.1
```
1    G:    . . .d'ju see me pull up?=
2    S:    =.hhh No:. I was trying you all day. =an' the
3          line was busy for like hours.
4    G:    Ohh:::::, ohh:::::, .hhhhhh We::ll, hhh I'm
5          gonna come over in a little while help yer
6          brother ou:t
7    S:    Goo[:d
8    G:       [.hhh 'cause I know he needs some he::lp,
9    S:    .hh Ye:ah. Yes he'd mention' that today.=
10   G:    =Mm hm,=
11   S:    =.hh Uh:m, .tlk .hhh Who were you ta:lking to.
```
(Frankel TC:I:1:2)

The transcript, slightly simplified here, is taken from an analysis by John Heritage (1990–1: 317) of the problems of identifying goals and intentions in ordinary talk. Heritage in turn takes it from a study by Anita Pomerantz (1980) of 'fishing', which is a conversational device by which a speaker may obtain information without overtly asking for it. The device is that of citing 'limited access' to something evidently known to the recipient (such as the recipient's age, address, or recent activities), with the possible consequence that the recipient will provide further details. In Extract 4.1, the 'fishing' is done by S's utterance in lines 2–3, 'I was trying you all day. =an' the <u>line</u> was busy for like <u>hours</u>.' This sets up a situation in which S has been trying and failing to contact G, who has been on the phone to some unknown (to S, but presumably not to G) person. S signals that there is something interesting or remarkable (literally) in G's unavailability, enhanced by the extremity of 'all day', and the puzzlement hinted at in 'for like <u>hours</u>'. G fails to reveal anything further, such as who else was on the line all that time, and S eventually asks directly, 'Who were you <u>ta</u>:lking to' (line 11). The fact that S goes on to ask this directly is part of Pomerantz's grounds for seeing the initial item as 'fishing' for it.

The issue that Heritage raises (and to which Pomerantz, 1980, is also cautiously sensitive)[16] is the status of participants' goals and intentions in this kind of analysis. Can we say that S was 'fishing' in some strategic, goal-oriented way, whether consciously or unconsciously? The distinction is between 'fishing' as something we can see going on in talk, through its sequential occurrence and turn-by-turn realization (given that, in lines 2–3, no overt request for information is made), and 'fishing' as something which we might attribute to S's will, plans, goals, mental states, or intentions-prior-to-speaking. Heritage undermines that psychologizing move by offering a revised analysis. He notes that lines 2–3 could be construed not as a bit of 'fishing', but as an account for calling:

> S has called G who lives across the street. . . . In this context, S's description of G's 'busy line' can stand as an explanation for how she came to be calling now, rather than as a piece of 'fishing'. (Heritage, 1990–1: 318)

So G's initial turn in line 1, 'd'ju see me <u>pull</u> up?', may itself be a bit of 'fishing', a prompt for S to provide a reason for calling. And that makes S's final utterance, 'Who were you <u>ta</u>:lking to', possibly a *first* inquiry about that, rather than a spelled-out, explicit second one.

Note that Heritage's analysis of Extract 4.1 does not imply that these kinds of alternative analyses are arbitrary or indefinitely alterable. In each case, the analysis is carefully grounded in the details of occurring talk, and might be resolved (or made more complicated) by further analysis. More importantly, the point is not that there are two irreconcilable analyses here, but, rather, that *whatever* participants are doing, by what they are saying, has this character, of being negotiated turn by turn out of ambiguities and potentialities. What is 'meant' by their talk is at stake for participants, and realized as they proceed, as a practical matter in the making, rather than something for analysts to worry about defining for each utterance psychologically, at the moment it occurs. As Heritage notes, 'complex questions arise . . . about specifying an exact moment at which we may claim that S formed an "intention" to find out who G was talking to' (1990–1: 318).

It is a matter not merely of suspending judgment *in this case* on speakers' intentions prior to speaking, but of treating such intentions more generally as speakers' active business in talking, as being at stake in talk's sequential trajectory and outcomes, rather than as being pre-formed psychologically in any sense that is analytically useful or necessary to pursue. It is not the wrongness of an 'intentional' treatment of speakers' meanings and communicative actions that undermines a communication model of speech acts. Rather, it is its conversational optionality for speakers, its interactionally managed and to-be-accomplished nature, and the potentially at-issue or contentious nature, for participants, of any formulation of what was 'meant' by what was said. CA focuses on how participants 'methodically construct their talk so as to produce a possible instance of an action or activity of some sort, and to provide for the possible occurrence next of various sorts of actions by others' (Schegloff, 1989a: 197).

Much of CA deals with something similar to what speech act theorists call 'indirection' (indirect speech acts are things such as using declaratives or interrogatives to make requests: Searle, 1969). CA's examples of indirection are acts such as 'fishing', in which information is obtainable without directly asking for it; we have seen how this sort of analytic category should not be equated to a goals-and-intentions model of talk. Schegloff (1989a, 1992b) lists a non-exhaustive set of nine analytic themes that recur in Harvey Sacks's early lectures, and all of them are to do with indirection. Eight are of the form 'How to do X without doing Y', and include such items as 'how to avoid giving help without refusing it (treat the circumstance as a joke)', and 'how to get an account without asking for it (offer some member of a class and get a correction)' (Schegloff, 1989a: 199). However, in contrast to Searle,

> Sacks' analytic strategy here is not a search for recipes, or rules, or definitions of types of action. He begins by taking note of an interactional effect actually achieved in a singular, real episode of interaction. . . . And he asks, was this outcome achieved methodically. (Schegloff, 1989a: 199)

In Sacks's analytic writings, speech act categories such as 'requests' or 'invitations' do feature, but tentatively, as common-sense and provisional ways of describing interpretative issues for particular stretches of talk that are to be resolved empirically in terms of local contingencies, sequential patterns, and uptakes.[17]

Conversation analysis does not, in the first instance at least, resolve the philosophical–psychological problem of intentionality, nor the relations between intentional states and talk. What it does is to pose a different question, by treating intentionality not as a metaphysical problem for analysts to wrestle with, but as a *practical matter for participants*. As Lena Jayyusi notes, 'the issue of intention, luck, chance, deliberation is of *programmatic relevance* in the organization of accounting practices . . . for the way that "outcomes" and thus actions and their agents, as well as their recipients, can get morally constituted' (1993: 443, original emphasis). Participants' goals and intentions feature in their discourse not only as overt topics, but as ways of talking, including ways of treating each other's talk as intention-implicative. Issues concerning intentions either *do not arise* as anything problematical or to-be-dealt-with, or else, if they do arise, they get resolved *practically* in some way, or topicalized, as part of the business of talk and social action. This applies to speakers' intentions in talking; to actors' goals, plans, and intentions in acting; and to actors' intentions (thoughts, reactions, etc.) in the actions being talked about. They are part of the common sense basis of participants' practices, and so, properly, part of our object of study rather than our explanatory framework.

A further difficulty in identifying speakers' intentions is that, as analysts, we need a principled way to *stop* doing it. Whatever our general views on the nature of human actions and intentions, *for any one instance of talk* we could go on for ever, attributing to participants all kinds of reasons for saying things, based on what reasons they tell us, or what kind of person we know them to be, in what role we assume they are acting, towards whom, in what institutional context, under what kind of pathology, or contingency, or utilitarian consideration, and so on. CA's practical solution is to look at how considerations such as 'reasons for talking' or 'bases for speaking' may arise in talk, or be oriented to in some way by participants, or if they do not arise, then examine what does. In some of Harold Garfinkel's classic 'breaching experiments', what was breached was the usual 'trust' that what people mean by what they say is, for general practical purposes, to be taken as normatively unproblematic and unworthy of close examination. Any insistence on detailed explication of meanings was harshly and abruptly sanctioned:

> The subject was telling the experimenter, a member of the subject's car pool, about having had a flat tire while going to work the previous day.
> S: I had a flat tire.
> E: What do you mean, you had a flat tire?
> She appeared momentarily stunned. Then she answered in hostile way: 'What do you mean? What do you mean? A flat tire is a flat tire. That is what I meant. Nothing special. What a crazy question!' (Garfinkel, 1967: 41)

This side-stepping move on intentionality and mental states that CA and ethnomethodology make is, as I have remarked, a methodological step done 'in the first instance'. It need be taken no further than that, a disciplined methodological agnosticism – a principle that, *as analysts*, we should adopt the kind of 'methodological relativism' towards mental states in discourse studies that sociologists of scientific knowledge have adopted towards truth and error in science (see Chapter 3). However, a more radical possibility also arises (Coulter, 1990a; Rorty, 1980) that this is all there is to intentionality after all. In a *two-stage* alternative to intentional accounts of meanings and actions, we might (1) side-step the metaphysical questions in favour of seeing how they may arise (if at all) as practical matters for participants; but then (2) consider that perhaps this is all there is to it. Perhaps 'practical matters' are precisely where the metaphysical–psychological question initially came from, and where it might safely remain. In other words, 'intentionality' might be considered a pseudo-question for theorists, an example of how we have extracted a practical issue from its workings in common-sense discourse, and distorted it into a generalizable theory of persons, and of the relations between thoughts and actions and talk.

Descriptions, actions, and subversion

John Austin's (1962) starting point for developing an action-performing approach to language was to draw an initial distinction between the kinds of statements that *do* things (for example, 'I [hereby] name this ship the Bismarck', 'I [hereby] promise to come'), which he called 'performatives', and those he called 'constatives' which simply describe things, and can therefore properly be considered true or false (for example, 'the capital of France is Paris', 'swimming with sharks is dangerous'). The result of Austin's subsequent analysis was to abandon the notion of mere description, and to see *all* propositions as performative of some kind of social or communicative action. Chapters 1 to 3 have emphasized the interactional business performed by descriptions (for example, the discussions of ethnography and ethnomethodology, of SSK, of Sacks's Navy pilot data, and of descriptions in psychological studies of child cognition and bystander intervention). One of the achievements of conversation analysis has been to promote detailed empirical study of such discursive actions, where particular descriptions are produced within interaction sequences, with regard to what is said before and after, and with regard to alternatives.[18]

In one of his early lectures, Sacks introduced a sample of recorded talk, from which the following is an extract, in which a man (B) had called a helpline and was talking about his troubles.

Extract 4.2
```
1    B:    . . . Well, she ((wife of B)) stepped between me and the child,
2          I got up to walk out the door. When she stepped between me
3          and the child, I went to move her out of the way. And then
4          about that time her sister had called the police. I don't know
5          how she . . . what she . . .
6    A:    Didn't you smack her one?
7    B:    No.
8    A:    You're not telling me the story, Mr B.
9    B:    Well, you see when you say smack you mean hit.
10   A:    Yeah, you shoved her. Is that it?
11   B:    Yeah, I shoved her.
```
(Sacks, 1992, vol. 1: 113, line numbers added)

Sacks was interested in how it was that A, receiving the call, could recognize (and bring off that recognition through prompting B) that there was more to the husband's story than he was saying, and how this hinged upon what kinds of actions might be treated as adequate grounds for the wife's sister having 'called the police' (line 4). I shall return to that sort of 'cultural knowledge' issue in chapters 6 to 10 (see also the further discussion of this extract, as

10.1). The main interest for now is how the interchange revolves around the work done by alternative descriptions (*move, smack, hit, shove*).

First, however, note what looks like a preliminary detail: B's 'I got up to walk out the door' (line 2). This ostensibly scene-setting description effectively specifies B's intentions prior to, and relevant to, the event in question (that is, in question *for them*, the hit/smack/shove event whose proper description A and B then pursue). B's intentions are descriptively produced in such a way as to counter an alternative, at issue in their talk, concerning B's violence towards his wife. The action of 'moving her' (or whatever) 'out of the way' (line 3) thus occurs as merely instrumental in this rather innocuous-looking intention 'to walk out the door'. So this is an example of the discursive management of actors' intentions in reported events. The kind of intention-management that I was canvassing earlier occurs here in the context of potential blame for a possible act of violence that, under at least one actor's apparent understanding of it, warranted calling the police. Note how, in pursuing a preferred alternative, B displays concern for A's intentional meanings as problematical – 'Well, you see when you say smack you mean hit' (line 9). By attending to what each other *means* by the words they say, the nature of the events at issue is negotiated, and along with that, the nature of B's culpability in those events. So this is an interactional context in which 'intentions' arise as a participants' concern, both for their talk and for the actions under discussion.

The at-issue descriptions – 'move her out of the way', 'shoved her', 'hit', 'smack her one' – feature for the speakers as alternatives for the same prior event. As alternatives, the choice between them is interactionally significant. The call receiver (A) signals a problem with the descriptive adequacy of 'move her out of the way' by offering a correction, 'Didn't you smack her one?' (line 6). As Sacks noted, B's description had not provided the kinds of grounds that one might expect for the police being called, and A's alternative provides such grounds, in the form of physical violence. That absence of grounds is marked in how A, who did not witness the events, can nevertheless accuse B, who obviously did, of 'not telling me the story'.[19]

Note again the work done by descriptive *details*. For example, 'smack her one' versus 'smack': this invokes various interpretative possibilities to do with particular kinds of hitting, and how the colloquiality of the expression seems to place A and B as co-members of a sub-culture that might use such an expression, and perhaps where such an action, so-described, has a recognizable place in the rough and tumble of interpersonal relationships, rather than being anything out of the ordinary. If that were so, then such a choice of description might help the husband to confess it; or if it were not so, then he might deny or correct it, and thereby be induced to address precisely what kind of violence took place (which is what he does). Note also how B delicately introduces the sister's calling the police as an action lacking a clearly intelligible basis or precise sequential coherence – 'about that time . . . I don't know how she . . . what she . . .' (lines 4–5). And of course, there are the more obvious alternatives here; 'shove' is preferred to 'smack' or 'hit' (which B treats as equivalent), while 'shove' is then treated by A and B as a jointly acceptable substitute for 'move out of the way'. It is a substitute that manages to down-play any violence in the husband's actions, while still providing a plausible basis for an over-reacting and possibly biased witness (relevantly identified as 'her sister') to call the police. As such, lines 9–11 are an interactional fix for line 8, the requirement for a more believable story.

The fact that descriptions work in this way, in their details, constructing the sense of events, implicating motive and intention, managing agency and culpability, working with regard to actual or possible alternatives, and managing credibility, is not a feature lost on participants, even though they might not explain it all in these terms themselves. Their talk is not automatically or accidentally like this, but appears to be *designed* with regard to such matters (indeed, these intricate patterns of description, alternative description, and the accountabilities thereby attended to, are pervasive in CA data corpora and analysis). Again, the point here is not to attribute particular conscious or unconscious plans to such designs, but to note it as a feature of how such talk *works* in the moment-to-moment performance of social actions. It is a corollary of the ethnomethodological principle concerning how actions in general are designed. As Heritage notes, Garfinkel

> views social action as designed with reference to how it will be recognized and described. Descriptions are no different. They are not to be regarded as disembodied commentaries on states of affairs. Rather, in the ways in which they (1) make reference to states of affairs and (2) occur in particular interactional and situational contexts, they will *unavoidably be understood as actions which are chosen and consequential*. (1984a: 140, emphasis added)

This allows for descriptions to be produced, but also *treated interactionally*, as designed for the actions they perform, and designed for particular inferences to be drawn (see, for example, Jefferson, 1985). Descriptions, narratives, accounts, and so on, are 'actions' precisely in that they construct one sense of events rather than another, and 'provide for' upshots, conclusions, and so on. This endemic second-level organization[20] permits everyday, mundane talk to be highly sophisticated.

The interactionally achieved 'visibility' of actions, which is also what makes analysis possible, links to what Sacks called *subversion*. This is an extraordinarily powerful notion, both for participation and for analysis. It consists in the *enlisting*, by participants, of actions' visibility, such that actions will be taken for what they appear to be: 'When a woman walks away from a supermarket with the baby carriage filled with a baby that's not hers, that's the sort of thing I'm talking about with "subversion". It's not seeable' (Sacks, 1992, vol. 1: 254). Sacks's example derives from his celebrated discussion of a child's story, taken from a published collection, which contained the sequence 'The baby cried. The mommy picked it up.' His analysis elaborates the kinds of cultural assumptions required to make that a coherent narrative, such as the category-incumbent activities expected of mommies and babies, their canonical kinds of relations, the likelihood that it was the baby's own mommy, and so on. Given that those sorts of things are treated as hearable and seeable by participants in talk and action, their subversion is possible. People can perform actions, and say things, for the kinds of actions they will be taken to be.

At this point, the term 'subversion' becomes a little misleading, in that what we have is an example of how social action per se works. It is a matter not so much of deception, machiavellianism, or insincerity (though it *can* be, or be taken to be), as of Garfinkel's dictum regarding the accountably-seen-to-be-done nature of social actions. In Sacks's words,

> . . . producers of activities could use seer's and hearer's maxims. That the seer's maxims are available to producers of actions, and are crucial to them in producing their activities, can at least in part be gotten at by locating those things which Members have available to them as things that can be done subversively under the very general usage of 'subversion' I offered . . . subversion is simply a consequence of seer's maxims, hearer's maxims and the like. (1992, vol. 1: 414)

So subversion becomes the norm, with the non-condemnatory sense that actions are produced with regard to their visibility-as-such. Even such a category as 'being ordinary' is something that people can 'do' (Sacks, 1992, vol. 2: 215; cf. Sacks, 1984), just as 'being phoney' is a notion that they can also apply (Sacks, 1992, vol. 1: 581).

Again, 'subversion' is not to be confused with a motivational theory of talk. It says nothing about speakers' motives, except that these may figure as participants' descriptions in the sense already defined. The crucial thing about social actions is their designed visibility, and the endemic procedures that ensure their publicly accomplished *recognition*. It is not that social actions are thought to be produced by some prior motive or intention, such as saving face or trying to influence, but that recognizability is a *constitutive feature of how social action works*, and participants do things with it.[21] Conversational exchange is the arena in which motives and intentional states are at stake for participants, and is therefore *analytically prior* to the mental states that supposedly precede it.

Whenever participants perform the discursive actions of revealing what they think, how they see things, what they understand of their situation, or of just describing the way things are, they inevitably do so in and for interaction. With regard to an ostensibly obvious and inconsequential description that occurred during a group therapy session, Sacks remarked:

> Members can't do pure formulating . . . you can't be engaged in 'merely' – non-consequentially, non-methodically, non-alternatively – saying 'This is, after all, a group therapy session.' To do that . . . is to do other things as well, e.g., put somebody down for something they just said, propose special relevancies, propose that some topic ought to be discussed or not be discussed, invoke a status hierarchy, etc . . . in each case . . . that's something that has some line of consequences, and some analyzable basis, for participants. (1992, vol. 1: 516)

Any such formulations are therefore candidates for 'subversion': that is, ways of *doing* all those ostensibly second-order social actions, and being treated as doing them.[22]

As Garfinkel also noted, descriptions can go on indefinitely. There are all kinds of ways to describe any given activity or scene, and any description could always, in principle, be further explicated or extended. So the selection or assembly of any *particular* description (where all descriptions are particular ones) may be inspected, by participants as well as by analysts, for its specificity from amongst an indefinite set of possibilities, and therefore as performing some action and making available some implication. Those actions and implications are not themselves another infinite set, but precisely the ones that participants' prior and subsequent talk does, in some manner, deal with. The sequential organization of 'next turns' is also our next topic. Later chapters will explore various ways in which participants' descriptions, generalizations, mental state predicates, and so on, figure within these kinds of sequential organizations, in the performance of discursive actions.

Sequential organization, intersubjectivity, and repair

In conversation analysis, sequential organization is the major basis of whatever talk does.[23] It is a rather obvious and, initially, unremarkable feature of talk-in-interaction, but it is the heart of talk's capacity for performing social actions. Sequential organization provides a practical scaffolding for 'intersubjectivity', in the sense of publicly realized shared understandings. Each utterance creates a context for the next, and each next utterance, in attending to the context created by its prior, thereby stands as a kind of participant's public reading of, or treating-as, whatever action that prior performed, or whatever implication it made relevant. So sequential organization is a major feature of what ethnomethodologists call the *indexicality* and *reflexivity* of social actions (including talk), which were introduced in Chapter 3. 'Indexicality' is a feature of talk-in-interaction in which the specific sense and reference of a word is relative to the precise context of its utterance. Whereas dictionary definitions and semantic models attempt to provide abstracted meanings that will cover all legitimate uses of a word, they can not handle the infinite ways in which, in actual use, words take on specific meanings and relevancies in specific contexts, such as we saw with 'hit', 'shove', 'move', 'sister', and indeed all the other words in Extract 4.2.

'Reflexivity' is the property of talk whereby it constructs or otherwise contributes to the sense of its own occasions and contexts. As Heritage puts it:

> [Talk is] context *shaped* and context *renewing* . . . [which] is a major, and unavoidable, procedure which hearers use and rely on to interpret conversational contributions and it is also something which speakers pervasively attend to in the design of what they say. (1984a: 242, original emphasis)

CA is essentially the explication of that sequential, turn-by-turn, public process. In fact, sequential organization is a major part of what makes analysis *possible*, in that participants 'make available to the analyst a basis in the data for claiming what the co-participants' understanding is of prior utterances, for as they display it to one another, we can see it too' (Schegloff, 1984: 38; cf. Sacks et al., 1974: 728–9).

Again, this is not to say that joint understandings are produced *cognitively*, in the sense of individuals possessing the same ideas or beliefs; nor that intersubjectivity is interactionally straightforward. It is to say that the phenomenon of mutually intelligible social interaction is a practically accomplished public production, and not a matter, outside of that, of people 'actually' (from a God's-eye point of view) understanding or misunderstanding each other. As we saw with speakers' intended meanings, the problem of 'actual' understandings and misunderstandings between speakers, when posed in that way by psychologists and philosophers, can be considered the abstraction of a theoretical conundrum out of the practical contingencies of everyday talk. Within talk's publicly managed procedures, whatever meanings are taken up turn-by-turn by participants (for example, in second speakers' turns) are also available for 'repair' by first speakers in subsequent (for example, third) turns. Given the turn-by-turn possibility of repair, its *absence* signals that participants are treating their talk as, by default, continuously coherent. So intersubjectivity is approachable as something oriented-to by participants, and researched by analysts, *as a practical matter*, handled to whatever degree is required (and no more) as part of talk's sequential organization, rather than being an actual and specifiable state of mind, of shared ideas, or of mutual beliefs about beliefs (as discussed in Smith, 1982; see also Chapter 5).

This availability of participants' 'readings' of each other's talk is what conversation analysts, following Sacks et al. (1974), call the 'proof procedure'. The idea is that the analysis of any turn at talk can be checked against, or based on, how participants themselves respond to it in subsequent turns. So, loosely speaking, a request is a request if somebody treats it as that, whether by complying with it, refusing it, questioning its propriety, or whatever; and any such 'treating it as a request' is immediately available to the first speaker as a basis for proceeding, or for 'repairing' meanings. Since 'meanings' are considered here features of social interaction, rather than speakers' intentions, what any utterance 'means' is the same thing as its interactional uptake and trajectory. Again, this is not to say that speakers' intentions are off the agenda, or that folk may not be 'misunderstood'. The notion that a hearer might misunderstand a speaker's intentions is not a counter to the 'proof procedure', but merely another interactional move. Hearers can signal difficulty with a prior turn at talk, or respond in ways that the original speaker may then move to 'repair' (Schegloff, 1992c; Schegloff, Jefferson, and Sacks, 1977). In other words, speakers' intentions, hearers' (mis)understandings, and the moment-to-moment establishment of intersubjectivity are all approachable analytically as participants' business, publicly performed.

Something of the nature of sequential organization, and the public

management of intersubjectivity, can be seen in the two brief data extracts
that were examined earlier in this chapter. In Extract 4.1 (reproduced
below), Pomerantz's analytic theme of 'fishing' and Heritage's notion of an
'account for calling' both hinge on the *relations between* utterances, rather
than on those utterances' intrinsic features.

Extract 4.1 (repeated)
```
1    G:    . . .d'ju see me pull up?=
2    S:    =.hhh No:. I was trying you all day. =an' the
3          line was busy for like hours.
4    G:    Ohh:::::, ohh:::::, .hhhhhh We::ll, hhh I'm
5          gonna come over in a little while help yer
6          brother ou:t
7    S:    Goo[:d
8    G:       [.hhh 'cause I know he needs some he::lp,
9    S:    .hh Ye:ah. Yes he'd mention' that today.=
10   G:    =Mm hm,=
11   S:    =.hh Uh:m, .tlk .hhh Who were you ta:lking to.
```
(Frankel TC:I:1:2)

The status of 'I was trying you all day. =an' the line was busy for like hours'
(lines 2–3), as either a fish for information (who was G was talking to?), or as
an account for S's calling G *both* rely on that utterance's sequential
relationship to prior and subsequent turns. Its status as an 'account' relies on
how 'd'ju see me pull up?' might be taken by S as a 'fish' for reasons for
calling. Its status as a possible 'fish' relies on its relation to G's subsequent
non-provision of to whom he was talking, and S's eventual direct asking for it
(line 11). So the interactional categories assigned to turns at talk are fixed
not by those turns' intrinsic contents, but by their relations to prior and
succeeding turns.

Similarly, in the analysis of Extract 4.2, A's utterance 'You're not telling
me the story, Mr B' (line 8, below) formulates as problematical B's *prior*
story and denial, and also simultaneously sets up the relevance, and *potential
for performing the action it does*, of A's next conversational move. In fact,
A's next turn (line 9) is analysable as initiating a *repair* of intersubjectivity,
which is then (in next turns) brought off by A and B jointly:

(From Extract 4.2)
```
6    A:    Didn't you smack her one?
7    B:    No.
8    A:    You're not telling me the story, Mr B.
9    B:    Well, you see when you say smack you mean hit.
10   A:    Yeah, you shoved her. Is that it?
11   B:    Yeah, I shoved her.
```

Note how any treatment of B's repair as *merely* a repair of joint
understandings, as merely 'informative', in the sense of individuals expressing their knowledge states, and communicatively updating them for
each other, misses the interactional point somewhat. B's repair performs

important business in *establishing* the nature of events, and, thereby, of his accountability in them. It would surely be naïve of us to hear all this as what B thinks, and what A thinks B thinks, and what B thinks A thinks B thinks, and so on. Bits of dialogue can have that status only when invented and put before us as having that status, by philosophers and psycholinguists.

Talk's sequential organization is also captured in utterance pairs such as question–answer pairs, invitation–acceptance pairs, request–compliance pairs, and the like, which have a special relatedness over and above the sequentiality that all utterances have. These are called 'adjacency pairs' (Sacks et al., 1974), and they have the following characteristics:

> (1) two utterance length; (2) adjacent positioning of component utterances; (3) different speakers producing each utterance . . . [there is] a typology in the speakers' production of the sequences... [which] partitions utterance types into 'first pair parts' (i.e., first parts of pairs) and 'second pair parts'. . . . A basic rule of adjacency pair operation is: given the recognizable production of a first pair part, on its first possible completion its speaker should stop and a next speaker should start and produce a second pair part from the pair type of which the first is recognizably a member. (Schegloff and Sacks, 1973: 295–6)

This 'rule' that specifies what speakers 'should' do is not a behavioural rule that people have to follow in order to make sense. Rather, in keeping with what we have noted about everyday social rules in Chapters 1 and 3, adjacency pairings are *normative* and *constitutive* kinds of rules. That is to say, they are sequential patterns that set up relevancies, or interpretational frames, for other actions to slot into, where the status of such 'relevancies' and 'interpretations' is a matter of what happens interactionally. An utterance that functions as an 'invitation' thereby functions as the first part of an invitation–acceptance or invitation–refusal sequence. It creates a relevance slot, in which any next turn can be produced and inspected (by participants and analysts) as a possible response – that is, relevantly, a possible acceptance or refusal. This can work backwards too, through the way in which utterances imply their own sequential coherence. A refusal effectively constitutes whatever preceded it as an invitation or offer, whereupon the first speaker has the option, in next (third) turn, of repairing any misunderstanding.[24]

Of course, by Sacks's principle of subversion, such an opportunity for 'repair' also provides a rather useful procedure for *treating* rejected offers *as* misunderstandings, and thus for managing psychological issues of intention-in-speaking, motive, or 'face'. Similarly, the *production* of what appear to be ambiguous or 'indirect' offers and invitations provides speakers with just that opportunity, of treating them later as not having been made. Whether or not 'actual' offers have been made and rejected and unmade, or shared states of mind 'actually' (psychologically) repaired, is not the point here; that would be to reintroduce an intentional and strategic, communication model of talk. What we are dealing with is an interactional 'machinery' (as Sacks called this kind of thing) for making all those psychological matters interactionally live for participants, as public, performative features of talk.[25]

Clearly, given its normative rather than mechanical operation, the ostensibly simple device of adjacency pairing is capable of sustaining some rather subtle interactional work. This is partly due to the fact that the relevancies set up by adjacency pairings are inescapable. Failing to produce an appropriate or intelligible 'second' is not a breakdown of communication, but a breach of 'conditional relevance', a contextually meaningful action, what Schegloff calls a 'notable absence':

> When one utterance (A) is conditionally relevant on another (S), then the occurrence of S provides for the relevance of the occurrence of A. If A occurs, it occurs (i.e. is produced and heard) as 'responsive to' S, i.e. in a serial or sequenced relation to it; and, if it does not occur, its non-occurrence is an event, i.e. it is not only non-occurring (as is each member of an indefinitely extendible list of possible occurrences), it is absent, or 'officially' or 'notably' absent. That is an event that can be seen not only from its 'noticeability,' but from its use as legitimate and recognizable grounds for a set of inferences (e.g. about the participant who failed to produce it). (Schegloff, 1972: 76)

Once again, a category such as 'notable absence' is first and foremost a participants' category before it is an analysts' one. Such absences, and the inferences they may engender, are recognizable by analysts insofar as they are oriented to as significant and accountable, and as available for inferences, and/or for repairing them, by participants.

Preference organization and accounts

One of the most important developments of the notion of adjacency pairs, and how they produce conditional relevance, is what conversation analysts call *preference organization* (Atkinson and Heritage, 1984). This is the notion that there is a normative[26] pattern in the production of second pair parts. Requests and proposals are normatively granted rather than refused (Davidson, 1984); invitations and offers are normatively accepted rather than rejected (Drew, 1984); agreement with some prior assessment of things is normatively preferred to disagreement, except when such assessments are self-deprecations (Pomerantz, 1978, 1984a); and there is a normative preference for self-correction (repair) rather than for others to do it (Schegloff et al., 1977). Again, despite the use of the term 'preference', it is important to distinguish between speakers' 'actual' wants or desires, and these normative structures. One key to that distinction is the fact that invitation refusals (etc.) are *generally* marked as non-normative, or 'dispreferred', irrespective of how welcome or repugnant the invitation may be.[27]

In the following extracts (from Heritage, 1984a: 258; and Drew, 1984: 135), 4.3 shows a preferred pattern for invitation acceptance, while 4.4 illustrates a dispreferred pattern for refusal.

Extract 4.3

```
1   B:   Why don't you come and see me some┌times
2   A:                                       └I would like to
3   B:   I would like you to
(SBL:10:12)
```

Extract 4.4

```
1   E:   Wanna come down'n ┌have a bite a l:unch with me:?=
2   N:                     └°(            )°
3   E:   =I got some bee:r an' stu:ff,
4        (0.2)
5   N:   Well you're real sweet hon:, uh::m
6        (.)
7   N:   ┌let-    I:   ha(v) ┐
8   E:   └or d'you have some ┘p'n el┌se (t')
9   N:                             └No:, I have to uh call
10       Rol's mother. .h I told 'er I'd ca:ll 'er this morning
(NB:II:2:14)
```

In Extract 4.3 the acceptance (line 2) is simple and immediate, even
occurring in overlap with the invitation's ending.[28] In contrast, in Extract 4.4
the refusal (line 9) is delayed, prefaced by an appreciation of the invitation
(line 5), and accompanied by an account for non-acceptance (lines 9–10).
Levinson (1983: 334–5) lists these and various other markers of dispreference (such as starting a response with 'well. . .'), though not all of
them have to occur for participants to produce and (interactionally)
recognize them.

The provision of an *account*, as part of a dispreferred turn, is particularly
important for the ways in which psychological business gets done in talk. It is
an interaction slot for the production of stories, versions of events,
descriptions of physical circumstances, mental states and dispositions, and
so on. Ethnomethodologists and conversation analysts, as we have noted,
emphasize the pervasive relevance of accountability in human conduct.
Dispreferred turns are a specific case, in that their 'account' components
attend to the specific moral and 'attributional' issues (Edwards and Potter,
1992a) that arise through the acts of rejection or refusal. Note, for instance,
how N's account (Extract 4.4, lines 9–10) specifies a conflicting obligation, a
promise to be fulfilled, and one that specifies the particular morning
in question, rather than any time ever. In rejecting invitations, offers,
self-deprecations, and so on, accountability issues are typically managed by
bringing off the rejection as due to obligations or outside circumstances,
beyond the speaker's agency, wishes, or control (Drew, 1984). So accounts
that 'externalize' responsibility for actions occur here, in these discursive
contexts, as local actions being done *in and through current talk*, rather than
having the status of persons' actual or enduring beliefs or all-purpose mental
representations of events.

Note that N's inability account is not only produced by N, but anticipated
by E (line 8). N's incipient production of an invitation refusal (the delay,

preface, etc.) *signals a dispreferred in the making*, not just to analysts but to the participants themselves, and we can see that in how E starts to join in its production. The analyst's notion of 'preference' is designed to identify conversational features that participants themselves orient to interactionally, as an essential feature of how they work, even though participants would not recognize the analyst's term 'preference' as a description of what they do. Preference organization, to the extent that it proves to be a robust conversational phenomenon, is not a mechanical or technical pattern picked out by the analyst, like observing billiard ball interactions, or the way astronomers describe planetary motion around the sun, or how bees communicate information about sources of nectar (Frisch, 1950). Of course, participants who are not also conversation analysts would not be able to categorize and name them as 'preference phenomena', but they use them and orient to them.[29]

Max Atkinson and Paul Drew (1979) reject the notion of a single, definitive, decontextualized 'account' of events that researchers must learn how to extract from people (cf. Gilbert and Mulkay, 1984; Potter and Wetherell, 1987). Rather, various accounts will be deployed in conversational contexts, and, further, accounts depend for their force upon their sequential placement, such as acceptances of self-blame, which may occur as the opening parts of dispreferred turns, followed by 'defences' which refute or mitigate the blame. This sort of sequential organization of accounts reveals a great deal of subtle interactional work being done, and militates against extracting singular 'accounts' from their conversational contexts and coding them for their putatively general functions (Scott and Lyman, 1968), or their causal-explanatory status with regard to the actions accounted for (Harré and Secord, 1972).

Of course, accounts also occur outside of dispreferreds. As Schegloff (1989a) has remarked, any account *of* events is likely to be produced and received as an account *for* them. That is to say, participants' event reports generally attend to causality, agency, and accountability for those events, as well as managing accountability for the current action done in the reporting (Edwards and Potter, 1993). More narrowly, there is a range of accountable actions which are those for which members routinely offer accounts. In telephone calls, for instance, 'by and large on the first opportunity to talk after greetings, the person who's called gives an account of how they happened to make the call' (Sacks, 1992, vol. 1: 73). It can then be taken as a sign of intimacy that these kinds of accounts, for uninvited visits, or phone calls, stop being necessary (1992, vol. 1: 73).[30] The sequential organization of conversation provides for participants' production of reports, stories, event descriptions, and mental state formulations, to occur as interactionally situated and occasioned phenomena, within an oriented-to normative order of accountability and social intelligibility. This contrasts starkly with the conventional treatment of such discourse phenomena in most of psychology and the social sciences, where they are taken to be the products, however indirectly or inadequately expressed (and therefore in need of specialized devices such as questionnaires, experimental controls, or standardized tests), of some kind of situation-transcendent, reflective sense-making that happens to be expressed in words.

Conclusions: speakers' meanings and talk's design

The notion of talk-as-action cautions against the assumptions of a 'communication model' of talk, in which talk is viewed as the expression of speakers' intentions and mental contents, and a kind of transmission between minds. Instead, intentions, goals, mental contents, and their intersubjective 'sharing' are analysed as kinds of business that talk attends to, rather than being the analyst's stock assumption concerning what is actually going on. This 'caution' does not preach denial of an intentional life of the mind, nor of its importance for talk and action, but concerns the different kinds of status those things may have for participants and for analysts. We can think of this in terms of one of the major principles of talk-in-interaction, its indexicality.

Analysis of talk-in-interaction immediately has to deal with how specific utterances, and parts of utterances, take on local and sequentially conditional meanings, and with how marvellously intricate and consequential the details of that seem to be for talk's interactional trajectory and upshots. However, rather than assuming all this to be going on under cognitive control or intentional planning (however fast or unconscious that may be), we might try considering it retrospectively, as a *consequence* of indexicality. That is to say, it is retrospectively inevitable, both for participants and for analysts, that at any moment *something specific got said*, and that, given the ways in which meanings are indexically realized, some local and specific sense is always available, especially when this sense is provisional, being conditional upon what is said next. So the detailed contextual design and precision of talk is at least partially conceivable as an inescapable design feature of it, rather than something that has to be built in to it mentally for each utterance, under the control of intentions and plans (Suchman, 1987).

Now, it is not that I want to replace a forward-planning model of talk with one based on the discursive equivalent of walking around backwards and seeing where you have been. Rather, the point is to loosen up the status of communicative goals-and-intentions as an obvious basis for analysts' explanations of discourse, and to encourage instead an analytical stance in which such matters are, in the first instance, participants' business. Again, this is the essence of the conversation analyst's 'proof procedure', not simply to replace a prospective, intention-based model of meaning with a retrospective, uptake-based one, but, rather, to take seriously the nature of talk-in-interaction, which means examining how meanings are interactionally accomplished. Rather than providing analysts with hard evidence of what prior speakers actually meant when they spoke, it is no more than the analyst's recognition that the object under analysis is *interaction*.[31] The proof procedure is, in the first instance, a *participants'* procedure.

The accusation is sometimes levelled at CA, and at CA-influenced discursive psychology (for example, by Neisser, 1992), that they are forms of 'behaviourism'. Such an accusation has a special appeal for cognitive psychologists, who (as we noted in Chapter 2) count themselves as having vanquished behaviourism already. In fact, what was vanquished was stimulus–response conditioning models of human behaviour, and especially their capacity to account for language (Chomsky, 1959; Gardner, 1985). CA and discursive psychology are nothing of that sort. The object under study is talk considered as social practice, analysed as intersubjectively constituted meanings rather than behavioural causes and effects, with the aim of explicating participants' own descriptive and explanatory practices, rather than ignoring those in favour of analysts' descriptions and causal explanations. One of the achievements of ethnomethodology and conversation analysis has been the development of analyses of 'action' in which the behaviour–action dichotomy itself features not as an analyst's conundrum, to be decided in principle, but as a participants' category, or basis for proceeding.

Distinctions between what is intentional or not, and meant or not, are deployed and at stake in talk, and are *thereby analytically available*. That is not the same thing as eschewing meaning and intention altogether, as the behaviourists did, nor of trying to discover for ourselves, as 'explanations', what real intentions lurk behind, explain, or precede the things people say (as cognitivists do). Intentionality is approached as something pervasively implicated in participants' descriptions and versions, but also arising as an overt topic in such contexts as doing repairs, dealing with disjunctures in versions of events, managing accountability, and, as we shall see in Chapter 11, in policing the boundaries between who is fully human, and who/what is not. Doing repair, for example, is a way of 'doing' or *accomplishing* intent, rather than of revealing or retrieving it, and need not coincide with any psychological state lying behind the original utterance. As such, repair becomes a 'subvertible' way of (re)writing, or (re)constituting intent, and of establishing it interactionally as such, rather than merely reiterating it.[32]

The claim to be analysing participants' understandings carries no expectation that participants will readily recognize a conversation *analysis* as a (proper) description of their talk (Schegloff, 1984). As Sacks suggested, a purely non-technical analysis of conversation was always likely to be a 'very short term possibility, so you'd better look while you can' (1966: 9). In any case, CA's claims about participants' understandings are not claims about speakers' cognitive states. Participants need only 'understand' (in the interactional, accomplished-and-repaired sense) *each other*, not the technical analyses of CA; those are for us academics to display *we* understand, in how we cite, use, summarize, and criticize them, and in how those citations, and so on, are received. In the next chapter I examine some instances of when conversational participants do, indeed, produce summarizing 'formulations' of their own talk, and of the kinds of locally situated, interactional business that such formulations manage.

Notes

1. As noted in Chapter 3, there is some dispute about whether CA is fully ethnomethodo-logical, and there is *also* a possibility of doing ethnomethodological studies of CA itself, viewed as a reality-producing social practice: 'to treat the science of conversation analysis as a recoverable order of literary practice . . . as the outcome of a specific set of literary technologies' (Bogen, 1992: 274). See also Atkinson (1990), Lynch and Bogen (1994), and Pollner (1991). The line taken here follows that of Heritage (1984a) and Schegloff (1992b), who present CA as grounded in ethnomethodology (see also Garfinkel and Sacks, 1970).

2. Major sources include: Atkinson and Heritage (1984); Boden and Zimmerman (1991); Button, Drew, and Heritage (1986); Button and Lee (1987); Drew and Heritage (1992); Goodwin and Heritage (1990); Heritage (1984a); Maynard (1987, 1988); Pomerantz (1993); Psathas (1979, 1990, 1995); Schenkein (1978); Sudnow (1972); ten Have and Psathas (1995). The journal *Research on Language and Social Interaction* is also largely CA-based.

3. It has to be acknowledged, however, that it may take an analyst as expert and subtle as Schegloff (1989c) to reveal how this participants' orientation to the nature of mundane talk is done. By and large, institutional talk is something that participants may pass judgments on, treat as justifiable or criticizable, and so on, while mundane conversation remains its normative backdrop or, in Garfinkel's terms, 'specifically uninteresting' and 'not matters for competent remarks' (Heritage, 1995: 395).

4. As the linguist Wallace Chafe put it, 'Language enables a speaker to transform configurations of ideas into configurations of sounds, and it enables a listener within his own mind to transform these sounds back into a reasonable facsimile of the ideas with which the speaker began' (1970: 15). This echoes the communication model of language and ideas outlined by the philosopher John Locke (1894). For a variety of critiques, see Derrida (1977a), Harris (1981, 1988), Reddy (1979), Schegloff (1989a), and Taylor (1992).

5. That is to say, organizations such as adjacency pairs, repair, the turn-taking system, preference structure, and so on, are found to operate as purely sequential phenomena, independently of variations across speaker and topic, and perhaps even across cultures (Moerman, 1988).

6. This is also disputed, of course. Chomsky's (1968) assumption of an idealized speaker–hearer, who intuitively knows the grammar of a homogenous speech community, contrasts with studies by sociolinguists (Labov, 1972) and critical linguists (Hodge and Kress, 1993) of the prevalence and social potency of variations and differences.

7. This is Garfinkel's (1967) term for how, within the workings of mundane common sense, those workings themselves remain an unremarkable backdrop until they are in some way 'breached' and/or made the focus of phenomenological or ethnomethodological inquiry.

8. For example, Sperber and Wilson (1982: 79) invite us to 'consider the following dialogue':

> *Ann*:   Will you have a glass of brandy?
> *Omar*: You know I am a good Moslem.

They point out how, possessed of some knowledge of Muslim restrictions on drinking alcohol, Ann would infer from Omar's response that he is declining her offer. The detailed ways in which offers are made and declined in naturally occurring talk, and the design of 'accounts' for refusals (such as Omar's), together with other considerations such as the constitutive nature of refusals and their uptakes in defining such things as 'offers' and participants' 'inferences', are among the issues addressed by conversation analysts (e.g., Davidson, 1984). See the comments on 'preference organization' later in this chapter.

9. Saussure (1922/1974) distinguished between the grammar or systematic organization of a language ('*langue*'), and speech, or language in use; his construction of a 'structural linguistics' was an effort to describe '*langue*'. As we noted in Chapter 1, Chomsky (1968) adapted this for a cognition-versus-behaviour dichotomy between 'competence' (the range of grammatical judgments that competent speakers are able to make) and 'performance'

(the messier, error-prone realm of actual speech). These kinds of distinctions proved powerfully persuasive in the development of linguistics, cognitive psychology, and the philosophy of mind in establishing a prime focus on grammatical rules and idealized knowledge states, and away from the contingencies of talk.

10. Note that the object of analysis has been 'sentences' rather than 'utterances' – that is, units defined grammatically, rather than units of talk or of social action. It is much less contentious to invent sentences, being objects defined by judgment, than to invent utterances, which are empirical.

11. This includes starting to notice not just instances but absences, where the analyst's knowledge of general conversational patterns may help identify something 'missing': 'Thus one looks for them and finds them "missing" if they are not there. The relevant "missing", however, is "missing for the participants", and one must then go back to the data to find evidence of the participants' orientation to something being awry' (Schegloff, 1995: 201).

12. The notion that language, or talk, is a kind of communication is deeply embedded in both technical and common-sense discourse. For example, the linguist John Lyons remarks that 'To say that language serves as an instrument of communication is to utter a truism' (1977: 32). It is the business of this chapter to define 'communication' as no more than an available *metaphor* in talk about talk.

13. Examples include Geertz's (1973, 1983) observations on the absence of the assumption of an agentive self in many non-Western cultures; Duranti's (1988) study of its absence with regard to intentional meanings in Western Samoa (cf. Ochs and Schieffelin, 1984); Rosaldo's (1982) similar use of Ilongot conversation to criticize speech act theory; various critiques based on Western patterns of talk and accountability, such as Harré (1987), the edited collection in Shotter and Gergen (1989), critiques by Levinson (1983) and Streeck (1980); empirical studies such as Linell, Alemyr, and Jönsson (1993) of the joint, or interactional, production of intentionality and responsibility in judicial settings; and Jayyusi's (1993) observations on intentionality versus happenstance as endemic issues in accounts of human activities.

14. For example, what a speaker 'meant to say' arose in some studies that Jonathan Potter and I did of a political dispute reported in the British press, in which the then Chancellor, Nigel Lawson, having been quoted 'verbatim' on controversial government plans to cut pensions, deployed a distinction between what he might have 'said' and what he plainly 'meant' as part of a counter-argument about inadequate and mischievous reporting (Edwards and Potter, 1992a, 1992b; Potter and Edwards, 1990). In CA, what a speaker 'meant' is also a *participants' concern*, and a means of conducting social relationships. It is handled in the turn-by-turn organization of talk, and sometimes addressed directly by participants as part of managing intersubjectivity, such as when talk is 'repaired' by a speaker in 'third turn' (Schegloff, 1992c). Intersubjectivity is discussed further below and in Chapter 5.

15. This is not to deny cultural differences, but to orient analysis to participants' discursive practices rather than the presence or absence of categories derived from Western philosophy, psychology, and social science. See also Michael Moerman's (1988) application of conversation analytical perspectives to talk in non-Western settings. Moerman concludes, with regard to a goals–intentions model of talk's actions, that 'No individual human actor is their author. We build our experienced, lived in, significant social reality out of a mesh of interactive processes too tiny and too quick for the thinking, planning "I" to handle' (1988: 30).

16. Pomerantz (1990–1) is nevertheless more willing than other conversation analysts are to attribute mental states to speakers. Heritage's analysis demonstrates the analytical difficulties of doing that; cf. Jefferson's (1989a) and Schegloff's (1988, 1989a) critiques of speech act theory.

17. CA's dispute with speech act theory extends beyond indirect speech acts to ostensibly direct ones (Levinson, 1983). For example, Schegloff's (1967) doctoral thesis 'disputes the claim that a greeting item in first position in a conversation is a method for doing greeting' (Schegloff, 1989a: 205). The notion of 'indirect speech acts' makes the false assumption

that linguistic form is the participants' primary interpretative resource unless overridden by other factors. Schegloff shows that speakers, in some cases at least, may orient primarily to the sequential location of an utterance. This raises the otherwise unforeseen problem of accounting for how grammatically defined 'interrogative' forms function interactionally as questions, never mind 'indirectly' as requests, or whatever. 'The point is that no analysis, grammatical, semantic, pragmatic, etc., of these utterances taken singly and out of sequence, will yield their import in use, will show what co-participants might make of them and do about them' (Schegloff, 1984: 31, based on Schegloff and Sacks, 1973: 313). Similarly, many 'indirect speech acts' can be explicated in terms of their sequential contexts of occurrence, as recognizable 'pre-sequences' to whatever act they are taken to indirectly perform. An example would be a 'pre-request' such as:

A: You don't have this number I don't suppose?
B: Sure. Cambridge 60385.
(Levinson, 1983: 360)

From a CA perspective, 'indirect speech acts' are decontextualized, and often conventional, kinds of pre-sequences whose sense is analysable in contexts of use via empirical, sequential analysis. See also the exchanges between Schegloff and Searle in Verscheuren (1992).

18. The way in which descriptions in conversation orient to actual and potential *alternative* descriptions is also a major feature of rhetorical social psychology (Billig, 1987; Billig et al., 1988; Edwards and Potter, 1993). When rhetorical and discursive psychologists invoke *rhetoric* as a pervasive feature of talk and text, and therefore also of analysis, we have in mind not only *argument*, in Billig's (1987) sense, but also this could-have-been-otherwise, attending-to-alternatives, nature of everyday descriptions. Rhetoric is not something that CA has ignored, because the ways in which participants attend to interactionally live alternatives has been a recurrent theme, but it has not been much topicalized as 'rhetoric'. It is a feature that has been named and highlighted much more in social psychologically oriented work, where it is set against its own rhetorical alternative. That alternative is conventional psychology's treatment of language and cognition, where language features as a methodological tool or dependent variable. That is to say, language is used in drawing up interview schedules, questionnaires, rating scales and experimental instructions, to which people's verbal or other responses tell us of their beliefs, attitudes, understandings of the world, and various other cognitive states.

19. Note how all these analytical notions – of what counts as sufficient grounds for knowing, of what B was in a position to know as a witness and A was not, the adequacy of B's story – are features that arise in the discourse itself, in how A and B orient to each other and to described events, rather than something the analyst introduces from outside of their talk to explain it; for instance, that B may have had a string of convictions for domestic violence, or whatever. While the analyst clearly needs to know more than is contained in the talk, such as what kind of folk the police are, and what kinds of things they may get called out for, the analytical issue is *the role that that kind of knowledge plays in analysis*. In CA, as I have emphasized, that role is not as an analyst's explanatory resource, but as a resource whose use is disciplined by the task of recognizing how and when it is made relevant by participants within particular stretches of talk.

20. This expression is meant to invoke the notion of 'second level signification' in semiotics (Barthes, 1972; see also Potter, 1996), where, once something gets to be a sign for something, it may in turn become something for which second-order signs can stand. This is a principle of (semiotic analyses of) advertising, where advertised products such as cosmetics or cigarettes are sold by association with signs of desirable identities and life-styles.

21. On ostensibly 'indirect' forms such as euphemisms and pro-terms, Sacks remarks: 'it seems to me that the things called "indirect reference" . . . are the most usual ways to talk. Where . . . the fundamental aim is to have proved, by the de facto understandability of what they've said, that the other, by understanding what you've said, sees that he's not in a

position to, need not, turn that utterance into a problem. That is to say, all that machinery for checking things out – why an utterance is said, why now, why did he do it, why did he refer that way, etc. – as much as is possible is *built into the structures for doing talk. And if talk is at all understandable, it solves those issues*' (1992, vol. 1: 545–6, emphasis added).

22. This claim for the normality, even primacy, of what Sacks calls 'subversion' finds an unexpected echo in Derrida's (1977b) ironic critique of the notion of 'indirect' speech acts, and the supposed primacy of directness and literal description. Similarly, the utterance 'This is, after all, a group therapy session' might be considered a challenge, of which Austin might have approved, to his initial 'constative–performative' distinction. Is it a mere description, which might be deemed true or false, or something more like 'I name this ship the *Bismarck*,' which performatively *makes* it so? Perhaps all descriptions are kinds of making-it-so namings, given that things could always be described otherwise, and do not come ready-labelled outside of human naming practices. In this sense, and in keeping with the constructionism outlined in Chapter 3, assigning 'proper names' are less *interestingly* 'performative' (or constitutive) than assigning everyday descriptions.

23. The following treatment of sequential organization is very brief, focusing on its implications for notions such as 'shared cognition,' and omitting altogether the 'turn-taking system' outlined in the classic paper on sequential organization: Sacks et al. (1974).

24. These kinds of conversational sequences have sometimes been misunderstood, especially in the cognitive science literature, as 'formal' rules that generate or constrain conversation, like rules of grammar are supposed to do. But recall the discussion of traffic rules, etc., in Chapter 1. It is a false presumption 'that ordinary language is constrained by a calculus of determining rules' (Button et al., 1995: 157). Rather, 'ironically for those who are offering up conversation analysis to computational linguistics, *it is exactly the contrary case that conversation analysis sustains*' (Button et al., 1995: 192, original emphasis).

25. There is much more to this important notion of 'repair' than I have indicated here. There are various analytic categories of it, based on by whom, and precisely when, repairs are initiated and dealt with. These include within turn repairs, by a current speaker, of the utterance in progress; next turn repair by a second speaker (which may be accepted or refused by the first speaker); and 'third turn' repair, in which the speaker of a first turn repairs a misunderstanding (and thus constitutes it as such) by a second speaker. Schegloff (1992c) refers to third turn repair as 'the last structurally provided defence of intersubjectivity in conversation'. For the other kinds of repair, see also Schegloff et al. (1977).

26. Again note the difference, introduced in Chapters 1 and 3, between 'normative' rules that people *orient* to as being in operation, and those that supposedly constrain or govern, or are statistically normal.

27. In an early discussion of 'preference' in question–answer pairs, Harvey Sacks introduced the term to refer to occasions when 'a question is built in such a way to exhibit a preference as between "yes" or "no"' (Sacks, 1987: 57, originally given as a lecture in 1973). Note even here how such 'exhibits' of preference are features 'built' into talk, rather than appeals to speakers' wishes or intentions, though clearly they provide bases for participants to infer such notions. An example of a 'no'-oriented question was 'Well is this really what you wanted?' (1987: 57). The notion of preference in subsequent CA studies has focused more on structural characteristics of second rather than first pair parts (see also Bilmes, 1987).

28. As Judy Davidson (1984) notes, first pair parts such as invitations, requests, and offers are generally recognizable as such prior to their completion as utterances. There may, therefore, be some time during which the first utterance is still in progress, which she calls a 'monitor space,' when acceptances are made, or else potential refusals start to be hearable, such that first speakers may then reformulate an offer, request, or invitation before it has been overtly rejected, or even anticipate the refuser's account for non-compliance (see, for example, line 8 in Extract 4.4). Again, this being so, it is something that can be 'subverted' to the extent that invitations (etc.) may be built or extended so as to possess monitor spaces within which overt rejections can be anticipated and forestalled. This is the kind of interactional subtlety that requires careful transcriptions for its analysis, including the recording of pauses, overlaps, and the like.

29. In another example of a receiver-orientation to a dispreferred, the receiver of a rejection-in-progress anticipates its basis: 'With "I don' know if it's possible, but" Donny adumbrates the conventional grounds of rejection of requests' (Schegloff, 1995: 200).

30. This is one way in which conversations can vary. There will be forms of talk where the kinds of norms and preferences that I have been summarizing seem to be contravened. People may refuse invitations abruptly, fail to provide 'accounts for calling,' and so on. Rather than standing as evidence that conversations are *not* as organized as CA proposes, it may be that they are understandable as ways of being rude, or of signalling intimacy, and so on, precisely because they *are* exceptions to norms that otherwise, or elsewhere, prevail. It is not that CA is then becoming immune from disproof, but, rather, that analysing talk in terms of norms, orientations, and preference is a way of explicating what we understand talk to be doing, including how we may form the impression that we are looking at rudeness or intimacy, while wondering how it is that we sense such things.

31. As Sacks, Schegloff, and Jefferson put it: 'Since it is the parties' understandings of prior turns' talk that is relevant to their construction of next turns, it is *their* understandings that are wanted for analysis' (1974: 726, original emphasis). The 'proof procedure' is not a mechanical acceptance, by the analyst, of uptakes as guarantees of what prior turns 'actually mean' psychologically, or intentionally. For example, see Schegloff (1995: 191), where a speaker is analysed as having 'not caught', in immediate next turn, the interactional trajectory of a first speaker's turn. But in Schegloff's analysis the second speaker's 'not getting it' is not a psychological judgment about the speaker, but, rather, an intrinsic part of the interaction itself, based on how it then unfolds. The crucial analytic point is the sequential organization and constitution of meaning-in-interaction, rather than the vain pursuit of speakers' true intentions (cf. Bilmes, 1986).

32. I am probably making much more of Sacks's notion of 'subversion' than his own brief use of it warrants, and I make more use of it in the chapters that follow. But it seems to be a pervasively relevant notion in how Sacks analyses social actions. For example, the following is surely a cautionary tale for those who would ignore subversion: 'Here's a marvellous thing by some absolutely inane fellow, in a book called African Suicide and Homicide. This guy wrote an article where he proposed that there's no problem finding out the correctness of the rate of suicide among some tribe, because when they kill themselves they all hang themselves' (Sacks, 1989: 245). Presumably, hanging someone would be a fine way to commit murder there, while suicide would be very easy to hide.

5

Shared Knowledge

'Shared knowledge' is a topic that invokes a wide range of concerns in philosophy, psychology, and social science. It plays a part in sub-disciplines such as social cognition, discourse comprehension, artificial intelligence, human–computer interaction, 'distributed cognition' (Engeström and Middleton, 1996), cultural psychology, as well as in sociological and anthropological notions of social order and culture itself, and more besides these. It also features as an analytic concern in discursive psychology, and this chapter outlines how.

The first part of the chapter takes some examples of work in psycho-linguistics, especially Herbert Clark's, in which psychological studies of shared knowledge have come closest to the study of everyday discourse. Various problems are raised with regard to the conception of discourse as 'conveying information' within an underlying 'communication model' of thought and language. This chapter argues for viewing shared (or 'given') information as a rhetorical category that participants actively construct and use, or treat as such, rather than its having the psychological status of things actually known in common, or even assumed by them to be known. That brings us to an examination of how participants sometimes explicitly 'formulate' the content of shared knowledge, and what they are doing when they do that. Finally, we examine the notions of consensus and agreement as discourse categories, and again, as concerns that participants orient to in their talk, rather than as a judgment that analysts have to make (such as by asking, 'Is there actually a consensus or agreement here?').

The notion of 'shared knowledge' has three senses that I shall use: (1) *Cultural knowledge* – things that people generally know about the world or can be expected to know, within a given speech community, and that they use across different occasions of talk. Examples include 'folk models' of various kinds (D'Andrade and Strauss, 1992; Holland and Quinn, 1987), cultural 'scripts' (Schank and Abelson, 1977), and the like. These will feature more in later chapters (especially Chapters 6 and 9). (2) *Mutual knowledge* – things that individuals in interactions assume each other knows, and think the other person knows they know (and so on), and that they update continuously as the conversation proceeds. (3) *Pragmatic intersub-jectivity* – shared knowledge as a participants' practical concern; what their talk *treats as* shared, and when, and how. This third sense, 'pragmatic intersubjectivity', is a continuation of how intersubjectivity was treated in Chapter 4, the kind of thing conversation analysts study. That continues to be the primary sense I shall use here. One of the arguments that runs through this book is that the study of pragmatic intersubjectivity, sense 3, overrides and subsumes the other two senses of 'shared knowledge'.

The main issue in this chapter is the tension between senses 2 and 3. We take up the argument that sense 2, despite its common-sense appeal, gives rise to conceptual and empirical difficulties that can be largely avoided by reformulating the issue in terms of sense 3, as talk's practical business. The issue of 'mutual knowledge' (sense 2: see Smith, 1982) can be related to the communication model of talk. It conceives of talk as a kind of communication between minds, where these minds already hold a large amount of information in common, and know (or believe, or assume) they do, and formulate messages on that basis. This commonality of mental contents is sometimes called, by psychologists of communication, 'common knowledge' or 'common ground' (for example, Clark, 1985; Krauss and Fussell, 1991).

Shared knowledge as 'common ground'

Herbert Clark's notion of 'common ground' is that which participants in interaction 'mutually know, believe, and suppose' (1985: 183). So, 'grounding' is 'the collective process by which the participants try to reach this mutual belief' (Clark and Brennan, 1991: 129; see also Clark and Schaefer, 1989). Grounding is a feature of communication-between-minds:

> Grounding is essential to communication. *Once we have formulated a message, we must do more than just send it off.* We need to assure ourselves that it has been understood as we intended it to be. Otherwise, we have little assurance that the discourse we are taking part in will proceed in an orderly way. (Clark and Brennan, 1991: 147, emphasis added)[1]

Among the linguistic devices that are used in such inter-mental coordinations are those of *deixis* and *anaphora* (see Lyons, 1977, for a useful summary). Broadly speaking, deictic words are the set of pronouns, adverbs, and demonstratives that shift their meaning according to context, requiring situational or contextual observations and knowledge in order for us to know what they refer to. So, an utterance such as 'Put that over there would you?' works on the basis that the addressee knows (or can see or infer) what 'that' is, and where 'over there' is (possibly by looking where the speaker is pointing to), and of course 'you' shifts its referent to whoever is being addressed.

Ragnar Rommetveit (1978) usefully distinguishes three dimensions of deictic reference: *person* (the speech act roles of 'I' the speaker, 'you' the listener, and various third parties: he, she, it, they, etc.); *place* ('here' is relatively close to the act of speaking, 'there' is contrastively distant); and *time* ('now' is close to the time of speaking, 'then' is again *contrastively* distant). Note how much these terms shift in their objective references, and how relative they are to the act and context of talk, and to the contrast being drawn. *Here*, for example, can mean anything from 'here where I want you to sign your name', as distinct from a few inches away (or, indeed, discriminations on an even smaller scale), to 'here in Western Europe', as distinct from, say, the USA (or even larger, galactic scales; cf. Miller and Johnson-Laird, 1976; Schegloff, 1972).

Anaphora, again broadly speaking, is the use of pronouns and other pro-terms (she, it, do [a pro-verb], we, etc.) to refer to items already, or about to be, identified in the text or talk. An example would be: 'John thanked Mary for giving *him* [John] a present.'[2] The tracing of anaphoric references by communication partners in laboratory experiments, and by computer programs designed to do it, is a feature of various studies by cognitive psychologists in the fields of psycholinguistics (for example, Anderson, Garrod, and Sanford, 1983; Clark and Wilkes-Gibbs, 1986), social cognition (for example, Krauss and Fussell, 1991), and artificial intelligence (for example, Winograd and Flores, 1986). These studies support the general conclusion that, in practice, comprehenders of talk and text quickly move from the actual words spoken or read, into inferences, mental models, and other 'knowledge representations' of the world described. This implies that, as far as current talk is concerned, there may be little psychological difference between deictic references to things outside the text, and anaphoric references to things actually said. People may soon forget what was said, but retain a conception of what was meant or referred to (Bransford, 1979; Johnson-Laird, 1983; Kintsch, 1974).[3]

Deixis and anaphora are linguistic devices that require and enable conversational participants to link the content of talk to its temporal, situational, and interpersonal settings. However, as we noted in Chapters 3 and 4, indexicality is a pervasive feature of discourse. *All* words are indexical in usage. In my invented example, 'John thanked Mary for giving him a present', all the *other* words (as well as the pronoun 'him') also take on specific local meanings. There will be a particular 'John' and 'Mary', a particular instantiation of 'thanking', of 'giving', and of 'present'. Each of these descriptors is an optional way of packaging the sense of events, and each provides a context for the others; if the 'present' were a motor car, say, or an annuity, or a fountain pen, then the 'giving' also might be different sorts of actions.

In conversation analysis and discursive psychology, the 'loose fit' between descriptions and their referents (Heritage, 1984a: 145) has to be understood as an essential feature of how language works, rather than an unfortunate lack of referential precision. The loose fit obviates the need for an infinitely detailed and extended descriptive mapping between words and the world which a more precise semantics starts to require. Fuzzy semantics provides the flexibility required for words to be *used to do things*, including the practical management of intersubjectivity: 'hearers must perform active contextualizing work in order to see what descriptions mean, and speakers rely upon hearers performing such work in order that their utterances will make definite sense' (Heritage, 1984a: 147–8).

A useful perspective on conversation analysis is to see it as the systematic study not only of how talk performs social actions, but of talk as the practical management of intersubjectivity (Drew, 1995). This incorporates much of talk's sequential organization, including the proof procedure, repair, turn organization, conditional relevance, and recipient design.[4] Conversation's sequential organization provides for the social actions that talk performs to be jointly, publicly understood activities, in Garfinkel's sense, where 'the appropriate image of a common understanding is . . . an operation rather than a common intersection of overlapping sets' (Garfinkel, 1967: 30). With this principle in mind, so to speak, we can return to the psycholinguistic notion of 'common ground', conceived as shared 'information', and explore the linguistic and psycholinguistic notions of 'given' and 'new' information, as these have been used in the work of Herbert Clark.

Common ground: 'information structure' as a way of talking

Clark (1985, 1992) offers a combination of 'individualist' and 'interactionist' approaches to language and meaning, in which talk is conceived as a 'coordination of action'. While drawing strongly on conversation analysis, he nevertheless retains the major elements of a communication model (or 'speech act theory') of talk, as expressing speakers' psychological states, such as their *goals* and *intentions*. Thus, 'when people utter sentences, they ask questions, make demands, offer apologies, and perform many other so-called speech acts. Their immediate purpose is to get certain listeners to do things in response' (1985: 180). By incorporating an interactionist perspective, Clark is able to mount a valuable critique of standard psychological approaches to sentences and texts, which treat them 'without regard for how speakers coordinate with listeners. . . . Stories, jokes, folk-tales, and other narratives are best viewed as specialized sections of conversations, as extended turns by a single speaker still genuinely interacting with his audience' (1985: 181).

The 'individualist' element retained in Clark's approach is evident in his use of invented as well as recorded dialogues, with accompanying imputations of speakers' intentions. Thus:

> When Helen tells Sam, 'The Bakers are on their way,' she may be indirectly requesting Sam to start dinner, to put more logs on the fire, to call the police for protection, or any number of other things. How does Sam infer what Helen means indirectly? That . . . is a matter of coordination – specifically, of Helen uttering the right words in the right circumstances, confident that Sam will understand her as she intended him to. (1985: 181)

We should note that the problems of 'coordination' faced by Helen and Sam arise very starkly here, precisely because this is all we are given of them, and indeed, up to now, being an invented couple, *all there is*. We have an utterance ('The Bakers are on their way') with all kinds of possible 'indirect' meanings, providing a puzzle to be solved, by them and by us (mostly by us, since 'they' are mere inventions). Presumably, in actual interactions, most of those possible meanings would not arise as relevant concerns.[5] And those that did arise would be *practically* resolved, in the sequential flow of interaction and repair, rather than being marooned as conceptual puzzles besetting theorists of 'mutual knowledge'.

The image is that of a society of marooned individuals, conceptually removed from the flow of situated interaction, but then placed *into* interactions where they find themselves beset by problems of inter-mental communication. It is an image applicable to a broad range of work in psycholinguistics and artificial intelligence. The problematics of discourse coordination are set up within the framework of the communication model, producing what is called the 'coordination problem' (Clark, 1985; Lewis, 1969; Schelling, 1960; Smith, 1982). This was originally articulated largely by the use of invented examples rather than through studies of talk-in-interaction, though it has subsequently been extended to such studies by Clark. We might call these *the problematics of the frozen moment*, a problem posed for individuals, considered psychologically as problem-solving minds, computing the sense of things at each of a series of moments in the action, like in a series of stills from a movie.

For Clark 'common ground' is *actual*. That is to say, it is something like a Venn diagram[6] of shared knowledge, pictured as intersecting cognitive states – factual information that participants both actually know, or actually believe they both know. It is based on

> three types of information. . . . *Linguistic evidence* . . . everything they have heard said as participants in the same conversation. . . . *Perceptual evidence* . . . all those experiences they have jointly had and are jointly having in each other's presence. . . . *Community membership* . . . all those things they take to be universally – or almost universally – known, believed, or supposed in the many communities and subcommunities to which they mutually believe the two of them to belong. (Clark, 1985: 183)

An appropriate way to conceive of all this is in AI (artificial intelligence) terms, as the kinds of knowledge that we would have to build into an information processing device (computer, person, etc.) to get it (her, him) to be able to take part in a conversation and keep track of its information flow.

What this notion of 'actual' shared knowledge underestimates, however, is how all those things (shared knowledge and experiences, notions of what has been said so far, etc.) are potentially capable of being described in variable ways. These things are not specifiable bits of 'information', but, rather, matters of concern, of possible relevance, of potential dispute; matters yet to be described. Of course, shared knowledge is just the kind of stuff that is *not* going to be put into words, but the thing at issue here is its nature as 'information'. The notion of 'information' elides the *constructive* work that has to be done when any such matters are 'formulated' (assigned a specific description), or otherwise made relevant at specific junctures in discourse.[7] However, rather than seeing common knowledge as inherently indeterminate, or interactionally at issue, Clark treats it as a reservoir of shared factual information which exists prior to, and is built up during, conversations: 'conversations can be viewed as the accumulation of information in the parties' common ground' (1985: 190). He sets aside, as abnormal, those occasions when people may 'lie, deceive, manipulate . . . and otherwise subvert the normal forms of coordination' (1985: 184). In Chapter 4, following Harvey Sacks, I argued that 'subversion' is part of talk's normal operation (just as rhetoric is – Billig, 1987), and by no means restricted to lies and deceptions. Let us explore this in terms of the notion of how common ground 'accumulates'.

The accumulation of common knowledge, in Clark's scheme, requires 'new' information to be added, by each succeeding utterance in a conversation, to old, or 'given' information. The linguistic structures that provide for this to be done make up what the linguist Michael Halliday (1967, 1970; cf. Chafe, 1970) has called 'information structure'. Thus, according to Clark (1985: 196):

> Most sentences can be divided into two parts, as in this example:
> • *Sentence*:   What Margaret did was go into the hospital.
> • *Given information*:   Margaret did X.
> • *New information*   X = go into the hospital.

So the sentence 'What Margaret did was go into the hospital' presupposes, as something already jointly known or 'given', that Margaret (a person jointly known and adequately identified by that name) did something; and it updates that shared knowledge by adding, as a bit of 'new' information that the speaker assumes the hearer does not already know, what it was that Margaret did. It is an example of how sentences of that general form ('What X did . . .') are designed to fit into conversations, as devices for accumulating shared information.

According to Clark, these and other structures (for example, uses of intonational stress or emphasis) provide the basis for a *given–new contract* (Clark and Haviland, 1977) between speaker and hearer. Under this contract, whatever information is placed into the linguistic categories *given* and *new* is, in normal and proper talk, appropriate to what is (believed to be) already mutually known. Some kind of given–new (or 'thematic') structure is a feature not merely of specialized types of sentences, but of *all* sentences. So in a sentence such as 'Where did you go for your vacation last year?' it is 'given', or presupposed, that the addressee went somewhere on vacation last year, and the request is for some 'new' information, in this case the location.

'Information structure' is certainly a useful way of taking a look at sentence grammar as function-oriented, and Clark and his colleagues have performed a number of convincing demonstrations that people are sensitive to those structures. But in Halliday's linguistics, 'given' and 'new' information are primarily signalled by *intonation*, by the use of stress or emphasis, and are therefore features of *talk*, rather than of the kinds of written sentence grammar that linguists and psycholinguists mostly deal with. Clark's treatment depends much more on grammatical structures and written sentences than Halliday's,[8] and this is a standard feature of most theoretical linguistics and experimental psycholinguistics. Halliday's focus on *spoken* language also coincides with a more action-oriented conception of what speakers are doing: 'These are options on the part of the speaker . . . what is new is in the last resort what the speaker chooses to *present* as new' (Halliday, 1967: 211, emphasis added). Similarly, 'one of the features of the "given–new" structure is its use for various rhetorical purposes, such as bullying the listener' (Halliday, 1970: 163). Of course, 'bullying' is a rather strong example of rhetorical use; one of the themes of discursive analysis is that discourse is *pervasively* rhetorical, not just abnormally or blame-worthily so. Truth and plain-speaking are just as constructed and inter-actionally 'defeasible' a pair of categories as are error and dissimulation.

Pressing Halliday's point further, the important thing is that these 'information structure' devices should be taken not as signs of actual or assumed knowledge states, but as *ways of talking*. Whether or not participants actually know things in common, and whether or not they believe each other to know things in common, these devices provide ways of *treating* various items *as* known in common, or as new, or, indeed, as mere 'information'. The notion that even their status as 'information' is not to be presumed relates back to the status of any verbal description as one of many possible ones, and therefore as providing an opportunity for constructive and rhetorical business to be done. These considerations do not merely add an extra variable to Clark's approach, an extra level of speakers' inten-tionality, nor an additional category of exceptional, manipulative, or deceitful talk. Rather, it is a matter of rethinking the base model of what talk is all about, and how it works. It is to include Sacks's notion of *subversion* as a pervasive feature of human interactions,[9] and to incorporate the central notion of the flexibility of descriptions, together with general ethno-methodological principles of how social actions work.

Clark's approach might be characterized as an attempt to incorporate into psycholinguistics as much as possible of the findings of conversation analysis, without letting go of the communication model of talk.[10] As Chapter 4 emphasized, intersubjectivity can be analysed as business that conversational participants *manage*, and do things with, rather than a state of actual shared knowledge and belief. Psycholinguistic approaches to intersubjectivity have been useful in identifying a range of devices by which that management is done. But they are also based on a rather mechanical and presumptively mentalistic notion of the process. The base metaphor is the communication model, which, as I have argued, generates for psycho-logical explanation the problematics of how two or more information processing devices (such as persons) are able to coordinate their talk and action in a rather robotically 'honest Joe' (or Jo) manner. But *what is linguistically 'given' need not be psychologically or inter-mentally given*, and that is a key to a wide range of relations between language and cognition in talk. Nor need 'new' be new: not actually, nor intentionally, nor inter-mentally. It is a way of talking. And it can be investigated empirically by studying samples of talk.

For example, consider Extract 5.1, which starts with Lottie answering a phone call from her close friend Emma. We can examine it for signs of new and given information.

Extract 5.1

```
 1     Lottie:   Hello:,
 2     Emma:     Good morning.
 3     Lottie:   How're you:::.=
 4  →  Emma:     =Oh: hi: honey we haven' gotten together have we.
 5     Lottie:   Oh:: gosh no: let's see: (.) Thurs:day night I
 6               went in town I came back Friday it was la:te,
 7               (0.5)
 8     Emma:     Oh you went in ↓Thursday ni:ght?
 9     Lottie:   Yea:h oh Earl had to get some stuff for: uh:::w
10               u- uh::m (0.2) working on a picture so I had to
11               go up there'n get it ['n : :
12     Emma:                          ['n you wor]ked Thursday too:?
13     Lottie:   Yeah (. . .)
```
(NB:I:6:R:1, slightly simplified)

In line 4 Emma's observation that she and Lottie have not 'gotten together' is problematic for a *linguistically* based analysis of given and new infor-mation. While Emma's 'we haven' gotten together' looks grammatically and intonationally like a news announcement, the following tag 'have we' suggests that Lottie might be (expected to be) in a position to ratify it as known. Presumably also, though this is a matter of general knowledge rather than grammar or intonation, we would expect a meeting between the two people concerned to be something they would both be aware of, which also makes it plausible that Emma is producing this non-meeting as a matter of common knowledge rather than news. But if it is common knowledge, or 'given information', where is the 'new' part? What is being *said*?[11]

Now consider line 4 sequentially, as something that follows line 3. Lottie's notably *emphatic* 'How're you:::.' (both stressed and elongated) could be taken as a rather exaggerated enquiry, signalling more than the routine interaction opener it might otherwise be (if unstressed), and perhaps a more serious enquiry after Emma's well-being. This in turn may imply that they have not seen each other for a while (however long, *for them*, such a 'while' might be), such that Lottie would not already know how Emma is.[12] So Emma's response in line 4 can be seen as attending to their non-meeting as something notable and possibly accountable (note that she does not respond by telling Lottie 'how she is'). Indeed, Lottie's subsequent turns construct a series of *accounts* for her part in not having gotten together with Emma. Now, how are we doing analytically, in terms of 'given' and 'new' information? My reading of the talk's sequential trajectory, and how it attends to interactional concerns, suggests that 'given' and 'new', in this instance at least, are not clear-cut categories of 'what people know', and nor are they adequately conceived as checks and updates on assumed shared knowledge. Rather, they begin to emerge as ways of packaging versions of the world, in the performance of talk's interactional business.

Consider line 5. Rather than acknowledging the 'given' nature of their not having met (lately), Lottie actually receives it as *news*, indeed exaggeratedly so: 'Oh:: gosh n<u>o</u>:'. But it is news that she treats as recognizably true (as something she knew, once made aware of it), and she immediately embarks on a discursive search-and-examination of her recent activities – 'Let's s<u>ee</u>:' (etc., lines 5–11). Lottie's talk in line 5 does not tell us that she actually, mentally, had not noticed that she and Emma had not met lately; nor that we and/or Emma would be mistaken in taking her enquiry in line 3 ('<u>How</u>'re you::::') as invoking that non-meeting. Rather, we can observe that, on a turn-by-turn basis, Lottie's 'news receipt' is a *way of talking* that *packages it as news*, at least as news-to-consciousness, and thus as something that, not being pre-formed in her mind, she now has to think about and 'see'.[13]

The distinction between the mental and the interactional, or *treated-as*, status of 'information' in discourse (as 'new' or 'given') is important not only in mundane conversation but also in formal settings such as law courts, interrogations, interviews, and in propaganda and advertising. It is common in such settings (and more widely) for potentially contentious claims or versions of events not to be marked or focused on as 'news', but, rather, to be packaged as 'given'. In a recently televised advertisement for the breakfast cereal Shredded Wheat, the ex-captain of England's Rugby Union team, Bill Beaumont, endorses the product while a television monitor in the background shows a video sequence of him, some years before, being carried triumphantly off the field on the shoulders of his team-mates. He says:

In those days I never really thought about why I ate Shredded Wheat . . .

– and proceeds to list what he now knows of its various nutritional virtues. In terms of information structure, the 'given' information (in the quoted sentence) is that he *ate Shredded Wheat* in those days; the 'new' part is that he never thought about why.

Now, if we examine the content of these 'information' categories, it quickly becomes doubtful that the audience already knows about Beaumont's erstwhile breakfast habits (that is, doubtful that they *actually are* common knowledge), or that Beaumont (or his script-writer) actually assumes we do. So what is it doing there, positioned as 'given'? Note that we can ask what it is doing there irrespective of whether or not Beaumont actually *is* a long-term Shredded Wheat eater, or thinks we know he is; this is not an investigation into the historical or psychological facts of the matter.

Let us start again; this is an advertisement, a product endorsement for which Beaumont is presumably being paid. As in any such advertising endorsement, an issue of 'stake' can arise that threatens to undermine its credibility (Edwards and Potter, 1992a): he may be endorsing it because he is being paid to. Of course, there are a variety of ways in which advertisers may deal with that difficulty, and work up an endorsement's authenticity. The device used here (an example of 'stake inoculation': Potter, 1996) is to project Beaumont's use and enjoyment of the product as pre-dating his endorsement of it.[14] Indeed, we might suppose that this is the advertisement's major persuasive content, at least as significant as the fact that the cereal is made from whole wheat, with no added salt or sugar, and so on. The beauty of packaging Beaumont's long-term consumption of the stuff as 'given information' is that we are invited to treat it as such, alongside the less contentious video-reminder of him as England's rugby captain, both as 'information' and as 'given', rather than as a contentious description doing persuasive business.[15]

Again, it is important not to think of this kind of information packaging as an abnormally strategic or machiavellian process restricted to advertisers, lawyers, politicians, and propagandists. As I have emphasized, rhetorical design is a pervasive feature of discourse in general, just as the deployment of alternative possible descriptions (but not necessarily contradictory ones) is a feature of mundane talk. Sacks's notion of *subversion* can be applied. Given that there are recognizable devices in talk and grammar that provide for the practical accomplishment of intersubjectivity, those devices are *available for use* in signalling and packaging the 'information status' of whatever content we insert into them. As we noted in the last chapter, it may be premature to consider that the 'normal' thing is straight, honest-to-goodness information coding and exchange. If subversion is the norm, in this pervasive and non-pejorative sense, then it may be that talk's devices, and the grammatical structures that support them, are designed for it.

Formulating what has been said

I have argued that the packaging of a piece of information as 'given' (or 'new') is no guarantee either that it is *psychologically* common (or new) knowledge, nor even that participants assume it to be. It has to be seen as a way of treating something as given, and even as 'information', rather than a particular and possibly contentious version of things. One of the ways in which shared knowledge is invoked in talk is when participants offer a 'formulation' of what has been said (Heritage and Watson, 1979). In Extract 5.2 a husband (Jimmy) and wife (Connie) have started recounting their marital troubles to a counsellor, including an incident two years prior to their current troubles when Jimmy 'walked out' following some disputed events in a pub.

Extract 5.2
```
 1  Counsellor:   the time of the first walk out, after the pub
 2                incident? .h wa::s t↑wo years ago did you sa↑:y?
 3  Connie:       Two years but now we:'ve had (.) problems,
 4                        [(      )]
 5  Jimmy:        [Well  ] LONG before that we've had things where
 6                I've (.) uh I'm going. I'd get in the car- an'
 7                       [go. ]
 8  Counsellor:   [Ten ] years. You've been walking out. ((sniffs))
 9  Connie:       No [:. No      ]
10  Jimmy:             [YEH yeh- ]
(DE–JF:C2:S1:5)
```

In lines 1–2 the counsellor, in information structure terms, treats it as given
that the 'walk out' happened, and was 'the first walk out', but treats as in
question, or in need of confirmation, *when* it happened. Connie's reply
confirms that time as 'two years' ago, but signals that there have also been
'problems'. Jimmy's version of those problems starts to upgrade them
towards walking-out status (lines 5–6), which the counsellor picks up and
explicates (line 8). By lines 9–10 Connie and Jimmy are flatly contradicting
each other on the 'given' status of the incident two years ago as the 'first' walk
out'.

This kind of example can be repeated many times, where a description is
offered as 'given' (and therefore as merely 'information'), but is then
resisted and reformulated; indeed, disputes may occur *before*, and not only
after, such treatments-as-given. This is likely to be the case here, in Extract
5.2. The status of Jimmy's walking out, and the recency or else the long
recurrence of such events in their marriage, are salient bases of disputation
in their discourse, and very likely something they have discussed many times
before coming for counselling. One of the major bones of contention
throughout their four sessions of counselling is Connie's claim that their
marital difficulties are relatively recent, following Jimmy's affair with
another woman, and Jimmy's counter-claim that their troubles are of long
standing, stemming from the day they met, and therefore more plausibly the
cause rather than the result of his affair. My reading of line 3, where
Connie's confirmation of the counsellor's formulation is immediately followed by 'but now we:'ve had (.) problems', is that this attends to Jimmy's
potential disagreement. Connie's term 'problems' is nicely vague here,
specifying no particular events, while providing a softened, non-walking-out
label for whatever long-term marital troubles Jimmy may cite.

The status of 'given information' has to be subsumed under the status of
descriptions in general, as part and parcel of talk's fact-constructive and
interaction-oriented business. As we have noted in earlier chapters, descriptions are ways of constructing the nature of events, and of implicating cause,
consequence, and accountability. This applies whether or not specific treatments of things as 'new' or 'given' become matters of open dispute between
participants, just as the constructive, could-have-been-otherwise nature of

everyday descriptions remains a salient feature of discourse, oriented-to as consequential by participants, even in the absence of overt disagreements.

One of Clark's sub-categories of shared knowledge or 'common ground', that we noted above, was '*Linguistic evidence* . . . everything they have heard said as participants in the same conversation' (1985: 183). It is unlikely, of course, that 'everything that has been said' is psychologically available to participants, like in some mental tape recording, and in any case, what they appear to keep track of is probably something more like its essence or 'gist'. Indeed, what people remember, infer, and use from what they have heard said has been a major issue in experimental cognitive psychology at least since Frederick Bartlett's (1932) pioneering studies. As we noted with regard to deixis and anaphora, participants in psychological experiments on memory for textual materials soon forget most of the specific linguistic details, retaining only their major meanings, or even a more schematic representation of the things described (Bransford, 1979; Sachs, 1974). In interaction analysis, however, the extent of participants' memories for talk may feature as an issue *for them*. Whereas participants sometimes appeal to what each other essentially 'meant' in spite of what they literally 'said', they also appeal to what each other 'actually said', and may even support such appeals by claiming an extraordinarily good verbatim memory (Edwards and Potter, 1992b; Lynch and Bogen, 1996).

Within the more general process of keeping track of what has been said, and orienting one's talk to it, people will sometimes *formulate* a version or gist of it. In their analysis of such formulations[16] John Heritage and Rod Watson (1979) demonstrate how these devices provide not merely matter-of-fact glosses or updates on shared information, but opportunities for performing constructive and consequential work on the content of prior talk. In extract 5.3 a solicitor is being interviewed on radio.

Extract 5.3

1	*Solicitor*:	The inescapable facts are these, er in nineteen thirty two
2		when he was er aged twenty three mister Harvey was er
3		committed to Rampton hospital under something called
4		the mental deficiency act nineteen thirteen which of course
5		is a statute that was swept away years ago and er he was
6		committed as far as I can er find out on an order by a
7		single magistrate er sitting I think in private.
8	*Interviewer*:	How long did he spend in Rampton
9	*Solicitor*:	Well he was in er Rampton and Moss-side hospitals er
10		alternatively er until nineteen sixty one
11 →	*Interviewer*:	That's the best part of <u>thirty</u> years
12	*Solicitor*:	That's right. Now in nineteen sixty one (. . .)

(Heritage and Watson, 1979: 130)

The interviewer's comment in line 11 is a formulation of what the solicitor has said. Heritage and Watson draw attention to three properties of such formulations in relation to the prior talk: *preservation*, *deletion*, and *transformation*:

It *preserves* the length of time Mr. Harvey was in hospital whilst simultaneously *deleting* such information as: the names of the hospitals involved, the Act of Parliament under which Mr. Harvey was committed . . . and so on. At the same time, the interviewer's utterance *transforms* some of the information furnished to him . . . re-describes or re-references parts of the information already delivered to him, thus preserving them 'in other words.' (1979: 130, original emphasis)

These three properties of formulations permit them to perform two kinds of functionally oriented work on prior content: *gists* and *upshots*. 'Gists' may be performed on one's own talk, or on that of another person, or on the conversation generally, or on some part of it. For example, when performed on another speaker's talk, gists may be offered as 'clarifications, or demonstrations of comprehension or in-touchness with the talk so far' (1979: 130). Examples include: 'So what you're saying is that you're self conscious', and 'You conform for the sake of conformity' (1979: 134, both spoken by a doctor to a patient). Note how the second example here is not explicitly a gist, and is identifiable as one only in the context (not provided here) in which it occurred, in relation to what preceded it, and how it was taken up and confirmed. 'Upshots', which may or may not follow gists, formulate consequences: 'So there might be another occasion on which you will use the law against unions' (1979: 134).

If I may offer a formulation of what Heritage and Watson are saying, it is that formulations essentially work like the rest of talk does, performing social actions, rather than merely reflecting the current cognitive status of a conversation-monitoring, information processing speaker–hearer. In the spirit of the phenomenon, my own formulation of formulations selectively works them into a statement about discourse, cognition, and shared knowledge. The important element is the constructive and interaction-oriented nature of formulations, the way they perform consequential work on preceding text or talk, proposing what is essential, or currently relevant, what is to be taken as jointly understood, and a basis on which to proceed. They do not merely reflect or express common knowledge, conceived as some state of joint cognition or understanding, nor even, necessarily, the speaker's best guess at it, but *construct* it in a manner fitted precisely to the occasion of its production, and for the interactional business such formulations accomplish.

The properties of conversational formulations are comparable to Bartlett's (1932) classic observations on serial reproduction remembering. One of Bartlett's procedures was to get people to examine an unfamiliar picture or read some text, such as a foreign and unfamiliar folk tale, and try to reproduce it later from memory. That reproduction would be passed to another person, who would also have to reproduce it from memory, and then that second reproduction would be passed to a third, and so on and on. Bartlett was interested in the changes that were introduced into each successive 'remembering', and what these changes tell us about how minds work, and how cultures work. The pictures and stories became more and more 'conventionalized' in the direction of images, symbols, and common-sense narratives and characters familiar in the participants' own culture.

Bartlett noted three main kinds of alterations in the successive reproductions: *additions*, *omissions*, and *transformations*. While these categories
do not precisely duplicate those of Heritage and Watson's 'formulations',
there is the same general phenomenon in which meaningful materials
(stories, pictures, talk) are 'reproduced' (under instructions to duplicate
them as well as possible) in ways that transform and embellish their
significance in some socially recognizable direction meaningful for the
reproducer. Despite Bartlett's major concern with the social and cultural
basis of memory and conventionalization, his findings have been treated by
cognitive psychologists primarily as foundational studies on the workings of
mind.[17] Heritage and Watson's more naturalistic and interaction-based
studies help to re-establish the intrinsically social and functional nature of
such reproductions, when they are things that people actually do in their
own time and as part of their own practices.

Formulations that perform institutional work

One of Harvey Sacks's earliest observations and interests was a conversational phenomenon he took from Plato's Socratic dialogues (such as the
Meno, which was discussed in Chapter 2), called 'adding them up'. From
examining a series of telephone calls between suicidal persons and
counsellors, Sacks concluded:

> . . . the person who is asking the questions seems to have first rights to perform an
> operation on the set of answers. You can call it 'draw a conclusion.' Socrates used
> the phrase 'add them up.' It was very basic this way of doing dialectic. He would go
> along and then say at some point, 'Well, let's see where we are. Let's add up the
> answers and draw some conclusions.' And it's that right that provides for a lot of
> what look like strugglings in conversations, where the attempt to move into the
> position of 'questioner' seems to be quite a thing that persons try to do. . . . As
> long as one is in the position of doing the questions, then in part they have control
> of the conversation. (1989: 289)

This early insight into the interactional dynamics of what came to be called
'formulations' was part of an interest Sacks shared with Emanuel Schegloff
in relations between psychodynamic theory and 'Platonic dialogue as a form
of discourse designed to control conduct' (Schegloff, 1989a: 188). In this
section we look briefly at some social settings in which formulating common
knowledge is a feature of how those settings work: these include courtrooms, classrooms, police interrogations, various kinds of interviews, and
counselling.

A characteristic of asymmetrically organized social relations, such as
teacher–pupil or lawyer–witness relations, and one that helps define the
nature of such relations, is an asymmetry in who performs various kinds of
formulations. In courtrooms, judges may do formal 'summings up', while
barristers are able to do that also in a more partisan way, and question
witnesses and 'formulate' their testimony.[18] Paul Drew (1990, 1992;

Atkinson and Drew, 1979) has analysed a variety of courtroom cross-examinations, including examples in which lawyers provide a summary of witnesses' testimony, which in turn may then be resisted and reformulated.

Extract 5.4

```
 1 Counsel:    Yesterday (0.6) when you testifie::d that (0.3) you been in the
 2             hospital (about) a half hour (.) a:nd (you were mistaken) (0.3)
 3             is that correct,
 4             (3.2)
 5             Remember testifying to that,
 6 Witness:    I remember yesterday's u:hm (.) it could've bin fiftee:n twenny
 7             it could've been a half hour I-y- a little more a little less
 8             (0.6)
 9 Counsel:    So. Instead of a half hour now between fifteen minutes and a
10             half hour (0.3) that's what (you led us to believe)
11             (0.4)
12 Defense     'jection
   Counsel:
13             (1.8)
14 Judge:      No it may stand
15 Counsel:    (        )
16 Witness:    (Yes)
17 Counsel:    Fifteen minutes to a half ho:ur (0.3) is that what it is now
18 Witness:    O:kay: (hh) (.) well uh::
19 Counsel:    You don' (know)
20 Witness:    Yes. (.) u-uh mean NO
21 Counsel:    No=
22 Witness:    =it was abou(t)-
23             (2.0)
24 Counsel:    Well how ⌈long
25 Witness:            ⌊Twenty minutes I'm not sure. (bu-) I don' know
26             how long it takes for anyone to get stitched up (. . .)
```
(Cheek: 35–3A, from Drew, 1990: 58, slightly simplified)

Drew (1990: 58) points out various salient features of this extract, and, in particular, how the cross-examining counsel works at producing and exploiting an inconsistency between what the witness had said the day before, and her current testimony (lines 1–3). The item in question is the 'half hour' (or however long) she claims to have spent in the hospital. The witness counters that imputation of inconsistency or error, in the precise details of her deceptively vague-looking response (lines 6–7). She includes the 'half hour' within 'a three-part list designed to convey the very approximate nature of her estimate' (Drew, 1990: 58), ranging between half an hour, fifteen, and twenty minutes, and also the overt claim to approximateness, 'a little more a little less'. The counsel again (re)formulates her talk (lines 17 and 19), using the extremes of the range she gave, as amounting to a confession of ignorance (line 19). Once more the witness asserts the approximate (rather than damagingly inaccurate or inconsistent) nature of her claim ('about . . . twenty minutes I'm not sure', lines 22–5), and provides a reasonable basis for that uncertainty: 'I don' know how long it takes for anyone to get stitched up' (lines 25–6). Her estimates of the time are now based not on anything such as checking her watch, say, and mis-remembering or getting it wrong, but on her inferences concerning how long such a technical procedure would be expected to take; a matter which she quite reasonably could only roughly estimate.

In 'going over' witnesses' testimony, lawyers are in a position to formulate and reformulate it, and thereby to 'expose' (that is, produce-as-such) errors, inconsistencies, implausibilities, and so on. Witnesses, in their subsequent turns, are in a position to resist and offer their own (re)formulations. It is hardly necessary to point out the highly rhetorical, interaction-oriented nature of all this; these formulations are not merely participants' best efforts at accurate remembering (though that may be exactly the grounds on which they are presented),[19] but are designed with regard to their implications and upshots. Again, this is not to be seen as merely a peculiar feature of such obviously adversarial talk; the interaction-oriented nature of formulations is a pervasive feature of them, including supportive or consensus-building ones (such as in Extract 5.3, line 11: 'That's the best part of <u>thirty</u> years').

Per Linell and Linda Jönsson present a study of police interrogations of crime suspects, in which 'the major objective of the policeman is to provide a written report, which is supposed to sum up the relevant and important aspects of the criminal actions and their background' (1991: 79). A feature of these settings is that suspects' stories are retold on successive occasions (again, echoing Bartlett's experiments), and are available for analysis as interactional and serial co-productions. The creation of a written statement is a particularly interesting aspect too, in that it exploits one of the major things that written texts afford, which is the establishment of authoritative, textually fixed, and for-the-record versions. Extract 5.5 is from an early phase of an interrogation, in which the policeman solicits 'identificatory' information for the slots on the interrogation form, prior to the interrogation proper.

Extract 5.5

```
 1 P:  How long did you have that job?
 2 S:  (...) the last job I had now we can take ((P: Mm)) it was at Lights
 3     Limited with the Ekbergs ((P: I see)), then I had both my hands in
 4     plaster, after an accident
 5 P:  Mm, we can leave that, I will just write what you have said
 6 S:  Yes
 7 P:  Ah healthy and fit for work we usually write, you know.
 8     You have no illnesses?
 9 S:  Noo, I hope not... No, illnesses, I have had a cold since last autumn
10     but ah ah ((P: Mm)) ((pause)) well, that counts as an illness, I guess
11 P:  Well, this is, they're referring to more serious illnesses
```
(Linell and Jönsson, 1991: 82, original language Swedish) (P = Policeman; S = Suspect)

What gets written, as the factual record, is clearly not merely what the suspect says, nor a straightforward summary of it. Nor is it determined by the ready-made boxes on the bureaucratic report form. Rather, and with regard to the requirements of those boxes, it is a joint production in which the policeman, to echo Bartlett again, *transforms*, *omits*, and *adds* to what the suspect says. The written record is *norm-oriented*, transforming talk's content into conventional formulae ('healthy and fit for work we usually write, you know', line 7), with normative criteria invoked, for *counts-as* definitions of relevant illnesses (lines 8–11). These (italicized) features link this study to other empirical work on how participants construct a shared or jointly produced version of facts and events (Edwards and Middleton, 1986a, 1986b).

There is also a range of studies of asymmetric, situated talk where joint versions, or versions for-the-record, are dialogically elicited or produced as part of institutional activities. These include the analysis of courtroom testimony (for example, Atkinson and Drew, 1979) and doctor–patient dialogue (for example, Heath, 1992; Silverman, 1987). Others include how calls to the emergency services are taken and responded to, where information is elicited and entered into pre-existing slots on a computer screen (Whalen, 1995); interviewing unemployed persons about job training possibilities, with information written into the categories on a pre-written form (Longman, 1995); a kindergarten teacher's construction of a written list, from talk she elicits from them, of what the children have learned about plant growth (Edwards, 1993); the range of procedures whereby 'common knowledge' is *produced as such* in classroom discourse, including the use of written records, the rehearsal of formulaic phrases that perform 'essential gists' of what is understood, the elicitation and conventionalization of descriptions of scientific findings, and so on (Edwards and Mercer, 1987, 1989); as well as the analysis of the *Meno* in Chapter 2 (and in Billig et al., 1988, where it is linked to the study of classroom discourse).

The studies of institutional talk that I have briefly listed (there are many more: see Drew and Heritage, 1992; Marková and Foppa, 1991) focus mainly on naturally occurring social interactions; that is to say, ones that happen irrespective of the researcher's need for data. But the elicitation of versions-for-the-record is also a widespread *research* tool in the human and social sciences, in the form of interview and questionnaire studies, ethnographic research, the elicitation of participant 'protocols', studies of oral narratives, autobiographical memories, and so on. One of the values of studying naturally occurring interactions is the critical insight such studies provide into those other kinds of research methods, by considering them as phenomena, as discursive interactions to be analysed as such, rather than as methods for eliciting, however carefully and cautiously, thought and fact (cf. Potter and Wetherell, 1987; Suchman and Jordan, 1990).

Consensus and agreement

The general topic of 'shared knowledge' includes categories such as *consensus* and *agreement*, as used both in everyday talk and as technical terms (such as in attribution theory, political analysis, or conversation analysis). Consensus and agreement[20] cut across the three types of shared knowledge with which this chapter began (cultural knowledge, mutual knowledge, and pragmatic intersubjectivity). They may be taken to include matters that people happen to believe or know in common without knowing that they do (the 'silent majority' kind of political consensus, for example, or what are called 'folk theories'), but also things people know they have actually told each other, or have built, negotiated, struggled and compromised over, or in some other way acknowledged overtly. They cut across our three types of shared knowledge because those are *preliminary* types, conceptual distinctions about shared knowledge that the study of discourse ultimately fails to uphold. What counts as cultural knowledge, when it is actually invoked, may be countered or put to specific practical uses – such as uses of proverbs and idioms (Billig, 1987; Drew and Holt, 1988; Sacks, 1992; and this volume, Chapter 9). What counts as consensus or agreement (including political appeals to what the 'silent majority' believes, for example) is a similarly pragmatic and rhetorical matter (McKinlay, Potter, and Wetherell, 1993; Potter and Edwards, 1990), and turns out to be another interactional category (in addition to what is 'given' or 'new') for packaging specific content and performing social actions (Button and Sharrock, 1992;[21] Pomerantz, 1984a).

Some instances of consensus and agreement have already been discussed, under such topics as 'grounding' and 'given information'. In those examples, the status of some matter as agreed or consensual was largely implicit, rather than being an overt topic for talk; part of what it means to treat some matter as 'given' or already known is to treat it as non-topical, as not requiring attention or discussion. Before considering agreement as an overt concern, it is worth looking at another common way in which a sense of consensus is brought off, and that is by successive speakers completing each other's talk, or by talking in unison. These are ways in which an orientation to agreed versions may be displayed, in collective story-telling or in pedagogic discourse (Edwards and Mercer, 1987; Lerner, 1995), though those are not their only functions. Note, however, the crucial point here, which is that such devices are analysed as ways of talking, ways of *constituting* something *as* consensual, rather than merely reflections of actual or assumed overlapping cognitive states.

Extract 5.6 is from a study of joint recall (Edwards and Middleton, 1986a) in which a group of students, as part of a class exercise in psychology, were recalling what happens in the movie *ET*, which they happened to have recently seen.

Extract 5.6

1	*K*:	Well he goes to the fridge to get something to eat <u>first</u>
2		doesn't he with the dog following him
3	*D*:	Yeh <u>that's it</u>
4	*K*:	Mm
5	*D*:	and he finds him feeding the dog

```
6     J:    AND THEN AND THEN he finds the beer
7     D:    AND THEN he finds the beer and what is it there's a link
8           between ⌈Elliot and ET=⌉
9     K:          │Elliot's at school│
10    J:          │telepathic link  │
11    D:    =that whatever happens to ET Elliot feels the same effects
12          and ET got paralytic ((laughs)) and so ET is sort of going
13 →  L:    all a bit drunk
14    T:    that's right I remember.
```
(Edwards and Middleton, 1986a: 435)

K's 'doesn't he' (line 2) signals that her narrative is being produced with regard to other participants who are in a position to agree, ratify, or disagree with her version of things. In lines 3–5 D agrees, has that agreement accepted by K, and tags on (with 'and') a further narrative event. The uses of 'and', 'and then', and 'and so' provide the sense of an unfolding narrative jointly produced from individual memories (lines 3, 14), with successive turns adding successive story elements to what others have contributed, or adding details that assist whoever is currently doing the telling (cf. Lerner, 1992). It is a consensual version in that it is *worked up and oriented to as such*, turn by turn.

One of the features of this study was how a strong orientation to producing a consensual and orderly narrative of the movie was a function of the task that the participants took themselves to have been given. That consensual orientation weakened as soon as the participants had finished the task of 'remembering' the movie together, after which they started to exchange views and opinions, agreeing and disagreeing, and no longer constraining their rememberings to the strict narrative order of events. That is to say, consensus was not only worked up as such in their talk (rather than simply existing mentally, behind or prior to it), but was worked up in a way that oriented to the talk's situated business, of doing a particular kind of practical exercise in class.

In line 13 (in Extract 5.6), L's contribution not only adds to, but *grammatically completes* D's sentence, a conversational phenomenon that has been studied, in a variety of naturally occurring materials, by Gene Lerner (1991; see also Sacks, 1992; C. Goodwin, 1979, 1981, 1995a; and M.H. Goodwin, 1980). Lerner examines completions as instances of the more general phenomena of conversational turn-taking, where participants monitor each other's talk for the kinds of 'turn constructional units' that are under way, these being various linguistic units such as sentences and their grammatical components (Sacks et al., 1974). Such 'monitoring' is displayed in how opportunities for taking turns are taken, or else overtly passed up (by using various gestures and vocalizations at those points), and also in phenomena such as completions. In other words, completions (of one person's talk by another) are part of the interactional 'machinery' of intersubjectivity, providing further options for various kinds of orientation towards the content and import of what is said.

Among the more obvious grammatical structures which provide for completions to be done are two-part formats such as 'if X – then Y' (or 'when X – then Y'), such that the 'if/when X' component can be taken to project a forthcoming 'then Y'. Examples (from Lerner, 1991: 445) include:

(a) *Rich*: if you bring it intuh them
    Carol: ih don't cost yuh nothing

(b) *David*: so if one person said he couldn't invest
    (.)
    Kerry: then I'd have ta wait

(c) *Dan*: when the group reconvenes in two weeks=
    Roger: =then they're gunna issue strait jackets

Further kinds of projectable and completable structures, to which Lerner draws attention, include three-part list completions (Jefferson, 1990), contrast structures, and preference structure phenomena. For example, given that 'dispreferred' responses are typically prefaced by components such as pauses, and 'Well . . .' (see Chapter 4), the occurrence of such prefaces signal what is coming, and clues to how to complete it. So the occurrence of completions is further evidence of the intersubjective status of 'preference' phenomena, as something not only observable by analysts, but interactionally used and oriented-to by participants.

Lest it be assumed that interactive completions are the overt expressions of some kind of mental communion, it has to be emphasized again that these are *ways of talking*. Completions are like formulations in this respect; they are opportunities for intersubjective display and repair,[22] and for accomplishing interactional business. Completions need not be just what the first speaker was going to say, even if such a thing were knowable. Nor need they be the second speaker's best guess at it. They are candidates for that status, which first speakers may then (in a third turn) ratify or not – but again, those ratifications are not psychological guarantees of joint intentionality either, but further interactional moves.

Sacks's pioneering work includes some studies of group therapy sessions in which a therapist ('Dan' in Lerner's completion item [c] above) talks with a group of teenagers who have been in some kind of trouble with the police. Sacks focuses on the following sequence, which immediately follows a new member's introduction to the group:

Extract 5.7
1 *Ken*:   We were in an automobile discussion
2 *Roger*: discussing the psychological motives for
3 ( ):   hhhhhhh
4 *Al*:   drag racing on the street.
(GTS: Sacks, 1992, vol. 1: 321)

What interested Sacks about this particular 'collaborative production' was its *non*-idiomatic, *not*-projectably-completable nature; it is not one of the structurally provided-for kinds of completions highlighted by Lerner. The fact that these folk could do it, therefore, and did it so smoothly and without hesitation or repair, is part of what it indexically performs – 'showing the new guy that this is a group. They do together what is among the most prototypical things that a single person would do' (1992, vol. 1: 321). Sacks remarks on how these kinds of 'speaking as one' sequences are used in literary works to signal interpersonal closeness or being in love (cf. Vygotsky, 1934/1987).

Sacks also explores its interactional dynamics. In natural dialogue, a second speaker (such as 'Roger' in Extract 5.7) can 'tie' an utterance to a prior one that grammatically did not need completing, and was not a 'first' part of a collaborative sequence until the second part retrospectively made it so. Collaborative sentence construction, like the other conversational devices we have examined in this chapter, is no passive index of a psychological joint mentality, but, rather, an interactive way of constructing and displaying such notions, and of performing social actions such as signalling agreement, irony, or accomplishing group membership.[23] In the 'automobile discussion' example above, those actions include showing the new member what kinds of things he would have to know about in order to take part (1992, vol. 1: 324).

We have noted that the discourse category *agreement* is an interactional category, a performative feature of talk rather than an actual matching of minds. The analytic task is not to examine the content of different people's talk and decide whether or not those contents match each other on some criterion. It is to examine talk and see how and where agreement or disagreement arises as a participants' concern. Anita Pomerantz (1978, 1984a) has studied how agreements and disagreements occur in the form of 'second assessments':

> When persons partake in social activities, they routinely make assessments . . . a summary of the actor's sense or experience of the event. . . . Second assessments are assessments produced by recipients of prior assessments in which the referents in the seconds are the same as those in the priors. (Pomerantz, 1984a: 57–9)

Second assessments are opportunities for displaying agreement or disagreement with priors; in this way, (dis)agreement can be examined as a sequentially occasioned conversational category (cf. Sacks, 1987).

The importance of second assessments, for notions such as shared knowledge or intersubjectivity, lies not only in the obvious relevance of agreement and disagreement, but also in the kinds of matters on which assessments are offered. Considerations apply, of what kinds of things each participant might know about, or have routine access to, or have witnessed separately or together, or know more about than the other does, or have privileged knowledge of, and so on. These considerations are not just background matters for analysts to ponder, but participants' concerns that feature strongly in how disagreements and agreements display 'preference organization'. As we noted in Chapter 4, disagreements are generally the 'dispreferred' option, the one marked by hesitation, prefaces, and accounts. One way in which a category such as 'insufficient knowledge' features interactionally is as an account for not providing immediate agreement.

Assessments are likely to be provided *on some basis*, with some orientation to their experiential or other knowledge grounds, and indeed the nature and occasions for providing such grounds are topics for systematic inquiry in their own right (Pomerantz, 1984b). As Pomerantz notes, assessments are a routine part of participating and witnessing, and these are activities that can provide 'bases for knowing', as in Extracts 5.8 and 5.9.

Extract 5.8
```
1  →   J:    We saw Midnight Cowboy yesterday -or
2            ⌈suh-Friday
3       L:   ⌊Oh?
4       J:   Didju s- you saw that, it's really good
```
(JS:II:61, from Pomerantz, 1984a: 59)

Extract 5.9
```
1       C:    Uh what's the condition of the building.
2  →    D:    Well, I haven't made an inspection of it.
3  →          But I've driven by it a few times, and uh
4             it doesn't appear to be too bad, (...)
```
(FD:1, from Pomerantz, 1984a: 59)

Here, assessments are offered on various claimed knowledge bases, marked by the arrows. Note line 3 in Extract 5.8, where L (J's wife) treats J's report as occasioning some kind of further remark, and how, in offering his assessment, J attends to whether L has seen the movie herself. In Extract 5.9, D's report on the building is prefaced by a specification of the limited extent of his grounds for knowing (lines 2–3), which nicely accounts for the limited nature of his report (line 4).

Again, invoking Sacks's notion of subversion, such matters as what is known, by whom, and on what basis are not merely the preconditions for talk, but part of talk's active business. Claims to knowledge and experience can be made in reverse as it were, by offering specific kinds of assessments that would imply them. Pomerantz (1984a) provides a rich series of examples, in which second assessments (in particular) are produced in ways that attend to interactional matters alive in the current talk, such as differential grounds for knowing, and the management of interpersonal relations. For instance, disagreements may include a component called 'weak agreement', in which the second speaker partially agrees as a preface to disagreeing. Extract 5.10 is from the same group therapy sessions that Sacks analysed. Note how Ken's disagreement is produced as a modification of Roger's description (cf. D in Extract 5.11), rather than as an abrupt counter to it. Such ways of doing disagreements provide ways of attending to interactional contingencies between speakers, and to similar contingencies with regard to the objects or persons assessed.

Extract 5.10
```
1   Roger:   But you admit he is having fun and you think
2            it's funny.
3   Ken:     I think it's funny, yeah. But it's a ridiculous funny.
```
(GTS 4:32, from Pomerantz, 1984a: 75)

Extract 5.11

1   C: (...) you've really both basically honestly gone
2   your own ways.
3   D: Essentially, except we've had a good relationship
4   at home.

(JG: II.1.15, from Pomerantz, 1984a: 75)

These features of disagreements are part of a 'dispreferred' design that can 'house disagreements when agreements are invited' (Pomerantz, 1984a: 75). Being recognizable to participants as such, together with other signals of forthcoming dispreference such as pauses and 'Well' prefaces, folk who offer initial assessments may step in quickly and modify their original assessments before any overt disagreement has been produced. While there is much more to these intricate conversational phenomena than I have discussed here (see, for example, Bilmes, 1987), the major point is their status for the analysis of shared knowledge. Assessments, agreements, disagreements, partial agreements, and the like, are features of talk-in-interaction whose precise design is part of a conversational and interactional precision, rather than a reflection of just how much people know, or what they pre-verbally think.

This has been a necessarily condensed and selective treatment of the discourse of consensus and agreement. It would be possible, after all, to organize the entire discussion of discourse and cognition under these headings, together with their corollaries and opposites, disagreement and opposition. Further discussion of consensus as a participants' category that is in various ways occasioned, constructed, rhetorically deployed and countered can be found in Edwards and Potter (1992a). In that work, studies of conversations and press reports of political disputes are set against some of the social-cognitive assumptions underlying attribution theory in particular, and cognitive psychology more generally. Significant studies of how conversational reports and assessments attend to difficulties of intersubjectivity and agreement include Robin Wooffitt's (1992) study of reportings of supernatural experiences, and Paul Drew and Elizabeth Holt (1988) on everyday uses of idioms (emblematic expressions of cultural knowledge) in the context of non-affiliative responses to complaints. The discursive status of cultural knowledge is discussed further in Chapters 7 to 10.

Conclusions: shared knowledge as a participants' concern

This chapter has dealt with a variety of ways in which issues such as 'shared knowledge' and 'intersubjectivity' can be approached as features of discourse. The essential analytic move has been to treat them as participants' concerns, and to examine a range of devices through which such matters are managed. Analysis focused on how participants work up, imply, formulate, and counter what is jointly known. This was applied to the workings of linguistic structures such as grammatical completions, and 'given' and 'new' information (including the status of some version of things as mere 'information'), through to overt formulations of what is jointly known or consensual. Matters of agreement and disagreement were also approached analytically as part of talk's practical business, rather than some kind of updated intersection of mental contents, existing objectively (or indeed subjectively) prior to or after talk.

Not only is the nature of shared knowledge a practical matter managed in discourse, but the details of that management are also performative of a range of social and rhetorical activities. These range from the mundane business of ordinary conversation, through various institutionally situated matters such as doing police work, classroom education, cross-examining witnesses in court, selling breakfast cereal, and political persuasion. These are not merely *contexts* within which conversational devices work, but, rather, it is part of talk's business to *realize* such institutional settings as the kinds of settings they are, recognizably doing the work they do (Drew and Heritage, 1992). As part of the workings of such settings, and indeed of any kind of ordinary talk, participants define what counts as given, new, agreed, just so, contextual, contentious, or 'common knowledge'. The analytic task is to identify those matters as participants' categories, and to examine how they perform interactional work at whatever juncture they are used or invoked.

The psycholinguistic approach to shared knowledge, as 'information' that discourse participants actually possess in common, or assume they possess in common, is sustainable only by virtue of two key elements. The first element is the communication model, which contains assumptions that are virtually built in to the entire practice of analysing discourse psychologically, as a matter of inter-mental transmission and coordination. I have argued that we have to re-conceptualize discourse as a domain of social action, with psychological knowledge states analysed as its business-in-hand. The second element is the range of methodological procedures that embody and sustain those built-in assumptions. The communication model gets built in to method when it is used as a blueprint for setting up experimental communication tasks, and defining criteria for their completion; when it is used as the basis for inventing (descriptively constructing) conceptual scenarios in which individuals, in their imagined 'frozen moments', are faced with communicative conundrums; and when discourse is treated as a domain best investigated, from the outset, via computer programming and interface design, where even fewer of the marooned individual's human resources are initially available. Such studies may be highly useful and can be done for a variety of good reasons. But they are a dangerous and unnecessary starting point for understanding what is going on when people ordinarily converse.

The analysis of intersubjectivity as a practical conversational accomplishment ties in to the notion of talk as action rather than communication. The communication model of talk, as a kind of inter-mental transmission of ideas, is certainly the simpler one. Unfortunately, that simplicity is bought at the expense of loading the explanatory burden onto a private and underlying life of the mind. The problem of intersubjectivity then gets defined in ways that stem from, rather than question, the presumption of minds-in-communication: the philosophical 'other minds' problem; the psychology of 'theory of mind'; the Piagetian notion of childhood 'egocentrism'; the symbolic interactionists' 'taking the role of the other'; and so on. It is not that we no longer need a psychology of interactional competence, but a matter of what it would have to deal with, and of its explanatory scope. By focusing on conversation's built-in procedures, on talk as action rather than communication, we reduce the explanatory burden on the putative mental states of speakers and listeners. In the next and subsequent chapters, this perspective is put to use in examining a variety of psychological themes, including the thought–language relationship, categorization, scripts and plans, emotions, event memory and personal narratives, 'folk psychology', and the cognitive competence of non-humans and non-adults.

Notes

1. The assumption that messages are first formulated and then 'sent off' in the direction of a recipient, who has to decode and retrieve them, derives of course from the communication model, which, as we have noted, has a long tradition in the philosophy of language and cognition, being formulated in these terms by John Locke: 'The comfort and advantage of society not being to be had without communication of thoughts, it was necessary that man should find out some external sensible signs, whereof those invisible ideas, which his thoughts are made up of, might be made known to others' (1894: 8, cited in Chafe, 1970: 16). Clark's approach to language and cognition is not only Lockian, but draws also on studies in conversation analysis; the point here is to identify its (problematically) simultaneous use of the communication metaphor. My use of Clark's work as a point of departure recognizes it as the most CA-aware work available in psycholinguistics, as the best of its kind, and for that reason especially worthy of critical attention.
2. A distinction is sometimes drawn between anaphora and *cataphora*, in which pro-terms refer forwards rather than backwards, to items not yet mentioned: e.g., *she* in 'She was a fine woman, your mother.' Lyons (1977: 659) cites Karl Bühler as the origin of the distinction, but chooses to use the term 'anaphora' generally for both senses.
3. Psycholinguistic studies, while helping to define the discourse functions of devices such as anaphoric pronouns, nevertheless promote an idealized conception of discourse founded mostly on artificial materials and exercises. This encourages a rather mechanically cognitive and interactionally unsophisticated notion of how discourse works, theorized in terms of mental representations and processes in 'working memory' (Barsalou, 1992: 257). The more interaction-oriented psycholinguistic work of Herbert Clark is highlighted in this chapter.
4. For a selection of CA work on how descriptions are 'recipient designed', see Atkinson and Drew (1979), Drew (1978, 1984), Pomerantz and Atkinson (1984), Sacks (1972a), Schegloff (1972), and Watson (1978). Some of CA's analytic terminology was introduced in Chapter 4.
5. This relates to the fact that psycholinguists seem to perceive much more difficulty with *ambiguity* than conversational participants do. Schegloff notes that 'the finding that the "same sentence" or "same component" can have "different meanings" across the imagined range of scenarios is the kernel of the problem of ambiguity. It is because actual participants in actual conversations do not encounter utterances as isolated sentences . . . that most theoretically or heuristically depictable ambiguities do not ever arise' (1984: 51).

6. I am referring here to the use of geometric shapes in set theory logic and mathematics, in which a couple of overlapping circles, say, would represent the categories A and B, with the overlapping part being an 'intersection' that includes everything that is both A *and* B (e.g., the two circles may represent women and professors, and the intersection would be women professors). If you are wondering why I have described and not drawn them for you, then I have a couple of confessions to make. One is that I started to do so and discovered I was not as adept with Microsoft Draw as I had hoped. The other, worse still for a discursive psychologist, is that I did not want to provide a highly memorable and rhetorically effective pictorial representation of the position I am arguing *against*.

7. Schegloff usefully points out that the information status of some item is in any case an insufficient basis for uttering it: 'because there is no limit to the utterables that can be informative and/or true, the informativeness or truth of an utterence is, by itself, no warrant or grounds for having uttered it or for having uttered it at a particular juncture in an occasion' (1995: 187).

8. Halliday (1967, 1970) distinguishes 'given' and 'new' from a variety of other kinds of thematic structure, including grammatical ones such as subject and predicate, and related notions such as theme and rheme, topic and comment.

9. Kenneth Gergen's social constructionist analysis of personal narratives makes a related point, concerning a possibly over-manipulative view of social action: 'Certainly the constructionist emphasis is on flexibility in self-identification, but this does not simultaneously imply that the individual is either duplicitous or scheming. To speak of duplicity is to presume that a "true telling" is otherwise available. We have found this view to be deeply problematic' (1994: 249). It is also a principle enshrined in SSK (see Chapter 3), of course, though often misunderstood, that to analyse the truth-defining practices of science is to study its ordinary procedures, rather than to undermine it as some kind of epistemic malpractice.

10. Since CA has traditionally directed its critique against standard sociological rather than psychological assumptions, there is plenty of scope for that kind of incorporation, in notions such as the 'proof procedure' and 'recipient design', which can easily be taken as routes into speakers' underlying knowledge states and communicative intentions. One of the aims of this book is to counter that incorporating move; see Chapter 4 on the interactional status of the proof procedure, and the more recent arguments by Schegloff (1988, 1989a, 1992d) against the kinds of speech act theory assumptions that Clark retains alongside CA. Clark's incorporation of CA tends to treat talk's *actions*, such as using 'continuers' (*mm, yes, quite, I see*, etc.) that work as non-interruption signals for the other speaker to continue (Schegloff, 1982), as the signs and products of cognitive states, actual understandings, beliefs, and intentions (Clark and Schaefer, 1989). This has the effect of relegating the interactional uses of such signals, which in CA are primary, to the status of side-effects, lies, or deceptions.

11. Note that, in Halliday's treatment, a 'given' element is optional whereas a 'new' element is obligatory: 'otherwise there would be no information' (Halliday, 1970: 163). This supports the analysis that Emma's 'we haven' gotten together' is presented as new linguistically, if not being actually, or even presumptively, psychologically new information for Lottie.

12. My tentativeness here, in 'could be taken as', and 'perhaps', is in recognition not of any special analytic difficulties with these materials, but, rather, of the principle that these possible meanings are first of all participants' matters, of what they take each other to be saying. The subsequent analysis is an effort to explore that as an interactional concern, rather than to decide on what they actually do or did mean.

13. Although I would not want to extend this analysis much further, one thing that Lottie's 'Oh gosh no:' and 'let's see:' may do, interactionally, is defuse any possiblity (should it arise) that Lottie had been concerned about, or wanting to complain about, the non-meeting. The notion of 'news to consciousness' as a matter of interpersonal display echoes Jefferson's (1978: 222) remarks on a further use by Lottie of 'Oh' as a 'display of sudden remembering'. Heritage has performed a systematic study of 'Oh' that includes how it performs interactional categories such as 'news receipt': 'the particle is *used to propose that*

its producer has undergone some kind of change of state in his or her locally current state of knowledge, information, orientation or awareness' (1984b: 299, emphasis added). Note that Heritage analyses such expressions as ways of talking, rather than indications of actually updated mental states. They are ways in which 'an alignment taken to events is displayed' (1984b: 300), such that 'the parties to the talk establish local identities of informed teller and uninformed recipient with respect to the matter in hand' (1984b: 304). This notion that news receivers may actively constitute themselves as such, using particles such as 'oh', parallels how news announcers may also use tokens such as 'guess what?' and other 'pre-announcements' (Schegloff, 1995; Terasaki, 1976). By the use of such conversational devices participants are able to define various upcoming content *as* news, while also monitoring its status as such in advance, and thus signalling an orientation to the norm of not telling people what they already know.

14. The Shredded Wheat example has a rhetorical design comparable to the Eurotunnel advert cited in Chapter 3: '. . . *having been a very strong sceptic before, I would now recommend it. Yes.*' Both examples manage credibility by means of a trade-off between reality and mind. Factual credibility is established by the actor-narrator's construction of a prior mental state: (1) doubt, which is subsequently overcome by experience, and (2) liking the breakfast cereal prior to endorsing it. See also the examples in Chapter 10, on projecting an 'authentic' social identity, and Chapter 11, where scepticism about the language capacity of apes is used as a preface to concluding in favour of their abilities. A favourable predisposition is cited as a preface to concluding the opposite. It is the *contrast* between expectations and findings rather than scepticism itself that constructs credibility, a contrast recognizable in the scientific rhetorics of 'falsification' and the 'counter-intuitive finding'.

15. Josef Goebbels, Hitler's propaganda minister, was notoriously an admirer of Hollywood, of how America's cinema worked as far more effective propaganda for American cultural and political values than the crudely anti-Semitic and pro-Nazi stuff favoured by the Führer himself. What made Hollywood work better was the way those messages were built in as assumptions, as what life (history, social achievement, etc.) happened to be like, rather than as overt, tub-thumping demagogy. Relatedly, old-fashioned 'Daz washes whiter' advertisements have largely been replaced by product placements within life-style image-manipulation, mini soap operas and the like, despite occasional nostalgic, stylized, or ironic echoes of the old-style campaigns. While these examples stretch the meaning of 'information structure' as a grammatical property of sentences, the important thing in selling and persuasion seems to be getting control not of the new, but of the given – getting to define what is taken as *common knowledge*, as uncontentious matters.

16. The term 'formulations', applied to these conversational occurrences, was suggested by Garfinkel and Sacks to cover not only gists of what has been said, but also a wider range of meta-comments on the kind of talk it is, or the kind of actions it performs – or 'saying-in-so-many-words-what-we-are-doing' (1970: 351).

17. See, for example, the use made of Bartlett's work in Ulric Neisser's (1967) seminal text, *Cognitive Psychology*. Arguments for recovering from Bartlett a more socio-cultural foundation for studies of remembering, linked to cultural and discursive psychology, include Edwards and Middleton (1986a, 1987), and Shotter (1990).

18. See, for example, Caesar-Wolf (1984); also various studies of police interrogations (e.g., Linell and Jönsson, 1991; Watson, 1990), all of which demonstrate the constructive and consequential nature of the formulations produced in such settings, and show how the nature and business of those settings is an oriented-to and produced-thereby feature of such talk.

19. For some studies of the interactional status of 'best efforts at remembering' in the context of cross-examinations, see Edwards and Potter (1992a, 1992b), Lynch and Bogen (1996), and also Chapter 10 of this book.

20. I am avoiding giving these terms precise definitions, though any dictionary would be a useful starting point. What they *precisely* mean is a matter for analysis: of how they are used, what they are contrasted with, and of whatever kinds of discourse phenomena analysts may find it useful to group under such headings.

21. Button and Sharrock (1992) offer an ethnomethodologically grounded critique of how the notions of agreement and consensus have been used in 'social constructionist' studies of science (SSK), which they claim exhibit an unfortunate 'cognitive turn'. This claim involves categorizing Gilbert and Mulkay's (1984) 'discursive repertoires' as cognitive operations. My own take on SSK work (see Chapter 3; cf. Potter and Wetherell, 1987) treats it alongside ethnomethodology as an anti-cognitivist enterprise, one in which cognition and reality are studied as participants' practical concerns. Indeed, the notion that SSK produces an '*intentionally* perverse picture of scientific investigations' (Button and Sharrock, 1992: 5, emphasis added) might reasonably be taken as a cognitivist analysis of how SSK folk's erroneous cognitivism is produced. The reader is invited to take this note as support for the defeasible, contingent, and brought-off nature of agreement and consensus (as well as cognition and perversity) as discourse categories.

22. Sacks (1992, vol. 1: 321) provides an example of multi-speaker repair:

Ken:	He looked like he was coming in here for uh . . .
Al:	kicks
Louise:	guidance. heh

Al's insertion is a 'candidate' completion, which Louise then repairs.

23. In further analysis of the group therapy data, Sacks also notes how the deictic tokens 'we' and 'us' are used in fomulations of prior talk in ways that construct alignment and collaboration, even for talk that was not, in the first instance, collaboratively produced. An example (in addition to '*we* were in an automobile discussion') is:

. . . after the statement 'Ken, face it. You're a poor little rich kid,' we get [from another speaker] 'Now you're a poor little rich kid *we've told you that*,' . . . [which] involves, it seems, formulating what was previously said as having been said representatively, and therefore incidentally said by the other guy, but said on behalf of us – even, perhaps, whether he knew it or not. (Sacks, 1992, vol. 1: 428, emphasis added)

6

Scripts and Dispositions

One of the types of shared knowledge mentioned in Chapter 5 is the notion of 'what we all know'. This can include all kinds of things, ranging from fundamental notions of how the world works, to more local kinds of knowledge about routine and familiar events and places. For example, the following is an extract from a counselling session in which Mary and Jeff are talking to the counsellor about their marital problems. Mary is recounting how she and Jeff had an argument after she went out one Friday night, while Jeff was at work.

Extract 6.1
```
1   Mary:   I went out Friday n↑i↓ght (.) and (.) Jeff was
2           ↓work↑ing (.) on call (.) and (.) um (2.2) the
3           place that I went to (.) like (.) c̲l̲o̲sed at half
4           past twe̲lve and I got home about one o'clo̲c̲k̲
(DE–JF:C1:S2:1)
```

There are various references in this extract which depend for their sense on cultural knowledge, like all discourse does. These include what kind of activity 'went out Friday night' might be (in contrast, say, to going out on a Tuesday morning), and, linked to that, what kind of 'place' Mary is probably referring to, and also what kind of thing 'working on call' might be.

As analysts we need to have some knowledge of these kinds of things, though the use we make of that knowledge is in trying to understand the talk, rather than in offering explanations of it. Also, we do not generally need to know precise details of participants' background knowledge unless these become relevant in the talk under scrutiny, and the talk itself is the best guide to that. I can tell you from my knowledge of the rest of this transcript that the 'place' that Mary refers to was a kind of bar or night-club,[1] where she had met the man with whom she had recently had (and apparently ended) an extra-marital affair, and that Jeff's learning about this (from Mary) was (according to them) a major precipitating event in their going for counselling.

The thing I want to pick out is Mary's mention of what time the 'place' she went to closed. This detail works to provide an account for Mary's late arrival home, 'late' according to Jeff at least, which got her into trouble with him. The accounting is accomplished by a simple narrative: the place 'c̲l̲o̲sed at half past twe̲lve and I got home about one o'clo̲c̲k̲' (lines 3–4). This is the basis of an externalizing, situational kind of account rather than, say, that she was enjoying herself and did not *want* to come home, let alone that she was enjoying the attentions of men, or even of the man with whom she had had the affair. Mary's getting home at one o'clock (a.m.) is provided as part of a narrative sequence of going somewhere that happened to close at 12:30.

It is an important feature of a wide range of psychological and sociological explanations, as well as a pervasive feature of everyday discourse, that people's actions are characterized as falling into routine, recognizable patterns, associated with particular kinds of social occasions, places, or settings. In psychology this is the domain of 'script theory' (Mandler, 1984; Schank and Abelson, 1977). While I shall have a few things to say about script theory, and especially how it contrasts with discursive analysis, it should be noted at the outset that these features of talk, in which events are categorized as routine and scripted, or as exceptions to such patterns, would be of immense importance even if cognitive script theory had never been invented. They are the site of some very significant and interactionally potent ways of constructing the sense of events, of persons, of their mental states, and of the causal and accountable bases of their actions.

In cognitive theory 'scripts' are generalized event representations, whose psychological nature is explained within the framework of perceptual–cognitive metatheory. According to Katherine Nelson, who has elaborated their implications for children's mental and social development, script schemas are 'derived from concrete experience of events and thus represent "how the world works". Nonetheless, they are very much abstractions from experienced reality' (1986: 8).[2] According to script theory, people perceive the world in terms of its regular, repeated features, and notice and learn from anomalies (that is, from expectation failures). Through repeated exposure to places such as restaurants, or to parents cooking food in the kitchen, or to school lessons, children and adults build mental schemas or models of what the world is like, and what to expect. A 'restaurant script', for example, would include a series of roles and props including tables, a menu, waiter, cashier (some such 'slots' are compulsory, some optional), and various sequentially expected actions such as ordering, eating, and paying.

Script theory assumes that events themselves (social events primarily) are more or less ordered and predictable, such that competence to perceive, recall, and take part in those events rests on our capacity as individuals to draw generalized abstractions across variations in experience, learning from exceptions, and updating our mental representations as we go.[3] Our scripted knowledge of what to do and what to expect when visiting restaurants, cinemas, dentists, or shopping in department stores, and so on, is thought to develop out of *personal scripts* (Nelson, 1981; Schank and Abelson, 1977). Children and adults form schematic understandings primarily through repeated experiences in their own lives, in the daily round of activities. Events that conform to script expectations start to pass largely unnoticed. The things we notice, remark on, and remember are the exceptions or anomalies, and these in turn can become, with sufficient regularity, the basis of new schematic scripts or sub-scripts. People come to possess broadly the same cultural scripts, according to perceptual–cognitive theory, mainly through living in the same culture and experiencing the same kinds of routine scenarios.

This kind of knowledge is clearly fundamental to any sort of cultural competence, and we surely use it in making sense of what people are doing, where, and why. However, discursive psychology takes a somewhat different position on the nature of such 'making sense' from how cognitive theory imagines it. The thing of interest, when we examine discourse, is how such notions of a particular kind of place, and of particular kinds of action sequences, are produced in specific and discursively occasioned ways, perhaps even as variable or contested descriptions. The status of scripted activities here is not perceptual, mental, or real, but in the first place discursive. In examining script talk, or 'script formulations' (Edwards, 1994b, 1995), it quickly becomes necessary to abandon any notion that what people are doing is 'expressing' some neutral, definitive, and ready-made sense of events produced through a process such as noticing what the world is like and then putting it into words. Script talk is far more interesting than that.

What we find in discourse is that participants *describe* the world in these ways. Through naming and narrating them, people descriptively construct events as following, or as departing from, some normative or expected order. And that opens up the possibility of looking to see, in discourse, what kinds of social-psychological business are being done by describing things in that way. The analytical focus moves away from how cognitive scripts are formed, with the usual assumption of a disinterested, 'naive scientist' (Heider, 1958) trying to form definitive, all-purpose models of reality, towards the study of how, on specific occasions, and specifically *for* those occasions, people descriptively construct activities as routine or anomalous. By examining scripted versions of events as pragmatic constructions, we are also able to deal empirically with the specific details of spontaneous talk.

The theme of this chapter, then, is how the routine or predictable nature of actions and events, and exceptions to such routines, feature as participants' discursive resources and concerns. Events are described *as* scripted, *as* instances of some general pattern, or *as* anomalies or exceptions. At stake in such descriptions are the normative basis of actions, and the accountability of the actors. That is to say, moral and normative issues of appropriateness, responsibility, and blame are at stake in how a person's actions or involvement is described, and thereby defined as the kinds of actions they are. And one of the ways in which all of this works is to describe actions in ways that build a picture of what kind of person the actor is – that is, his or her personality, disposition,[4] or mental state.

Several of this chapter's analytic themes can be anticipated by returning to Mary's account of her Friday night out. We noted that Mary's description of how the place 'closed at half past twelve and I got home about one o'clock' (Extract 6.1, lines 3–4) performs some crucial causal accounting. It provides for a situational cause, set rhetorically against Jeff's blaming of her for the late homecoming (see Extract 6.1a below, lines 23–5). It achieves that via ostensibly straightforward narrative event reporting, deploying a script fragment tied to notions of place. In fact, this rhetorical, attributional (causal accounting), and script-invoking citation of place names is a very common discourse phenomenon that has been analysed in a variety of settings, including casual talk, counselling, and courtroom cross-examinations (for example, Drew, 1978, 1992; Edwards, 1994b, 1995; Schegloff, 1972; Widdicombe and Wooffitt, 1995).

Let us consider briefly some other features of Mary's story, which continues in Extract 6.1a (some intervening lines have been omitted).

Extract 6.1a (continued from 6.1)

14	*Mary*:	(. . .) and um so I <u>went</u> out (.) <u>came</u> back at about
15		one o'clock and I phoned (.) <u>phoned</u> him at <u>work</u> (.)
16		which I <u>don't</u> normally <u>do</u> but I thought I <u>wanted</u> to
17		phone him .hh to say that I was back <u>home</u> (.) and
18		(.) um (2.0) and that he could <u>trust</u> me and (.) uh
19		it was just my way of (0.4) like (.) saying (.)
20		that I was (.) youknow
21	*Counsellor*:	Hm.
22	*Mary*:	I was at home .hh and um (0.4) and then we had an
23		ar:gument didn't we (.) Jeff said what do you think
24		(0.2) what <u>hour</u> do you think this is and (.) you
25		shouldn't be home this late and (.)and <u>I</u> said >at
26		least I had the decency to <u>phone</u> yuh I coulda <u>lied</u><
27		(0.6) and >and I didn't <u>wanna</u> lie< (0.5) because I
28		thought there was no:: (.) <u>point</u> in lying to him
29		I don't <u>wanna</u> (1.2) <u>keep</u> on lying well I <u>never</u> used
30		to lie but (.) <u>since</u> I had this affair I <u>did</u> start
31		to <u>lie</u> obviously.

Note Mary's further routine-invoking descriptions: her phoning Jeff at work was something 'I <u>don't</u> normally <u>do</u>' (line 16). Similarly she '<u>never</u> used to lie' to him, but started to do so once the affair began, '<u>ob</u>viously' (lines 29–31).[5] It is important to recognize these avowed norm-breaches as *descriptions* that Mary produces at specific junctures in her talk; it is not that we assume they are true or false, nor that she or Jeff or anyone else would have to describe things that way every time. That being so, we can ask, what discursive business do these *actual* formulations perform?

Mary's norm-breaching telephone call serves as the occasion for a motive account, a link between action and intention. Since she did not usually call her husband, this makes relevant and accountable why she did so on this occasion – a personal, internal attributional account (this relation between norms and accountability is a pervasive feature in conversation analytical studies: Heritage, 1984a). The account offered is that she '<u>wanted</u> to phone him' (lines 16–17), and this stands as evidence of her consideration of him, and of her trustworthiness (line 18). Indeed, Mary presents a series of things as what she *wanted* (lines 16, 27, 29), each produced in rhetorical contrast to

Jeff's blamings. They work to undermine Jeff's basis for mistrust of her. In contrast to that mistrust (a theme developed extensively in the rest of these data) Mary cites her honesty in phoning Jeff, who was at work, of course, and would not personally witness her late homecoming. In confessing her lateness ('I coulda lied', line 26), Mary constructs her status as a reliable truth-teller.

She also deals somewhat (even in this extract) with the outstanding grounds of her husband's mistrust – her recent extra-marital affair. The affair is introduced here not as a damning piece of evidence against her trustworthiness, but, on the contrary, as a recognizable ('obviously', line 31) account for her past lies being a temporary, out-of-character aberration, something she would not, in the normal course of things, want to do. Mary's deployment of script formulations for various places and actions works rhetorically with regard to her general accountability, as a contrast to Jeff's alternative story (which is only minimally glimpsed in the extracts given), and with regard to various closely related implications concerning psychological states such as understandings, motives, intentions, and trust. In the following sections we encounter an extraordinary degree of finely tuned precision in these discursive activities, in ordinary people's conversational descriptions and inferences, that may surprise anyone unfamiliar with the detailed analysis of ordinary talk-in-interaction.

Script formulations

People do sometimes narrate their experiences in restaurants. We need take no special interest in how they do that, but since the 'restaurant script' has become the classic example since Schank and Abelson's (1977) original treatment, it may be useful to look at a couple of examples (Extracts 6.2 and 6.3) of restaurant talk. These are taken from the 'NB' series of telephone calls transcribed by Gail Jefferson, and used as the basis for an extended discussion of script talk (Edwards, 1994b). In Extract 6.2 Lottie is telling Emma about her visit to 'a nice hotel in the Spa'.

Extract 6.2

```
 1  Lottie:   (. . .) 'n we ha:d lunch there?  she 'ad two martinis
 2            'n we had the be:st?  ↓uh::: .hhhhh oh chicken
 3            sa:la⌈d  uh↓::::.⌉
 4  Emma:           ⌊M m : : :⌋ ::::.
 5  Lottie:   it-it- Oh: great big sa:lad=
 6  Emma:     =Isn' that a pretty place that Spa:, sn⌈f  f  f   .snff ⌉
 7  Lottie:                                          ⌊Ye:ah. Gee an'⌋
 8            we just had a ba:ll in there an' the gir:l (.) the:
 9            waitress was so nice evrything we ordered they were
10            ou:t of youknow an' it w⌈as a big  ⌉ ih-: got rea:l=
11  Emma:                             ⌊°Mm hm°⌋
12  Lottie:   =funny but we didn' care =youkno⌈w, .hmhhht.hhhh
13  Emma:                                     ⌊M m : hm:
```
(NB:IV:10:R:51)

Extract 6.2 contains a number of features that cognitive script theory would recognize: lunch details, 'the' waitress (lines 8–9), the ordering of food, and so on, all delivered as expectable items, with specific or newsworthy details nicely attached (the *especially* good chicken salad, the niceness of the waitress, the absence of ordered items, lines 9–10, and how 'ih-: got rea:l funny', lines 10–12). The food and the waitress were so good that the lack of menu items was funny and forgivable ('we didn' care', line 12). These kinds of details, while not exactly predictable, make sense in both perceptual and discursive terms, both as the script-relevant kinds of things that would be noticeable, and also as the kinds of things that would be interactionally relevant in an evaluation-oriented narrative about good and bad places to eat.

In Extract 6.3 the restaurant under discussion is evaluated less favourably. This story occurred at an earlier point in the same long telephone conversation; the two eating places were not directly compared by the participants, and did not occur within the same topical sequence.

Extract 6.3

```
 1  Lottie:  (. . .) we went in: to the ((Name)) place on the way
 2           back an; uh e-had (.) uh: they ah an a:fter dinner
 3           dri:nk 'n God there wasn' a sou:l ih We were the only
 4           ones at the bar an' there was about two parties in
 5           th⌈e dining⌉ room .p.hhhhh
 6  Emma:     ⌊°Ye:h.°⌋
 7  Lottie:  An' I didn' wanna say-eh: A:dcline said she a'ways
 8           wanted uh see it so .hnhh I never said anything
 9           but- uh: Claude said today he says wasn' that the
10           dirtiest place?=
11  Emma:    =⌈ Ye:s⌉
12  Lottie:  =⌊'n I s⌋ ai:d you know? (.) I: felt the same thing
13           but I didn't wanna say anything to you but I jus'
14           fe⌈:lt=⌉
15  Emma:     ⌊Ya: ⌋h
16  Lottie:  =dirty when I walked on the ca:r↓p*et.h .hh
17  Emma:    Well you know we were there in ↑Ju:ne
18           youknow Bud played go:lf inna (.) when the air
19           conditioner went o::ff? .hhh An' we're about (.)
20           the only ones that ha:d an air conditioned room
21           the ↑rest of 'em were bro:ken. .hhh An' we went down
22           to breakfast 'n there was only about ↑two people to
23           help for breakfast with all these guys goin' to pla:y
24           go:lf. They were a:ll teed o:ff:.
25  Lottie:  Ye⌈:ah?
26  Emma:     ⌊.hhhhh Because (.) °*uy°
27           ↑Bud u-couldn' e:ven eat his breakfast. He o:rdered
28           he waited forty five minutes 'n he had to be out
29           there to tee off so I gave it to uh: (.) Karen's:
30           little bo:y.
31           (0.7)
```

```
32   Emma:    ((swallow)) I mean that's how bad the service ↓w*as
33            .hh (.) °It's gone to pot.°
34   Lottie:  u-Oh*::: (.) e-[Y e : : a h. Ye<]
35   Emma:                  [°But it's a° beauti]ful ↓go:lf
36            ↓°course.°
```
(NB:IV:10:R:35)

The complaint details in Extract 6.3 are recognizably produced with regard to the standards expected of hotels and restaurants, and yet I would suggest that they are not easily accommodated by cognitive script theory. The reason for this is that the participants not only produce their specific descriptions of the restaurant with regard to standard items such as menus, tables, waiters, and so on, but also work up various other script-relevant criteria that, unless we start to specify a large number of additional scripted features, would be difficult to anticipate. While Bud certainly should get to eat his breakfast (line 27), the exceptional items here also include things like how many people would be expected to be in the bar (lines 3–4), carpet cleanliness (line 16), an adequate number of waiters or cooks (lines 22–3), a reasonable waiting time for receiving the food (line 28), and the general quality of service (line 32). These are produced not merely as non-scripted items that might be noticeable for that reason, like if the waiter had burst into song, or not having to pay for the food, or whatever. They are produced as the kinds of script-invoking 'expectation failures' that signal those features that restaurants should normally, according to Extract 6.3, provide.

We could, of course, proceed to build these details into a cognitive script model and use that as the basis on which those details are perceptually noticed and linguistically generated – if only we could imagine or discover how many such items and criteria there are. Or perhaps we could specify a higher-level set of requirements for efficiency and cleanliness in service industries and elsewhere, though this would have to become non-specific for actual places. The trouble is, any such exercise becomes a post hoc procedure consequent on analysing these sorts of conversations, while for specifying general purpose *plan-based* cognitive models it would be difficult to know when to stop adding details. We could find ourselves having to specify a very large amount of script-relevant knowledge which, for any actual conversation or interaction, overspecifies it and fails to show up as relevant.

There could be a potentially endless list of these kinds of features, even excluding as a special case the need to serve breakfast in time for the golfers to go out and play (Extract 6.3, lines 23–9). And in any case, any such analytic move would side-step the basic and contentious idea that those details should have the status of mere 'noticings', rather than being descriptions constructed, from an indefinitely large set of possibilities, to perform and warrant the action of complaining. Note that the same kinds of features could plausibly figure, with a different kind of discursive gloss, as characteristics of a desirably folksy, laid-back, informal sort of restaurant that contrasts favourably with places that are antiseptic, regimented, and characterless.[6] It emerges that cognitive script theory, therefore, may have endemically serious problems in dealing with the specifics of conversational script and breach formulations.

An alternative approach is to make a virtue of these problems and consider script-relevant descriptive details as inventively produced and *made* relevant as part of the production of situated accounts. In the context of producing a complaint, details are descriptively worked up and built into script-relevant formulations, where their status as accurate depictions and as recognizable complaints is interactionally accomplished on-the-fly rather than existing as pre-written cognitive contents, dumped from memory storage into talk. Note the corroborating appeals to what Claude independently said (Extract 6.3, lines 9–10), and Emma's affiliating interjections. The interactional, evaluating, and complaint-relevant nature of the discourse is further reinforced by what the place is then unfavourably compared to; not another restaurant, as script theory might predict, but the compensating attractions of its own golf course (Extract 6.3, lines 35–6). It is notable that Extract 6.3 occurs within an extended narrative sequence in which the places evaluated are not a set of disconnected restaurants, but the set of places (a new shopping mall, a restaurant, a golf course) that Lottie happened to have visited recently, with Emma's made-relevant reminiscences interspersed. The thread is discursive and interactional, joint narrative and evaluation (cf. Edwards and Middleton, 1986a), rather than a conceptualization of what kinds of restaurants there are in the world.

Episodes, instances, and dispositions

A major issue, both for perceptual–cognitive script theory and for discourse theory, is how people move from *episodes* (singular events that happen, or that are described as such), to the status of these as *instances* of a more general pattern, to *script formulations* of what kind of pattern that is. Script formulations can be fleshed out or warranted by detailed episode descriptions, just as episodic events can be described and scripted up into generalizations. Another feature of everyday event descriptions is how they make inferentially available particular dispositional states of the actors; their moral character, personality, or state of mind (Edwards, 1995; Smith, 1978). For all these features, the issue addressed here is the kind of analytic framework we need in order to make sense of the specific details of situated descriptions. In particular, we shall be looking at what might be called 'scripts in the making', not ready-made cultural examples such as restaurant routines, but at a series of personal 'observations' on recurrent patterns of activities that people offer in their talk, and that are presumably the kinds of perceptual 'noticings' from which cognitive script representations are assumed to be built.

For example, consider this piece of data from Dorothy Smith's influential study of the descriptive construction of a person, 'K', as 'mentally ill': 'K was

unable to put on a teapot cover correctly, she would not reverse its position
to make it fit, but would simply keep slamming it down on the pot'
(1978: 46). The specification of K as 'unable' provides a dispositional basis
for a series of actions that are formulated as regular and repeated by the use
of *would*; she 'would not reverse its position', and 'would simply keep
slamming it down on the pot'. The use of *keep* reinforces the repetitive
nature of the action and, together with *simply*, helps build a picture of
irrationality and compulsion. It is through these kinds of linguistic details
that links are produced between a specified set of recurrent actions and the
status of these patterns as documenting the actor's inner disposition
(pathological, in K's case) to act in those ways.

In the following sections we examine how this interplay between episodes,
instances, and scripted generalities provides discursive resources for
building dispositional descriptions of persons, including moral, personal,
and pathological traits. Extract 6.4 deals with the character of an apparently
troublesome neighbour.

Extract 6.4
```
 1   Emma:    (. . .) 'n then I went 'n saw Na:ncy? 'n .hhhh (.)
 2            Jesus I guess there was a mess youknow that little
 3            (0.3) whorey thing that lives across from me
 4            that Pa:m youknow⌈: that talk to the homosexual=
 5   Lottie:                   ⌊Ya:h,
 6   Emma:    =there was a great big FI:GHT there Monday night 'n
 7            the police: were the:re an' .hhuhhhh she was SO:BBI:NG
 8            YOUKNO:W that she wa::nted to come in: Nancy wouldn'
 9            let her come in an' th't she woke up everybody::
10            y'know I guess it was a b:lurry mess I dunno whether
11            ⌈uh somebody tried to beat her u:p=
12   Lottie:  ⌊Mhm
13   Emma:    =er'e w- (.) .t.hhh.hhh he was too big for her he was
14            too: oversexed or something I don'kno:w but (.)
15            .hnhhhh God we gotta get her ou::tta there hhh
16            (.) She distu:rbs me I just ul:oa: the every time I
17            s:ee her.
18            (0.5)
19            .tch 'N I live right across from her you ↓know
20            .hm⌈hhh
21   Lottie:     ⌊°Oo::°
22            (.)
23   Emma:    .hh Dirty f:ilthy thing an' Nancy says .hhh she hit
24            the ironing board up there on the wa:ll °n*:-n*:°
25            night before la:st was goin o:n (.) °n*:° I dunno
26            what the hell they do they play on the floor 'n they
27            go take sho:wers 'n poor Nancy's tryin' a sleep 'n
28            go to ↓wor:k youkno:w 'n
29   Lottie:  Ye:a:h.
```
(NB:IV:13:R:22)

The neighbour Pam's character and identity are categorized and presented for recognition ('youknow'), as 'that little (0.3) whorey thing . . . that talk to the homosexual' (lines 2–4). The event descriptions that follow establish a basis for this description of Pam's character, and for the thus-warranted notion that Emma and her friends would be justified in trying to get Pam evicted (line 15). First come some episodic descriptions, the recent events which are the occasion for this passed-on report from Nancy: a disturbance in the night, a big fight, the police, a 'b:lurry mess' (lines 2, 6–10), together with indications of abnormal sexual activity and violence (lines 11–14). But all of this is to be understood as no singular, exceptional occasion; it is part of a regular pattern. Character and consequence (complaint, possible eviction) are built through generalization and script formulation.

The reported events are depicted as part of a pattern, where Emma's routine response to Pam (lines 16–17), described now as a 'Dirty f:ilthy thing' (line 23), is warranted first by an additional episode with an ironing board (lines 23–4), and then by a scripted account of what *routinely* goes on in Pam's apartment (lines 25–7), while next door 'poor Nancy' is engaged in the contrastingly proper business of trying to get some sleep and go to work. The script details are interesting, in that it is the *conversational* context that provides for their specific formulation. Playing on the floor and taking showers are difficult to see as generally applicable anomalies for what people get up to in their apartments. In another context they might sound legitimate and harmless, or not be mentioned at all, or not in that way. Note how 'I dunno what the hell they do' (lines 25–6) works to create this impression of mysterious misdeeds going on behind closed doors, with 'I dunno' providing at the same time for the fact that Emma does not have a lot of precise and damning details to offer. Extract 6.4 demonstrates, therefore, how event items, cross-event comparisons, and scripted event formulations can be descriptively built as part of the warranting of character or personality descriptions, orchestrated for their current interactional upshots and consequences.

Much of Emma's and Lottie's talk is of people and events of which they share a lot of experience. These include Emma's husband Bud, the news here for Lottie being that Bud has just 'walked out' on Emma, leaving her with the uncertainty of who is going to be coming for Thanksgiving dinner. In Extract 6.5 Emma offers one of several reports to Lottie of what happened.

Extract 6.5

```
1  Emma:   An' then when 'e c-came in when ah-uh from fishin'
2          an' I said gee look 'at I: did a:ll the hhh things
3          with aw- va:cuum cleaner I've been all over the f::-
4          well .hhh (.) he says Well hhow could you do i:t.
5          uh: ↓uh Did you do a good jo::b,h.hh .hhh well that
6          tee:d me o::ff,hh
7          (.)
```

```
 8  Lottie:   hkhh °hhuh huh ⌈he:h,°⌉
 9  Emma:                  ⌊.hh.hh⌋ So HE↑PACKED HIS CLO:THES
10            'N'E WENT an' he says he won't ev'n be down for
11            Thanksgi↓ving. So I think I'll ca:ll Barbara 'n
12            cancel the who:le thing. °°hmhh°°
13            (2.2)
14            Isn' this ri:diculous ↑an' u-an BILL'N GLADYS WAITIN'
15            OUT THERE TO GO TO DINNER 'N I: had to go tell 'em
16            ↑Isn'he ri:diculous?
17            (1.0)
18  Lottie:   He's cra:z↓y.
(NB:IV:4:R:2)
```

Extract 6.5 provides an apparent exception to the linking of episode–script–disposition, in that the events described are not directly treated as scripted, but are singular events which nevertheless result in Bud being described as 'ridiculous' and 'crazy'. However, script formulations are not far away. There is already some script-relevance in that Bud's leaving is produced as being precipitate, and provoked by very little on Emma's part. It is the *absence* of any normatively recognizable basis for Bud's actions that provides the grounds for blaming him. Note also how Bud's character is built up from episodic details, to 'this' being ridiculous (line 14), then Bud himself being ridiculous (line 16), and then to Lottie's upgrading of that to 'He's cra:z↓y' (line 18). Dispositions *are* built from and warranted by generalized action formulations, and from norm-exceptions; it is just that the order of presentation of episodes, scripts, and dispositions can be varied, or that elements can be treated as understood. What counts is that participants produce these elements as linked, as bases for talking about a coherent world, and for formulating upshots and consequences.

In Extract 6.5a we start to see how the scriptedness of Bud's actions plays a more overt part.

Extract 6.5a (continuing from Extract 6.5)

```
20  Emma:    ↑ Oh: Go:d dammit. I said it's ↑too bad the boat didn't
21           sink yesterday an' tha:t m-guh thah- I shouldn' o' said
22           ↓ th*a:t. But .t.k.hhhh ↑Lottie I: can't do anything
23           ri:ght honest to Go:d I ca:n't. e- ↑Here I↑ worked
24           ha:rd va::cuumi:ng 'nd hh (.) .hhh he got up 'n fe:lt
25           it to see if there wa:s any du:st, hhh
26           (0.8)
27           'NIS RI:DI:cu↑lous?
28           (0.4)
29  Lottie:  °Oh: he's crazy.°
```

Lines 22–3 place Bud's actions into a more general pattern where Emma, in Bud's eyes, 'can't do anything ri:ght'. The episodic actions of Extract 6.5 are now identified as part of that repeated pattern, in which Bud unreasonably finds fault with Emma, such that Bud's looking for dust (lines 24–5) is offered not only as episode, but as *instance*. Shortly afterwards, even the action of walking out is scripted up:

Extract 6.6 (a page on from 6.5a)
1   *Emma*:   ↑ This is buh ↑Youknow he's ↓good at wa:lkin' out
2   ↓on me like tha:t.↓ (.) Youknow takin' 'is clo:thes
3   'n leavin',

And again later:

Extract 6.7
1   *Emma*:   Buh YOUKNOW HE e-he ↑ does this so many ti:mes.
2   'E k-.hhhhh He PA:CKS UP'n LEA↓:ves youkno:w
3   'e did it up (.) to me in the apartment
4   he gets if he doesn' like someth'n I sa:y
(NB:IV:4:R:14)

Bud's actions are now script-formulated and *recognizable as* such; Emma says something, Bud takes unreasonable exception to it, Bud packs his clothes and leaves. It is the kind of thing he routinely does ('so many ti:mes', Extract 6.7, line 1), with other instances starting to be introduced that warrant the generalization (lines 3–4). Apart from noting the rhetorically organized script-building and disposition-warranting work being done in these extracts, we can note also the relevant sense of descriptive details. The formulations 'takin' 'is clo:thes 'n leavin'' and 'He PA:CKS UP'n LEA↓:ves' (Extracts 6.6 and 6.7) provide just the details required to specify what *kind of* activity it is. Clothes packing is a sufficient particular to identify it as a leaving-to-go-and-stay-somewhere-else, a walking out, and *that* constitutes the nature of the repeated activity.

Actions and events are available to be characterized as episodic items, instances, exceptions, or routines. Such descriptions attend to interactional concerns in the events and in their reporting (cf. the model of attributional reasoning in Edwards and Potter, 1993). Specific details are reported not in automatic accordance to their status as perceptual anomalies or expectation failures, but with regard to interactive and rhetorical contingencies (such that the status of being an expectation failure is *itself* discursively produced). The implicative relations between script and anomaly (breach) formu-lations, and personality or mental state formulations, are such that activities can be described, and responded to on this basis, precisely *for* those implications. All of this is a far cry from the disinterested perceivers, making their best sense of the world, that script theory presumes. While cognitive theorists might wish to distance themselves from participants' interactive and rhetorical business, and speculate about a purely sense-making cognitive being, to do so would be to remove the theory from one of its major domains of applicability, which is everyday discourse.

Script rhetoric and reciprocity

Having examined some ways in which Emma builds script-and-disposition complaints to Lottie about her husband Bud, we return now to counselling materials such as the Mary and Jeff data in which both parties (in these cases, husbands and wives) are present and in a position to reciprocate. The advantage of these materials is that they help to develop further a *rhetorical* analysis of personal narratives, and in particular the ways in which stories are told with regard to possible or actual alternatives, together with alternative and reciprocating implications for accountability, and how all this may be accomplished with a remarkable degree of subtlety and precision.[7]

In Extracts 6.8 and 6.8a Connie and Jimmy, an Irish couple living in England, respond in turn to the counsellor's invitation to provide some historical background to their problems. Connie begins by characterizing their marriage as having been, up to now, 'rock solid'.

Extract 6.8

```
 1  Counsellor:  Whe:n: (.) before you moved over here hhow was
 2               the marriage.
 3               (0.4)
 4  Connie:      ↑O↓h. (0.2) I- (.) to me: all alo:ng, (.)right
 5               up to now, (0.2) my marriage was rock solid.
 6               (0.8) Rock solid. = We had arguments like
 7               everybody else had arguments, (0.4) buthh (0.2)
 8               to me there was no major problems. Y'know?
 9               That's (0.2) my way of thinking but (0.4)
10               Jimmy's thinking is very very different.
     (DE–JF:C2:S1:7)[8]
```

Connie's description 'rock solid' offers a picture of strong marital stability, maintained 'all alo:ng', and 'right up to now', which is to say, right up to their present difficulties. Their 'arguments' (lines 6–7) are depicted as the routine sort, the kind that everyone has, the normal kind that are observable and expectable in close relationships, and that say nothing against the general rock solid stability of her marriage to Jimmy. This acknowledgement of past difficulties, as the routine sort, is an important way of claiming that the relationship was *essentially* good, as it makes that claim more difficult to refute merely by citing any such difficulties.

Rhetorical design is signalled also by the uses of extreme formulations such as 'rock solid', 'all alo:ng', and 'right up to now', which, as Pomerantz (1986) has noted, tend to occur when claims are being bolstered against doubt or disagreement. Such disagreement is not far away, as Connie states in lines 9–10; this is her version, and Jimmy's 'thinking is very very different'. The interesting thing here is how Connie attends to what Jimmy might say (he is sitting next to her, and presumably they have argued these matters somewhat before coming for counselling). She does so in lines 6–7; note the latching (or rush-through[9]) marked by the 'equals' sign, the immediate attachment of the statement about arguments to the claim about rock solidity. Jimmy's versions of their marriage, with which Connie is familiar, focus on its *lack* of solidity, as evidenced by the frequency and severity of such arguments.

Jimmy's contrasting account builds those 'arguments' (Connie's term) as recurrent and severe, and a pervasive feature of their relationship right from the start. The episode he starts to cite is from the beginning of their relationship, and from that time on 'We were at each other the who:le time' (lines 16–17).

Extract 6.8a (continuing Extract 6.8)
```
10   Connie:   Jimmy's thinking is ve⌈ry very different.⌉
11   Jimmy:              ⌊Well (1.0)       ⌋ Bein: (0.8)
12             a jealous person, (0.8) u:m, (0.6) we go back- (.)
13             back to: (0.6) when we were datin'(1.0) when we were
14             dating first (0.8) well we met in this: particular pub.
15             (1.0) >When we start'd datin' we was in there,< <EV'ry
16             single week> we'd fight. (0.2) We were at each other
17             the who:le time.
```

Connie's formulation of a rock solid marriage interspersed with routine and unremarkable 'arguments' is countered by Jimmy's alternative account, an equally script-formulated version ('<EV'ry single week>', 'the who:le time', lines 15–17), but one of perpetual conflict. The attention that both give to the scripted nature of events is part of their factual accounting; these are offered as long-term observations, covering many individual events, and provide the basis for a generalized characterization of the relationship itself. Note the specific contrast with what Connie characterizes as routine 'arguments', the sort that 'everybody else' has (Extract 6.8, line 7). Jimmy also works up their repeated nature, but not as a means of normalizing them. Rather, he emphasizes their *excessive* frequency ('<EV'ry single week>', 'the who:le time'), and also their severity, replacing Connie's term 'argument' with 'fight' (Extract 6.8a, line 16). In these ways he produces a pathologizing, rather than normalizing kind of scriptedness, indeed more like the way K's mental illness was documented (Smith, 1978).[10]

We can begin to see that these are not merely different and inconsistent accounts, the stuff of communication failures and misunderstandings, say, that are often assumed to underlie relationship disputes.[11] They are *contrasting* accounts constructed precisely in relation to an actual alternative, in that they display an awareness of that alternative and its evidential–rhetorical grounds. Jimmy's self-avowal as 'a jealous person' (Extract 6.8a, line 12) picks up from something Connie had said earlier. One of the key features of their talk is the way in which each deploys dispositional characterizations of the other, supported by script-formulated accounts of the sorts of behaviour they each routinely get up to. As with the stories of their prior relationship, we focus on the reciprocal design of those dispositional formulations.

Jimmy's 'jealousy' is descriptively built by Connie, both directly and evidentially, in terms of his recurrent actions. She describes it as an enduring feature of him, notably again something he 'Has a:lways ↓been, from the da:y we met' (Extract 6.9, line 3).

Extract 6.9

```
1    Connie:    At that poi:nt, (0.6) Jimmy ha- (.) my- Jimmy
2               is extremely jealous. Ex- extremely jealous
3               per:son. Has a:lways ↓been, from the da:y we met.
(DE–JF:C2:S1:4)
```

Connie describes Jimmy as possessing a deep-rooted personality disposition (not just jealous, but a jealous *person*) which is both extreme and enduring. It has been so 'from the da:y we met', which places it prior to any subsequent marital difficulties. Connie thus provides an enduring basis *inside* Jimmy that accounts for his recurrent behaviour during their marriage, and for a variety of difficulties, including the recurrent 'arguments' or 'fights' to which both have alluded. Such recurrent patterns are exemplified by an *instance*, given in the form of a specific narrated episode.

Extract 6.9a (continuing from 6.9)

```
 4   Connie:      Y'know? An' at that point in time, there was an
 5                episo:de, with (.) a bloke, (.) in a pub, y'know?
 6                And me: having a few drinks and messin'. (0.8)
 7                That was it. (0.4) Right? And this (0.4) got all
 8                out of hand to Jimmy according to Jimmy I was
 9                a:lways doin' it and .hhh y'know a:lways
10                aggravating him. He was a jealous person I:
11                aggravated the situation. .h And he walked out
12                that ti:me. To me it was (.) totally ridiculous
13                the way he (0.8) goes o:n (0.4) through this
14                problem that he ha:s.
15                (0.2)
16                And [(he) (   )]
17   Counsellor:      [Was that ] the time that you left?=
18                ((Apparently to Jimmy))
19   Connie:      =He left the:n that was (.) [two ye]ars ago. He=
20   Jimmy:                                   [°Yeh.°]
21   Connie:      =walked out then. Just (.) literally walked out.
```

Connie's narration of a single 'episo:de' (Extract 6.9a, line 5) is used as the basis of a more generalized, scripted account of the kind of thing that Jimmy can be routinely expected to do (line 13, 'the way he (0.8) goes o:n'), again deploying the continuous or iterative present tense ('goes o:n'), and a characteristic activity generalizer ('the way'). Jimmy's extreme jealousy is cited as an explanation of this patterned conduct; he behaves that way 'through this problem that he ha:s' (lines 13–14).

Jimmy's dispositional jealousy is descriptively grounded, not only in the scripted nature of his actions, but also by the specific details of Connie's episodic example. The incident involved 'a bloke' (Extract 6.9a, line 5), an anonymous, impersonal, anybody-would-do sort of category; 'in a pub' rather than anywhere more intimate, and indeed a recognizably category-bound kind of place where people might be expected to socialize somewhat (cf. examples in Drew, 1992, and in Widdicombe and Wooffitt, 1995).

Indeed Connie's specific activity was restricted to 'having a few drinks and messin'. (0.8) <u>That</u> was <u>it</u>' (lines 6–7). Messing is a nicely vague sort of description that accomplishes some rather precise rhetoric. While characterizing her actions as some sort of pub-typical harmless play, *messing* is vague enough to cover a wide variety of specific behaviours of which she might be accused, while countering any suggestion that she was engaged in anything sufficient to occasion a strongly jealous reaction from her husband. His leaving was therefore (like Bud's) precipitate, inadequately caused by anything Connie did: 'He <u>walked out</u> then. Just (.) <u>literally</u> walked out' (Extract 6.9a, lines 19–21; the 'just' is a lovely little device here). All this leaves Jimmy with quite a lot of work to do if he is to counter that story and reverse the direction of blame. We soon see how he goes about that.

The analysis thus far shows that Jimmy's jealousy, as depicted by Connie, provides a damaging, pervasively applicable way of pathologizing his behaviour and blaming him for various marital difficulties. The important thing, for the current analysis, is how Connie's discourse possesses a reflexive, *rhetorically symmetrical* design of blaming Jimmy while at the same time protecting her own conduct from blame. Jealousy underlies not only his unreasonable behaviour, but also his false accounts of *her* actions. And yet, it is an ascription that Jimmy himself sometimes endorses (including its pathological, endemic nature in him; this is in talk not examined here). Jimmy's jealousy offers grounds for interactional delicacy beyond merely blaming him. Connie variously treats Jimmy's jealousy as a 'sickness' that needs to be recognized and understood.

An insight into Jimmy's rhetorical use of it is provided by Connie in the form of a succinct characterization of the kind of thing Jimmy says:

```
(From Extract 6.9a)
 8   Connie:    (. . .) according to Jimmy I was
 9              a:lways doin' it and .hhh y'know a:lways
10              aggravating him. He was a jealous person I:
11              aggravated the situation.
```

It appears that being a pathologically jealous kind of person is not only something that Jimmy *counters*, but he may also on occasions assert and make rhetorical use of it. Later in the same session he refers to it himself, as something that 'hurts inside 'n it gives me: <u>ba:d pains</u>. (.) Uh I <u>I</u> feel (.) if Connie does something to me I can- I'm <u>hurt</u> real bad' (DE-JF:C2:S1:27). His jealousy being a predictable reaction, and painful *to him*, can be turned around as a way of excusing him (he would not *want* to be in pain) and of blaming his wife. He is a deeply jealous man, constitutionally so from way back (as Connie asserts), and can do nothing about it; so *she* ought to take that into account and not go aggravating the situation by flirting with other men. So it can be *her* fault when *he* has an unreasonable fit of jealousy, for getting him going, causing him pain (Extract 6.9a, line 10, '<u>aggravating</u> <u>him</u>'). If it is a predictable script in Connie's eyes, then that places her in a position, and with a responsibility, to predict and avoid it.

The notion that Connie flirts with other men is not hers but Jimmy's, and it is countered by her as the product of his jealous imagination. This is the rhetorical symmetry again; accusations of unreasonable jealousy provide an account for the jealous husband's perception that his wife is an incorrigible flirt, and vice versa. Again, what we have is a personality disposition (this time one for Connie, being flirtatious) that relies for its credibility on the flexibility of specific event descriptions and generalized script formulations. Jimmy produces his own detailed narrative, not fully reproduced here, of the pub episode mentioned in Extract 6.9a, in which what Connie called *messing* is reworked as a sustained flirtation with a 'bit of a la:d' called Dave.

Extract 6.10

```
 1   Jimmy:   Connie had a short skirt on I don't know. (1.0)
 2            And I knew this- (0.6) uh ah- maybe I had met him.
 3            (1.0) Ye:h. (.) I musta met Da:ve before. (0.8)
 4            But I'd heard he was a bit of a la:d (    ).
 5            He didn't care: (1.0) who he (0.2) chatted up
 6            (. . .)
 7            So Connie stood up (0.8) pulled her skirt right
 8            up her side (0.6) and she was looking straight
 9            at Da:ve (.) >°like that°< (0.6) and then turned
10            and looked at me (1.2) and then she said w- (.)
11            turned and then (.) back to Dave and said (.)
12            by the way that wasn't for you.
```
(DE–JF:C2:S1:10)

Jimmy's extended narrative, only partially reproduced here, counters Connie's by reformulating her story in various ways. We join Jimmy's narrative where Connie's anonymous 'bloke, (.) in a pub, y'know?' (Extract 6.9a, line 5) is fleshed out more personally as Dave, someone they had known previously and of whom Jimmy had 'heard he was a bit of a la:d' (Extract 6.10, line 4). This appeal by Jimmy to Dave's *reputation*, known also for his tendency to 'chat up' women indiscriminately (lines 4–5), helps objectify this judgment of Dave's character, as stemming not merely from Jimmy's subjective viewpoint. Jimmy's description of Connie's 'short skirt' and what she did with it (lines 1, 7–12) helps build an image of her also as flirtatious, in how she dresses and acts. Dave is introduced as a person to whom Jimmy has paid no specific attention, in that he signals an initial uncertainty about whether he had previously met him (lines 2–3). Similarly with Connie's short skirt, while managing to introduce such telling details, Jimmy nevertheless displays himself as not particularly zealous in monitoring them (line 1, 'Connie had a short skirt on *I don't know*'), which works to counter any notion of a watchful and suspicious jealousy.

We have seen that Jimmy may occasionally deploy a picture of himself as dispositionally, irrationally, and extremely jealous, just as Connie does, though he does so as part of a different rhetoric. But Jimmy also counters that image. He does so by building a counter-narrative of events in which his eventual emotional outburst occurs as a sequentially intelligible and appropriate reaction to her behaviour.

Extract 6.10a (continuing shortly after 6.10)
```
27   Jimmy:    then we went back to the house (.) >°Connie and we
28             all went back to the house at this point°< (0.6)
29             Uh: (0.5) went back there 'n I was- I was si- um
30             (.) John and Caroline were together (   ) and
31             Dave (0.2) and Connie were sitting. (0.4) °Talking.°
32             (0.8) I was sitting on the floor playing records.
33             (0.8) I sat there for (.) two 'n a half hours (0.8)
34             uh (.) and no one come over (.) not once did they-
35             (0.4) .h ANYthing. (.) Just sat there. (.) Talking.
36             (0.6) I was just completely ignored the whole time.
```

Connie's intimacy with Dave is further enhanced by its reported continuation throughout the evening. During this time Jimmy himself is contrastingly excluded, sitting alone on the floor, not by choice, but by being 'completely ignored' (line 36) for a rather precisely specified (and thus credible) 'two 'n a half hours' (line 33). So he was not engaged, say, in any *social* interaction that might provide a basis for Connie's neglect of him.

Lines 30–2 include a specific formulation of intimate couples. 'John and Caroline' are Connie's sister and her husband, a ready-made couple. Note how Jimmy describes them as 'together', providing a category for how we hear about Dave and Connie:

(From Extract 6.10a)
```
30   Jimmy:    (.) John and Caroline were together (   ) and
31             Dave (0.2) and Connie were sitting. (0.4) °Talking.°
32             (0.8) I was sitting on the floor playing records.
```

The picture is of two couples, paired off as intimate twosomes, with Jimmy contrastively sitting alone, not even listening, watching, sulking, or whatever else he might be described as doing, but, rather, performing the host's duty of putting the records on.

Jimmy's narrative then reaches the point where, having prepared some rational grounds for them, he introduces his own (re)actions, the ones that Connie has complained of, and offered as evidence of his extreme, irrational, and dispositional jealousy.

Extract 6.10b (continuing shortly after 6.10a)
```
42   Jimmy:    Uh: I was (.) boiling at this stage and I was real
43             angry with Connie (   ). And uh went up to bed 'n
44             (.) I lay on the bed. (0.7) °got into bed.° (0.6)
45             I- uh (.) could hear giggling ('n all that)
46             downstairs and then (0.5) the music changed (0.5)
47             slow records. (1.2) And um: (1.2) >and then they
48             changed to slow records< (0.8) I could hea::r (1.0)
49             that Connie was dancing with (0.2) this blo:ke
50             downstairs. (1.0) And Caroline turned round and
51             said (.) something (.) about it (it was wha-) it
52             was oh Connie look out I'm going to tell (.)
53             Jimmy on you. (1.0) And (.) next thing I hear is
```

54		(.) °what he doesn't know (doesn't) hurt him.°
55		(0.2)
56	*Counsellor*:	°I'm sorry?°
57	*Jimmy*:	What he: doesn't kno͟w: doesn't hu͟rt him. (0.8)
58		Soon as I heard tha͟t I went- (1.6) strai͟ght down
59		the stairs. (0.8) 'n uh (0.6) threw them out.
60		(1.2) Took Co͟nnie up the sta͟irs and thre͟w her on
61		the be͟d. (1.6) I ke͟pt trying to ru͟:n to ju͟mp out
62		the window. (1.6) Bu͟t y'know: I I cou͟ldn't. (.)
63		I cou͟ldn't (.) ge͟t myself (0.4) to go ou͟t. (.) I
64		cou͟ldn't (.) do͟ it.
65	*Counsellor*:	So that's what you fe͟lt like.
66	*Jimmy*:	Oh ye:h.

Jimmy's eventual actions (lines 58–64) are displayed as an understandable result of sustained provocation by Connie over the course of a long evening. Both its sequential placing in the story, and the expression 'at this stage' (line 42), identify Jimmy's 'boiling' anger as following a series of provocations. His anger builds up event by event (lines 42–3, 58–64), as a reaction to events; 'at this stage' and 'soon as I heard that'. The extremity of Jimmy's response, including an aborted leap from an upstairs window, serves as an index of the extremity of that provocation. The failed leap from the window not only displays the genuineness and intensity of his emotional state,[12] but its self-destructive nature would also detract from any alternative category that might arise here, such as that of a bad-tempered wife beater. The counsellor (line 65) picks up its indexical import as evidence of Jimmy's (reactive) emotional state, and Jimmy confirms that (line 66). The upshot is that these are not actions that tell us about him as a person; they are *re*actions to provocations by Connie, which tell of the emotional states he gets into through having a wife who behaves like that. So Connie's scripted-and-instanced depiction of Jimmy, as problematically and extremely jealous, is countered by Jimmy's detailed narrative, whose rhetorical force is to provide an alternative specification of events, as a sequence of provocation and understandable reaction.

The thrust and counter-thrust of episodic narrative, scripted sequences, and dispositional upshots do not end with Jimmy's story. Connie, in turn, counters the notion that she is dispositionally flirtatious. Apart from providing alternative accounts of the same events, she works as Jimmy does to establish alternative stories as *emblematic instances* of general patterns, from which a different and more valid (both factually and morally correct) characterization of her as a person can be drawn. Extract 6.11 shows how Connie's script-instancing and dispositional work on Jimmy accomplishes some fine-grained rhetorical business with regard to the specific alternative stories and implications that he produces.

Extract 6.11

1	*Connie*:	Uh I mean if some͟body came up- I'm no͟t the type
2		that can- (0.4) I'll te͟ll you just a quick

```
 3              instance now. A couple of weeks ago we went out
 4              (0.6) and he went up to the bar to get a drink
 5              and he said if anyone comes over (0.4) tell them
 6              to get lo:st or something like that. Right? (0.2)
 7              I was sitting there, he had s↑aid it to me and
 8              stated it to me. (0.2) Goin' up, .hh I was
 9              sitting there and there was (.) three blokes
10              standin- (0.6) to the side, (0.2) they had (.)
11              similar shirts (.) and they were lau:ghing at
12              one another saying something about- and the bloke
13              said something to me: and I was c- talking (0.2)
14              and (.) Jimmy came dow:n and he (0.2) he nearly
15              went ↑ma↓:d >he said< I ↑told you not to ta- .h=
16   Jimmy:     =It's not what I said.
17   Connie:    Well i- you say it.
18   Jimmy:     S- you (.) you jus- (.)
19   Connie:    I'M N↑OT THE TYPE that'd turn round and ignore
20              somebody. (.) Regardless who they are. I I jus'
21              can't do it.
```
(DE–JF:C2:S1:28)

Connie frames her narrative in Extract 6.11 rhetorically, as a denial of a counter-proposition about her (lines 1–2, 'I'm not the type that can-', and again in line 19). The narrative produced in support of that denial is offered as 'a quick instance' (lines 2–3) of events in general, in other words a *script instance*. Both Connie's and Jimmy's reported actions are offered as emblematic instances of general action sequences. Note *how* the scripting is done – 'if somebody came up- I'm not the type that can-'. The conditional *if* clause refers here to an action routine, *if X happens then I do/don't do Y*. The expression 'I'm *not* the type' also performs scripting work, reflexively via the close folk-logical connection that obtains between scripts and dispositions; reference to a 'type' of person provides a dispositional basis for associated patterns of conduct and reaction.

Connie's direct quotation of Jimmy's words (Extract 6.11, lines 5–6), and her emphatic repetition that this is what he 's↑aid' and 'stated' to her (lines 7–8), draws attention to Jimmy's strong position on these matters and to the notion that this is a ready-made, in-advance position of Jimmy's, said 'goin' up' to the bar, prior to and not therefore merely a reaction to events. Rather than doing anything provocative, Connie also repeats that she had been merely 'sitting there' (lines 7, 9). Her interaction with the men was responsive, not initiative (lines 12–13). Note also the nicely relationship-neutral formulations for that interaction: 'said something to me' and 'talking' (line 13: cf. Drew, 1992). The brief description of the men is interesting too. It is emphatically 'three blokes' (line 9) rather than a one-to-one encounter, and their 'similar shirts' (line 11) further homogen-izes them as individually unremarkable and undifferentiated.

The scripted upshot of Connie's narrative is that if she talks in response to people who are merely being friendly (lines 9–12, three anonymous 'blokes' who were 'lau:ghing at one another'), then she catches some highly charged trouble from Jimmy (lines 14–15, 'he nearly went ↑ma↓:d'), who was primed for trouble before anything happened. If she obeys Jimmy and ignores them, then she is forced into being rude, refusing a common courtesy, which is not in her nature. Note how the specific object of that refused courtesy is formulated as 'somebody. (.) Regardless of who they are' (line 20), which again works against any notion that Connie may be singling out individuals for sexual interest. The detail 'turn round and' (line 19) nicely specifies the action, that ignoring such people who talk to her would be abrupt, unoccasioned, or rude. Her *inability* (lines 1–2, 19–21) to comply with Jimmy's requirements, which is (under a different description of it) Jimmy's ground for criticizing her flirtatiousness, is precisely her own basis for an alternative dispositional account of herself as ordinarily sociable and polite, to folk in general no matter whom, and not at all flirty with flirty men.

The rhetorical organization in the details of Connie's story, with regard to Jimmy's, is remarkably precise and finely wrought, building a detailed series of contrasts between her actions and his perceptions. In the course of her narrative Connie provides a descriptive basis, in terms of scripted action patterns and emblematic instances, not only for her own character but, reciprocally, for Jimmy's too. It is her sociability that he takes objection to, and the factual status of that sociability, underwritten by graphic narrative detail, is precisely what constitutes his reaction as one of unreasonable jealousy. Stories and counter-stories, generalizations and counter-generalizations, upshots and counter-upshots, are produced in ways that attend, in sensitive detail, to what the other partner may and does say, and to a clear-cut set of implications. That is to say, they display an interaction-orientation and rhetorical design that is realized at the level of fine-grained descriptive details.

In looking at Connie's and Jimmy's opposed stories, with their opposed script and breach formulations, and psychological ascriptions, it may be supposed that we are looking at something exceptional, a case where there is an obvious dispute, while for most people most of the time these matters are simply agreed, jointly assumed, or, indeed, straightforward expressions of cognitive schemas. Maybe troubles talk provides a soft case for a rhetoric of personality ascriptions. It should be emphasized, however, that building inferential links between episodes, scripted sequences, and dispositions is a pervasive feature of both everyday and technical discourse. The counsellors themselves do it, not *in spite of* their (worked-at) neutrality, but as part of it, such as when formulating the routine and recognizable ways in which couples typically get themselves into relationships troubles, and how they might be helped out of them (Edwards, 1995).[13]

The objection that the counselling data are a 'soft case' for a *rhetoric* of script and dispositions also fails to recognize that *consensus* is also a worked-up rhetorical category (Potter and Edwards, 1990; see also Chapter 5), together with 'given' information. Similarly, *all* descriptions are produced from an indefinite set of potential alternatives, and often against locally relevant specific ones, and are therefore interactionally potent without overt disagreement necessarily breaking out. The choice of the counselling materials serves to open up this kind of rhetorical organization with a clear case in which the categories of action, event, description, inference, regularity, disposition, mental states, and so on, are contended. An appropriate procedure would be to work back from these materials towards ostensibly more straightforward discourse (if this can be found) and ask, do we *ever* reach a point where things are just so, as described, doing nothing, all there is to say, mere 'honest Jo(e)' talk, where consensual descriptions and inferences can be taken by the analyst as tokens of fact or cognition? The treatment of script talk in this chapter is part of a general approach to discourse as *performative*, where honesty, straightforwardness, and the reality behind versions are just as much participants' business as are deception and error.[14]

Conclusions: scripts, cognition, and discourse

The problem with trying to account for the orderliness of eating out in restaurants by invoking mental scripts is that it is not clear when, if ever, we come to the point where plans are adequate to handle contingencies (Suchman, 1987). Since rules do not specify their applications (Collins, 1990; Dreyfus, 1992; Wittgenstein, 1958, 1967), except by invoking further rules to which the restriction must also apply, there always arises the problem of accounting for the contingencies of situated actions (cf. Dresher and Hornstein, 1976). The issue here is that there may well be a form of competence for dealing with situated actions that, to the extent that it works in practice, may manage at the same time to account for much of the orderliness of action and understanding that the 'script' concept was invented for.[15]

Restaurants have served as a useful topic for explications of cognitive script theory. They stand somewhere between more highly scripted routines such as catechisms and ritual ceremonies, on the one hand, and the one-off vagaries of existence, on the other. But script theory is designed to be applicable not only to very formalized routines, which are easily specified but highly restricted, but also to the more messy, partial, in-the-making ways in which people deal with, and start to build up perceptions of, the routine features of everyday life. Indeed, these are supposedly the developmental root and origin of scripts, the starting point for perceptual orderliness and for noticeable anomalies. They have also been the focus of the analyses provided in this chapter.

Script theory is clearly dealing with something psychologically important. Everyday activities are performed and narrated with regard to criteria of orderliness, and are intelligible to participants as more or less routine or exceptional. People surely do form generalized expectations, and treat actions as planful, and plan things. Script theory seeks to formalize such common-sense resources, and place the scripted, planful nature of actions prior to accounts. In contrast, discourse theory treats scripts and plans as discursive productions – ways in which people project, reconstruct, and render intelligible those activities as part of their performance, and when producing accounts of them. The discourse approach reverses the reality–cognition relation found in script theory, by reversing the mediating nature of language. Discourse is viewed as primary, with cognition and reality its topics, or matters-in-hand. The empirical advantage of a shift from abstracted perceptual models to specific script *formulations* is that it retains (but reworks) the explanatory power of script formulations as ways in which people make sense of the world, while managing to deal with the specific detail, contingency, and functionality of how they actually do so on particular occasions.

In Harvey Sacks's (1992) studies, people deal with the world as basically orderly and recognizable, but Sacks's treatment differs in important ways from those of schema and script theory. Sacks uses a notion related to that of a mental/cultural script when analysing a data sample in which the receiver of a telephone helpline call to a psychiatric hospital said, 'May I help you?' Sacks offers, as a 'base environment' for such sayings, a department store, where 'it's pretty much the case that for a customer, the question of whether some person "can help" is a matter of the department store having made them the person who does that' (1992, vol. 1: 9). This way of drawing on his own cultural knowledge of such places is reminiscent of Roger Schank's use of remembered and imagined routines in restaurants (Schank, 1982; Schank and Abelson, 1977). However, Sacks draws on such knowledge as a resource for dealing with specific segments of naturally occurring talk, such that whatever cultural knowledge is introduced to help the explication of talk immediately takes on a contingent and flexible character.

This flexibility is different from Schank's. For script theory it is *cognitive* – a matter for analysts of identifying categories of restaurants (etc.) that are more or less typical, and for participants, of learning from experiential variations across visits to restaurants and accordingly having their schematic knowledge structures (automatically) updated. In Sacks's analysis, the flexibility is *pragmatic*, to do with the interactional contingencies of speaking. Indeed, Sacks emphasizes how robust and *normative* such cultural knowledge is, and how impervious it is to the dictates of personal experience (Sacks, 1992, vol. 1: 62). He argues that it is strongly 'protected against induction . . . it isn't automatically modified if events occur which it doesn't characterize' (1992, vol. 1: 196). It is the very robustness of such knowledge that permits its flexible invocation, such that Sacks argues explicitly *against* a 'model of how it might get modified . . . [in which] you store up a bunch of exceptions, saving each one, remembering them, and when you get a whole bunch of them, you're forced now to say that what you supposed were so is not so' (1992, vol. 1: 196).[16]

The normative knowledge that is invoked in conversation should not, as I have argued in other chapters, be equated with statistical frequency, or perceptual normality. It is not that a 'base environment' has to be one that is frequently encountered, and alters in the mind each time it is encountered. Rather, its use is in accounting for actions. So, the 'may I help you' formula, since it normatively implies a person who has the credentials to use it, can be flexibly used outside of any obviously scripted scene. To do so need not imply error, nor provide data for updating mental scripts, but, rather, may perform the action of invoking those kinds of credentials, together with whatever routine, standardized implications may be attached to them. That being the case, we can reconsider even the 'base environment' example as a participants' accomplishment. It is a way of providing a particular inter- pretative trajectory for interaction. In other words, it is a way of 'subverting', indeed of making it so, that a certain kind of interaction is being done, a certain kind of status being claimed. Such flexibility of usage *requires* that cultural norms are more robust against experiential variations than a perceptually based theory tends to assume.

Sacks's treatment of naturally occurring conversational materials reveals subtleties that pre-programmed, plan-based devices cannot feasibly handle. It is not merely more subtle or complicated, but a different basis of assumption. The intelligible orderliness of social life stems not from a set of updatable knowledge structures in a sense-making cognitive being, but from how social actions flexibly unfold, as situated performances. This is also the argument in an influential study by Lucy Suchman (1987), which contrasts plan-based cognitive models of human actions with an ethnomethodo- logically inspired notion of 'situated actions'.

Suchman begins with an example taken from an anthropological study by Thomas Gladwin (1964), and from a discussion of it by Gerald Berreman (1966), of how Trukese navigation methods contrast with European chart-following methods. Apparently, the Trukese (inhabitants of Truk, a Micronesian island in the western Pacific) navigate the open seas in an ad hoc manner, adjusting course according to various signs and conditions on the way (wind, waves, tides, current, stars, clouds, etc.) rather than following a predetermined route. 'If asked, he can point to his objective at any moment, but he cannot describe his course' (Berreman, 1966: 347, cited in Suchman, 1987: vii). In contrast, for chart-following European navigators 'the comparable account . . . seems to be already in hand, in the form of the very plan that is assumed to guide his actions' (Suchman, 1987: vii–viii). It is the one-sided European model that serves as the primary metaphor for standard cognitive science, for how cognitive plans are supposed to work in human actions and cognitions, universally, as programs or blueprints that generate actions and understandings.

Suchman considers various options, including the possibility that there are two different kinds of organization for human actions (the Trukese and the European), available to different kinds of people, or perhaps to everybody all the time. But she argues otherwise. After a careful theoretical and empirical analysis (of the practices of photocopier repair technicians), Suchman concludes that *all* actions are of the 'situated' kind, and do not proceed from plans, even those for which plans are available (cf. Suchman, 1992; Whalen, 1995):

> . . . plans are best viewed as a weak resource for what is primarily ad hoc activity. It is only when we are pressed to account for the rationality of our actions, given the biases of European culture, that we invoke the guidance of a plan. *Stated in advance*, plans are necessarily vague, insofar as they must accommodate the unforeseeable contingencies of particular situations. *Reconstructed in retrospect*, plans systematically filter out precisely the particularity of detail that characterizes situated actions, in favor of those aspects of the actions that can be seen to accord with the plan. (Suchman, 1987: ix, emphasis added)

The crucial notion here is that plans themselves can become parts of situated actions, the actions of talking and accounting for conduct. They arise as things said and done 'in advance' of the actions they refer to, or 'in retrospect'. But 'as *ways of talking* about action, plans as such neither determine the actual course of situated action nor adequately reconstruct it' (Suchman, 1987: 3, emphasis added). As categories of talk they work like script formulations do, providing a basis for accountability, rather than a program for generating the activity itself. We should add that they may also be invoked reflexively *within* action sequences as formulations of the kind of activity it is,[17] as a criterion for what to do next, or for what has gone wrong. But each time they occur in these ways they feature as actions in their own right, in the form of situated descriptions, again just as script formulations do. The anticipatory, reflexive, and retrospective relationships between accounts and activities are features of participants' talk and, *as such*, suitable objects for analysis.

This chapter has demonstrated how the routine, recurrent, and recognizable nature of everyday life is approachable empirically through the analysis of discourse, as a participants' practical concern. Event descriptions are constructed with regard to what is expectable or exceptional about them. Analysis has focused on the way such 'script' features are built into events in descriptions, where descriptions themselves are consequential activities performed in the telling, and designed for the occasion of their production. Part of the analytic interest in such discursive productions is the ways in which they are oriented to alternative possible (or actual) descriptions, and to the alternative implications and upshots they produce.

Some of these implications and upshots concern the dispositions of the actors involved in events and in event tellings, such that script and breach formulations may be produced, and taken interactionally, to imply personal or mental states. The reverse happens too, where disposition formulations provide explanatory bases for how people (are reported to) behave in predictable ways. The discursive–performative approach to such phenomena and their inferential upshots contrasts with prevailing cognitive and 'social cognition' approaches, such as schema and script theory, in which event descriptions correspond to knowledge representations of a perceptually apprehended external world. But even without the rhetorical foil provided by cognitive script theory, it would have to be a prime concern of discursive psychology to examine the ways in which event regularities, patterns of conduct, personality and mental states, exceptions, expectation failures, and so forth, are produced as such and contended in talk.

The next chapter focuses on emotion discourse, which is an important part of dispositional and mental state descriptions, and of narratives about human activities. There is a direct link, both in everyday talk and in psychological theories, between scripted patterns of action and reaction, and the emotions or emotion descriptions that go with them. The discussion of emotion discourse takes us into psychological, anthropological, and social constructionist theories of emotions. We examine various discursive uses of emotion terms, including the rhetoric performed by contrasting emotion with rationally grounded thought and action.

Notes

1. The various counselling data used in this book were obtained without background ethnographic information, and with no independent knowledge of any of the participants apart from my having met one of the two counsellors (Jeff's and Mary's). All that is known of them is derived from the recorded sessions.

2. Script theory, as a variety of schema theory, originated in artificial intelligence and has been influential in social, cognitive, and developmental psychology, in the study of memory, comprehension, social cognition, and the development of children's language and knowledge. See, for examples, Bower, Black, and Turner (1979), Nelson (1986), and Schank (1982).

3. Script theory is not a single, precisely specifiable thing. Schank's (1982) revision of the initial theory dealt with objections to its brittleness and redundancy, by disassembling the classic routines such as restaurant and dentist-visiting scripts into more widely and efficiently usable components, while introducing higher-level principles for reassembling them for a greater variety of situations. Nevertheless, the essential principles of perceptually derived schemas, planned actions, and a reliance on artificial textual representations, have remained in place. A foundational 'perceptual–cognitive' meta-theory is retained across variations and developments in basic principles (Abelson, 1981; Schank, 1982; Schank and Abelson, 1977), and throughout its various extensions from cognitive science into experimental, developmental, and social psychology.

4. The treatment of mental states and personality traits as 'dispositions' echoes Gilbert Ryle's (1949) use of this term, in his celebrated critique of Cartesian 'ghost in the machine' concepts of mind. For Ryle, many everyday terms for mental states, personality traits, etc., can be analysed as dispositions to act or behave in various ways. The materials discussed in this chapter demonstrate a specific domain of action–disposition inferences as ones *participants themselves* construct and deploy. Ryle also distinguished between 'episodes' and 'dispositions' in a way that somewhat prefigures the discussion in this chapter and the next of references to anger, jealousy, and flirtatiousness. My own more empirical (rather than philosophical) analysis suggests that mental state descriptions are not semantically fixed in their 'dispositional' or 'episodic' implications, but can be to some extent *worked up* discursively, on occasions, as one kind or another. This links 'mental state' terms to a Wittgensteinian notion of how they function as tokens in everyday 'language games', but also to a requirement to study them empirically, in use. The prospect for combining conceptual analysis and ethnomethodological principles in analysing the discourse of mental life owes much to the pioneering work of the sociologist and philosopher Jeff Coulter (1979, 1983, 1990a; see also Bilmes, 1986; Button et al., 1995).

5. Mary's 'obviously' acknowledges her lying as known (though it had earlier been hidden from Jeff). In the context of normative accountability, it may also perform a bit of script work, normalizing her past lying as the kind of thing that spouses having affairs are generally expected to do, rather than implying that they are, outside of that, disposed (as persons) to telling lies.

6. For example, bare floors and tables, spartan décor, surly waiters, and even a bit of dust about the place might give it a kind of rustic or inner city authenticity, while taking a long time over delivering the food is citable as a sign of its having been freshly prepared and cooked, in preference to pre-cooked, prepared from frozen, stale, and so on.

7. Coulter has noted how 'Researchers working in spouse-abuse clinics . . . report that a curious symmetry can arise in which, e.g., the personality attribution of one spouse is matched by a counter-attribution from the other in terms which potentially undermine the original attribution by tacitly furnishing criteria for its possible defeat (and vice versa). Thus, one spouse characterizes the other as, e.g., "a poor listener," while the other makes an attribution of "a persistent nag." Or again, one party calls the other "a lazy s.o.b.," while the other party calls the first a "hyperactive bitch."' (1990a: 106).

8. A technical note on transcription: it is conventional in CA transcripts to place a pause such as the one in line 6, where it occurs at an intonationally marked 'possible completion point', on a line of its own, like the pause in line 3, rather than effectively assigning it to one or another participant, like in line 7, where it occurs more obviously within an uncompleted turn at talk. This is a transcription detail relevant to notions of whose turn it is, and what might count as an interruption or an overlap. One of the features of the counselling data is that individuals get to take very long turns with lots of abnormally lengthy pauses (see Jefferson, 1989b), yet without having to fend off interruptions. This is a general feature of story-telling (Jefferson, 1978; Sacks, 1992; see also Chapter 10), where long turns are conversationally set up and provided for, and also of how 'counselling' is oriented to as being done, where getting to tell your full story, your side of things, is something participants treat as normative in that setting. In the various transcripts provided of the couple counselling data I have included many such within-story pauses as within-turn.

9. See Schegloff (1982) on the 'rush-through' as a device used in avoiding interrruptions.

10. The difference between a normalizing and a pathologizing script formulation seems in this case to inhere in the specific details and discursive context of each description. The possibility of a systematic pattern in such differences must await further study.

11. Analyses of descriptions and accounts in these settings contradict some prevalent 'social cognition' assumptions concerning relationships, relationship troubles, and couples therapy (e.g., Bubenzer and West, 1993; Duck, 1993). Social cognition theories, currently the dominant paradigm in social psychology (Augoustinos and Walker, 1995; Fiske and Taylor, 1991), assume that people act generally, and in relationships, on the basis of their perceptions and understandings, including such mental constructs as scripts and plans (Berger, 1993). The discovery of a precisely calibrated rhetorical reciprocity in competing accounts can be set against the familiar 'mismatch between minds' assumption underlying many studies of interpersonal troubles. Rather than treating differential perceptions as causing relationship troubles, it may be fruitful to treat perceptions and cognitions as discourse *topics*, as features of how relationship troubles are descriptively constructed, interactionally managed, and accounted for, for example in (and for) counselling. For further analysis and discussion of these matters see Edwards (1995), which is a major source of the materials used in this chapter.

12. See also the discussion in Chapter 7 of an extension of this sequence (Extract 7.2), which focuses on Jimmy's emotions. As Buttny (1993: 94) noted, 'affect avowals' in discourse can serve as 'shorthand formulations' to invoke a variety of culturally understood grounds for emotional reactions.

13. A 'technical' example of the pervasive nature of script-and-disposition inferences is what is called the 'correspondent inference model' of causal attribution (Jones and Davis, 1965), a development of causal attribution theory, which is a major sub-field of 'social cognition' (Fiske and Taylor, 1991). This claims that people form character judgments about other

people on the basis of perceiving the routine ways they behave in various circumstances. When comparing those personality judgments to a person's current actions, that person is seen to be behaving 'in character' or not. If they are behaving in character, then their current actions will be explained 'internally' by reference to their dispositions or character. If out of character, their actions will be explained as due to external circumstances. In discursive psychology these kinds of inferences and causal explanations are reworked as matters constructed and managed in situated talk (Edwards and Potter, 1992a, 1993).

14. Button et al. also object to what they call a 'spectatorist' approach to discourse: 'It is as if we first observed other people engaged in a host of activities, and *then* required some terms with which to describe and explain the regularities in what they do' (1995: 218, original emphasis).

15. Perhaps restaurants are not such good base models for cognitive theory after all. In fact, there are worries about the necessity of cognitive models from other, non-discursive perspectives. For example, there may be situational, 'ecological' cues available in any setting that help specify what to do (and which therefore require less elaborate mental models and plans to deal with them: cf. Rogoff and Lave, 1984). It may even be that the only things that *can* vary *will* vary, such that the orderliness of the restaurant script, once we start dealing with a number of eating places, is either necessary or definitional. Either it is necessary (you have to gain access to the food before you can eat it; you have to enter the restaurant before you leave it; you have to go to your table before you can sit down at it), or else it is semantically defined, by what we mean by 'restaurant' (such as a place where you can pay for and eat prepared meals). Apart from those things, everything that is neither necessary nor definitional may turn out to be variable, such as when to pay, whether there is a waiter, whether 'service' (compulsory tipping) is included in the price, and all the obviously variable things that any particular restaurant will possess that no script model was ever designed to include.

16. 'Odd events, by and large, are just not added together . . . in part by way of the fact that what is normal gets incorporated into things like proverbs and becomes very stable, odd events are just sloughed off. They don't get incorporated. . . . What you get is, "Those things happen, sure, but . . ."' (Sacks, 1992, vol. 1:62). Cf. the rhetorical status of 'commonplaces' (Billig, 1987), and of idiomatic expressions (Drew and Holt, 1988). Sacks notes that 'one thing about odd events, then, is that they're very hard to report. This fact can occasion the relevance of a category that this society has, called "believing"' (1992, vol. 1: 62). See also Wooffitt (1991), on participants' credibility concerns in the reporting of unusual experiences, and the discussion in Chapter 3 of this volume.

17. The reflexive character of talk, in constituting and not just commenting on the activities in which it occurs, was discussed in Chapters 3 and 4. Recall particularly Sacks's remarks on the utterance 'This is, after all, a group therapy session' (1992, vol. 1:516). Sacks notes that 'members can't do pure formulating', and that such a thing cannot be said 'non-consequentially'.

7

Emotion

The emotions are often defined in contrast to rational thought. They are conceived to be natural bodily experiences and expressions, older than language, irrational and subjective, unconscious rather than deliberate, genuine rather than artificial, feelings rather than thoughts, indeed anything but central topics for a book on 'discourse and cognition'. Yet these categories and contrasts are precisely what signal their importance for discursive psychology. Their significance is in how they are *conceived*, how they may be *defined*, and especially in how various emotion categories contrast with alternative emotions, with non-emotional states, with rational conduct, and so on, within the discursive construction of reality and mind. Emotion discourse is rich and various, full of contrasts and alternatives, and marvellously useful in working up descriptions of human actions, inter-personal relations, and in handling accountability.

The discursive psychology of emotion deals with how people talk about emotions, whether 'avowing' their own or 'ascribing' them to other people, and how they use emotion categories when talking about other things.[1] Emotion discourse is an integral feature of talk about events, mental states, mind and body, personal dispositions, and social relations. It is used to construct thoughts and actions as irrational, but, alternatively, emotions themselves may be treated as sensible and rationally based. Emotion categories are used in assigning causes and motives to actions, in blamings, excuses, and accounts. Emotional states may figure as things to be *accounted for* (in terms of prior causal events or dispositional tendencies, say), as *accounts* (of subsequent actions and events), and also as evidence of what *kind of events or actions* precede or follow them. For example, anger or exasperation, whether performed bodily or evoked linguistically, can be used/taken to signal that something is wrong or problematic about whatever they are directed at, functioning as 'shorthand formulations *of the event*' (Buttny, 1993: 90, altered emphasis).

Emotions are not only *contrasted* with cognitions (whether rational or not), both in 'folk' and professional psychology, but there are also cognitive theories *of* emotions, and indeed cognitive models that virtually do away with, or explain away, emotion categories altogether. But there are also emotion-based explanations of cognition, of what people think, what they think about, and why they think one thing rather than another (envy, jealousy, prejudice, obsession, etc.: see Oatley and Jenkins, 1996, for a general review). At stake in both lay and professional discourse, therefore, are not only the distinct uses of various emotion terms, but also the status of 'the emotions' as a superordinate and explanatory category. A major theme of this chapter is the rhetorical design and use of emotion categories. This theme is developed empirically, through the analysis of various conversational and textual materials, and also critically, through an examination of semantic and cognitive approaches to emotion discourse, together with various historical and anthropological perspectives.

An appropriate place to start, if we have not started already, is where we left off the previous chapter, with scripts and dispositions.[2] Recall Jimmy's description of his 'boiling' anger (Extract 6.10b), and its relationship to his possibly pathological jealousy (Extract 6.9). The focus now is on what kinds of descriptions those are, their rhetorical organization, what they say about actors and events, how they figure in building credible narratives and moral accountability, how they are produced and defended as accurate descriptions (or countered as false): generally what kinds of business such descriptions perform at the juncture they are introduced, both in the reported events and in the discourse that reports them.

The scripted and extreme nature of Jimmy's jealousy was used discursively in depicting his actions as irrational; that is, as stemming not from an objective perception of Connie's behaviour but, on the contrary, from something within him that biased and clouded his vision. The rhetorical reciprocity of Connie's and Jimmy's accounts (analysed in Chapter 6) was sustained partly through the use of emotion talk. It played upon the capacity of emotion descriptions to provide a *contrast to rational thought* (Jimmy's unreasonable jealousy), but also to provide a *rationally sensible* story of coherent, understandable reactions to provocation (Jimmy's anger). This was what Jimmy's 'boiling' anger did; his extreme emotions were, under his description of them rather than Connie's, responsive to a storied sequence of clear provocations, documenting not so much his own irrational mental state, as her unreasonable behaviour with Dave.

Again, part of the intelligibility of those contrasting stories lay in the construction of *scripted event sequences* in which the various emotion descriptions were rendered coherent as parts of normatively intelligible actions, or else stood out as deviant and unreasonable (cf. Smith, 1978). The link between emotions and scripted scenes or 'scenarios' is one that recurs not only in everyday talk and counselling discourse, but also in psychological and anthropological theories of emotion. Since 'cognitive scenarios' are a major feature of cognitive approaches to emotions, and also feature (as discourse categories) in everyday talk, we shall give them close attention in this chapter.

First, again as a glimpse at the kinds of phenomena under analysis, consider something Mary said about Jeff. It is a snippet from her story about the events leading up to their coming for counselling (these personal narratives are examined in Chapter 10). The counsellor has asked them both 'why: uh you went to Relate in the first place', and Mary's version is told first.

Extract 7.1

```
1        Mary:    (...) so that's when I decided to (.) you know
2                 to tell him. (1.0) U::m (1.0) and then::, (.)
3   →             obviously you went through your a:ngry stage,
4                 didn't you?
5                 (.)
6   →             Ve:ry upset obviously, .hh an:d uh, (0.6)
7                 we: started ar:guing a lot, an:d (0.6)
8                 just drifted awa:y.
```
(DE–JF:C1:S1:4)

Mary provides, as part of her narrative, a time and place for, and specification of, Jeff's emotions on hearing about his wife's affair with another man (lines 3 and 6). He was 'a:ngry' and 've:ry upset'. These descriptions characterize Jeff's reactions *as* emotional rather than, say, as having come to a damning but rational appraisal of Mary's actions and character. But the details I want to focus on are 'obviously' and 'stage'. The 'obviously' normalizes and somewhat endorses those emotional reactions as expectable, and sequentially proper within the story as told. Mary is displaying (here) an understanding, uncritical position on Jeff's reactions (though elsewhere, and soon after, she is more condemnatory).

The phrase 'your a:ngry stage' is exquisite. It employs a notion of anger as a temporary state with its proper occasions and durations. While Jeff's anger is proper in its place, one would not expect it to go on for ever, to endure unreasonably, beyond its 'stage'. Mary makes rhetorical room here for something she exploits soon afterwards, which is the notion that Jeff's reactions are starting to get in the way of progress, starting to become (instead of her infidelity, as Jeff insists) 'the problem' they have in their relationship. Indeed the *next thing she says* in her narrative (and implicationally, therefore, what not only follows but follows *from* Jeff's reactions), is how 'we: started ar:guing a lot, an:d (0.6) just drifted awa:y' (lines 7–8). Their problems are now described as joint ones, arguments, and a kind of non-agentive, non-blaming, 'just' drifting apart. The implication that Mary develops in her subsequent discourse is that Jeff's reactions should end at some reasonable point. His 'stage' is already past tense ('you went through your a:ngry stage, didn't you?') and he starts to become accountable for continuing to be 'upset'.

Now, I have glossed in a condensed way quite a lot of what is going on between Jeff and Mary, rather than producing all of that through an analysis of further extracts from their talk. This is in order to succinctly point up the kinds of interactional business that emotion talk can perform. Emotions and cognitions (and the differences between them) are not just sitting there, inside Jeff's head and actions, waiting to be reported on. 'Anger' and 'upset' are *descriptions* that, first and easily missable, can be used to construct reactions *as* reactions, and *as* emotional ones, rather than, say, as something like coming to a view or an opinion. One of the uses of such talk is that emotions such as 'anger' and getting 'upset' permit talk of stages, of temporary inflammations of the passions, rather than the more enduring states of mind we might expect of things like conclusions or beliefs, or even 'the way things were' – events themselves. Similarly, emotion categories provide for rational (sequentially understandable, in Garfinkel's sense) accountability, though they can also be used to contrast with rational thought, to label behaviour as spontaneous and sequentially incoherent (unjustified by events), and even to pathologize it.

I have emphasized the *flexibility* of emotion discourse in providing the sense of events, of states of mind, and for managing issues of accountability. This is one of the advantages of examining emotion discourse *in use*, rather than relying solely on conceptual analysis or idealized cognitive models. Consider, for example, the notion that emotions lend themselves to talking of temporary rather than enduring mental states. The point is that this is a way of talking, and that it can (but need not) be used and worked up on occasions. There are alternative categories of emotion that conceptually lend themselves to more enduring dispositional statements, and imply that something more cognitive and analytical is going on; jealousy and resentment, for instance (Coulter, 1986). However, there appear to be no strict constraints here on how we have to talk. We can talk of *dispositionally* angry[3] or fearful people, and, conversely, of sudden pangs of jealousy or resentment (even if we use 'sensation' words such as *pangs* to do that – Coulter, 1986: 123–4). Emotion categories provide a flexible resource for situated discourse, including the potential for rhetorical opposites and contrasts, rather than a set of semantic templates that will mean or imply the same things about actors and events whenever used. With that warning, we shall examine some claimed relations between emotions and standardized cognitive event scenarios.

Emotions, semantic universals, and cognitive scenarios

I shall not offer here a general review of psychological theories of emotion (for brief but instructive histories of 'emotion' in psychology, see Averill, 1990; Gergen, 1995; and Soyland, 1994). The focus is on emotion *discourse*. Nevertheless, there are points on which a discursive approach fits better with some kinds of psychology than with others. Narrowing the range to language-oriented approaches to emotions, discursive psychology is broadly compatible with social constructionist work (Harré, 1986a; Harré and Gillett, 1994), and less happy with cognitive–semantic models (Lakoff, 1987; Wierzbicka, 1992). But one prominent feature of both cognitive–semantic *and* social constructionist approaches (for example, K.J. Gergen, 1994) is the link between emotions and 'scripts' or 'scenarios'. This is the notion that emotions can be defined and differentiated in terms of the standard kinds of event sequences (or cognitively represented event sequences), or dialogue sequences, in which they occur.[4] We have seen how everyday emotion discourse is bound up with event descriptions, script formulations, and disposition and mental state attributions. Since it might be presumed that this is evidence of the explanatory power of a scripts-and-semantics model of emotion talk, we shall explore some comparisons and differences.

There has been considerable disquiet in the cognitive and social constructionist literature concerning a thesis popular since Darwin (1871) and recently championed by Paul Ekman (1992, 1993) which claims the existence of a set of 'basic' and 'universal' emotions and emotional expressions that can be found across cultures and that is due to innate human physiology. Ekman's list of 'basic emotions' is supported mainly by cross-cultural comparisons of the perception of facial expressions. The list has varied somewhat, but includes *anger, fear, disgust, sadness, enjoyment*, and (though recently omitted) *surprise*. The disquiet about it is based on anthropological and social constructionist studies of cultural variability (for example, Harré, 1986b; Heelas, 1986; Lutz and Abu-Lughod, 1990), and on forceful critiques of the assumption that there is widespread cross-cultural agreement about the meanings of emotional expressions, both linguistic and facial (Russell, 1991, 1994). Part of the worry is that English emotion words may have been arbitrarily built into theory and method as the criteria for cross-cultural comparisons: 'English words like *anger* or *sadness* are cultural artefacts of the English language, not culture-free analytic tools' (Wierzbicka, 1995: 227). Indeed, this is a worry that reaches far beyond claims about universals, and is applicable also to work that emphasizes cultural and linguistic differences.

James Russell and others (for example, Harris, 1992; Wierzbicka, 1992, 1994) prefer an analysis which links emotions to *action scripts*. This forms part of a cognitive theory of emotions, where cognitions precede feelings. For example, *happiness* is linked to a scenario in which 'I think: something good is happening; I feel something good because of this' (Wierzbicka, 1995: 240; cf. Lakoff, 1987, on *anger*). Anna Wierzbicka's (1995) cognitive approach to emotion words attempts to avoid the common ethnocentric tendency of treating all the world's emotion terms as greater or lesser approximations to the emotion vocabulary of English. She does this by defining the meanings of emotion words, in any language, in terms of a strictly defined set of semantic universals, derived from systematic cross-linguistic study (Goddard and Wierzbicka, 1994). These semantic universals, or 'conceptual primitives', are used as the building blocks for the 'cognitive scenarios' that define the meaning of any emotion term in any language. According to this scheme, it is not (necessarily) the emotions or the emotion terms that are universal, but the conceptual primitives from which their definitions can be assembled. Thus, 'the use of conceptual primitives allows us to explore human emotions (or any other conceptual domain) from a universal, language-independent perspective' (Wierzbicka, 1995: 236).

Wierzbicka (1995: 251–2) provides the following 'full set of hypothesized conceptual primitives':

[substantives] *I, you, someone, something, people*
[determiners, quantifiers] *this, the same, other, one, two, some, much/many, little/few, all*
[mental predicates] *know, want, think, feel, see, hear*
[speech] *say*
[action, event, movement] *do, happen, move*
[existence, life] *there is, live*
[evaluators] *good, bad*
[descriptors] *big, small*
[space] *where, side, inside, far, near, above, under*
[time] *when, after, before, a long time, a short time*
[taxonomy, partonymy] *kind, of, part of*
[intensifier] *very, more*
[similarity] *like*
[clause linkers] *if, if . . . would, because*
[clause operators] *not, maybe*
[metapredicate] *can*

I am in no position to dispute the cross-linguistic evidence on which these universal primitives are claimed. However, the implication is that not only would we expect to find these concepts (given here in English) lexicalized in all languages, but that they would all mean precisely the same thing in all languages, in which case we may as well use English. Be that as it may, here are some 'cognitive scenarios' for *surprise* and *sadness*, assembled from the conceptual primitives (Wierzbicka, 1995: 245, 253):

X was *surprised* =
 X thought something like this:
  'something is happening now
  before this time, I didn't think this would happen
  I want to know more about it'
 X felt something because of this

X was *sad* =
 X thought something like this:
  'something bad happened
  if I didn't know that it had happened I would say: "I don't want this"
  I don't say this now
  because I know I can't do anything'
 X feels something bad because of this

Wierzbicka claims that, whereas bodily sensations and mental states may vary for any particular 'emotion', or be difficult to pin down and define, 'it is the cognitive scenario associated with an emotion term . . . which allows us to distinguish one presumed emotion from another' (1995: 232). Different but similar emotions in English (such as *sadness, grief, distress, sorrow*), and similar kinds of sets in other languages, invoke 'different (but overlapping) cognitive scenarios' (1995: 242). The aim in defining scenarios for emotions (or any other concepts) like this, using the highly restricted vocabulary of conceptual primitives, is 'to identify and compare emotions without using any "names" ' (1995: 250). The 'names' to be avoided are emotion words, of course, none of which figure in the list of universal primitives.

Wierzbicka's cognitive scenarios, built using the conceptual primitives, are provided as if they were in some sense non-descriptions, not actually sentences of English, nor of any particular language, not things anyone might say, but pictures of abstract and universally understandable semantic representations. They are reminiscent of the idealized, transcendent, occasion-free 'restaurant script' (see Chapter 6),[5] though much more abstract still, being composed of (putative) universals rather than of obviously culture-specific objects such as waiters and menus. Although definitions of scripts and scenarios are certainly recognizable, and relevant to an analysis of what people mean by what they say, they have only an idealized and possibly misleading application to everyday discourse. They obscure rather than reveal the flexibility of situated uses through which talk performs its interactional and world-building business.

Let us examine briefly how these very abstract scenarios can nevertheless be recognizable as specifications of various emotions. Note that, included in the list of conceptual primitives, is the philosophically notorious word *feel*. Given the difficulty of defining precisely what this word means in English,[6] its occurrence in a list of semantic universals is surprising. It is difficult to imagine what it takes to perform an adequate multi-lingual conceptual analysis for such a claim. However that may be, its presence in the list of 'primitives' conveniently allows a series of 'X felt something' statements to be inserted at the end of each scenario. I would suggest that what we do when reading these scenarios is to *read in* the English emotion word given at the top (*surprise*, *sadness*, etc.), and let our ordinary understanding of that word inform the scenario definition of it (rather than vice versa), including both the events in the scenario, and what we are supposed to be 'feeling'. Some such process is necessary, given that the semantic primitives are so semantically *impoverished*, being largely a list of pro-terms, prepositions, and deictic expressions (see Chapter 5 on these).

Heavy use is made of the conceptual primitives *good* and *bad*: precipitating events are 'something good' or 'something bad', and the resulting feelings are 'feel something', 'feel good', 'feel bad'. It is a kind of Legoland model of the emotions; simple outlines made from a small set of basic and identical building bricks that require knowledge of the originals (buildings etc.) to know what they are supposed to be. Now, it may well be that when we try to specify[7] semantic universals what we end up with is something like this list of very generally applicable primitives. And it is a coherent argument that any universals of emotion meanings would have to be a sub-set, or a combination, of those. But it might also be that when we try to produce those combinations they are too crude to adequately capture the meaning of any emotion word in any language. If it comes down to events and feelings being 'good' and 'bad', then it is not at all clear that the pursuit of emotion universals has proven fruitful. The presence of such 'evaluators' in a language is no guarantee of the range of their application, nor of their specific, local sense (Winegar, 1995).

Wierzbicka's scenarios are not merely permutations or sub-sets of the semantic primitives. They contain other words too, and combine them into sentences, and take English *tenses* like '*had* happened', and modals like '*would* happen'; are *these* primitive too? Does the conceptual 'clause linker' *if . . . would* encompass the use of the English modal auxiliary *would* even when it is used without the conditional *if*, in order to define *surprise*?[8] How free are we to add other words and (English) grammatical devices to the primitives when constructing scenarios? How essential are the actual tenses that Wierzbicka uses, such as *sadness* being triggered by something that 'happened'? Does that rule out being sad about things happening now (Josephs, 1995), or by thoughts of the future? The fact that it is *possible* to provide recognizable but very generalized scenarios for any emotion word in any language, using only the items available in a small set of 'universal primitives', carries no assurance that it is *sufficient* to do so. Such a procedure carries no guarantee that it will capture the bases on which those words are selected and used, or how they relate and differ from alternatives in that language.

Coincidentally, when telling the story of his boiling anger at Connie's provocative flirtations with Dave, Jimmy directly appeals to a rather literally scenario-like image of what he was doing, as 'like (.) something that you see from a film' (lines 68–9 below). Extract 7.2 is a continuation of Extract 6.10b, including a few lines of overlap with it.

Extract 7.2

57	*Jimmy*:	What he: doesn't kn<u>ow</u>: doesn't hurt him. (0.8)
58		Soon as I heard <u>that</u> I went- (1.6) str<u>aight</u> down
59		the stairs. (0.8) 'n uh (0.6) threw them out.
60		(1.2) Took <u>Connie</u> up the <u>stairs</u> and <u>threw</u> her on
61		the <u>bed</u>. (1.6) I <u>kept</u> trying to ru:n to <u>jump</u> out
62		the <u>window</u>. (1.6) <u>But</u> y'know: I I <u>couldn't</u>. (.)
63		I <u>couldn't</u> (.) get myself (0.4) to go <u>out</u>. (.) I
64		couldn't (.) <u>do</u> it.
65	*Counsellor*:	So that's what you f<u>elt</u> like.
66	*Jimmy*:	Oh ye:h.= =I kept (.) g<u>oing</u> <u>o</u>ver as far as the <u>window</u>.
67		I was well a a- (1.0) I <u>knew</u> I was like (0.5) a
68		<u>madman</u>. (0.2) I mean I was <u>really</u> like something that
69		you see from a f<u>ilm</u>. (0.8) An' I <u>put</u> my fist through
70		the <u>door</u>, (0.4) u:m, (1.0) I d<u>idn't</u> hit you >or
71		anythin',<
72	*Connie*:	°ooh no:.°
73		(0.8)
74	*Jimmy*:	U:m (.) >I d<u>on't</u> hit h<u>er</u> anyway.<
75	*Connie*:	((coughs))
76		(1.0)
77	*Jimmy*:	<u>So</u>:, (1.8) th<u>at</u> was like (.) <u>that</u> was the st<u>art</u> of
78		(0.2) the reason why I left the la:st time.

(DE–JF:C2:S1:12)

The idea that conversational participants might *use* the scenario-like nature of their actions, in other words *construct* them as scenario-like and *do something with* that, reminds us of the analysis of script formulations in Chapter 6. As we noted there, Jimmy's story attends to a number of interactionally sensitive issues concerning his accountability: do his marital problems stem primarily from his irrational and excessive disposition to jealousy and anger, or are his angry actions coherent as understandable responses, recountable in sequentially ordered detail, to unreasonable provocations from Connie? We have noted that Jimmy both endorses and, on occasions, counters the notion of his excessive jealousy. In Extract 7.2 we see him orienting rather delicately to all these things in how he elaborates his story.

Jimmy recounts his actions as the result of an extended build-up of provocations ('soon as I heard that', line 58 above; see also the discussion of Extract 6.10b in Chapter 6), in which the accumulation of provocations provides a step-by-step causal account for the build-up and nature of his emotions. He provides a sense of watching himself doing these things, like watching a scene from a movie, recognizable but unreal, acting 'like (0.5) a mad̲man' (lines 67–8), but as much self-destructively as violently towards Connie. Indeed, wanting to throw himself from the upstairs window, and putting his fist through the door, are hearable as somewhat more violent kinds of actions than throwing her on the bed. Jimmy distinguishes his violent actions from any suspicion of wife beating, and obtains Connie's corroboration on that (lines 70–4). He pictures himself as a man striving to control violent emotions, directing them at himself and at physical objects rather than (and explicitly rather than) at the woman who provoked them. The emphatic 'stra̲ight down the stairs' (lines 58–9) conveys his emotional reactions as *immediate*. This fits a *non-cognitive* version of what drove his actions; they were immediate, uncalculated, unconsidered kinds of responses, yet still available to conscious reflection ('I k̲new I was like (0.5) a mad̲man', lines 67–8), and to retrospective narration, and not so wild or uncontrolled as to spill over into 'hitting' Connie.

So we get the sense of Jimmy watching himself acting out a scene, where his movie-like madness is viewed by another, thinking and spectating Jimmy, not only now but then. The narrative construction of himself acting out this scene manages to incorporate and render coherent a series of potentially contradictory elements: his violent anger; his extreme jealousy; his rational accountability; his simultaneous loss and retention of control; Connie's provocation; his recognition that he can act crazily. Jimmy constructs himself as essentially normatively accountable: as one who, even when provoked to the utmost, is still capable of control and reflection, while the excesses of Jimmy the madman are in some sense on view and movie-like, rather than being done by the real him, who is there to ensure that no real harm is done, and to tell us the tale afterwards.

It would be unfair to criticize Wierzbicka for failing to do something she is not attempting to do, such as to specify the conceptual base for complex *situated uses* of emotion terms. She is certainly not offering useful definitions of what people, in actual discourse, do with the words they say. Rather, it is an exercise in universal cognitive semantics, part of the pursuit of universals of mind, linked in turn to iconic elements of facial expressions, towards a possible 'semantics of the human face' (Wierzbicka, 1995: 227). Such a pursuit may well be an entirely different matter from analysing discourse. But I assume that it is also supposed to be relevant to the psychology of speaking and doing things with words – certainly the various emotions and emotion words invoke potent social interactions – just as the analysis of discourse can have something to say about the nature of semantic categories (Edwards, 1991).

In contrast to Wierzbicka's semantic–conceptual method the discursive approach examines samples of talk and text for how various kinds of functional, social interactional business is attended to (such as blamings, reasons, excuses, accounts, etc.), and looks for how 'emotion words', and even their roles in scripted sequences or scenarios, figure in those discursive activities. Within any language the terms available for talking about social accountability, action and reaction, thought and emotion, and so on, are likely to be a set of contrasts and alternatives (Josephs, 1995; cf. Saussure, 1922/1974): this reaction rather than that, this mental state rather than that. We can expect such a patterning in terms of contrasts and discriminations from the basic 'action performative' principles of discourse and rhetoric. The analyst's construction of idealized cognitive scenarios, assembled one at a time out of semantic primitives, obscures the situated, rhetorical use of emotion terms. And yet the semantic primitives it uses are presumably not *incidentally* a list of contrasts and opposites (*many* and *few*, *above* and *below*, *big* and *small*, *good* and *bad*, etc.), designed just as ideally for situated rhetoric, one might suppose, as for abstracted conceptual discrimination. The argument that semantic categories may be designed primarily for functional and rhetorical deployment, rather than for encoding perceptual discriminations, is developed in this chapter and the next.

Emotional etymology

Social constructionist studies of emotion can be grouped into three related kinds: historical, anthropological, and discursive. Each of these is concerned with exploring 'the ontological, conceptual, and temporal priority of the public realm' (Harré, 1983: 114). No clear distinction is drawn between emotion 'discourse' and emotions 'themselves', given that what emotions *are* is equivalent to what emotions are taken to be, how they are conceptualized, talked about, and interpreted, as intelligible social performances: 'look to see how the psychological vocabulary is actually used – then we will know of what it is used!' (Harré, 1983: 115; cf. Coulter, 1979, 1986). Both 'folk' psychology and its technical, professional counterpart are approachable as a set of practices, descriptions, and explanations that have their own cultural and historical trajectory, available to a constructionist analysis (Gergen, 1995).

Rom Harré notes that, whereas some emotions in current use can be historically dated to fairly recent times (he cites romantic love as an example, cf. Gillis, 1988), 'some emotions and moods[9] which once had great importance for us have become extinct or obsolete . . . [for example] the extinct emotion *accidie* and the obsolete mood *melancholy*' (1983: 126). He goes on to draw a telling comparison and contrast between melancholy and 'one of its modern descendants, clinical depression' (1983: 126). Harré's argument is that the origin and extinction of emotions and emotion terms are at the same time rearrangements of the patterning of moral orders, social relations, and accountability. These are not just changes of vocabulary, while our inner (or outer) emotional life remains the same. Emotions 'themselves' are socially and historically defined.

Accidie was a mediaeval emotion, related to the religious sin *sloth*. It was associated with idleness and misery (or something approximating what those words now mean to us), with regard to the neglect of one's duties to God. The association between idleness and misery was part of a notion that performing one's duties to God ought to be a joyful matter, and not just a reluctant obligation, so that getting up and doing things and not being *behaviourally* slothful was not enough. The growth, change, and decline of the emotion was intrinsically linked to social patterns and religious beliefs (Wenzel, 1960), and defined with regard to a changing religious–moral order. So, 'idleness and procrastination are still amongst our failings but our emotions are differently engaged, defined against the background of a different moral order, roughly the ethics of a material production' (Harré, 1983: 129). Again, it is not merely that we feel the same things, but learn to call them by different names. It is that emotions and the names we call them are intrinsically tied to social conditions, rights, and responsibilities, which change historically and differ across cultures.

Historical studies of the changing meanings of emotion terms in English (Stearns and Stearns, 1988) are important in establishing the cultural relativity and specificity not only of current sets of emotion terms, but also of the general 'emotionology' that is built into psychology's most modern, technical 'models' (Gergen, 1995). For example, there is a common-sense notion, which can be traced etymologically, of emotions as private, subjective feelings that are expressed outwardly (and somewhat ambiguously, and subject to disguise) in behaviour.

A perusal of the marvellously informative *Oxford English Dictionary* (1994) reveals that subjective meanings of the word 'emotion' (from Latin *emovere* 'to move out') were preceded by physical, bodily and geographical meanings:

1. A moving out, migration, transference from one place to another. *Obs.*
1603 Knolles *Hist. Turks* (1621) 3 The divers emotions of that people [the Turks].
1695 Woodward *Nat. Hist. Earth* i. (1723) 45 Some accidental Emotion . . . of the Center of Gravity.

2. A moving, stirring, agitation, perturbation (in physical sense). *Obs.*

1692 Locke *Educ.* 7 When exercise has left any Emotion in his Blood or Pulse.

1708 O. Bridgman in *Phil. Trans.* XXVI. 138 Thunder . . . caused so great an Emotion in the Air.

1758 Ibid. L. 647 The waters continuing in the caverns . . . caused the emotion or earth-quake.

3. *transf.* A political or social agitation; a tumult, popular disturbance. *Obs.*

1579 Fenton *Guicciard.* ii, There were . . . great stirres and emocions in Lombardye.

1709 Addison *Tatler* No. 24 313 Accounts of Publick Emotions, occasion'd by the Want of Corn.

4. a. *fig.* Any agitation or disturbance of mind, feeling, passion; any vehement or excited mental state.

1762 Kames *Elem. Crit.* ii. §2. (1833) 37 The joy of gratification is properly called an emotion.

1785 Reid *Int. Powers* 725 The emotion raised by grand objects is awful.

1828 Scott *F.M. Perth*, Desirous that his emotion should not be read upon his countenance.

The current 'psychological' meaning[10] is given as originating in the late eighteenth century, as follows:

> *Psychology.* A mental 'feeling' or 'affection' (*e.g.* of pleasure or pain, desire or aversion, surprise, hope or fear, etc.), as distinguished from cognitive or volitional states of consciousness. Also *abstr.* 'feeling' as distinguished from the other classes of mental phenomena.

1808 *Med. Jrnl.* XIX. 422 Sea-sickness . . . is greatly under the dominion of emotion.

1841–4 Emerson *Ess. Friendship* Wks. (Bohn) I. 81 In poetry . . . the emotions of benevolence and complacency . . . are likened to the material effects of fire.

1842 Kingsley *Lett.* (1878) I. 61 The intellect is stilled, and the Emotions alone perform their . . . involuntary functions.

1875 Jowett *Plato* (ed. 2) I. 249 The . . . emotions of pity, wonder, sternness, stamped upon their countenances.

The original sense of 'emotion' is that of physical movement (cf. Harré and Gillett, 1994), such that the way the word has become associated with inner feelings would appear to be almost a historical recapitulation of Wittgenstein: felt emotions are the kinds of subjective experiences that have become descriptively associated with publicly described activities. The notion of a general class of 'emotions' as 'involuntary functions' of an inner mental life, conceptually distinguished from cognitive and volitional states, and 'stamped upon their countenances' coincides with the origins of psychology in the nineteenth century as a laboratory discipline founded in philosophical categories and the common-sense assumptions of contemporary linguistic usage.

Specific emotion words in English show a similar historical transformation, from overt social actions and public performances, to the inner life of the psyche. The following are summaries of the *OED* entries for *worry* and *surprise*.[11]

WORRY stems from Old English and Old Dutch words (cf. German *würgen*) for *kill*, *strangle*, or *throttle*. Earliest quotations, from AD725–1483, have the transitive meaning 'to kill (a person or animal) by compressing the throat; to strangle'. Then there are intransitive forms from the 13th to the 17th century, 'to choke (a person or animal) with a mouthful of food...; hence "to be worried", or "worry oneself, on" = to devour greedily'. The current 'dogs worrying sheep' sense of the term is cited from 1380, 'to seize by the throat with the teeth and tear or lacerate; to kill or injure by biting and shaking'. From the 16th century we find 'to bite at or upon (an object); to kiss or hug vehemently; to utter (one's words) with the teeth nearly closed, as if biting or champing them', alongside 'to harass by rough or severe treatment, by repeated aggression or attack; to assail with hostile or menacing speech'. Current colloquial usage in the USA develops also during this period: 'to get or bring into a specified condition by harassing treatment, persistent aggression, or dogged effort'. From the early 19th century we find 'to *irritate* (an animal) by a repetition of *feigned attacks*', which starts to introduce the notion of worry as a state of mind thus caused. It is followed by 'to cause distress of mind to; to afflict with mental trouble or agitation; to make anxious and ill at ease', until 'worried' appears from 1863, 'denoting a state of mind', though still with detectable connections to earlier uses.[12]

SURPRISE derives from Old French, Italian and Spanish *sorpresa*, meaning 'the (or an) act of assailing or *attacking unexpectedly or without warning*, or of taking by this means; sudden attack or capture of a fort, a body of troops, etc. that is unprepared; formerly also in more general sense, seizure (of a person, a place, or spoil)'. From this came the Shakespearean and subsequent use (up to the 19th century), 'the (or an) act of coming upon one unexpectedly, or of taking unawares; a sudden attack', and thence the expression 'to take by surprise'. The subjective feeling is given, from Shakespeare onwards, as 'the feeling or emotion excited by something unexpected, or for which one is unprepared', though the sense persists into the 19th century, as a feeling appropriate to dire straits: 'alarm, terror, or perplexity, caused by a sudden attack, calamity, or the like'. The modern psychological definition is more benign: 'the feeling or mental state, akin to astonishment and wonder, caused by an unexpected occurrence or circumstance'.

It is important not to confuse a word's etymology with its current meaning. There is no suggestion that speakers of a language possess and use knowledge of its earlier history. Nevertheless, as Bakhtin (1981) has taught us, the past uses of a word leave residues in how it is currently used and understood, while the historical tracing of such meanings (even a study as casually performed as looking them up in an etymological dictionary) can be as informative as anthropological studies are in gaining a sense of cultural differences. Past meanings also bring the special bonus of looking 'developmentally' at how words for mental states might derive from situations of use with regard to public activities. According to Wittgensteinian and social constructionist perspectives on words, minds, and meanings, what we find in the etymological dictionary reflects an important principle of how all words, including mental process ones, come to mean things, and indeed are *learnable*. They are the coins of social exchange, used in the performance of social actions.[13] It is only in and through that basic function that they can ever come to mean something ostensibly other than that, such as referring to a private, experiential, or personal subjectivity.

Cultural models, narrative, and rhetoric

In addition to historical perspectives, there is an extensive tradition of anthropological studies of emotion and emotion terms. (See Harré, 1986b; Lutz and Abu-Lughod, 1990; and Shweder and Levine, 1984, for useful collections.) Catherine Lutz (1988, 1990a) focuses on the 'emotion theories' of the Ifaluk people of Micronesia, in the Western Pacific. The notion that members of cultures possess 'theories' of how the world works, including an 'ethnopsychology' of persons and how they work, is a popular one in anthropology (see, for examples, D'Andrade and Strauss, 1992; Heelas and Lock, 1981; Holland and Quinn, 1987; White and Kirkpatrick, 1985). Research on 'folk theories' examines how people talk about matters such as self, emotion, social relations, and the physical world, and constructs out of the patterns of that talk a coherent underlying cognitive model of local thought and social structure. We shall consider the status of 'folk theories' later in this chapter and the next; our first concern is with what such investigations reveal about the everyday discourse of emotion.

Lutz shows how the Ifaluk concept *song*, roughly translated as a kind of indignant and justified anger, functions within a hierarchically organized social life:

> . . . the everyday understanding of this emotion does not simply occur as a form of reflection on experience, but emerges as people justify and negotiate both cultural values and the prerogatives of power that some members of this society currently hold. (1990a: 204)

Song expresses a moral judgment on another person's improper actions, generally when they have violated a social rule (such as against shouting aloud, spreading false rumours, or failing to share resources with others). Its very meaning is tied into, and reinforces, ideological patterns of power, obligation, and ownership: 'the direction in which "justifiable anger" flows is predominantly *down* the social scale' (1990a: 218, original emphasis). *Song* is an emotion inseparable from the norms, expectations, and patterns of accountability of Ifaluk society; if you are not a member of that society, essentially you cannot have the emotion.[14] In fact, it is part of a set of *inter-related* emotions specific to that culture, and the implication is that Western and other cultural patterns of emotions may be culturally systemic like that too, though we tend to think of them as basic, natural, and separate, merely because they are all we know.

For instance, *song* is an emotion Ifaluk people may express when something bad happens to a person for whom they feel *fago*, where *fago* is something like compassion, but not quite. It is felt for people who need help, or have suffered misfortune, and are socially subordinate, or are considered close to the kind of ideal Ifaluk sort of person – calm-natured and generous – so that, feeling *fago* for them, if something bad happens to them you feel *song*. Or you *should*, this being a moral or normative matter in Ifaluk society, just like English-speaking people are supposed to feel (or display) admiration, embarrassment, grief, or anger in some circumstances and not others.

The emotional interconnections multiply. Ifaluk people work to avoid the possibility of other people expressing *song* with regard to their conduct. But that work is undermined by displaying *ker* (a kind of excited happiness), in that *ker* conflicts with *metagu*, which is the sort of 'fear' that *song* properly elicits in those to whom it is applied. *Ker* is therefore subject to disapproval and moral condemnation, despite (from a Western point of view) its rough translation as 'happiness'. I imagine, therefore, that *ker* may provide problems for Wierzbicka's 'good feeling/bad feeling' categories of emotions, quite apart from its conceptual dependence on other emotion terms rather than on a set of entirely non-emotional semantic primitives. But more importantly, Lutz's analysis provides an important insight into emotion terms as an interdependent set; one would probably have to understand *ker* and *metagu* (etc.) in order to experience *song*.

Lutz emphasizes the way *song* works as a description, as a word used on occasions of speaking. It is something people publicly *claim* to experience, and in doing so place a meaning on events that 'must be *negotiated* with the audience of such claims' (1990a: 205, original emphasis). Thus for an Ifaluk person to display or report his or her *song* with regard to some state of affairs is to place a morally loaded construction on that state of affairs, and one that may be contested. Overt confrontation is nevertheless mostly avoided by means of a constant orientation to the possibility of *song*, such as when scarce resources are publicly evenly shared out: 'The daily anticipation of the "justifiable anger" of others is a fundamental regulator of the behaviour of individuals and a basic factor in the maintenance of the value of sharing' (1990a: 211). This 'anticipation' of *song* is not merely Lutz's theory of underlying mental processes, but a feature of Ifaluk discourse in and of the events in question. Although the constellations of relationships and emotional alternatives are not the same, we can start to see a general parallel with the contentious, blaming, and mitigating business done by Jeff and Mary, and by Jimmy and Connie, in their talk of emotions and events.

I have noted that much current anthropological work describes cultural life and language in terms of 'folk models', including appeals to people's understandings of standardized 'scripts' or 'scenarios'. This notion stems from the dominance that cognitive anthropology has enjoyed especially in the USA, paralleling that of cognitive psychology, since the 1950s (Gardner, 1985). The appeal to cognitive models comes not only from cognitive linguists such as Anna Wierzbicka, but from a wide range of theorists and field researchers, including Catherine Lutz and Geoffrey White. Lutz summarizes her discussion of Ifaluk emotions thus:

> Each word in a language evokes, for the native speaker, an elaborate 'scene' replete with actors, props and event sequences (Fillmore, 1977). The scene that the term *song*, or 'justifiable anger', paints is one in which (1) there is a rule or value violation; (2) it is pointed out by someone, (3) who simultaneously calls for the condemnation of the act, and (4) the perpetrator reacts in fear [*metagu*] to that anger, (5) amending his or her ways. Almost all of the hundreds of uses of the term 'justifiable anger' that I recorded evoked this scene, making reference to the violation of the widely shared Ifaluk value system. By examining the contexts in which 'justifiable anger' is used, therefore, it is possible to draw the outlines of the Ifaluk worldview. (1990a: 207)

However, Lutz also emphasizes the importance of *discourse* in how such scripted routines are invoked, made relevant, and sometimes disputed. The *song* 'script' is not Lutz's description of actual events or social interactions, nor even of how Ifaluk folk may perceive them. Rather, it formulates a *normative* criterion for events that participants orient to as such in their talk:

> Each time a person declares 'I am *song*' . . . is an opening gambit or bid in an effort to install a particular interpretation of events as the definition of that situation to be accepted by others. . . . The theory of 'justifiable anger' and the social course it follows is thus a script, *creatively used*, for use in achieving individual goals. (Lutz, 1990a: 211 and 225, emphasis added)

The link between related sets of emotions in a culture, canonical cultural scenarios, and the *rhetorical uses* to which those are put has also been explored by Geoffrey White (1990). In a statement reminiscent of Wierzbicka's cognitive scenarios, White suggests:

> Culturally defined emotions are embedded in complex understandings about identities and scenarios of action, especially concerning the sorts of events that evoke it, the relations it is appropriate to, and the responses expected to follow from it. (1990: 47)

However, White's actual analyses move us away from semantic universals and, further even than Lutz's work does, towards the study of situated rhetoric. He emphasizes a feature of everyday talk that 'conceptual models' theories tend to play down (in their pursuit of coherence and consistency): that the same events are subject to alternative descriptions, and alternative 'emotional' readings.

White takes three verbal expressions used in a Solomon Islands community on Santa Isabel, and provides rough English translations: *di'a tagna* (anger), *di'a nagnafa* (sad), and the practice of *graurutha* (disentangling).[15] 'Disentangling' an institutionalized procedure on Santa Isabel for sorting out interpersonal problems and resentments by talking them through. It bears cautious comparison, therefore, to the kinds of 'couple counselling' data we have examined (including notions such as 'opening up', and 'talking out' bad feelings: White, 1990: 54). One of the ways 'disentangling' is done, and social harmony established or oriented-to, is by talking about events and reactions in terms of 'sadness' rather than 'anger'. 'Anger' is associated with an event cycle represented schematically (1990: 48) as:

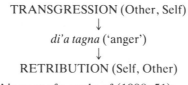

TRANSGRESSION (Other, Self)
↓
di'a tagna ('anger')
↓
RETRIBUTION (Self, Other)

In contrast, 'sadness' is part of a cycle of (1990: 51):

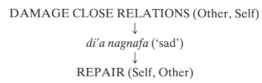

DAMAGE CLOSE RELATIONS (Other, Self)
↓
di'a nagnafa ('sad')
↓
REPAIR (Self, Other)

A discourse of 'anger' invokes a prior event as a 'moral breach . . . implying the need for corrective action' (1990: 49). In contrast, describing reactions in terms of 'sadness' is part of the practices of reconciliation and repairing community solidarity. It is important to understand that these terms, and the 'disentangling' process itself, are (as with Ifaluk *song*) public expressions that are available to be heard for their moral implications, and for their consequences for social life. 'Anger' publicly threatens community solidarity, while 'sadness' invokes repair, and signals a positive orientation towards community values.

In White's analysis the rhetorical organization of emotion talk is based on the availability of alternative descriptions which can be, and are, plausibly applied to the same circumstances or events. This rhetorical process *constitutes* 'disentangling': 'by engaging in disentangling, speakers tacitly acknowledge the prior value of community solidarity, ritually closing the conflict episode as a source of disruptive thoughts and actions' (White, 1990: 53). The availability of alternative emotional discourses for 'the same eliciting event' is captured in another diagram (1990: 50):

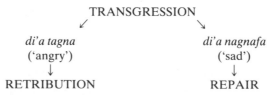

TRANSGRESSION
↙   ↘
di'a tagna   *di'a nagnafa*
('angry')   ('sad')
↓   ↓
RETRIBUTION   REPAIR

The advantage of Lutz's and White's analyses over Wierzbicka's is that they start to decouple talk and event scenarios from events themselves, and even from perceptions of events. The application of one description rather than another, or one scenario rather than another, is systematically oriented to the performance of local discursive business, rather than simply standing as the document of how a speaker 'saw' things, or of cultural differences.

The same, or ostensibly similar, events are not only differently *perceived* according to a person's cognitive constructs, but differently *described*, even by the same person on successive occasions, according to the rhetorical, action-performative work being done on those occasions. That is to say, Lutz and White, despite their generalized cognitive theorizing, emphasize the discursive action-performing nature of descriptions. Their studies support the notion of an indeterminate relation between events and how they are described, together with the rhetorical, could-have-been-otherwise orientation of descriptions when studied as things people actually *say* on occasions (rather than purportedly *think*).

Rather than analysing talk in terms of a set of events prior to their description, a standard cognitive scenario that represents their sense, and an appropriate emotional description that expresses it, one of the functions of emotion discourse (as we saw with Lutz's work, and in our discussion of the counselling data) is to *work back upon the nature of prior events*, and constitute them as events of a certain kind.

> Thus, when Tom asserts that the banishment of his brother made him 'sad', he is implying, in this context, that the rejection is an instance of a certain kind of social action – one that damages close relations, that is, the sort of thing that evokes 'sadness'. (White, 1990: 60)

So, a 'sad'-oriented reporting is also *itself* a kind of social action that performs indexical work on the reporter: 'he implicitly claims that his response of telling off the offending parties was an attempt at withdrawal rather than some kind of "angry" getting even' (1990: 60). As part of the speech event of 'disentangling', 'sad' talk not only constructs the sense of the events at issue, but simultaneously attends to current requirements for doing reconciliation.[16]

White's and Lutz's ethnographic observations demonstrate the cultural workings of what we would call a discourse of the 'emotions': the use of verbal formulae for actions, feelings, and motives (our terms again), with regard to interpersonal judgments and attitudes, located within local moral orders of authority and responsibility. A key feature of emotion discourse is its deployment inside *narrative* and *rhetoric*. Emotion terms occur not merely as one-off descriptions of specific acts or reactions, but as parts of interrelated sets of terms that implicate each other in narrative sequences, and also in rhetorically potent contrasts between alternative descriptions. Narrative sequence and rhetorical contrast are *ways of talking* about things that perform social actions on the occasion of their production. Those social actions are discursive ones of a (by now) familiar kind: constructing the sense of events, orienting to normative and moral orders, to responsibility and blame, intentionality, and social evaluation. Emotion categories are not graspable merely as individual feelings or expressions, and nor is their discursive deployment reducible to a kind of detached, cognitive sense-making. They are discursive phenomena and need to be studied as such, as part of how talk performs social actions.

The narrative functions of emotion discourse are appreciated in the cognitive psychology and anthropology of emotions much more readily than the rhetorical functions.[17] This is because narrative organizations are at least partially subsumable to the notion of standardized scripts or scenarios. While the 'script' notion is important in the conceptual definition of different emotion terms, it surely underestimates narrative invention, and quickly loses sight of the specifics of actual stories and tellings (see also the discussion of narratology in Chapter 10). The rhetorical dimension is less easily assimilated to cognitive models, in that it requires contradictions and inconsistencies[18] (which tend to be filtered out when cognitive models are constructed), and is much more at odds (than narrative is) with the metacognitive assumption of a disinterested, sense-making perceiver of events.

Emotion metaphors as discursive resources

Emotion discourse includes not only terms such as *anger, surprise, fear*, and so on, but also a rich set of metaphors, such as Jimmy's 'boiling' (Extract 6.10b). The notion of 'boiling' belongs to a set of anger metaphors, mainly to do with heat and internal pressure, that George Lakoff (1987) and Zoltan Kovecses (1986) have identified in American English, and which they trace to the emotion's bodily experience and physical manifestations. Lakoff endorses Ekman's view of anger as one of several universal 'basic emotions' rooted in the activity of the autonomic nervous system (ANS) (Ekman, Levenson, and Friesen, 1983). Thus, anger metaphors are 'motivated by ANS activity that corresponds to the emotions as felt' (Lakoff, 1987: 39).

We have noted that Ekman's universal emotions thesis has a controversial status (Russell, 1991, 1994; Wierzbicka, 1995), and certainly we would not be justified in extending metaphors of English *anger* to notions such as Ifaluk *song*. Nevertheless, emotion metaphors can be considered *conceptual resources* that, where they occur in any language, whatever the metaphorical base, are available for discursive deployment. The concepts of anger as bodily heat, pressure, and agitation, for example, provide for a range of expressions such as (from Lakoff, 1987: 381–5): 'hot under the collar', 'burst a blood vessel', 'losing his cool', 'a heated argument', 'red with rage', 'hopping mad'. Then there are associations with distorted vision: 'blind with rage', 'see red', 'so mad I couldn't see straight'. Some metaphors are based on bodies imagined as strained containers: 'filled with anger', 'brimming with rage', 'bursting with anger', 'bottled up', 'outbursts', 'exploded'.

This is only a small part of anger's metaphorical thesaurus. But as well as raising questions about their conceptual origins, as Lakoff and Kovecses do, it is also useful to inquire into their discursive uses. The various metaphors are not equivalent and interchangeable, even those that are closely related, such that we should consider the grounds for choosing one rather than another, and what kinds of discursive business such choices may perform. Apart from heat, pressure, and container metaphors for anger, Lakoff (1987) lists madness, struggle, and dangerous animal metaphors. While it is possible to devise conceptual relationships between all these, they also have their own narrative implications and rhetorical uses. 'Contained heat' metaphors such as 'boiling with rage' are unlike wild animal metaphors such as 'bit her head off'. Raymond Gibbs (1994) suggests that different anger metaphors encode different parts of a complex cognitive model, suitable for use on different discursive occasions. For example, note that 'bit her head off' is explicitly active and object-directed, while 'boiling with rage' is more passive and experiential. The choice between such alternatives may be useful for constructing alternative narratives of causal attribution and accountability.

The point of all those alternative metaphorical expressions is, surely, to enable certain things to be *said* and not just *thought* (Edwards, 1991), such that the proliferation of metaphors may be motivated not only by their conceptual sense (as suggested by Gibbs, 1994, and Lakoff, 1987), but by what they allow us to say and do. Jimmy's 'boiling' anger, for example, *formulates it as extreme*, and plays a nicely *timed* part in his narrative of a gradually building emotional state ('at this stage'), with its 'boiling' extremity an index, as we have noted, of the extremity of Connie's provocations. Jimmy's selection of this 'heat and pressure building' metaphor performs interactionally significant narrative and rhetorical work. Also, specifying anger in such graphic (experiential and visual) detail provides the kind of warrant, the kind of document of experiential recall, of 'being there' (Geertz, 1988), that bolsters the validity of all kinds of stories and descriptions when they are in danger of being countered (Edwards and Potter, 1992a; Potter, 1996; Wooffitt, 1992).

In order to develop this notion of how emotion concepts and metaphors may be designed and selected for their deployment, we need to examine them in use, and preferably in spontaneous use ('natural discourse'), rather than in scenarios invented to illustrate what we think we know. Most of the spontaneous discourse analysed in this book is conversational interaction, but 'conceptual resources' can be identified at work in any kind of discourse. The materials in Extract 7.3 below are taken from a newspaper commentary on an infamous incident involving the French international footballer Eric Cantona, when playing for Manchester United at Selhurst Park in London, in January 1995. Cantona was accused (and convicted in court, on the basis of witnesses' testimony and live television coverage) of a physical attack on a member of the crowd, who was allegedly taunting him while Cantona was leaving the field, having been 'sent off' for a foul on another player. Our interest in this incident is the use of emotional descriptions in the reporting of it, and in particular, the kinds of conceptual resources that those uses display. The selected extracts are those that deployed emotional expressions.

Extract 7.3

Text above the main headline:
1   After Selhurst Park's night of French with jeers,
2   the future is uncertain for a troubled soul whose
3   fiery act of spontaneous combustion has echoes
4   in other moments of madness

Text from the article:
5   No true lover of the game likes the idea of an artist
6   being provoked beyond his level of tolerance, even
7   one as low as Cantona's.
8   (...)
9   Graham Kelly [of the Football Association] rightly, sensitively,
10 spoke of the stunned expressions of young spectators.
11 Football had an example to set.
12 (...)
13 He [Cantona] has always seemed consumed by a
14 dangerous self-belief masquerading as hatred of
15 injustice (which, after all, most of us would claim to share).
16 (...)
17 Maybe now, shocked, we will achieve a sense of proportion.
18 Football induces anger. It induces sadness, too, but
19 not the real thing. That was in the newspaper photographs
20 of Cantona's wife and their son Raphael as they emerged from
21 their home to go to work and school on Thursday morning.

(Patrick Barclay, 'Rage of the Red Devil May Stretch Loyalty of Fans'.
The Observer, 29 January 1995, Sports tabloid, p. 16)

To begin with the article's headline, 'rage of the red devil', plays on the
fact that one of Manchester United's nicknames is 'the red devils' (they play
in red and black). That reference works nicely here, in invoking Cantona's
team membership simultaneously with devilment and the 'red with rage'
metaphor for excessive anger. It is a simple point, but worth making;
Cantona is not called this merely because his team *are* the 'red devils'; it is an
identity category nicely fitted to the context of its use, the moral-evaluative
discourse of action and emotion. Like 'red devil', 'a troubled soul' (line 2; we
are still in the headlines, not yet the story's main text) sets up Cantona
dispositionally. It specifies the kind of person he is, such that the incident in
question is no one-off, but an instance of the kind of thing he does ('in other
moments of madness', line 4; 'has always seemed consumed', line 13). We
are in the realm of script instances and disposition formulations, of course
(see Chapter 6), where emotions are not merely transitory states (which they
can be descriptively rendered as), but also attributable as long-term, and
sometimes pathological, behavioural tendencies.

Cantona's 'fiery act of spontaneous combustion' (line 3) deploys an
internal heat metaphor. But the notion of 'spontaneous combustion'
introduces a further important element of the conceptual repertoire of
emotions, their spontaneity. Emotion talk is useful for making rhetorical

contrasts with planned actions and rational conduct. Spontaneous combustion is that which has no detectable or sufficient external cause; it happens of itself, from within. As with Connie's versions of Jimmy's fits of jealousy, Cantona's anger is descriptively worked up here as unprovoked, insufficiently caused, internal, irrational. It is a discourse of emotion that side-steps what is generally considered in philosophical analysis to be its defining feature – its 'intensionality'; we are angry *at* things, fearful *of* things, and so on, rather than just in a 'mood' of some kind (Harré, 1983; see also note 2 for this chapter). Of course, those intensional objects are readily available, for Jimmy and for Cantona, but there are ways of doing emotion talk that can leave them out of account, play them down, or treat them as insufficient cause. 'Emotions' can be discursively produced as internal states similar to 'moods', and this is a further example of their flexibility.

The reference to what 'no *true lover* of the game likes' (Extract 7.3, line 5) raises another rhetorical theme in emotion discourse, closely related to spontaneity, which is genuineness. A 'true lover' is genuine, without artifice, the real thing. But for there to be true lovers, there also (conceptually and rhetorically) have to be false ones. False love (or false anger) would be, by contrast, simulation, artifice, not spontaneous but planful and deliberate, cognitive and contemplated. Indeed, there are examples in Extract 7.3: Cantona's 'self-belief *masquerading as hatred* of injustice' (lines 14–15), and 'sadness . . . but *not the real thing*' (lines 18–19). Here emotions are unreal, not genuine reflections of the true life of experience, but, rather, simulacra of it, mere pretence. Cantona's ostensible 'hatred of injustice' masks something truer beneath, a form of vanity, while true sadness is to be found in poignant pictures of his innocent family, trying vainly, one infers, to continue their ordinary lives. Note how the contrast is drawn, between *passive* emotional truth (his self-belief is something he 'has always seemed *consumed by*') and *active* falsity ('masquerading').

The concept of emotions as basically honest and spontaneous responses relates to the popular assumption, and experimental research finding, that body signals can betray the true feelings of people who are trying to disguise them. Emotions and attitudes may 'leak' past a person's more consciously controlled gestures and words (Ekman and Friesen, 1969). But the possibly contrary status of emotional displays, as artificial performances, provides scope for description and counter-description. It is also a rhetorical opposition that reflexively works back upon the speaker/writer. In appealing to what 'no true lover of the game likes', the author manages to align himself with true lovers of the game, and thereby to define as false those who might disagree with him. The writer constructs himself as truth-teller, partly at least by his deployment of emotion discourse. He is by implication a true lover of the game, 'shocked' into 'a sense of proportion' (line 17), just as he is a member of we who share a hatred of injustice (line 15), whose pronouncements on Cantona are based on repeated observations of what he 'has always seemed' to be (line 13), rather than a conclusion jumped to on the basis of this one incident. Again, as we noted with script formulations, they not only specify robust patterns of events, but reflexively construct the observer/teller as coming to considered and careful conclusions. In that process, rationality does not merely contrast with emotion, but may result from it; we can be 'shocked' into it.

Despite Cantona's scripted-up depiction as a 'troubled soul', 'consumed' and prone to this fit of 'spontaneous combustion', the actions in question are also described as 'provoked' (line 6). The potential contradiction here, between spontaneity and provocation, is discursively managed via the notion of 'an artist being provoked beyond his level of tolerance' (lines 5–6). So there can be an inner determination, but also an outer cause, the net effect being triggered by crossing some kind of threshold of tolerance, Cantona's being relatively low (line 7). Cantona's reactions are thus rendered excessive but situationally understandable. It seems that the conceptual repertoire for emotion discourse in evidence here can potentially have it all ways: spontaneous, provoked, or a bit of both; enduring trait or moment of madness; active or passive; honesty or masquerade. While such conceptual oppositions and inconsistencies, especially in a single text, might threaten an internally consistent cognitive model of the emotions (or just of anger, or even just of Cantona's one angry reaction), they are marvellously designed for 'witcraft' – for the rhetoric of alternative descriptions.

Lastly, consider the 'stunned expressions of young spectators' (line 10). Emotions are given here as readable in facial expressions. But what exactly does *stunned* look like? Is it definitively, and for all the spectators equally, and for all observers of them, different from, say, *agog*, *amazed*, even *thrilled*? The discourse of facial expressions is discourse nevertheless when such expressions are put into words. Of course, *stunned* performs rhetorical work, reinforcing the sense of a kind of chorus of young innocents,[19] viewing with ingenuous dismay Cantona's (thus further rendered) extraordinary display. And note the 'footing' (Goffman, 1979) here; the report is given indirectly, not as the author's but as that of Graham Kelly, chief executive of the Football Association. Indeed there is an embedded series of footings; the writer's judgment ('rightly, sensitively', line 9, and of the events generally) is solidified, externalized, corroborated, by this being not just his, but another (authoritative) person's reaction. And Kelly's reaction is not to the Cantona incident itself, but to another displaced reaction, the 'stunned expressions of young spectators'. These 'footing' devices provide the sense of the event in a way that deflects from any artifice or subjectivity on the writer's part, had he just told us what *he thought* about it all. The discursive point is how the whole thing is constructed up like this, via category choice, narrative, footing, and the rhetoric of emotion.

Conclusions: emotion concepts and their rhetorical uses

We have examined two basic kinds of phenomena with regard to emotion discourse: word meanings (concepts), and samples of talk and text (situated usage). Each kind of analysis informs the other. Words provide conceptual resources that permit discursive uses, while empirical studies reveal a flexibility and rhetorical organization that semantic or conceptual analyses generally underestimate. Conceptual analysis is necessary in that it aims to clarify what words mean, rather than proposing theories of their referents. Thus, the difference between 'emotions' and 'sensations' helps rid us of too close an association between emotions and subjective mental or bodily experiences (Bedford, 1962; Wittgenstein, 1958), and points us towards the moral[20] nexus of action and accountability, and, therefore, towards what people are doing when they *use* emotion words.

The use of emotion words (like any other words) invokes other elements of meaning and culture, such as the range of alternative emotions, dispositions, or mental states that they might be distinguished from, and the kinds of things they might properly be directed at. We do not receive an insult and feel *pride* – not, that is, without some special circumstances that would restore the senses of 'insult' and 'pride', such as being insulted as some kind of teasing, ironic compliment by a friend, or insulted by someone whose values and judgment we detest. To analyse meanings conceptually is not to propose or deny a particular psychological theory of emotions, nor of their pathology (though it may fit some better than others). Nor does the notion of 'intensional objects' deny that people can experience emotions and 'not know why'. What it does is to explicate how these words can be used intelligibly (cf. Coulter, 1990a), including why 'not knowing why' might be something to remark on and account for.

Nevertheless, models of word meanings, whether semantic, etymological, monolingual, universalistic, cognitively modelled, or derived from conceptual analysis, tend to aim for *coherence*, as if the word's meaning was always that whole package, scenario and all, and it all gets wheeled out for use on each occasion. But the rich variety of emotion metaphors, and empirical studies of discourse, suggest something more like a set of *rhetorical affordances*, in which different parts or potentials of meaning, even contrasting ones, may be worked up and deployed, on and for occasions. This conceptual and rhetorical flexibility (cf. Averill, 1990), although plainly a nuisance to semantic and cognitive model-making, is ideal for the action-performing, accountability-oriented, rhetorical 'witcraft' of discourse.

It is possible to spell out a range of discursive resources concerning emotions, based on the examples and discussions in this chapter, in the form of a set of rhetorical positions and contrasts. These are not definitions of what emotion words 'mean',[21] neither generally nor for individual words. Rather, they point to a range of things that emotion discourse can do, in everyday narrative and rhetoric (and, of course, in fiction), in discourses of events and accountability. They are not a definitive or discrete set. I am not proposing that there have to be ten of them, for instance, nor that they might be worked up into some kind of formal model. Their interrelatedness and flexibility are important features of how they work.

1   *Emotion versus cognition* – there is flexibility in how people's activities
    are described. Emotional descriptions are optional. We can formulate
    people's actions and words as expressions of their thoughts, their
    opinions, how they feel, and so on.

2   *Emotions as irrational versus rational* – emotions are not just ir-
    rational, they are an integral part of rational accountability; for ex-
    ample, Jimmy's pathological jealousy or Cantona's spontaneous
    combustion versus Jimmy's intelligible responses to Connie as flirt, or
    the indignant anger of Ifaluk *song*.[22]

3   *Emotion as cognitively grounded and/or cognitively consequential* –
    Ifaluk *song*, and Jimmy's 'soon as I heard that . . .' imply prior cog-
    nitive assessments; cognitive *consequences* are given in the Cantona
    report's 'shocked, we will achieve a sense of proportion', and in how
    di'a nagnafa on Santa Isabel 'disentangles' conflicting perspectives.

4   *Event-driven versus dispositional* – Jimmy's justified and reactive
    anger versus his dispositional jealousy; Cantona's aggression as pro-
    voked, or as stemming from his flawed character.

5   *Dispositions versus temporary states* – Jimmy as an enduringly 'jealous
    person'; versus 'I was boiling at this stage' and Jeff's 'angry stage'.

6   Emotional behaviour as *controllable action or passive reaction* – the
    notion of emotions as 'feelings' that are 'expressed' or 'acted out'
    lends itself to a dichotomy between how someone felt and what he or
    she did about it; to the notion of controlling one's passions, and so on.
    Having emotional reactions can thus be split into how you unaccoun-
    tably feel, and what you accountably do.

7   *Spontaneous versus externally caused* – 'spontaneous com-
    bustion . . .'; 'football induces anger . . .'. Note the marvellous
    flexibility here. The fact that emotions take intensional objects pro-
    vides for ways of assigning causes: being angry *at* something can imply
    being angry *because* of it. But there is rhetorical scope for 'internal'
    and other causes to be induced: 'I can be . . . angry *at* little things *be-
    cause* I am suffering from dyspepsia, where to know its object is not
    thereby to understand its cause' (Coulter, 1986: 129, original em-
    phasis).

8   *Natural versus moral* – unconscious, automatic, bodily reactions
    versus social judgments; rather than these being parts of a comprehen-
    sive analysis of emotion terms, they can be selectively worked up and
    used.

9   *Internal states versus external behaviour: private* ('feelings') *versus
    public* ('expressions', 'displays') – a person's 'true' emotions can be
    those avowed on the basis of personal experience, as privileged re-
    ports from the inner life of the mind, or else ascriptions based on overt
    behaviour, which may be adduced to refute such avowals.

10 *Honest* (spontaneous, reactive) *versus faked*, artful, not 'true' – 'true
    lover'; 'self-belief masquerading as hatred'; 'sadness . . . but not the
    real thing'.

These sets of oppositions and contrasts are used discursively to construct (whether cooperatively or contentiously) the sense of events and their causes, and (thereby) to manage accountability. They may be used in various combinations. For example, the public–private dichotomy may be used in relation to active–passive and honest–fake. Thus, 'true' emotions may be those avowed from private experience, denying any impression based on superficial appearances. But such confessions might also be treated as fake, on the grounds that they contrast with actions (which can speak louder than words); or again, actions may be treated as insincere when they conflict with (ascribed) inner feelings.

These rhetorical oppositions challenge the assumption of consistency that is implied in notions such as 'cognitive models' and 'folk theories' of the emotions. For example, Richard Buttny (1993) analyses conversational sequences in which 'negative affect ascriptions' are denied. That is to say, these are occasions when person A, accused of some emotion within a 'blame' sequence, denies it. Denying that you are angry, according to Buttny, relies on 'a folk logic of privileged access to one's own emotional states' (1993: 96) – the fact that you have privileged access to your own internal feelings puts you in a position to deny other people's descriptions of you. But of course, as Buttny recognizes, these avowals are not automatically accepted. We also have available to us a contrary 'folk logic' of emotions being matters of display, visible to others, not secret or hidden, and this is part of how actions can be treated as reliable indicators of a person's true feelings, as distinct from what they may tell us about their private experiences. In the couple counselling data, for example, both husbands (Jeff and Jimmy) claim not to prevent their wives going out alone at night, but both wives (Mary and Connie) counter those claims, in terms of how their husbands signal very clearly, in bodily expression and other actions, their disapproval.[23]

It is a principle of ethological and experimental studies of non-verbal communication (Argyle, 1988) that emotions are matters of public display, part of a rich interchange of verbal expressions and bodily signals. An interesting feature of studying situated discourse is that this notion of 'public display' may occur as a participants' descriptive category and interactional concern, rather than just what emotional life happens to be like. We see this in how people in relationship disputes claim to know each other's real feelings, and in the rhetorical use made of the 'stunned expressions of young spectators' in Extract 7.3. A person's emotions can be treated discursively as private experiences, or as *anything but* his or her own private domain, and may even be strongly contrasted with cognition and language in this respect, such as in the popular idea that you can keep your thoughts to yourself, but not so easily your emotions.

What Buttny (1993: 88) calls a 'folk logic of affect' – experiences that happen to us beyond our control, and, thereby, prevent or inhibit adequate performance – is not so consistent and worked out as the term 'logic' implies.

It might better be called a folk *rhetoric*. People may blame themselves, and be blamed, for having emotions, for 'expressing' them and for not expressing them, for not 'controlling' them or being too much in control, or for being emotionally insincere. Emotions can be distinguished from their expression or control, and people can exploit their privacy and do things with 'confession'. The conceptual resources concerning emotions that are available for emotion discourse permit much more indexical and rhetorical variation than is implied by notions such as folk logic, folk theory, conceptual models, cognitive scenarios, and such. It is precisely because people's emotion displays can be treated either as involuntary reactions, or as under agentive control or rational accountability, that emotion discourse can perform flexible, accountability-oriented, rhetorical work. These are just the sorts of conceptual resources that people require for doing talk's business – inconsistent, contradictory, fuzzy, to-be-indexically-specified, rather than some kind of coherent cognitive model of the emotions.

It is a futile psychological enterprise to work up these conceptual resources into competing hypotheses about the true nature of emotional life and seek to choose between them. That misses the point of how all these fuzzy, overlapping, and contrastive resources are like that precisely so they can be put to work in locally specified ways, in situated talk. A discursive psychology of the emotions must try to examine, conceptually and empirically, the nature and uses of emotion discourse, rather than imagining that it adds up to something that could be called a folk theory, as if capable in some way of being not a very good one, and waiting to be improved on by professional psychology. From the perspective of discursive psychology, emotion talk is part of how people live their lives, rather than some kind of abstracted amateur theorizing. They cannot be 'wrong' about it, they can only do it differently.[24]

It appears from the etymological evidence that the English word *emotion* has only recently acquired its current status as a *superordinate* category under which other words such as *anger*, *indignation*, *jealousy*, and *surprise* can be grouped together. As a historically modern concept (at least in English), the word *emotion* starts to look a dubious category under which to group all the ways that other cultures (including our own, in other times) talk about feelings, reactions, attitudinal judgments (if we can use all *these* terms), and related matters. It may be inappropriate to render them all as theories or discourses 'of emotion'; that would be to select and group their discourse into the superordinate categories of ours.

That can be dangerous not only for the intellectual damage it may do to our understanding of how words work, but also for the nexus of social relations in which that work is done. Discursive constructions of cognition and emotion, and their associated rhetorical oppositions and uses, are a reflexive part of the relationships they describe, setting up categories and contrasts within what Lila Abu-Lughod and Catherine Lutz (1990) and John Shotter (1993b) call the 'politics of everyday life'. For example, couple counselling discourse is also, to an extent, gender relationship discourse. Matters under negotiation, in these mundane discourses of emotion and rationality, include the warranting of restrictions on outside relationships, on what it is proper to do and feel, and when, and for how long, and on the differences between what each partner is allowed to do, within and beyond the relationship (cf. Stenner, 1993).

Lutz notes that 'one important aspect of that category [emotion] is its association with the female, so that qualities that define the emotional also define women' (1990b: 69; cf. Hekman, 1990; Pringle, 1988). Emotion discourse, whether or not gendered, deploys a set of rhetorical oppositions for talking about events, understandings, mental states, issues of personal control and interpersonal relations:

> As both an analytic and an everyday concept in the West, emotion, like the female, has typically been viewed as something natural rather than cultural, irrational rather than rational, chaotic rather than ordered, subjective rather than universal, physical rather than mental or intellectual, unintended and uncontrollable, and hence often dangerous. . . . Another and competing theme . . . contrasts emotion with cold alienation. Emotion, in this view, is life to its absence's death, is interpersonal connection or relationship to an unemotional estrangement, is a glorified and free nature against a shackling civilization. (Lutz, 1990b: 69)

Though not selected deliberately to redress this imbalance, most of the examples of emotionality in this chapter have been men (though admittedly more often angry than, say, compassionate).

The argument that English emotion words, and even the superordinate category 'emotion' itself, may provide an insecure and ethnocentric basis for cross-cultural and historical comparisons raises issues that take us far beyond emotion discourse. In the next chapter, we look at 'categorization' more generally, including efforts to use cross-linguistic comparisons and differences to define causal relationships between language and thought. Again, a functional perspective on discourse and rhetoric, including talk-in-interaction, is developed and contrasted with the perceptual–cognitive assumptions of much of the psychological and linguistic work in that area.

Notes

1. In addition to avowals and ascriptions (cf. Coulter, 1989), Richard Buttny includes emotion *displays* within a useful study of 'the sequential organization of affect discourse in accountability practices' (1993: 89). Displays of emotion can serve to intensify verbal content: thus, 'an accusation may be intensified by the accuser's show of anger' (1993: 85). However, including affect displays within an analysis of discourse is by no means straightforward: 'A problem for the analyst is how to *identify* the emotions as exhibited in and through these non-verbal or vocal cues. There is no one-to-one relationship between a particular non-verbal or vocal component and emotion' (1993: 103, emphasis added). The problem of 'identifying' emotions is, of course, a discursive one; the analyst has to choose a *description* for the emotion, and that is precisely the kind of contentious and interactionally consequential business that the participants themselves are engaged in. The idea that a

participant is definitively, and not alternatively-describably, *angry* (rather than miffed, annoyed, pissed off, being ironic, upset, etc.), is an interpretatively contentious thing for the analyst to build into the phenomena under analysis. Despite the importance of affect displays for talk-in-interaction, this chapter focuses on avowals and ascriptions – that is, on emotions as discourse categories.

2. It might be assumed that a better way to start would be to define what 'emotions' are, how they differ (psychologically and semantically) from 'cognitions', 'motives', and 'sensations', for example. However, while semantic or conceptual analysis plays an essential part in the analysis of emotion words and their uses (e.g., Bedford, 1962; Coulter, 1986; Ryle, 1949; Wittgenstein, 1958), the meanings and contrasts invoked in everyday and professional 'emotion talk' are also matters for empirical analysis, rather than matters to be legislated in advance of it. For example, we shall see that, while emotions can be conceptually distinguished from sensations in how they take 'intensional objects' (we are not just afraid but afraid *of* things), one of the rhetorical uses of emotion words is to focus on inner feelings *rather than* events in the external world, just as talk of emotional reactions can also be a way of specifying the nature of the events that provoke them. Following the practice adopted by Button et al. (1995), I use the spelling 'intensional' for how some mental state predicates 'take objects'. The spelling 'intentional' is reserved for the everyday notion of deliberateness, voluntariness, 'on purpose', etc.

3. Following the success in the 1950s of John Osborne's play *Look Back in Anger*, a whole generation of dissatisfied 'angry young men' were brought into British public awareness (revealed, named, invented, or whatever), alongside James Dean's brooding *Rebel Without a Cause*.

4. The defining importance of actors' understandings of social scenarios to the meaning or use of emotion terms is also a feature of conceptual analysis: 'To say, for instance, that a man acted out of resentment is to relate his currently problematic conduct to the way in which he has appraised the situation in relation to prior social experiences; it is to assert of him that he knows or believes that someone or some institution or group has done something that has affected him adversely and that his present behaviour is informed by that knowledge or belief. Conversely, one could use the category to account for the absence of some otherwise conventionally required conduct on the part of the person' (Coulter, 1986: 126). Note, however, the crucial role Coulter gives to how such categories are *used* to *account* for conduct *in discourse*, rather than standing merely as documents of how people see things.

5. Wierzbicka's 'conceptual primitives' are also comparable to Schank's (1985) 'semantic primitives', which he proposed as conceptual building blocks for computer analysis of sentence meanings.

6. I am referring to a host of analyses of the language of mental and bodily experiences, from Hume to Wittgenstein and beyond, from treatments (e.g., Hume, 1739/1969) which specify experiential feelings as the prime identifying criteria of emotional states, to those in which subjective feelings are something incidental to, different from, or irrelevant to how emotions are defined (Armon-Jones, 1986; Bedford, 1962; Ryle, 1949; Wittgenstein, 1958).

7. The term 'specify' rather than 'discover' points up the constructed nature of these 'universals'. They are the result of an analytic method designed to produce them, in which core meanings are obtained by abstracting what is common and stripping away what is not. There is no guarantee that the results of such a process will produce what people 'mean' when they actually say things; it may even grossly distort it. It is a procedure reminiscent of the perceptual–cognitivist metatheory used in script theory, attribution theory, and so on, where perceptual invariances are thought to be distilled out from many different experiences. Cognitivist methods and theory are, like behaviourist ones, and indeed discursive ones, mutually sustaining.

8. Note the presence, in Wierzbicka's scenario for *surprise*, of the crucial clause 'I didn't think this would happen'. But all kinds of things can 'happen' that are not predicted without causing surprise. I assume Wierzbicka means 'I thought this would not happen'. Still, even with the clause grammatically corrected, what we have is something put together in English

grammar, where it matters precisely how we do that, and where the modal *would* is crucial. Do all languages contain something like *would*, or a European language 'subjunctive' of that kind, with precisely that meaning, and that kind of cognitive relation between linear time, perceived events, and mental expectations?

9. 'Emotions' such as *anger* and *fear* can be conceptually distinguished from 'moods' such as *joviality* and *frivolity*, on the grounds that emotions take 'intensional objects' and moods do not; we are angry *at* things, fearful *of* things, but can be simply jovial or frivolous. But the emotion–mood distinction is not an absolute one. Harré suggests that *sadness* comes somewhere between – 'we can be "sad about . . .", or just plain sad' (1983: 127). I prefer to treat the emotion–mood dichotomy as primarily a *participants'* discursive resource, or explanatory repertoire, rather than being semantically built into each word. For example, Jimmy's jealousy and anger were constructed as either reactive or endogenous, on (and for) occasions.

10. These historical changes in the meanings of emotion words clearly bear upon philosophical discussions of the nature of emotions. The two-way nature of relations between academic discourses and historical events is addressed in Foucauldian and 'social representations' theories (e.g., Foucault, 1973; Jodelet, 1991). According to the eighteenth-century philosopher David Hume, emotions could be defined exclusively experientially: 'when I am angry, I am actually possessed with the passion, and in that emotion have no more reference to any other object, than when I am thirsty, or sick, or more than five feet tall' (1739/1969, cited in Coulter, 1986: 121).

11. Further delights of the *OED* include how *anger* originated in Old Norse as a reference to trouble or affliction, i.e., *that which* afflicts, and hence irritates. *Happy* has the same stem as *happen*, and *happenstance*, being what comes by luck or chance, and then good luck or lucky, like in 'many happy returns' and so could come to label the mental state of one so fortunate.

12. Examples include, from 1863, 'I am sure, dear Mama, you are worried to death about it'; and from George Eliot's *Middlemarch*, 1871 (xxiii. II. 25), 'He felt a little worried and wearied, perhaps with mental debate.'

13. Kenneth Gergen provides a typically clear summary of the Wittgensteinian position: 'On this view, mental predicates acquire their meaning through various language games embedded within cultural forms of life. Mental language is rendered significant not by virtue of its capacity to reveal, mark, or describe mental states, but from its function in social interchange' (1995: 3). The psychology of emotions has thus been a 'tradition in which we mistakenly treat the putative objects of our mental vocabulary as palpable, where it is the names themselves that possess more indubitable properties' (1995: 2). Chapter 11 of this volume takes up the 'learnability' issue.

14. *Song* is not the only Ifaluk word for (roughly) 'anger'. Lutz (1988) produces a detailed comparison and contrast between Ifaluk *song* and American English *anger*, as well as a list of other Ifaluk words from which *song* is differentiated, including terms for emotions produced by frustration, and notions similar to 'annoyance'.

15. I use the English terms in these condensed summaries, given that my interest is more in the *kind* of analysis White offers, and what it says about how to analyse emotion discourse in general, rather than in the specifics of Polynesian linguistics and anthropology. The continued use of 'scare quotes' signals that it is the Santa Isabel terms that are being referenced.

16. Again, a cautious parallel with the counselling data is irresistible here, where counsellors and their clients orient to the normative criteria of cooperatively (being seen to be) doing counselling and being counselled (Edwards, 1995).

17. Emotion 'rhetoric' is not merely a South Sea Islands phenomenon, of course. Recall the use of emotion talk by Jeff and Mary, and Connie and Jimmy, in constructing alternative stories. Nor is it the case that one emotion will always be contrasted with a specific other; there is considerable scope for invention, for what Billig (1987) calls 'witcraft'. Jimmy builds a contrast between justified anger and an irrational, dispositional jealousy. For the ghost of Hamlet's father, 'more in sorrow than in anger' was the distinction, and from that

(without getting much into Shakespearean analysis) stemmed the themes of Claudius's possible villainy, Hamlet's struggle over what to do, his balked revenge, and the ambiguous role of his father's ghost as maybe having (effectively) prompted him to it.

18. This contrast between the pursuit of consistency as a feature of cognitive theory and methods, and the celebration of contrast, inconsistency, and opposition in discursive and rhetorical psychology, is a strong feature of 'Loughborough group' work such as Billig (1987, 1991), Billig et al. (1988), Edwards and Potter (1992a), Middleton and Edwards (1990a), and Potter and Wetherell (1987).

19. Note how 'young spectators' is, in producing such an effect, very different from possible alternatives such as 'gang of lads', or numerous other derogatory descriptions to be found of young football supporters in the British press.

20. The moral significance of emotions is invoked not only for their display, but for their absence in appropriate circumstances. Similarly, emotions may be ascribed on the basis of other kinds of non-occurring actions: 'we often use *fear, jealousy*, and so on, not to explain actions, but to signify emotional states that explain a failure to act appropriately' (Mischel, 1969: 263, cited in Coulter, 1986: 126).

21. I have used the word 'meaning' rather casually throughout this chapter, avoiding theoretical distinctions such as 'reference' or 'extension' versus 'sense' or 'intension', and 'semantic meaning' versus 'intentional meaning' (cf. Wittgenstein's German *bedeuten* and *meinen*, both generally translated as 'to mean'). One everyday meaning of 'meaning' is indeed intention, as in 'I meant to mow the lawn, but I forgot'. Rather than attempting to nail down such important conceptual distinctions, I have allowed the meaning of 'meaning' to shift indexically with the issue under consideration. These include semantic definitions (such as dictionary entries), underlying scenarios, metaphors, speech act intentions, and whatever semantic packages, contrasts, and affordances words bring to their particular discursive occasions. Jack Bilmes (1986) provides a useful discussion of 'meaning' with regard to what he calls 'discursive sociology' (see also Bilmes, 1992; Coulter, 1992).

22. Buttny (1993: 94) provides the following example of how an emotion can be treated interactionally as subject to rational accountability.

    Mother: Well you don't sound like you're too exc̲ited about it.

    Daughter: .h Well no: I think it's fi̲ne I just don't want to get my
                ho̲pes up real high and ha̲ve it turn out to be some old
                gu̲:y that's gonna try to hi:re (0.4) you know for no̲thin'

The mother's observation concerning her daughter's lack of 'excitement' about some prospective event implies an assessment of that event on the daughter's part, and is itself an assessment of the daughter's state of mind. 'Instead of directly asking her, the mother makes this ascription which makes relevant an explanation' (Buttny, 1993: 95).

23. For example, Mary tells of the difficulty she has in going out without incurring Jeff's disapproval.

    Mary: I just thought to myself w- .hh youkno:w I
                shouldn't be sto̲pped.
                (0.8)
                I shouldn't ⌈need to be stopped.
    Jeff: ⌊I've ne̲ver stopped you y-
                (.) I wou̲ldn't stop you would I?
                (0.2)
    Mary: Well I kno̲w but that .h but (.) I .hh the wa̲y
                you sto̲p me is by (.) be- is is by: (.) um
                sending me to Coventry. Or- (.) well yo̲u know
                by not ta̲lking to me (.) and being fu̲nny

24. This may be a principle applicable even to professional, psychological theories. John Soyland suggests, in his examination of psychological theories of emotion considered as kinds of metaphor, that 'the variety of theories . . . could be used to undermine any particular account. But the working psychologist or philosopher should not see these accounts as requiring a kind of crucial experiment that will decide on the validity of any

particular instance. Rather, these accounts involve assumptions that are fundamentally antagonistic . . .' (1994: 102). As with the metaphors of everyday emotion talk, what we find in psychological and 'folk' theories alike may be distillations of one-sided positions extracted from the rich rhetoric of everyday discourse, treated as potentially definitive theories.

8

Categories I: Language and Perception

The previous chapter, on emotion discourse, introduced the idea that talk and text deploy *conceptual resources*. Whatever discourse does, it does it with resources that are to some extent ready-made and available for use, 'already "there", deeply entrenched in culture and language' (Bruner, 1990: 11). The focus of this chapter and the next is on word meanings. The aim is to explore some ways in which words, considered as conceptual resources for talk, 'categorize' mental experience and the external world. This opening paragraph is full of just the kinds of conceptual categories at issue, including the presumption that there are three separate realms: linguistic meanings, mental experience, and external reality. Perhaps not all cultures and languages make those distinctions, nor all members of my own culture, or perhaps they draw the lines at different places. But *all* the text of this paragraph, and of this book, deploys conceptual categories and distinctions.

It is one of the major difficulties in raising this topic at all, as we saw with the notion of 'emotions', that to do so involves using a set of categories of precisely the kind supposedly under examination. Furthermore, it may be that the least obvious, least noticed of those categories are the most insidiously potent (Whorf, 1956). With those reflexive joys and dangers in mind (so to speak), we are looking for an approach to categorial 'resources' that has them ready-made enough to make discourse intelligible, while flexible enough to let it perform the kinds of indexical and occasioned work that has been highlighted in previous chapters. We begin with a brief look at three approaches to verbal categories: classical, natural, and discursive.

Consider a well-known categorial definition: humans can be classed (however frivolously) as *featherless bipeds*.[1] We are the only species that walks around on two legs while also, to set us apart from birds, lacking feathers. It is the kind of definition that aims to include all human beings equally, while excluding everything else (whether it completely achieves this, without omitting various lizards and dinosaurs, is not the point here).[2] However whimsical, it is an example of what cognitive linguists call a *classical category* (Gibbs, 1994; Lakoff, 1987). That is to say, it is the kind of category used in logic and algebra, where there are meant to be clear boundaries, within which all instances of the category are equivalent. When we reason logically or mathematically about A and B (for example, 'all A's are B's', or '3a + 2b = c'), we do so on the basis that all A's (etc.) are equivalent to each other, that it is a clearly defined set, with no fuzzy edges or dubious members. While categories of that kind are necessary for basic logic and algebra to work, they are not the kinds of categories we generally find in natural language. We can explore that with the case of 'featherless biped'.

Note that the two terms in 'featherless biped' are technical rather than everyday ones. 'Biped' is recognizable as an anatomical and zoological term, but 'featherless' is technical too, when we consider what it is meant to include. Plucked turkeys are not included, any more than new-born, amputated, or tarred-and-feathered humans are excluded. To the extent that it works as a definition, it refers to something ideal, such as biological design, not to actual folk we know. But the concepts that abound in everyday discourse are generally not so precisely defined, outside of specific occasions of use, and this has to be understood as no fault or inadequacy that needs fixing, but (as previous chapters have argued) an important feature of how words work.

Take *chair*, for example. In ordinary talk, not all members of that category are equally clear or 'good'. Some objects are more clearly 'chairs' than others, and it is difficult to produce a hard and fast definition that will cover all instances that we may encounter and name.[3] Neither form nor function is easily stated; chairs may or may not have arm rests and 'legs' (for example, some tubular frame and bent wood chairs), and not everything used or made 'for sitting on' will count (floor cushions, for instance). There are objects close to the boundaries with *benches*, *sofas*, and *stools*, where we may have to decide what to call them, let alone derived meanings such as 'professorship'. Chairs are an example of what Eleanor Rosch (for example, Rosch, Mervis, Gray, Johnson, and Boyes-Braem, 1976) has called *natural categories*, to distinguish them from the artificial, 'classical' categories invented for doing logic and algebra.

The notion of natural categories has been an important development in the psychology of thought and language, helping to move theory and investigation away from how classical categories such as 'all the large triangles that are not blue' are comprehended, 'attained', or talked about (for example, Bruner, Goodnow, and Austin, 1956; Winograd, 1972), towards the study of ordinary language (Gibbs, 1994; Lakoff, 1987; Lakoff and Johnson, 1980). The latter studies have also argued in favour of a shift in cognitive psychology, away from 'literal description' towards a focus on the central importance of metaphor. Cognitive psychology has mostly assumed the primacy of literal description, the idea that the normal business of language is to describe the world directly, whereas metaphorical language could be set aside as some kind of derived, secondary, poetic, or abnormal usage. While accepting the critique of 'literal description', and the importance of metaphor, I argue in this chapter and the next that these important cognitive studies still have some way to go towards dealing with category use in everyday discourse.

There is another feature of 'featherless biped' that brings my argument closer still to the study of everyday discourse. Notice how strange it is, how we have to think about it to make it work, to understand how it defines humankind. There is a cognitive arbitrariness: it is unlikely that using and comprehending the word 'human' involves mentally computing an absence of feathers. But there is a discursive and rhetorical arbitrariness too. The issue of our lack of feathers does not arise; we never lost them. Contrast this with 'the penguin is a flightless bird'. It is not just that birds generally fly, or that people generally think they do, but that anybody *saying such a thing on some occasion* would thereby be doing something interactive and rhetorical. As an assertion, it addresses a possible misunderstanding, denies a plausible or presumed alternative, or, as we noted in Chapter 5, *treats* that alternative as plausible or presumed, as part of the action of denying it.

The awkwardness of 'featherless biped' lies in the fact that, removed from any discursive or rhetorical context, it did not arise that someone was supposing or suggesting that we might be quadrupeds, or have feathers. This *argumentative context* (Billig, 1987) is missing from cognitive–linguistic theories of 'natural categories', where the nature of categories is defined not with regard to how discourse performs social actions, but in relation to individuals' bodily experience and, through that, to the nature of the external world. In 'natural category' theory, perception and bodily experience come first, as ways of engaging with and apprehending the world, and language follows. Natural categories are primarily 'real world' ones defined by action and usage – material action and usage, not linguistic: what chairs are used for, rather than what the word *chair* is used for. But if categorization makes things equivalent, discursive categorization can be understood as a device for linguistically *treating things* as equivalent, as a *way of talking*. We shall examine the notion of 'natural categories' further in Chapter 9. Before that, we look at the work that led up to it: the much abused 'linguistic relativity hypothesis'.

Linguistic relativity: gas drums and snow

Psychologists' discussions of categories in language and thought have largely hinged on the direction of effects: does language impose categories upon our knowledge and experience of the world, or do the categories that we find in language reflect something prior to language, such as the way the world actually is, or how we perceive and understand it? The notion that language shapes thought, and that different languages shape thought according to their specific grammatical and conceptual structures, is called 'linguistic relativity', or the 'Sapir–Whorf hypothesis' (henceforth SWH), named after the linguists Edward Sapir and Benjamin Lee Whorf. For a comprehensive review of this venerable thesis, its critics, and a critique of its critics, see John Lucy's (1992) scholarly work, which has influenced the following discussion, even though the direction I take is somewhat different from Lucy's.[4]

Discussions of linguistic relativity include two notorious and emblematic examples: the number of words 'Eskimos' have for 'snow' (a discussion originated by Franz Boas, 1911/1966), to which I shall return, and the case of Whorf and the empty gasoline drum. Whorf worked throughout his career in anthropological linguistics as a fire prevention engineer for the Hartford Insurance Company in Connecticut. In addition to a series of studies on Native American languages such as Hopi and Apache, Whorf recounts how a large number of cases of accidental fires and explosions seemed to involve the workings of language. The term *empty*, because of its semantic associations with 'null and void, negative, inert' (Whorf, 1956: 135), led to *so-called* empty drums, which were actually filled with explosive vapour from the remains of petroleum, bursting into flames when a cigarette stub was thrown into them. This and other fire-causing examples (including how so-called 'scrap lead', which contained paraffin between the sheets, got dumped near a fire melting pot) were used to support the contention that applying language categories to a situation can structure and affect how we think and act.

The key factor was 'the linguistic description commonly applied to the situation' (Whorf, 1956: 135) which, for gasoline drums whose contents had been poured out of them, was *empty*. Whorf analyses *empty* as having two meanings: 'null and void, negative, inert', and also a less precise, everyday sort of reference to containers whose contents have been removed (emptied), but 'without regard to, e.g., vapor, liquid vestiges, or stray rubbish, in the container' (1956: 135). The use of the same word for both kinds of circumstances provides a linguistic basis for people to apply the word to potentially dangerous objects such as emptied petrol drums that contain residual explosive vapour.

Whorf's claim that the exploding gasoline drum demonstrates an effect of language upon thought was challenged by Eric Lenneberg (1953) in an influential and damaging rebuttal of Whorf's entire thesis. Lenneberg pointed out that gas drums do not have to be called 'empty'; it is also easy to say in English 'filled with explosive vapour', proving that the culprit's error was not caused by the semantics or grammar of his language. What Lenneberg is addressing here, as Whorf also went on to do, is the relationship between a language and the range of concepts available to speakers of that language – what people are *able* to say. But there is a feature of Whorf's gas drum analysis which is easily overlooked. He does not claim that the drums *had to be* described as empty, or *could not* have been otherwise described, but that this is how they *were* described and, moreover, how they were habitually described. So there is a tension here concerning what the relevant phenomena are, and what kind of explanation is appropriate for them; are we dealing with conceptual categories in the abstract (the linguistic system), or with general patterns of habitual usage, or with specific examples of situated talk?

Let us keep that tension in mind while exploring a second one, which was raised also in Chapter 7, concerning cross-cultural concepts of emotions. It is the use of categories of English as criteria for either promoting or disputing the presence of cross-linguistic differences. According to Boas (1911/ 1966: 22), writing on Eskimo words for 'snow': 'here we find one word, *aput*, expressing "snow on the ground"; another one, *qana*, "falling snow"; a third one, *piqsirpoq*, "drifting snow"; and a fourth one, *qimuqsuq*, "a snowdrift".' Lucy (1992) points out how this and numerous subsequent discussions of Eskimos and snow[5] implicitly use English as a metalanguage for reality. They treat what in English is called 'snow' as the objective domain in question, this domain of reality being supposedly sub-divided in another language, rather than constituted differently, or separately, and despite the lack of any evidence that those things are conceived by Eskimo people as 'varieties of the same thing' (1992: 149). The result of such assumptions across a wide variety of cultural, theoretical, and experimental studies on language and thought has been a systematic underestimation of the radical nature of Whorf's and Sapir's proposals on linguistic relativity, and especially the reflexive implications of those proposals for academic discussions of the issue. Since that underestimation is part of a current orthodoxy in mainstream psychology, where perception and action are pervasively given pride of place as generating concepts prior to language, it is worth pursuing further.

The Sapir–Whorf hypothesis (SWH)

The work of Sapir, Whorf, and various other American linguists was an 'anti-evolutionary project' (Lucy, 1992: 1) in anthropological studies that promoted cultural equivalence in place of presumptions of Western superiority and advancement. It was a project designed to appreciate the immense diversity and richness of languages that had mistakenly been considered primitive. What is now called the Sapir–Whorf hypothesis is more or less an invention by psychologists (see Carroll, 1956: 27), seeking to derive from that linguistic programme a simple statement about the direction of effects between language and cognition, that could be subjected to experimental testing. The SWH was derived from statements such as the following:

> We cut nature up, organize it into concepts, and ascribe significances as we do, largely because we are parties to an agreement to organize it in this way – an agreement that holds throughout our speech community and is codified in the patterns of our language. The agreement is, of course, an implicit and unstated one, *but its terms are absolutely obligatory*; we cannot talk at all except by subscribing to the organization and classification of data which the agreement decrees. (Whorf, 1956: 213–14, original emphasis)

The notion that different languages 'cut nature up' differently is not merely an argument for differences, but also an argument for equivalence: 'no language is "primitive"' (1956: 260). All languages are fully fledged systems that *leave nothing out*, even if they might categorize things differently. As Sapir put it:

> The outstanding fact about language is its formal completeness . . . a language is so constructed that no matter what any speaker of it may desire to communicate . . . the language is prepared to do this work. . . . The world of linguistic forms, held

within the framework of a given language, is a complete system of reference. (1924/1949, cited in Lucy, 1992: 17)

Similarly Whorf noted that 'the Hopi language is capable of accounting for and describing correctly, in a pragmatic or operational sense, all observable phenomena of the universe' (1956: 58). Whorf's interest was not so much in one-to-one correspondences between specific items of language and their corresponding concepts, but in how languages embodied general 'world views', cosmologies of time and space, of matter and form, of the material and spiritual worlds. The notion that Hopi descriptions were correct 'in a pragmatic or operational sense' nevertheless allowed for the possibility, sometimes invoked by Whorf, that objectively correct descriptions of the world could be provided in a culture-free manner by science. But he also considered scientific concepts themselves to be influenced by the categories of language (Whorf, 1956).[6]

Whorf's object of study was not isolated bits and pieces of language, specific semantic categories, or grammatical rules, but pervasive and important patterns of conceptualization. These patterns of conceptualization were general and far-reaching enough for him to lump together English and other historically related languages as 'SAE' ('Standard Average European', Whorf, 1956: 138), for the purpose of drawing contrasts with the grossly different conceptualizations he found in (and between) Native American languages.

Take, for example, the SAE distinction between 'mass' nouns that label unbounded kinds of stuff such as *sugar*, *water*, *wood*, and *sand*, and 'count' (or 'individual') nouns that label discrete entities, such as *a tree*, *a man*, *a hill*, *a stick* (Whorf, 1956: 140). Whorf argued that these differences are not in the first instance matters of reality or perception, but of how language categorizes things. Whereas *wood* is a mass noun, for instance, we typically encounter it perceptually in discrete, bounded pieces, unlike *sand*.[7] Non-SAE languages sub-categorize things differently or do not use the distinction at all, while in SAE languages the distinction is (according to Whorf) very far-reaching, making up a general pattern of conceptualization that extends to how we ordinarily conceive and talk about time, as a mass substance divided into countable units.

These observations on mass and count nouns, and on linguistic categories of time, were linked to differences between SAE and Hopi conceptions of time, memory, planning for the future, and historical record keeping. Keeping records is a less obvious necessity if the past is thought to be already written into the present. For the Hopi, 'it is as if the return of the day were felt as the return of the same person, a little older but with all the impresses of yesterday, not [as in SAE] "another day," i.e., like an entirely different person' (Whorf, 1956: 151). Just as the present bears the impress of the past, so what we do in the present will affect the future, indeed will *become* the future, and this underlies a variety of Hopi 'magical' (as we would say) beliefs and rituals.

Whorf argued that the way we count units of time in English, such as *days* and *hours*, like we count *men*, provides the basis for a pattern of 'habitual thought' that he called 'objectification' (1956: 140), in which the continuum of time is treated as a set of discrete, object-like items. Unlike physical objects, or even units of length 'visibly marked off into inches' on a ruler, both of which are 'perceptible spatial aggregates' (1956: 139), Whorf claimed that SAE units of time are 'imaginary' and 'metaphorical'. But there is a problem with Whorf's claims here. Whence comes the notion that time is objectively continuous? Do not the events of light and dark, day and night, sunrise and sunset, breakfast and lunch, start to demarcate time for ordinary SAE speakers into perceptually available units, something like marks on a ruler? What Whorf did was to use Western, technical notions of temporal measurement to tell him what 'time' is *actually* like (a continuum, with arbitrary units of measurement), as a baseline for the analytic category of 'objectification'.[8] He ignored his *own* objectification procedure, done also in English, though referenced to Hopi, that classifies time as one kind of stuff, and visible objects in 'perceptible space' as another.

According to Whorf, the Hopi language contains 'no general notion or intuition of time as a smooth flowing continuum in which everything in the universe proceeds at an equal rate, out of a future, through a present, into a past. . . . Hence the Hopi language contains no reference to "time", either explicit or implicit' (1956: 58). The notion of time as a 'smooth flowing continuum' is, he supposes, how SAE speakers think of it. In contrast, Hopi thought and language conceive a distinction closer to, what we might call in English, subjective and objective events. The Hopi verb system marks events not as past, present, or future, but, rather, with regard to considerations such as duration and certainty, as part of the 'manifest' realm of recent and current events, or else as part of an 'unmanifest' remote past, near future, or imaginary world of wishes and possibilities. In such a system (whose difference from SAE is underestimated here by having to use English terms for it), a past event of which the speaker is uncertain might be coded similarly to a future one not yet known.

But there is again a problem with Whorf's comparison between Hopi and SAE time. Not only has Whorf presumed rather than investigated the everyday notions of time used by SAE speakers, he has also presumed rather than examined the grammar of English (Chomsky, 1973). Whereas some European languages have a future tense (for example, Latin, French, and Spanish), English does not. English makes past tenses by adding '-ed' to regular verb stems (walked, kicked, kissed), and by altering the form of irregular ones (ran, left, ate). But there is no such inflection for future events. The 'future tenses' of other languages are usually translated into English by using the separate auxiliary verb *will*, as in 'will go', 'will eat', 'will run'. But *will* is merely one of a number of modal auxiliaries including *might*, *may*, *would*, *could*, and *should*. Taken as a group, what they appear to express is something like degrees of subjective certainty and moral compunction. In other words, the danger courted by Whorf is that of adopting an idealized notion of how people talk and think, based on a study of Hopi grammar, based in turn on interviews with a native informant living in New York City (Carroll, 1956: 17). Whorf's study of Hopi grammar was not matched by an equivalent study of SAE (the very category 'Standard Average European' signals Whorf's lack of concern with the specific structures of European languages when drawing contrasts with Hopi), nor by any sort of systematic ethnography of thought, practice, and discourse in any of the languages at issue.

The psychologists' critique of Whorf

Some of the critical comments I have made of Whorf's work accord with what has become a standard critique of the SWH in the psychology of thought and language, but I want to distance myself from that too. The rejection of the SWH by cognitive-experimental psychologists since the 1950s has led to a gross underestimation of the importance of language, and a corresponding overemphasis on perception, external reality, and bodily experience, in shaping its conceptual categories. Recent work in that cognitivist tradition will be examined later in this chapter and the next. But first we examine the often misplaced and circular critique of Whorf that paved the way for the new 'cognitive linguistics'.

One popular observation is that a 'strong' version of the SWH is both absurd and untestable. A strong SWH would be that language creates and determines the categories of thought and perception; a 'weaker' version would be that language *influences* thought, perception, or perhaps just our memories of what we thought we perceived (Miller and McNeill, 1969), a notion far more amenable to the cause-and-effect methodology of experimental testing. Reasons for ridiculing the 'strong' version include the fact that it becomes impossible to demonstrate, let alone test, the hypothesis. Whorf's efforts to show the differences between Hopi and English reduce to translations of Hopi into funny-looking English to show how strange they are, while remaining translations into English nevertheless. So either they are distortions, or else they disprove the hypothesis by demonstrating how the two languages are actually interchangeable (Lenneberg, 1953). A related absurdity is what we might call the 'lucky' theory of language and thought, that Eskimos have more words for snow than speakers of English or Arabic do, while Arabic has lots of words for horses and camels. If language were truly prior to thought and perception, it would be merely fortunate that the Eskimos (or Inuit, to use their own name)[9] do not find themselves in possession of a host of useless categories of camels.

It is important to realize that Sapir and Whorf were not that stupid. Neither of them proposed (outside of decontextualized popular quotations) that language actually brings into being either the world we see or the bio-perceptual apparatus we perceive it with. In fact, both Whorf and Sapir were careful to set aside various basic features of human psychology as not deriving from language.[10] The reason that critical discussions focus on Whorf rather than on Sapir is that the SWH, as a unidirectional statement about language and thought, reflects Whorf rather better than his mentor. Sapir saw language as both constraining cognition and constrained by it,[11] and partly as irrelevant to it. But even Whorf did not propose the SWH as crudely as it has been formulated for laboratory testing.

Whorf's focus on generalized, cosmological categories of conceptual thought has not been reflected in experimental studies, which have mostly tested whether capacities such as the perception of shape or colour are dependent on shape and colour categories in language. Not only do such studies risk missing the cosmological mark somewhat, they also ignore Whorf's explicit proposal that basic perceptual categories, what he knew at the time as Gestalt perception, might provide (like Wierzbicka's 'semantic primitives' – see Chapter 7) a non-linguistic, universal, and innate baseline for cross-linguistic comparisons: 'modern configurative or Gestalt psychology gives us a canon of reference for all observers, irrespective of their languages or scientific jargons' (Whorf, 1956: 163). As we have noted, Whorf set aside not only basic perceptual processes, but also scientific findings (including Gestalt perception, and his own linguistics), as standing outside of the relativism of specific languages.

Whorf's translations of Hopi and other languages were designed *not* to serve as adequate translations of the kind required by delegates to the UN or the EU, by book translators, or by tourists on vacation, but as an academic exercise to show what kind of reality construction was being done. They were produced in order to show how different and arbitrary those meanings would look when taken out of one language and culture (Hopi, say) and put 'literally' into another (English). It is obviously a silly, hopeless contradiction to translate proposition X into language Y and then to claim that X *cannot* be said in Y. It is much more sensible to claim that X is not said in Y, or did not get said, or would not be said in the same circumstances, or is not habitually said, or that something quite different would be said.

The point Whorf makes, by the use of translation, is the same point as he makes within English, with the example of the explosive gasoline drums. It is that different groups of people habitually say different things, formulate the world differently from how it might otherwise be formulated (sometimes, from how it might objectively be formulated!), and that this has consequences for what they understand and do. In looking at different languages, he sought to show how such differences in habitual conceptualizations had got built into grammar.

The major critique of Whorf, often recycled subsequently, was provided by Eric Lenneberg (1953). A flavour of that critique can be gained from his treatment of Whorf's analysis of a sentence in Apache. Whorf examined how in Apache one would describe something for which we might say in English, 'it is a dripping spring'. He came up with something that, translated morpheme by morpheme[12] back into English, would be 'as water, or springs, whiteness moves downward at a place'. Whorf used this example to suggest the presence of deep conceptual differences between Apache and English. Lenneberg argued that the peculiarity of that so-called Apache description is merely an artefact of how Whorf chose to translate it, morpheme by morpheme. First, the fact that it can be translated *at all* supports Lenneberg's claim that we can say more or less the same things in any language, though less efficiently in one than another (1953: 467). Second, the proper translation should in any case be 'it is a dripping spring', rather than the peculiar monstrosity constructed by Whorf. We should translate 'colloquially', which is to say we should substitute for what they say what we would say in the same circumstances.

This seems perfectly reasonable, in that it has the advantage of avoiding a temptation to depict foreigners as strange folk, while also conforming to the norms for proper translation between European languages, where the French 'J'ai faim' is rendered not as 'I have hunger', but as 'I am hungry'. The trouble is, of course, that colloquial translation ruins Whorf's entire point, not by disproving it, but by ignoring it. The product (if not the effort) of colloquial translation makes semantic differences impossible to find; it becomes impossible for speakers of different languages ever to mean anything much different from each other. That makes it just as circular a process as Whorf's efforts were accused of being, in showing the differences in meanings between languages by doing funny-looking translations of them. But he would *have to* do something like that after all, if he were not to rely on his academic readers all being proficient speakers of Hopi and Apache! As I have noted, Whorf's aims were different from what a translator at the United Nations would be trying to achieve.

Lenneberg's critique of Whorf reduces to the fact that they started with a radically different set of assumptions about language, mind, and reality. The notion of colloquial translation assumes, rather than proves, that sentences in different languages express the same meanings, and solidifies that assumption every time it is done. People are imagined as universal individuals, each viewing with the same cognitive apparatus the same objective world, and each endowed with a language capable of expressing it, capable of saying more or less the same things, in however superficially different a manner. This can be identified as a very common assumption in modern cognitive psychology, and it is precisely what Whorf attempted to undermine. It is worth remembering that one of the principles of Whorf's project, indeed of early anthropological linguistics generally, was to avoid using our own language and culture as the criterion for others.[13]

As I argued in Chapter 7 on 'emotion', the tendency to assume the universal adequacy of English is not merely an outdated 'evolutionary' ideology of cultural development that accompanied nineteenth-century imperialism, but an insidious tendency that still threatens theory and practice in modern cross-cultural research. If we can and should translate anything from any language colloquially into English, in order to obtain its meaning, then, of course, no real harm is done by retaining English as a criterion language for all comparisons. So English is installed as a neutral language for academic work of any kind, including relations between thought and language, and almost inevitably, given the methodological reduction of 'language' to English, we start discovering 'universals' (as with emotions). The psychologists' trick in refuting Whorf is precisely the one that Whorf questioned: the insertion of a notion of 'reality' prior to cognition, and of cognition prior to language, that 'uses [English] categories as the metalanguage for "objectively" describing the nature of referents purportedly independently of any language' (Lucy, 1992: 146).

Lenneberg's idea of what an English speaker would say in the same circumstances was expressed in the psychological argot of the time as 'equivalent verbal responses to the same stimulus situations' (1953: 465). This ignores the notion of descriptive indeterminacy that is foundational in ethnomethodology, SSK, CA, social constructionism, and discourse analysis, and that we have explored at some length in previous chapters. Descriptions are grossly under-determined by any notion of 'the same circumstances', or objective events. What would Lenneberg's position make of contradictory, or merely different but not contradictory, eyewitness reports? Which of them reflects just the way things were, just what any proper and honest reporter would say, in just those words and not any others? What about stories of 'anger' versus 'sadness' on Santa Isabel (White, 1990: see this volume, Chapter 7)? As alternative versions of the same stimulus conditions, is one right and the other wrong? Similarly, how do we deal with alternative *scientific* descriptions of the 'same phenomena'? In the study of situated discourse, the notion of 'equivalent verbal responses to the same stimulus conditions' fails at the first hurdle; it is the business of descriptions to say what the phenomena are (Edwards and Potter, 1992a; Potter, 1996).

Perhaps the most telling and influential objection that Lenneberg made against him was that Whorf provided no *independent measures of cognition*. No amount of observations about language, Lenneberg argued, can tell us about the relations between language and cognition, if there are no independent, corresponding measures of cognition. That is the rationale for an extended series of experimental studies (for example, Brown and Lenneberg, 1954; Carroll and Casagrande, 1958; Heider, 1972; Rosch and Mervis, 1975), all of which have attempted to test the SWH against non-linguistic criteria. Yet, reasonable as the call for independent cognitive measures appears to be, it also suffers from circularity. It is an objection that relies for its force on the notion that language and cognition, and in particular the kinds of cognition that language is said to shape, are separate realms, independently measurable. In order to appreciate the problems with this assumption, and how far-reaching they are for any cognitive psychology of language and meaning, we shall examine the major domain in which those independent measures have been pursued – that is, colour categories.

The colour studies

Colour seemed to provide an ideal domain for testing the SWH for a number of reasons. (1) It is a domain of the physical world that can be objectively measured; different colours correspond to different wavelengths and intensities of light. (2) The spectrum of wavelengths is a smooth continuum, onto which verbal categories such as 'red', green', and 'blue' are superimposed; this is unlike other domains of reference such as types of plants and animals, tables and chairs, and so on. (3) All normal human beings live in coloured worlds and possess colour vision. (4) Just about all the world's languages possess some colour words, but the number of colour words in any language is very small compared to the millions of gradations of colour we are able to discriminate visually. So a set of important conditions for doing experiments is in place. We can examine how different languages sub-categorize the objective colour spectrum by assigning names to different parts of it, and we can perform psychological tests of whether those colour names correspond to psychological effects in the perception or memory of actual colours.

A variety of anthropological studies had established that different languages do indeed sub-divide the colour spectrum at different points, sometimes making no distinction between yellow and orange, for example, or between green and blue, and placing other dividing lines at places on the spectrum different from English (Hoijer, 1954). In any language the huge range of visually discriminable colours could be considered more or less 'codable' (Brown and Lenneberg, 1954), according to how closely they correspond to colour words in that language (straightforward 'red', say, rather than 'a kind of pale bluish green'). Experimental studies by Roger Brown and Eric Lenneberg (1954) and by Lenneberg and John Roberts (1956) demonstrated that, for English speakers and also for monolingual Zuni (a group of Native Americans), the 'codability' of a colour in the language was a good predictor of memory – of how well they could pick out, from an array of alternatives, those colours they had been shown some time previously. These results supported a 'weak' form of the SWH, that language categories can influence memory. But the explanation for how it came about that some colours got to be more 'codable' than others in the first place was a two-way process, in which having names for things makes them psychologically salient, but also the salience of various categories, like with Eskimo types of snow, reflects something non-linguistic and ecological, 'the importance of snow in the Eskimo's life' (Brown and Lenneberg, 1954: 456).

The colour studies took a much sharper turn against the SWH with the work of Brent Berlin and Paul Kay (1969), and of Eleanor Rosch (Heider, 1972; Rosch, 1974), on what they called 'basic' or 'focal' colours. Basic colours were defined linguistically, by a series of criteria designed to restrict the list of 'colour words' to an essential set. Basic colour terms had to be single morphemes (units of meaning – see note 12), such as *red, green, blue,* and not *reddish* or *dark blue.* They had to name only colour and not some other thing (thus excluding *gold* and *silver*), or some restricted set of objects (which also eliminates *blond*). They had to be in general usage (no *magenta* or *cyan*), not recent imports from other languages (no *turquoise*), and not sub-categories of other terms (so *crimson* and *scarlet* are omitted, being sub-categories of basic *red*). That left for English a set of eleven basic colour terms, including the three 'achromatic' terms *black*, *white*, and *grey*, and eight chromatic hues: *red*, *yellow*, *green*, *blue*, *pink*, *orange*, *brown*, and *purple*. These eleven happened also to be the maximum number found in any language, and the basis for claims about a universal set of colour terms in all languages. The fact that English had the full set was, I shall argue, not just a lucky coincidence.

This linguistically defined set of basic colour terms was then put to the test, to see if it had psychological correlates. Berlin and Kay (1969) began by asking twenty foreign students (foreign in and to the USA), whose native language was not English, to identify on a large two-dimensional array of colours the range of reference for the basic colour words of their native language. They were asked to do this in two ways: (1) by marking where the boundaries between different colour words fell, and (2) by identifying the *best example* of each colour word. There was a lot of variation, even between speakers of the same language, and by the same individuals on different occasions, in where the boundaries were drawn. But the 'best examples' were much more consistently chosen, not only within languages, but across them.

Berlin and Kay suggested that the basic colours (whatever further research might refine these to be) were a universal set. Although various languages might not possess words for some members of the set, there was a pattern in the words they did have, according to an 'evolutionary' order of emergence. A 'stage 1' language would simply distinguish dark colours from light ones, a 'stage 2' language would also pick out focal red, and further developments of the colour lexicon would start to distinguish green and yellow, then blue, then brown, and then (by stage 7) the rest. This notion of 'stages' inevitably (whatever the authors' intentions) invokes an impression of progress from primitive colour systems to more advanced ones, leading up to English as the prime example of a fully developed lexicon of colour.

Studies by Rosch (then named Heider, 1972) supported the claim that focal colours were cognitively universal and prior to language. Rosch visited the Dani, a stone age people of New Guinea, and tested their recognition memory for focal and non-focal colours. The Dani's 'basic' colour vocabulary is 'stage 1', consisting of the two words *mili* (for dark, cool shades of all hues) and *mola* (for light, warm shades). The Dani were able to remember or recognize focal colours better than non-focal ones (just as a sample of American students did), despite possessing no words in their language for those colours. So the colour studies had come full circle. Having started as demonstrations of the influence of language on memory, weak though even that support might be for the SWH, they eventually came to suggest the presence of universal categories of perceptual experience that were prior to language, physiologically based (Brown, 1976; Kay and McDaniel, 1978), and that imposed themselves onto linguistic categories whenever languages got around to naming them.

Colour: too good to be true?

At the start of my summary of the colour studies, I said that colour *seemed* to provide an ideal domain for testing the SWH. Let us now consider some objections to that assumption. The finding that colour categories are dominated by the universal physiology of perception suggests that the SWH has failed. The main counter-argument to that is that it has not been tested. We have noted that Whorf explicitly (though not every time he wrote) set aside basic perceptual processes as being beyond the shaping influence of language, and focused his theories on higher-level concepts and wide-reaching cosmological ideas. The entire programme of empirical testing using colour memory and perception, whatever its intrinsic merits in informing us about colour, may therefore have scant relevance to the major thrust of Whorf's work, and even to the so-called SWH. But there are other criticisms of the colour studies that have much wider implications, and these are the main reason for my discussing them at some length here, in a book whose primary topic is neither psychological experiments nor isolated items of vocabulary, but discourse.

As John Lucy very thoroughly argues, the procedure used by Lenneberg, Brown, and other critics and experimenters was to 'psychologize' Whorf's and Sapir's interest in culture and habitual usage, 'by redirecting concern to processing potential' (Lucy, 1992: 129). The question became, not how do people ordinarily talk and think, but, rather, what are their cognitive–linguistic abilities. This altered question was in turn transformed into a testable hypothesis about the referential relations between language, mind and reality: how do the categories of a language map onto the things in the world that those categories refer to, and which we can objectively measure? Again, Lucy emphasizes what a huge and presumptive *translation* (ironically enough) this was. Lenneberg's starting point was the assumption that reality, cognition, and language could each be defined independently of the other, and compared. The SWH was effectively reinvented, translated into a comparison between categories and reality, with English the criterion for which categories of reality to study. Whorf's vision of a constructive, rather than mapping, relationship between language, mind, and world was side-stepped from the start.

The role of English as a criterion was hidden by the scientific objectivity of the major test domain chosen – colour. The choice of colour was justified on the basis that it could be objectively measured, independently of linguistic categories. But that justification pays no attention to the kinds of linguistic criteria Whorf used. In fact, it was based on something that educated English speakers may easily take for granted and overlook, which is the close relationship between the English (and other European languages) terms for colours and the isolation of 'colour' itself as a superordinate, distinct, and technically specified domain of the world. 'The only fact about English that could possibly have motivated the selection of this domain is the existence of the English [word] *color*, which suggests that there is a referential experience that has some unity for English speakers' (Lucy, 1992: 150). Many languages do not possess a word for 'colour'.

This is where the circularity enters. What the colour studies eventually did was to rediscover the technical basis of colour terms in modern English (or, as Whorf would say, in SAE). 'Basic terms' for colours are not simply tokens of ordinary discourse. What they do is to isolate and define categories of a technical, scientifically based notion of 'colour', as a domain separate from other ways of describing the appearance of things, a domain specifiable in terms of wavelengths of light, and developed for doing physics, dying wool, making photographs, films, and television sets. The omission of words such as *blond*, *bright*, *tawny*, *crimson*, *sallow*, *ruddy*, *gaudy*, and so on, from the list of 'basic' colour terms in English is the use not only of a linguistic criterion, but of a technical–scientific one. The notion that some of those terms are not strictly and uniquely 'colours' only takes us away from studying how people actually describe things, and pulls us back to what 'colour' objectively is. As Lucy noted, it is a word of English, and lots of other (non-SAE) languages do not have an equivalent.

The *Oxford English Dictionary* (1994) is once again informative here, but in a rather perverse manner. For the superordinate category *colour* it offers the following:

> The particular colour of a body depends upon the molecular constitution of its surface, as determining the character and number of the light-vibrations which it reflects. Subjectively, colour may be viewed as the particular sensation produced by the stimulation of the optic nerve by particular light-vibrations. . . .

The dictionary then proceeds to list examples of the word, commencing in the year 1398! For the notion of 'colour' as meaning one particular colour versus another, it gives 'A particular hue or tint, being one of the constituents into which white or "colourless" light can be decomposed, the series of which constitutes the *spectrum*; also any mixture of these' – and lists examples from the year 1290. Of course, these definitions can only be modern ones, technically specified, and retrospectively applied. They no more define what fourteenth-century speakers 'meant' by the word (conceptually or psychologically, that is)[14] than they do for most folk today. The worry that this raises about the colour experiments, and the pursuit of 'independent objective criteria' of reference, is that those studies may also have effectively side-stepped looking at what people mean by what they say, including what they do, interactionally, with the words they use.

Regarding what words are used for, and it is time that we returned to that, it is reasonable to suppose that it would be no use having one colour word and no others. Even a 'stage 1' language is supposed to have two contrastive terms, something like 'dark' and 'light'. Given the position I adopt here, that languages are designed so that people can relevantly say one thing to each other rather than another (rather than just putting perceptual labels on things because they *can*), it would presumably be no use having a third term 'red' either, without alternatives. In a 'stage 2' language, one wonders, what is 'red' (or whatever term is locally used) alternative to? Perhaps it joins 'dark' and 'light', as an additional descriptive option. Or perhaps there are other, non-'basic' contrasts lurking here uninvestigated, linked to flora and fauna, life and death, danger and safety, ritual and adornment, or whatever. Whatever those may be, the criteria for 'basic colours' excludes them from consideration. But we would have to investigate how people *use contrasts and alternatives in discourse*, irrespective of the formal criteria for 'focal colours', before we could know what, for those people, the relevant conceptual domains are – just as we argued for emotion words (Chapter 7).

The same argument applies to the superordinate category 'colour' itself. In modern English we use the word 'colour' to distinguish sets of objects from their 'monochrome', 'black-and-white', or just 'white' versions. We use it for making distinctions between kinds of film and photograph, types of television sets and movies, film processing chemicals and procedures, kinds of washing powder and coded machine wash cycles, and human races – all categories not merely visually discriminable in some experimental test, but pragmatically important for how we use them, what we do about them, what they cost, how we think and act with regard to them (cf. Sahlins, 1976). Note that all these examples are modern kinds of objects or concepts. Presumably in the fourteenth century the point was not to distinguish 'colour' from what we now call 'black and white'. Whatever they used the concept of 'colour' for, it need not have been the same as distinguishing 'chromatic' (another modern, technical term), from 'monochromatic'. The word was presumably used for things we could still call coloured (kinds of heraldry, flags, flora and fauna, clothing, etc.), but the modern definition of chromatic colour was only later extracted from those things as the essential property being labelled, after pragmatically useful distinctions got to be drawn between what was coloured and what was not.

So the definition of 'colour' used in all the experimental studies corresponds to the scientifically defined *modern English meta-category 'colour'*. Citing Conklin (1955) and Newman (1954), Lucy (1992: 151, 168) notes that other languages have words that (to use English terms for these things) include 'colour' criteria along with other attributes, including surface reflectivity, that in English we might separate out as non-chromatic attributes such as 'wet', 'shiny', 'dry', or 'dull'; or they mix reference to colour with types of objects and other properties. The North American Zuni language, for example, uses different words for the yellow of skin, of paint, of leaves, and for labelling things such as the appearance of ripened fruit.

Of course, English also has words of this kind that are associated with objects and their states (*blond*, *ruddy*, etc.), but these got excluded from SWH experiments as not proper (basic) colours. Yet object-specificity is a feature that applies also to the major 'focal' colours, when we consider them in use. Take *red*, for example. Herbert Clark notes that the colour denoted by *red* varies according to the object described: 'the reds in red hair, red potatoes, red cabbage, red bell peppers, red onions, red grapes, red beans, red wine, and red skin are very different from the blood red of the focal red Munsell chip'[15] (1992: 372). Clark emphasizes that the precise reference of *red* (and all other words for that matter) depends indexically on the context in which it is used, with regard to the range of linguistic and conceptual possibilities that are interactionally at issue on any such occasion.

Clark's insight into English *red* suggests that what English speakers mean and do when talking of 'colour' has been subsumed far too readily within a technical framework of objective reference. It also reminds us that *other* languages are likely to have rich vocabularies, within which 'colour' figures as a partial, object-sensitive, and indexically variable criterion, but which have been ruled out of consideration in the colour studies by technical criteria of what colour *actually is*. The complete reliance of those criteria on objective methods reflects and reinforces a perceptual-realist approach to language and mind. It shifts our attention away from descriptive practices, and depicts many of the world's languages as possessing impoverished vocabularies of basic perceptual appearances, when compared to (especially) English. The colour studies virtually lost sight of the Whorfian project altogether, the project of investigating the conceptual status of language in cultures and patterns of habitual usage. Lucy notes that the choice of colour for testing the SWH 'replicates exactly the treatment . . . of the category "snow", where the English [word] was taken as the guide (the metacategory) for characterizing the objective referential domain' (1992: 152). Ironically, therefore, the experimenters failed to consider how the SWH might actually apply to the very domain chosen as its ostensibly independent criterion, 'colour' itself.

The fact that 'colour' could be given a technical, objective definition obscured the presence of a kind of cultural–linguistic bias that is much more obvious where no such objective definitions are available. Cultural anthropology has long grappled with the problems of asking what is another culture's or historical period's religion, form of marriage, moral code, conception of love, or whatever. These are difficult questions to ask in any neutral way, since 'religion', 'morality', 'love', 'marriage' (and so on), are elements of our own cultural life, conceptually distinguished from a range of alternative kinds of feelings, relationships, rules, and social institutions in our own culture. But the task of Western anthropology is not to measure other cultures by our own criteria, but to discover what *their* criteria are, while still describing them in ways we can understand and compare to our own. Unlike with 'colour', there is no plausible candidate for a scientific, language-independent, culture-independent criterion of 'love' or 'religion'. That is both the joy and the horror of doing anthropology. Yet colour can be objectively, 'independently' specified for cross-linguistic purposes only on the assumption that our category 'colour', and the measurement of light, correspond to *what members of other cultures are thinking and doing when they use words that we translate into our colour lexicon*. That assumption does not test Whorf's hypothesis, but falls for it.

All of this leaves us in a quandary. What else can we do, if our best efforts at defining an independent, objective criterion for studying thought–language relations have failed? The solution, I would suggest, is to rethink the whole issue. The colour experiments were based, like all of the empirical studies of the Sapir–Whorf hypothesis, on the assumption of a clear dichotomy between cognition and language. This is the basis of Lenneberg's (1953) critique, that Whorf deals only with language, and omits an independent study of cognition. Language and cognition are assumed to be separately measurable, independently definable, such that we can then map one onto the other and see how they match up. But it can be argued that, on further examination, this entire approach is circular, *itself* boiling down to a disputable theory and metaphor – the use of a 'mapping' notion of the relationship between language, mind, and world.

Let us begin again from a different assumption, which is that we do not have to, or indeed cannot, study the thought–language relationship by measuring cognition separately from language and then matching the results. This is not to say that we cannot study non-verbal cognition – of course we can, and do, in adults, infants, and animals – though even here, the domain is purely 'non-verbal' only for the subjects of study, animals and infants, and not for the investigators themselves, who necessarily adopt verbal categories and labels for it (see also Chapters 2 and 11). But the issue is the logic of studying the Sapir–Whorf hypothesis, which Lenneberg (1953) and Chomsky (1973) have claimed must entail an independent study of cognition. The reason we can reject that separation is that it relies on a discredited 'picture' or 'mapping' theory of meaning (Austin, 1962; Harris, 1981; Wittgenstein, 1958).

What we call 'language' in these discussions of linguistic relativity is more or less equivalent to the *meanings* of words and grammatical constructions. So the aim of the SWH-testers is to map meaning onto independent measures of cognition and reality. But in the SWH, meaning is *already* the relation between words and the world, or between words and cognitions about the world. That makes it difficult to study relations between meanings and reality or cognition in anything other than a presumptive and circular way; they are not independent matters. Whorf did not simply omit to study cognition; he treated the *cognitive* differences between two statements or formulations as intrinsic to their *meanings*. Words and sentences construct the nature of things, relations, and events in the world. We perform the cognitive construction in the same process as we understand the language. We do not need to ask also, as if it were a separate matter, how the world is conceptually constructed by these sentences.

Lenneberg forced a strong distinction between *what* is expressed, that is, message content ('we can say anything we wish in any language' – 1953: 467), and *how* it is expressed, which he called 'codification'.

His argument involved first drawing a distinction between message and code, thus immediately minimizing the importance of code–message interactions of the sort Whorf sought to emphasize. . . . Finally, he interprets the question of codes in terms of different ways of handling the same messages, or, as we might say, the same reality. (Lucy, 1992: 141)

Languages were assumed to differ in codification, in how easily they can express various concepts. Lenneberg's influential critique of Whorf rested (ironically, given the nature of the Whorfian hypothesis) on crucial a priori conceptual distinctions, based on a kind of cognitive–perceptual realism. What the colour experiments eventually did was to come full circle and 'discover' those assumptions in the form of empirical findings. Language was eventually reduced to a reflection of reality guided by the biology of perception, in which 'the possibility that a language plays a role in *constituting* a speaker's reality is essentially dissolved' (Lucy, 1992: 141, original emphasis).

As we shall see in Chapter 9, colour is not the only domain of language and experience that has been mapped out in this perception-and-reality kind of way. The importance of the pioneering studies on focal colours lies not in the importance of colour, but in how the principles of those colour studies have been extended to account for meanings and metaphors in general. There are focal chairs and tables, emotions and democracies, while perception and bodily experience provide a rich metaphorical base, rooted in realistic perception and action, for meanings of all kinds (Gibbs, 1994; Lakoff, 1987; Rosch et al., 1976). But even the simpler domain of colour terminology is one that we should not relinquish lightly to theories of that sort. If we turn our attention away from the linear, causal hypothesis of thought–language effects, and towards situated practices, then we can ask, how are such terms actually deployed? People do not normally sit around under experimental conditions, in a vacuum of non-action, judging objects to be red or yellowish green. These are categorizations that are deployed, when they are deployed, on and for occasions.

We have noted how the word 'colour' figures in modern discourse in various pragmatic contrasts with 'black-and-white' (film, television, washing powders, etc.). Similarly, specific colour terms, when descriptive of people ('black', 'white', and 'coloured' in the old South Africa; 'redskins', 'palefaces', 'people of colour' elsewhere), are not simply determined by perceptual accuracy (actual skin hues etc.), but are richly embedded in social practices, consequential for how such 'named objects' are to be discriminated, thought of, and acted upon, and they are namings that perform social actions in their very utterance. But the 'cognitive category' studies have conceived the whole issue in terms of 'naturalness', of biology and objectivity, of categories as reflections of perceived reality. What is required if we are to understand the nature of the conceptual resources used in discourse is an analysis of their use within descriptive practices. While that seems obvious for the politically charged business of describing people, I suggest that it is equally applicable to the less obvious case of describing objects. In art and advertising, in commerce and everyday conversation, the empirical issue becomes the construction and interactional dynamics of actual, defeasible (could be otherwise), rhetorically potent descriptions.

Words and images: a cautionary tale

One common-sense objection to the SWH is that, obviously, language is not everything. We understood the world non-verbally before we ever acquired language, both ontogenetically (as children) and phylogenetically (as a developing animal species), and we continue to do so as adult human beings. So perception *must* be prior to language. And therefore, it seems plausible that language follows the older categories and contours of bodily experience, rather than vice versa. A picture, after all, is worth a thousand words, is it not? But there we go again, coining verbal formulae about the priority of the non-verbal. How do we get beyond language in the very act of using it to do so? What about the non-verbal itself; cannot experiences, or images, speak for themselves?

Note first that pictures and images, such as those in art and photography, in newspapers and magazines, on television and on the pages of scientific articles, are not brute reality (even when 'realistic'), but artefacts that depict things. Clearly there are things images do other than 'depict things', but it is their representative function that is at issue here, their capacity to 'speak' directly to us about the world without need of language. They can themselves be analysed, in words of course, for their function, rhetoric, message content, and reality effects (for example, Barthes, 1981; Goodwin, 1995b; Kress and Van Leeuwen, 1990; Lynch and Woolgar, 1990; Myers, 1990). Not only are pictures themselves semiotic artefacts, but they can be worked up and presented as mere reflections of reality just as descriptions can, and often work along with descriptions, in documentaries, press pictures, laboratory work, scientific diagrams, and the like. Since I cannot find a picture to demonstrate the limits of the pictorial (without having to say that that is what it is for), and because I have not allowed myself the space here to discuss this topic more fully, I shall discuss it by way of a (verbal) anecdote.

I recently attended a seminar (by John Corner, at Loughborough University on 30 November 1994) on the topic of television documentaries. The speaker made a remark concerning a sequence from the popular BBC programme *999*, which is a dramatized event 'reconstruction' programme on the work of the emergency services. The sequence contained visual (filmed, simulated action) footage of a reconstructed rescue operation, and a verbal comment from a television commentator well known for his association with factual/news programmes (Michael Buerk). Buerk said that what the rescuers were doing was 'dangerous'. The speaker suggested that this comment was redundant, in that the depicted scene was *obviously* dangerous, and we did not need Buerk to point that out to us.[16] This notion that images can speak for themselves, that certain descriptions may be obvious or redundant, that some things do not need saying, is worthy of scrutiny for a number of reasons. It lies at the heart of discussions of the nature and cognitive origins of semantic categories, for example (discussed in Chapters 7, 8, and 9 of this volume), and of 'thought without language' (see Chapter 2).

Three problems can be raised with 'dangerous' and its obviousness. First, the televised events were flagged as *simulated*, such that their 'dangerous' quality was at best artificial, and quite possibly something of which the audience might appropriately be reminded, so that they should treat what they were looking at as the real event simulated, rather than the perform-ance acted out on screen. They ought not to be responding to the sequence as if it were a purely fictional scene.

Second, such a description might be *deniable*, even for such a scene. It is not unknown, or unreasonable, for protagonists in such scenes to play down or deny the danger. They may claim that proper professional training makes of it a routine job of work; that knowledge and understanding reduce danger; or even that the danger is more apparent than real. Of course, the 'reality behind appearances' is an effective descriptive device for countering the visually obvious (Pollner, 1987), and it is also one that young children have to learn.[17] I was reminded of another television programme which I saw the same week, in which Rod and Valerie Taylor (renowned for their films of shark behaviour, including contributions to the Great White footage used in *Jaws*, and themselves victims of attacks) were in the water with dozens of sharks, testing some new device for getting close to these 'obviously' terrifying animals (my own description), while verbally (on the soundtrack) playing down the danger. They pointed out that many shark species are not as dangerous as people think, emphasized their own professionalism and knowledgeable precautions, and advocated the cessation of off-shore nets on Australian bathing beaches because these endanger the sharks. So on both these first two grounds (simulation and deniability), perhaps 'danger-ous' was not so obvious or redundant a description of the 999 sequences. At least, 'dangerous' can be descriptively built up or played down, and contended.

But a third, more interesting problem arises if we set aside these (nit-picking?) disagreements and go along with the notion that, by any normal criteria, it was obviously a pretty dangerous situation. The point here is that, while 'dangerous' may well be a perfectly reasonable and agreeable description, from which hardly any sane viewer would demur, it is *not the only such description*. Equally acceptable candidates might include 'frightening', 'terrifying', 'confusing', 'hazardous', 'exciting', 'harrowing', and so on. A person can be frightened without being in danger (such as when waking from a bad dream), and in danger without being frightened (by being professional, brave, stupid, or whatever). Even 'hazardous' is different, implying something less active perhaps than 'dangerous': I would more likely call sharks dangerous than hazardous. A useful question to ask is what does the description 'dangerous' do that 'frightening' and the rest do not? One possibility is that it makes relevant just that set of notions I mentioned, such as bravery, professionalism, and so on, which may well be significant in a generally laudatory programme on the work of the emergency services.

Now, I think there is a profound point here concerning the nature of descriptions and their relation to the world and to visual representations or appearances. The world, and visual images of it, do not translate automatically into descriptions (unless they are specifically designed or coded to do so). Since an indefinitely large number of reasonable, agreeable descriptions can be offered for any ordinary scene or event, each of which may be appropriate but somewhat different from the rest, any such description can be examined for the particular semantic and interactional (pragmatic, rhetorical) business it may perform (see Chapter 4). This is not a matter of market researching your descriptions to see how far people may *agree* with them – we are not concerned here with how many people would agree that 'dangerous' was an appropriate description in this case. Descriptions can be countered; that is plain enough, and instructive. But the fact that a specific description is perfectly agreeable is *just the point at which it deserves our most careful analytic scrutiny*, because it is precisely at this point that we are most disposed to accept it as obvious, natural, a reflection of the scene itself, and therefore as doing nothing. The very last thing we want to conclude is that such a description is redundant; that would be merely to fall for it, and to fail analytically.

It is contrasts such as 'dangerous' versus 'frightening' that are hardest to see, both by participants and by analysts, rather than ones like 'dangerous' versus 'safe'. Semantic opposites are a restricted basis for considering the workings of rhetoric.[18] We have to examine the particular range of consequential alternatives that may be at work in actual discourse, and especially the range of close, equally acceptable, but not actually chosen descriptions, in order to grasp what actions are being done by the particular words we find; this is the lesson of conversation analysis. It is as if, as soon as we (participants and analysts) hear a description that is *acceptable*, we tend to go along with it. That makes it a very powerful position to be in, to get your mundane, unobjectionable description in first, to be the one who provides the just-so, unobjected-to version of events, the one whose version stands as the criterion against which considering alternatives has to look like nit-picking.

This is not to deny that images are, in their own right, powerful signifiers. It is just that they do not determine, nor translate into, descriptions. That would be another version of the 'information' fallacy (see Chapter 5), the cognitivist presumption that words 'code' and communicate perceptual categories. My argument is designed to celebrate the fuzzy, overlapping, and referentially inconsistent nature of the words at our disposal. This is not something to be generally improved on (though new words are welcome) by simplifying, clarifying, or systematizing the language, nor by inventing a technical vocabulary for events and psychological processes, nor by

attempting a non-interpretative discourse for non-linguistic images. Referential flexibility is what enables us to do things with words – creatively,
adaptively, deniably, indexically. It is just the way language is, and has to be,
to serve as the resource it is for everyday use.

Conclusions: categories in thought and talk

I have argued that the description 'dangerous', even when so unobjectionable as to seem redundant (perhaps *especially* then), is a defeasible category.
That is to say, it is always one of a range of alternative and potentially
objectionable descriptions, the choice amongst which is likely to be
interactionally potent. This brings us back to Whorf and the notorious
gasoline drums which, despite being objectively 'dangerous' (Whorf,
1956: 135), got described as 'empty'. We can now develop a further element
of Whorf's anecdote that he did not. The cases Whorf described were ones
that occurred in the context of insurance claims, where we can assume that
issues of culpability versus accident were important. Descriptions of objects
and events provide for the accountability of actions, generate excuses, and
deal generally with 'attributional' issues of cause, intention, and responsibility (Edwards and Potter, 1992a). Whorf provided no detailed ethnography, but describing the drums as *empty* might provide for an actor's
accountability, in accidentally, but understandably and excusably, causing a
fire. Verbal categories are resources with which speakers perform discursive
actions; they are not just reflections of how they see things, or the way things
are.

One of the major problems underlying the colour studies is that colour is
very probably *not* the meta-category under which other language users
generally describe the appearance of things. They are probably not, most of
the time, outside of highly specialized contexts, concerned with nothing but
the hue, saturation, and brightness of reflected light. The cross-cultural
colour experiments, from Lenneberg to Rosch, became tests of various
possibly universal features of human perception, rather than studies that
sprang from an interest in how, why, and when people ordinarily describe
things. Alternative hues measured on objective dimensions need not
correspond to the range of interactionally relevant descriptive categories,
even when colour words are used. There are no studies, in the SWH-testing
psychological tradition, of the discourse of colour.

The critique of the colour studies helps us to ground and generalize the
discussion of emotion categories in Chapter 7. The pursuit of cultural
universals and differences in concepts of emotion has assumed that, when
members of other cultures use words that we would roughly translate as
'anger', 'sadness', and so on, they are also using sub-categories of what we
call 'emotions'. As with colour categories, the pursuit of the semantics of
emotion has brought us to the discovery of physiologically based universals,
for which descriptions in English seem happily to suffice. The whole notion

of semantic universals seems ridden with cognitivist assumption and method, the hegemonic English language, and a disregard of the way conceptual meanings work within discursive practices.

The modern English meta-category of 'emotion' informs and is informed by a long tradition in philosophy and psychology (Gergen, 1995; Harré, 1986b), including efforts to distinguish and isolate categories of mental faculties, and to provide psychological explanations of actions (cf. the meta-category 'colour' in relation to science and technology). Rather than asking, what do 'emotion' words do in discourse, the question has been, what do these words uniquely refer to? What would be their best dictionary definition, if dictionaries could be informed by a science of what they refer to (like the modern definitions of 'colour' in the *OED*)? It is not only Whorf's critics, but Whorf himself who commits this referential fallacy. His notion of 'time', for example, conflates what SAE speakers habitually say and think with an idealized, technical kind of 'clock' time, linear and even. No study is offered either of the complexity of temporal reference in English, or of the rich domain of references to time that can be found in everyday discourse.

The ordinary discourse of time is surely a promising line of investigation, just as it is in phenomenology, narratology, history, physics, and anthropology. For example, consider various details from the transcripts used in Chapter 6: the general implication of time in script routines, in formulating recurrent actions, and the causal implications of temporal sequence in narratives (see also Chapter 10); Mary's reference to what time the club closed, with regard to what time she got home, and its reasonableness versus her husband's reaction to her coming home 'late' (Extract 6.1); Emma's implication of Thanksgiving as a normative time for families to be together, and, therefore, for her estranged husband Bud to come home (Edwards, 1994b); Emma's use of the notion of a reasonable time for food to be served in a restaurant (Extract 6.3); Connie's and Jimmy's concerns with specifying the time from which their troubles started, and the relevance of that within the narrative accountability for those troubles (Extracts 6.8 and 6.8a); and, of course, Jeff's 'angry stage', which we focused on in Chapter 7. These are just a few quick and dirty examples, but they indicate the possibility of a systematic study of the discursive psychology of time, where references to time are flexibly specifiable and action-performative, on and for the occasions when they are used.

The 'occasioned' nature of discourse is itself a temporal concept, which reminds me of one more tantalizing conversational snippet. Harvey Sacks observed how asking 'What time is it?' can be used to close a social encounter.

> This provides for some kind of gearing into the rest of the world; a world that's organized apart from this conversation, like one has an appointment. . . . And given that 'What time is it?' is very frequently used in that way, the notion that our society is constrained by the clock may not be altogether true, since the clock can be a freeing device also. (1989: 223)

So merely asking and telling the time, like the rest of descriptive discourse, is, in Sacks's sense, 'subvertible' for social action (see Chapter 4). For Sacks, of course, the analytic object was not 'language'. That is what linguists and psycholinguists generally study. It was talk-in-interaction, which (to invoke Whorf and Lenneberg again) is *not* another label for the same thing.

Discursive psychology moves away from the SWH's concern with how static and coherent linguistic systems embody static and coherent world views, and starts to examine: (1) how particular versions of the world construct it variably; (2) how linguistic categories provide descriptive resources for such constructions; and (3) how specific constructions perform local actions, on and for the occasions of their production. The study of the linguistic system is useful not for how it displays a theory of the world, but for how it provides a conceptual and functional resource kit out of which constructions of reality can be fashioned within the pragmatics of discourse (cf. Fairclough, 1992; Fowler, 1991; Hodge and Kress, 1993; Van Dijk, 1993).[19]

Lenneberg described his research programme on the language of colour as that of 'mapping color terms into the color space' (1967: 339). This *mapping* metaphor for meaning is closely linked to the decontextualization of 'language' from discourse, and the eventual circular rediscovery of its own assumptions. As John Lee has succinctly remarked,

> . . . given the removal of the sentence, phrase, word, or utterance from a context, and therefore from whatever role it might have been playing, then its meaning must reside in the correspondence between the structure and what it mirrors, represents, or stands for. (1991: 210)

'Language' is an abstraction from practices, and most linguistic and psychological treatments of it depend on extracting it from practices.

If we go to where the mapping metaphor comes from, to geography and navigation, it turns out that mapping is in any case more like pragmatic natural language than the pursuit of literal correspondences. A map is not merely a once and for all, decontextualized representation of the world (Barnes, 1977); nor indeed is an aerial photograph, and a map is not one of those either. The classic London Underground map distorts scale, direction, and distance for the sake of functional readability, omitting an infinity of possible detail. More generally, it is no use asking a geographer for a map, or *the* map, of an area, unless, by chance, there were only one available. But even that single map would have been made for some kind of use. The first question would have to be, what do you want it for? A map for rambling around hill and dale, marking stiles and footpaths, marshy ground, public rights of way, public houses and such is not the same as a motorists' route map, nor a geologist's survey of the terrain.

Note also that, with geographical maps, you cannot get back from the map to the terrain. It is a one-way reduction and coding of information – except, that is, in situated usage, when the rambler, motorist, or geologist, map in hand, looks to see how it relates to the physical setting it is supposed to represent. Then map use becomes like situated language use, relying on indexicality and whatever action/journey, from an infinite range of possibilities, it is being used for. Indeed, it is precisely that indexicality, the actual situated use of the map, that the thing is designed for, just like language. So maps are something like plans and scripts, but like plans and scripts under the treatment of them in Chapter 6 (recall also Suchman's, 1987, discussion of Trukese navigation).

The 'mapping' metaphor is starting to look more attractive, but only subject to these functional reconceptions of it. In the next chapter we examine how psycholinguistic studies of conceptual categories have been extended beyond colour perception, to encompass concepts and metaphors of all kinds, yet still based in notions of more or less realistic perceptual and bodily experience. An appreciative but critical analysis of those studies is developed from the perspective of discursive psychology.

Notes

1. This memorable expression possesses an ancient philosophical pedigree, in discussions of reference and logic: 'In defining the human being as a featherless biped, the Greeks were not simply providing a succinct definition of their own species. They were exemplifying their belief that common objects of the world can be classified into groups, and that these groups can be defined by certain criterial attributes' (Gardner, 1985: 340). Aristotle also provided less frivolous definitions of humankind, as the 'rational', or 'political' animal; my discussion of 'featherless biped' can be applied to those too. Michael Billig managed to find me something more: 'I tracked down something about featherless bipeds. According to Diogenes Laertius, the definition was one of Plato's. Diogenes of Sinope (a piss-taker who lived in a bath) apparently plucked a live chicken and threw it at Plato, telling him that this was another human being he could talk to. After that, the accepted definition was altered: a featherless biped with smooth fingernails' (personal communication).
2. Actually it *is* the point, or it will be shortly. One of the problems in conceiving of everyday human categorization in terms of logical, 'classical' categories of this kind, as we shall see, is the trouble we have in keeping all the category members nicely and unambiguously contained within their categorial boundaries. That same referential messiness was a major reason for the invention of a specialist philosophical vocabulary for doing 'formal logic'. With regard to the domain of featherless bipeds, the ancient Greeks were of course unfamiliar with dinosaurs.
3. The *Oxford English Dictionary* (1994) offers for *chair* this mixture of form, function, and custom: 'A seat for one person (always implying more or less of comfort and ease); now the common name for the movable four-legged seat with a rest for the back, which constitutes, in many forms of rudeness or elegance, an ordinary article of household furniture, and is also used in gardens or wherever it is usual to sit.' The principal component of that definition, the word *seat*, is itself given functionally (among various other definitions) as 'Place or thing to sit upon'.
4. Whereas Lucy develops a methodology for analysing conceptual differences in the grammars of different languages, the direction I pursue is more critical of Whorf and takes us towards the study of categories as items deployed, within a single language, in situated discourse. Lucy follows Whorf in operationalizing 'habitual usage' as the study of *grammar* and cross-linguistic grammatical differences, rather than studying situated discourse. The aim is that of 'linking distinctive language patterns to distinctive habitual behavior or belief at the level of the *aggregable individual social actors*' (Lucy, 1992: 7, emphasis added). He

also retains the notion that the SWH requires independent measures of cognition; work that derives cognitive models from linguistic patterns 'begs the issue of the relation of language and thought' (Lucy, 1992: 184). I argue that studying discourse practices is *already* a study of culture and cognition, rather than something to be compared with how people actually behave and think (cf. Edwards, 1993). In any case, doing cross-cultural translations and comparisons are themselves cultural practices, and all the more evidently so, the more historical distance and critical perspective scholars such as Lucy manage to bring to them. Michael Moerman notes the tendency, in citations of Whorf and linguistic relativity, 'to glide from "language" to assertions, affirmations, and communication' (1988: 103). Like Moerman, I am trying to shift the analytic focus from the linguistic system (grammar) to studies of situated discourse.

5. The literature since Boas has turned the number of Eskimo words for 'snow' into an emblem of cultural differences, celebrating a wide range of estimates from three to 'hundreds' (via four, seven, and twenty-two, for instance), and based on virtually no empirical research at all (Martin, 1986).

6. Whorf's ambivalence concerning science's objectivity can probably be related to a common-sense distinction between truth, on the one hand, and various errors and influences, on the other (see also Chapter 3 of this volume). Truths are, by common-sense definition, non-relative, whereas errors, or impedances on truth-discovery, might be due to biases in the conceptual schemes of the scientist's language. Einstein's relativity theory, for example, while somewhat counter-intuitive for SAE speakers, nevertheless has 'a basis in . . . the fact that these languages use many space words and patterns for dealing with time' (Whorf, 1956: 266). But Whorf's ambivalence about science probably related also to the issue that prompted his interest in linguistics, which was the apparent clash between science, especially the theory of evolution, and his deep religious convictions. He supposed that a solution to that conflict 'might lie in a penetrating linguistic exegesis of the Old Testament. For this reason, in 1924 he turned his mind to the study of Hebrew' (Carroll, 1956: 7).

7. Whorf also drew attention to the systematic use of grammatical devices through which 'mass' nouns can be given 'individual' status. We combine them with count nouns as in 'stick of wood', 'lump of coal', 'piece of cloth', 'bar of soap', etc., or as bounded within countable containers, as in 'cup of tea', 'bag of flour', 'bottle of beer', and so on. Note that this kind of descriptive flexibility provides for *options in situated usage*, rather than suggesting mechanical effects of grammar on cognition.

8. It might be noted that Whorf's notion of objective linear time, demarcated into measurable units, is closer to his own training as an engineer than, say, to theoretical physics, or even to the phenomenology or ordinary discourse of time. In the latter, time is something that may pass faster or slower on occasions, that will 'tell', that we can run out of, or have none of, or lose, or take, or fall victim to, or be healed by, and so on. I come back to this observation later in the chapter.

9. The following information is from Microsoft's *Encarta 95* CD-ROM: 'Inuit, also called Eskimo: people of Arctic Mongoloid stock inhabiting small enclaves in the coastal areas of Greenland, Arctic North America, and extreme Northeastern Siberia. Their name for themselves is Inuit (in Siberian and some Alaskan speech, Yuit), meaning "the people." The name Eskimo comes from the descriptive term for "eaters of raw flesh", inaccurately applied to them by an Algonquinian people.'

10. This is reminiscent of Vygotsky's distinction, itself influenced by his reading of Sapir, between 'natural' psychological functions, biologically provided for, and their transformation into 'higher mental functions' derived from language and other forms of cultural–semiotic mediation (Vygotsky, 1934/1987; Wertsch, 1985).

11. For example: '[Language] categories . . . are, of course, derivative of experience at last analysis, but, *once abstracted from experience*, they are systematically elaborated in language and are not so much discovered in experience as imposed upon it because of the tyrannical hold that linguistic form has upon our orientation in the world' (Sapir, 1931/1964: 128, cited in Lucy, 1992: 20, emphasis added).

12. 'Morphemes' are the units of meaning from which word meanings are made. Thus, 'write' contains one morpheme, but 'writer' contains two (both the action and the actor). Similarly, 'dog' is one morpheme, while 'dogs' is two (dog + plural). Both 'walked' and 'ran' have two morphemes (action + past tense), despite the fact that the past tense of the irregular 'ran' is not realized by a phonetically separable suffix like in the '-ed' of 'walked'. Lenneberg argued that Whorf's practice of translating morpheme-by-morpheme *produces* weird distortions of meanings, and that we should translate things into colloquial, sensible-looking English.

13. This is not to say that such a principle has always been championed or accomplished in actual studies. Rather, it is identifiable as anthropology's deepest tension and most pervasively compromising goal (Geertz, 1973).

14. It is possible of course to argue, against the position I take in this book, for a hard-line referential theory of meaning, such that what people mean by 'colour' becomes what 'colour' objectively is, whether they understand it or not. So while folk of the fourteenth century have long stopped talking, science will continue to redefine what they meant. Fortunately none of the positions taken seriously in this book, including those of cognitive linguistics and experimental psychology, take such a view.

15. 'Munsell chip' refers to the set of several hundred colour chips, varying through precisely measured equidistant intervals, developed by the Munsell Color Company and used as objective referential criteria in the experiments by Brown, Lenneberg, Berlin and Kay, Rosch, and others.

16. I do not want to take issue with John Corner here, or attribute these remarks contentiously, because what I am concerned with is the thought–language issue lying behind that remark, rather than the main focus of Corner's own excellent analysis of how television documentaries work.

17. Understanding the reality behind appearances has been a basic theme in science and philosophy since Plato. It features in the classic cognitive developmental psychology of Jean Piaget and Jerome Bruner. See also Flavell, Flavell, and Green (1983), and studies of children's grasp of illusion and deception (Leslie, 1987, 1988). My concern here, however, is not with the notion that there actually is a reality behind appearances, nor that folk think there is, but, rather, with 'appearance–reality' distinctions as discourse practices, effective in supporting and countering knowledge claims based on appearances.

18. 'The significance of what is said depends on what is not said. . . . The fact that "excellent", "splendid", and the like are available and yet not employed serves to determine the significance of "that is a good painting"' (Ziff, 1960: 147, cited in Bilmes, 1986: 119; cf. Billig, 1987). The significance of close but not equivalent alternative meanings has been a major theme of semiotic analyses since Saussure (1922/1974) and Barthes (1964).

19. These studies deploy what is called 'critical linguistics' or, more recently, 'critical discourse analysis' (Fairclough, 1992). They analyse how various linguistic devices are used, especially in the mass media, to reify and reinforce established patterns of social power. The main differences between those studies and the approach I take in this book is that they draw on functional linguistics (Halliday, 1985) rather than conversation analysis for their ideas about language, and they install, as an explanatory backdrop for discourse phenomena, a mostly taken-for-granted approach to power and social reality. The term 'critical' invokes political critique, rather than academic, though its users would probably reject that distinction. One particularly relevant insight for the present discussion is a brief criticism of the SWH for its holistic, unitary view of language, as 'a homogeneous entity uniting a harmonious society' (Hodge and Kress, 1993: 14). For critical linguists, modern societies and their discourses are divided and conflictual, which is an important theme also greatly developed by feminist writers (e.g., Wilkinson and Kitzinger, 1995), and in rhetorical–ideological analysis (e.g., Billig, 1992, 1995).

9

Categories II: Bodily Experience and Folk Psychology

In cognitive psychology, categorization is a fundamental process. It converts sensory input into perceptions of objects and events, groups individual objects and events into recognizable types, and thus renders the world of experience intelligible and describable. 'Categories' include recognizable objects such as chairs, houses, and persons; units of language itself (words, phonemes, etc.); and complex cognitive representations such as abstract concepts and scripted event sequences (see Chapter 6). Categorization is basic sense-making. It is not restricted to language, nor even to human cognition, but is 'one of the most basic functions of all organisms' (Rosch et al., 1976: 382). Similarly, 'without any categorization an organism could not interact profitably with the infinitely distinguishable objects and events it experiences' (Mervis and Rosch, 1981: 94).

Categorization is therefore older than language, older than discourse, older even than *Homo sapiens*. This ultimately biological and perceptual notion of categorization, as something that pre-exists and shapes language, is retained in current cognitive theories of the nature and origins of linguistic categories (Gibbs, 1994; Lakoff, 1987). The concepts that are carried in the meanings of words, including their discursive uses and metaphorical meanings, are thought to derive from the nature of bodily experience. Further, the fact that bodily experience is rooted in activities in the real world, a world that exists beyond what anyone might want to say about it, guarantees effective, sensible linkages between language (or discourse), human experience, and the external world. We do not, and could not, get away with saying and thinking anything we like. So the scope for 'linguistic relativity' is severely constrained by human bodies, their actions, perceptual capacities, and experiences.

The links between language, mind, and world are conceived and investigated by cognitive psychologists as matters of individual psychological functioning. There are two features of this approach, familiar to us from earlier discussions in this book: perceptual-cognitivism, and the communication model. The world is apprehended through the actions and perceptions of individual organisms, and represented mentally (at least in higher mammals and humans) in the form of abstracted categories of information: 'concepts or conceptual categories . . . are mental representations of objects, entities or events stored in memory' (Roth, 1995: 19). The base model is the lone, sense-making perceiver, extracting sensory information, recognizing patterns, storing mental representations of things in the world, and (then) talking about them: 'without conceptual categories, it would be extremely difficult to communicate about objects such as chairs' (Roth, 1995: 20).

We have also noted that this eminently sensible-seeming approach to language, cognition, and reality is subject to critique.[1] There are three main strands of that critique:

1   One foundation of the perceptual-cognitive approach to categorization is the well-established rejection of linguistic relativity (the Sapir–Whorf hypothesis), and its replacement by perceptually derived categories of experience. The discussion in Chapters 7 and 8 of this book weakens that rejection (cf. Lucy, 1992).

2   Another line of critique was introduced in Chapters 2 and 3. The notions of a real world that possesses a definitive (uniquely describable) nature, and of a realm of perceptual experience that is prior to concepts and language, deploy in their very formulations a series of conceptual categories. Distinctions between reality and experience, and all the sub-sets of those distinctions, are themselves categories, produced in and for common-sense reasoning and human descriptive practices, including the academic disciplines of philosophy and psychology. They are, therefore, *anything but* pre-human, pre-conceptual, or pre-linguistic (cf. Edwards et al., 1995).

3   There is also the argument developed in Chapters 4, 5, and 6 concerning the action-performative nature of descriptions. This counters the presumptions that language is best, or neutrally, approached as mental representation, and as a convenient currency for communication between minds. The performative nature of descriptions is also the focus of discursive critiques of categorization theories in cognitive social psychology, which '[fail] to examine categorization as a social practice involving certain sorts of language use' (Potter and Wetherell, 1987: 120). Cognitivist categorization theories are themselves approaches that use categories and metaphors, picturing 'the thinker as obedient bureaucrat' (Billig, 1987: 137). As Michael Billig also remarks, 'there is much we do *not* share with all other organisms, such as disputation, gossip, and oratory' (1987: 123, emphasis added).

Natural categories

Eleanor Rosch's studies of the universal properties of colour categories, as we noted in Chapter 8, were subsequently extended to the study of 'natural categories' in general (Rosch, 1978). That extended work established what we might call psychology's current categories of categories. The notions of 'prototypes', 'typical features', 'fuzzy categories' and 'basic level categories' have been hugely influential in cognitive, developmental, and social psychology, and are now familiar items in standard textbooks.

'Basic level' categories are determined by principles of perception and action, coupled with 'cognitive economy'. *Chairs* and *tables* are basic level, while *furniture* is superordinate, and *dining chair* subordinate. Basic level categories are the ones that are used most frequently, and learned first and most readily, and which correspond to distinctive bodily actions: we sit in chairs, but we do not perform similar activities with all kinds of furniture (Rosch, 1978). Roger Brown, in an early and influential paper, similarly noted that 'flowers are marked by sniffing actions, but there are no actions that distinguish one species of flower from another' (1965: 318).[2] Basic level categories are thus 'human-sized. They depend not on objects themselves, independent of people, but on the way people interact with objects: the way they perceive them, image them, organize information about them, and behave toward them with their bodies' (Lakoff, 1987: 51).

'Prototypes' are defined as best examples. That is to say, they are mental abstractions of the essential properties of best examples. A more refined way of defining 'best' is 'most typical' (Rosch and Mervis, 1975). Given any natural category, whether basic level or not, people are able to judge that some instances or members of that category are more typical or central than others (see Roth, 1995, for an exceptionally clear treatment of experimental studies on this). For example, chairs and tables are more typical members of the superordinate category *furniture* than are table lamps and filing cabinets. Sparrows and robins are more typical members of the basic category *birds* than are chickens, ostriches and penguins. These intuitions are well supported by a large number and variety of empirical studies that use rating scales, free recall, recognition reaction times, developmental observations, and other methods.

Table 9.1 is a useful summary, provided by Ilona Roth (1995: 51), of three approaches to conceptual categories following Rosch's pioneering work. In each case, new 'instances' of category members (such as a 'chair' that we have not seen before) are recognized by comparing them to some kind of mental representation stored in memory. The differences between the three approaches are in what those stored representations are thought to be like (column 2). In addition to Rosch's 'prototype' and 'typical features' proposals is a third approach based on 'exemplars' (Barsalou, 1992; Smith and Medin, 1981). Exemplars are stored representations of actual instances of a category, rather than of their abstracted features. For example, the category 'chair', instead of being represented mentally by a list of its defining or typical features, will include specific instances such as 'the chair in my study', 'my dining chair', 'my dressing table chair', and so on. This approach has an obviously direct link to the world of experience, but risks losing what many theorists consider the major psychological function of categorization, which is the reduction of massive sensory variety to a much smaller, descriptively powerful set of general features.

Each approach solves a theoretical problem in specifying what exactly is

Table 9.1   *'Fuzzy concept approaches'*

Approach	Nature of representation	How an instance is categorized	Which empirical findings are explained	Theoretical problems
Original prototype	Composite abstraction based on most typical members	By measuring overall similarity of instance to category prototypes	Typicality ratings; typicality effects (e.g., speed of categorization); context effects	Nature of prototype not clear
Typical feature model	List of features abstracted from typical instances and weighted according to strength of association	By comparing features of instance with feature lists for categories and computing the sum of cue validities for the instance	Typicality ratings; typicality effects (e.g., speed of categorization); context effects	Feature lists do not represent relations between features or components of features
Exemplar model	Individual representations of exemplars the person has encountered	By comparing the instance to the multiple exemplar representations for different categories and assigning to the category those exemplars it most closely resembles	The 'limited' exemplar model explains: typicality ratings; typicality effects (e.g., speed of categorization); context effects	How are exemplars actually stored?

Source: Roth, 1995: 51

mentally stored, but immediately generates further problems of its own (Table 9.1, column 4). I shall not pursue those specific problems of mental representation here, because I consider them to be largely self-generated by the assumptions of the perceptual–cognitive metatheory which underlies all three models. They are generated by the notion that human concepts are, in the first place, a matter of abstracting information from perceptual experience, storing mental representations of it, and comparing new sensory input to those stored representations. It is the kind of perceptual–cognitive metatheory that underlies the colour studies reviewed in Chapter 8, and script theory (Chapter 6), and also causal attribution theory and studies of event memory (Edwards and Potter, 1992a, 1993), and it is susceptible to the same kind of critique and reformulation.

For example, the three approaches summarized in Table 9.1, while offered as models of pre-linguistic perceptual processing, are all circularly dependent on language. This becomes evident as soon as we ask, what is a prototype supposedly a prototype *of*? A typical *what*? An exemplar of *what*? The categories at issue (chairs, birds, furniture, triangles) are ones available in the experimenter's language, and just as we found in the 'colour' studies, in discussions of 'words for snow', and 'words for emotions', those *categories as such* are assumed to be *natural objects in the world*. In the 'exemplar' model for instance, what else is it, outside of what we call 'chairs', that defines all those objects *as* exemplars of something? Defining a new instance of the category 'chair' is the same thing as calling it one. We are trading in concepts, word meanings, right from the start. And once again, the English language takes on the status in cognitive methods of the natural world's natural language. There is a deep circularity in the perceptual–cognitive metatheory employed in cognitive studies of categorization, just as we found in the SWH-colour studies (Chapter 8). The perceptual processes that supposedly produce and define verbal categories are themselves dependent on those categories, in order to identify what should *count as an instance or exemplar*.

Of course there *is* another possibility that might take us beyond linguistic practices, which is to move theory in the same direction that the colour studies and the emotion studies eventually took: that the categories used in natural languages, and in English especially, reflect natural, pre-conceptual divisions *in the world*. That would imply that there actually are, objectively in the world, prior to description, perceptually available categories for the things we routinely distinguish in English. But this kind of semantic realism, while attractively economical for theorists, is contentious, especially when other languages use different categories and superordinates even for ordinary, mundane matters such as colours, animals, and emotions. Experimental studies on natural categories have routinely used English words ('furniture', 'dining chair', 'places of interest to visit', etc.) with scant concern for their status as linguistic items or situated, could-have-been-otherwise descriptions. It is also an unfortunate direction to take to assume that linguistic categories reflect objective reality, when the whole attraction of working with 'fuzzy categories' such as everyday words was that they did not have to have common features. It was partly the fact that everyday words and objects could *not* be defined in the 'classical categories' manner, exclusively and definitively, but were based instead on assemblies of 'family resemblances' (Lakoff, 1987; Rosch, 1975; via Wittgenstein, 1958), that prompted the drive towards studying 'natural categories'.

The problem I am pointing to here – that for psychologists themselves, verbal categories methodologically pre-exist perceptual studies of them – seems at first to be no problem at all, because of a subtle feature of experimental design and reporting. The use of a word to define the relevant instances or exemplars is done *off stage*, in methodology and theorizing, rather than treated as part of the empirical topic under investigation. How else might it be done? Two directions out of this quandary are possible. One direction is to make discourse practices a far more central topic of study, which is the direction I recommend. The second is some form of realism, in which once again the English language, and the construction of idealized, decontextualized examples and scenarios, stand in for the nature of the world. Psychologists have been (despite appearances) insufficiently interested in language, far too committed to explaining it as mental product and process, while using it as a transparent feature of method and theory. In particular, we have been blind to the language *we* use to define and discuss the very phenomena that are assumed to require psychological (and generally non-linguistic) explanations.

Some features of experimental studies of categories point to the neglected importance of discourse practices, even though that is not what they were designed to do. Lawrence Barsalou (1983, 1991) distinguishes between 'taxonomic' categories, which are basically nameable (birds, furniture, chairs, etc.), and 'goal-directed' categories, which are constructed 'ad hoc', as part of planned actions. Examples of the latter include 'things to take on a picnic', and 'places of interest to visit'. Most cognitive studies of categories have been studies of taxonomic ones, largely dependent, as I have argued, and as the term 'taxonomic' implies, on the presence of names for them in English. Barsalou's (1991) experimental studies suggest that 'typicality' judgments for ad hoc categories appeal to 'ideal' criteria. People select items for 'foods to eat on a slimming diet', not according to what slimmers mostly eat, but according to what they ideally ought to eat. In other words, these judgments are norm-oriented, rather than merely reflective of direct experience, and that is held to distinguish them from how 'taxonomic' categories are used and understood.

From a discourse perspective, the distinction between 'taxonomic' and 'ad hoc' categories seems a little forced. Given that the major examples of ad hoc categories are 'goal-directed' human activities such as going on picnics and visiting places (rather than, say, temporary categories for new observational phenomena in astronomy),[3] the role of ideals or norms is somewhat built in to the examples studied. Furthermore, even 'ad hoc' categorizations are constructed out of taxonomic items, such as 'picnic'. And taxonomic items themselves, *if considered in contexts of use*, will always be part of whatever actions such discourse performs, invoking all the norm-referenced accountability that pervades the analysis of discourse and conversation (see especially Chapters 4 to 7). Arguably, it is only because conceptual categories have been studied as decontextualized items, in psychological experiments and in linguistic theorizing, that their norm-relevant, action-oriented functions are not already among the basic findings reported for them.

Although discourse theorists have been critical of cognitive category theory (Billig, 1987; Potter and Wetherell, 1987), there are some attractions to it, especially its advances over 'classical' category theory (see Chapter 8) for modelling everyday thinking. Cognitive category theory could be said to meet discursive psychology half-way. Despite the treatment of categories in a decontextualized and idealized fashion, it portrays word meanings in a way that lends them to situated, rhetorical practices. It makes for opportunities to *define* things *as* more or less central exemplars, to construct and organize descriptions *so as* to centralize, marginalize, or mark as exceptional whatever is described. In other words, precisely because things and events do not automatically call for single, unique descriptions, 'typicality' can be imposed upon talk's topics via the choice of categorial descriptions; and category theory can be seen as articulating how words can be used, as conceptual resources, to typicalize the world. Unfortunately cognitive category *theory* faces in the opposite direction, away from discursive practices, and towards the biological foundations of individual experience.

In any case, discourse does not deploy verbal categories merely as ready-made resources. Centrality of membership is itself a participants' concern: that is to say, something that participants orient to in their talk, rather than just being an analyst's explanatory idea. It may be dealt with indexically, or as a matter of disputation, and this is true even for birds and chairs: 'If, in a pencil and paper test situation, I am asked to "name some typical birds", I may very likely mention robins and sparrows. . . . But neither is at all likely to come to mind when I am greeted at the door with: "I've just put the bird in the oven"' (Heritage, 1984a: 149). Similarly, and rhetorically: 'With imagination one could envisage a situation where the choice between terms such as "armchair" and "chair" might be keenly contested: this could be a situation involving law courts and allegations of broken contractual agreements between furniture manufacturers and wholesalers' (Billig, 1987: 136).

Another interesting feature of semantic categories, in addition to centrality of membership, is their sometimes *contrastive* organization. Categories are not merely sets of perceptual distinctions, but are often organized into contrasting pairs: black or white, male or female, good or bad, and so on. 'Categories are organized into systems with contrasting elements', such that the same speakers will draw upon 'two different and inconsistent understandings of one real-world situation' (Lakoff, 1987: 133). The linguist and semiotician Roman Jakobson considered this a fundamental feature not only of semantics but of language in general, and not only of language, but of human cognition. We naturally organize things into binary contrasts. As Howard Gardner remarks:

> On Jakobson's account, because human beings tend to perceive things in terms of polarities, many important distinctions in language also prove to be binary. Phonemes are constituted of distinctive features, with each distinctive feature either being present . . . or absent. . . . Other aspects of language, including grammar and meaning, can also be seen in terms of the presence or absence of various binary features. (1985: 236)

It may be that, for some items at least, there are *built-in* binary oppositions, like in phonology where the English sound category /b/ differs from /p/ by being 'voiced' rather than 'unvoiced'. Yet binary opposition is not a feature of perception generally, nor of language; it is not merely how human beings must see things.

In discourse, binary oppositions can be manufactured, and they lend themselves to rhetoric. Even when they *are* ready made, people do not have to select them. As we have noted, there is huge flexibility available in descriptive discourse. Harvey Sacks tentatively suggested that 'many of these classes are, or *can be built as*, two-set classes. Sex is a two-set class. Race can be formulated as a two-set class; for example, non-whites and whites. And there's a rich and poor, old and young, et cetera' (1989: 280, emphasis added). Sacks noted how this two-set organization lends itself to comparisons and contrasts, such that 'formulating in terms of two-class sets is a method of doing things' (1989: 280–1).

It is not just a matter of there being two classes of things, but two opposed or opposable classes of things. This establishes *contrast structures* as not only inherent in the semantics of a language, but also as usable and constructable for any topic. It is not simply a built-in feature of cognitive sense-making, nor a reflection of how the world itself happens to fall naturally into two-set classes. Rather, it is a powerful, general-purpose discursive device for constructing the world *as* such. That makes it ideally suited to ideological, dilemmatic, and rhetorical discourse (Billig et al., 1988), and to the mundane, situated production of contrasts and alternatives (Atkinson and Drew, 1979; Smith, 1978).

The term 'contrast structures' was coined by Dorothy Smith (1978; cf. Atkinson, 1984), in her celebrated article 'K is Mentally Ill' (see also Chapter 6). Smith noted how, in descriptions constructing K's behaviour as anomalous, 'a description of K's behaviour is preceded by a statement which supplies the instructions for how to see that behaviour anomalous' (1978: 39). Examples included:

1   When asked casually to help in a friend's garden, she went at it for hours, never stopping, barely looking up
2   She would take baths religiously every night and pin up her hair, but she would leave the bath dirty
3   When something had gone radically wrong, obviously her doing, she would blandly deny all knowledge

Examples 2 and 3 are what I have called 'script formulations'; example 1 is constructed as a one-off, but also provided as an *instance* of what K would generally do, one episode from a series of instances. The pathologizing work is done, in these cases, by presenting them contrastively against an implied norm.

Smith's examples show that the discursive practice of formulating things into contrasts and oppositions is not just a matter of deploying ready-made conceptual resources that are built into semantic categories, but something people can do flexibly and inventively, for just about any set of objects or events. It is not difficult to imagine K's gardening activities being described non-anomalously, or even contrastively as a sign of diligence and selfless-ness. The presence in languages of more conventional or even semantically ready-made contrast sets may be a function of the rhetorical uses of discourse. As I have argued with regard to 'emotion' and other examples, it may be that conceptual categories are designed in this way *for talk*, for performing talk's business.[4] That is starting to seem more likely than the invention, by socially marooned individuals, of classification systems whose prime purpose is to first code and sort their mental libraries of objects and events, and then talk about them.

Experiential realism: the Lakoff–Gibbs hypothesis

Rosch, unlike many psychologists who have taken up her ideas on the perceptual basis of conceptual categories, has been parsimonious in her interpretation of what 'prototypes' imply about cognition. She limits the notion to the status of an important empirical discovery (Rosch, 1978: 40–1), rather than claiming it as a direct model of mental representation. George Lakoff develops this further, arguing that 'prototype effects . . . are superficial phenomena which may have many sources' (1987: 56). Lakoff identifies the major sources as 'idealized cognitive models' (ICMs). ICMs are kinds of cognitive schemas[5] based upon bodily or perceptual experience, and its metaphorical extension to other things in the world.

Lakoff proposes that 'reason is made possible by the body' (1987: xv), a position he calls 'experiential realism' or 'experientialism'. The 'realism' element is the assumption that human categorizations are based upon, or metaphorical extensions of, bodily experience, which is in turn constrained by reality. Thus, as we saw in Chapter 7, metaphorical conceptions of *anger* are based upon the subjective experience of autonomic nervous system physiology, coupled with the operation of appropriate cognitive models to do with heat, containment, pressure, agitation, and so on. Likewise *mother* is a category that invokes a cluster of cognitive models, based upon the different conceptual domains of biological inheritance, genealogy, birth, nurturance, and marriage. Experiential realism is a position intermediate between 'metaphysical realism' (Lakoff, 1987: 260), in which reality is independent of human embodiment, and its opposite, the mental solipsism of 'total relativism'.[6]

In Lakoff's thesis, categorizations work via ICMs. These are generalized understandings (folk theories, or conceptual models) of how the world works, including how categories such as *anger* or *mother* are conceptually involved with other things and actions in the world, such as standard emotional scenarios (see Chapter 7), or kinds of kinship relations. But, underlying ICMs, the primary basis for conceptual understandings is *bodily experience*. This provides the grounding for a host of metaphorical analogies and extensions, which people use to conceptualize everything from emotions and human relationships, to abstract concepts and scientific theories. Raymond Gibbs (1994) extends Lakoff's work into a sustained and effective critique of the presumption in most of cognitive science that 'literal' representations of the world, in thought and language, are basic, while figurative, metaphorical, or poetic representations are distortions and secondary. On the contrary, 'much of what we normally see as literal thought or literal language is itself constituted by fundamental processes of figuration' (Gibbs, 1994: 20).

Gibbs takes as his topic 'how people naturally think in poetic ways to make sense of their ordinary experiences and how poetic thought gives rise to the language we employ to express our thoughts, feelings and experiences' (1994: 15). He avows 'a commitment to make my account of human language consistent with what is generally known about human cognition' (1994: 15). Although many of their arguments are directed at positions within the cognitive sciences, Lakoff and Gibbs remain committed to cognitive science. Thus, Gibbs endorses a 'conception of mind as being fundamentally constituted by various figurative processes that are *then linguistically communicated* by speakers/listeners and authors/readers in socially shared *environments*' (1994: 27, emphasis added). So thoughts are mentally conceived, and then transmitted, within communicative contexts that are merely 'shared environments'. Despite this being offered as a Wittgenstein-inspired radical alternative to conventional cognitive theories, because of its emphasis on metaphor, it nevertheless retains the major elements of a conventional cognitive psychology of thought and language – the primacy of mental representation, and the communication model of discourse.

Gibbs offers 'love as a nutrient' as a paradigm example for his ideas about how metaphors derive from experientially derived ICMs: 'conceptual metaphors arise when we try to understand difficult, complex, abstract, or less delineated concepts, such as love, in terms of familiar ideas, such as different kinds of nutrients' (1994: 6). Examples of 'love as a nutrient' include various poetic and everyday expressions: *I was given new strength by her love*; *I thrive on love*; *He's sustained by love*; *I'm starved for your affection*; *I taste a liquor never brewed* (Gibbs, 1994: 5–6; the last example is from a poem by Emily Dickinson). By applying the notion of nutrition to love, people are able to generate an indefinitely large variety of metaphorical expressions. But nutrition is not the only metaphor for love, as shown in other examples that Gibbs cites: *He was burning with love*; *I am crazy about her*; *We are one*; *The magic is gone*; *Don't ever let me go*; *She pursued him relentlessly* (1994: 5, citing Kovecses, 1986, and Lakoff and Johnson, 1980). The sheer variety of metaphors and models in everyday use shows that, at the very least, these are not fixed ways of thinking, nor evidence of a predictable pathway from experience, through cognition, to language. That is a feature that cognitive linguists such as Gibbs and Lakoff recognize but, I shall argue, undervalue.

Gibbs, Lakoff, and other cognitive linguists provide rich and extended analyses of metaphors and meanings based on cognitive models and bodily experience. They construct a formidable challenge to the common presumption that 'literal' mappings between language, mind, and world are psychologically the more basic. Indeed they criticize, as this book also does, the tradition in cognitive psychology and linguistics that proceeds according to the 'objectivist' assumption that 'reality comes with a preferred description'

(Gibbs, 1994: 4; cf. Lakoff, 1990).[7] Yet I would argue that an objectivist element is retained in these theories of metaphor, in the form of appeals to bodily experience (Lakoff's 'experiential realism'), and in the notion of how 'abstract' ideas are expressed by more concrete or 'familiar' analogies. My unease stems also from what the cognitive linguists *insert between* 'language' and 'reality', in order to loosen up the objectivist (or 'literal') relation that otherwise might hold between them. What they insert are not discursive practices, as I would do, but individual cognitive processes. I shall deal first with the residual objectivism in the Lakoff–Gibbs hypothesis,[8] and then consider the cognitivist rather than discursive basis of it.

Note how *nutrient* is assumed to be a simpler, less abstract, more 'familiar' notion than *love* (Gibbs, 1994: 6). Despite its initial plausibility, this assumption is dubious. 'Nutrition' is arguably a technical abstraction, a generalization about the biology of organisms and diets, no more familiar an idea for most people, I imagine, than 'love' itself. It seems more sensible to talk of experiencing love than nutrition. But perhaps this is nit-picking; 'nutrition' may be simply Gibbs's gloss on something pre-conceptual, like the experiences of eating and drinking and going hungry.[9] The theory states very clearly that 'metaphorical understanding is grounded in *nonmetaphorical preconceptual structures* that arise from everyday bodily experience' (Gibbs, 1994: 17, emphasis added). But eating, drinking, and going hungry (etc.) are, surely, subjectively different experiences. It is precisely the use of the superordinate category *nutrient* that enables Gibbs to group together all the various metaphors for love that he does (thriving, starving, giving strength, etc.), while excluding the others (burning, magic, holding, etc.) as not stemming from the 'same' experiential base. 'Nutrient' is Gibbs's own categorization, grouping together all the specific metaphors that he places under it.

In any case, it is not entirely clear that *nutrient* is the best superordinate term for the poetic line 'a liquor never brewed'. Are brewed drinks such as tea, or alcohol, *nutritious*? Do we (all) even *think* they are?[10] Gibbs's use of the term *nutrient* is reminiscent of the cognitive studies of *colour* and *emotion* (Chapters 7 and 8). It is the insertion, into the analysis of everyday meanings, of a technical, scientifically specifiable category, and therefore one that we are disposed to take as objectively (bodily, pre-conceptually) natural. The problem stems from the assumption that 'nutrition', or the properties of 'heated fluid in a container' (Lakoff's, 1987, metaphorical base for *anger*), and so on, are pre-conceptual, or experiential. Common-sense objects, processes, and experiences, *as labelled* by ordinary or technical words, are taken unreflectingly as tokens of a world prior to its description, and used as criteria even for studies and theories that claim to refute the presumption of literal meanings and objectivity. Studies of this kind appear alive to everybody else's conceptual metaphors but their own. They deploy the very conflation between descriptive categories and presumptions of non-linguistic reality that Whorf, long since abandoned in cognitive theory (Lakoff, 1987), tried to explore.

The perceptual–cognitive theory of categories depends on circular assumptions concerning what is 'conceptually more basic'. The analytic procedure is to identify a series of instances in which A is being used as a metaphor for B, and then devise some way in which A is more basic. That usually involves introducing a further, *superordinate* (rather than more primitive) category that possesses technical or scientific status (colour, emotion, nutrition, human physiology, 'semantic primitives'), which provides the possibility of anchoring the analysis of metaphor and meaning in something ostensibly objective and literal. My criticism of the Lakoff–Gibbs thesis is directed not at its specific metaphorical analyses, but at the presumption of cognitive metatheory. It does not take the analysis far enough. Lakoff and Gibbs fail to consider their own linguistic formulations of what they take to be 'pre-conceptual'.

The argument that cognitive linguists omit from consideration the role of language in constituting the categories of the non-linguistic, or pre-conceptual, brings metaphors closer to *all* descriptions. If there is no literal description, no one-to-one mapping between words and things, then *all* descriptions are, in a sense, metaphors. All verbal categories are devices for treating one thing as like another, in just the respect labelled.[11] Calling something a 'chair' is an action we perform on occasions that implies an object's co-membership with other things so-called. Cognitive theorists, in disputing the primacy of the literal or the metaphorical, lack an account of description per se. Cognitivism, through its most basic assumptions, incorporates a blind spot to the fundamentally *performative* nature of descriptions, to how the range of possible descriptions is a function of the work that can be done, on occasions of talking, by saying one thing rather than another.

Categories as performative descriptions

In focusing on our cognitive abilities to conceptualize, Lakoff, Gibbs, and other cognitive linguists have illuminated how metaphors and idioms are understandable and usable, and how they can be grouped into general and superordinate schemas. The limitations of their approach are the same as those that John Lucy (1992) has identified for cognitive tests of the Whorfian hypothesis: the 'psychologizing' move towards conceptual 'ability' rather than discursive practices, together with the treatment of discourse as secondary, an expression and reflection of thought (see Chapter 8). Thus, even 'our ability to speak and comprehend ironic *discourse* is a direct reflection of our ability to *see* situations ironically' (Gibbs, 1994: 22–3, emphasis added). This misses the active role of discourse, including irony, in constructing how things are 'seen'. It retains the 'communication model' of thought and language, in which pre-formed, perceptually based thoughts are expressed and transmitted.

The Lakoff–Gibbs hypothesis is directed not, for the most part, at naturally occurring discourse, but at 'what we all know' about it: 'American speakers often talk of love in the following ways . . .' (Gibbs, 1994: 5). In contrast, it is one of the basic themes of discourse and conversation analysis, of Harvey Sacks's (1992) empirical project, that presuming we know how people talk is analytically dangerous. It tends to produce circular confirmations and illustrations of analytic assumptions, and is no substitute for detailed empirical study of text and talk. That is not to imply that the various tropes and metaphors analysed by cognitive linguists do not occur; nor that analysis of empirical materials can itself proceed without some kind of conceptual or semantic analysis. Rather, it proposes that all such analyses are best done not *in vacuo*, but with regard to the indexical, performative business of talk-in-interaction.

Conceptual categories are pervasive in discourse. Inevitably, therefore, many of the examples and analyses offered in previous chapters are *already* studies of categories-in-use. In any stretch of discourse people recount events, categorize them, objectify them, explain them, narrate action sequences, script-formulate or particularize them, manage accountability, reject alternatives, orient to intersubjectivity, and so on, all more or less at the same time. Those are analytical topics, not discrete activities. Recall, for example, the use of the category 'military target' in Sacks's Navy pilot story (Chapter 1) and in contested descriptions of the bombing of Baghdad during the Gulf War (Edwards and Potter, 1992a, and below); the discussion of 'move', 'smack', 'hit', and 'shove' in Chapter 4 (Extract 4.2); Connie's and Jimmy's alternative categorial descriptions of events (Chapters 5 and 6); the formulation 'healthy and fit for work' (Linell and Jönsson, 1991) cited in Extract 5.5; the formulations of emotions, actions, and dispositions examined in Chapters 6 and 7; and the category 'dangerous' (versus 'frightening' etc.) in Chapter 8. These and other examples, while providing bases for discussions of how intersubjectivity is managed, of script formulations, the uses of emotion discourse, and so on, are also and simultaneously materials for a discursive study of categorization.

Sacks (1972b) provides a celebrated analysis of the normative background of a child's story which contained the sequence 'The baby cried. The mommy picked it up.' His discussion has much in common with Lakoff's notion of ICMs (idealized cognitive models); it involves how we make sense of the text in terms of the typical kinds of (scripted) things that mothers and babies are expected to do. But as we noted in Chapter 4, with regard to this example, it is not simply that talk realizes the structure of an underlying cognitive model. Rather, it *references* that structure in a way that allows the speaker to have something to say. Normatively shared assumptions about mothers and babies are also the backdrop to statements like 'I don't even want babies; I think they're horrible, smelly, dirty little things.' This is extracted from a young woman's talk studied by Elizabeth Barrett (1990: 260). It is part of a discussion that disagreed with a suggestion that mothers should stay at home to look after their children. It by no means refutes Lakoff's notion of ICMs. Indeed, the status of such models as 'idealized' allows them to operate normatively in just this way. But it is only by studying how such normative assumptions are oriented to in talk, in the adoption of rhetorical positions, that we can make sense of how particular categorizations are constructed on occasions, so that idealized cognitive models do not slip into becoming idealized models of cognition.

George Lakoff complains that:

> Possibly the most boring thing a linguistics professor has to suffer at the hands of eager undergraduates is the interminable discussion of the 22 (or however many) words for snow in Eskimo. This shows almost nothing about a conceptual system . . . When an entire culture is expert in a domain . . . they have a suitably large vocabulary. It's no surprise, and it's no big deal. It is no more surprising than that. . . . Americans have lots of names for cars. (1987: 308)

The essays may be boring but, as we noted in Chapter 8, the issue need not be. It may well be that examining the range of kinds of snow, or of American cars, for their perceptually distinct and behaviourally consequential characteristics would be a psychologically trivial exercise. But the various makes and marques of motor cars carry powerful semiotic significances, over and above perceptual distinctiveness and bodily use, and it is no great insight to suggest that it is precisely *for* such significances, for what it means to own and drive a Porsche, a safety-conscious Volvo, or the top of the range model within a fleet of company cars, that the different models are produced, badged, and marketed. For motor cars, the categories may well exist, in just the way they exist, and are named, and advertised, *so that* they can be socially deployed, such that it is only the fact of their perceptual distinctiveness which is trivial.

Sacks (1979) provides a brief but revealing study of some naming practices of American car users: specifically, a group of 1960s teenagers. He shows how the choice of terms like 'hotrod' and 'Pontiac station wagon' are opposed, and operate as alternative descriptions that indexically display social positions and identities, both for the objects and persons described and, through that, for the producers of those descriptions. Similarly, 'hotrodder' and 'teenager' are contrasted as adults' versus members' categories, applied to the same sets of persons, invented and used in order to make distinctions in the world, to define membership in ways that are relevant to the accountability of actions. They do not reflect distinctions that are already there. Category terms, for both objects and persons, are used in ways *designed* to perform social actions, not only in current talk, but in a historical sense, being invented precisely for such uses. It would not be possible to establish the existence of named objects, bodily actions, and significances in the physical world, or in behaviour, prior to the construction of such naming practices, since it is essentially through and for those practices that the categories are brought into existence. This does not deny that named objects had better be distinguishable, whether they are motor cars, varieties of 'snow', or regions of the colour spectrum.

One theme that has recurred in discursive studies of description and categorization (including several in this book) is interpersonal violence. For example, Kate Clark (1992) shows how descriptions in the *Sun* newspaper of acts of violence against women often manage to blame the victim. The category of rape, when contested by police questioning and in court, proves notoriously difficult to define clearly in terms of specific actions and intentions, themselves subject to alternative descriptive categorizations (Drew, 1990). Victims themselves may work to avoid the category: '. . . it's a fine line, isn't it, between saying yes, whether you want to or not, to somebody like that [sexually violent], that I didn't want to go to bed with. . . . He didn't rape me, because I more or less consented' (quoted by Nicola Gavey, 1992: 336). The now (in Britain) legally recognized category of 'marital rape' is also frequently avoided by its victims, by the use of alternative event descriptions (Russell, 1990). Margareta Hydén and Imelda McCarthy (1994) analyse husbands' and wives' contrasting accounts of 'wife battering', in terms of their orientation to accountability, and to disclaiming responsibility. As argued in Chapter 3, reality is approachable as what *counts as* reality, which is to say, whatever description of it may prevail – where 'prevailing' is also a matter of the discursive management of shared knowledge (see Chapter 5).

Let us look a little closer at one discursive study of interpersonal violence. Timothy Auburn, Sue Drake, and Carla Willig (1995) analysed audio-taped police interviews with people accused of interpersonal violence. Police officers were found to orient to the production of 'preferred versions' of criminal acts (cf. Linell and Jönsson, 1991, discussed in Chapter 5 of this volume), in which, typically under a presumption of guilt, a definitive account of events is pursued which 'constructs a person suspected of committing a crime as responsible for the actions and of intending to carry them out' (Auburn et al., 1995: 357). 'Suspects' typically resist those preferred versions, providing alternative (contrasting or mitigating) descriptions (1995: 361; cf. Drew, 1990). Auburn et al. use a 'discursive action model' of causal attributional reasoning (derived from Edwards and Potter, 1992a, 1993) to examine descriptions and accusations as discursive attributions.

In Extract 9.1 the suspect/interviewee ('I') is telling the police officer ('PO') of his involvement in a 'fight'. The interviewee has been accused of starting the fight by 'punching' another man on the head.

Extract 9.1

1	*I*:	'cos I was off dancing and I was just dancing around and I was
2		dancing with this girl and like I've just clipped this boy's head
3		(1.0) and as I as I've clipped him I've gone oh sorry mate
4	*PO*:	when you say you've clipped by accident d'you mean
5	*I*:	yeah well I'm not gonna hit someone on the head on purpose am I
6	*PO*:	Yeah
7	*I*:	and he's come across all like that and I've gone all right there's
8		no need to be like that and he pushed me so we just started fighting
9		and his mates got up and there was about four of them I think

(Auburn et al., 1995: 375)

As Auburn et al. (1995: 375) note, the interviewee's 'reformulation' of his action from 'punch' to 'clip', and the contrast between 'clip' and 'hit' (line 5), are part of the activity of disclaiming intentional responsibility, a highly significant inference for the business at hand that the police officer picks up, and the interviewee ratifies (lines 4–5). 'Clip' also downgrades the nature of the action and its effects to something more slight. The accidental nature of the 'clip', and its status as undeserving of the escalated fighting that followed, is built by a *narrative sequencing of descriptive categories* (including an apology, line 3). The interviewee was emphatically (repetitively) 'just dancing' when the event happened, and therefore not at all looking for trouble.[12] The category 'hit someone on the head' is script-formulated as an unlikely thing he (or, inferentially, anyone) is *gonna* do in the circumstances. Again, his own agency in the ensuing fight is downgraded not only to retaliation (after being 'pushed'), but to something he acted to avoid (lines 7–8), and to joint rather than individual action ('we just started fighting').

What we have here is a set of specific conceptual categories deployed in situated event descriptions. Note that they do not form the kind of idealized, neatly organized set that might be obtained by imagining, or eliciting out of context, lists of types of violence. It is a restricted and specific range of action descriptions (hit, push, fight, clip, dance), whose relations to each other are *narrative* (one action following another in a coherent event sequence) and/or *rhetorical* (one contrasted with another). Further, the contrasts are indexically specific and *locally* contrastive, rather than available in a dictionary of antonyms (dancing rather than fighting, clipping rather than hitting). They work with and against each other, in rhetorically oriented narratives, as locally relevant alternatives for the interactional issues at hand – the management of credibility and accountability, in the face of alternative versions of specific events. As we have seen, other sets of terms may be deployed in closely related kinds of activities and descriptions: for example, 'hit', 'shove', 'move her out of the way', 'smack', and 'smack her one' (Chapter 4, Extract 4.2), which were also occasioned by a 'when you say X you mean Y' kind of repair. In order to understand how *specifically these* sets of categories function as alternative descriptions for specifying the nature of events, we have had to examine them in use.[13]

This emphasis on the flexibility of conceptual alternatives in discourse is not an effort to deny conceptual order, nor the importance of wide-ranging metaphorical resources such as those identified by Lakoff and Gibbs. Rather, it is an attempt to locate and examine those resources in the empirical study of discourse. As I argued in Chapter 8, the analyst's task is to identify how such resources are ready-made enough for discourse to be intelligible for its users, but flexible enough for it to perform (with considerable invention or 'witcraft' – Billig, 1987) an unending variety of locally managed, indexically specified, situated actions. The danger for cognitive theorists is that of building conceptual models, on the basis of idealized meta-categories, that say nothing about how and why a specific way of saying something is chosen, and does something, on occasions – and thereby to miss, perhaps, an important basis for its existence (as a way of talking), and for the psychology of its production.

How do we deal with the sheer number and variety of metaphors, tropes, and devices? One way is to collect a quantity of them and consider them all together, as making up some kind of map of a conceptual terrain, and organize them into conceptual sets, as Gibbs, Johnson, Lakoff, and others have done. That is a useful thing to do, up to a point. But I am worried about the kinds of theorizing it leads to, and that lead to it. My worry is that the practice of collecting, inventing, and remembering sets of decontextualized exemplars reinforces a broader tendency to treat language in that way, as conceptual categories divorced from occasions of use.[14] It reinforces rather than resolves the problematics of cognitivism, those of mental representation and communication. It defines the issue of how people intelligibly converse as a matter of how they code experience and transmit messages between minds. I have argued throughout this book that that is not a good starting point for the psychology of situated discourse.

Experience and reality

Lakoff's 'experiential realism' is a cognitivist position that lies, as we have noted, somewhere between realism and relativism. Human knowledge is considered relative to the schematizing influence of bodily experience, but bodily experience itself is situated in a real world that exists beyond it, *in ways that can be neutrally described, by science, or by reference to mundane experience*. It is the latter, italicized bit that does the damage. We are dealing here with an issue close to the heart of cognitivist versus discursive approaches to language, mind, and reality, so I want to discuss it a little. In particular it makes relevant to the present discussion of categorization the earlier discussion in Chapter 3 of discourse and reality.

Lakoff recognizes that social and other 'human' categories may be constructive rather than reflective of reality, but draws a sharp distinction (cf. Collins, 1990) between mundane physical objects and human institutions:

> Trees and rocks may exist independently of the human mind. Governments do not. . . . An enormous number of the products of the human mind exist, but not in the way that trees and rocks exist. In the case of social and cultural reality, epistemology precedes metaphysics. . . . (Lakoff, 1987: 208)

Ignoring the psychological reduction of governments to 'products of the human mind', we can still ask, if trees and rocks exist outside of epistemology and discursive practices, do 'trees' and 'rocks' so exist? In other words, like we asked of snow, emotions, and colours in Chapter 8, do these things exist *as* 'trees' and 'rocks', thus categorized?

Social institutions, and the names we give them, are obviously *both* cultural inventions. With trees and rocks it is not so obvious. But physical objects are by no means immune from linguistic conceptualization. Distinctions such as animate and inanimate, plant and animal, are items of culture and vocabulary. Trees and rocks are parts of human cultures (Ayers Rock, American Redwoods, the English Oak, etc.), and the practices of naming them are not passively descriptive (Edwards et al., 1995). The physical things that we encounter and talk about are either artificial, like cars, houses, and furniture, or meaningfully incorporated into human designs, like tropical rainforest ecosystems or cloudy weather.[15] Jonathan Potter and I have discussed examples of descriptions of actions in the Gulf War (Edwards and Potter, 1992a). The selection of categorial descriptions such as 'civilian shelter' or 'military bunker' for a building in which several hundred Iraqi people were killed by aerial bombing displayed not merely a perceiver's best sense of events, but a speaker's rhetorically performative choice of terms. Even the terms 'building' and 'events' have rhetorical force. As Michael Billig notes, 'even a choice of ostentatiously neutral terms would indicate a position, for neutrality in the midst of conflict is every bit as much a position – and a controversial one at that – as is partisanship' (1987: 143).

Political discourse might be considered a soft test for a rhetorical approach to categorial descriptions. But studies of scientific texts, as we saw in Chapter 3, display those also as argumentative:

> When we approach the places where facts . . . are made, we get into the midst of controversies. The closer we are, the more controversial they become. When we go from 'daily life' to scientific activity, from the man in the street to the men in the laboratory, from politics to expert opinion, we do not go from noise to quiet, from passion to reason, from heat to cold. We go from controversies to fiercer controversies . . . *when debates are so exacerbated that they become scientific and technical*. (Latour, 1987: 30, emphasis added)

Philosophers from Plato to Kant have argued for a world of reality or 'substance' that lies behind or beyond the phenomena of sensory experiences. Sensory experiences can be considered the basis of all true knowledge, as the empiricists argued, or else they can be argumentatively worked up as a potential source of error, mere perception, the shadows of a more substantial world beyond appearances. Such philosophical positions are echoed in mundane talk,[16] where categories of perceptual experience may be deployed to construct an *effect* of objective reality independent of talk. Experientialism can operate as a rhetorical device: as a basis for intelligible, but disputable, *claims* about reality. A description's experiential grounding is a discursive accomplishment, and it is rhetorically potent.

Recall the discussion in Chapter 3 of Pollner's work on 'mundane reason', and Sacks, Jefferson, and Wooffitt on the 'At first I thought' device, together with the use of perceptually vivid descriptions and detailed 'I-witnessing' (Geertz, 1988) accounts and testimony. These were features of John Dean's testimony to the Watergate hearings (Edwards and Potter, 1992a, 1992b; Neisser, 1981); of Oliver North's testimony in the Irangate hearings (Lynch and Bogen, 1996); of political and journalistic disputations about consequential events (Edwards and Potter, 1992a, 1992b; Potter and Edwards, 1990); and they feature in reports of disputable events generally (Wooffitt, 1992). Their status is that of participants' resources for dealing with knowledge claims, not mere reflections of how people apprehend reality. Experiential realism makes a lot of sense as part of a theory of language, of how talk is intelligible and of how claims about reality are accomplished, but this does not establish it as any kind of discourse-free guarantee about the world.

The link between perception and reality is, in everyday talk as in philosophy, open to reversal. The 'At first I thought' device of mundane conversation plays upon this possibility. It is also a feature of accounts of both truth and error in science (Ashmore, 1993; Gilbert and Mulkay, 1984; Woolgar, 1988a), and a topic for explanations of children's cognitive development (Bruner, 1974; Flavell et al., 1983). In rhetoric, perceptual appearance can be discursively deployed both as a warrant and as a noticeable feature of things or events that figures as a preface to their denial. In conversation, people sometimes warrant accounts or pursue rhetorical aims by producing a distinction between superficial appearance and an underlying reality which represents the true situation, or a preferred version. 'Appearance' will often be couched as a perceptual metacognition: what things look, sound, or seem like. The appearance–reality distinction is rhetorically effective in that it recognizes the obviousness of appearances, and so acknowledges the basis for one's own or the other person's (defective) understanding. At the same time, it subverts that impression, in favour of a purportedly more insightful and adequate analysis (cf. Eglin, 1979; Potter, 1987, 1988). Like experiential realism, which trades off the link between perception and reality, the contrary *distinction* between appearance and reality functions in ordinary talk as a rhetorical resource for claims and counter-claims.

In discourse, therefore, people deploy what we might call *referential* experientialism, which means that bodily experience offers a basis for a set of images, metaphors, and other devices by which things are described. This is what Lakoff provides in his summary of work such as Claudia Brugman's (1983) on body imagery in the semantics of Chalcatongo Mixtec, a language of Western Mexico (Lakoff, 1987: 313), and in most of his analyses of metaphors in English. We should distinguish this from *epistemological* experientialism, which is a philosophical and psychological theory of knowledge, of what we know and how we know it. It is this second sense of experientialism that is problematical – experientialism as a philosophical position adopted by the analyst, rather than a participants' discursive practice. Evidence for the practices of referential experientialism, which is abundant as Lakoff shows, demonstrates something about the basis on which claims to knowledge are made, sustained, and defended. It does not constitute a general case for realism; not unless we go outside of descriptive practices and disputations, and are willing to settle the matter of reality over the heads of participants. This is exactly what Lakoff does, by appealing to science.

Lakoff recognizes that science is a human practice in which bodily experience plays a shaping role, as for example in the case of Linnaeus and the taxonomy of plants, where the defining taxonomic characteristics of plants are shown to be closely referenced to what could be seen and done with them (Lakoff, 1987: 35). But what happens when scientists disagree? Lakoff's position allows no legitimate room for debate, only for difference and error. When people disagree or offer inconsistent versions of the world they are simply applying different cognitive models. Argument, despite the fact that Lakoff's entire text is couched as one, appears to be a residual, unnecessary, and futile pursuit. Lakoff's realism can be sustained only by appeal to some criterion that is capable of transcending the experiential and metaphorical domain of folk understandings: science itself. But in order to serve such a purpose, scientific argument has to be quietened and reduced to cognitive difference, made 'cold' (Latour, 1987).

In a demonstration of the explanatory value of ICMs, Lakoff discusses 'the heated disputes between two groups of biologists, the cladists and the pheneticists' (1987: 119), as portrayed by Stephen Jay Gould (1983). Despite Gould's efforts to sustain the dispute, Lakoff prefers the notion that the opposing camps merely possess conflicting taxonomic models 'that reflect different aspects of reality' (Lakoff, 1987: 121), implying that there is no genuine basis for disputation. Unfortunately the biologists, including Gould, want to continue arguing, and this is for a good reason. It is that the very 'reality' which Lakoff wants to say they each partially perceive is precisely what is under dispute. Biological reality, as in all science, is the outcome not the precedent of disputation (Woolgar, 1988a; Yearley, 1986), and cannot be appealed to, over the heads of the biologists, as a criterion for ending their debate. As with the notion of experiential realism, there is a great difference between showing how models of reality operate and accepting their veridicality.

Similarly, and with considerable rhetorical flair, Lakoff uses scientific findings as a basis for dismissing classical category theory. He claims that this theory fails to capture not only the nature of human categorization processes, but also the nature of 'categories in the world' (1987: 371). The latter turn out to be what science tells us exists: 'the only kind of evidence that has a bearing on the question of what exists *external to human beings* is scientific evidence' (1987: 185, emphasis added). Again, Lakoff recruits the fact that the cladists and the pheneticists disagree about how to classify species (according to evolutionary descent versus similarity), such that each will occasionally place particular species into different taxonomic categories. Since each side is considered to have captured a different aspect of reality, this shows that there are no singular and objective, once and for all, natural kinds of animals. While we might want to agree with the conclusion, we do not have to agree with the reasoning. It depends upon a notion of science as revealing the nature of the world, which conflicts with a notion of science, also used by Lakoff, as an experientially oriented human practice.

However, we now have two contrasting models of science, to go with the two models for the taxonomy of species. We may ask, do these models of science also reflect different aspects of reality, of what *science* is really like? Whether or not they do, it is again instructive to look at how they are rhetorically organized, how they are contrasted and related, and how they are occasioned and deployed (cf. Gilbert and Mulkay, 1984). They feature in Lakoff's text as rhetorically organized positions, constructed in debate rather than just happening to find themselves at odds with each other. Lakoff develops both versions of science and deploys them rhetorically, using the experientialist, multiple-perspectives version to object to objectivism, and the realist version to object to classical category theory.

Categories and folk psychology

Approaches to categories and categorization are closely linked to notions of cultural knowledge. Cultural knowledge includes what are called 'folk theories' (or 'lay theories' – Furnham, 1988), 'cultural models' (D'Andrade and Strauss, 1992; Holland and Quinn, 1987), and 'folk psychology' (Stich, 1983). These are defined in psychology, philosophy, and anthropology as the ways in which ordinary people categorize and understand things and events, including human actions and mental experiences. Just as any culture may possess a folk botany, and a folk zoology, there are folk psychologies (Heelas and Lock, 1981). Folk psychology, like other domains of folk theory, is generally conceived cognitively as people's *mental models and representations* of human life: 'a cultural model is a cognitive schema that is intersubjectively shared by a social group' (D'Andrade, 1990: 99). Given that professional psychology is aimed at producing its own, scientific, *non*-common-sense models of mental life, 'folk psychology' is often depicted as some kind of primitive and flawed precursor to it (Greenwood, 1991). Just as Berlin and Kay (1969) did with colour terms, studies of folk categories typically measure their relativity against what science tells us are the botanical, zoological, psychological (etc.) facts of the matter.

Much discussion of 'folk theories' proceeds on the basis that analysts already know (from their own common sense) what these are, and can summarize them and define their properties. This takes the form of putting folk understandings into words, or narratives, and then explicating those narratives. Rather than reiterating my reservations about the danger of conceptual circularity in that kind of analytic practice, I shall focus here on empirical studies. Roy D'Andrade (1990: 94) describes a 'frame elicitation technique' for eliciting cultural belief statements about illness (cf. D'Andrade, Quinn, Nerlove, and Romney, 1972). Statements about illness are obtained from informants, and from these statements 'frames' are constructed with blank slots for illnesses, such as 'It is safer to have ____ as a child and get it over with'. A variety of common diseases are then inserted into a series of such frames, and people are asked to rate the statements as true or false. 'The modal response was then taken as culturally representative' (D'Andrade, 1990: 94).

So folk knowledge is constituted by method, rather like attitude scales constitute the nature of attitudes (Potter and Wetherell, 1987), systematically decontextualizing statements from occasions, constructing statements that nobody has said in any circumstances at all, and removing variability by the use of statistical procedures. Although there is no doubt that such studies tell us something about how people think, it is by no means clear how such findings bear upon how ordinary people talk about illness (for a rhetorically oriented contrast, see Alan Radley's contribution to Billig et al., 1988, Chapter 6; and Harré, 1991). Indeed, important features of common-sense understanding are systematically obscured, such that we are left with nothing but abstracted cognitive sense-making to explain the data – in other words, with the assumptions about language and cognition that the methods presupposed.

Quinn and Holland (1987) argue for a greater use of natural discourse in empirical research. However, their approach is directly allied to Lakoff's and D'Andrade's schema theories of categorization, and uses discourse more or less as a treasure trove of cognitions. Transcripts are trawled for statements and descriptive terms which are extracted, coded, and systematized into sets of metaphorical schemas. For example, Quinn (1987) uses a technique which reformulates the content of transcribed discourse according to the cognitive model assumed to underlie it, thus rendering the talk more coherent and logical than it first appeared to be (that is, to a cognitivist analyst/reader; cf. Hutchins, 1980).

D'Andrade notes that studies of cultural belief systems, such as myths, 'fail to make clear exactly what individual natives really believe' (1990: 108), and recommends psychological methods such as those used by Shweder and Bourne (1984). The latter is a study of cross-cultural differences in concepts of the person. Descriptions of close acquaintances were elicited from informants, and broken down into a set of more than 3,000 subject–predicate–object phrases. These were then coded for their conceptual content, and compared across cultures. Although the results are interesting and revealing about cultural differences, their status as studies of 'what people think' is limited. What these kinds of studies provide is information about the kinds of linguistic and explanatory resources that people may use in talk. As far as explicating ordinary talk and social practices, and even situated cognition, is concerned, they once again conflate theory and method, and obstruct any analysis of the flexibility of personality and attributional discourse (Edwards and Potter, 1992a, 1993; Shotter and Gergen, 1989). The consistency and cognitive basis of categories are not *discoveries* of studies of that kind, but, rather, assumptions that are built into method.

D'Andrade notes that 'one of the persistent problems in cognitive

anthropology is individual variability . . . when human groups are systematically surveyed, there is considerable disagreement about most items. . . .
One way to avoid this problem is to treat the most frequently held items – the
modal items – as if they were *the* culture of the group' (1990: 118, original
emphasis). The worry that this might result in a statistical artefact possessing
little psychological reality is assuaged by an assurance that 'persons who are
more likely to give modal responses on a task are more likely to be reliable,
that is, to give the same responses if the task is presented at a later time. . . .
[And] are more likely to give responses that are consistent with each other'
(1990: 119). So different measures of consistency are taken as warrants for
each other.

Unfortunately, it turns out that the consistent informants are also those
who are 'better educated . . . judged more intelligent . . . and tend to have
more experience in that task domain' (1990: 120). D'Andrade ignores the
circularity of such task-related judgments of intelligence, and also the
possibility that these 'informants' are precisely those who are more
sophisticated when it comes to figuring out what sorts of answers the
questioner wants. Rather, it is simply concluded that 'those who give the
more modal responses display the behavioral characteristics of an expert'
(1990: 121), so that all the rich variation in the data, all those *other voices*,
can be discarded in favour of a selected set of 'representative' and consistent
responses. Again the abstracted, consistent, and discursively disembedded
nature of conceptual knowledge is the product of assumptions and methods
that prevent it from looking any different.

Discursive psychology suggests that variability, both across and within
individual participants' conceptualizations and versions of things, is best
examined as a *key phenomenon* rather than removed by statistical procedures that result in a single, consistent, 'modal response'. In order to
understand variability we have to look at the pragmatics of situational usage.
And doing that brings us into conflict with any idea that categorization, as
something people do, can be handled by appeal to categories as merely
reflecting speakers' understandings. The study of situated descriptions leads
us directly into examining categorizations in terms of the rhetoric they
accomplish. The same white New Zealanders could say of Maoris that
'they're proud' and 'they've lost their pride and dignity', describe them as a
'lazy race' and 'such hard working people', possessing a 'lack of greed' and
being 'quite selfish and greedy' (Potter and Wetherell, 1987: 124–5). It is
only by replacing such categorizations within their specific discursive
settings that orderliness returns; and the order is that of discursive action,
rather than perceptual sense-making. Again, it is not that there is no order of
a cognitive sort. If words did not carry categorial implications, if we did not
know what *greedy* means, they would be unable to serve rhetorical
purposes. The argument is that it is only through examining the pragmatics
of situated talk that we can discover what those categorial implications are,
their scope and flexibility, and the principles of their deployment.

According to the Lakoff–Gibbs hypothesis, experiential ICMs operate not as direct representations of actual things or events, but as idealizations of them, defining what is prototypical, exceptional, or expected. In this regard ICMs are allied with folk theories (Lakoff, 1987: 118). One of the problems for ICMs and folk theories is that, since they are abstracted and idealized, it is not clear how *actual* objects and events are apprehended. In fact, ICMs are sources of error. Idealized models 'may or may not fit the world well', may 'conflict . . . with some piece of knowledge that we have' (1987: 130–4), and will not precisely 'fit the actual worlds of the objects being categorized' (D'Andrade, 1990: 93). So there appears to be another kind of knowledge at work, by which an actual and real world, which the ICMs and folk theories do not fit, is known, and according to which the degree of fit is calibrated. But if cognitive models are not themselves how we do it, how exactly do we know what the world is like? Lakoff suggests that we need 'two cognitive models . . . one needs the concept of "fitting" one's ICMs to one's understanding of a given situation and keeping track of the respects in which the fit is imperfect' (1987: 71).

But if we adopt an individualist, perception-and-action notion of cognition, one has to wonder, if this second form of cognition is available, which grasps and keeps track of the world in finer detail and serves as the measure of ICMs, why we need ICMs at all. It seems of little value to have devices that simplify and codify reality when they can only be applied in company with a process that still has to perform all that specific reality-apprehending work anyway.[17] It is reasonable to suggest, therefore, that verbal categorizations are designed for the social actions of talking, describing, taking positions, and so on. In discursive psychology there can be no process of 'reality checking' that is independent of descriptions, except as a rhetorical device in itself, deployed both in science and in ordinary talk, for 'externalizing' descriptions *as* mere reflections of reality (Woolgar, 1980).

Lakoff's second kind of cognition is a device that inserts reality back into mind, deployed to maintain the doctrine of 'basic realism', with reality playing a crucial but back-stage role as criterion for the very knowledge structures that are otherwise supposed to apprehend it. It seems to rest on the possibility of direct, unmediated bodily experience – 'real experiences in a very real world with very real bodies' (Lakoff, 1987: 206). So it joins in the discursive glide between *noumena* and *phenomena*, between apprehensions and reality.

Another device for escaping the cognitive conundrum of reality and its apprehension is, as we have seen, to appeal to *science* not only as revealing the real nature of cognitions (cognitive science), but also as criterion and supplanter of folk theories of the world (physics, biology, etc.: cf. the contrast between 'folk taxonomies' and 'true scientific taxonomies' – D'Andrade, 1990: 87). But this assumes a relationship between science and the world that transcends human sense-making and discursive practices, and a relationship between discourse and knowledge such that when people produce versions of the world, these are primitive efforts at what scientists are supposed to be doing when they produce generalized explanations

(Churchland, 1988; Stich, 1983). These assumptions are probably false, both about science and about folk explanations, in that they ignore the contextualized, constructive, and rhetorical dimensions in how *all* versions of the world are produced.

Proverbs, idioms, and stating the obvious

Proverbs and idioms are often treated, in psychology, philosophy, and the social sciences, as distillations of some kind of generalized folk wisdom, expressions of an underlying folk theory of life and the universe. In a lecture on proverbs Harvey Sacks (1989: 366) cites various psychologists on how the notoriously *contradictory* nature of proverbs is evidence of cognitive 'confusion'. We advise each other to look before we leap, although he who hesitates is lost, and we should strike whilst the iron is hot; many hands make light work, although, of course, too many cooks spoil the broth. Sacks notes that it is 'a very usual use of proverbs amongst academics' to employ them as evidence of the inadequacy of everyday thinking, in preference to a proper psychological or anthropological study of thinking: 'to refer to them as "propositions" and to suppose that it then goes without saying that the corpus of proverbs is subjectable to the same kind of treatment as, for example, is scientific knowledge' (1989: 366). In contrast to treating such proverbial statements as decontextualized folk efforts at generalized theories, Sacks argues for, and makes a start on, 'considering proverbs in terms of their situations of use' (1989: 367).

Sacks identifies the kinds of commonly held assumptions about marriage, divorce, suicide, death, and so on, that he is talking of as 'lay theories'. But he contrasts these very interestingly with scientific theories, or, rather, with 'our prototype of a scientific theory' (1989: 269), and it is not the kind of contrast that we find in cognitive science, where lay theories are seen as merely poor versions of scientific theories.

> If you consider our prototype of a scientific theory, then, if some object doesn't conform to what the theory proposes about the object, then the theory has to be revised. This world [of lay theories] has been constructed in a rather more exquisite way. What goes on is the following. A large class of lay theories are properly called 'programmatic theories.' If they don't describe your circumstances then it's up to you to change. And if they don't provide for you as a Member, then it's up to you to rid yourself of being a Member, for example to kill yourself. In that way you keep the theories going as descriptive. (1989: 289)[18]

In other words, lay theories are produced for their relevance to particular actions, and their relevance is normative ('programmatic') rather than objectively descriptive (see previous chapters of this volume, especially 1, 3, 4, and 6). Common sense looks like bad theory only because it is not theory at all. Its contradictions and inconsistencies are its virtues, not its faults, because vagueness and inconsistency are precisely what are required for flexible application to, and in, situations of use,[19] where the rhetoric of alternative descriptions, rather than singular word–world truth correspondences, are the stuff of discourse.

In Sacks's work (cf. Drew and Holt, 1988), proverbial formulations are also interactionally occasioned productions with regard to locally relevant topics, including talk itself. They are implicative about what should be done, rather than being hypotheses about the world in general, to be altered by how events turn out.[20] Proverbs are stable linguistic formulae, but indexically flexible in use. The analyst's task is to examine how such formulations *work* (cf. the more ad hoc kinds of generalizations done in 'script formulations' – Chapter 6), not to agree or disagree with them. Like conversation analysts, we discursive and rhetorical psychologists (for example, Billig, 1987) avoid finding ourselves in the position of wondering whether, in general, too many cooks actually do, in fact, spoil the broth; and we avoid finding people stupid for saying so.

Proverbial formulae such as 'seeing is believing', and 'the proof of the pudding is in the eating' make available ways of saying, on relevant occasions, that proper knowledge derives from direct perception and experience. They are useful, say, as cautions against overblown expectations and first impressions. Alternatively, and for argument's sake, and specifically with relevance to some actual, local issue, we can say things like 'beauty is in the eye of the beholder', or 'they can't see the wood for the trees', which are ways of saying that direct perception and experience need *not* deliver accurate knowledge. It makes little sense for analysts to point out that a producer of any such expression has, on some other occasion, said the opposite. That is what these things are for, to enable us to say one thing or another on occasions, *for* occasions, while endowing our judgments with the status of folk wisdom. That is the kind of rhetorical use we can make of common-sense idioms, conventional metaphors, and proverbs. They are, in the first instance, ways of talking.[21]

Proverbs and idioms, in use, share features with less pre-formulated items such as script formulations, tautologies, and various ways of 'stating the obvious'. These pick up the theme of Chapter 5, on the status of 'shared knowledge' as a participants' concern, and provide a link from that discussion to this, on folk wisdom. Folk wisdom, folk theories, common sense, proverbs, and idioms are all categories of shared knowledge, and they are all available for various degrees of flexible formulation and situated use. Sacks (1989: 277) notes how tautological statements such as 'boys will be boys', while appearing on logical grounds to be saying nothing, are useful, along with other ways of 'stating the obvious', in invoking the idea that *category definitive features can be applied*. They are ways we can 'flip in and provide that in the last analysis he's like the others' (1989: 277). And it is not only that those category definitive features already exist mentally, or in the world, ready to be applied. Context can be relied on to fill in what the relevant features are. So category work can be done inversely, by treating a topic as one that this device can be applied to. For example, the content and issue that are the context for an utterance such as 'women will be women' will specify just what 'womanly' features are being adduced as definitive. The rhetorical force of this device is that it appears to be invoking self-evident, undeniable, obvious knowledge, while at the same time accomplishing things as so, and doing some potentially objectionable local business in a manner that makes denial difficult. Category features and membership are thus contextually constructed in talk, as we have noted, and not just invoked from ready-made resources.

Here is an empirical example of 'stating the obvious', taken from an *Observer* newspaper front page report (20 October 1991) on a forthcoming USA-sponsored Arab–Israeli peace conference in Madrid. Senator James Baker was reported to be tentative about the conference's possible success: 'He said: "I prefer not to put odds on this or give percentages at this stage. . . . *We are dealing with the Middle East*"' (omission in original; emphasis added, and the quote and topic finish there). Note that: (1) it voices a bit of obvious common sense, like tautologies, idioms, and proverbs do. Nobody needed *informing* that they were dealing with the Middle East. (2) It serves to invoke ready-made categorial knowledge about the Middle East. (3) Its implications, about the nature of the Middle East, are in fact not simply 'given', but are partially constructed by this context, that political negotiation outcomes and Arab–Israeli politics are notoriously unpredictable, or predictably volatile, or whatever. The same statement ('We are dealing with the Middle East') might have very different implications if defending a company's record on exports, or attacking a Western government's record on arms shipments. (4) Its rhetorical force is to *claim* for one's own particular, current argument the status of common knowledge, and thus render it hard to deny. These kinds of generalized devices make it difficult to refute the more specific positions they are used to protect. (5) Statements of this kind, possessing a robustly undeniable design, far from being beyond argument, are themselves constructed (in their indexicality for an actual topic) and rhetorically deployed (in an argument).

Conclusions: concepts and their uses

The Lakoff–Gibbs hypothesis rejects the assumption that literal meanings are primary, and precede and underlie metaphorical ones. Nevertheless it trades on that very presumption, in the form of 'experiential realism', a kind of phenomenological bedrock driven by perception and physiology that provides an interpretative anchor for the words we use, and enables us to understand each other. Without that literal bedrock, metaphors might drift and fall, like kinds of snow, or castles in the air, without limit – total 'anything goes' relativism. That seems a horrendous prospect, to be avoided at all costs, in that it seems to make communication impossible. How could we ever understand each other, if it were not that the words we use rest upon shared experiences?[22] I have argued that such a prospect looks very different when viewed as a *practical* matter for discourse users (see also Chapters 4 and 5), rather than a theoretical problem engendered by a representation-and-communication approach to language and thought. The horrors arise only on the assumption that meanings are made in minds, and have to be safely transmitted, like letters through the post, in case they get lost.

The argument from body to language is just as circular as Whorf's efforts were at demonstrating the SWH by doing translations (see Chapter 8). Brute experience has to be categorized, put into words, in order to argue that it is pre-categorized or pre-representational. So experiential realism falls, ironically, into *Whorf's dilemma*, translation. What is pre-conceptual about 'heat', 'pressure', or 'nutrition'? We might recall here SSK's processes of *splitting* and *inversion* (Latour and Woolgar, 1986; see Chapter 3 of this volume), in which a phenomenon, once labelled and constructed as such, is placed prior to its description as a feature of the world. The reflexive danger is precisely Whorf's topic, dilemma, and bane. How do we describe without describing, or translate without translating? The solution is not to seek safety in experiential bedrock, but to abandon cognitivist metatheory as a worn out metaphor for thought and talk, and adopt an alternative, which is the study of talk-as-action. We have to avoid answering the question as posed, in terms of divisions and relations between language, thought, and reality. Those merely force us into the absurdity of constructing linguistic categories of the non-linguistic – into doing what we ought to be studying. We have to stop underestimating what language does, and study how it works, in discourse, where most of the time what it does is precisely to define what lies beyond it, the nature of the world and of human experience.

Insofar as the Lakoff–Gibbs hypothesis deals with the semantic content of categories, rather than with the actions performed in situated discourse, it is tempting to put those two approaches together, in a kind of division of labour. While the discursive approach says little about how words come to have systematic semantic properties, the cognitive approach fails to explicate how actual categorizations, things that are said, function as actions fitted for their occasions. Thus, Lakoff might be seen as explicating the nature and origins of the linguistic resources from which people construct discourse. However, things are not quite so easy. The discursive approach requires categories to be flexible, not merely in the sense of containing non-central members and having fuzzy boundaries, but in the sense of taking meaning indexically, and in indefinitely many specific ways, from contexts of use: 'the building blocks of our many versions of the social world . . . have to be moulded in discourse for use in different accounts' (Potter and Wetherell, 1987: 137; cf. Heritage, 1984a). We need to explore the *relationship* between 'resources' and situated talk, and, indeed, this is the major point at issue. It is a matter of how the burden of explanation is to be shared.

Important features of categorization, such as prototype structures, indefiniteness of membership, indexicality of application, and contrastive organization, can be viewed as features designed for the business performed by discourse, rather than for displaying a person's abstracted understanding of the world. Take, for example, the flexible, constructible, rhetorically oriented nature of contrasts and oppositions. There are examples in this and other chapters: Harvey Sacks on how we often organize items into contrasting pairs, such as cars and hotrods, Bonnevilles and Pontiac station wagons; contrasts not only between dangerous and safe, but between dangerous and frightening (which are not ready-made opposites); 'boiling' metaphors for anger, versus animal metaphors;[23] contrasts between shoving and hitting, fighting and dancing; and so on. These contrasts are constructible and applicable for specific instances, just as scriptedness is constructible for specific actions and events.

Cognitive theories, while providing important insights into semantic organization, manage to sustain the explanatory primacy of perception and cognition only through the use of methods that systematically remove from view the flexibility and action orientation of discourse. Only by studying discourse, rather than imagined scenarios, and tropes *in vacuo*, can the range, specificity, and flexibility of idioms and metaphors be understood. Why do we have so many tropes if they all seem to derive from the same 'few' basic conceptual roots? Why multiply them so much, why so many, why so inconsistent, overlapping, and contradictory, if they don't really add to how things are conceptually 'understood'? The reason is that they are required (like all words are) for doing specific, different, contrasting, and nuanced work in discourse.

Consider, as an example of a binary opposition, a specific instance of a gender category in use. Gender categories lend themselves to binary contrasts, even though there are a very large range of gender descriptions available. So they are partly ready-made, but still constructible (not only as binaries of course), and selectable for use on occasions. Sacks provides some data from a group therapy session with teenagers. Dan is the therapist.

Extract 9.2
1	*Ken*:	So did Louise call or anything this morning?
2	*Dan*:	Why, didju expect her t'call?
3	*Ken*:	No, I was just kinda hoping that she might be able to figure out
4		some way t-to come to the meetings and still be able t'work.
5		C'z she did seem like she d-wanted to come back, but uh she
6		didn't think she could.
7	*Dan*:	D'you miss her?
8	*Ken*:	Well in some ways yes, it's- it was uh nice having- having the
9		opposite sex in-in the room, you know, havin' a chick in here.

(Sacks, 1992, vol. 1: 597)

Sacks focuses on Ken's switch from a named individual ('Louise') to a generalized gender category (lines 8–9, 'the opposite sex . . . a chick') to account for his concern for her absence. This effectively forestalls any inference that his concern might have been personal: 'he wasn't going to say he likes her or anything like that' (1992, vol. 1: 60). The gender categorizations work on the basis that Louise, as the only girl in the group, is uniquely, if impersonally, identifiable by gender,[24] and that gender is picked out by Ken as the *relevant thing about her*. Further, Sacks examines how it functions as a 'safe compliment' categorization, in that it attends to the possible perceptions of other group members, who are all male. He imagines how something like 'it was nice having someone smart in the room' might invoke unfavourable implications for the rest of the group, smartness being one of 'a whole range of categories which also *can* apply to any other person in the room' (1992, vol. 1: 60, original emphasis). The interaction-orientation of a specific contrastive category manages, in this case, a subtle kind of motivational accountability.

So categories are not just available sense-making devices that get triggered by events; that kind of theory grossly under-specifies situated talk. People have considerable flexibility in their choice and deployment of words. Particular choices of words perform subtle interactional work. Even in the case of ostensibly ready-made sets such as gender categories, we find the generalized category 'the opposite sex . . . a chick' being used to refer to a particular individual, while invoking that general category as the relevant feature of that individual, while also performing indexical work on the speaker's own perceptions and motives. Is it just a fortunate feature of verbal categories, derived from perceptual laws, that they make all of this possible? I suggest not. We need to approach language as designed for discourse, for public performances, rather than having public actions as a kind of lucky consequence of people representing things mentally, in what happens to be a fortuitously shared meaning system.

It is useful to show that categorizations such as *chair*, *things to sit on*, and *things to take on a picnic* have prototype properties, with typical and central members. Discursively, one can imagine being blamed on a picnic for leaving behind the drinks or the bottle opener more reasonably than the newspaper or the dictionary. But these are intuitions that draw upon *imagined social practices*. Without some principle by which descriptive categorizations are located within, and are themselves, social practices, it is easy to glide between studies of language and theories of knowledge, between collecting or inventing bits of language, imagining them as bits of talk, and treating them as telling us what the speaker understands about the talk's topic. Folk theories are analytically abstracted from imagined discourse practices, and treated as a separate explanatory realm. It is then an easy matter both to overextend and to underestimate the range of phenomena that a cognitive theory has to account for. Asking how people ordinarily categorize things is not the same as asking how they make abstracted judgments of category membership. It is decontextualization from situated practices that makes culture look like grammar, discourse like cognition, versions like theories.

Notes

1. One reason why this individualistic, cognitive–perceptual species of 'experiential realism' (Lakoff, 1987) seems so sensible is that it *incorporates* important categories of common-sense reasoning concerning persons, minds, the world, and language that (I have

argued) ought to be our prime *topic* for investigation. There is some irony, therefore, in the popular notion that cognitive science is poised to replace common-sense, 'folk' psychology (Stich, 1983).

2. I have to conclude from this remark that Brown is probably as inept a gardener as I am.

3. For some studies of how descriptive categories for new phenomena in astronomy and biochemistry are formulated and deployed in the development of scientific knowledge, see Garfinkel et al. (1981), Latour and Woolgar (1986), Lynch (1985).

4. John Lee notes that Lévi-Strauss's structural semiotics made much of binary and opposite categories in language, but in an idealized and abstracted manner: 'Even his so-called binary oppositional categories, such as "left" and "right", or "black" and "white", cannot be said to be "opposites" outside an organizational context in which they are produced and provided for as opposites' (1991: 199).

5. A schema is 'a spatially and/or temporally organized cognitive structure in which the parts are connected on the basis of contiguities that have been experienced in time or space' (Mandler, 1979: 263). Schemas include not only conceptual categories but also scripts (see Chapter 6), conceived cognitively as generalized event schemas. In a wide range of cognitive theory from Piaget to Bartlett to Schank, schemas are the cognitive organizing principles for perception, memory, and action.

6. The widely held notion that 'total relativism' is a kind of self-refuting, inward-looking, navel-gazing nonsense is not a necessary conclusion, but one based largely on the prior acceptance of an alternative set of the assumptions, including those of realism, individualism, and the communication model of mind and language. For defences of varieties of relativism, see Edwards et al. (1995), Feyerabend (1975), K.J Gergen (1994), Potter (1996), Rorty (1991), Smith (1988), and the extensive literature cited therein.

7. See Chapter 3 of this volume, on SSK and ethnomethodology. Critiques of objectivism are available across such a large literature in post-Wittgensteinian philosophy, the social sciences, and the humanities that it is arbitrary to pick out just a few. But see Geertz (1988), Lynch (1993), Potter (1996) and Rorty (1991) for discussions particularly relevant to the position I take here.

8. I have coined this term, fairly obviously, to set 'experiential realism' in opposition to the more relativistic 'Sapir–Whorf hypothesis' (SWH). As with the SWH, there are of course a number of other important exponents of experiential metaphor theory, including Mark Johnson (1987), Zoltan Kovecses (1986), and Eve Sweetser (1990). Richard Cromer defined the first clear alternative to the SWH in 1974, and called it the 'cognition hypothesis' (see Cromer, 1991).

9. Of course I am conceding a lot here, in letting *even these* words stand for pre-linguistic experiences that are bounded and interrelated in *precisely* the ways that the concepts 'eating', 'drinking', and 'going hungry' are. It is impossible, of course, to write about pre-conceptual experiences without conceptualizing them. But rather than treating this as an unavoidable nuisance, or an unfair criticism of theorists who have no choice in the matter, I am arguing for its fundamental and overlooked importance in psychological treatments of language and cognition.

10. It may be recalled, by those old enough, that the venerable advertising slogan 'Guinness is good for you' had to be dropped as a misleading factual claim.

11. My suggestion that all descriptions are 'metaphorical' echoes Roman Jakobson's distinction between 'metaphor' and 'metonymy' (Jakobson and Halle, 1956), and Ferdinand de Saussure's (1922/1974) 'paradigmatic' versus 'syntagmatic' relations between categories. For Jakobson, 'metaphor' concerns the selection of one word rather than another, whereas 'metonymy' is the combination of words (etc.) in sentences. The retention by Lakoff and Gibbs of a residual 'literal' bedrock of meaning relies on the more common-sense notion of metaphor which implies a contrast with the literal: 'The figure of speech in which a name or descriptive term is transferred to some object different from, but analogous to, that *to which it is properly applicable*' (*OED*, 1994). The common stricture against using 'mixed metaphors' may also be understood as something imposed by the notion that there should not be more than one concrete, real world.

12. Cf. 'I got up to walk out the door' in Chapter 4, Extract 4.2. This was also a narrative detail, prior to a disputed act of violence, that helped construct that act as different in kind from a 'hitting', and as not premeditated.

13. These comments on the interactional business that is managed by the choice of one 'simple' description rather than another can be related to a critique of cognitive–linguistic approaches to causal attribution. For example, it has been suggested that 'direct action verbs' such as *punch* are straightforward, interpretation-free descriptions of events (Semin and Fiedler, 1988). For a discursive critique and alternative, see Edwards and Potter (1992a, 1993). Note how the 'accidental' notion of 'clipped' versus intentional 'hit' in Extract 9.1 is contextually variable; people can fall and 'hit' the floor (accidentally), whereas there is nothing accidental when a child gets 'clipped round the ear' for some misdemeanour.

14. An exception to the usual manner of heavily inventive metaphorical analysis is George Lakoff's (1991) study of the metaphors, including commercial and fairy tale motifs, underlying American government and media discourse prior to the Gulf War. As an analysis offered in the first instance (via networked email) as a piece of political action (trying to prevent the war), rather than an exercise in cognitive theory, it can be read with or without a background of cognitivist metatheory. In fact it fits equally well an approach to language that takes as its starting point not mental representations of experience, but an analytic orientation to what actually occurring discourse *does*.

15. This very distinction between the artificial and the natural worlds is also defeasible. Parks and gardens, from the wildest to the most cultivated, just like artificial kinds of 'intelligence' and domesticated animals, might be (for argument's sake) placed into a category of 'hybrids' (cf. Callon, 1986; Haraway, 1991; Latour, 1993). See also Chapter 11, on children, animals, and machines.

16. Whether common-sense reasoning is influenced by philosophy, or philosophy is a distillation of oppositions extracted from common-sense reasoning, I cannot say. Probably there is two-way traffic, though I suspect that philosophy derives more from everyday discourse than vice versa. The term *phenomena*, a Greek term in educated English (and German) usage prior to Kant, was refined by Kant as referring to things directly experienced by the senses. He introduced the contrasting term *noumena* for objects of conception and reality, but possessing no experiential attributes. Despite Kant, mundane discourse has found little use for distinguishing *noumena* from *phenomena*, though there are, and surely there have long been, everyday (and religious) notions of a reality beyond sensory appearances.

17. This is a quandary faced by all efforts to illuminate one thing by invoking another – all analogies, metaphors, and explanatory models including the 'theatrical' and 'game' models of social life (Billig, 1987), and even the use of children, animals, machines, and members of other cultures as 'mirrors' to help us understand 'our' nature (whoever 'we' may be). See Chapter 11 of this volume. The quandary for analogies of these kinds is, how can using analogy A for object O substitute for, or constitute an understanding of O, when it requires an independent grasp of O in order for us to see its application and evaluate its success? (Cf. Harré, 1988, on artificial intelligence.) One way of resolving that quandary is to see *all* descriptions as metaphorical and implicitly comparative, and all analogies as primarily *discursive* devices rather than cognitive ones. They come into their own in situated usage, in activities such as persuading, explaining, arguing, and educating, rather than merely in one-off perceptual sense-making.

18. The rather stark option of 'killing yourself' arises in Sacks's data, these being calls to a psychiatric help line for people contemplating suicide.

19. The indexically specified nature of proverbial expressions is captured in Sacks's comment, 'you can have these potential descriptions and see them as "correct for something", where what it would be correct for remains to be seen' (1989: 373). Sacks also notes how a proverb loses effectiveness when paraphrased, or when concretized into one of its specific applications – as when 'a rolling stone gathers no moss' becomes 'a man who doesn't settle down doesn't gather possessions' (1989: 372). It then becomes 'questionable' as an

empirical claim, whereas in proverbial form, though its particular relevance might be questioned, people do not say, of moss and rolling stones, 'Is that so? What is your evidence for that?' As Sacks puts it, 'proverbs are in the first place correct' (1989: 372).

20. Cf. Paul Feyerabend, siding with Protagoras against Plato on the meanings of generaliz-ations and rule statements: 'a statement such as [Man is the measure of all things . . .] can be interpreted in (at least) two ways: as a premise "entailing" well defined and unambiguous consequences; or as a rule of thumb adumbrating an outlook without giving a precise description of it. In the first case (which is the one favoured by logicians) the meaning of the statement must be established *before* it is applied, or argued about; in the second case (which characterizes most fruitful discussions, in the sciences and elsewhere) interpreting the statement is part of applying it, or arguing about it' (Feyerabend, 1987: 45). This is echoed in CA's principle that meaning is interactionally and indexically accomplished, and that this is what discourse *is like*, rather than being an inadequacy of language that needs fixing. See Chapter 4.

21. Paul Drew and Elizabeth Holt (1988) note how idiomatic expressions function sequentially to end topics and start new ones, especially at junctures when an addressee is 'withholding affiliation'. This relates to Sacks's observation that 'members are so committed to their correctness – that if you undercut one, exactly what you've undercut is not clear. And one doesn't know exactly how we can continue talking' (1989: 251). Also, 'the problem [of proverbs] is not, on any given one's use, is it true relative to other proverbial expressions, but, does it, as something one understands with, understand what it applies to?' (1992, vol. 2: 422).

22. As we noted in Chapter 5, this was the conceptual problem that the philosopher John Locke (1894) sought to resolve, a problem not so much solved as reformulated by Wittgenstein (1958), through his notion of meaning as use, rather than representation. The radical implications of a Wittgensteinian approach to language and meaning for psychology and the social sciences are still, slowly, being defined and appreciated.

23. The point here is that 'boiling' and other 'heated fluid in a container' metaphors are useful for depicting specific instances of anger as passively experienced and externally caused, while 'dangerous animal' metaphors such as 'don't bite my head off' are useful for construing emotions as agentive and blameworthy: see Chapter 7.

24. 'Chick' is one of a variety of gender categorizations available to this group, so its choice signals something further about the speaker than merely his choice of a gender category. Sacks does not pursue that here. However, while the term is available as an index of the *speaker's* gendered attitude, we should be wary of reading the talk of 1960s Californians in the light of a subsequent history of awareness of language and feminism. Its use today might signal something different; irony, or opposition, perhaps. Note that Sacks understands the remark as, locally, part of a compliment.

10
Narrative: Stories and Rememberings

One of the things that people do in discourse is recall and recount events in their lives. We have seen plenty of examples of this already, in the various conversational extracts used in other Chapters. It does not have to be a special 'story time' kind of talk, nor anything so worked up as a diary or an autobiography, but, rather, it occurs as a routine part of everyday discourse. It is also an activity that blurs any easy distinctions we might be tempted to draw between fact and fiction, memory and discourse, explanation and narrative. Factual and fictional stories share many of the same kinds of textual devices for constructing credible descriptions, building plausible or unusual event sequences, attending to causes and consequences, agency and blame, character and circumstance. The study of factual narratives, such as those found in histories, biographies, and ethnographic texts, blends into the study of fictional literature (Geertz, 1988; White, 1973), while the psychology of memory can be only crudely separated from literary, conversational, and other cultural forms of discourse, records, mementoes, and narratives (see, for example, Bartlett, 1932; Bruner, 1990; Freeman, 1993; Lowenthal, 1985; Middleton and Edwards, 1990b). The aim of this chapter is to examine the nature of stories and storied rememberings *as discursive phenomena*. There is a vast literature relevant to this topic, so any path through it has to be a selective one.

Let us start by recalling examples of stories encountered in previous chapters, in order to get a feel for the kinds of phenomena at issue here. Most of the extracts we have examined, for whatever analytic interest they had at that point, are also candidates for a study of 'narrative' or of 'remembering'. These include Harvey Sacks's (1992) 'Navy pilot' newspaper story and Bill Buford's (1991) ethnographic reportage on football riots in Chapter 1; Robin Wooffitt's (1992) tale of the unexpected in Chapter 3; Lottie's account for not having gotten together with Emma (Extract 5.1); Paul Drew's (1990) example of courtroom cross-examination, concerning precisely how long a witness said she had spent in the hospital (Extract 5.4); other stories told in testimony to the police (Extracts 5.5 and 9.1); Lottie's and Emma's stories of trips to restaurants, the scripted instances of Bud's unreasonableness, and all the rest of those episodes and story formulations discussed in Chapter 6, including Connie's and Jimmy's and Jeff's and Mary's competing stories of marital strife. There was Mary's account of what time she got home (Extract 6.1), Connie's and Jimmy's contrasting stories of the 'pub episode' and Jimmy's ensuing 'boiling anger' (Extracts 6.9 through

6.10, and 7.2), and the narrative emotionology of Jeff's 'angry stage' (Extract 7.1). We might include also, at a pinch, the story-definitions of emotions in Micronesia and the British press (Lutz, 1990a; White, 1990; see Chapter 7).

My point in recalling all these examples is to make them relevant here not only as examples of conversational narratives, but also as examples of the *kind of analysis* that can be applied to them. In every case, it is the general approach and analytic framework of discursive psychology and conversation analysis that have been brought to bear, rather than any specifically 'narrative' theory or method. In this chapter, I shall consider narratives and narrative analysis in the light of that same general perspective.

Let us take another look at Extract 4.2, reproduced here as 10.1.

Extract 10.1

1	*B*:	. . . Well, she *((wife of B))* stepped between me and the child,
2 →		I got up to walk out the door. When she stepped between me
3		and the child, I went to move her out of the way. And then
4		about that time her sister had called the police. I don't know
5		how she . . . what she . . .
6	*A*:	Didn't you smack her one?
7	*B*:	No.
8 →	*A*:	You're not telling me the story, Mr B.
9	*B*:	Well, you see when you say smack you mean hit.
10	*A*:	Yeah, you shoved her. Is that it?
11	*B*:	Yeah, I shoved her.

(Sacks, 1992, vol. 1: 113, line numbers added)

Consider again lines 2 and 8, from the point of view of analysing stories. As we noted in Chapter 4, 'I got up to walk out the door' (line 2) might be taken to be a kind of scene-setting detail (performing what narrative analyst William Labov, 1972, calls 'orientation'). Or else it might be treated as just another narrated act-in-sequence, one item in a chain of events, like any other act. But it also bears crucially on the rest of the story, and on the kinds of actions being done in the *telling* of the story. It establishes the husband's (B's) intentions as essentially innocent, as oriented towards leaving the scene rather than looking for trouble, let alone intending violence.

There is a similar instance in Connie's story of the disputed 'pub episode' in which, following the extracts presented in Chapter 6, she provides a description of Jimmy's attitude before it all happened:

> You were a:ll annoy:ed and everything else going out the doo::r becau:se you didn't want to go:.

Again, what Connie manages to do here is produce a specific narrative detail which can be heard as a kind of interpretative frame for what happened later. Jimmy's emotional outburst, his anger, and (allegedly) unreasonable jealousy can now be seen as *in the offing*, and attributable to *him*, before she did anything, indeed before they even got to the pub. It is also a detail that, being produced after Jimmy's counter-narrative to Connie's own version of the incident, works to *counter* Jimmy's version. It is a rhetorically potent detail, both in its specific content and in its positioning in the dialogue. What I want to do is leave these narrative details here as a marker, and return to them later when we consider various category schemes for narrative analysis.

Now, as another marker, consider also the marvellous line 8 (in Extract 10.1), which is what Sacks himself was most concerned with: 'You're not telling me the story, Mr B'. One interesting thing here is that telling a story is clearly a participants' category of talk, and one for which they may assert criteria of adequacy. In other words, participants themselves, and not only analysts of 'narrative structures', display a sensitivity to what might count as a proper, 'well-formed' instance of a story. It is not that participants are expressing any kind of interest in narratology; they are not about to resolve whether or not Mr B is telling the story by invoking narrative theory or consulting a book on the subject. The point of A's remark is that there is something quite specific (line 6) that is hearably wrong with, or missing from, B's story, and B recognizes the sense of that (line 9), and A and B confirm it (lines 10–11) as some kind of interpretably violent act, adopting the less violent description 'shove' (all of which is the focus of discussion in Chapter 4).

But note now the *nature* of that missing element concerning, as Sacks notes, adequate grounds for someone's having called the police. There are three important points here with regard to analysing narratives. First, a matter such as 'adequate grounds for calling the police' is not something that has to depend on knowing the special conventions of literary forms such as detective novels, police movies, or television police soaps (though those conventions might well arise). Rather, it is the same kind of common-sense knowledge we would use in life (cf. Garnham, 1985), just like good reasons for not (yet) having washed the dishes, or whatever. Second, it is not a pre-ordained item, a definite verbal formula, that fills the inferential gap, but something negotiably or rhetorically adequate; if 'went to move her out of the way' was insufficient, then 'smack her one' might fit better, but not necessarily, and 'shoved her' eventually proves, in a practical sense, satisfactory. The specific verbal details are crucial for the story's acceptability to both participants, and they are delicate choices between semantically similar-looking words (cf. the discussion of 'dangerous' in Chapter 8). Third, note what all this talk *does*. It is not just some kind of set-aside story time, told out of interest or as disembedded sense-making, but an integral part of talk-in-interaction. Accountability is being managed, on two levels, both in the story itself, and in the current interaction (cf. Edwards and Potter, 1992a, 1993), with regard to culpability, reasons for actions, and reasons for describing them, precisely, one way or another.

The analysis of narratives in the human and social sciences has mostly ignored the interactional business that people might be doing in telling them. This stems partly from the adoption of analytic concepts and methods derived from studies of set-piece written literature, such as novels and autobiographies. But it is also a feature of cognitive psychological approaches to narrative which display scant awareness of those literary traditions, but where the study of language as mental representation, rather than the study of discourse as social action, is a built-in and natural-seeming disciplinary commitment. Studies of narrative, both in cognitive psychology and in literary 'narratology', have tended to pursue generalized types and categories of narrative *structure*, rather than dealing with how specific story content, produced on and for occasions of talk, may perform social actions in-the-telling.

The cognitive psychology of life's events

Cognitive psychology has a way of dealing with the sense that people make of events in their lives. It conceives such 'sense' as a mental process and subdivides its attention to different features of that process (event memory, story schemas, script theory, autobiographical memory, attribution theory, etc.). It retains, across all of these topics, the basic model of the individual, sense-making perceiver. Psychological work on 'story schemas',[1] for example, has mostly used brief written vignettes, specially invented as stimulus materials for an experiment or simulation, and designed to contain whatever features or omissions are under experimental variation or control, and relevant to a particular hypothesis. Typically absent from such procedures (being obviated by psychology's standard assumptions about language and thought) are speakers and speech events. There is scant interest in the notion that any such stories as are used were *never told* by anyone anywhere, and often bear gross dissimilarities to such stories as *are* produced in ordinary conversation, or even in written literature. This traditional lack of interest amongst psychologists in discourse as a natural phenomenon or social production has resulted in cognitive models of discourse and discourse processing which treat text as the result of neural or computational information processing, an expression of thought, or evidence of minds-at-work (for example, Graesser, 1993; Kintsch and Van Dijk, 1983).

In a useful overview of psychological work on 'autobiographical memory', Martin Conway (1990) locates it within the conceptual and explanatory framework provided by mainstream cognitive psychology. He charts its overlaps and relevancies to issues of accuracy, pathology, information storage and processing, retention and forgetting, mental representations, computational and script models, cognition and emotion, and various sub-categories of memory such as 'episodic' and 'semantic' (Tulving, 1972). One popular theme in studies of autobiographical memory is the use of diaries. Typically, diaries are treated not as forms of record-making and remembering in their own right, but as a source of biographical materials which can be pressed into service as criteria for testing later recall of their contents (for example, Smith, 1952). Additionally, and advantageously according to the criteria of experimental control, the 'diaries' used in such research may even be *written for that purpose*, precisely in order to provide suitable materials for later recall, and therefore may include various standardized requirements for what to include (for example, Linton, 1982; White, 1982), with memory assessed by standard criteria for recall, such as percentage accuracy scores.

For example, Willem Wagenaar (1986) recorded events in his life over a six-year period, under four categories (*who*, *what*, *where*, and *when*), designed to serve as subsequent criteria for recall. This ensured a basis of comparability so that recall could be measured according to standard criteria, in that all recorded events would contain a specific entry under all four headings. The analytical part of the study focused on how much could later be recalled, under each category, over different periods, under varying amounts and types of cueing or prompting. The specific findings of these studies are not at issue here; they surely do make a useful contribution to the standard psychological approach to memory. The thing of interest is how such studies treat diaries, and discourse more generally. Essentially, there is virtually no interest at all in *diaries*. These are treated as available, or constructible as required, records of life events that can be substituted for the input materials used in a standard memory experiment.

But despite such studies, ordinary diaries are particular kinds of texts with their own characteristics, with varying criteria of content, personal uses, privacy norms, and so on (Linde, 1993; Wiener and Rosenwald, 1993). Similarly, written autobiographies are not merely mental reflections on a life lived, but instances of a culturally and historically located textual genre. As such, they are part of the same individualism in Western culture that is embodied in psychology itself, and may even be partly responsible for that individualism (see Freeman, 1993, on the nature and influence of St Augustine's writings; cf. Weintraub, 1978). This makes 'autobiographical memory' an attractive topic for psychologists who are interested in non-laboratory 'ecological' studies, while not wishing to challenge too severely the discipline's traditional topics, theoretical commitments, and methods. Autobiography embodies a notion attractive to standard psychological assumptions of a reflective, sense-making self or mind, pausing to take stock, and to tell a tale of self-realization (or otherwise), of trials and tribulations, accomplishment, career. As a specialized literary genre (however heterogeneous), autobiography is somewhat dangerous, I would suggest, as a metaphor for what we are doing when we recount life's events in ordinary talk.

One important difference between diaries and autobiographies is captured in Hayden White's (1973) distinction between a *chronicle* (a sequential record of events) and a *history* (events worked up into an explanatory narrative). If diaries are chronicles, then autobiographies are histories. But let me strike a note of caution about idealized distinctions of this kind, because the literature on 'narrative' is full of them. Diaries and chronicles are likely to be written not just blindly from day to day, but constructed in ways that attend to the sequentiality of events, to 'points' or upshots, moral evaluations, and so on, with an explanation-relevant view to what is important, just as histories and narratives generally permit a reconstruction of the chronological order of events, the underlying 'story'.

There are various bipolar contrasts of this kind in literary studies, each somewhat different, but echoing something like the distinction between the temporal sequence of events and a worked-up discourse of those events. These include the Russian formalists' notions of *sjuzet* and *fabula* (used, for example, by Bruner, 1986), also *histoire* and *récit* (Genette, 1988), and *taleworld* and *storyrealm* (Young, 1989). None of these corresponds very well, however, to the simple realism that courtrooms and psychologists generally entertain, between actual events that happen in the world and people's memories or stories of them (see also Edwards and Potter, 1992a). For Katherine Young, for example, the taleworld of sequential events is something that the storyrealm of discourse 'conjures up' (1989: 153) – a world *as if* beyond the text (whether fact or fiction), in which the storied events supposedly transpire. For a sense of how worlds and lives can be *conjured up* by stories of them (see also Chapter 3), we turn to narratology and narrative psychology.

Narratology and narrative psychology

Narrative psychology (for example, Bruner, 1990; Murray, 1995; Sarbin, 1986a) is an extension of 'narratology' (for example, Bal, 1985; Frye, 1957; Prince, 1982; Propp, 1928/1968; Todorov, 1969) from its origins in literary theory, into the psychological study of how people make sense of their lives. Narratology, the study of stories, defines general categories and types of narrative based on literary genres. Classic studies include Vladimir Propp's (1928/1968) analysis of the structures of Russian fairy tales, and Northrop Frye's (1957) four literary genres *comedy*, *tragedy*, *romance*, and *satire*. Hayden White (1973) and others have claimed Frye's fourfold typology (itself stemming from a long tradition in literary theory) as deeply entrenched cultural models that people in Western cultures use and recognize, in anything from the writing and understanding of history, to everyday personal story-telling. Narrative categories include types *of* stories, such as Frye's, and also categories *within* stories that define their internal components and organization. This concern with identifying types and structures is also a feature of sociolinguistic studies of oral narratives, such as those by William Labov (1972; Labov and Waletsky, 1967; cf. Longacre, 1976).[2]

Narratology and narrative psychology take the view that narrative is not merely a collection of literary genres, nor merely a particular category of talk, but something much more profound – a basic, perhaps *the* basic, mode of human understanding: 'the primary scheme by means of which human existence is rendered meaningful' (Polkinghorne, 1988: 11). Narrative psychology is part of the broad 'discursive turn' in the human and social sciences, the rejection of mental mechanisms and 'laws-and-causes social physics' (Geertz, 1983: 3) in favour of how people make meanings. In Theodore Sarbin's (1986b) view, narrative can be promoted as a 'root metaphor' for psychology, capable of replacing other root metaphors such as the computer, the naïve scientist, the laboratory rat, and so on.

The focus of much narrative psychology up to now has remained somewhat cognitivist in its theoretical orientation, using the notion that individuals *reflect upon* their experiences of life through constructing and understanding stories. Jerome Bruner's (1990) narrative psychology, for example, is presented as an effort to restore the original programme of the 'first cognitive revolution' of the late 1950s and 1960s, to restore culture and 'meaning' to a discipline that has become dominated by the root metaphor of information processing, and the pursuit of computational and neuro-physiological models of information flow.[3] Thus, for Bruner, narrative is not merely a kind of discourse, but a mode of thought and action describable in terms that can be related to cognitive plans and representations. It is the means by which 'people organize their experience in, knowledge of, and transactions with the social world' (Bruner, 1990: 35).

Much more narrowly cognitivist than that is Wallace Chafe's formulation: narratives are 'overt manifestations of the mind in action . . . windows to both the content of the mind and its ongoing operations' (1990: 79). But even outside of such overtly cognitivist terminology as Chafe's, narrative psychology is an approach largely allied to autobiographical case studies (Bruner, 1990; Freeman, 1993; Plummer, 1995), and concerned with self, identity, or subjectivity (Sarbin, 1986a; Shotter and Gergen, 1989; Young, 1987), including feminist approaches to women's lives and identities (for example, Gergen and Gergen, 1993; M.M. Gergen, 1994; Henwood and Coughlan, 1993; Personal Narratives Group, 1989; Riessman, 1993; Young, 1987), pathology (Keen, 1986), and psychotherapy (Schafer, 1976, 1982). In therapy, for instance, individuals may be helped to locate themselves within an alternative, more agentive and optimistic story of their lives – to start living a better story.

But as Kevin Murray notes, 'both psychoanalysis and the cognitive school offer narrative a place in the head of an isolated individual. There is no allowance here for the *actual telling of the story*' (1995: 185, emphasis added). Many studies of personal narratives do indeed study *actually told stories*, rather than the artificial inventions used in laboratory psychology and artificial intelligence. But they generally extract those stories from the occasions of their telling, or play down the importance of such occasions by collecting stories through research interviews, or in the form of written autobiographies, and examining these for how their authors 'see', or 'make sense' of, things (Cortazzi, 1993). The more discourse-oriented studies emphasize the active nature of narratives in 'constructing' rather than expressing identity (Harré, 1983; Shotter and Gergen, 1989), while also promoting a much more rhetorical and interaction-managing treatment of discourse as something produced in, and for, its occasions (Edwards and Potter, 1992a).

The flexible and occasioned nature of discourse tends to be understated in studies of narratives, which deal largely with set-piece stories culled from written autobiographies or ethnographic interviews. The risk of such studies is that of replacing the familiar cognitivist trope of rational, sense-making honest Joe (or Jo) with a merely more imaginative, or romantic, literary version. It risks treating discourse as a kind of storied 'sense-making', an author's or speaker's best efforts at self-exploration. In Mark Freeman's approach to written autobiographies, these are efforts at 'rewriting the self', a process 'in which we survey and explore our own histories, toward the end of making and remaking sense of who and what we are' (1993: 6; cf. 'as I gaze back and try to understand how I have gotten to be here, doing what I am', 1993: 14). However self-*constructive* that textual process may be, there appears to be little or no interaction-oriented business going on in the telling.

Of course, this is what written texts such as autobiographies lend themselves to: providing unique, for-the-record, best-effort, stand-alone versions of things. And that is precisely what restricts their usefulness as points of departure for discursive psychology. Literary narratives distract analytic attention and theory from the performance contingencies that become much more evident when examining spoken discourse, such as in the stories we have seen generated in telephone calls, courtrooms, and couple counselling. As Kenneth Gergen remarks, self narratives, even written ones, should be understood as 'forms of social accounting or public discourse' (1994: 188).

Autobiographical discourse is likely to share much with everyday discourse in general – a realm of persons, actions, thoughts, feelings, intentions, circumstances, influences, choices, relationships, outcomes, and so on. Discursive psychology's analytic job is not to enter that world and adopt its tropes and explanations (let alone its factual or subjective authority), nor indeed to disagree with it like the hard-line opponents of 'folk psychology' suggest (for example, Churchland, 1988; Stich, 1983). Rather, the task is to examine and explicate its workings. This may appear to some to be a disrespectful way of approaching people's often painfully wrought life stories. But I am not proposing that we treat these texts as fiction instead of fact, dishonest as opposed to sincere, manipulative as opposed to hermeneutic. Rather, it is a matter of treating *both sides* of those dichotomies as part of the phenomena: as oriented-to discursive concerns, issues, and accomplishments. The business done *in* talk and text *includes* attending to their status as factual or sincere, self-serving or objective. The alternative to a discourse analytic stance (see Chapter 3 on 'methodological relativism' and 'ethnomethodological indifference') is not a greater personal respect for talkers and writers, but the pervasive model of discourse whose inadequacies this book has sought to point up. That is, discourse as representation, expression, communication, best sense, best efforts, decontextualized, doing-nothing pictures of mind and world: reflection on activities, rather than activity itself.

Written autobiographies are interesting documents in their own right, and proper objects of discursive study. Narratological work often recognizes the differences between literary and oral sources, even though it may play down the status of stories as interactionally produced and potentially flexible phenomena. For example, Charlotte Linde, in a study of life stories mostly given in interview, emphasizes the oral nature of her materials, in contrast to written autobiography, which 'constitutes a literary genre with its own history, its own demands, and its own market' (1993: 38). Similarly, Luk Van Langenhove and Rom Harré warn of the dangers of using the norms of written texts as a model for spoken life stories, given the different natures, functions, and cultural–historical traditions of oral and written discourse: 'though seldom telling complete biographical stories, people are constantly engaged in all kinds of self-positioning in which self-narratives occur that are not modelled by any literary plots' (1993: 94). Rather than rejecting the usefulness for psychology of studying written autobiographies, or even stories given in interview, I am warning against their use as a general basis for narrative psychology and analysis.

One feature of the study of literary autobiographies that *has* been important, and which accords with studies of conversational discourse, is their orientation to accountability. Autobiographies mix event reports with explanations, attending to the trade-offs between fact and interest, just as conversational reports do (Edwards and Potter, 1992a, 1993). They recount successes and failures, rites of passage, lessons learned, potentials realized or thwarted, and so on. As Freeman notes, autobiographies can be read as 'a kind of apologia for who and what one has been' (1993: 20, cf. Edwards and Middleton, 1988, and Edwards and Potter, 1992a). For that reason we have no business, as analysts, reading *through* them to the life beyond, any more than we can read through discourse of any kind, to recover the world it purports to represent. Rather, they have to be read reflexively, in the ethnomethodological sense, as part of, as moves in, and as constituting the lives they are ostensibly 'about'.

Narrative analysis: structures and schemas

Before considering specific kinds of narrative analysis, it may be useful to reiterate, in this context, the basic analytical theme of this book. There are three kinds of objects at which any analysis of narratives might be aimed: (1) the nature of the *events* narrated; (2) people's perception or *understanding* of events; and (3) the *discourse* of such understandings and events. We can think of these as three crudely separated kinds of analysis.

Type 1: pictures of events
Type 2: pictures of mind
Type 3: discursive actions

Of course, these are ways of approaching any discourse, not just narrative, and they resonate with many of the discussions in earlier chapters.

Type 1 corresponds to the basic aims of ethnography and oral histories, in which stories and descriptions are collected as a route (however compromised) to the things that are their topic – to matters and events beyond the talk. It is also part of common-sense practices, in ordinary talk, texts, courtrooms, classrooms, and scientific publications, that discourse about events is produced as, and taken to be, a way of telling and finding out about those events, with due caution for lies and errors. Type 2 takes one step back from events themselves, and takes a psychological interest in the speaker. It treats people's discourse as how they 'see' things (again, through a glass however darkly), whether as representatives of groups or cultures, or as individuals. This corresponds to much of cognitive and narrative psychology and cognitive anthropology.

Type 3 focuses on discourse itself, as a performative domain of social action. Both the nature of events (type 1), and the nature of people's perspectives on events (type 2), are considered to be *at stake* here (worked up, managed, topicalized, implied, and so on), rather than simply available, in the discourse. Type 3 is broadly characteristic of the kind of discursive psychology pursued in this book, and of conversation analysis, rhetorical analysis, SSK, and some varieties of narratology.[4] Type 3 essentially reverses the order of the three. Discourse is, analytically, what we have got, what we start with. Whereas we might assume, common-sensically, that events come first, followed by (distorted) understandings of them, followed by (distorted) verbal expressions of those understandings, type 3 inverts that, and treats both understandings and events themselves as participants' concerns – the stuff the talk works up and deals with.

With these three types in mind[5] we may turn to some ways of defining and analysing narrative, starting with Jerome Bruner's.

> Narrative requires . . . four crucial grammatical constituents if it is to be effectively carried out. It requires, first, a means for emphasizing human '*agentivity*' – action directed toward goals controlled by agents. It requires, secondly, that a sequential order be established and maintained – that events and states be '*linearized*' in a standard way. Narrative, thirdly, also requires a sensitivity to what is *canonical* and what violates canonicality in human interaction. Finally, narrative requires something approximating a narrator's *perspective*: it cannot, in the jargon of narratology, be 'voiceless'. (Bruner, 1990: 77, emphasis added)

Bruner's broad definition is a useful place to start, in that it is specifically oriented to narrative *psychology*, and because it includes elements of various other descriptive schemes and definitions, such as Kenneth Burke's (1945). Burke suggested a scheme which he called 'dramatism', which deals with matters such as motives, persuasion, stories, and so on, by defining five elements that make up a well-formed story: 'What was done (act), when or where it was done (scene), who did it (agent), how he [*sic*] did it (agency), and why (purpose)' (1945: xv). Bruner (1990) glosses these five elements as: Action, Scene, Actor, Instrument, and Goal. Into these elements is then inserted Trouble, in the form of some kind of imbalance or conflict between the five elements, and this is what gives rise to the subsequent actions, events, and resolutions that make up a coherent, bounded narrative.

A related set of criteria is provided by Kenneth Gergen (1994: 189–90). Well-formed narratives have (1) a valued endpoint, goal, or 'point'; (2) an ordering of events, not necessarily told in the order in which they occur (flashbacks, insertions, etc., are possible); (3) stable identities for the main characters, which may develop; (4) causal links and explained outcomes; (5) demarcation signs – in conversations especially, marking where stories start and end. Gergen's list is clearly similar to Bruner's and to Burke's, and there are others which also draw on general narratology, but none of them are identical. Why not? Are the differences minor and terminological, or are they matters that the authors might insist on? How might the differences be resolved, or, alternatively, by what criteria should we prefer one definition to another? It is not simply a matter of pointing to actual instances of stories and showing that one definition fits better than another, because each definition specifies, somewhat circularly, what would count as a good ('well-formed') example.

Definitions of this kind can be understood as analysts' efforts at nailing down common-sense categories: efforts at defining what a story or narrative is, as distinct from, say, a sermon, lecture, scientific explanation, or any other discourse category. As we saw in Extract 10.1, the participants themselves displayed a sensitivity to what *that* story should contain, and one imagines that Bruner's, Burke's, and Gergen's lists accord with those kinds of participants' sensibilities, although that would be a matter for research rather than stipulation. But note what it was that occasioned and resolved line 8 in Extract 10.1 ('You're not telling me the story, Mr B'). It was not the absence of some required general category such as actors, goals, scenes, and such, but, rather, an objection to *something very specific*, that insufficient reason had been provided for somebody, plausibly, calling the police. While that might be classified under a category such as 'goal', 'causal link', 'canonicality', or 'purpose' (but note how different *those* categories are), it was the participants themselves (rather than narrative analysis) who raised and resolved the notion that such details had not been adequately provided. None of the definitions of well-formed narratives that anybody has suggested get anywhere near specifying in advance what should count, generally or for anyone in particular, as adequate reasons for calling the police.

It is not that Bruner's, Burke's, or Gergen's definitions would be improved by including details of that kind. In fact, they would be considerably *less* useful if they did. The more detailed such definitions of narrative become, then the more specific they are to particular genres (for example, Propp, 1928/1968) or events, and the less generally applicable they are as analytic schemes. On the other hand, the looser their definition, the more they dissolve into the tropes, concerns, and devices of discourse in general. The problem of too broad a definition, of seeing virtually all discourse as narrative, is that it starts to lose explanatory power. As Kenneth

Gergen suggests, definitions of narrative can only be definitions of specific cultural forms: 'rather than seek a definitive account [of narrative structure] . . . there is a virtual infinity of possible story forms, but due to the exigencies of social co-ordination, certain modalities are favored over others in various historical periods' (1994: 195).

Narratology deals with the internal structures of narratives, with distinctions between narratives of different kinds, and also with distinctions between narratives and other kinds of discourse. As we have noted, Hayden White (1973) takes from literary theory four basic categories, *tragedy*, *comedy*, *romance*, and *satire*, and suggests that these are appropriate labels for a wide range of literary, historical, and everyday narratives. The four categories have been taken up and applied in a variety of psychologically oriented treatments of personal narratives, including Gergen and Gergen (1988), Murray (1989), and Schafer (1976). Kevin Murray provides a concise summary, which I condense a little further here:

> . . . *comedy* involves the victory of youth and desire over age and death. . . . *Romance* concerns the restoration of the honoured past through a series of events that involve a struggle . . . between a hero and forces of evil. . . . In *tragedy* the individual fails to conquer evil and is excluded from the social unit. The nobility of this failure is contrasted with the satire of *irony*, which deals in the discovery that comedy, romance, and tragedy are mere schemes of mortals to control experience: individuals are not so pure, nor is the social order so healthy. (1989: 181–2)

It is easy to see how these categories might be applied to actual instances. But even literary works, let alone ordinary talk, have to be *fitted* to the four types, giving rise to various sub-types, overlaps, and mixtures. The problem for narrative analysis is that of *idealization* – the adoption of an analytic category scheme in advance of examining specific instances, perhaps even a scheme whose original domain of application was different (in this case, literary genres), and seeing how something such as stories collected in interviews can be fitted to them.

In order to illustrate the problems of applying category schemes, let us briefly consider a particularly influential one that is widely used in narrative analysis: that of William Labov (1972; Labov and Waletsky, 1967). Labov's categories of the structure and functions of oral narratives are shown in Extract 10.2, which is an example provided by Catherine Kohler Riessman (1993: 59) in a book on the methodology of narrative analysis. Riessman presents the example positively, as one to which Labov's categories can be usefully applied (Riessman uses the scheme in her own research), rather than as one of the 'many narratives [that] do not lend themselves to Labov's framework' (1993: 59).

Labov's categories[6] are signalled by the letter codes assigned to each numbered line. The codes, as glossed by Riessman, are as follows: 'to provide an Abstract for what follows (A), Orient the listener (O), carry the Complicating Action (CA), Evaluate its meaning (E), and Resolve the action (R)' (1993: 59; note that Labov's scheme also specifies an optional sixth item, a 'Coda' that brings us back to the present). Extract 10.2 is taken from a husband's talk about incidents leading up to a divorce. So it has a thematic resemblance to many other examples of discourse on relationship troubles we have considered in this book.

Extract 10.2 (Applying Labov's categories)

30	and (.) finally, ah, it's, this is actually a crucial incident	A
31	because I <u>finally</u> got up and (.)	CA
32	and (.) went into the other room	CA
33	(.) she was in the laundry room with the door closed and	O
34	(.) knocked on the door and said	CA
35	'When are you going to be done with this?'	CA
36	'cause we, we were going to talk.	O
37	And she kind of held up her hand like this and went 'no'.	CA
38	And I got absolutely bullshit	E
39	I put my <u>fist</u> through the door ((*Interviewer*: uh-huh))	R
40	which is not the kind of stuff that I, that I do, you know	E
41	I'm <u>not</u> a real physically violent person at <u>all</u>.	E

(Riessman, 1993: 59, untimed pauses)

Some of the problems of *applying* Labov's categories *as an analytic scheme*, and by extension other related pre-defined analytic codes and categories, can be seen in this example. The thing to do is to try assigning alternative categories, and see how plausible, or strained, that becomes. Of course, this leaves aside the appropriateness of having subdivided the talk into precisely those twelve discrete 'clauses' (the twelve lines) in the first place. Line 30 is coded as an 'Abstract', although 'a crucial incident' might reasonably be judged an Evaluation rather than a summary of events. Less obviously, try considering line 31 as an Evaluation. The expression 'because I <u>finally</u> got up', including the emphasis on 'finally', surely reinforces the notion of a 'crucial incident' having just taken place, together with a sense of the narrator's judgment (evaluation) of that incident – enough to 'finally' make him get up. Again, it is not clear why 'And I got absolutely bullshit' (line 38) is not a next occurrence or Complicating Action (CA) rather than an Evaluation (E), unless all emotion descriptions are automatically considered Evaluations. Part of the problem here is that the single category 'Complicating Action' (CA) seems to contain the bulk of what one might common-sensically assume is the basic storyline, the sequence of events, which means that, as an analytic scheme for stories, much of the content must remain largely unanalysed.

The category 'Orientation', in Labov's scheme, supposedly informs the listener of the circumstances of the action, a kind of contextual scene-setting – time, place, situation, participants. But surely this under-specifies what is going on in lines 33 and 36. The narrative sense of 'she was in the laundry room with the door closed' is not merely circumstantial; she was not doing the laundry. Rather, it helps define the nature of the wife's actions at that juncture, making a secretive and illicit phone call (she was 'talking to her lover on the phone', Riessman, 1993: 59), just as 'we were going to talk' establishes, in contrast to that, the less objectionable activity she was (according to him) supposed to be doing at that time with her husband. These 'Orientations' are reminiscent of the examples reviewed and placed as 'markers' near the start of this Chapter, such as B's 'I got up to walk out the door' (Extract 10.1), and Connie's 'You were a:ll annoy:ed and everything else going out the doo::r becau:se you didn't want to go:'. What matters with these utterances is not that we categorize them under Orientation, or Complicating Action, or Evaluation, or whatever, and then deal with those categories, but, rather, that we grasp what they are doing, as specific, precisely worded, occasioned formulations.

Without labouring the point, similar kinds of reassignments and complications are possible for the rest of the narrative in Extract 10.2. 'Evaluation' is likely to be a pervasively relevant concern in story-telling, rather than something exclusively coded in a specific item or slot, while the inclusion of an Abstract and Orientation are in any case considered optional in oral narratives (Labov, 1972), again leaving 'Complicating Action' with a very heavy and rather uninformative analytic burden. 'Orientation' includes the kinds of story details that can occur anywhere in a narrative, and perform significant business (see Drew, 1978, and Schegloff, 1972, on 'formulating place'). In other words, when we come to dealing with specific story details, we are immediately dealing with the contingencies of discourse per se, of descriptions, reports, accounts, and so on, rather than something specific about narrative. It is by collecting stories through interviews, taking them out of the interactional (and rhetorical) contexts of their production, and formulating check-list categories of their structural components that we obtain a rather idealized notion of how they work.

The identification of general story schemas across a wide range of stories is clearly an important analytic goal. But despite being derived from and for empirical analysis, Labov's categories are idealized as well as empirical. That is, they define the kinds of things a story *ought* to contain, theoretically, in order to count as a story. They become less useful when used as a set of pre-coded analytic slots into which we should try to place an actual story's contents. The temptation for analysts using the scheme is to start with the categories and see how the things people say can be fitted into them, and, having coded everything as one category or another, to call that the analysis, and then compare it to other findings. In that role, as a coding scheme, these kinds of structural categories impose rather than reveal, obscuring the particularity of specific details, and how that particularity is crucial for the occasioned, action-performative workings of discourse (cf. discussions in Langellier, 1989: 248; Linde, 1993: 66).

Competing stories

One of the features of the stories examined in Chapter 6, where we were concerned with script and disposition formulations, was the way in which stories may be rhetorically designed to manage their own credibility, and to counter alternatives. We examined various ways in which that may be done, specifically with regard to what Bruner (1990: 77) calls the 'canonical' in narrative – the notion of what is usual, routine, or exceptional – and with regard to Kenneth Gergen's (1994: 189) notion of 'character' and its development. The point I want to emphasize here, which both Bruner and (more emphatically) Gergen also appreciate, is the rhetorical, interaction-oriented nature not only of those kinds of formulations, but of narratives generally.

A basic issue in telling a story of events in your life is where to begin: 'Where one chooses to begin and end a narrative can profoundly alter its shape and meaning' (Riessman, 1993: 18). Where to start a story is a major, and rhetorically potent, way of managing causality and accountability. It is an issue not only for personal narratives, but for accounts of all kinds, including histories of nation states, and stories of immigration and ethnicity: who actually belongs where? Starting when? Whose country *is* it? From Britain to Bosnia to New Zealand (Wetherell and Potter, 1992), and the so-called 'Indian' natives of North America (Cronon, 1992), alternative narratives compete in terms of precisely when and where they start.

Then there is what to include: which words/categories to use? To whom, for whom, for what, and at what juncture is the story told? What alternatives are being countered or aligned with? What current interactional business is being managed? It is not just a matter of possessing a narrative mind, whose mental operations turn events into best-sense personal stories. Telling stories is discursive action doing discursive business. This certainly emerges when studying research interviews, but those essentially work *against* interactional considerations, because they tend to substitute, for the ordinary occasions on which stories might be told, got-up occasions for set-piece performances-for-interview. It is better to collect samples of natural talk, where possible, if we want to see how talk performs interactional work other than informing researchers who are interested in narratives, in family relations, in violence, or social attitudes, or whatever.[7]

As an example of 'where to start', consider Extract 10.3, which occurs near the beginning of Jeff's and Mary's first session with their relationship counsellor. Jeff, it may be noted (for brevity's sake), places his wife's recent affair with another man as the origin of their current marital difficulties. But it is Mary who takes the first opportunity to outline their troubles.

Extract 10.3

```
1   Counsellor:   (. . .) P'haps (.) uh in in in your words
2                 or (.) either of your words you better (0.8)
3                 st↑art from the beginning as to why:, you
4                 went to Relate in the first place, (0.6)
5                 and then the difference between the[:n and now.
6   Jeff:                                            [Shall I
7                 (      ) start now or (    )?=
8   Mary:         =Uh? (.)
```

```
 9   Jeff:        °'n you jus (.) keep on  going.°
10                (.)
11   Mary:        Yeh. (.) U:m (3.0) well. What happened,
12                Jeff started doing some exa:ms (.) which (.)
13                la:sted abou:t (0.2) four years.= And before that,
14                (0.8) >this is when we were living in the
15                hospital,< (.) we was always doing some exa:ms,
16                (1.0) since we've me:t, (0.5) at some point, (.)
17                which has lasted some time.
18                (0.8)
19                Anyway Jeff was doing u:m (.) a degree:, (.) that
20                (0.3) la:sted must've bee:n about (0.5) we were
21                just coming to the e:nd. (0.7) Just last summer.
22                (1.0)
23                A:nd during that time I felt that, (0.8) u:m (1.0)
24                he didn't pay any attention to me: that (0.4) um
25                (0.2) ↑alth↑ough we had a s- we still had a fairly
26                good relationship, .hh I didn't feel there was
27                anything wro:ng, .h but (.) at the time, (.)
28                I ↑didn't really think anything too much abou:t
29                (0.2) these pr↑oblems, (0.6) but (.) it must have
30                all like come to a head. (0.8) Then I felt like
31                he was neglecting me:, he didn't wanna know,
32                I was working too har:d, .hh u:m, (0.8) and then
33                I had the two children I felt I was being left on
34                my ow:n, (0.8) uhh (.) an' the:n (.) I started
35                going round with my friends quite a bit, (1.6)
36                u:m, (0.4) ↑just to get out of the house.
37                (0.4)
38                For some rel↑ief.
39                (1.0)
40                And then: I met °somebody e:lse,° (0.8) an:d u:m
41                (1.4) had (0.6) an affair, (.) uh (.) and then I
(DE–JF:C1:S1:2)
```

Rather than starting with her recent affair, Mary starts several years back (lines 12–17) with events that (according to her) led up to it, and therefore somewhat account for it. According to Mary, Jeff's continual and long-term exam preparations led to her feeling neglected (lines 30–1), even though she herself was 'working too har:d' (line 32) and had the children to look after. Mary's own hard work stands as a counter to any suggestion (which Jeff actually develops later) that he was doing all the work for the family while she went off and indulged herself. The affair itself is offered by Mary as an understandable event-in-sequence, a sequence culpably implicating Jeff, and an unlooked-for consequence of her going out with friends, '↑just to get out of the house. (0.4) For some rel↑ief' (lines 34–8).

The rhetorical design of Mary's story (which continues beyond the extract provided) is clear, even without a full interactional analysis of her various accounts, and of Jeff's, which I shall not provide here. In starting her story with events prior to the affair, and in formulating those events in specific ways, Mary manages to provide an accountable basis for her actions, while at the same time attending to likely (and no doubt familiar, and in any case forthcoming) counter-versions from Jeff. Any notion of an irresponsible *neglect* of her family (a notion which Jeff later develops) is countered, ahead of its production in counselling, by an account of *his prior* neglect of her. Any notion that their problems are those of a *happy marriage* spoiled by a wife's sexual adventures (another of Jeff's themes) are countered by the prior problems she outlines. And, should Jeff try to claim that everything was *basically* fine between them prior to the affair (which he does), Mary attends to that ('we still had a fairly good rel_ationship, .hh I didn't feel there was anything wro:ng', lines 25–7), while recounting the underlying, partly unnoticed (and therefore uncomplained-of, should he point that out) pattern of neglect. There is an interaction-oriented exquisiteness in the detail and subtlety of these kinds of stories (and more that I have not picked out here) that is easily missed on a first reading, and missable altogether where stories of this kind are collected and analysed structurally, and in isolation, or as reflections of events or cognitions.

Narrative truth and authenticity

In the social and human sciences, in anthropological, ethnographic, psychological, and other research domains, narrative analysis is generally a matter of collecting interviews about particular kinds of life experiences (for example Linde, 1993, recorded interviews on choice of profession), and fitting them to various analytical categories and schemas.

> The purpose is to see how respondents in interviews impose order on the flow of experience to make sense of events and actions in their lives. The methodological approach examines the informant's story and analyses how it is put together, the linguistic and cultural resources it draws on, and how it persuades a listener of authenticity. (Riessman, 1993: 2)

These notions of 'persuasion' and 'authenticity' reflect a recurrent theme in narrative theory, which is the interpersonal functions of story-telling. Despite that theme, interactional orientations tend to be underplayed *in actual analyses* of narratives, by virtue of the focus on structural story schemas, data from interviews and written literature, and in the location of narrative studies within the theoretical domains of self, identity, and personal growth.

As Riessman (1993) notes, in the 'life story method' (for example, Bruner, 1990; Josselson and Lieblich, 1993; Murray, 1989; Plummer, 1995) the usual thing is to mix analysis and data, and blur the distinction. Rather than focusing analysis on transcribed materials and their interactional settings, the analyst uses quotations from informants' talk as illustrations of analysts' summaries, gists, generalizations, and glosses. This glosses-and-quotes treatment of discourse materials is reminiscent of essays on works of literature,[8] though sometimes transcripts are also used (Linde, 1993; Young, 1987). Generally, the analyst's 'authorial voice and interpretative commentary knit the disparate elements together and determine how readers are to understand [the informant's] experience. . . . Illustrative quotes from the interview provide evidence for the investigator's interpretation of the plot twists' (Riessman, 1993: 30).

One advantage of interviewing-for-narratives is that it allows participants to develop long turns and tell things 'in their own way', in contrast to the more question–answer kinds of format used in other interview research, where personal narratives and 'anecdotal' replies may even be systematically prevented from developing. More structured research methods (questionnaires, experiments, structured interviews, etc.) may treat personal stories as some kind of noise or nuisance, to be discouraged by the use of standard questions, fixed topics, a fixed range of possible responses, and/or analytic methods that break up and lose whatever conversational or narrative flow might still have been captured on audiotape. Nevertheless, narrative interviewing is still interviewing, and 'in their own way' tends to be treated as definitive of how respondents 'see' things, rather than an instance of interaction-oriented talk.

'Authenticity' in life story interview studies is generally taken not as a participants' concerted accomplishment, something discursively constructed, but, rather, as some kind of built-in feature bequeathed by the methodology of collecting personal stories (in contrast to more impersonal methodologies). *Non*-authenticity in such settings may be treated as a kind of forgivable *aberration*, behind which may nevertheless lie a deeper, and recoverable, psychological truth: 'When talking about their lives, people lie sometimes, forget a lot, exaggerate, become confused, and get things wrong. Yet they *are* revealing truths. These truths don't reveal the past "as it actually was", aspiring to a standard of objectivity. They give us instead the truths of our experiences' (Personal Narratives Group, 1989: 261, original emphasis).

This is a 'type 2' treatment of discourse, approaching it as a kind of window on participants' perspectives. Again, it is essential to separate the notion I am promoting here of discourse's action-orientation from any notion that this is a cynical and mistrusting way to deal with people. It is neither to trust nor to mistrust, but to analyse. It is to treat *all* talk as performative, as action-oriented, as doing something, such that issues of sincerity, truth, honest confession, lies, errors, confabulations, and so on, are matters that talk itself must manage, and *does* manage, in analysable ways. The management of authenticity, as a participants' concern or accomplishment, is explored in a wide variety of discourse studies. These include Edwards and Potter (1992a), Lynch and Bogen (1996), and Wooffitt (1992) on factual authenticity and the credibility of reports; Widdicombe (1993) and Widdicombe and Wooffitt (1995) on persons as authentic members, holders of, or spokespersons for a particular social identity; and Whalen and Zimmerman (1990) on how those two things (personal identity and the authenticity of reports) may be managed simultaneously.

For example, Sue Widdicombe and Robin Wooffitt (1995) are concerned with the discourse of social identity. In their materials, 'authenticity' is at stake with regard to membership (and therefore speakers' rights to talk *as* members) of a youth sub-culture whose appearance, tastes, and other preferences might be taken as signs of mere conformity to a standard group image. Respondents deal with that issue by telling fragments of life stories that build authentic membership in terms of self-expression or personal choice. Like Mary does with regard to Jeff (Extract 10.3 above), and Jimmy does with regard to Connie (Chapter 6, Extract 6.8a), one way they do it is to place decisive details *further back* in the 'taleworld' of events than the rhetorical alternative would require. In Extract 10.4, 'MR1' is a 'goth' talking to an interviewer, 'I'. The important notion here, in the context of analysing personal narratives, is how the notion of a 'true self' is discursively managed, rather than being something that is simply available in this kind of talk, lying behind and generating it.

Extract 10.4

```
 1   MR1:   yeah 'cos I started wearing make up, and I
 2            didn't even know about other people wearing it
 3            I st- I star- I just started wearing it and
 4            putting on these black clothes and things like
 5            that an' then ⌈I went
 6   I:                     ⌊ahha
 7   MR1:   I went into town one week because like I was
 8            considered really freaky by everybody (.)
 9            because .hh all these people who lived on this
10            estate hadn't ever seen anybody like me before (.)
11            I went into town one evening an' walked by this
12            pub an' saw loads of people with hair, spiked up
13            an' things like that an' er a lot more way out than
14            me even though I was considered the biggest freak
15            of the area- they were a lot more way out than me-
```
(3G:2M/1F:T17SA [KHS]) from Widdicombe and Wooffitt (1995: 148)

Widdicombe and Wooffitt focus on how, in snatches of 'autobiography', respondent 'MR1' manages his authenticity, both as an independent agent, and also as a member of a sub-cultural group. His narrated change of appearance, in the way it is described as personal and spontaneous, and in its sequential placing prior to his knowledge of other people looking similar (lines 1–4), follows a pattern of narrative accountability found across a range of other interviews. MR1's story rhetorically counters any 'negative inferences regarding the reasons for that change . . . that speakers were copying or influenced by others, or conforming to a particular image' (1995: 149). The narrative in lines 7 to 15 (which runs on after line 15) is produced as a specific episode within a larger pattern of events, in which the speaker had already started, spontaneously, to adopt the persona that would eventually make him identifiable as a member of a group.

Widdicombe's and Wooffitt's analysis brings out the way in which autobiographical stories are intrinsically, and in detail, interaction-oriented and rhetorical. Personal stories attend to motive and accountability, to alternative readings, alternative identities. Bruner suggests that young children learn to narrate events within the context of family relations, disputes, and the negotiation of identities, where 'narrative becomes an instrument for telling not only what happened but also why it justified the action recounted . . . narrating becomes not only an expository act but a rhetorical one' (1990: 86–7). This should not be thought of as something restricted to people with especially delicate identities to manage. It is an issue also even for the most literary and interactionally marooned of written autobiographies (Freeman, 1993), although the interaction-oriented nature of autobiographical discourse emerges most clearly in spoken interaction, and through applying the kinds of discursive and conversation analytic methods used by Widdicombe and Wooffitt.

Stories, mental states, and memory

As we have noted, in both cognitive and narrative psychology, whatever their theoretical and methodological differences, memory for events is closely bound to the phenomena and organization (whether mental or discursive) of story-telling. From a discursive perspective, relations between narrative and memory can be studied in two related ways. First, narrative accounts can be studied *as* acts of remembering, as the discursive equivalent to what people do in memory experiments when they recall events (Edwards and Middleton, 1986a, 1986b). Second, we can study memory as a participants' concern, examining the situated uses of words such as 'remember', 'forget', and so on. And we can study how those two things go together, how appeals to notions such as remembering and forgetting feature in the dynamics of event reporting, and vice versa. Relations between narrative accounts and references to remembering are part of how ordinary discourse deals with relations between mind and world: in this case, with events in relation to memory. Memory and events, mind and world, feature in discourse as mutually defining and delimiting categories, just as we saw in Connie's and Jimmy's discourse of emotional states, clouded perceptions, and disputed event descriptions (Chapter 6; cf. Goodwin, 1987, on forgetting; and Drew, 1989, on recall). So Extract 10.4 can be considered a piece of narrative *remembering*, in that it recounts specific events in the speaker's past life, offered as recalled experiences.

Another feature of Extract 10.4 is the various direct invocations of cognitive processes: 'I *didn't even know* about other people wearing it' (lines 1–2); 'I was *considered* really freaky' (lines 7–8). Mental states, including knowledge and belief, and claims to remember or forget, feature in stories as an intrinsic part of the actions recounted, as well as performing evaluations of those actions, and dealing with an actor-narrator's accountability. Mental state descriptions feature in how narrators attend to factual authenticity, and create a sense of conveying genuine personal experiences. In doing all of that (rather than as some separate business) they also attend to interactional concerns in the telling, and this can be something very delicately managed.

According to Wittgenstein, words such as 'remember' and 'forget', which psychologists may take to label private mental processes, are best analysed in terms of their public uses. This focus on public uses is not a matter of denying the existence of inner mental processes. Rather, 'what we deny is that the picture of the inner process gives us the correct idea of the use of the word "to remember"' (Wittgenstein, 1958: §305). The way words such as 'remember' are used, and the common-sense assumptions that go with them, are available for analysis as public practices. The issue becomes, what are people *doing* when they talk like this? The topic for investigation becomes 'the intersubjective conventions and constraints in the ratification of the ascription of such predicates by self or other' (Coulter, 1985: 129).

Among a rich and suggestive series of observations, Coulter notes that the discourse of memory and forgetting permits *retrospective knowledge claims* to be handled in interactionally sensitive ways. For example, 'I forget X' can be used to imply that X was previously known, whereas the ostensibly similar 'I don't remember X' need imply no such prior knowledge, making such an expression useful, for example, as a courtroom 'evasion device' (Coulter, 1985: 132). Indeed, as we noted in discussions of categories in general (Chapters 7–9), it is likely to be *for* such discursive uses that verbal categories are coined.

This very distinction between forgetting and not remembering was a recurrent trope used by witnesses in the Iran–Contra hearings (Bogen and Lynch, 1989; Lynch and Bogen, 1996). Based on an analysis of Oliver North's testimony (and other examples), Michael Lynch and David Bogen suggest that '"I don't remember" is not a report on a speaker's cognitive state any more than the terms yes and no act as reports on mental states of agreement or disagreement' (1996: 182). The *performative* nature of the discourse of mental and intersubjective states is, of course, something I have emphasized throughout this book. The claim to 'not remember' something is perfectly designed to avoid the yes–no strategy of interrogation, while avoiding blame for avoiding it, and retaining options to go either way according to how future questioning, testimony, and emerging evidence may develop. The much repeated response along the lines of 'I don't recall' became notorious as a possibly evasive manoeuvre, especially in the testimonies of Oliver North and of ex-President Reagan.

Extract 10.5

1	*Nields*:	Did you suggest to the Attorney General that maybe the
2		diversion memorandum and the fact that there was a
3		diversion need not ever come out?
4	*North*:	Again, I don't recall that specific conversation at all, but

5   I'm not saying it didn't happen.
6 *Nields*:   You don't deny it?
7 *North*:   No.
8 *Nields*:   You don't deny suggesting to the Attorney General of the
9   United States that he just figure out a way of keeping this
10   diversion document secret?
11 *North*:   I don't deny that I said it. I'm not saying I remember it either.
(as cited in Lynch and Bogen, 1996: 195, line numbers added)

Lynch and Bogen note how North's claim (lines 4 and 11) that he cannot remember something functions to make him 'practically unavailable' as a witness.[9] His responses provide a way of balking the progress of a line of interrogation (whether or not successfully), and avoiding both an incriminating confession and a potentially troublesome denial if later evidence and testimony should undermine such a denial. The examiner's use of the title 'Attorney General of the United States' (lines 8–9), rather than the name (Edward Meese) of North's conversational partner, not only builds the seriousness of what is at stake ('just' in line 9 is surely ironic – 'that he just figure out a way of keeping this document secret'), but also the unlikelihood of North's inability to remember it.[10]

One of the themes of Lynch and Bogen's analysis is the function of common-sense appeals to what people may be expected, or entitled, to remember or forget: 'the interrogator and witness engage in an agonistic struggle . . . in which both parties try to invoke public standards of memorability in order to specify convincingly for an audience what *could* make up the contents of the witness's past' (1996: 196, original emphasis). Memory and forgetting are thus referred to criteria of public accountability (cf. Shotter, 1990). They are essentially 'visible' in the general sense used by Wittgenstein, Garfinkel, and Sacks, in that they are used as tokens of intelligible, describable, and norm-oriented public practices.

Claiming an exceptionally good memory, or possessing such a reputation, is as rhetorically flexible a matter as being forgetful. In the Watergate hearings for example, John Dean's rhetorical use of his reputedly exceptional memory was to provide a credible basis for the provision of a remarkably (and remarked on) large range of precise details in his testimony (Edwards and Potter, 1992a, 1992b; Neisser, 1981). On the other hand, 'judges sometimes rule that a witness's testimony is too detailed, or too consistent with independent records of the facts, and that it therefore has the appearance of being concocted or rehearsed, as opposed to being remembered' (Lynch and Bogen, 1996: 190; cf. Edwards and Potter, 1992b, on a politician's rebuttal of a consensus of journalistic reports on what he purportedly said).

In the Iran–Contra hearings, Admiral Poindexter arrived with the potentially unfortunate reputation of being a man of high intelligence and academic training (a PhD in nuclear physics), and of possessing a virtually photographic memory (Lynch and Bogen, 1996: 188). In the context of those hearings, and the notorious inability of several key witnesses to recall events, this threatened to make it very difficult for Poindexter if he was also to deny being able to remember a number of potentially incriminating details of his, and other high-profile people's, activities. What he did was to use his 'good memory' to rhetorical effect as a basis for his *inability* to provide details:

> Poindexter: (. . .) I want to obviously be very careful as to what I attribute to the President and what I don't. It's obviously an important issue, and so, unless I can remember something very specific, I'm reluctant to- to- uhm attribute things to the President, uh ih- either things he said or- or things I think he knows. (1996: 188)

Being such an able and careful recaller, and in contrast to anyone for whom remembering details might be a more fuzzy and insecure sort of activity, Poindexter could appeal to that special scope for accuracy as grounds on which he might sift between those precise details of which he was sure, and those of which he was not. The significance of the issues at stake, for the culpability of the President, indeed the very thing that made his testimony so important, became useful as grounds for withholding anything of which he could not guarantee total accuracy. The potentially undermining notion that his rememberings might selectively favour the President was produced as a feature of that necessary care and importance. Additionally, it provided grounds for Poindexter's reluctance to provide the 'gist' or 'tenor' of whatever he could not recall in detail.

Inability to recall certain details may also provide a way of implying that those details were not worth remembering. This can imply that, despite the significance they might obtain later, as relevant to a subsequent crime or misdemeanour perhaps (Drew, 1990), they did not have that significance at the time for the person now remembering, and this in turn can signal an innocent involvement in those events. This kind of status for an item in a report-from-memory can be quite subtly accomplished. Look back, for instance, to the discussion of Extract 6.10, in which Jimmy's 'she had a short skirt on *I don't know*' (the part italicized here) delicately signals his lack of concern about such things at the time, and counters Connie's picture of a pathologically suspicious and watchful husband. Public criteria for the workings of mind and memory are, in Sacks's sense, discursively 'subverted'.

If and *then*: narrative versus paradigmatic thinking

Bruner's approach to narrative adopts it as the essential feature of 'folk psychology', the common-sense understandings by which people of all cultures, in their different ways, live their lives. Folk psychology is concerned with 'how human beings, in interacting with one another, form a sense of the canonical and ordinary as a background against which to interpret and give narrative meaning to breaches in and deviations from "normal" states of the human condition' (Bruner, 1990: 67). This links narrative psychology to Heider's (1958) common-sense 'attribution theory', and to script theory (Schank and Abelson, 1977), as modes of cognition and action by which people understand and account for what is routine and exceptional.

In defining the nature and importance of narrative understanding, Bruner (1986) draws a distinction between narrative and 'paradigmatic' modes of thought. Paradigmatic thought is the abstracted, generalized, logical mode of discourse used in philosophy and science. Similar kinds of distinctions between common-sense language and thinking, on the one hand, and formal or analytic kinds of thought, on the other, can be found in academic discussions of diverse matters such as literate versus oral discourse (Havelock, 1963; Olson, 1977; Ong, 1982); formal education versus its absence (Scribner and Cole, 1981); working-class versus middle-class modes of speech (Bernstein, 1971); human language versus animal communication (Bronowski and Bellugi, 1980; Hockett, 1960); and the thinking of young children versus older ones (Bruner, 1964; Inhelder and Piaget, 1958). Various critiques of those distinctions have made at least some of them look like theoretical idealizations rather than empirically sustainable oppositions (Donaldson, 1978; Labov, 1970; Street, 1984).

Narrative is a category of discourse that comes into its own, as any other category does, when contrasted with alternatives. Narrative is defined contrastively as virtually any non-paradigmatic text, though Bruner's base model of it seems to be literary fiction, and narratology's ideal types and schemas. However, in drawing that contrast, the definition of narrative becomes very broad indeed, in recognition of the sheer variety of types, including modern and postmodern literary works, and condenses merely to 'narrative deals with the vicissitudes of intention' (Bruner, 1986: 16–17). Examined more closely, the narrative/paradigmatic dichotomy blurs the ways in which science and philosophy work as discourses. It draws on an idealization of science; something more like philosophical stipulations of what science ought to be, rather than SSK's descriptions of science as social and discursive practices. For example, Gilbert and Mulkay (1984) propose the 'contingent repertoire' (a narrative mode of scientific talk: see Chapter 3) as an *integral part* of science, used in constructing and accounting for scientific error. On the other hand, even everyday narratives deploy generalized analytic categories, such as types of persons, actions, events, and dispositions (see Chapters 4–9, on the explanation-oriented nature of everyday descriptions, script and disposition formulations, and the deployment of categories in everyday discourse).

In pursuing the virtues of narrative against a widespread academic and educational bias in favour of paradigmatic thinking, Bruner draws a rather stark dichotomy. There are 'two modes of cognitive functioning, two modes of thought, each providing distinct ways of ordering experience, of constructing reality. . . . They function differently . . . and the structure of a well-formed logical argument differs radically from that of a well-wrought story' (Bruner, 1986: 11). Bruner defines the differences here 'as baldly as possible' (1986: 11) for clarity's sake, though what we are left with is the difference, the stark dichotomy, rather than any kind of rapprochement, which is resisted: they are 'complementary' and 'irreducible to one another' (1986: 11).

Bruner offers a neat illustration of the distinction, using the word 'then', which is a central term both in logical reasoning and in story-telling. 'The term *then* functions differently in the logical proposition "if x, then y" and in the narrative *recit* "The king died, and then the queen died". One leads to a search for universal truth conditions, the other for likely particular connections between two events' (1986: 11–12). It seems churlish to try to upset such an agreeable distinction, though we could start to do so by suggesting that the two meanings of 'then' are simply different, that they are two words that happen to share the same phonetic form, making it an artificial exercise to put them together like this. Alternatively, we could argue that the differences are overplayed. For example, which kind of connection is this, narrative or logic? – 'If you go back there, then I shall think you the worst person I have ever met.'

Interestingly, the *Oxford English Dictionary* (1994) puts the two meanings of *then* squarely together, listing, among other references to 'sequence in time, order, consequence, incidence, inference':

> In that case; in those circumstances; if that be (or were) the fact; if so, when that happens. Often correl. to *if* or *when. what then?* (ellipt.) what happens (or would happen) in that case? what of that?

The *OED* illustrates this mixture of sequential events and rational inferences by examples all the way from the seventh-century *Laws of Wihtræd*, through Shakespeare's narrative-conditional 'O had they in that darkesome prison died, Then had they seene the period of their ill', to A.J. Ayer's 'Can it reasonably be held that knowledge is always knowledge that something is the case? If knowing that something is the case is taken to involve the making of a conscious judgment, then plainly it cannot.' In the *OED*, no strong distinction is drawn, etymologically or semantically, between logical and temporal uses of 'then', despite the fact that, as Bruner shows, we can choose examples that polarize such differences, and make them look like two different words.[11]

Let us pursue the similarities, then, rather than the differences, and consider how the *relations* between a logical and narrative 'then' might prove useful in ordinary talk. My rather strained, invented example is a start: 'If you go back there, then I shall think you the worst person I have ever met.' Considering this as something perhaps *said* somewhere, I can hear a couple of things (at least) possibly being done. It serves as a kind of prediction and warning of how actual events (in *narrative* sequence) will follow each other: 'do X and after that I will think Y of you'. At the same time, there is a kind of rational accountability built in for the speaker: thinking Y of you is offered as a reasonable conclusion, a *rational inference*, an example of the kinds of action–disposition links that people draw between the things people do (X) and their personal characters (Y).

Those rational links are the basis, for example, of a 'correspondent inference theory' of everyday attributional reasoning (Jones and Davis, 1965), in which common-sense reasoners compute people's traits and personalities from consistencies in their actions across situations, and then use those inferred personality profiles in order to explain their actions. In Chapter 6 we examined ways in which such inferences, including the use of *if–then* kinds of constructions, were discursively and rhetorically produced. For example, there was Jimmy's 'Uh I I feel (.) if Connie does something to me I can- I'm <u>hurt</u> real bad', and also Connie in Extract 6.11: 'if <u>some</u>body came up- I'm <u>not</u> the type that can-' (see the discussion of that sequence in Chapter 6). *If–then* structures are useful as general scripting devices (Edwards, 1995), and can perform the disposition-implicative work that such devices do. Rudyard Kipling's renowned homily of Victorian virtue (the poem 'If') can be understood as a sustained example of this, a plan formula for budding manhood: 'If you can keep your head when all about you/Are losing theirs and blaming it on you . . . [etc.], you'll be a Man, my son!'). It tells what to do, in terms of a series of scripted vignettes (narratives), while simultaneously offering a logical definition (paradigm) of what, properly speaking, a 'Man' is.

In other words, it may be that the *close relations* between temporal and logical connections can serve as *discursive resources* for telling stories, for treating events and actions as expectable, and for drawing inferences, in which temporal sequence, causality, and rational accountability are mutually implicative. If that is so, then distinctions between paradigmatic and narrative modes of thought, again, start to look like theoretical idealizations of how people think, based on polarized examples of formally defined types of text (formal logic versus literary narratives).

Second stories: cognitive and discursive approaches

The essential difference between cognitive and discursive approaches to narrative (or stories) is that cognitive approaches treat them as expressions of how people understand things, whereas discursive approaches treat them as interaction-oriented productions. In discourse, 'how people understand things' dissolves into discourse practices. 'Narrative psychology' entertains both these notions, cognitive and discursive, though the tensions between them generally remain unexplored. Those tensions tend to remain in the background when the materials under analysis are one-off, definitive kinds of productions, such as autobiographies, literary works, responses elicited in interview, or the analyst's own schematic reconstruction of a story's underlying structure. The tensions come to the fore, however, when we start to examine narratives produced in conversation, including when research interviews are conducted and analysed as social interactions, rather than as elicitations. Couple counselling is an obvious context in which successive stories are produced which attend, in form and detail, to agreements and contrasts with competing stories (see especially Chapter 6). But even in much less obviously confrontational settings, we have seen how stories attend to interactional concerns such as the management of personal identity, authenticity, and factual credibility.

In conversation analysis, one feature of stories is that they are kinds of *long turns* that people can take, and the analytic interest is partly in how stories are begun and ended, including how the ordinary norms of conversational turn-taking are oriented-to so that stories can be told without constant interruption.[12] Stories may be 'proposed' or 'pre-announced' (for example, 'Guess what? . . .'), or invited or otherwise provided for in special kinds of social interactions such as interviews, courtroom testimony, or counselling. See, for example, lines 1–11 in Extract 10.3 above, where the counsellor invites Mary and Jeff to tell their stories, and how they sort out who will go first, including Jeff's suggestion that Mary 'jus (.) keep on going'. But a large part of the interest here is not simply in turn-taking procedures per se, but in how, *as* turns of talk-in-interaction, stories can be analysed as *participants' own discourse categories*; in how the specific content of stories is tailored to current interactional concerns; and in how stories are contextually 'occasioned' and 'received'.

One way in which a story may be 'received' is through the production of a second one that, in various ways, matches or contrasts with it. These 'second stories' (Sacks, 1992) provide a useful basis for showing how cognitive and discursive approaches can take widely divergent analytic and theoretical paths. We can appreciate the similarities and differences by looking at how Harvey Sacks (the conversation analyst) and Roger Schank (the cognitive scientist) have gone about analysing them.

Schank (1982: 185), in discussing the basis for script theory (see Chapter 6 of this volume), recounts a series of stories of 'suckering experiences', exchanged between himself and fellow cognitive scientist Don Norman, in a university cafeteria. Apparently Schank had noticed some attractive-looking meat being carved, and had ordered some, only to be given some inferior stuff that had been sliced previously. He returned with it to his table with Norman, and told what had happened, saying 'Boy, have I been suckered!' Norman denied that this was a proper example of suckering on the grounds that there was no 'serious attempt to defraud', and proceeded to tell a second story, recounting how he (Norman) had bought some food and wine from a little Spanish village store, 'run by someone who looked just like a gypsy lady' (1982: 185), only to find later, on opening the package, that it contained nothing but 'carefully wrapped up garbage', adding 'now that was a suckering experience' (1982: 185). That led on to further 'suckering' stories by Schank and then again Norman. The thing of interest here is the kind of theory that Schank provides for these instances, and the contrasts that can be drawn with how conversation analysts treat 'second stories'.

Consider first the kind of data we are dealing with. Schank's stories are presented as anecdotal summaries of what Schank and Norman said to each other, rather than being transcribed recordings of talk; and I have produced my own further summaries of Schank's. In conversation analysis, in contrast, we would be dealing with transcribed audio recordings, in which specific details (as we have seen) can be crucial for the analysis. Second, consider the kind of analysis offered. Schank describes the succession of stories as a series of 'remindings', each story triggering another similar one, based on similarities between how the events were perceived and understood at the time they happened. The stories are taken to be expressions of similar cognitive representations of generalized (scripted) event sequences.

In contrast to a talk-as-action approach (such as CA itself, and various kinds of discursive and rhetorical analysis), there is no notion of *invention* in Schank's treatment. There is no notion of telling stories so as to *make* them fit each other; no notion of upstaging, of designing stories *for* such relevant secondings, and so on. Indeed this is where it matters that it is *not* an audio recording that we are dealing with. What we are given is a post hoc reconstruction of dialogue, reproduced precisely for how it illustrates the workings of shared cognitive representations. The succession of stories might take on a different status if transcribed and analysed *as an interaction* between Schank and Norman. In a discursive analysis, something would surely be made of significant details, such as the difference between 'the server, a young woman' who gave Schank the carved meat, and the woman 'who looked just like a gypsy lady' who more severely, and seriously, 'suckered' Norman, and of the related *upgrading* of Schank's story done by Norman's story – of how subsequent stories are *told so as to* fit, but build relevantly (as partial contrasts, upgrades, 'cappings', etc.) on prior ones.

For Schank, hearing a story *triggers an automatic cognitive response*, a 'reminding', a reactivation of the perceptual–cognitive schemas that presumably processed the original event. Conversational remindings are therefore an index of the common (scripted) features of mental representations. In conversation analysis, producing second stories is a kind of *performative activity*. The kinds of interactional business that second stories can do are illustrated in an analysis offered by Harvey Sacks of an example that, like Schank's, also focuses on failed expectations of a sort.

Sacks (1992, vol. 2: 459ff) analyses a piece of everyday autobiographic story swapping between two participants with regard to matters of job careers and prospects. In Sacks's analysis, there emerges a clear sense of the stories being generated very precisely for the occasion of their production, and with regard to the current concerns of the interaction in which they are told. It is a rich transcript and analysis which I shall not reproduce here. But one specific segment is a report concerning an acquaintance of the speaker who, a long time previously, had 'said he went to acting school with Kirk Douglas. And I [the speaker, not Sacks] believe him.' Sacks analyses this as a 'failed-prospects' story, whose relevance in the conversation in which it occurs is that *its* general topic is the current speaker's own failed prospects, which in some way parallel those of the could-have-been actor. Sacks remarks:

> Kirk Douglas is a very relevant object for that, in two related ways. The one obvious way is that if he went to acting school with Kirk Douglas, Kirk Douglas now being somebody plainly a success, then the fact that Kirk Douglas is a success and he isn't, makes for that he did, indeed, fail. But also . . . turns that he is a failure into . . . a failure given that one had prospects. . . . He [the teller] also puts in, 'He was a nice looking guy' . . . [as if] to say 'I now looking at him, I can see how he could have been an actor . . . ' The question is whether one could say 'I always wanted to be an actor and now I end up an insurance man' and someone could believe that you are now someone who had failed prospects in a way that's relevant to their own failed prospects. (1992, vol. 2: 461–2)

Again, it is a Schankian 'remindings' sort of example of everyday narrative, but developed by Sacks in terms not of the automatic triggering of story schemas, but of how such stories are methodically assembled in conversations. They are put together in ways that *accomplish* relevance to each other (what Sacks calls, with emphasis, 'an *achieved similarity* . . . that B produced this story in such a way that its similarity to A's will be seeable', 1992, vol. 2: 4), and in doing so, manage current interactional concerns. That being the case, Sacks raises the intriguing possibility that events might be understood, and stories told, precisely so that they can be *used* like this, to accomplish interactional business in various tellings, rather than simply to code experience once and for all.

For Sacks, second stories are actively designed as matching versions, thereby performing a kind of *receipt* of first stories, exhibiting 'understanding' of them, of their point or relevance, and so on. Second stories are kinds of *next turns* that, whatever else they do, manage and develop conversational intersubjectivity. Intersubjectivity, as Chapter 5 demonstrates, involves contrasts and oppositions as much as similarities and agreements, and is analysable as public conversational business. Sacks provides an example of how he approaches these matters that contrasts directly with a standard kind of psychological approach to memory and comprehension:

> A typical device is if somebody tells a story, you give a hearer ten minutes and ask them to retell the story. . . . Now what's impressive here is, instead of saying 'Let's find a way of seeing whether people understand what somebody else says', we've asked 'Is there some procedure *people use* which has as its product a showing that they heard and understood?' (1992, vol. 2: 30–1, emphases added)

This is a question that can be addressed empirically with conversational materials (for example, Buchanan and Middleton, 1995).

Let us finally, to the extent it is possible with the materials Schank provides, see how a discursive analysis might start to deal with them. Schank cites 'President Carter's statements in 1979 about the Russian presence in Afghanistan. He alluded then to the Munich conference of 1938. "No appeasement this time – stop them now" seemed to be the point'(1982: 63). Schank's analysis starts by asking the question, 'How is an input processed so as to draw out the *appeasement led to disaster* episode from memory?' (1982: 63–4). So Carter's drawing of a parallel between Russian activity in Afghanistan and the Nazi invasion of Europe is treated as a cognitively triggered 'reminding', rather than, say, as an artfully *worked-up* parallel, a powerfully evocative piece of political rhetoric that might serve to justify current presidential foreign policy with regard to non-interference alternatives. One wonders whether opponents of that policy would be, or would claim to be, similarly 'reminded'. Indeed, we should start to consider what statements such as 'that reminds me' can *do*, when uttered in discourse. It is clearly a useful, 'subvertible' idea that you are saying something on the basis that it just occurred to you, rather than that you are working it up rhetorically, for its occasion, or have been trying to find a place to say it, or that it has got any interactional business hanging on it.

In objecting to a perceptual–cognitive treatment of story-telling, I am not claiming that involuntary, perception-based remindings do not happen, or are not psychologically important. It is just that, whatever the nature and status of such things, they are *a perverse basis for analysing discourse*. Clearly some kind of event-pattern-matching process is going on when people tell stories and second stories. But Schank's specification of it as a series of triggered conceptual remindings grossly misses the action-performative, interaction-oriented, nature of discourse. Schank's notion of remindings adopts the model of the lone cognitive perceiver whose talk is a window upon, or expression of, 'best sense' cognitive processes that crank out automatically behind it: 'An intelligent understander is seeking to learn from his experiences, to draw new conclusions, to make sense of the world' (Schank, 1982: 63). It is a cognitivist mode of explanation, moving from perception through cognition to discourse, that, whatever its virtues as a model of cognitive information processing, fails to explicate what people are doing when they narrate events.

Notes

1. See, for examples, Brewer and Lichtenstein (1981, 1982), Kintsch and Van Dijk (1983), Mandler (1984), Mandler and Johnson (1977), Rumelhart (1975, 1977), and Thorndyke (1977). For critical discussions see Black and Wilensky (1984), Brewer (1985), Brown and Yule (1983), Cortazzi (1993), and Garnham (1983).
2. One feature of the type-and-structure approach is to draw distinctions of various kinds between 'stories' and 'narratives', usually as part of an effort to legislate about what should count as a proper, 'well-formed' example (e.g., Labov, 1972). Since I develop reservations in this chapter about the analytic usefulness of typological approaches, I use these terms more or less interchangeably, or use whichever term the study in question used. A common-sense notion of 'stories' is perfectly adequate at this point (cf. Sacks, 1972b); I consider some formal definitions later in the chapter.
3. Rather than reviving the first cognitive revolution, Rom Harré (1993; also Harré and Gillett, 1994) celebrates the growth of a contrasting 'second cognitive revolution', exemplified by discursive psychology. Bruner's new psychology has much in common with Harré's vision, but the notion that narrative psychology, rather than information

processing, captures the spirit and intention of the 'first' revolution seems at odds with the views of George Miller, who was Bruner's co-founder in 1960 of the influential Harvard Center for Cognitive Studies. Miller, a long advocate of information processing approaches, sketches the ideal preparation for a career in the psychology of cognition and language: 'I would try to learn everything I could about biology and computers. A psychologist who masters either one of these fields will be uniquely prepared for the future; a psychologist who mastered them both, in addition to psychology, would be a scientific superman' (1990: 13).

4. Bruner's discussions of narrative move mostly between types 2 and 3, treating narratives as expressions of mind but also, and apparently without contradiction, as a form of 'praxis'. For example, he suggests that it is thought, not reality (type 2 not type 1), that narratives express: 'it does not matter whether the account conforms to what others might say who were witnesses, nor are we in pursuit of such ontologically obscure issues as whether the account is "self-deceptive" or "true". Our interest, rather, is only in what the person *thought* he did, what he *thought* he was doing it for, what kinds of plights he *thought* he was in, and so on' (Bruner, 1990: 119–20, emphasis added).

5. Lest it be thought that I am contradicting the anti-cognitive perspective for which I argue by using expressions in my own writing such as 'with these three types *in mind*', I should state that I use them as coherent and familiar *ways of talking*. I could say instead, 'having reviewed these three types', or 'having established their relevance', or some such thing, but I prefer to write with the same rhetorical and common-sense freedom of expression as everyone else.

6. See Longacre (1976) for a related, though independently formulated, set of structural categories: Aperture (opening, or pre-announcement), Stage (setting, scene, etc.), Episode (event, conflicts, disequilibrium), Dénouement (resolution), Conclusion (upshot, point, moral), Finis (closing).

7. As Charlotte Linde (1993) points out, interviews are useful when you want to pursue specific topics (attitudes to X, stories about Y, etc.), and cannot wait for ever to hear them come up spontaneously. But the risk is that of analytically *ignoring* contexts and occasions, of imposing in their place those of mere research methodology, and of treating responses as what people think, or know, or as what actually happened. Although the disadvantages of interviews can be effectively countered by adopting a more interaction-based analytic stance towards them, one that treats them as interactions rather than elicitations, this remains largely a matter of making a virtue of necessity or convenience. Clearly it is possible to analyse research interviews *as kinds of social interactions*, and to reveal various kinds of interactional business being attended to (see, for some useful discussions and examples, Mishler, 1986a, 1986b; Potter and Mulkay, 1985; Rosenthal, 1993; Wetherell and Potter, 1992; Widdicombe and Wooffitt, 1995). And of course there are studies which focus specifically on various kinds of interviews themselves as the phenomena at issue (e.g., Greatbatch, 1986; Schegloff, 1989c; Suchman and Jordan, 1990). The point is that, if personal stories are constructed with regard to managing interactional concerns *in the telling*, then the interactional contingencies of their production are a crucially important matter for analysts to study, rather than subvert.

8. Note, however, that readers of essays on literary works can consult the originals for themselves and dispute any analysis offered. Likewise it is a foundational aim of conversation analysis that 'the reader has as much information as the author, and can reproduce the analysis' (Sacks, 1992, vol. 1: 27).

9. Lynch and Bogen (1996: 183) note that 'the pragmatic uses of nonrecall have long been recognized by legal scholars', and cite an article by Michael Graham (1978) as the source of the notion of a witness's 'practical unavailability'.

10. This is comparable to an instance from John Dean's testimony to the Watergate hearings, in which Dean warranted the accuracy of his rememberings by appealing to how 'you tend to remember what *the President of the United States* says when you have a conversation with him' (Edwards and Potter, 1992b: 8, emphasis added). Try substituting 'Nixon' for the italicized part. Similarly, Lynch and Bogen (1996: 195) cite a counter-value report to the

effect that Meese's involvement was not in his capacity as Attorney General, but as 'friend of the President'.

11. In addition to 'then' there are other semantic concurrences between logic and narrative, such as the notion of 'what follows', and of 'conditions'.

12. See, for examples, C. Goodwin (1984), M.H. Goodwin (1990), Jefferson (1978), Lerner (1992), Ryave (1978), and Sacks (1974, 1986, 1992). We might note again at this point how, in the counselling materials we have examined, speakers engage in long turns full of pauses and other potential points at which others might ordinarily start to talk ('transition relevance places', or TRPs), but are generally allowed to continue talking, with due allowance for 'backchannel' reactions and hearer-prompted clarifications or repetitions (Goodwin, 1984). This feature makes counselling recognizable and producible as a form of social interaction in which folk can 'have their say'.

11

Membership: Children, Animals, and Machines

The analysis of everyday discourse generally proceeds on the assumption that participants, analysts, and readers are co-members of an essentially common culture. The kinds of textual and conversational materials used in this book generally present no initial problems in understanding them. Many are quite mundane, and only start to become interesting under analysis. Even politically oriented 'critical' discourse studies (for example, Fairclough, 1992; Hodge and Kress, 1993; Parker, 1992), which emphasize the conflictual, power-wielding and class-ridden nature of discourse, present their data samples as ones that the producers and recipients, as well as the analysts and readers, can readily grasp. Indeed, it is precisely the presumption that discourse is generally straightforwardly *understood* (that is, setting aside what *analysis* might claim to reveal about how it achieves its effects) that permits it to carry any kind of influence or power at all.

But co-membership can also be at stake, rather than presumed. We caught a glimpse of this in Chapter 10, where 'authentic' identity, or group membership, arose as something *at issue* in talk. Deeper assumptions of a common culture and common understanding, at least between analysts and participants, had to be suspended while we examined the Whorf hypothesis and categorization in Chapters 8 and 9, and various cross-cultural and historical studies of 'emotion' in Chapter 7 (and see Moerman, 1988, 1993). Also I have emphasized throughout this book that joint understandings are a worked-up, at-issue accomplishment, rather than a prerequisite or 'effect' of conversational interactions (see especially Chapters 4 and 5). In this chapter we return to co-membership as the matter at issue, specifically with regard to animals (especially apes), machines (especially computers), and human children (especially infants), all of which/whom are subject to conflicting claims concerning cognition and discourse, including their status as co-members (or not) of a society of thinking, talking, mutually understanding, 'human' beings.

Co-membership can be recognized or granted in at least two discursive domains: either by experts, in academic research papers and discussions, or by ordinary folk who interact with, and say things about, both human and non-human 'others'. Part of the interest is in the relations between those two domains. Some 'folk' may be disposed to treat animals, infants, and machines as agentive, mindful beings, whereas (some) academics may dispute those beliefs and practices, just as they may dispute the practice of taking horoscopes seriously. Everyday concepts and practices are invoked *in* academic discussions (and vice versa), whether in rejecting them in favour of something better (scientific or logically superior judgments), or as something to recruit and align with. Academics of various kinds (psychologists, cognitive scientists, philosophers, etc.) may propose that a proper, objective analysis of how computers work, or how programs work, or how human minds or languages are structured, is capable of resolving the issue of co-membership, whatever ordinary (or any other) folk may naïvely say. On the other hand, those folk may be precisely the ones whose concepts and concerns are being spoken for, and whose criteria of membership is at issue. There are tensions, therefore, not only between membership and exclusion, but between expert judgments on the issue, and everyday discourse practices.

The 'socialization problem'

It is an intrinsic feature of cultures that the way they work is *learnable*. This requires that discursive and other cultural practices are, in the ethnomethodological sense I have been using, 'visible'. As Jerome Bruner puts it, 'by virtue of participation in culture, meaning is rendered public and shared . . . we live publicly by public meanings and by shared procedures of interpretation and negotiation' (1990: 12–13). These cultural–discursive practices include the subject matter of discursive psychology – the ways in which psychological states, actions, events, beliefs, dispositions, motives, and so on, are conceptualized, invoked, and talked of. In contrast to conceiving of those matters discursively, psychologists and philosophers have traditionally started with individual persons and their individual minds and experiences, and then formulated various problems of knowledge and of language based on an individualized 'communication model' of discourse and cognition. Discursive psychology prefers to start with public, social practices.

The 'learnability' of discursive and other cultural practices stems from their visibility, or public nature. I have analysed emotion words and other mental predicates as *ways of talking*. As Jeff Coulter notes, echoing Wittgenstein, 'it is only because, for example, I have exhibited a public reaction to a pain I have that I give others a basis for training me in the language for sensations' (1990a: 69). Contrast that with cognitive scientist Roger Schank: 'there's only one place to get ideas about intelligence, and that's from thinking about myself' (quoted in Turkle, 1984: 256). The notion pursued here, that psychological discourse is possible, learnable, and works as an element of public practices, is an approach shared by ethnomethodology, conversation analysis, and the kind of 'ordinary language philosophy' promoted by Ryle (1949) and Wittgenstein (1958; see also Button et al., 1995). It was also outlined by the sociologist C. Wright Mills in a classic paper on 'motive' discourse, in which he also addressed learnability:

> . . . motives are imputed by others before they are avowed by self. The mother controls the child: 'Do not do that, it is greedy.' Not only does the child learn what to do, what not to do, but he is given standardized motives which promote prescribed actions and dissuade those proscribed. Along with rules and norms of action for various situations, we learn vocabularies of motives appropriate to them. (1940/1967: 360)

What Harvey Sacks (1972a, 1992) called the *socialization problem* covered his various discussions of children, psychotics, and others as analytic foils for the study of everyday social interaction. Any *analysis* of social interaction would have to be one which allowed for 'members', including new ones, to see how to take part. That entails studying 'how it is that a human gets built who will produce his activities such that they're graspable in this way' (Sacks, 1989: 386). Children and psychotics could also be used to point up the nature and scope of ordinary social norms, making them analytically apparent, rather like Garfinkel's (1967) 'breaching' experiments did, and how rules are 'proven' (tested and shown to be in force) by exceptions to them. Although Sacks did not take it up as a serious empirical project, he saw it as necessary and insightful to consider how any kind of adult competence could possibly be acquired, and was *designed to be acquirable*, and how such a developmentally relevant interactional design was a built-in feature of the public, 'visible' nature of conversational competence (cf. Lock, 1978; Vygotsky, 1934/1987).

For example, Sacks (1992, vol. 1) distinguishes two classes of 'accountable actions'. Class 1 includes items such as not putting your hands on a hot stove, whereas Class 2 includes the kinds of moral prescriptions or advice we can 'get away with', in that their consequences do not flow directly from them. He discusses adults' rules for children (a basis of what psychologists call 'moral development') in terms of how children need to acquire these different concepts of causation, and of how certain kinds of neurosis or psychopathy are definable as an inadequate grasp of the difference (1992, vol. 1: 327–30). Sacks also notes how the two classes can be subverted by both parents and children. Parents can categorize and account for their own Class 2 actions as Class 1, such as characterizing spankings as things that just 'have to be done', and by deploying a concept of immanent justice as a way of getting children to behave themselves when not being supervised. It is a device that can serve to externalize the need for punishment ('you brought this on yourself', etc.).

Sacks (1992, vol. 1: 388) also cites from an observational record of a child's behaviour during one whole day, from a study by Barker and Wright (1951), to show how 'subversion' may be learned. In a manner reminiscent of Vygotsky (1934/1987), whom he had approvingly read,[1] Sacks notes that children can learn, from their parents' reactions, which aspects of their behaviour are *visible* and are *evidence of* their prior actions or intentions, and can thus become able to 'subvert' such interpretations by producing their behaviour *for* those reactions. Another example Sacks offers is biblical, from Genesis, where Adam learns that his moral character is potentially visible; God sees the fig leaf, and infers that Adam has eaten the forbidden fruit (Sacks, 1992, vol. 1: 388). Note also how Adam handles accountability, via descriptive event reporting: 'And the man said, the woman whom thou gavest to be with me, she gave me of the tree, and I did eat.' So it was Eve's fault from the start, as gender-aware readers will have noted. And God is implicated too, quite wonderfully, by having given her to Adam in the first place – 'the woman *whom thou gavest me*', as if there was any other woman on earth it could have been. Adam learned fast. The inferential visibility of moral conduct, the evidenced nature of what you have done, is exactly what gets subverted into the rhetoric of description. So Sacks was providing clues for a developmental psychology of conversational competence, one that goes beyond mere socio-linguistic skills, and into the heart of what we call cognition and personality, one that could link up with the sophisticated, conversation analytic study of adult life that Sacks was starting to establish.

Rather than pursuing that developmental psychology here, I want to remain on the boundaries of it, and explore 'membership' more broadly as a feature intrinsic to social interactions and discourse in general. The way I am going to do that is by examining various ways in which membership is discussed in the psychological literature with regard to marginal candidates, including human infants (and occasionally other categories of humans), but mainly animals and 'intelligent' computers. Again, apart from the intrinsic interest of these categories, a major concern is with what such studies, and the debates around them, tell us about everyday discourse in which co-membership is not overtly at issue.

The analytic topic is what happens when ordinary people, and behavioural or cognitive scientists, contentiously attribute to animals, machines, and so on, the kinds of mental states or competencies that they attribute to each other, and the grounds on which they do so. In the academic literature the prime topics are language and thinking, and the objects (or subjects) in question are often apes, computers, or infants. The question typically posed is, can animals or machines 'think' and 'converse' the way *we* do? My aim is not to *resolve* that question but to examine some ways in which it is generally posed and argued, or even rejected as meaningless (Button et al., 1995). The focus is on how various criteria of human 'co-membership' work, including the candidates' overt performances, inner workings, intentionality, interactions with bona fide humans, and the notion of 'imitation'. While this might look like a side-step, a focus on the debate in preference to its topic, the position I take is that the operation of these criteria, both in ordinary discourse and in the scientific literature, is the substance of it all.

Looking in the mirror

The most common trope for these concerns with non-members and candidate members must be the 'mirror to Man'. We study apes in their capacity as 'those amazing creatures that can teach us so much about ourselves' (Goodall, 1971: 14). Similarly, 'discovery of extraterrestrial life would utterly transform our own view of ourselves as a species' (*The Observer*, 29 July 1990, quoting Professor Martin Rees, Director of Cambridge University's Institute of Astronomy). Technology in general may also be seen as a kind of mirror to human nature (Woolgar, 1987: 312), or, at least, computer-based 'artificial intelligence' (AI) may be. 'After all, the pursuit of artificial intelligence means uncovering the unbelievably complex layers of our own thought processes' (Crevier, 1993: xi). Indeed, some ambitious projections of AI produce mirrored reflections indistinguishable from the human original: 'if machines do come to simulate all of our internal cognitive activities, to the last computational detail, to deny them the status of genuine persons would be nothing but a new form of racism' (Churchland, 1988: 120).

On the other hand what the mirrors reveal, as Snow White's wicked stepmother discovered, may not be as welcome, or as accurate, or informative, as anticipated. Some critics reject the trope, or want the mirror broken. Despite hopes for informative reflections, it may all be a flawed exercise in domination and hubris, a wrong analogy: 'Western primatology is Simian orientalism' (Haraway, 1989: 10, drawing a further analogy to Said, 1979), a hall of dark and distorted mirrors where neither ape nor human is clearly seen. It turns into an *imposition* of cultural assumptions, indeed a reification of them in the form of science, mere confirmation rather than transformation of our view of ourselves. Looking into Man's (*sic*) mirror, from this critical perspective, guarantees no clear vision, neither of the object nor of ourselves looking back. It is an issue not only for the contentious humanity of 'marginal objects' (Turkle, 1984) such as apes and machines, but for human studies too, and especially social anthropology, a more obviously cultural sort of mirror 'for displacing the dulling sense of familiarity with which the mysteriousness of our own ability to relate to one another is concealed from us' (Geertz, 1973: 14).[2]

Sherry Turkle's (1984) notion of 'marginal objects' invokes the sense of a to-be-defined set of proto-human, or 'almost human' (Strum, 1987; Yerkes, 1925), beings at the margins of full membership with, let us say, 'us'.[3] 'We search for ways to see ourselves. The computer is a new mirror, the first psychological machine. Beyond its nature as an analytical engine lies its second nature as an evocative object' (Turkle, 1984: 306). Such evocative objects, or beings, are both similar to and different from us, in ways to be defined, investigated, and *changed*. Apes are also, like computers, considered a good choice for comparisons because they seem the most like us, yet sufficiently unlike us to make the project interesting. They are the closest modern equivalents to the creatures in Clarke/Kubrick's *2001: A Space*

Odyssey, seemingly on the verge of humanity, just needing (as Adam did) a little external help, the breath of God, or the 'gift' of language. The (un)likeness varies across descriptions. On the one hand, the 'anthropoid' apes may deceptively look like and imitate us, but what we cannot immediately see is the underlying biological and intellectual chasm that separates us language-using humans from our signal-swapping cousins. Or, in contrast, perhaps we and they 'do not *look* like sibling species' at all, but are closer *beneath* appearances, where 'Man/Ape protein structure is practically identical' (Desmond, 1979: 14–15).

The same sorts of contrary opposites are available for androids and humans: computers, brains, and minds (for example, Dreyfus, 1992; Hofstadter, 1979; Searle, 1980). They are available also for the other senses of 'marginal', the moral outsiders, the not-us, the beings upon which/whom efforts are expended or wasted, contentiously, to make them more like us. We put animals through the conceptual categories of our own pre-history, from wild, to domesticated, to virtually human, 'an epochal unfolding of animal to man, from instinct to consciousness' (Haraway, 1989: 60). Talking apes and thought-simulating computers are of our making, whether by manufacture or by description, made in our image as God made us. But they are also *monsters* that may, like Frankenstein's creation ('that nightmare about the crushing failure of the project of man', Haraway, 1989: 31), and the wicked Queen's reflection, threaten our sense of our own unique worth. Yet amongst all this there is the sense also of *ourselves* as cultural beings, inventions, artefacts, of our own if not of God's making – but then, in whose image? Artificial intelligence may yet be the only kind there is.

Imitation and artifice

'Imitation' is a rich conceptual resource for the rhetoric of membership. In use, it resonates with contradictions. It is both the aim and the critique of simulation. Displaced by the psychology of 'cognitive development' from its role as behavioural explanation of how children become competent adults, imitation becomes available for dismissing cognitive inadequacies, as superficial copies, mere imitations. Children's language is contrasted with that of trained apes such as Washoe, Sarah, Lana, Nim, and Kanzi[4] on the grounds that, unlike theirs, child talk is non-imitative, non-aped; it is produced creatively from grammar (Brown, 1973; Chomsky, 1991; Terrace, 1979). The exceptions are held to be just that: exceptional, one-offs, capable of alternative, more parsimonious explanations;[5] they prove the rule. So ape language (that is, apes' uses of parts of human language that have been taught to them) is like but unlike, *too much* of a copy yet not close enough. Similarly, however closely computers can be made to function like people, failure is guaranteed by the conceptual failure of imitation itself: 'so long as they are not members of our society . . . they cannot imitate our intelligent activities' (Collins, 1990: 18). Of course, this begs the question of what it takes to be counted as a member, and whether there is anything to that, for bona fide members like us, apart from being counted-as, and being the ones whose counting counts.

Imitation is available as a category for *dis*-counting things. Apes' efforts at acquiring human language, or, rather, humans' efforts to train them to use it, are dismissed as either too loosely documented or too tightly constrained. Either they babble without grammatical structure (the apes, that is), or they converse in routines, fixed by imitation and rehearsal (Brown, 1973). Rote learning produces routines without understanding, behaviour without competence. 'Overlearned' laboratory tricks are responsible for a *semblance* of grammar, the mere product of a long training session.[6] Or else the semblance of productive spontaneity in less rigid ape–human interactions merely hides an *imitative* pattern revealed by close scrutiny of videotaped sequences (Terrace, 1979). Methods of quoting, presenting, and analysing ape language are said to have exaggerated its human-likeness, by obscuring its routine and imitative nature, and by 'trimming' repetitive strings of signs, transforming them into 'data' that 'manufacture a human-like end product' (Desmond, 1979: 49).

The notion that imitation-based talk is not proper talk is also part of a dispute between behaviourism and cognitive psychology. Allen and Beatrice Gardner, who trained Washoe in sign language (Gardner and Gardner, 1969), were explicitly engaged in an argument against Noam Chomsky (1959) over the merits of behavioural methods and conceptions of human competence, including language. It was not, from their perspective, an error or oversight that Washoe's performance was based on imitation and behavioural training, but an important point of principle and practice. The imitative character of Washoe's signing was a product of how they shaped her hands into gestures, and rewarded her for getting them right. Imitation was built into performance, a feature of the behavioural scientist's equation of control with understanding.[7] Laboratory animals are like artificial intelligence devices in this respect, '*designed* . . . in short, engineered, to answer human queries' (Haraway, 1989: 62, original emphasis) in the pursuit of the perfectibility of 'Man'. Apes and computers have to be *made into* mirrors.

Imitation works as a *descriptive* category; the making into mirrors can be a discursive construction, as well as an engineering one. Harvey Sacks describes how, in early American ethnographies, 'again and again I found references to the activities of Negroes as "imitating whites". And they were characterized as being "marvelous imitators". Such reports are very similar to the way the behavior of children is characterized' (Sacks, 1992, vol. 1: 70). Sacks makes sense of this in terms of how classes of persons are seen as 'entitled' to behave:

> 'Imitation' seems to involve a way of characterizing some action which somebody does when they are unentitled to do that class of action. And if you watch the way the Negro slaves got talked about, or the way the emerging Negro is talked about [this was a 1964–5 lecture], you can see how marvelous a category 'imitation' is,

because it turns out that everything whites can do Negroes can imitate, but they
can't *do* any of these things that whites can do. (1992, vol. 1: 70, original emphasis)

So attribution can precede evidence; you categorize the actors, and that
provides for how to interpret their actions. Imitation is a way of describing,
and thus constituting as such, the actions of entities that are not proper, fully
fledged, members or persons. That is not to say that it is a false category, or
that some actions are not imitations; and *this* is not to say that some are.
Rather, it is to say that it *is* a category, a form of description, and it has its
attributional and rhetorical uses. As Sacks remarks, 'such categories as
"imitation" and "phoney" . . . serve as boundary categories around the term
"Member"' (1992, vol. 1: 70).

There are several linked senses of 'imitation'. There is the behaviour
itself, and also its ersatz product, such as imitation antique furniture. There
is also an *intentional* sort of usage, invoked by 'phoney', or 'artifice', in which
imitating is a kind of deceptive, goal-oriented action. In critiques of what
apes, children, computers, and even 'Negroes' can do, 'imitation' is
dismissive, a way of discounting some performance as not genuine, less than
the original, not produced by the same mechanism, *mere* imitation. This is
the sense used also in critiques of behavioural theories – that invoking
imitation, like other behavioural routines, as explanations leaves out what is
definitive about human nature, that people can do things creatively and
intentionally, as proper persons, and not merely by imitation. A fruitful
place to look for other uses and ironies of imitation might be in European
and American comparative representations of Japanese education and
manufacturing since the 1950s, and Japan's replacement in that role by the
more recent economic emergence of Taiwan and Malaysia. While Far
Eastern businesses 'copied' or 'cloned' the West's products, the reverse
process seems more a rational adoption of efficient business practices and
global new technologies; not insincerity or the production of counterfeit,
but, on the contrary, the sincerest form of flattery.

If imitative apes were to be described as *passing themselves off* as human,
or computers to be *dis*-simulating, the conceptual implications would also be
reversed. Deception or artifice is taken to be a hallmark of sophistication, of
mind, intelligence, even of 'mindreading' (Baron-Cohen, 1995; Whiten,
1991), a capacity claimed to be not beyond baboons, apes, and pre-linguistic
children. For example, the Gardners provide accounts of Washoe embar-
rassing new project members, new to sign language, by signing particularly
slowly and carefully for them (Gardner and Gardner, 1974). These
observations are, in the first instance, like Sacks's, matters of description.[8]
Whereas distinctions between actions on the grounds of intentionality *can be
made* between human and non-human, or animal and machine, or one
animal and another, or one human action and another (Collins, 1990), these
are attributive descriptions of the sort that participants in interactions might
themselves deploy or counter (Edwards and Potter, 1992a). The problem
for analysis would then be, as Chapter 4 argued, how are actions
behaviourally or descriptively *brought off* as intentional or not?

In an effort to draw a line between what people (can) do, and the *ostensibly similar* performances of computers, Harry Collins (1990) discusses a class of 'behaviour-specific actions'. These include army parade ground drill, which is about as similar to programmed routines as humans are likely to produce. But even these are performances that machines only mimic. The crucial difference for Collins is again 'intention', these being actions that people are *trying* to perform in precisely the same way every time. Even if people were described as *not* trying, or not trying hard enough, or whatever, Collins's point is presumably that 'trying' is an appropriately at-issue (intentional, moral) descriptive category for what people do, but not for what machines or programmed computers do. The trouble with this argument is that it proceeds *by definition*, by assuming at the outset the very matter supposedly at issue. The notion that people can try and machines can't is treated as something we already know, either about those objects or about those words. Yet when we consider actual descriptive practices, we may find that people *do* use intentional language to describe what machines do.

The issue then becomes, on what grounds can we say those people are wrong? Is it that they do not understand machines well enough, or that they do not understand their own language well enough? The latter choice seems to me circular and preposterous; whose language is it? The former possibility, that they do not understand how the machines work, at first seems to settle the matter. But it suffers from the assumption that, when people ordinarily use an intentional vocabulary, *even for each other*, they do so on the basis of some kind of technical, psychological, physiological, or whatever, knowledge of how (human) actions are *actually* produced. But of course they don't. As I have argued throughout this book, intentional language is a way of talking, a common-sense way of conducting and describing human relations, not something based on expert knowledge, nor to be assessed according to whether it is objectively correct. Collins may sensibly object to people's use of intentional language when they talk about machines. But he does so as a cultural participant, in the same way as people may object to supernatural or religious beliefs, meat eating, astrology, quantum mechanics, and so on. People are not simply wrong by definition, at the outset, on matters of that kind.

In a similar manner to Collins, Button et al. distinguish 'authentic' performances from artificial ones: 'what suffices to establish that a proper or correct performance is an authentic expression or manifestation of understanding is that *it issues from a human being*' (1995: 148, original emphasis). In contrast, 'computers cannot think because they are machines' (1995: 149). Again, the trouble here is that not only are the relevant categories ('thinking' and 'understanding') treated as known and amenable to conceptual explication (which indeed they are), but so also are the *things in the world that are capable of doing them, whatever people may say*. There is no room here for defeasible counts-as practices. All it takes to dismiss the Turing test[9] for machine intelligence is to side-step it altogether and look behind the curtain. One worry about that is that it leaves us with little

purchase on epistemically similar, but more obviously arbitrary, discriminations *between human beings*, such as how we need to know only that
someone is a woman, Negro, servant, idiot, or child to know that they
obviously can't think or understand the way 'we' do. 'We' would know such
things, not according to any specification of what talking and thinking are,
but by reference to who or what is producing them; just like in Sacks's
examples of 'imitation'. It is a dangerous and flawed argument when taken
out of Turing's imaginary laboratory.

The notion of *authentic* performances is illustrated by the example of
forged and genuine banknotes. Despite physical identity in all respects, the
genuine note is nevertheless the one legitimately issued by the appropriate
authorities (Button et al., 1995: 146–7). That is certainly a good way to
define, conceptually, the difference between the genuine and fake articles,
but this kind of conceptual discussion can only work via these kinds of
made-up scenarios. In life, in *practical* matters, the thing at issue is not only
what a 'forgery' *is*, conceptually, but precisely *which one* is the forgery. The
issue is how is such a judgment actually made? As authors of their own
example, Button et al. can simply write it in, make it so by *fiat*, that one of
them actually is the true banknote. But back in the world where descriptions
are produced, and lives are lived, this is presumably precisely the issue, and
there is nobody to inform us, outside of whatever practical procedures can
be applied, which is which. The condition of human interaction, and of its
socialization, is more like that of the subjects in the Turing test than like the
possibility of looking behind the curtain. Looking behind the curtain simply
misses the point, in that it presumes that, for any cases where descriptions
are *actually at issue*, there is a straightforward, beyond-dispute procedure
for getting them right, which is to be equated with sorting your concepts out,
and/or letting reality speak for itself.

However, Collins (1990) argues that there *is* a genuine (and empirical-
looking) criterion of mere simulation, at least for artificial intelligence. In
order to demonstrate how the Turing test must *ultimately* fail (however
human-like the computer might at first appear to be), Collins invents a
parallel humans-only case, one that would be sure to unmask the imitator.
The imagined case is that of a cold war British spy who is arrested and
interrogated by the KGB, having been trained in London to impersonate a
native of Semipalatinsk. The KGB's task, like that of the interrogator in the
Turing test, is to cross-examine and try to unmask him.

> The agent has learned the history and geography of Semipalatinsk from books,
> atlases, town guides, photographs, and long conversations with a defector who was
> once himself a native of the town. He has undergone long sessions of mock
> interrogation by this defector until he is word perfect in his responses to every
> question. His documents are in order. . . . The moment of crisis occurs for our
> hero when an interrogator enters who is himself a native of the town. . . .
> However good his training, we know that the spy will not survive cross-
> examination by a native of Semipalatinsk. (Collins, 1990: 6)

Collins invokes a form of 'tacit' knowledge that can be acquired only from experience, and not from instruction, such that however much the spy's trainer had told him, it could never be fully programmed into him:

> . . . there is much more to this than can be explicitly described even in a lifetime . . . he cannot know everything that the trainer knows, nor everything that the native interrogator knows . . . Is there an area of the town – near the river, perhaps, or going toward the forest, or just beyond the tanning factory – that is quite distinctive to a native, but the distinctiveness of which cannot or has not quite been put into words or cannot quite be captured even in films and photographs? (1990: 7)

Sooner or later, the spy will be caught out. And so also, therefore, must the programmed computer behind Turing's screen.[10]

I accept Collins's distinction between the two kinds of knowledge, one based on experience, the other on instruction. But as a possible empirical test, rather than a conceptual exercise, there are two things that his example underestimates. The first is an implication of his own remarks concerning how the personal nature of experience combines with the unending possibilities of description. It is not clear to what extent 'genuine' natives of Semipalatinsk are interchangeable with each other, such that even they, or their spy-catcher colleagues, could be sure of what exactly another native would absolutely have to know. And given the vagaries of description, there ought to be as much uncertainty moving back from accounts to experiences as forwards; at what point would the spy's description be bound to fail? Whatever 'cannot or has not quite been put into words' (1990: 7) cuts both ways.

The second problem is more severe. What one would like to know, as with the banknote forgery, are the empirical grounds on which the *true* native of Semipalatinsk got counted as such. Presumably it was something more than that his documents were in order, that he claimed to come from there, knew a lot about the place, and so on. The production of a further set of corroborating witnesses from Semipalatinsk, *real* natives, would only regress the problem. We can imagine the final scenes of the movie, when it turns out that the KGB interrogator was herself a British spy, a case of double agency, and another hall of mirrors. The analytic trick here is, again, to be the *author* of all this stuff (Edwards et al., 1995). Collins *informs* us that the successful interrogator *really was* what the spy could only contentiously claim to be, just as we are informed about what actually lies behind Turing's curtain, and that one of two banknotes is genuine. The Turing test requires that everything is obvious when we pull back the curtain and look; but how sophisticated an android are we allowed to find before the discriminatory issue comes back full circle? We are back to author's privilege, the usurpation by the author of the participants' problem of description and attribution. The empirical issue is how people are able to make these judgments when nobody is writing their lines. Writing their own lines (discourse, descriptions, attributions) is, of course, the core phenomenon.

Members only: anthropomorphism and rapport

There is plenty of evidence that ordinary people do, routinely, attribute mental states and motives to animals and machines. Pet owners are notorious for it, as are the parents of new-born or even pre-natal infants (Macfarlane, 1977).[11] 'Anthropomorphism' is the tendency to attribute human characteristics to non-human beings – in its original uses, to God or the gods. As the term implies, it is something people do; not just 'ordinary' folk but, mostly according to their critics, scientists and experts of various kinds too. Michael Lynch (1988) implies that it is a very solid and recognizable feature (whether 'correct' or not is another matter) of common-sense conceptions of animals. He distinguishes a category of 'analytic animals' used in laboratory research from what he calls 'naturalistic animals':

> By 'naturalistic animal' I mean the animal in ordinary perception and interaction; the animal of common sense, the animal as it is viewed and acted upon in the world of everyday life . . . to which human-like 'feelings', perceptions, sensitivities, and even 'thoughts' are attributed. . . . The naturalistic animal . . . is assumed to possess a subjective basis of behaviour. . . . Interaction with animals in the naturalistic mode, such as between a pet and its owner, is rich with actual and assumed elements of reciprocity, empathic understanding, and emotional attachment. . . . Perhaps many of these references ultimately are little more than a shorthand way of dealing with 'complex mechanisms', analogous with the way computer 'hackers' ordinarily act toward their computers and speak of them as though they were endowed with moods, emotions, and other forms of reactive subjectivity. (Lynch, 1988: 267–8)

Not only hackers speak that way (again, irrespective of what they say they 'believe'). Joseph Weizenbaum (1984), Sherry Turkle (1984), and others have reported how 'ordinary' folk, while interacting with computers, attribute to them all manner of psychological states and actions.[12]

There is at least a superficial resemblance between the Turing test and Harold Garfinkel's (1967) so-called 'student counselling experiment', which was another of his ethnomethodological 'breaching' studies (see Chapter 3). Participants (undergraduates) were asked to describe the background to some personal problems, and then formulate at least ten yes–no questions for communication via an intercom to a 'counsellor' in the next room. After each answer was received, the participants privately tape-recorded their reactions. The 'counsellor' was a stooge with a set of pre-arranged randomly ordered answers. The participants nevertheless managed to make coherent sense of the answers, constructing them as motivated advice, and developed a sense of the overall 'pattern' of advice as each new answer came in, set against a background of normative values and expectations for such settings. Their sense-making was ad hoc and inventive, responsive to each next 'answer'. It seems to be an intrinsic feature of human interactions that interactants treat each other as inescapably interpretable, if not necessarily as normal. And it seems to be something that humans are ready to apply (even if they may also argue about it) to any category of interactant, human or not.

While analysts and commentators of various kinds examine, promote, or criticize notions such as 'thinking machines' or 'talking animals', the thing that is typically sitting unexamined in the background is the basis on which we attribute thoughts, intentions, cognitions, and other mental states *to each other*. Discussions of the ways in which computers and their programs actually work, or of the ways in which animals have been trained, fail to take account of the fact that it is not by examining each other's inner workings, or life histories, that we treat each other, in ordinary social interactions, as bona fide conversational partners. We do it on the hoof, as we go, attributionally, generously perhaps (or else not), but always as part of what 'having a conversation' *is*. On what basis we do that, and when, and when not, are matters for investigation and for political engagement. This brings us back to the 'socialization problem', including the 'membership problem' that co-constitutes it.

We can object that 'anthropomorphic' practices are misguided and inappropriate, but only on technical grounds, by examining how computers (etc.) actually work and declaring it different from how people work. But as we have noted, it is not on technical grounds that people predicate mental states *of each other*. Mental state predicates are ways of talking, features of common-sense discursive practices, produced in, and as part of, ways of life. In that sense, as ordinary language users, folk are doing something we need to study, not (in the first instance, at least) to correct. We may indeed, as co-members of a culture, want to disagree with such attributions and offer arguments about how mistaken those practices are. Other co-members certainly do that. But to do so is to *enter the fray* as conversational participants and arbiters of common sense, rather than remaining analysts of it.

The term 'anthropomorphism' is generally used in the fray, critically, in accusations and rebuttals. With regard to animals and machines, anthropomorphism is the *error* of describing what they do in terms first designed, and properly reserved, for what people do. A large part of the critique of any claims concerning ape 'language' or machine 'intelligence' is that any such notions are mere anthropomorphism. Yet I have argued that there is something unanalysed here, which is the basis or manner in which we *accord to each other* membership of the club of properly human beings. It may be that the same kind of social and discursive practices by which we (falsely?) accord human attributes to non-humans play an essential part in our everyday interactions with each other. Perhaps anthropomorphism is not so much an attributional error as an intrinsic feature of human social relations. If that is so, then, again, it becomes something we have to study, rather than telling people when and when not to do it.

It seems strange, inappropriate, or tautological even, to think of human–human interactions as 'anthropomorphic' – what else should they be? Yet it becomes less strange on closer examination. For example, the line is not easily drawn at the boundary of the species *Homo sapiens*. Not all species members are automatically considered social, linguistic, conversational members (the new-born, the brain damaged, the autistic, etc.). What does it take to be included? Consider human infants. According to the Vygotskian tradition in developmental psychology (see Chapter 2), one of the ways in which human infants are thought to *become* agentive, enculturated, language-using persons is by being *treated as* such (Bruner, 1983; Lock, 1978; Shotter, 1993a; Vygotsky, 1934/1987). This 'treated-as' procedure is considered not merely an error that starts off wrong and happens to end up right, but as a developmental, socializing, making-it-so sort of business. So my earlier distinction between discursive and engineering kinds of 'construction' (see also Chapter 3), drawn for the making of mirrors, must now be re-examined. On the 'engineering' side, when it comes to the 'manufacture' of agents, whether humans, apes, computers, or the secret service variety, then the discursive, descriptive activity (treating-as and counting-as) may figure as an important part of that, with conversational interaction the fulcrum of it all. It is the same *discursive* procedure for inclusion into the club of agentive members that accomplishes the human 'engineering', or socialization.

All of this is becoming unfortunate for any lingering hopes of *definitively resolving* the issue of whether non-human creatures/creations can properly be said, in fact or in principle, to talk and think. Among our most promising analytical tools, or descriptive categories, for sorting out that issue are distinctions between the real thing and mere imitation, or reality and attribution. Those dichotomies go together. When mere imitation is unmasked as such, the mistake of treating it as the real article is an attributional error. This can be especially persuasive when the unmasker is also the creator, as when Victor Frankenstein rejected his creation (and Mary Shelley authored it so), and when Joseph Weizenbaum authoritatively dismissed his early interactive program ELIZA as 'the simplest mechanical parody' (1984: 6). Weizenbaum reports, as we have noted, that he was 'startled to see how quickly and how very deeply people conversing with DOCTOR [a version of ELIZA] became emotionally involved with the computer and how unequivocally they anthropomorphized it' (1984: 6). This was not considered a product of the particular gullibility of the persons concerned. Weizenbaum noted the 'enormously exaggerated attributions an even well-educated audience is capable of making, even strives to make, to a technology it does not understand', and how the same process was at work for more sophisticated AI products: 'the subsequent, much more elegant, and surely more important work of Winograd . . . is currently being misinterpreted just as ELIZA was' (1984: 7)[13] But if anthropomorphism cuts deeply into what human agency *is*, then the distinction between reality and its attribution is blurred. The creator/author is making it so, not 'merely' describing it so.

Anthropomorphism is linked to *rapport*, which is also a concept that cuts both ways. Too much of it, when dealing with machines and animals, leads to subjective involvement and anthropomorphic errors. Yet the kind of rapport that ELIZA's human interactants felt, which so astonished Weizenbaum, is routinely recommended by ape trainers as essential for establishing successful communications with them. Allen and Beatrice Gardner (1969) stressed the need to develop close social relations with the chimpanzee 'Washoe' (to whom they tried to teach deaf sign language), so that she would have something to say and find them worth talking to. It is a view repeated by Duane Rumbaugh (1977) and his colleagues with regard to 'Lana', by Francine Patterson (Patterson and Linden, 1981) with regard to 'Koko', and Sue Savage-Rumbaugh (Savage-Rumbaugh and Lewin, 1994) with regard to 'Kanzi'. One of the objections to Herbert Terrace's (1979) chimpanzee 'Nim', whom Terrace declared merely 'imitative', was that his 'battery of caretakers and trainers' (Desmond, 1979: 47) failed to establish the right kind of rapport, making Nim a disturbed and untypical animal.[14]

It has been suggested that the *dangers* of rapport might be lessened by employing an expert in interaction micro-analysis (Umiker-Sebeok and Sebeok, 1980) to spot when false attributions are occurring. This compares to the stage magician and fraud-buster James Randi's (1975) recommendations for testing Uri Geller's spoon-bending claims; Geller apparently also requires the establishment of rapport with his audience. The classic debunking was performed a century ago by Oskar Pfungst (1911/1965) on the horse Clever Hans. The horse was apparently able to perform feats of mental arithmetic by tapping out answers with his hoof. Pfungst showed that Hans was unable to do this when the questioner did not know the answer, or was sceptical or inattentive, and reasoned that gestural cues were inadvertently being given. The counter to the requirement for rapport is, of course, the danger of subjectivity, of anthropomorphic attributions: 'enthusiastic observers of animals are constantly in danger of interpreting their behaviour in more complex terms than is necessary or correct' (Griffin, 1976: 72).

On the opposite side again to *that*, of course, there are the dangers of treating some performances as *less* 'complex' than they deserve. Echoing Sacks's discussion of imitation, Donna Haraway notes how, in colonial stories and early anthropological works, 'if a black person accomplished some exceptional feat of intelligence or daring, the explanation was that he (or she?) was inspired, literally moved, by the spirit of the master' (1989: 52). Haraway cites several examples, including this from Mary Jobe Akeley, where attribution, empathy, and the descriptive classes of savages and animals are rolled together to bring off a piece of patronizingly well-meant membership exclusion from the class of proper persons:

> Now with few exceptions our Kivu savages, lower in the scale of intelligence than any others I had seen in Equatorial Africa, proved kindly men . . . how deeply their sympathy affected me! As I think of them, I am reminded of the only playmate and companion of my early childhood, a collie dog. . . . (Cited in Haraway, 1989: 52)

This is a kind of reattribution, a reapportioning of responsibility for some performance, where its ostensible producer (ape, savage, infant, machine) is a mere butt or conduit for the agentive work being done by someone else. This 'other' is one of *us*, standing in front or behind: the agent who wrote, controls, made, or designed it, or else the attributing perceiver, potentially tricked by appearances.

But this also is a conceptualizing move, one that splits the producer of a message from its recipient. If we adopt the kind of interactive, performative perspective on discourse that I have promoted in this book, rather than the standard 'minds-in-communication' model of thought and talk, then it becomes less convincing to make the distinction between what the ape, machine, infant, and so on, can *really* do, and what it is *interactionally treated* as doing. Once ape–human, infant–human, and machine–human inter-actions are admitted as such, as *interactions*, then it may make as little sense to extract the non-human partner's contributions from that matrix as it would for those of a human partner. If participants' meanings are those received, treated as meaningful, oriented to, and taken up for their interactional value, then we should stay with interactions, where uptakes provide analysts with 'proof procedures' for meanings (Sacks et al., 1974; see also Chapters 4 and 5). The ape trainers, ELIZA's dialogical partners, and anthropomorphic human parents become constitutively correct, in the sense of being producers of analysable practices. We could, of course, refuse to go along with any of this, and declare that neither academics nor ordinary folk have any proper grounds for conceptually treating apes, babies, and machines in the ways we treat adult humans. But we would have to find some other, 'essential', non-interactional basis for that. And those efforts trip up over the problems of description.

Description and translation: Whorf's dilemma revisited

The issue of non-human thought, language, mental attributes, or intentional agency hangs on how the actors/actants and their activities are *described*. Descriptions of animals, machines, or of ordinary human activities are not simply the way things are, but the way things are said and written. This is very easy to ignore when we are writing texts and engaging in arguments, as we saw with the story about the native of Semipalatinsk. We ignore it when we accept the challenge of explaining Washoe's calling a duck *water bird* (Fouts, 1974); or accept that people mistook ELIZA for a sympathetic listener (Weizenbaum, 1984); or accept that a computer program counts as a piece of AI because it 'fits the facts' of human psychology (Johnson-Laird, 1988: 26). It is not that these descriptions are wrong, but that they build into the ostensibly given world the very thing that is at issue (Woolgar, 1987). If we knew 'the facts' of human psychology well enough that they could stand as criterion for the output of computer simulations, then the claims of those simulations to be providing a superior sort of psychology would start to look circular. Take, for example, Paul Churchland's description of AI that, 'generally speaking, the system proposed must do what the creature at issue succeeds in doing, or what its selected faculty does' (1988: 93). How are those criteria and successes defined, except by non-computational criteria? AI would seem dependent upon the same common-sense or conventional psychological accounts it sometimes aims to replace.

Similarly, descriptions of Washoe's behaviour are already translations of it; not merely that Washoe signed something translatable as *water bird*, but that when she did so she was 'calling a duck' something. Similarly, whereas Lana is quoted as tapping on the idiograms on her computer console the sentence 'Please machine give fruit' (Rumbaugh, 1977), Chomsky (1979) cites a similar, ironic translation for the sequence of four coloured buttons that a pigeon, rewarded by food, and subject to no claims about language, learned to tap with its beak. In another retranslation study, Lenneberg (1975) trained a couple of schoolchildren to use the same sorts of magnetized plastic symbols by which the chimpanzee 'Sarah' (Premack and Premack, 1972) demonstrated impressive grammatical prowess. The children performed even better than Sarah, but were unable to translate the 'sentences' into English, having formed the impression that it was a kind of puzzle game rather than a kind of language.

Since the apes' performances are ones that use pictorial and gestural signs, or behavioural responses to words spoken to them, these signs and performances have to be *rendered into English* (or whatever written language) for the requirements of reporting and theorizing them, in academic treatises, as examples of language. Objections have been mounted not only to specific descriptions and translations, but to the general use of linguistic terms. Even for human children, the description of their early utterances as instances of 'language development' is a concession provided by the same anthropomorphic generosity that grants and anticipates their membership of the club of proper humans: 'What goes before "language" in development is only linguistic by courtesy of its continuity with a system which in fully elaborated form is indeed a language' (Brown, 1970. 37). According to this sort of argument, a child and a chimpanzee might produce observationally identical kinds of actions, but only in the case of the child would we be looking at language learning. The ape researchers were unimpressed:

> Dispatches from the Gardners' front line suggested that linguists were having their cake and eating it, while denying ape researchers even a glance at the edibles. A child's variable word order argued its innate mastery of grammar; an ape's condemned it irretrievably. (Desmond, 1979: 44)

The claims on both sides are similar, and are a classic form of scientific disputation. Each analyst claims that his or her opponent views some action, formulates a theoretical account of it, attributes that account to the actor/ actant, and builds it into the action's description.

In similar vein, Button et al. (1995) object to how Jerry Fodor (1975) describes the 'linguistic' and 'symbolic' operations of computers:

> . . . Fodor literalizes the metaphoric expressions which are employed in talk about computers in order to make it sound as though there are some actual linguistic

operations involved. . . . Thus he speaks of language which computers 'use', of computers 'talking to themselves' and of 'translation' between input/output codes and their machine language. . . . [Cognitive scientists] slip into the use of concepts that are appropriate for human reasoning when describing computer processing. We are invited to view the computer as an interpreting machine . . . [which] is then offered as a model or theory of human understanding. (Button et al., 1995: 99 and 162–3)

This echoes not only the discussion of cognitive psychology, computational models, and descriptions of infant cognition in Chapter 2, but also the discussion in Chapters 8 and 9 of *Whorf's dilemma*. One of the criticisms of Whorf was the fact that, in order to make his argument, he had to translate Hopi and Apache into peculiar-looking English sentences, and compare *those* to more ordinary-looking English sentences. Lenneberg (1953) and others pointed out the paradox in doing this. Either Whorf's argument was vitiated by the success of his translations (proving that the meanings of one language could indeed be rendered in another), or else the translations were constitutive of the peculiarity attributed to Hopi and Apache, and what he should have done was to translate them colloquially, which again would ruin his argument. When we are assessing the possibly agentive, intelligent, or linguistic productions of 'marginal objects', we are dealing with matters of translation.[15] In fact the description or 'translation' problem is especially severe for what goes on inside computers, given that those processes are not already, in the first place, utterances in a human language such as Hopi, or the sign language of the deaf.

Adrian Desmond refers to 'the distinct and distasteful possibility of cannibalizing the living chimpanzee body for makeshift human counter-parts' (1979: 15), that is, organ transplants. The category 'cannibalizing' places humans and chimpanzees into the same species of creature. Similarly, when chimpanzees were reported to have complex relations with baboons, including living alongside, playing with, hunting and eating them, this was described as 'a form of racism since, to chimpanzees, baboons are a sort of semi-conspecific' (Kortland, 1975: 302). Jane Goodall's (1979, 1986) descriptions of wild chimpanzees are full of notions defined first for human practices, such as murder, war, kidnapping, cannibalism, hunting, shyness, nurturing, sharing, and so on. Desmond is more wary of anthropomorphism when drawing *distinctions* between apes and humans, such as when questioning reports of Washoe's and Koko's 'swearing', which seemed to him suspiciously modern-looking: 'The apes are too up to date. I wondered whether in fact we were not reading too much into their outbursts' (1979: 27). But this is not a problem that can be cured by being more careful with particular descriptions and translations, or by excluding specific cases of rendered ape language. It is intrinsic to the entire exercise.

The trainers who work with these apes are typically also the same people who record and describe what they do and 'say', provide glosses of it in English, and write scientific and popular reports about it. Especially with the more heavily interaction-oriented work, with 'signing' apes such as Washoe, and with the 'conversational' Kanzi, the analyst's engagement in situated interactions, and ad hoc moment-to-moment interpretations with the ape, is intrinsic to how the ape's communications occur, and are constituted as meaningful. The data themselves are largely actor–observer–ethnographers' accomplishments of ape-as-communicator, rather than behavioural facts awaiting a possibly linguistic interpretation. Of course, this is similar to how it is with human infants and their anthropomorphic parents. But with human children, who generally go on to become fully fledged 'members', the process of interaction-and-gloss is all part of the *phenomenon* of becoming human and enculturated. For the ape studies, the problem for researcher and critic alike is that the same process is confounded with what the whole project purportedly sets out to test – how far can apes be made to be like us? This 'confounding' is not merely a scientific error that should be avoided. It is part of the nature of human social engagement, the name of the game. There is no *external* criterion, outside of how that game is played, for who is allowed to take part.

Even when we are defining the apes' non-linguistic actions (as Goodall does), or defining what they do to be *non*-human, we tend to deploy terms that describe alternative sorts of human actions and meanings:

> True, gorillas and chimps *do* readily learn the word 'sorry'. But again, we must shout *beware*: 'sorry' signed by an ape . . . does not necessarily imply remorse, as does *sorry* said in English. . . . It transpires Nim signed 'sorry' most frequently while under imminent threat of punishment . . . a ritual device to thwart an attack, not a symptom of deep remorse. . . . [But] I dare say that with a master-stroke of conditioning something *resembling it* might be attained. (Desmond, 1979: 201–3, original emphasis)

The trouble here is that saying *sorry* ritually and without remorse is not merely an ape's imitative shadow of what humans do, but a perfectly recognizable human option. Indeed it is a variety of options, redescribable in ways ranging from insincerity or deception through to the normal etiquette of ritualized 'remedial interchanges' (Goffman, 1971). It is no use judging what apes and machines do against a human standard if that human standard has not itself been investigated. As I have often noted in this book, there is a common but erroneous presumption in much academic discussion of language and mind that we know intuitively, without careful investigation, how people ordinarily talk. Those presumptions include relations between language and mind. But once analysts resist mapping talk onto putative internal states, even for *human* discourse (Coulter, 1990a; Wittgenstein, 1958), we are left with a domain of talk-in-interaction (Schegloff, 1989a), where the legitimacy of taking *anybody's* individual utterances as diagnostic of 'mind' is questionable. This applies to apes, infants, and computers too, therefore, whether it is done by proponents or critics of their human-likeness.

Anthropomorphism is arguably at its most potent when we are displaying caution, doing critique, and aiming for objectivity. It is plain to see in descriptions such as the following: 'impressionable adolescents or young adults setting out to make their mark on chimpanzee society', 'these shy creatures', 'as baboons became bolder', 'political chicanery of community life' (Desmond, 1979: 225–8). But it is present also here, even with the scare quotes:

> Melissa, partially crippled by polio and brutally beaten by Passion and Pam, extending her hand to Passion for 'forgiveness' and reassurance – even as Passion eats her still-warm infant – *is not an act we readily understand*. (Desmond, 1979: 244, drawing on descriptions by Goodall; emphasis added)

It is, however, a description written out in *words* that we readily understand. Further, the effect of empathy or of alienation from other persons is not unknown in descriptions of purely human conduct, where descriptions may either unite us all in a common sensibility (cf. Geertz, 1988, on the anthropology of Evans-Pritchard), or emphasize difference (Said, 1979, on 'orientalism'). Even the details of Melissa's[16] alien behaviour invite comparison with human experiences, such as the requirement for Victorian children to thank their fathers and schoolmasters for a beating, and (contentious) descriptions of the feelings of concentration camp victims for their guards (Bettelheim, 1943).

Descriptions of what computers or apes (whether language-trained or wild) are able to do cannot escape Whorf's dilemma. To try to avoid translation altogether runs into a further conundrum: 'if a lion could talk, we could not understand him' (Wittgenstein, 1958: 223). The idea that humans and animals might 'mean' different things, however, may be only a more severe, and not a qualitatively different, problem from that which besets humans alone. According to Wittgenstein (1958), we do not know, except by playing the same public language games, what *each other* means. But the fact that we are able to play those games provides no guarantee, as if one were needed, of sharing an inner life of the mind. It is, rather, as I argued in Chapters 4 and 5 on conversational intersubjectivity, what that sharing amounts to. So, while sharing a form of life with the lions is not altogether out of the question (as the 1966 Columbia Pictures movie *Born Free* implies), the various rich interactions between humans and apes might be considered ape–human forms of life, with their ape–human languages. The problems occur when representing those ape–human forms of life within the forms of another – human discourse, academic reports and debates – where only one (human) partner plays both games, and represents the first (ape–human relations) as a diagnostic test for the apes' possible membership of the second (human discourse and society).

Small steps, giant leaps

In a classic paper criticizing the usefulness of the Turing test for deciding whether machines can properly be said to converse or think, the philosopher John Searle (1980) imagines a scenario in which questions and answers might be coherently produced, and the test passed, but with no 'understanding' whatsoever. The scenario is the 'Chinese room', in which a person who does not understand Chinese receives from outside the room pieces of paper with various Chinese symbols written on them. The person in the room then consults various lists of symbols and rules, and uses them to construct a written response from the same symbol set. So we have coherent Chinese input and output, but the room itself, and the person in it, understand nothing. So whatever success an analogous machine in a Turing test might have, it remains a mere simulation, and not a demonstration of human-like understanding.

There are various arguments for and against Searle's scenario, and the negative inferences he draws from it concerning the possibility of machine intelligence. I shall not review all those here (see Button et al., 1995, for a useful Wittgensteinian discussion). But one objection to Searle's argument is the way in which he reduces what the *machine* does to a series of small mechanical steps that themselves possess no understanding of Chinese.[17] Presumably, if we did something similar for a bona fide Chinese speaker, we would end up with neuronal impulses that also, themselves, do not understand Chinese. But *the speaker* does! Button et al. (1995) point out that the whole discussion hinges on what we take 'understanding' to be. Rather than some kind of internal process of mind or brain, reducible to its internal operations, they argue that 'understanding' is, like other mental predicates (including emotions, beliefs, etc.), a concept we use in conducting and talking about human activities and relations. Its sense remains at that level, and is not reducible to the small steps performed by brain states, electrical impulses, or blindly shuffling symbols around. I have made similar arguments in this book, especially in Chapter 2, about the relations between discourse and cognition, and between discursive and cognitive psychology.

There is also a further argument that critics of artificial and animal intelligence make, and that is to state that the 'small steps' that can be programmed into animals and machines are, in any case, the wrong sort. According to this argument, when animal trainers and cognitive scientists take some facet of human discourse or understanding, and break it down into the kinds of step-by-step routines that might be performed by electrical switches or non-human animals, what they invariably do is *alter the whole basis* of those performances. Following Gary Kasparov's recent defeat in a chess game by IBM's computer 'Deep Blue', Ray Monk commented:

> The way they [digital computers] play chess is actually rather dumb. They look at one position after another, evaluating them according to inflexible rules. They treat bad and brilliant moves with the same degree of seriousness. It is an inefficient, stupid way to play chess, which, if adopted by humans, would make it impossible to move within the time allowed. A computer's power lies in its ability to carry out this moronic process very quickly. (1996: 3)

This is reminiscent of how ostensibly human-like animal performances, including 'linguistic' ones (Brown, 1973; Chomsky, 1979), are dismissed as the mere products of rote learning and conditioning, in contrast to how persons generate their performances through creativity and understanding. Similarly,

> Turing contrived a method for breaking down calculations into such remarkably simplified steps that they could be carried out according to a series of instructions whose following did not involve any understanding of the mathematical operations thereby being carried out. (Button et al., 1995: 17)

So Turing's computers, like the 'talking' apes, do not perform calculations like we do, but by another, mechanical process *instead*. What Turing had invented was 'a new way of doing calculations' (Button et al., 1995: 139) – that is, a new way in which *people* can do calculations, by *using* computers.[18]

Arguments of this kind, which contrast bona fide human accomplishments with those of machines and animals, are also arguments against reductionism. The first reductionist step is hardly even noticed, being the adoption of the standard psychological paradigm – the individualist, in-the-head conception of what everyday notions such as thinking, believing, and knowing 'refer to'. Having conceived them as *actual* internal, mental processes, rather than as *ways of talking*, the second step is a much shorter one, which is to assume that they can be specified and reduced to the step-by-step internal operations of mind, brain, or program. The reason that those small step operations are 'the wrong sort' is that the nature of everyday discourse, and its repertoire of mental concepts, have been misconceived at the outset.

Similar conceptual problems arise for efforts to 'eliminate' folk psychology in favour of neurophysiology (for example, Churchland, 1988; Stich, 1983; see also Chapters 7 to 10). Those efforts are founded on the assumption that neurophysiology will eventually provide a full scientific description of the causal bases of human actions and experiences, and will therefore be able to replace the muddled, inadequate, common-sense ways in which we currently describe them. Fortunately that awful prospect is unlikely to arise, and not only because 'folk psychology' has been misconceived. As we noted for AI, if neurophysiology were to replace common-sense ways of talking, then not only would neuro-descriptions have to be adequate in their own terms, as descriptions of physiological processes, but they would also have to be mapped onto an adequate set of *non*-neurological descriptions of everyday life and discourse, if only to permit us to see how neuro-descriptions properly account for them.

Rom Harré links this kind of objection directly to the 'socialization problem', using Wittgenstein as a guide:

> There has also been a failure to consider how a neurophysiological language would or could be taught. What the physiological language games that linked neurophysiology to public manifestations would be like has not been addressed. If these were concepts overlapping in identical ways with ours, for example 'pain' and 'discharges in the c-fibres', could we seriously teach an infant c-fibre talk? What would that possibility presuppose? Well, at least a prior scientific education and skill with a microscope. If that is not presumed, we have just translated the word

'pain' or given a synonym for it. So there is a dilemma: if a new language, of the sort envisaged by the Churchlands, did come into existence, it would be unteachable, and if it were teachable it could not be new, at least not in the fashion they envisage. (Harré, 1989: 21)

The 'socialization problem' brings us back to the matter of how the ordinary, everyday, competent activities of bona fide 'members' are analysed and described. The major problem that besets efforts to simulate those competencies, whether on machines or animals, has been the lack of an adequate analysis of what it is we are trying to simulate – 'us', and the social bases of our own membership of the 'folk' club; we who are counted as (and counters as) already, genuinely, obviously, members. The task is to study how everyday psychological descriptions and attributions are assigned to persons and things, which includes, as a corollary, how 'persons and things' are defined and distinguished. We should not presume to know that already, prior to ethnomethodological and discourse analytical investigation.

Conclusions

The arguments presented in this chapter suggest the futility of trying to resolve the issue of non-human thought and language as a problem of *ontology*, of what kinds of beings there are in the world. Rather, it has to be understood as a discursive matter – a matter of social, conceptual, and especially descriptive practices. Further, these descriptive practices include not only those of participants in interactions, but also those of the writers of research reports, and all constructors of lay and academic dichotomies and distinctions.

The distinction that I have used between everyday and academic discourse has been useful in pointing up various problems and dilemmas in how this whole area is conceptualized and discussed. But the distinction is a superficial one. It is not so much a contrast between the ontological disputes of academic texts (whether or not apes, infants, and computers *actually can* think and talk like us) and the 'counts-as' operations of common-sense reasoning (computers and apes 'think' and 'talk' if people treat them as doing so). The thing to remember is that the professional, academic discussions and criteria, including whatever tests and invented scenarios are applied, are themselves 'counts-as' procedures too. As Chapters 2 and 3 argued, there is nothing in the world outside the scope of counts-as procedures.

Let us review some of the themes we have discussed. First, there is Whorf's dilemma: the reflexive problems of description. Accounts of, and data on, human/non-human communications are themselves examples of discourse, of the thing under analysis: the capacity of anyone to render themselves in human language, or otherwise make themselves intelligible. These kinds of descriptions become available for analysis (for further description) like any other text, as forms of social action. For example, descriptions of non-humans as agentive or non-agentive figure prominently in justifications for treating them as such (see Haraway, 1989, on the intimate relations between primate studies, eugenics, medical research, racism, and constructions of gender). Meanwhile, we must not forget that analysis of human–human interactions is founded on the same competence as participation (Heritage, 1984a), and both are constituted in the 'writing-up' (Ashmore, 1989; Geertz, 1988).

Second, there is Malinowski's dilemma (Geertz, 1988), the attribution/ anthropomorphism quandary: the need for both rapport and objectivity. This is not merely a problem of how best to do participant observation, but a deeper issue of what kind of thing participation and its description *are*. The ontology of us-and-them dissolves into text and description. Anthropomorphic attribution is as plausibly about the *constitution* of human relations, the formation of persons and their proper description, as it is a matter of truth and error concerning what already exists. Its application to non-humans is as much a matter of social practice, a participants' making-it-so procedure, as is its application to us. These are the practices that mark 'us' out.

Third, there is the futility of what we might call the 'impossibility argument', that there is no way *in principle* that non-humans can ever cross the conceptual divide that marks out true 'thinkers' and 'conversers' from the rest. The impossibility argument sustains, by definition, an ontological or conceptual distinction between what humans and non-humans can do. Partly the futility stems from the Whorf and Malinowski conundrums, where reality is what counts-as. What counts-as can change, without the conceptual criteria having to change, just as excluded people can get to be counted as fully fledged, intelligent, and agentive members of a society, without intelligence and agency being redefined. Indeed, that is the point, that new members are included, rather than old meanings altered. Whereas we can reasonably doubt the capacity of machines and animals to enter into human 'physiognomic language games' (Harré, 1988; Hintikka and Hintikka, 1986), there is no reason to insist that humans and non-humans *cannot* engage together in forms of life, of interaction, nor that some kind of language, even some of what we use already, could not serve to mediate those interactions.

If we turn to constructions of commonality rather than difference, the impossibility argument refuses to countenance or take seriously Haraway's category of 'boundary objects' called 'cyborgs' (Haraway, 1991). These are ways of describing *us*, not merely androids, hoaxes, or fictional inventions.

> A cyborg is a hybrid creature, composed of organism and machine . . . entities made of, first, ourselves and other organic creatures in our unchosen 'high-technological' guise as information systems, texts, and ergonomically controlled laboring, desiring, and reproducing systems. The second essential ingredient in cyborgs is machines in their guise, also, as communications systems, texts, and self-acting, ergonomically designed apparatuses. (Haraway, 1991: 1)

Haraway's description decomposes the cyborg into organism and machine, but only to put them together again. The argument emphasizes their fusion, as with Latour's (1987) 'actants', where the division of labour is finally obscured between subject and object, knower and known, agent and artefact.

The argument of this chapter, and of the book it is part of, does not end with the primacy of attribution. That would merely shift the explanatory focus from object to attributer, with mind and agency displaced and reapportioned from one to the other. Rather, it is an argument for the further step of dissolving these categories (object and attributer) into those of interaction and description. Attributions of agency, intelligence, mental states, and their attendant problems are *in the first place* participants' categories and concerns (manifested in descriptions, accusations, claims, error accounts, membership disputes, etc.), just as much as reality, imitation, and authenticity are. The first analytic task in the study of discourse and cognition is to *study* those attributions, before disputing them.

Notes

1. Some confusion is possible here over the dates of various publications that I am citing. Vygotsky's classic text *Thought and Language* was first published in English in 1962, followed by a fuller version in 1987, having appeared posthumously in Russian in 1934. Sacks (1992) is a collection of lectures (also posthumously published) delivered between 1964 and 1972. The lectures I am drawing on here are from the early 1964–5 collection, also published as Sacks (1989). Sacks's approval of Vygotsky specifically concerned his treatment of 'scientific concepts' as embedded in social practices. There is also in Sacks's work (e.g., 1972b) a discussion of the social-interactional basis of learning how to 'refer' to things, which bears comparison to the classic Vygotsky–Bruner approach (Bruner, 1983).

2. It has been noted that, for human out-groups as well as for apes, the most forceful distinctions are often drawn closest to home. With regard to apes, 'man's closest and homeliest relative has in history been the most vilified of all creatures: the wretch of creation' (Desmond, 1979: 18). See also Charles Taylor (1989) on how personhood can be withheld from, and define the status of, members of various out-groups. Such categoriz-ations work via *similarities* as much as differences. For example the use of rats, both in Nazi anti-Semitic propaganda and as standard laboratory animals, is helped by their capacity to provoke human comparisons, both social and biological, as well as their 'traditional reputation as "vermin" with minimal human sympathy' (Lynch, 1988: 281). They are close enough to 'us' to be useful as experimental substitutes and human analogies, but verminous enough to kill; both close enough and distant enough for comparison, though not as close as apes, and perhaps computers, which can (reputedly) 'think' and 'talk like you and me' (Reichman, 1985).

3. This is at least my fourth use of this pronoun ('us') so far, but here it is becoming provisional and ironic. It is, in a sense, the point at issue: 'The pronouns embedded in sentences about contestations for what may count as nature are themselves political tools, expressing hopes, fears, and contradictory histories. Grammar is politics by other means' (Haraway, 1991: 3). Note, for example, Turkle's use of them in the quotation that follows.

4. For an excellent collection of the early research reports and critiques, see Sebeok and Umiker-Sebeok (1980); on Kanzi, see Savage-Rumbaugh (1993) and Savage-Rumbaugh and Lewin (1994).

5. Various examples have been offered of non-imitative, creative language production by chimpanzees and gorillas, including Washoe's *water bird* for a duck, and *rock berry* for a Brazil nut (Fouts, 1974); Lana's *finger bracelet* for a ring (Rumbaugh, Gill, Glasersfeld,

Warner, and Pisani, 1975); Lucy's *cry hurt food* for radishes (Temerlin, 1975); and Koko's *white tiger* for a zebra (Patterson and Linden, 1981). Rejections of such evidence are based on their untypicality, selective reporting, and indeterminacy of situational reference (Desmond, 1979). I am reminded of the *iron horse* of the old Wild West movies, the stock 'Indian' term for steam locomotives, strange but inventive, like children, though in this case more an emblem of difference rather than sameness to 'us'.

6. Roger Brown's version of this 'rote learning' objection is delightfully mechanical, in the context of non-human agency in general, and a change from his usually highly readable prose: 'possible dependence of terminal accomplishments on specific atomic preliminary programs' (1973: 48). For examples of what the criticism may apply to, see Premack and Premack (1972) and Rumbaugh (1977).

7. The *forced* relations between control and understanding cut deeply into these matters. The laboratory control of animals, and the possibility of giving them verbal instructions, have not escaped the attention of the military. This is even more the case with artificial intelligence, as the 'smart bombs' and television-monitored guided missiles of the Gulf War so vividly demonstrated, both to the watching public, and to the world's arms traders: 'AI research is, at least in the United States, first and foremost a military affair' (Crevier, 1993: 313). It was DARPA, the US government's 'Defense Advanced Research Projects Agency', that established for military uses what has now become the Internet, and it is DARPA that has underwritten, and occasionally pulled the plug on, AI research in the USA.

8. It is claimed even for the chimpanzee Nim, whose imitative behaviour became the basis for rejecting his and other apes' spontaneous grammaticality, that he displayed a human-like orientation to intersubjectivity: 'he was alive to new discoveries, and just had to share them; he would drag his flatmate [Laura Petitto] outside to point out planes or birds' (Desmond, 1979: 231). Again, this is in the first place a description, a motive-attributing *narrative account*, in which the activity and its interpretation are descriptively conjoined. Thorpe (1972) cites evidence of 'prevarication' in birds, such as feigning a damaged wing to lure a predator away from the eggs. How far such activities are intentional or automatic begs the question, of course, of the appropriateness of words such as 'prevarication', and the purposive little word *to* in 'to lure', for what birds do. 'When Herb Terrace concluded that Nim was just imitating his trainer, he was implying that it's a very low-level ability. Experiments like these [by Sue Savage-Rumbaugh with Kanzi] have shown that imitation, understanding the goal and achieving it by the same method as the demonstrator, is a very sophisticated skill' (Jones, 1993). Note again the cognitivist, purposive gloss on imitation. Terrace's study was itself sophisticatedly imitative (or not, depending which side you are on) – it was a *replication* of earlier studies.

9. The 'Turing test' (Turing, 1950) is the classic definition of the point at which AI will have succeeded in simulating human intelligence. Its criterion is the (in)ability of a human interactant/interrogator to distinguish between the conversational output of a machine and another human being. In Alan Turing's version, the machine and other person are situated behind a screen, and communication is by means of typed input and printouts. See also Chapter 2 of this volume.

10. Collins's argument parallels Rom Harré's (1988) insistence on the importance for human language and intelligence of possessing a human body, upon which human 'physiognomic language games' are predicated. Joseph Weizenbaum makes a similar case, adding that 'however much intelligence computers may attain, now or in the future, theirs must always be an intelligence alien to genuine human problems and concerns' (1984: 213).

11. As Bruner notes, 'Mothers will tell you that they don't *really* believe the baby understands. But they go on talking that way in spite of what they say. They assign meanings to what their infants are doing, and respond accordingly. And in time . . . they create formats of interaction, *jointly constructed* little worlds in which they *interact* according to the social realities that they have created in their exchanges' (Bruner, 1986: 114–15, original plus added emphasis). However, the extent to which adults anthropomorphize babies appears to be culturally variable. Samoan caregivers are reported to avoid assigning intentional

meanings to infants' acts and vocalizations, and treat them more as natural reflexes or physiological states (Ochs, 1982).

12. Some people talk at, and about, computers when operating them. Here is a programmer reacting to his bugged chess program: 'When it feels threatened, under attack, it wants to advance its king. It confuses value and power, and this leads to self-destructive behavior' (quoted in Turkle, 1984: 16). Of course, the anthropomorphic traffic goes both ways. Not only are computers humanized, but cognitive psychology treats humans as computational. Ordinary folk may do so too: '"My God," says the mother, "she treats that thing like a person. Do you suppose she thinks that persons are like machines?"' (Turkle, 1984: 14). It also applies both ways with regard to animals, not only for naïve everyday folk, but for scientific researchers. Animal behaviour is, for sociobiologists, a source of insight into the 'human animal'. In the other direction, 'a researcher, who worked with ants in maze experiments, confided that experimental success depended, in part, on his abilities to monitor the "emotions" of his ant subjects. He learned to interpret whether or not his subjects were agitated or "calm" enough to undergo maze tests by examining positions and movements of their antennae' (Lynch, 1988: 280).

13. Weizenbaum is referring to Terry Winograd's (1972) celebrated AI program SHRDLU, which greatly impressed the worlds of AI and cognitive psychology with its ability to engage in seemingly natural conversation. Unfortunately SHRDLU's conversational abilities were restricted to a highly constrained 'Blocks Micro World' in which blocks of various clear-cut 'classical category' types (see Chapter 8) – small red pyramid, large green cube, etc. – were moved around. Daniel Crevier remarks, 'For all its brilliance, SHRDLU was but a shooting star in the firmament of AI. It soon became clear that it could not be extended beyond the Blocks Micro World. The simplicity, logic, and isolation of this domain allowed the appearance of intelligent dialogue by simply dodging difficult language issues' (1993: 102). The difficult issues dodged are precisely those discussed throughout this book. These include the action-performative nature of discourse (addressed somewhat in Winograd and Flores, 1986); the constructive, 'categorizing' work of everyday descriptions, where the world does not come definitively pre-described; and the rule-oriented rather than rule-governed nature of talk (see also Button et al., 1995).

14. This description of Nim can be contrasted with other ways of discounting Terrace's claims, noted above, in which even Nim's 'imitations' could be described as highly sophisticated sorts of actions.

15. Whorf's dilemma enters the description not only of linguistic and gestural performances, but of their developmental trajectories. With children, for example, an argument for the pre-linguistic structuring of infant activity and interaction, as a foundation for language, is much aided by the analyst's description of those *pre-linguistic* activities in terms derived from the analysis of language and speech acts (Bruner, 1983; Edwards, 1973), or from narratology (Bruner, 1990). See also the discussion of 'infant cognition' in Chapter 2, where a similar 'Whig history' of how children acquire adult competencies is discussed. Relatedly, one of the tropes for animal language research is the idea of bringing up an ape just like a child, 'as far as possible'. This is an issue of substance, inserted as method. If we could, precisely (and this is where the 'as far as possible' bites), bring up an ape as we bring up a child, and make the ape's interactional environment 'the same as' that of a child, then ape and child would be interactionally indistinguishable. The ape would effectively have passed the Turing test in the report's Method section, before we get to see the Results.

16. The naming of apes is itself a feature of their transformation into proto-humans, just as it is for human infants. For the apes observed in the wild, these remain observers' names. Washoe and other trained apes apparently learned them as labels for themselves.

17. This is reminiscent of the discussion, in Chapter 2, of Plato's *Meno*, in which Socrates leads the slave boy through a series of very small steps towards a definition of Pythagoras's theorem. But whatever the slave boy already knew, or was possibly taught, the imaginary person in the Chinese room understands nothing.

18. As Wittgenstein noted, 'it is the use outside mathematics . . . that makes the sign-game into mathematics' (1978: V, paragraph 2). Similarly, 'an account of the program can only

explicate why the machine produced its results: not whether they were correct . . . the rules of calculation . . . are antecedent to the machine's operations' (Shanker, 1987: 639, cited in Coulter, 1991: 183).

Appendix: Transcription Symbols

The following list defines the main transcription conventions, as used in this book, that have been developed by Gail Jefferson for the purposes of conversation analysis (see Atkinson and Heritage, 1984). They reflect the requirements of analysing talk as a social activity rather than, for example, as an expression of ideas, phonetics, or grammar.

Data extracts are cited as coming either from published sources or from data corpora used in my own and other people's analytic work. Citations from data corpora specify the data set and the place of the extract within it. Thus, 'Frankel' specifies a body of counselling talk transcribed by Richard Frankel, although my access to those materials is through published papers. Other extracts cite the extensive 'NB' (place name) telephone conversation data transcribed by Gail Jefferson. A citation such as 'DE–JF: C2:S1:23' (see Chapter 6) specifies couple counselling data transcribed by myself (DE) and Jonsanto Fong, couple 2, session 1, page 23 in the transcript. Person and place names within the data are altered to preserve anonymity.

The initial difficulty of reading CA transcripts is largely a matter of our overwhelming familiarity with conventional written text. However, as suggested in Chapter 4, we should not be fooled by that familiarity into imagining that conventional orthography is in any sense a neutral or preferable way of representing talk. The advantage of reading and producing formal transcripts is that it encourages and permits the kind of analytic stance towards language that is promoted in this book; an orientation towards talk as discourse, as performing actions, rather than expressing and communicating thoughts. Note that many of the symbols are familiar as punctuation marks, but that here they signify intonation or speech delivery rather than grammar.

[ ]	Square brackets mark the start and end of overlapping speech.
↑ ↓	Vertical arrows precede marked pitch movement.
→	Side arrows are not transcription features, but draw analytic attention to particular lines of text.
Underlining	signals emphasis; the extent of underlining within individual words locates emphasis, but also indicates how heavy it is.
CAPITALS	mark speech that is obviously louder than surrounding speech.

°↑I know it,°	Raised circles ('degree' signs) enclose obviously quieter speech.
*	Asterisks signal a 'squeaky' vocal delivery.
(0.4)	Numbers in round brackets measure pauses in seconds (in this case, four-tenths of a second).
(.)	A micropause, hearable but too short to measure.
((text))	Additional comments from the transcriber.
she wa::nted	Colons show degrees of elongation of the prior sound; the more colons, the more elongation.
hhh	Aspiration (out-breaths); proportionally as for colons.
.hhh	Inspiration (in-breaths).
Yeh,	Commas mark weak rising intonation, as used sometimes in enunciating lists.
y'know?	Question marks signal stronger, 'questioning' intonation, irrespective of grammar.
Yeh.	Periods (stops) mark falling, stopping intonation, irrespective of grammar.
bu-u-	Hyphens mark a cut-off of the preceding sound.
>he said<	'Greater than' and 'lesser than' signs enclose speeded-up talk.
solid.= We had	'Equals' signs mark the immediate 'latching' of successive talk, whether of one or more speakers, with no interval.
(. . .)	This shows where some talk has been omitted from a data extract.

References

Abelson, R.P. (1981). The psychological status of the script concept. *American Psychologist*, 36, 715–29.

Abu-Lughod, L. and Lutz, C.A. (1990). Introduction: Emotion, discourse, and the politics of everyday life. In C.A. Lutz and L. Abu-Lughod (Eds.), *Language and the Politics of Emotion*. Cambridge: Cambridge University Press.

Anderson, A., Garrod, S.C. and Sanford, A.J. (1983). The accessibility of pronominal antecedents as a function of episode shifts in narrative texts. *Quarterly Journal of Experimental Psychology*, 35A, 427–40.

Argyle, M. (1988). *Bodily Communication* (2nd Edn). London: Routledge.

Armon-Jones, C. (1986). The social functions of emotion. In R. Harré (Ed.), *The Social Construction of Emotions*. Oxford: Blackwell.

Ashmore, M. (1989). *The Reflexive Thesis: Wrighting Sociology of Scientific Knowledge*. Chicago: University of Chicago Press.

Ashmore, M. (1993). The theatre of the blind: Starring a Promethean prankster, a phoney phenomenon, a prism, a pocket, and a piece of Wood. *Social Studies of Science*, 23, 67–106.

Atkinson, J.M. (1984). *Our Master's Voices: the Language and Body Language of Politics*. London: Methuen.

Atkinson, J.M. and Drew, P. (1979). *Order in Court: the Organization of Verbal Interaction in Judicial Settings*. London: Macmillan.

Atkinson, J.M. and Heritage, J.C. (Eds.) (1984). *Structures of Social Action: Studies in Conversation Analysis*. Cambridge: Cambridge University Press.

Atkinson, P. (1990). *The Ethnographic Imagination: the Textual Construction of Reality*. London: Routledge.

Auburn, T., Drake, S. and Willig, C. (1995). 'You punched him, didn't you?': Versions of violence in accusatory interviews. *Discourse and Society*, 6 (3), 353–86.

Augoustinos, M. and Walker, I. (1995). *Social Cognition: an Integrated Introduction*. London: Sage.

Austin, J.L. (1962). *How to Do Things with Words*. Oxford: Clarendon.

Averill, J.R. (1990). Inner feelings, works of the flesh, the beast within, diseases of the mind, driving force, and putting on a show: Six metaphors of emotion and their theoretical extensions. In D.E. Leary (Ed.), *Metaphors in the History of Psychology*. Cambridge: Cambridge University Press.

Bakhtin, M.M. (1981). *The Dialogic Imagination*. Austin, TX: University of Texas Press.

Bal, M. (1985). *Narratology: Introduction to the Theory of Narrative*. Toronto: University of Toronto Press.

Banaji, M. (1992). The lures of ecological realism. *The Psychologist*, 5, 448.

Barker, R.G. and Wright, H.F. (1951). *One Boy's Day: a Specimen Record of Behavior*. New York: Harper and Row.

Barnes, B. (1977). *Interests and the Growth of Knowledge*. London: Routledge.

Baron-Cohen, S. (1995). *Mindblindness: an Essay on Autism and Theory of Mind*. Cambridge, MA: Bradford/MIT Press.

Barrett, E.A. (1990). Discourses of femininity: Studies in the social psychology of gender. Unpublished doctoral dissertation, Loughborough University.

Barsalou, L.W. (1983). Ad hoc categories. *Memory and Cognition*, 11, 211–27.

Barsalou, L.W. (1991). Deriving categories to achieve goals. In G.H. Bower (Ed.), *The*

Psychology of Learning and Motivation: Advances in Research and Theory. New York: Academic Press.

Barsalou, L.W. (1992). *Cognitive Psychology: an Overview for Cognitive Scientists.* Hillsdale, NJ: Erlbaum.

Barthes, R. (1964). *Elements of Semiology.* New York: Hill and Wang.

Barthes, R. (1972). *Mythologies.* London: Paladin.

Barthes, R. (1981). *Camera Lucida: Reflections on Photography.* New York: Hill and Wang.

Bartlett, F.C. (1932). *Remembering: a Study in Experimental and Social Psychology.* Cambridge: Cambridge University Press.

Bedford, E. (1962). Emotions. In V.C. Chappell (Ed.), *The Philosophy of Mind.* Englewood Cliffs, NJ: Prentice Hall.

Berger, C.R. (1993). Goals, plans, and mutual understanding in relationships. In S. Duck (Ed.), *Individuals in Relationships.* Newbury Park, CA: Sage.

Berlin, B. and Kay, P. (1969). *Basic Color Terms: Their Universality and Evolution.* Berkeley, CA: University of California Press.

Berne, E. (1968). *Games People Play.* Harmondsworth: Penguin.

Bernstein, B. (1971). *Class, Codes and Control.* Volume 1. London: Routledge and Kegan Paul.

Berreman, G. (1966). Anemic and emetic analyses in social anthropology. *American Anthropologist, 68* (2), 346–54.

Bettelheim, B. (1943). Individual and mass behavior in extreme situations. *Journal of Abnormal and Social Psychology, 38,* 417–52.

Billig, M. (1987). *Arguing and Thinking: a Rhetorical Approach to Social Psychology.* Cambridge: Cambridge University Press.

Billig, M. (1991). *Ideologies and Opinions.* London: Sage.

Billig, M. (1992). *Talking of the Royal Family.* London: Routledge.

Billig, M. (1995). *Banal Nationalism.* London: Sage.

Billig, M., Condor, S., Edwards, D., Gane, M., Middleton, D.J. and Radley, A.R. (1988). *Ideological Dilemmas: a Social Psychology of Everyday Thinking.* London: Sage.

Bilmes, J. (1986). *Discourse and Behavior.* New York: Plenum Press.

Bilmes, J. (1987). The concept of preference in conversation analysis. *Language in Society, 17,* 161–81.

Bilmes, J. (1992). Referring to internal occurrences: A reply to Coulter. *Journal for the Theory of Social Behaviour, 22* (3), 253–62.

Black, J.B. and Wilensky, R. (1984). An evaluation of story grammars. *Cognitive Science, 3,* 213–29.

Bloor, D. (1976). *Knowledge and Social Imagery.* London: Routledge and Kegan Paul.

Boas, F. (1911/1966). Introduction. *Bureau of American Ethnology Bulletin, 40* (1), 1–83. Reprinted in F. Boas (Ed.), *Handbook of American Indian Languages.* Lincoln, NE: University of Nebraska Press.

Boden, D. (1995). *The Business of Talk.* Cambridge: Polity.

Boden, D. and Zimmerman, D. (Eds.) (1991). *Talk and Social Structure: Studies in Ethnomethodology and Conversation Analysis.* Cambridge: Polity.

Bogen, D. (1992). The organization of talk. *Qualitative Sociology, 15* (3), 273–95.

Bogen, D. and Lynch, M. (1989). Taking account of the hostile native: Plausible deniability and the production of conventional history in the Iran–Contra hearings. *Social Problems, 36* (3), 197–224.

Bower, G.H., Black, J.B. and Turner, T.J. (1979). Scripts in text comprehension and memory. *Cognitive Psychology, 11,* 177–220.

Bowers, J.M. (1991). Time, representation and power/knowledge: Towards a critique of cognitive science as a knowledge-producing practice. *Theory and Psychology, 1* (4), 543–69.

Brannigan, A. (1981). *The Social Basis of Scientific Discoveries.* Cambridge: Cambridge University Press.

Bransford, J.D. (1979). *Human Cognition: Learning, Understanding, and Remembering.* Belmont, CA: Wadsworth.

Brewer, W.F. (1985). The story schema: Universal and culture specific properties. In D.A. Olson, N. Torrance, and A. Hildyard (Eds.), *Literacy, Language and Learning*. Cambridge: Cambridge University Press.

Brewer, W.F. and Lichtenstein, E.H. (1981). Event schemas, story schemas and story grammars. In J. Long and A. Baddeley (Eds.), *Attention and Performance*. Volume 9. Hillsdale, NJ: Erlbaum.

Brewer, W.F. and Lichtenstein, E.H. (1982). Stories are to entertain: A structural-affect theory of stories. *Journal of Pragmatics, 6*, 473–86.

Bronowski, J. and Bellugi, U. (1980). Language, name, and concept. In T.A. Sebeok and J. Umiker-Sebeok (Eds.), *Speaking of Apes: a Critical Anthology of Two-Way Communication with Man*. New York: Plenum.

Brown, G. and Yule, G. (1983). *Discourse Analysis*. Cambridge: Cambridge University Press.

Brown, R.W. (1965). *Social Psychology*. New York: Macmillan.

Brown, R.W. (1970). *Psycholinguistics: Selected Papers by Roger Brown*. New York: Free Press.

Brown, R.W. (1973). *A First Language: the Early Stages*. London: George Allen and Unwin.

Brown, R.W. (1976). Reference: In memorial tribute to Eric Lenneberg. *Cognition, 4*, 125–53.

Brown, R.W. and Lenneberg, E.H. (1954). A study in language and cognition. *Journal of Abnormal and Social Psychology, 49*, 454–62.

Brugman, C. (1983). The use of body-part terms as locatives in Chalcatongo Mixtec. In *Report No. 4 of the Survey of California and Other Indian Languages*, pp. 235–90. University of California, Berkeley.

Bruner, J.S. (1964). The course of cognitive growth. *American Psychologist, 19*, 1–16.

Bruner, J.S. (1974). *Beyond the Information Given* (Ed. J.M. Anglin). London: Allen and Unwin.

Bruner, J.S. (1983). *Child's Talk*. Oxford: Oxford University Press.

Bruner, J.S. (1986). *Actual Minds, Possible Worlds*. Cambridge, MA: Harvard University Press.

Bruner, J.S. (1990). *Acts of Meaning*. Cambridge, MA: Harvard University Press.

Bruner, J.S., Goodnow, J.J. and Austin, G.A. (1956). *A Study of Thinking*. New York: Wiley.

Bubenzer, D.L. and West, J.D. (1993). *Counselling Couples*. London: Sage.

Buchanan, K. and Middleton, D. (1995). Voices of experience: Talk, identity and membership in reminiscence groups. *Ageing and Society, 15*, 449–57.

Buford, B. (1991). *Among the Thugs*. London: Martin, Secker and Warburg.

Burke, K. (1945). *A Grammar of Motives*. New York: Prentice Hall.

Butterworth, G. and Grover, L. (1988). The origins of referential communication in human infancy. In L. Weiskrantz (Ed.), *Thought without Language*. Oxford: Clarendon.

Butterworth, G. and Light, P. (1982). *Social Cognition: Studies of the Development of Understanding*. Brighton: Harvester.

Buttny, R. (1993). *Social Accountability in Communication*. London: Sage.

Button, G. (Ed.) (1991). *Ethnomethodology and the Human Sciences*. Cambridge: Cambridge University Press.

Button, G., Coulter, J., Lee, J. and Sharrock, W. (1995). *Computers, Minds and Conduct*. Oxford: Polity.

Button, G., Drew, P. and Heritage, J.C. (Eds.) (1986). *Interaction and Language Use*. Special issue of *Human Studies, 9* (2 and 3).

Button, G. and Lee, J.R.E. (1987). *Talk and Social Organization*. Clevedon: Multilingual Matters.

Button, G. and Sharrock, W. (1992). A disagreement over agreement and consensus in constructionist sociology. *Journal for the Theory of Social Behaviour, 23* (1), 1–25.

Caesar-Wolf, B. (1984). The construction of 'adjudicable' evidence in a West German civil hearing. *Text, 4*, 193–224.

Callon, M. (1986). Some elements in a sociology of translation: Domestication of the scallops and fishermen of St. Brieuc Bay. In J. Law (Ed.), *Power, Action and Belief*. London: Routledge and Kegan Paul.

Carey, S. (1985). *Conceptual Change in Childhood*. Cambridge, MA: Bradford/MIT Press.

Carroll, J.B. (1956). Introduction. In J.B. Carroll (Ed.), *Language, Thought and Reality: Selected Writings of Benjamin Lee Whorf*. Cambridge, MA: MIT Press.

Carroll, J.B. and Casagrande, J.B. (1958). The function of language classifications in behavior. In E.E. Maccoby, T.M. Newcombe, and E.L. Hartley (Eds.), *Readings in Social Psychology*. New York: Henry Holt.

Chafe, W.L. (1970). *Meaning and the Structure of Language*. Chicago: University of Chicago Press.

Chafe, W.L. (1990). Some things that narratives tell us about the mind. In B.K. Britton and A.D. Pellegrini (Eds.), *Narrative Thought and Narrative Language*. Hillsdale, NJ: Erlbaum.

Chomsky, N. (1959). A review of *Verbal Behavior* by B.F. Skinner. *Language*, *35*, 26–58.

Chomsky, N. (1965). *Aspects of the Theory of Syntax*. Cambridge, MA: MIT Press.

Chomsky, N. (1966). *Cartesian Linguistics: a Chapter in the History of Rationalist Thought*. New York: Harper and Row.

Chomsky, N. (1968). *Language and Mind*. New York: Harcourt, Brace and World.

Chomsky, N. (1973). Introduction. In A. Schaff, *Language and Cognition*. New York: McGraw-Hill.

Chomsky, N. (1979). Human language and other semiotic systems. *Semiotica*, *25*, 31–44.

Chomsky, N. (1991). Clever Kanzi. *Discover*, March, p. 20.

Churchland, P.M. (1988). *Matter and Consciousness: a Contemporary Introduction to the Philosophy of Mind*. Cambridge, MA: MIT Press.

Clark, H.H. (1985). Language use and language users. In G. Lindzey and E. Aronson (Eds.), *Handbook of Social Psychology*. Volume 2 (3rd Edn). New York: Random House.

Clark, H.H. (1992). *Arenas of Language Use*. Chicago: University of Chicago Press.

Clark, H.H. and Brennan, S.E. (1991). Grounding in communication. In L.B. Resnick, J.M. Levine, and S.D. Teasley (Eds.), *Perspectives on Socially Shared Cognition*. Washington, DC: American Psychological Association.

Clark, H.H. and Haviland, S.E. (1977). Comprehension and the given-new contract. In R.O. Freedle (Ed.), *Discourse Production and Comprehension*. Norwood, NJ: Ablex.

Clark H.H. and Schaefer, E.F. (1989). Contributing to discourse. *Cognitive Science*, *13*, 259–94.

Clark, H.H. and Wilkes-Gibbs, D. (1986). Referring as a collaborative process. *Cognition*, *22*, 1–39.

Clark, K. (1992). The linguistics of blame: Representations of women in *The Sun*'s reporting of crimes of sexual violence. In M. Toolan (Ed.), *Language, Text and Context: Essays in Stylistics*. London: Routledge.

Clifford, J. (1988). *The Predicament of Culture: Twentieth-Century Ethnography, Literature, and Art*. Cambridge, MA: Harvard University Press.

Clifford, J. and Marcus, G.E. (Eds.) (1986). *Writing Culture: the Poetics and Politics of Ethnography*. Berkeley, CA: University of California Press.

Cole, M. (1994). Culture and cognitive development: From cross-cultural research to creating systems of cultural mediation. *Culture and Psychology*, *1*, 25–54.

Collins, H.M. (1974). The TEA set: Tacit knowledge and scientific networks. *Science Studies*, *4*, 165–86.

Collins, H.M. (1982). Special relativism: The natural attitude. *Social Studies of Science*, *12*, 139–43.

Collins, H.M. (1985). *Changing Order: Replication and Induction in Scientific Practice*. London: Sage.

Collins, H.M. (1990). *Artificial Experts: Social Knowledge and Intelligent Machines*. Cambridge, MA: MIT Press.

Collins, H.M. and Yearley, S. (1992). Epistemological chicken. In A. Pickering (Ed.), *Science as Practice and Culture*. Chicago: University of Chicago Press.

Conklin, H. (1955). Hanunóo color categories. *Southwest Journal of Anthropology, 11*, 339–44.

Conway, M.A. (1990). *Autobiographical Memory: an Introduction*. Buckingham: Open University Press.

Cortazzi, M. (1993). *Narrative Analysis*. London: Falmer Press.

Costall, A. and Still, A. (1991). Introduction: Cognitivism as an approach to cognition. In A. Still and A. Costall (Eds.), *Against Cognitivism: Alternative Foundations for Cognitive Psychology*. Hemel Hempstead: Harvester Wheatsheaf.

Coulter, J. (1979). *The Social Construction of Mind: Studies in Ethnomethodology and Linguistic Philosophy*. London: Macmillan.

Coulter, J. (1983). *Rethinking Cognitive Theory*. London: Macmillan.

Coulter, J. (1985). Two concepts of the mental. In K.J. Gergen and K.E. Davis (Eds.), *The Social Construction of the Person*. New York: Springer-Verlag.

Coulter, J. (1986). Affect and social context: Emotion definition as a social task. In R. Harré (Ed.), *The Social Construction of Emotions*. Oxford: Blackwell.

Coulter, J. (1989). Cognitive 'penetrability' and the emotions. In D.D. Franks and E.D. McCarthy (Eds.), *The Sociology of the Emotions*. Greenwich, CT: JAI Press.

Coulter, J. (1990a). *Mind in Action*. Oxford: Polity.

Coulter, J. (Ed.) (1990b). *Ethnomethodological Sociology*. Aldershot: Edward Elgar.

Coulter, J. (1990c) Introduction. In J. Coulter (Ed.), *Ethnomethodological Sociology*. Aldershot: Edward Elgar.

Coulter, J. (1991). Cognition: Cognition in an ethnomethodological mode. In G. Button (Ed.), *Ethnomethodology and the Human Sciences*. Cambridge: Cambridge University Press.

Coulter, J. (1992). Bilmes on 'internal states': A critical commentary. *Journal for the Theory of Social Behaviour, 22* (3), 239–52.

Crevier, D. (1993). *AI: the Tumultuous History of the Search for Artificial Intelligence*. New York: Basic Books.

Cromer, R.F. (1991). *Language and Thought in Normal and Handicapped Children*. Oxford: Blackwell.

Cronon, W. (1992). A place for stories: Nature, history, and narrative. *Journal of American History, 78* (4), 1347–76.

D'Andrade, R.G. (1981). The cultural part of cognition. *Cognitive Science, 5*, 179–95.

D'Andrade, R.G. (1990). Some propositions about the relations between culture and human cognition. In J.W. Stigler, R.A. Shweder, and G. Herdt (Eds.), *Cultural Psychology*. Cambridge: Cambridge University Press.

D'Andrade, R.G., Quinn, N., Nerlove, S.B. and Romney, A.K. (1972). Categories of disease in American-English and Mexican-Spanish. In A.K. Romney, R.N. Shepard, and S.B. Nerlove (Eds.), *Multidimensional Scaling*. Volume 2. New York: Seminar Press.

D'Andrade, R.G. and Strauss, C. (Eds.) (1992). *Human Motives and Cultural Models*. Cambridge: Cambridge University Press.

Darwin, C. (1871). *The Expression of Emotions in Animals and Man*. London: John Murray.

Davidson, J. (1984). Subsequent versions of invitations, offers, requests, and proposals dealing with potential or actual rejection. In J.M. Atkinson and J. Heritage (Eds.), *Structures of Social Action: Studies in Conversation Analysis*. Cambridge: Cambridge University Press.

Deaux, K. and Wrightsman, L. (1988). *Social Psychology* (5th Edn). Belmont, CA: Wadsworth.

Derrida, J. (1977a). Signature event context. *Glyph, I*, 172–97.

Derrida, J. (1977b). Limited Inc. abc . . . *Glyph, II*, 162–254.

Desmond, A. (1979). *The Ape's Reflexion*. London: Blond and Briggs.

Donaldson, M. (1978). *Children's Minds*. London: Fontana.

Dresher, B.E. and Hornstein, N.H. (1976). On some supposed contributions of artificial intelligence to the scientific study of language. *Cognition, 4*, 321–98.

Drew, P. (1978). Accusations: The occasioned use of members' knowledge of 'religious geography' in describing events. *Sociology, 12*, 1–22.

Drew, P. (1984). Speakers' reportings in invitation sequences. In J.M. Atkinson and J.C.

Heritage (Eds.), *Structures of Social Action: Studies in Conversation Analysis*. Cambridge: Cambridge University Press.

Drew, P. (1989). Recalling someone from the past. In D. Roger and P. Bull (Eds.), *Conversation*. Clevedon: Multilingual Matters.

Drew, P. (1990). Strategies in the contest between lawyers and witnesses. In J.N. Levi and A.G. Walker (Eds.), *Language in the Judicial Process*. New York: Plenum.

Drew, P. (1992). Contested evidence in courtroom cross-examination: The case of a trial for rape. In P. Drew and J. Heritage (Eds.), *Talk at Work: Interaction in Institutional Settings*. Cambridge: Cambridge University Press.

Drew, P. (1995). Conversation analysis. In J.A. Smith, R. Harré, & L. Van Langenhove (Eds.), *Rethinking Methods in Psychology*. London: Sage.

Drew, P. and Heritage, J.C. (Eds.) (1992). *Talk at Work: Interaction in Institutional Settings*. Cambridge: University of Cambridge Press.

Drew, P. and Holt, E. (1988). Complainable matters: The use of idiomatic expressions in making complaints. *Social Problems*, *35*, 398–417.

Dreyfus, H.L (1992). *What Computers Still Can't Do: A Critique of Artificial Reason*. Cambridge, MA: MIT Press.

Duck, S. (Ed.) (1993). *Individuals in Relationships*. Newbury Park, CA: Sage.

Duranti, A. (1988). Intentions, language, and social action in a Samoan context. *Journal of Pragmatics*, *12*, 13–33.

Edwards, D. (1973). Sensory-motor intelligence and semantic relations in early child grammar. *Cognition*, *2*, 395–434.

Edwards, D. (1991). Categories are for talking: On the cognitive and discursive bases of categorization. *Theory and Psychology*, *1* (4), 515–42.

Edwards, D. (1993). But what do children really think? Discourse analysis and conceptual content in children's talk. *Cognition and Instruction*, *11* (3 and 4), 207–25.

Edwards, D. (1994a). Imitation and artifice in apes, humans, and machines. *American Behavioral Scientist*, *37* (6), 754–71.

Edwards, D. (1994b). Script formulations: A study of event descriptions in conversation. *Journal of Language and Social Psychology*, *13* (3), 211–47.

Edwards, D. (1995). Two to tango: Script formulations, dispositions, and rhetorical symmetry in relationship troubles talk. *Research on Language and Social Interaction*, *28* (4), 319–50.

Edwards, D., Ashmore, M. and Potter, J. (1995). Death and furniture: The rhetoric, politics, and theology of bottom line arguments against relativism. *History of the Human Sciences*, *8* (2), 25–49.

Edwards, D. and Mercer, N.M. (1987). *Common Knowledge: the Development of Understanding in the Classroom*. London: Routledge.

Edwards, D. and Mercer, N.M. (1989). Reconstructing context: The conventionalization of classroom knowledge. *Discourse Processes*, *12*, 91–104.

Edwards, D. and Middleton, D. (1986a). Joint remembering: Constructing an account of shared experience through conversational discourse. *Discourse Processes*, *9*, 423–59.

Edwards, D. and Middleton, D. (1986b). Text for memory: Joint recall with a scribe. *Human Learning*, *5*, 125–38.

Edwards, D. and Middleton, D. (1987). Conversation and remembering: Bartlett revisited. *Applied Cognitive Psychology*, *1* (2), 77–92.

Edwards, D. and Middleton, D. (1988). Conversational remembering and family relationships: How children learn to remember. *Journal of Social and Personal Relationships*, *5*, 3–25.

Edwards, D. and Potter, J. (1992a). *Discursive Psychology*. London: Sage.

Edwards, D. and Potter, J. (1992b). The chancellor's memory: Rhetoric and truth in discursive remembering. *Applied Cognitive Psychology*, *6*, 187–215.

Edwards, D. and Potter, J. (1993). Language and causation: A discursive action model of description and attribution. *Psychological Review*, *100* (1), 23–41.

Eglin, P. (1979). Resolving reality junctures on telegraph avenue: A study of practical reasoning. *Canadian Journal of Sociology*, *4*, 359–77.

Eiser, J.R. (1978). Cooperation and competition between individuals. In H. Tajfel and C. Fraser (Eds.), *Introducing Social Psychology*. Harmondsworth: Penguin.

Ekman, P. (1992). Are there basic emotions? *Psychological Review*, *99* (3), 550–3.

Ekman, P. (1993). Facial expression and emotion. *American Psychologist*, *48* (4), 384–92.

Ekman, P. and Friesen, W.V. (1969). Nonverbal leakage and clues to deception. *Psychiatry*, *31* (1), 88–106.

Ekman, P., Levenson, R.W. and Friesen, W.V. (1983). Autonomic nervous system activity distinguishes among emotions. *Science*, *221*, 1208–10.

Engeström, Y. and Middleton, D. (Eds.) (1996). *Cognition and Communication at Work*. Cambridge: Cambridge University Press.

Evans-Pritchard, E.E. (1937). *Witchcraft, Oracles, and Magic among the Azande*. Oxford: Clarendon.

Fairclough, N. (1992). *Discourse and Social Change*. Cambridge: Polity.

Feyerabend, P.K. (1975). *Against Method*. London: New Left Books.

Feyerabend, P.K. (1987). *Farewell to Reason*. London: Verso.

Fillmore, C.J. (1977). Topics in lexical semantics. In R.W. Cole (Ed.), *Current Issues in Linguistic Theory*. Bloomington: Indiana University Press.

Fiske, S.T. and Taylor, S.E. (1991). *Social Cognition* (2nd Edn). New York: McGraw-Hill.

Flavell, J.H., Flavell, E. and Green, F. (1983). Development of the appearance–reality distinction. *Cognitive Psychology*, *15* (1), 91–120.

Fodor, J.A. (1975). *The Language of Thought*. New York: Thomas Y. Crowell.

Foucault, M. (1973). *The Birth of the Clinic*. London: Tavistock.

Fouts, R.S. (1974). Language: Origins, definitions, and chimpanzees. *Journal of Human Evolution*, *3*, 475–82.

Fowler, R. (1991). *Language in the News: Discourse and Ideology in the Press*. London: Routledge.

Freeman, M. (1993). *Rewriting the Self: History, Memory, Narrative*. London: Routledge.

Frisch, K. von (1950). *Bees: Their Vision, Chemical Sense, and Language*. Ithaca, NY: Cornell University Press.

Frye, N. (1957). *Anatomy of Criticism*. Princeton, NJ: Princeton University Press.

Furnham, A.F. (1988). *Lay Theories: Everyday Understanding of Problems in the Social Sciences*. Oxford: Pergamon.

Gardner, B.T. and Gardner, R.A. (1974). Comparing the early utterances of child and chimpanzee. In A. Pick (Ed.), *Minnesota Symposium on Child Psychology*. Volume 8. Minneapolis: University of Minnesota Press.

Gardner, H. (1985). *The Mind's New Science*. New York: Basic Books.

Gardner, R.A. and Gardner, B.T. (1969). Teaching sign language to a chimpanzee. *Science*, *165*, 664–72.

Garfinkel, H. (1963). A conception of, and experiments with, 'trust' as a condition of stable concerted actions. In O.J. Harvey (Ed.), *Motivation and Social Interaction*. New York: Ronald Press.

Garfinkel, H. (1967). *Studies in Ethnomethodology*. Englewood Cliffs, NJ: Prentice Hall.

Garfinkel. H., Lynch, M. and Livingston, E. (1981). The work of a discovering science construed with material from the optically discovered pulsar. *Philosophy of the Social Sciences*, *11*, 131–58.

Garfinkel, H. and Sacks, H. (1970). On formal structures of practical actions. In J.C. McKinney and E.A. Tiryakian (Eds.), *Theoretical Sociology: Perspectives and Developments*. New York: Appleton-Century-Crofts.

Garnham, A. (1983). What's wrong with story grammars. *Cognition*, *15*, 145–54.

Garnham, A. (1985). *Psycholinguistics: Central Topics*. London: Methuen.

Gavey, N. (1992). Technologies and effects of heterosexual coercion. *Feminism and Psychology*, *2* (3), 325–51.

Geertz, C. (1973). *The Interpretation of Cultures*. New York: Basic Books.

Geertz, C. (1983). *Local Knowledge: Further Essays in Interpretive Anthropology*. New York: Basic Books.

Geertz, C. (1988). *Works and Lives: the Anthropologist as Author*. Oxford: Polity.

Genette, G. (1988). *Narrative Discourse Revisited*. Ithaca, NY: Cornell University Press.

Gergen, K.J. (1985). Social constructionist inquiry: Context and implications. In K.J. Gergen and K.E. Davis (Eds.), *The Social Construction of the Person*. New York: Springer-Verlag.

Gergen, K.J. (1994). *Realities and Relationships*. Cambridge, MA: Harvard University Press.

Gergen, K.J. (1995). Metaphor and monophony in the 20th-century psychology of emotions. *History of the Human Sciences*, *8* (2), 1–23.

Gergen, K.J. and Gergen, M.M. (1988). Narrative and self as relationship. In L. Berkowitz (Ed.), *Advances in Experimental Social Psychology*. New York: Academic Press.

Gergen, M.M. (1994). The social construction of personal histories: Gendered lives in popular autobiographies. In T.R. Sarbin and J.I. Kitsuse (Eds.), *Constructing the Social*. London: Sage.

Gergen, M.M. and Gergen, K.J. (1993). Autobiographies and the shaping of gendered lives. In N. Coupland and J.F. Nussbaum (Eds.), *Discourse and Lifespan Identity*. London: Sage.

Gibbs, R.W. (1994). *The Poetics of Mind: Figurative Thought, Language, and Understanding*. Cambridge: Cambridge University Press.

Gilbert, G.N. and Mulkay, M. (1984). *Opening Pandora's Box: a Sociological Analysis of Scientists' Discourse*. Cambridge: Cambridge University Press.

Gillis, J.R. (1988). From ritual to romance. In C.Z. Stearns and P.W. Stearns (Eds.), *Emotions and Social Change: Towards a New Psychohistory*. New York: Holmes and Meier.

Gladwin, T. (1964). Culture and logical process. In W. Goodenough (Ed.), *Explorations in Cultural Anthropology: Essays Presented to George Peter Murdock*. New York: McGraw-Hill.

Goddard, C. and Wierzbicka, A. (1994). *Semantic and Lexical Universals: Theory and Empirical Findings*. Amsterdam: Benjamins.

Goffman, E. (1955). On face work. *Psychiatry*, *18*, 213–31.

Goffman, E. (1959). *The Presentation of Self in Everyday Life*. Harmondsworth: Penguin.

Goffman, E. (1971). *Relations in Public: Microstudies of the Public Order*. Harmondsworth: Penguin.

Goffman, E. (1979). Footing. *Semiotica*, *25*, 1–29.

Goodall, J. (1971). *In the Shadow of Man*. Boston: Houghton Mifflin.

Goodall, J. (1979). Life and death at Gombe. *National Geographic*, *155* (5), 592–621.

Goodall, J. (1986). *The Chimpanzees of Gombe: Patterns of Behavior*. Cambridge, MA: Harvard University Press.

Goodwin, C. (1979). The interactive construction of a sentence in natural conversation. In G. Psathas (Ed.), *Everyday Language: Studies in Ethnomethodology*. New York: Irvington.

Goodwin, C. (1981). *Conversational Organization: Interaction between Speakers and Hearers*. New York: Academic Press.

Goodwin, C. (1984). Notes on story structure and the organization of participation. In J.M. Atkinson and J. Heritage (Eds.), *Structures of Social Action: Studies in Conversation Analysis*. Cambridge: Cambridge University Press.

Goodwin, C. (1987). Forgetfulness as an interactive resource. *Social Psychology Quarterly*, *50*, 115–30.

Goodwin, C. (1995a). Sentence construction within interaction. In U.M. Quasthoff (Ed.), *Aspects of Oral Communication*. New York: de Gruyter.

Goodwin, C. (1995b). Seeing in depth. *Social Studies of Science*, *25*, 237–74.

Goodwin, C. and Heritage, J.C. (1990). Conversation analysis. *Annual Review of Anthropology*, *19*, 283–307.

Goodwin, M.H. (1980). Processes of mutual monitoring implicated in the production of description sequences. *Sociological Inquiry*, *50*, 303–17.

Goodwin, M.H. (1990). *He-said She-said: Talk as Social Organization among Black Children*. Bloomington: Indiana University Press.

Gould, S.J. (1983). *Hen's Teeth and Horse's Toes*. New York: Norton.

Graesser, A.C. (Ed.) (1993). *Inference generation during text comprehension*. Special issue of *Discourse Processes*, *16* (1 and 2).

Graham, M.H. (1978). The confrontation clause, the hearsay rule, and the forgetful witness. *Texas Law Review*, 56, 170.

Greatbatch, D. (1986). Aspects of topical organization in news interviews: The use of agenda-shifting procedures by interviewees. *Media, Culture and Society*, 8, 44–56.

Greenwood, J.D. (Ed.) (1991). *The Future of Folk Psychology: Intentionality and Cognitive Science*. Cambridge: Cambridge University Press.

Griffin, D.R. (1976). *The Question of Animal Awareness: Evolutionary Continuity of Mental Experiences*. New York: Rockefeller Press.

Gusfield, J. (1976). The literary rhetoric of science: Comedy and pathos in drinking driver research. *American Sociological Review*, 41, 16–34.

Guthrie, W.K.C. (1956). *Plato, Protagoras and Meno*. Harmondsworth: Penguin.

Guthrie, W.K.C. (1975). *A History of Greek Philosophy*. Volume 4. Cambridge: Cambridge University Press.

Halliday, M.A.K. (1967). Notes on transitivity and theme in English: Part 2. *Journal of Linguistics*, 3, 199–244.

Halliday, M.A.K. (1970). Language structure and language function. In J. Lyons (Ed.), *New Horizons in Linguistics*. Harmondsworth: Penguin.

Halliday, M.A.K. (1985). *An Introduction to Functional Grammar*. London: Edward Arnold.

Hamlyn, D.W. (1990). *In and Out of the Black Box: on the Philosophy of Cognition*. Oxford: Blackwell.

Haraway, D. (1989). *Primate Visions: Gender, Race and Nature in the World of Modern Science*. London: Routledge.

Haraway, D. (1991). *Simians, Cyborgs, and Women: the Reinvention of Nature*. London: Free Association Books.

Harré, R. (1979). *Social Being: a Theory for Social Psychology*. Oxford: Blackwell.

Harré, R. (1983). *Personal Being: a Theory for Individual Psychology*. Oxford: Blackwell.

Harré, R. (1986a). An outline of the social constructionist viewpoint. In R. Harré (Ed.), *The Social Construction of Emotions*. Oxford: Blackwell.

Harré, R. (Ed.) (1986b). *The Social Construction of Emotions*. Oxford: Blackwell.

Harré, R. (1987). The social construction of selves. In K. Yardley and T. Honess (Eds.), *Self and Identity: Psychosocial Perspectives*. Chichester: Wiley.

Harré, R. (1988). Wittgenstein and artificial intelligence. *Philosophical Psychology*, 1 (1), 105–15.

Harré, R. (1989). Language games and the texts of identity. In J. Shotter and K.J. Gergen (Eds.), *Texts of Identity*. London: Sage.

Harré, R. (1990). Exploring the human Umwelt. In R. Bhaskar (Ed.), *Harré and His Critics: Essays in Honour of Rom Harré With His Commentary on Them*. Oxford: Blackwell.

Harré, R. (1991). *Physical Being: a Theory for Corporeal Psychology*. Oxford: Blackwell.

Harré, R. (1993). The second cognitive revolution. *American Behavioral Scientist*, 36 (1), 5–7.

Harré, R. (1995). Review of *Discursive Psychology* by D. Edwards and J. Potter. *British Journal of Psychology*, 86, 301–13.

Harré, R. and Gillett, G. (1994). *The Discursive Mind*. London: Sage.

Harré, R. and Secord, P.F. (1972). *The Explanation of Social Behaviour*. Oxford: Blackwell.

Harris, P. (1992). *Children and Emotion: the Development of Psychological Understanding*. Oxford: Blackwell.

Harris, R. (1981). *The Language Myth*. London: Duckworth.

Harris, R. (1988). *Language, Saussure and Wittgenstein: How to Play Games with Words*. London: Routledge.

Havelock, E. (1963). *Preface to Plato*. Cambridge MA: Harvard University Press.

Heath, C. (1992). The delivery and reception of diagnosis in the general-practice consultation. In P. Drew and J. Heritage (Eds.), *Talk at Work: Interaction in Institutional Settings*. Cambridge: Cambridge University Press.

Heelas, P. (1986). Emotion talk across cultures. In R. Harré (Ed.), *The Social Construction of Emotions*. Oxford: Blackwell.

Heelas, P. and Lock, A. (Eds.) (1981). *Indigenous Psychologies: the Anthropology of the Self*. London: Academic Press.

Heider, E.R. (1972). Universals in colour naming and memory. *Journal of Experimental Psychology*, *93* (1), 10–20.

Heider, F. (1958). *The Psychology of Interpersonal Relations*. New York: Wiley.

Hekman, S.J. (1990). *Gender and Knowledge*. Cambridge: Polity.

Henriques, J., Hollway, W., Urwin, C., Venn, C. and Walkerdine, V. (1984). *Changing the Subject: Psychology, Social Regulation and Subjectivity*. London: Methuen.

Henwood, K. and Coughlan, G. (1993). The construction of 'closeness' in mother–daughter relationships across the lifespan. In N. Coupland and J.F. Nussbaum (Eds.), *Discourse and Lifespan Identity*. London: Sage.

Heritage, J.C. (1984a). *Garfinkel and Ethnomethodology*. Cambridge: Polity.

Heritage, J.C. (1984b). A change-of-state token and aspects of its sequential placement. In J.M. Atkinson and J. Heritage (Eds.), *Structures of Social Action: Studies in Conversation Analysis*. Cambridge: Cambridge University Press.

Heritage, J.C. (1989). Current developments in conversation analysis. In D. Roger and P. Bull (Eds.), *Conversation: an Interdisciplinary Approach*. Clevedon: Multilingual Matters.

Heritage, J.C. (1990–1). Intention, meaning and strategy: Observations on constraints in interaction analysis. *Research on Language and Social Interaction*, *24*, 311–32.

Heritage, J.C. (1995). Conversation analysis: Methodological aspects. In U. Quasthoff (Ed.), *Aspects of Oral Communication*. New York: de Gruyter.

Heritage, J.C. and Atkinson, J.M. (1984). Introduction. In J.M. Atkinson and J. Heritage, *Structures of Social Action: Studies in Conversation Analysis*. Cambridge: Cambridge University Press.

Heritage, J.C. and Watson, D.R. (1979). Formulations as conversational objects. In G. Psathas (Ed.), *Everyday Language: Studies in Ethnomethodology*. New York: Irvington.

Hintikka, M.B.C. and Hintikka, J. (1986). *Investigating Wittgenstein*. Oxford: Blackwell.

Hockett, C.F. (1960). The origin of speech. *Scientific American*, *203* (3), 89–96.

Hodge, B. and Kress, G.R. (1993). *Language as Ideology* (2nd Edn). London: Routledge.

Hofstadter, D.R. (1979). *Gödel, Escher, Bach: an Eternal Golden Braid*. New York: Basic Books.

Hoijer, H. (1954). The Sapir–Whorf hypothesis. In H. Hoijer (Ed.), *Language in Culture*. Chicago: University of Chicago Press.

Holland, D. and Quinn, N. (Eds.) (1987). *Cultural Models in Language and Thought*. Cambridge: Cambridge University Press.

Hume, D. (1739/1969). *A Treatise of Human Nature* (Ed. E.C. Mossner). Harmondsworth: Penguin.

Husserl, E. (1965). *Phenomenology and the Crisis of Philosophy*. New York: Harper Torchbooks.

Hutchins, E. (1980). *Culture and Inference: a Trobriand Case Study*. Cambridge, MA: Harvard University Press.

Hydén, M. and McCarthy, I.C. (1994). Women battering and father–daughter incest disclosure: Discourses of denial and acknowledgement. *Discourse and Society*, *5* (4), 543–65.

Inhelder, B. and Piaget, J. (1958). *The Growth of Logical Thinking from Childhood to Adolescence*. New York: Basic Books.

Jaggar, A.M. (1983). *Feminist Politics and Human Nature*. Brighton: Harvester.

Jakobson, R. and Halle, M. (1956). *Fundamentals of Language*. The Hague: Mouton.

Jayyusi, L. (1993). Premeditation and happenstance: The social construction of intention, action, and knowledge. *Human Studies*, *16* (4), 435–54.

Jefferson, G. (1978). Sequential aspects of storytelling in conversation. In J. Schenkein (Ed.), *Studies in the Organization of Conversational Interaction*. New York: Academic Press.

Jefferson, G. (1984). 'At first I thought . . .': A normalizing device for extraordinary events. Unpublished manuscript, Katholieke Hogeschool Tilburg.

Jefferson, G. (1985). On the interactional unpackaging of a gloss. *Language and Society*, 435–63.

Jefferson, G. (1989a). Letter to the editor re: Anita Pomerantz's epilogue to the special issue on sequential organization of conversational activities. *Western Journal of Speech Communication*, 53, 427–9.

Jefferson, G. (1989b). Preliminary notes on a possible metric which provides for a 'standard maximum' silence of approximately one second in conversation. In D. Roger and P. Bull (Eds.), *Conversation: an Interdisciplinary Perspective*. Clevedon: Multilingual Matters.

Jefferson, G. (1990). List construction as a task and resource. In G. Psathas (Ed.), *Interaction Competence*. Lanham, MD: University Press of America.

Jodelet, D. (1991). *Madness and Social Representations*. Hemel Hempstead: Harvester Wheatsheaf.

Johnson, M. (1987). *The Body in the Mind: the Bodily Basis of Reason and Imagination*. Chicago: University of Chicago Press.

Johnson-Laird, P.N. (1983). *Mental Models: Toward a Cognitive Science of Language, Inference and Consciousness*. Cambridge: Cambridge University Press.

Johnson-Laird, P.N. (1988). *The Computer and the Mind: an Introduction to Cognitive Science*. London: Fontana.

Jones, E.E. and Davis, K.E. (1965). From acts to dispositions: The attributional process in person perception. In L. Berkowitz (Ed.), *Advances in Experimental Social Psychology*. Volume 2. New York: Academic Press.

Jones, J. (1993). *Chimp Talk: Text Adapted from the Programme Transmitted 21st June 1993*. London: BBC/BSS publications.

Josephs, I.E. (1995). The problem of emotions from the perspective of psychological semantics. *Culture and Psychology*, 1 (2), 279–88.

Josselson, R. and Lieblich, A. (Eds.) (1993). *The Narrative Study of Lives*. Volume 1. London: Sage.

Kay, P. and McDaniel, C.K. (1978). The linguistic significance of the meanings of Basic Colour Terms. *Language*, 54, 610–46.

Keen, E. (1986). Paranoia and cataclysmic narratives. In T.S. Sarbin (Ed.), *Narrative Psychology: the Storied Nature of Human Conduct*. New York: Praeger.

Keil, F.C. (1986). On the structure-dependent nature of stages of cognitive development. In I. Levin (Ed.), *Stage and Structure: Reopening the Debate*. Norwood, NJ: Ablex.

Kelly, G.A. (1955). *A Theory of Personality: the Psychology of Personal Constructs*. New York: Norton.

Kintsch, W. (1974). *The Representation of Meaning in Memory*. Hillsdale, NJ: Erlbaum.

Kintsch, W. and Van Dijk, T.A. (1983). *Strategies of Discourse Comprehension*. New York: Academic Press.

Knorr-Cetina, K.D. (1981). *The Manufacture of Knowledge: an Essay on the Constructivist and Contextual Nature of Science*. Oxford: Pergamon.

Kortland, A. (1975). Discussion. In R.H. Tuttle (Ed.), *Socioecology and Psychology of Primates*. The Hague: Mouton.

Kovecses, Z. (1986). *Metaphors of Anger, Pride, and Love*. Philadelphia: John Benjamins.

Krauss, R.M. and Fussell, S.R. (1991). Constructing shared communicative environments. In L.B. Resnick, J.M. Levine, and S.D. Teasley (Eds.), *Perspectives on Socially Shared Cognition*. Washington, DC: American Psychological Association.

Kress, G.R. and Van Leeuwen, T. (1990). *Reading Images: a Grammar of Visual Communication*. Geelong, Australia: Deakin University Press.

Labov, W. (1970). The logic of nonstandard English. In F. Williams (Ed.), *Language and Poverty*. Chicago: Markham.

Labov, W. (1972). *Language of the Inner City*. Philadelphia: Philadelphia University Press.

Labov, W. and Waletsky, J. (1967). Narrative analysis: Oral versions of personal experience. In J. Helm (Ed.), *Essays on the Verbal and Visual Arts*. Seattle: University of Washington Press.

Lakoff, G. (1987). *Women, Fire and Dangerous Things: What Categories Reveal about the Mind*. Chicago: University of Chicago Press.

Lakoff, G. (1990). The invariance hypothesis: Is abstract reason based on image-schemas? *Cognitive Linguistics*, 1, 39–74.

Lakoff, G. (1991). Metaphor and war: The metaphor system used to justify war in the Gulf. In B. Hallet (Ed.), *Engulfed in War: Just War and the Persian Gulf*. Honolulu: Matsunaga Institute for Peace.

Lakoff, G. and Johnson, M. (1980). *Metaphors We Live By*. Chicago: University of Chicago Press.

Langellier, K.M. (1989). Personal narratives: Perspectives on theory and research. *Text and Performance Quarterly*, 9 (4), 243–76.

Latané, B. and Darley, J.M. (1970). *The Unresponsive Bystander: Why Doesn't He Help?* Englewood Cliffs, NJ: Prentice Hall.

Latour, B. (1987). *Science in Action*. Milton Keynes: Open University Press.

Latour, B. (alias Johnson, J.) (1988). Mixing humans and non- humans together: The sociology of a door-closer. *Social Problems*, 35, 298–310.

Latour, B. (1993). *We Have Never Been Modern*. Hemel Hempstead: Harvester Wheatsheaf.

Latour, B. and Woolgar, S. (1979). *Laboratory Life: the Social Construction of Scientific Facts*. London: Sage.

Latour, B. and Woolgar, S. (1986). *Laboratory Life: the Construction of Scientific Facts* (2nd Edn). Princeton, NJ: Princeton University Press.

Lave, J. (1988). *Cognition in Practice: Mind, Mathematics and Culture in Everyday Life*. Cambridge: Cambridge University Press.

LCHC (Laboratory of Comparative Human Cognition) (1983). Culture and cognitive development. In W. Kessen (Ed.), *Carmichael's Manual of Child Psychology: History, Theories and Methods*. New York: Wiley.

Le Bon, G. (1896). *The Crowd: a Study of the Popular Mind*. London: Ernest Benn.

Lee, J.R.E. (1991). Language and culture: The linguistic analysis of culture. In G. Button (Ed.), *Ethnomethodology and the Human Sciences*. Cambridge: Cambridge University Press.

Lenneberg, E.H. (1953). Cognition in ethnolinguistics. *Language*, 29, 463–71.

Lenneberg, E.H. (1967). *Biological Foundations of Language*. New York: Wiley.

Lenneberg, E.H. (1975). A neuropsychological comparison between man, chimpanzee and monkey. *Neuropsychologia*, 13, 125.

Lenneberg, E.H. and Roberts, J.M. (1956). The language of experience: A study in methodology. *International Journal of American Linguistics*, 22 (2, part 2, Memoir 13).

Lerner, G.H. (1991). On the syntax of sentences-in-progress. *Language in Society*, 20, 441–58.

Lerner, G.H. (1992). Assisted storytelling: Deploying shared knowledge as a practical matter. *Qualitative Sociology*, 15 (3), 247–71.

Lerner, G.H. (1995). Turn design and the organization of participation in instructional activities. *Discourse Processes*, 19, 111–31.

Leslie, A.L. (1987). Pretense and representation: The origins of 'theory of mind'. *Psychological Review*, 94, 412–26.

Leslie, A.L. (1988). The necessity of illusion: Perception and thought in infancy. In L. Weiskrantz (Ed.), *Thought Without Language*. Oxford: Clarendon.

Leslie, A.L. and Keeble, S. (1987). Do six-month-old infants perceive causality? *Cognition*, 25, 265–88.

Levinson, S.C. (1983). *Pragmatics*. Cambridge: Cambridge University Press.

Lewis, D.K. (1969). *Convention*. Cambridge, MA: Harvard University Press.

Linde, C. (1993). *Life Stories: the Creation of Coherence*. Oxford: Oxford University Press.

Lindsay, P.H. and Norman, D.A. (1972). *Human Information Processing: an Introduction to Psychology*. New York: Academic Press.

Linell, P. (1988). The impact of literacy on the conception of language: The case of linguistics. In R. Säljö (Ed.), *The Written World*. Berlin: Springer.

Linell, P., Alemyr, L. and Jönsson, L. (1993). Admission of guilt as a communicative project in judicial settings. *Journal of Pragmatics*, 19, 153–76.

Linell, P. and Jönsson, L. (1991). Suspect stories: On perspective setting in an asymmetrical situation. In I. Marková and K. Foppa (Eds.), *Asymmetries in Dialogue*. Hemel Hempstead: Harvester Wheatsheaf.

Linton, M. (1982). Transformations of memory in everyday life. In U. Neisser (Ed.), *Memory Observed: Remembering in Natural Contexts*. Oxford: W.H. Freeman.

Lock, A.J. (Ed.) (1978). *Action, Gesture and Symbol: the Emergence of Language*. London: Academic Press.

Locke, J. (1894). *An Essay Concerning Human Understanding*. Volume 2 (Ed. A. Frazer). Oxford: Clarendon.

Longacre, R. (1976). *An Anatomy of Speech Notions*. Lisse: Peter de Ridder.

Longman, J.M. (1995). Talking heads: An analysis of the talk in vocational training interviews with the long-term unemployed. Unpublished doctoral dissertation, Open University.

Longuet-Higgins, H.C. (1981). Artificial intelligence – a new theoretical psychology? *Cognition*, *10*, 197–200.

Lowenthal, D. (1985). *The Past is a Foreign Country*. Cambridge: Cambridge University Press.

Lucy, J.A. (1992). *Language Diversity and Thought: a Reformulation of the Linguistic Relativity Hypothesis*. Cambridge: Cambridge University Press.

Lutz, C.A. (1988). *Unnatural Emotions: Everyday Sentiments on a Micronesian Atoll and Their Challenge to Western Theory*. Chicago: University of Chicago Press.

Lutz, C.A. (1990a). Morality, domination and understandings of 'justifiable' anger among the Ifaluk. In G.R. Semin and K.J. Gergen (Eds.), *Everyday Understanding: Social and Scientific Implications*. London: Sage.

Lutz, C.A. (1990b). Engendered emotion: Gender, power, and the rhetoric of emotional control in American discourse. In C.A. Lutz and L. Abu-Lughod (Eds.), *Language and the Politics of Emotion*. Cambridge: Cambridge University Press.

Lutz, C.A. and Abu-Lughod, L. (Eds.) (1990). *Language and the Politics of Emotion*. Cambridge: Cambridge University Press.

Lynch, M. (1985). *Art and Artifact in Laboratory Science: a Study of Shop Work and Shop Talk in a Research Laboratory*. London: Routledge and Kegan Paul.

Lynch, M. (1988). Sacrifice and the transformation of the animal body into a scientific object: Laboratory culture and ritual practice in the neurosciences. *Social Studies of Science*, *18*, 265–89.

Lynch, M. (1993). *Scientific Practice and Ordinary Action: Ethnomethodology and Social Studies of Science*. Cambridge: Cambridge University Press.

Lynch, M. and Bogen, D. (1994). Harvey Sacks's primitive natural science. *Theory, Culture and Society*, *11*, 65–104.

Lynch, M. and Bogen, D. (1996). *The Spectacle of History: Speech, Text, and Memory at the Iran–Contra Hearings*. Durham, NC: Duke University Press.

Lynch, M. and Woolgar, S. (Eds.) (1990). *Representation in Scientific Practice*. Cambridge, MA: MIT Press.

Lyons, J. (1977). *Semantics*. Cambridge: Cambridge University Press.

Macfarlane, A. (1977). *The Psychology of Childbirth*. Cambridge, MA: Harvard University Press.

McKinlay, A., Potter, J. and Wetherell, M. (1993). Discourse analysis and social representations. In G. Breakwell and D. Cantor (Eds.), *Empirical Approaches to Social Representations*. Oxford: Open University Press.

Mandler, J.M. (1979). Categorical and schematic organization in memory. In C.R. Puff (Ed.), *Memory Organization and Structure*. New York: Academic Press.

Mandler, J.M. (1984). *Scripts, Stories and Scenes: Aspects of Schema Theory*. Hillsdale, NJ: Erlbaum.

Mandler, J.M. and Johnson, N.S. (1977). Remembrance of things parsed: Story structure and recall. *Cognitive Psychology*, *9*, 111–51.

Marková, I. and Foppa, K. (Eds.) (1991). *Asymmetries in Dialogue*. Hemel Hempstead: Harvester Wheatsheaf.

Martin, L. (1986). 'Eskimo words for snow': A case study in the genesis and decay of an anthropological example. *American Anthropologist*, *88*, 418–23.

Maynard, D.W. (Ed.) (1987). *Language and Social Interaction*. Special issue of *Social Psychology Quarterly*, *50* (2).

Maynard, D.W. (Ed.) (1988). *Language, Interaction, and Social Problems*. Special issue of *Social Problems*, *35* (4).

Merton, R. (1973). *The Sociology of Science*. Chicago: University of Chicago Press.

Mervis, C. and Rosch, E. (1981). Categorization of natural objects. *Annual Review of Psychology*, *32*, 89–115.

Michotte, A. (1963). *The Perception of Causality*. London: Methuen.

Middleton, D. and Edwards, D. (1990a). Conversational remembering: A social psychological approach. In D. Middleton and D. Edwards (Eds.), *Collective Remembering*. London: Sage.

Middleton, D. and Edwards, D. (Eds.) (1990b). *Collective Remembering*. London: Sage.

Miller, G.A. (1990). The place of language in a scientific psychology. *Psychological Science*, *1*, 7–14.

Miller, G.A., Galanter, E. and Pribram, K.H. (1960). *Plans and the Structure of Behavior*. New York: Henry Holt.

Miller, G.A. and Johnson-Laird, P.N. (1976). *Language and Perception*. Cambridge, MA: Harvard University Press.

Miller, G.A. and McNeill, D. (1969). Psycholinguistics. In G. Lindzey and A. Aronson (Eds.), *Handbook of Social Psychology*. Volume 3 (2nd Edn). Reading, MA: Addison-Wesley.

Mills, C.W. (1940/1967). Situated actions and vocabularies of motive. *American Sociological Review*, *5*, 904–13. Reprinted in J.G. Manis and B.N Meltzer (Eds.), *Symbolic Interactionism: a Reader in Social Psychology*. Boston: Allyn and Bacon.

Mischel, T. (1969). Epilogue. In T. Mischel (Ed.), *Human Action: Conceptual and Empirical Issues*. New York: Academic Press.

Mishler, E.G. (1986a). *Research Interviewing: Context and Narrative*. Cambridge, MA: Harvard University Press.

Mishler, E.G. (1986b). The analysis of interview-narratives. In T.R. Sarbin (Ed.), *Narrative Psychology: the Storied Nature of Human Conduct*. New York: Praeger.

Moerman, M. (1988). *Talking Culture: Ethnography and Conversation Analysis*. Philadelphia: University of Pennsylvania Press.

Moerman, M. (1993). Ariadne's thread and Indra's net: Reflections on ethnography, ethnicity, identity, culture, and interaction. *Research on Language and Social Interaction*, *26* (1), 85–98.

Monk, R. (1996). Morons from inner space. *The Observer*, 18 February, Review section, p. 3.

Mulkay, M. (1979a). Interpretation and the use of rules: The case of norms in science. In T.F. Gieryn (Ed.), *Science and Social Structure*. Transactions of the New York Academy of Sciences, Series III, 39, 111–25.

Mulkay, M. (1979b). *Science and the Sociology of Knowledge*. London: Allen and Unwin.

Mulkay, M. (1981). Action, belief, or scientific discourse? A possible way of ending intellectual vassalage in social studies of science. *Philosophy of the Social Sciences*, *11*, 163–71.

Mulkay, M. (1985). *The Word and the World: Explorations in the Form of Sociological Analysis*. London: Allen and Unwin.

Mulkay, M. and Gilbert, G.N. (1982). Accounting for error: How scientists construct their social world when they account for correct and incorrect belief. *Sociology*, *16*, 165–83.

Mulkay, M. and Gilbert, G.N. (1983). Scientists' theory talk. *Canadian Journal of Sociology*, *8*, 179–97.

Murray, K.D. (1989). The construction of identity in the narratives of romance and comedy. In J. Shotter and K.J. Gergen (Eds.), *Texts of Identity*. London: Sage.

Murray, K.D. (1995). Narratology. In J.A. Smith, R. Harré, and L. Van Langenhove (Eds.), *Rethinking Psychology*. London: Sage.

Myers, G. (1990). *Writing Biology: Texts in the Construction of Scientific Knowledge*. Madison: University of Wisconsin Press.

Neisser, U. (1967). *Cognitive Psychology*. New York: Appleton-Century-Crofts.

Neisser, U. (1976). *Cognition and Reality*. San Francisco: W.H. Freeman.

Neisser, U. (1981). John Dean's memory: A case study. *Cognition*, *9*, 1–22.

Neisser, U. (1982). *Memory Observed: Remembering in Natural Contexts*. Oxford: W.H. Freeman.

Neisser, U. (1992). The psychology of memory and the sociolinguistics of remembering. *The Psychologist*, *5*, 451–2.

Nelson, C.K. (1994). Ethnomethodological positions on the use of ethnographic data in conversation analytic research. *Journal of Contemporary Ethnography*, *23* (3), 307–29.

Nelson, K. (1981). Social cognition in a script framework. In J.H. Flavell and L. Ross (Eds.), *Social Cognitive Development: Frontiers and Possible Futures*. Cambridge: Cambridge University Press.

Nelson, K. (Ed.) (1986). *Event Knowledge: Structure and Function in Development*. Hillsdale, NJ: Erlbaum.

Newman, S. (1954). Semantic problems in grammatical systems and lexemes: A search for method. In H. Hoijer (Ed.), *Language in Culture*. Chicago: University of Chicago Press.

Nofsinger, R.E. (1991). *Everyday Conversation*. London: Sage.

Oatley, K. and Jenkins, J.M. (1996). *Understanding Emotions*. Oxford: Blackwell.

Ochs, E. (1982). Talking to children in Western Samoa. *Language in Society*, *11*, 77–104.

Ochs, E. and Schieffelin, B. (1984). Language acquisition and socialization: Three developmental stories. In R. Shweder and R. Levine (Eds.), *Culture Theory: Essays on Mind, Self, and Emotion*. Cambridge: Cambridge University Press.

Olson, D.R. (1977). Oral and written language and the cognitive processes of children. *Journal of Communication*, *27* (3), 10–26.

Ong, W.J. (1982). *Orality and Literacy: the Technologizing of the Word*. London: Methuen.

Oxford English Dictionary (1994). (2nd Edn) on CD-ROM. Oxford: Oxford University Press.

Parker, I. (1992). *Discourse Dynamics: Critical Analysis for Social and Individual Psychology*. London: Routledge.

Patterson, F. and Linden, E. (1981). *The Education of Koko*. New York: Holt, Rinehart and Winston.

Pavlov, I.P. (1941). *Lectures on Conditioned Reflexes*. Volume 2 (Ed. and trans. W.H. Gantt). London: Lawrence and Wishart.

Pearce, W.B. and Chen, V. (1989). Ethnography as sermonic: The rhetorics of Clifford Geertz and James Clifford. In H. Simons (Ed.), *Rhetoric in the Human Sciences*. London and Beverly Hills, CA: Sage.

Personal Narratives Group (Eds.) (1989). *Interpreting Women's Lives: Feminist Theory and Personal Narratives*. Indianapolis: Indiana University Press.

Pfungst. O. (1911/1965). *Clever Hans (the Horse of Mr. von Osten)* (Ed. R. Rosenthal). New York: Holt, Rinehart and Winston.

Piaget, J. (1926). *The Language and Thought of the Child*. London: Routledge and Kegan Paul.

Piaget, J. (1952). *The Origins of Intelligence in Children*. London: Routledge and Kegan Paul.

Piaget, J. (1954). *The Construction of Reality in the Child*. London: Routledge and Kegan Paul.

Piaget, J. (1971). *Insights and Illusions of Philosophy*. London: Routledge and Kegan Paul.

Pickering, A. (Ed.) (1992). *Science as Practice and Culture*. Chicago: Chicago University Press.

Pike, K.L. (1954). *Language in Relation to a Unified Theory of Human Behavior*. The Hague: Mouton.

Plummer, K. (1995). Life story research. In J.A. Smith, R. Harré, and L. Van Langenhove (Eds.), *Rethinking Methods in Psychology*. London: Sage.

Polanyi, M. (1964). *Personal Knowledge: Towards a Post-Critical Philosophy*. New York: Harper Torchbooks.

Polkinghorne, D.E. (1988). *Narrative Knowing and the Human Sciences*. Albany, NY: State University of New York Press.

Pollner, M. (1974). Mundane reasoning. *Philosophy of the Social Sciences*, *4*, 35–54.

Pollner, M. (1987). *Mundane Reason: Reality in Everyday and Sociological Discourse*. Cambridge: Cambridge University Press.

Pollner, M. (1991). Left of ethnomethodology: The rise and decline of radical reflexivity. *American Sociological Review*, *56*, 370–80.

Pomerantz, A.M. (1978). Compliment responses: Notes on the co-operation of multiple constraints. In J. Schenkein (Ed.), *Studies in the Organization of Conversational Interaction*. London: Academic Press.

Pomerantz, A.M. (1980). Telling my side: 'Limited access' as a fishing device. *Sociological Inquiry*, *50* (3 and 4), 186–98.

Pomerantz, A.M. (1984a). Agreeing and disagreeing with assessments: Some features of preferred/dispreferred turn shapes. In J.M. Atkinson and J. Heritage (Eds.), *Structures of Social Action: Studies in Conversation Analysis*. Cambridge: Cambridge University Press.

Pomerantz, A.M. (1984b). Giving a source or basis: The practice in conversation of telling 'how I know'. *Journal of Pragmatics*, *8*, 607–25.

Pomerantz, A.M. (1986). Extreme case formulations: A new way of legitimating claims. *Human Studies*, *9*, 219–30.

Pomerantz, A.M. (1990–1). Mental concepts in the analysis of social action. *Research on Language and Social Interaction*, *24*, 299–310.

Pomerantz, A.M. (Ed.) (1993). *New Directions in Conversation Analysis*. Special issue of *Text*, *13* (2). Berlin: Mouton/de Gruyter.

Pomerantz, A.M. and Atkinson, J.M. (1984). Ethnomethodology, conversation analysis and the study of courtroom interaction. In D.J. Muller, D.E. Blackman, and A.J. Chapman (Eds.), *Topics in Psychology and Law*. Chichester: Wiley.

Potter, J. (1987). Reading repertoires: A preliminary study of some techniques that scientists use to construct readings. *Science and Technology Studies*, *5*, 112–21.

Potter, J. (1988). Cutting cakes: A study of psychologists' social categorizations. *Philosophical Psychology*, *1*, 17–33.

Potter, J. (1996). *Representing Reality: Discourse, Rhetoric, and Social Construction*. London: Sage.

Potter, J. and Edwards, D. (1990). Nigel Lawson's tent: Discourse analysis, attribution theory and the social psychology of fact. *European Journal of Social Psychology*, *20*, 405–24.

Potter, J. and Mulkay, M. (1985). Scientists' interview talk: Interviews as a technique for revealing participants' interpretative practices. In M. Brenner, J. Brown, and D. Canter (Eds.), *The Research Interview: Uses and Approaches*. London: Academic Press.

Potter, J. and Reicher, S. (1987). Discourses of community and conflict: The organization of social categories in accounts of a 'riot'. *British Journal of Social Psychology*, *26*, 25–40.

Potter, J. and Wetherell, M. (1987). *Discourse and Social Psychology: Beyond Attitudes and Behaviour*. London: Sage.

Premack, A.J. and Premack, D. (1972). Teaching language to an ape. *Scientific American*, *227*, 92–9.

Prince, G. (1982). *Narratology: the Form and Function of Narrative*. The Hague: Mouton.

Pringle, R. (1988). *Secretaries Talk*. London: Verso.

Propp, V.J. (1928/1968). *Morphology of the Folktale*. Austin, TX: University of Texas Press.

Psathas, G. (Ed.) (1979). *Everyday Language: Studies in Ethnomethodology*. New York: Irvington.

Psathas, G. (Ed.) (1990). *Interaction Competence*. Washington, DC: University Press of America.

Psathas, G. (1995). *Conversation Analysis: the Study of Talk-In-Interaction*. London: Sage.

Quinn, N. (1987). Convergent evidence for a cultural model of American marriage. In D. Holland and N. Quinn (Eds.), *Cultural Models in Language and Thought*. Cambridge: Cambridge University Press.

Quinn, N. and Holland, D. (1987). Culture and cognition. In D. Holland and N. Quinn (Eds.), *Cultural Models in Language and Thought*. Cambridge: Cambridge University Press.

Rabinow, P. (1986). Representations are social facts: Modernity and post-modernity in anthropology. In J. Clifford and G.E. Marcus (Eds.), *Writing Culture: the Poetics and Politics of Ethnography*. Berkeley, CA: University of California Press.

Randi, J. (1975). *The Magic of Uri Geller*. New York: Ballantine.

Reddy, M. (1979). The conduit metaphor – a case of frame conflict in our language about language. In A. Ortony (Ed.), *Metaphor and Thought*. Cambridge: Cambridge University Press.

Reicher, S. (In press). 'The crowd' century: Reconciling practical success with theoretical failure. *British Journal of Social Psychology*.

Reichman, R. (1985). *Getting Computers to Talk Like You and Me: Discourse Context, Focus, and Semantics*. Cambridge, MA: MIT Press.

Riessman, C.K. (1993). *Narrative Analysis*. London: Sage.

Rogoff, B. (1990). *Apprenticeship in Thinking: Cognitive Development in Social Context*. Oxford: Oxford University Press.

Rogoff, B. and Lave, J. (1984). *Everyday Cognition: its Development in Social Context*. Cambridge, MA: Harvard University Press.

Rommetveit, R. (1978). The architecture of intersubjectivity. In I. Marková (Ed.), *The Social Context of Language*. New York: Wiley.

Rorty, R. (1980). *Philosophy and the Mirror of Nature*. Princeton, NJ: Princeton University Press.

Rorty, R. (1991). *Objectivity, Relativism, and Truth: Philosophical Papers*. Volume 1. Cambridge: Cambridge University Press.

Rosaldo, M.Z. (1982). The things we do with words: Ilongot speech acts and speech act theory in philosophy. *Language in Society, 11*, 203–37.

Rosch, E.R. (1974). Linguistic relativity. In A. Silverstein (Ed.), *Human Communication: Theoretical Perspectives*. New York: Halsted Press.

Rosch, E.R. (1975). Cognitive representations of semantic categories. *Journal of Experimental Psychology: General, 104* (3), 192–233.

Rosch, E.R. (1978). Principles of categorization. In E. Rosch and B. Lloyd (Eds.), *Cognition and Categorization*. Hillsdale, NJ: Erlbaum.

Rosch, E.R. and Mervis, C. (1975). Family resemblances: Studies in the internal structure of categories. *Cognitive Psychology, 7*, 573–605.

Rosch, E.R., Mervis, C.B., Gray, W.D., Johnson, D. and Boyes-Braem, P. (1976). Basic objects in natural categories. *Cognitive Psychology, 8*, 382–439.

Rosenthal, A.M. (1964). *Thirty-Eight Witnesses*. New York: McGraw-Hill.

Rosenthal, G. (1993). Reconstruction of life stories: Principles of selection in generating stories for narrative biographical interviews. In R. Josselson and A. Lieblich (Eds.), *The Narrative Study of Lives*. Volume 1. London: Sage.

Roth, I. (1995). Part I: Conceptual categories. In I. Roth and V. Bruce, *Perception and Representation: Current Issues*. Buckingham: Open University Press.

Rumbaugh, D.M. (Ed.) (1977). *Language Learning by a Chimpanzee: the Lana Project*. New York: Academic Press.

Rumbaugh, D.M., Gill, T., Glasersfeld, E. von, Warner, H. and Pisani, P. (1975). Conversations with a chimpanzee in a computer-controlled environment. *Biological Psychiatry, 10*, 627–41.

Rumelhart, D.E. (1975). Notes on a schema for stories. In D.G. Bobrow and A.M. Collins (Eds.), *Representation and Understanding: Studies in Cognitive Science*. New York: Academic Press.

Rumelhart, D.E. (1977). Understanding and summarizing brief stories. In D. LaBerge and S.J. Samuels (Eds.), *Basic Processes in Reading: Perception and Comprehension*. New York: Wiley.

Russell, D.E.H. (1990). *Rape in Marriage*. Bloomington: Indiana University Press.

Russell, J.A. (1991). Culture and the categorization of emotions. *Psychological Bulletin, 110*, 426–50.

Russell, J.A. (1994). Is there universal recognition of emotion from facial expression? A review of the cross-cultural studies. *Psychological Bulletin, 115*, 102–41.

Ryave, A. (1978). On the achievement of a series of stories. In J. Schenkein (Ed.), *Studies in the Organization of Conversational Interaction*. London and New York: Academic Press.

Ryle, G. (1949). *The Concept of Mind*. London: Hutchinson.

Sachs, J.D.S. (1974). Memory in reading and listening to discourse. *Memory and Cognition, 2*, 95–100.

Sacks, H. (1966). The search for help: No one to turn to. Unpublished doctoral dissertation, University of California, Berkeley.

Sacks, H. (1972a). An initial investigation of the usability of conversational data for doing sociology. In D. Sudnow (Ed.), *Studies in Social Interaction*. Glencoe, IL: Free Press.

Sacks, H. (1972b). On the analyzability of stories by children. In J.J. Gumperz and D. Hymes (Eds.), *Directions in Sociolinguistics: the Ethnography of Communication*. New York: Holt, Rinehart and Winston.

Sacks, H. (1974). An analysis of the course of a joke's telling in conversation. In R. Bauman and J.F. Sherzer (Eds.), *Explorations in the Ethnography of Speaking*. Cambridge: Cambridge University Press.

Sacks, H. (1979). Hotrodder: A revolutionary category. In G. Psathas (Ed.), *Everyday Language: Studies in Ethnomethodology*. New York: Irvington.

Sacks, H. (1984). On doing 'being ordinary'. In J.M. Atkinson and J. Heritage (Eds.), *Structures of Social Action: Studies in Conversation Analysis*. Cambridge: Cambridge University Press.

Sacks, H. (1986). Some considerations of a story told in ordinary conversations, (Ed. G. Jefferson). In U. Quasthoff and E. Gulich (Eds.), *Narrative Analysis: An Interdisciplinary Dialogue*. Special issue of *Poetics, 15*, 127–38.

Sacks, H. (1987). On the preferences for agreement and contiguity in sequences in conversation. In G. Button and J.R.E. Lee (Eds.), *Talk and Social Organization*. Clevedon: Multilingual Matters.

Sacks, H. (1989). *Harvey Sacks – Lectures 1964–1965* (Ed. G. Jefferson). Special issue of *Human Studies, 12* (3–4), 183–404.

Sacks, H. (1992). *Lectures on Conversation*. 2 volumes (Ed. G. Jefferson). Oxford: Blackwell.

Sacks, H., Schegloff, E.A. and Jefferson, G. (1974). A simplest systematics for the organization of turn-taking for conversation. *Language, 50* (4), 696–735.

Sahlins, M. (1976). Colors and cultures. *Semiotica, 16*, 1–22.

Said, E.W. (1979). *Orientalism*. New York: Random House.

Sapir, E. (1924/1949). The grammarian and his language. *American Mercury, 1*, 149–55. Reprinted in G. Mandelbaum (Ed.), *The Selected Writings of Edward Sapir in Language, Culture and Personality*. Berkeley, CA: University of California Press.

Sapir, E. (1931/1964). Conceptual categories in primitive languages. Reprinted in D.H. Hymes (Ed.), *Language in Culture and Society: a Reader in Linguistics and Anthropology*. New York: Harper and Row.

Sarbin, T.R. (Ed.) (1986a). *Narrative Psychology: the Storied Nature of Human Conduct*. New York: Praeger.

Sarbin, T.R. (1986b). The narrative as root metaphor for psychology. In T.R. Sarbin (Ed.), *Narrative Psychology: the Storied Nature of Human Conduct*. New York: Praeger.

Saussure, F. de (1922/1974). *Course in General Linguistics*. London: Fontana.

Savage-Rumbaugh, E.S. (Ed.) (1993). Language comprehension in ape and child. *Monographs of the Society for Research in Child Development, 58* (3–4).

Savage-Rumbaugh, E.S. and Lewin, R. (1994). *Kanzi: the Ape at the Brink of the Human Mind*. London: Doubleday.

Scaife, M. and Bruner, J.S. (1975). The capacity for joint visual attention in the infant. *Nature, 253*, 265–6.

Schafer, R. (1976). *A New Language for Psychoanalysis*. New Haven, CT: Yale University Press.

Schafer, R. (1982). *Retelling a Life: Narration and Dialogue in Psychoanalysis*. New York: Basic Books.

Schank, R.C. (1982). *Dynamic Memory: a Theory of Reminding and Learning in Computers and People*. Cambridge: Cambridge University Press.

Schank, R.C. (1985). *The Cognitive Computer: on Language, Learning and Artificial Intelligence*. Reading, MA: Addison-Wesley.

Schank, R.C. and Abelson, R. (1977). *Scripts, Plans, Goals and Understanding*. Hillsdale, NJ: Erlbaum.

Schegloff, E.A. (1967). The first five seconds: the order of conversational openings. PhD dissertation, Department of Sociology, University of California, Berkeley.

Schegloff, E.A. (1972). Notes on a conversational practice: Formulating place. In D. Sudnow (Ed.), *Studies in Social Interaction*. Glencoe, IL: Free Press.

Schegloff, E.A. (1982). Discourse as an interactional achievement: Some uses of 'uh huh' and other things that come between sentences. In D. Tannen (Ed.), *Georgetown University Round Table on Language and Linguistics, 1981: Text and Talk*. Washington, DC: Georgetown University Press.

Schegloff, E.A. (1984). On some questions and ambiguities in conversation. In J.M. Atkinson and J. Heritage (Eds.), *Structures of Social Action: Studies in Conversation Analysis*. Cambridge: Cambridge University Press.

Schegloff, E.A. (1988). Presequences and indirection: Applying speech act theory to ordinary conversation. *Journal of Pragmatics, 12*, 55–62.

Schegloff, E.A. (1989a). Harvey Sacks – lectures 1964–1965: An introduction/memoir. *Human Studies, 12* (3–4), 185–209.

Schegloff, E.A. (1989b). Reflections on language, development and the interactional character of talk-in-interaction. In M. Bornstein and J.S. Bruner (Eds.), *Interaction in Human Development*. Hillsdale, NJ: Erlbaum.

Schegloff, E.A. (1989c). From interview to confrontation: Observations on the Bush/Rather encounter. *Research on Language and Social Action, 22*, 215–40.

Schegloff, E.A. (1991). Conversation analysis and socially shared cognition. In L.B. Resnick, J.M. Levine, and S.D. Teasley (Eds.), *Perspectives on Socially Shared Cognition*. Washington, DC: American Psychological Association.

Schegloff, E.A. (1992a). On talk and its institutional occasions. In P. Drew and J. Heritage (Eds.), *Talk at Work: Interaction in Institutional Settings*. Cambridge: Cambridge University Press.

Schegloff, E.A. (1992b). Introduction. In G. Jefferson (Ed.), *Harvey Sacks, Lectures on Conversation*. Volume 1. Oxford: Blackwell.

Schegloff, E.A. (1992c). Repair after next turn: The last structurally provided defence of intersubjectivity in conversation. *American Journal of Sociology, 97* (5), 1295–345.

Schegloff, E.A. (1992d). To Searle on conversation: A note in return. In J. Verscheuren (Ed.), *On Conversation*. Amsterdam: John Benjamins.

Schegloff, E.A. (1995). Discourse as an interactional achievement III: The omnirelevance of action. *Research on Language and Social Interaction, 28* (3), 185–211.

Schegloff, E.A., Jefferson, G. and Sacks, H. (1977). The preference for self-correction in the organization of repair in conversation. *Language, 53* (2), 361–82.

Schegloff, E.A. and Sacks, H. (1973). Opening up closings. *Semiotica, 7*, 289–327.

Schelling, T.C. (1960). *The Strategy of Conflict*. Cambridge, MA: Harvard University Press.

Schenkein, J. (Ed.) (1978). *Studies in the Organization of Conversational Interaction*. New York: Academic Press.

Scott, M.B. and Lyman, S.M. (1968). Accounts. *American Sociological Review, 33*, 46–62.

Scribner, S. and Cole, M. (1981). *The Psychology of Literacy*. London: Harvard University Press.

Searle, J.R. (1969). *Speech Acts: an Essay in the Philosophy of Language*. Cambridge: Cambridge University Press.

Searle, J.R. (1979). *Expression and Meaning: Studies in the Theory of Speech Acts*. Cambridge: Cambridge University Press.

Searle, J.R. (1980). Minds, brains and programs. *The Behavioral and Brain Sciences, 3*, 417–24.

Searle, J.R. (1983). *Intentionality: an Essay in the Philosophy of Mind*. Cambridge: Cambridge University Press.

Sebeok, T.A. and Umiker-Sebeok, J. (Eds.) (1980). *Speaking of Apes: a Critical Anthology of Two-Way Communication with Man*. New York: Plenum.

Semin, G. and Fiedler, K. (1988). The cognitive functions of linguistic categories in describing persons: Social cognition and language. *Journal of Personality and Social Psychology, 54* (4), 558–68.

Shanker, S.G. (1987). Wittgenstein versus Turing on the nature of Church's thesis. *Notre Dame Journal of Formal Logic, 23* (4).

Shotter, J. (1990). The social construction of remembering and forgetting. In D. Middleton and D. Edwards (Eds.), *Collective Remembering*. London: Sage.

Shotter, J. (1993a). *Conversational Realities: Constructing Life through Language*. London: Sage.

Shotter, J. (1993b). *Cultural Politics of Everyday Life: Social Constructionism, Rhetoric and Knowing of the Third Kind*. Buckingham: Open University Press.

Shotter, J. and Gergen, K.J. (Eds.) (1989). *Texts of Identity*. London: Sage.

Shweder, R.A. and Bourne, E.J. (1984). Does the concept of the person vary cross-culturally? In R.A. Shweder and R. Levine (Eds.), *Culture Theory: Essays on Mind, Self and Emotion*. Cambridge: Cambridge University Press.

Shweder, R.A. and Levine, R. (Eds.) (1984). *Culture Theory: Essays on Mind, Self, and Emotion*. Cambridge: Cambridge University Press.

Silverman, D. (1987). *Communication and Medical Practice*. London: Sage.

Skinner, B.F. (1957). *Verbal Behavior*. New York: Appleton-Century-Crofts.

Smith, B.H. (1988). *Contingencies of Value: Alternative Perspectives for Critical Theory*. Cambridge, MA: Harvard University Press.

Smith, D. (1978). K is mentally ill: The anatomy of a factual account. *Sociology, 12*, 23–53.

Smith, E.E. and Medin, D.L. (1981). *Categories and Concepts*. Cambridge, MA: Harvard University Press.

Smith, M.E. (1952). Childhood memories compared with those of adult life. *Journal of Genetic Psychology, 80*, 151–82.

Smith, N.V. (Ed.) (1982). *Mutual Knowledge*. London: Academic Press.

Soyland, A.J. (1994). *Psychology as Metaphor*. London: Sage.

Sperber, D. and Wilson, D. (1982). Mutual knowledge and relevance in theories of comprehension. In N. Smith (Ed.), *Mutual Knowledge*. London: Academic Press.

Stearns, C.Z. and Stearns, P.N. (Eds.) (1988). *Emotions and Social Change: Towards a New Psychohistory*. New York: Holmes and Meier.

Stenner, P. (1993). Discoursing jealousy. In E. Burman and I. Parker (Eds.), *Discourse Analytic Research: Repertoires and Readings of Texts in Action*. London: Routledge.

Stich, S. (1983). *From Folk Psychology to Cognitive Science: the Case Against Belief*. Cambridge, MA: MIT Press.

Stigler, J.W., Shweder, R.A. and Herdt, G. (Eds.) (1990). *Cultural Psychology: Essays on Comparative Human Development*. Cambridge: Cambridge University Press.

Still, A. and Costall, A. (Eds.) (1991). *Against Cognitivism: Alternative Foundations for Cognitive Psychology*. Hemel Hempstead: Harvester Wheatsheaf.

Streeck, J. (1980). Speech acts in interaction: A critique of Searle. *Discourse Processes, 3*, 133–53.

Street, B.V. (1984). *Literacy in Theory and Practice*. Cambridge: Cambridge University Press.

Strum, S. (1987). *Almost Human: a Journey into the World of Baboons*. New York: Random House.

Suchman, L.A. (1987). *Plans and Situated Actions: the Problem of Human–Machine Interaction*. Cambridge: Cambridge University Press.

Suchman, L.A. (1992). Technologies of accountability. Paper presented at the Conference for Sociocultural Research, Madrid, September.

Suchman, L.A. and Jordan, B. (1990). Interactional troubles in face-to-face survey interviews. *Journal of the American Statistical Association, 85*, 232–41.

Sudnow, D.N. (Ed.) (1972). *Studies in Social Interaction*. New York: Free Press.

Sweetser, E.E. (1990). *From Etymology to Pragmatics: the Mind–Body Metaphor in Semantic Structure and Semantic Change*. Cambridge: Cambridge University Press.

Taylor, C. (1989). *Sources of the Self*. Cambridge, MA: Harvard University Press.

Taylor, T.J. (1992). *Mutual Misunderstanding: Scepticism and the Theorizing of Language and Interpretation*. London: Routledge.

Temerlin, M.K. (1975). *Lucy: Growing up Human: a Chimpanzee Daughter in a Psychotherapist's Family*. Palo Alto, CA: Science and Behavior.

ten Have, P. and Psathas, G. (Eds.) (1995). *Situated Order: Studies in the Social Organization of Talk and Embodied Activities*. Washington, DC: University Press of America.

Terasaki, A.K. (1976). *Pre-Announcement Sequences in Conversation* (Social Science Working Paper no. 99). Irvine: University of California, School of Social Sciences.

Terrace, H.S. (1979). *Nim, a Chimpanzee Who Learned Sign Language*. New York: Knopf.

Thorndyke, P.W. (1977). Cognitive structures in comprehension and memory of narrative discourse. *Cognitive Psychology*, 9, 77–110.

Thorpe, W.H. (1972). The comparison of vocal communication in animals and man. In R.A. Hinde (Ed.), *Non-Verbal Communication*. Cambridge: Cambridge University Press.

Todorov, T. (1969). *Grammaire du Décameron*. The Hague: Mouton.

Tronick, E.Z. (Ed.) (1982). *Social Interchange in Infancy: Affect, Cognition, Communication*. Baltimore: University Park Press.

Tulving, E. (1972). Episodic and semantic memory. In E. Tulving and W. Donaldson (Eds.), *Organization of Memory*. New York: Academic Press.

Turing, A.M. (1950). Computing machinery and intelligence. *Mind*, 59, 433–60.

Turkle, S. (1984). *The Second Self: Computers and the Human Spirit*. New York: Simon and Schuster.

Turner, R. (1974a). *Ethnomethodology*. Harmondsworth: Penguin.

Turner, R. (1974b). Introduction. In R. Turner (Ed.), *Ethnomethodology*. Harmondsworth: Penguin.

Umiker-Sebeok, J. and Sebeok, T.A. (1980). Introduction: Questioning apes. In T.A. Sebeok and J. Umiker-Sebeok (Eds.), *Speaking of Apes: a Critical Anthology of Two-Way Communication with Man*. New York: Plenum.

Van Dijk, T.A. (1993). Principles of critical discourse analysis. *Discourse and Society*, 4 (2), 249–83.

Van Langenhove, L. and Harré, R. (1993). Positioning and autobiography: Telling your life. In N. Coupland and J.F. Nussbaum (Eds.), *Discourse and Lifespan Identity*. London: Sage.

Verscheuren, J. (Ed.) (1992). *On Conversation*. Amsterdam: John Benjamins.

Vygotsky, L.S. (1934/1987). *Thought and Language* (Ed. A. Kozulin). Cambridge, MA: MIT Press.

Wagenaar, W.A. (1986). My memory: A study of autobiographical memory over six years. *Cognitive Psychology*, 18, 225–52.

Wason, P.C. and Johnson-Laird, P.N. (1972). *Psychology of Reasoning: Structure and Content*. London: B.T. Batsford Ltd.

Watson, D.R. (1978). Categorization, authorization and blame-negotiation in conversation. *Sociology*, 12, 105–13.

Watson, D.R. (1990). Some features of the elicitation of confessions in murder interrogations. In G. Psathas (Ed.), *Interaction Competence*. Washington, DC: University Press of America.

Watson, G. (1994). A comparison of social constructionist and ethnomethodological descriptions of how a judge distinguished between the erotic and the obscene. *Philosophy of the Social Sciences*, 24 (4), 405–25.

Weintraub, K. (1978). *The Value of the Individual: Self and Circumstance in Autobiography*. Chicago: University of Chicago Press.

Weiskrantz, L. (Ed.) (1988). *Thought Without Language*. Oxford: Clarendon.

Weizenbaum, J. (1984). *Computer Power and Human Reason*. London: Allen Lane.

Wenzel, S. (1960). *The Sin of Sloth: Acedia in Medieval Thought and Literature*. Chapel Hill, NC: University of North Carolina Press.

Wertsch, J.V. (1985). *Vygotsky and the Social Formation of Mind*. Cambridge, MA: Harvard University Press.

Wertsch, J.V. (1991). *Voices of the Mind: a Sociocultural Approach to Mediated Action*. Hemel Hempstead: Harvester Wheatsheaf.

Wetherell, M. and Potter, J. (1992). *Mapping the Language of Racism: Discourse and the Legitimation of Exploitation*. Hemel Hempstead: Harvester Wheatsheaf.

Whalen, J. (1995). A technology of order production: Computer-aided dispatch in public safety communications. In P. ten Have and G. Psathas (Eds.), *Situated Order: Studies in the Social*

Organization of Talk and Embodied Activities. Washington, DC: University Press of America.

Whalen, M.R. and Zimmerman, D.H. (1990). Describing trouble: Practical epistemology in citizen calls to the police. *Language in Society*, *19*, 465–92.

White, G.M. (1990). Moral discourse and the rhetoric of emotions. In C.A Lutz and L. Abu-Lughod (Eds.), *Language and the Politics of Emotion*. Cambridge: Cambridge University Press.

White, G.M. and Kirkpatrick, J. (1985). *Person, Self and Experience: Exploring Pacific Ethnopsychologies*. Berkeley, CA: University of California Press.

White, H. (1973). *Metahistory: the Historical Imagination in Nineteenth Century Europe*. Baltimore: Johns Hopkins University Press.

White, H. (1987). *The Content of the Form: Narrative Discourse and Historical Representation*. Baltimore: Johns Hopkins University Press.

White, R.T. (1982). Memory for personal events. *Human Learning*, *1*, 171–83.

Whiten, A. (Ed.) (1991). *Natural Theories of Mind: Evolution, Development and Simulation of Everyday Mindreading*. Oxford: Blackwell.

Whorf, B.L. (1956). *Language, Thought and Reality: Selected Writings of Benjamin Lee Whorf* (Ed. J.B. Carroll). Cambridge, MA: MIT Press.

Widdicombe, S. (1993). Autobiography and change: Rhetoric and authenticity of 'gothic' style. In E. Burman and I. Parker (Eds.), *Discourse Analytic Research: Repertoires and Readings of Texts in Action*. London: Routledge.

Widdicombe, S. and Wooffitt, R. (1995). *The Language of Youth Subcultures: Social Identity in Action*. Hemel Hempstead: Harvester Wheatsheaf.

Wieder, D.L. (1974). Telling the code. In R. Turner (Ed.), *Ethnomethodology*. Harmondsworth: Penguin.

Wieder, D.L. (1988). From resource to topic: Some aims of conversation analysis. In J. Anderson (Ed.), *Communication Yearbook 11*. London: Sage.

Wiener, W.J. and Rosenwald, G.C. (1993). A moment's monument: The psychology of keeping a diary. In R. Josselson and A. Lieblich (Eds.), *The Narrative Study of Lives*. Volume 1. London: Sage.

Wierzbicka, A. (1992). *Semantics, Culture and Cognition: Universal Human Concepts in Culture-Specific Configurations*. New York: Oxford University Press.

Wierzbicka, A. (1994). Emotion, language, and cultural scripts. In S. Kitayama and H. Markus (Eds.), *Emotion and Culture: Empirical Studies of Mutual Influence*. Washington, DC: American Psychological Association.

Wierzbicka, A. (1995). Emotion and facial expression: A semantic perspective. *Culture and Psychology*, *1* (2), 227–58.

Wilkinson, S. and Kitzinger, C. (1995). *Feminism and Discourse: Psychological Perspectives*. London: Sage.

Winch, P. (1958). *The Idea of a Social Science and its Relation to Philosophy*. London: Routledge and Kegan Paul.

Winegar, L.T. (1995). Moving toward culture-inclusive theories of emotion. *Culture and Psychology*, *1* (2), 269–78.

Winograd, T. (1972). *Understanding Natural Language*. New York: Academic Press.

Winograd, T. and Flores, F. (1986). *Understanding Computers and Cognition: a New Foundation for Design*. Norwood, NJ: Addison-Wesley.

Wittgenstein, L. (1922/1972). *Tractatus Logico-Philosophicus*. London: Routledge and Kegan Paul.

Wittgenstein, L. (1958). *Philosophical Investigations* (2nd Edn). Oxford: Blackwell.

Wittgenstein, L. (1967). *Zettel*. Oxford: Blackwell.

Wittgenstein, L. (1978). *Remarks on the Foundations of Mathematics* (3rd Edn). Oxford: Oxford University Press.

Wooffitt, R.C. (1990). On the analysis of interaction: An introduction to conversation analysis. In P. Luff, D. Frohlich, and G.N. Gilbert (Eds.), *Computers and Conversation*. New York: Academic Press.

Wooffitt, R.C. (1991). 'I was just doing X . . . when Y': Some inferential properties of a device in accounts of paranormal experiences. *Text, 11*, 267–88.

Wooffitt, R.C. (1992). *Telling Tales of the Unexpected: the Organization of Factual Discourse*. Hemel Hempstead: Harvester Wheatsheaf.

Woolgar, S. (1980). Discovery: Logic and sequence in a scientific text. In K. Knorr, R. Krohn, and R. Whitley (Eds.), *The Social Process of Scientific Investigation*. Dordrecht: Reidel.

Woolgar, S. (1987). Reconstructing man and machine: A note on sociological critiques of cognitivism. In W.E. Bijker, T. Hughes, and T. Pinch (Eds.), *The Social Construction of Technological Systems*. Cambridge, MA: MIT Press.

Woolgar, S. (1988a). *Science: the Very Idea*. Chichester: Ellis Horwood.

Woolgar, S. (Ed.) (1988b). *Knowledge and Reflexivity: New Frontiers in the Sociology of Science*. London: Sage.

Wundt, W. (1900–20). *Volkerpsychologie*. Volumes 1–10. London: Allen and Unwin.

Yearley, S. (1981). Textual persuasion: The role of social accounting in the construction of scientific arguments. *Philosophy of the Social Sciences, 11*, 409–35.

Yearley, S. (1986). Interactive-orientation and argumentation in scientific texts. In J. Law (Ed.), *Power, Action and Belief: a New Sociology of Knowledge*. London: Routledge.

Yerkes, R.M. (1925). *Almost Human*. New York: Century.

Young, K.G. (1987). *Taleworlds and Storyrealms: the Phenomenology of Narrative*. Dordrecht: Martinus Nijhoff.

Young, K.G. (1989). Narrative embodiments: Enclaves of the self in the realm of medicine. In J. Shotter and K.J. Gergen (Eds.), *Texts of Identity*. London: Sage.

Ziff, P. (1960). *Semantic Analysis*. Ithaca, NY: Cornell University Press

Zimmerman, D.H. (1971). The practicalities of rule use. In J. Douglas (Ed.), *Understanding Everyday Life*. London: Routledge and Kegan Paul.

Zimmerman, D.H. (1988). On conversation: The conversation analytic perspective. In J. Anderson (Ed.), *Communication Yearbook 11*. London: Sage.

Index